REFERENCE

This book is presented to:

_____

Books
Are
Wings

LIVE UNITED

United
Way

United Way of Rhode Island
Women's Leadership Council

Interdisciplinary Encyclopedia of Marine Sciences

EDITED BY

James W. Nybakken, Editor in Chief

William W. Broenkow and Tracy L. Vallier

Volume 2
G–O

GROLIER ACADEMIC REFERENCE, AN IMPRINT OF SCHOLASTIC LIBRARY PUBLISHING
DANBURY, CONNECTICUT

Published by Grolier Academic Reference, an imprint of Scholastic Library Publishing, Danbury, Connecticut

© 2003 by The Moschovitis Group, Inc.
339 Fifth Avenue, New York, New York 10010

Library of Congress Cataloging-in-Publication Data

Interdisciplinary encyclopedia of marine sciences / edited by James W. Nybakken, William W. Broenkow, Tracy L. Vallier.
    p. cm.
   Includes bibliographical references and index.
   ISBN 0-7172-5946-3 (set : alk. paper)
   1. Marine sciences–Encyclopedias. 2. Oceanography. I. Nybakken, James Willard. II. Broenkow, William W., 1939-III. Vallier, T. L. (Tracy L.)

GC9 .I58 2002
551.46'003–dc21

2002192707

Printed and Manufactured in the United States of America

♾ The paper used in this publication meets the minimum requirements of the American National Standard for Information Sciences—Permanence of Paper for Printed Library Materials, ANSI Z39.48-1984.

G

~

Gabbro

Gabbro is a dark, medium- to coarse-grained plutonic rock that consists of mafic (iron and magnesium enriched) minerals and is the chemical equivalent of basalt. Although basalt is the most common rock on the surface of Earth, gabbro is relatively uncommon. Due to the variable nature of both the chemistry and the mineral composition, gabbro lies within a family or clan that ranges from anorthosite to ultramafic to diorite to quartz diorite. Gabbro occurs as dikes, sills, plugs, and small plutons, and as *cumulate* (layered) and *noncumulate* (nonlayered) bodies. Cumulate phases are volumetrically larger than noncumulate phases. Gabbro is relatively rare on continents but much more common as oceanic lithosphere.

Gabbro consists of the minerals plagioclase, clinopyroxene (with or without hypersthene), olivine, hornblende, biotite, and rarely orthoclase and quartz. Accessory minerals include ilmenite, magnetite, apatite, and rarely chromite. Chemically, gabbro contains less than 50 percent silica; fractionation trends vary from alkalic (sodium rich) to tholeiitic (quartz normative), with high-aluminum and high-magnesium varieties.

On continents, the majority of gabbro bodies are found in large cumulate intrusions such as the Muskox, Bushveld, Stillwater, or Skaergaard. Gabbro forms bodies beneath pooling basalt magma reservoirs at shallow depths. Processes important in the formation of cumulative gabbro bodies include crystal sorting, crystal settling, convection, and precipitation of mineral grains in the stagnant magma pool. As these processes change, the cumulate minerals will alter; changes in mineralogy develop vertically through the layered body.

Fractionation of the magma controls the composition of the mineral phases formed, and this fractionation results in different rock types. By removing material from the magma, layering causes the rocks to become enriched in silica, iron, and sodium relative to magnesium and calcium from the bottom of the layered intrusion to the top. An idealized section from the base to the top is pyroxenite/peridotite, olivine gabbro, normal gabbro, ferrogabbro, and ferrogranophyre.

Cumulate textures of the layered intrusions have no single feature that is common throughout but are most easily recognized by layering in the outcrop. If only one phase of mineral is being precipitated, the contrast between the magma and the mineral layer produces a sharp and recognizable layer. If several phases are present in the cumulus, the gabbroic texture develops where grains are anhedral with intergrown irregular boundaries but retain overall subhedral outlines.

Gabbro forms at oceanic spreading centers as part of ocean crust development. At these spreading centers, the magma chamber is elongated parallel with the spreading ridge. Magma rises from the asthenosphere to the crust and erupts through the roof of the magma chamber as sheeted dikes and lava flows. Magma that coalesces on the roof and wall of the magma chamber forms noncumulate gabbro, whereas magma near the chamber floor accumulates into layers. The cumulate layer dips toward the chamber center and overlies the sheared, noncumulate serpentinite and ultramafic rocks of the asthenosphere below the spreading center.

David L. White

FURTHER READING

Barker, Daniel S. *Igneous Rocks.* Engelwood Cliffs, N.J.: Prentice Hall, 1983.

Hughes, C. J. *Igneous Petrology.* Amsterdam and New York: Elsevier Scientific, 1982.

Middlemost, Eric A. K. *Magmas and Magmatic Rocks.* London and New York: Longman, 1985.

Williams, Howell, Francis J. Turner, and Charles M. Gilbert. *Petrography: An Introduction to the Study of Rocks in Thin Sections.* San Francisco: W. H. Freeman, 1958; 2nd ed., 1982.

RELATED ARTICLES

Oceanic Crust; Oceanic Volcanic Rock; Ophiolite

Gaia Hypothesis

The Gaia hypothesis was proposed in the early 1970s by British inventor and scientist James E. Lovelock (1919–) in collaboration with U.S. microbiologist Lynn Margulis (1938–). Central to the Gaia hypothesis is the notion that Earth, as a whole, behaves as if it were a superorganism. Most particularly, the biosphere is seen as self-sustaining insofar as the totality of life on the planet maintains environmental conditions suitable for its continued existence. A proposition of the hypothesis is that feedback systems—operating through biogeochemical cycles—regulate environmental conditions on Earth in a superficially similar manner to the way in which homeostatic mechanisms operate in the human body.

The Gaia hypothesis has its roots in Lovelock's work with NASA in the 1960s, when he was employed as a consultant to the team of scientists planning the two Viking expeditions to Mars. Lovelock was commissioned to advise on instrumentation for discovering whether life was present on Mars. Lovelock's analysis as to what life is—and what are signs of life—led him to conclude that organisms evolving on other cosmic bodies may be rather different than those on Earth. He concluded, however, that all living things—irrespective of their precise chemical nature—alter their environment above and beyond the changes expected by chemical and physical processes alone. For example, organisms process chemicals to obtain the raw materials and energy they require to construct and maintain their bodies. They excrete modified chemicals. The metabolism of organisms thus alters environmental conditions from those predicted by physical and chemical processes alone. In particular, the presence of life leaves its "fingerprint" on a planet's atmospheric composition. Lovelock, working with others, concluded that this departure from chemical equilibrium would be readily detectable at a distance with the use of infrared telescopes, without the need to actually visit a planet.

Such thinking led Lovelock to appreciate the profound impact of living organisms on a planet's environment. In reflecting on the 3.5-billion-year-long history of life on Earth, Lovelock noted that the Sun had increased its energy output by some 30 percent during that time, but that Earth's surface had not warmed correspondingly and had fluctuated within a fairly narrow range. Lovelock surmised that the activities of living organisms were maintaining a climate favorable to them. For example, by extracting the greenhouse-gas carbon dioxide from the atmosphere, they were reducing the greenhouse effect and so were countering temperature rises.

Lovelock's 1979 book *Gaia: A New Look at Life on Earth* outlined his developing ideas on the biological regulation of the environment. In it, he defined Gaia as "a complex entity involving the Earth's biosphere, atmosphere, oceans and soil; the totality constituting a feedback or cybernetic system which seeks an optimal physical and chemical environment for life on this planet." The book—and its thesis—came under criticism from the scientific establishment, especially biologists. Scientists took exception to the poetic name "Gaia" (in Greek mythology, derived from "Ge," meaning Earth, the setting for Greek gods); biologists disliked the notion of Earth as akin to a superorganism. Evolutionary biologists criticized the Gaia hypothesis because they could not see how Darwinian evolution of individuals and populations could lead to regulation of the planetary environment for the benefit of living organisms as a whole.

Despite such criticisms, the Gaia hypothesis remains highly influential. Testing the hypothesis has led to important scientific advances. For example, in 1987, atmospheric chemist R. J. Charlson and others, working with Lovelock, published a paper in *Nature* showing how the release of dimethyl sulfide by marine phytoplankton seeds clouds. Other studies, including the use of computer models such as *Daisyworld*, have lent support to the notion that organisms might regulate climate. Testing Gaia has promoted interdisciplinary research and has helped put biology center stage in the study of biogeochemical cycles. By the late 1980s, the Gaian study of Earth had become *geophysiology*. By the late 1990s, some evolutionary biologists, including W. D. Hamilton (1936–2000) of the University of Oxford in the United Kingdom, were beginning to accept the idea that Darwinian evolution of populations could give rise to climate regulation.

Trevor Day

FURTHER READING
Charlson, R. J., J. E. Lovelock, M. O. Andreae, and S. G. Warren. "Oceanic Phytoplankton, Atmospheric Sulphur, Cloud Albedo, and Climate." *Nature*, Vol. 274 (1987), pp. 246–248.
Hunt, Lynn. "Send in the Clouds." *New Scientist*, 30 May 1998, pp. 28–33.
Joseph, Lawrence E. *Gaia: The Growth of an Idea*. New York: St. Martin's Press, 1990.
Lovelock, James. *Gaia: A New Look at Life on Earth*. New York: Oxford University Press, 1979.
———. *The Ages of Gaia: A Biography of Our Living Earth*. Oxford: Oxford University Press, 1989; New York: W. W. Norton, 1995.
———. *Gaia: The Practical Science of Planetary Medicine*. London: Gaia Books, 1991; rev. ed., Oxford: Oxford University Press, 2000.
Volk, Tyler. *Gaia's Body: Toward a Physiology of Earth*. New York: Copernicus, 1998.

RELATED ARTICLES
Biogeochemical Cycle; Biosphere

Galápagos Spreading Center

The Galápagos Spreading Center is located near the equator in the eastern Pacific Ocean. The Galápagos Islands are the subaerial manifestation of a much larger spreading center system. Tectonically, the spreading center and islands are associated with the East Pacific Rise west of Ecuador and are thought to be the product of a long-lived mantle plume. Hydrothermal vent communities existing along this spreading system were first sighted and reported from the Galápagos Spreading Center.

Scientists onboard the submersible *Alvin* discovered the hydrothermal vent community in 1977. The hydrothermal vent field is located within the central rift zone. The water depth is 2500 meters (8200 feet), and the temperature of the water ranges from 8 to 12°C (46 to 54°F). The increased temperature of the water, plus the gases and particles that emanate from the vent field, allows nutrients to be plentiful. Most organisms derive their energy by processes of chemosynthesis.

A combined team of researchers from the U.S. Navy and Princeton University investigated the

Galápagos Spreading Center during the late 1960s and 1970s. They learned that the Galápagos Spreading Center contains a central rift zone that is cut by deep valleys that trend parallel to the axis of the rift zone. The central rift is a graben that exceeds the depth of the continental Grand Canyon in the United States. Results from magnetic surveys show a pattern that is similar to that of other spreading centers. This and other combined evidence indicate that there is plate motion away from a complex triple junction. Movement of the Galápagos Spreading Center is slow, similar to the Afar region of eastern Africa and the Mid-Atlantic Ridge.

The Galápagos Spreading Center is thought to have been very influential in the formation of the Isthmus of Panama and other parts of Central America. A series of east–west rifts and associated ridge systems are located north of the Galápagos Islands. The northward motion of spreading drove the oceanic plate under the Middle America Trench. Uplift of the sediments and crust from the trench and the seafloor created what is now Central America. Tectonic activity continues in the region today. Evidence from railroad surveys in Costa Rica indicates

Cocos and Nazca Plates forming the Galápagos Spreading Center. The Pacific Plate (not shown on the map), located farther to the west, completes the triple junction and pushes northwest away from the spreading center.

that annual uplift of several centimeters presently occurs along its Pacific coast.

West of the Galápagos Islands a special situation exists where three spreading ridges (ridge–ridge–ridge triple junction) radiate outward from a central point. This geometry indicates that a rising mantle plume is present beneath the oceanic crust at this location. The radiating plates are the Pacific Plate, the Cocos Plate, and the Nazca Plate. The Pacific Plate is driven northwest by motion along the East Pacific Rise. The Cocos Plate is moving northeast toward Central America by motion from the Galápagos Spreading Center. The Nazca Plate is being carried from the East Pacific Rise toward South America. This diverging triple junction causes the overlying lithosphere to thin. Displaced material is replaced by upwelling mantle material derived from melting within the asthenosphere.

David L. White

FURTHER READING

Condie, Kent C. *Plate Tectonics and Crustal Evolution.* New York: Pergamon Press, 1976; 4th ed., Oxford and Boston: Butterworth-Heinemann, 1997.

Sullivan, Walter. *Continents in Motion: The New Earth Debate.* New York: McGraw-Hill, 1974; 2nd ed., New York: American Institute of Physics, 1991.

Thurman, Harold V. *Essentials of Oceanography.* Columbus, Ohio: Charles E. Merrill, 1983; 6th ed., with Alan P. Trujillo, Upper Saddle River, N.J.: Prentice Hall, 1999.

RELATED ARTICLES

Chemosynthesis; Cocos Plate; Hydrothermal Vent; Mantle Plume; Nazca Plate; Pacific Plate; Plate Tectonics

Gas Hydrate

A gas hydrate is composed of ice and natural gas. Natural gas generally refers to methane (CH_4), although other hydrocarbon gases, such as ethane, propane, and butane, are also present in most natural-gas mixtures. Methane is a simple hydrocarbon molecule with one carbon molecule surrounded by four oxygen molecules. Methane occurs in variable quantities in the atmosphere, water, and sediment and rock layers. Gas hydrate is very common beneath the upper layers of deep-sea sediment and both onland and offshore in cold polar regions.

Gas hydrate, also known as *clathrate*, is a naturally occurring solid composed of water molecules (H_2O) that form a rigid lattice of cages, each containing a molecule of natural gas, mostly methane, although ethane, carbon dioxide, hydrogen sulfide, propane, and isobutane can occur in very small quantities. The water is crystallized to ice in an isometric crystallographic system that forms a latticelike structure that encloses molecules of gas. The methane is packed at densities 160 times greater than those at normal pressures. A fully saturated methane hydrate generally has one molecule of methane for every six molecules of water. At standard temperature and pressure (STP) it is theoretically possible that 1 cubic meter (35 cubic feet) of methane hydrate can contain up to 164 cubic meters (5790 cubic feet) of methane gas and 0.8 cubic meter (28 cubic feet) of water. Salt crystals are excluded from the ice lattices as shown by low chlorinity values. Chlorinity is a measure of the total weight of chlorine, bromine, and iodine in water and may be used to calculate salinity [salinity in practical salinity units (psu) = 1.80655 × chlorinity in parts per thousand (ppt)]. Chlorinity in seawater is about 19.5 to 19.8 ppt and the chlorinity of gas hydrate samples is much lower, ranging from 0.4 to 8.0 ppt.

Sources of Methane

Methane forms by three natural processes: (1) *biogenic,* which is related to the expulsion of gas from microorganisms (microbial—mostly bacteria) during digestion of organic compounds; (2) *thermogenic,* whereby the decomposition of organic matter occurs because of heat and pressure; and (3) *abiogenic,* which is related to reaction of deep crustal gases with minerals or seepage of

hydrogen- and carbon-rich primordial gas from Earth's interior.

Methane in gas hydrates is predominantly (greater than 99 percent) microbial in origin, based on isotopic and molecular composition. Carbon isotope results are particularly helpful and indicate a microbial origin consistent with the reduction of carbon dioxide derived from organic matter. There are places, however, as on the continental margin of the Gulf of Mexico and in some locations on the continental margin of the U.S. east coast, where some thermogenic methane occurs that migrated from great depths in the sedimentary piles.

Biogenic methane results from the decomposition of organic matter by methanogens, which are methane-producing microorganisms (mostly bacteria) that are particularly abundant in the near surface of Earth's crust in regions devoid of oxygen and where temperatures do not exceed 97°C (207°F). The amount of organic matter required is large, possibly as high as 2.0 to 3.5 percent by volume in the sediment if the methane forms in situ. The intestines of animals are sites where methanogens flourish.

Detection of Gas Hydrate Accumulations in Deep-Sea Sediment

Gas hydrates can cement or partially cement a near-surface layer of sediment as much as 1000 meters (3280 feet) thick, limited at the base by increasing temperature. They are detected by observation in drill cores and by acoustic methods, mostly by studying seismic-reflection profiles.

Drill cores containing gas hydrate have been recovered from several parts of deep continental margins, mostly by the Ocean Drilling Program (ODP). Special coring tools are needed to recover gas hydrate intact because it can easily melt during the coring and recovery process. Gas hydrate in cores is similar to dry ice (frozen carbon dioxide) that is packed around perishables to keep them frozen at STP.

Acoustic methods are used to identify gas hydrate accumulations because it forms an acoustic layer with a high sound velocity [up to 3.3 kilometers (2 miles) per second] relative to surrounding sediments which have transmitted sound velocities of 1.5 kilometers (0.9 miles) per second (speed of sound in seawater) to perhaps 1.65 kilometers (1 mile) per second. Sediments below the hydrate zone have lower velocities; if they are gas charged, the velocities are even lower. The base of the hydrate zone, because of the large difference in velocity, forms a strong acoustic reflector. The change in sound velocity near the top of the hydrate zone is more gradual and does not form a strong acoustic reflector.

The presence of a gas hydrate accumulation can therefore be inferred from seismic-reflection profiles where a pronounced bottom-simulating-reflector (BSR) coincides with depths predicted from theoretical phase diagram studies of the gas hydrate stability zone. The BSR is a seafloor-paralleling reflector that in places cuts across other acoustic layering that is caused by changes in sediment properties. In essence, BSRs mark the boundary, or interface, between higher-velocity sound waves in hydrate-cemented sediment above, and lower-velocity uncemented sediment below. Quantitative studies indicate that above the BSR is a high-velocity layer about 10 to 30 meters (33 to 98 feet) thick with about 30 percent of its pore space filled with gas hydrate. In this case, the BSR records an interface between sediment with gas hydrate (above) and sediment without gas hydrate (below).

Characteristics that allow hydrate detection in seismic profiles are (1) a bottom-simulating reflector (BSR) that is reflected from the base of the hydrate layer, (2) a velocity inversion in which the velocity of hydrate-cemented sediment above the BSR is observed to have higher velocity than that of the sediment below, and (3) a reduction in the amplitude of reflections within the hydrate-cemented zone, known as *blanking*. Blanking occurs on those parts of a seismic-reflection profile directly above the BSR. This decrease in amplitude weakens the reflections that occur in the seismic-reflection profile.

Controls and Models

Gas hydrate occurrences are controlled by temperature, pressure, and composition. Temperature is low, pressure is relatively high, and organic material is abundant, particularly in continental margin sediment. The hydrates are stable at temperature and pressure conditions that occur near and just beneath the seafloor, where water depths exceed 300 to 500 meters (985 to 1640 feet).

Best estimates indicate that the upper depth limit of methane hydrate is about 150 meters (490 feet) in polar regions, where surface temperatures are below 0°C (32°F). In ocean sediment, gas hydrate occurs where the bottom-water temperature approaches 0°C and water depth exceeds about 300 meters (985 feet). The lower limit in deep-sea sediment is at a maximum of about 2000 meters (6560 feet) below the ocean floor.

The most important control, however, appears to be the rate of sedimentation whereby abundant organic carbon can accumulate and bacteria have opportunities to create methane. Faults can form channelways for the passage of gas upward in the hydrate layer. Gas hydrate will form when about 90 percent of the clathrate cages are filled, which is about 150 volumes of methane at STP per volume of water. Methane solubility in seawater is very low and the amount of methane required for gas hydrate greatly exceeds the solubility of methane in water. Therefore, the requirement for large amounts of methane limits the regions on Earth where gas hydrate can be expected to form to those having significant sources of methane.

Two major models have been proposed to account for gas-hydrate formation and the development of BSRs. One predicts free gas below the BSR, and the other predicts no free gas below the BSR.

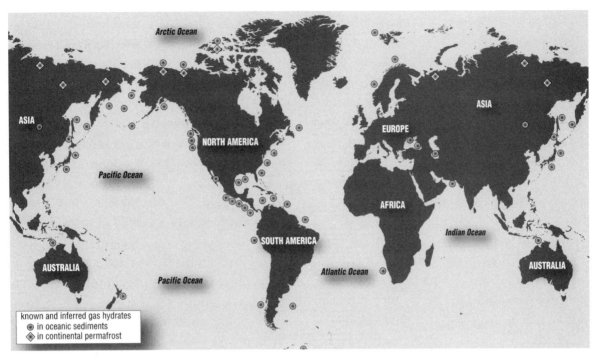

Distribution of known and inferred gas hydrates in oceanic sediments and in regions of continental permafrost. (Adapted from Kvenvolden, 1988.)

1. Methane is generated microbially from organic matter within the zone of gas-hydrate stability. It occurs during sedimentation. The zone thickens and deepens its base, thereby subsiding into a temperature region where the gas hydrate is unstable. Gas hydrate would occur throughout the zone of gas-hydrate stability, and free gas may or may not be present beneath the BSR.

2. Gas hydrate is formed by the removal of methane from rising pore fluids as they pass from below into the gas-hydrate stability zone. This model infers that most of the methane is generated microbially at depths below the stability zone but not at depths sufficient for the formation of thermogenic (deep) methane. In this model, gas hydrate is concentrated at the base of the stability zone near the BSR, and free gas is not expected below the BSR.

Locations of Gas Hydrate Accumulations

Gas hydrate accumulations are very common in the world but are restricted to polar regions, both onshore and offshore, and to deep oceans near continents (see figure). Permafrost and gas hydrate are associated in polar regions, whereas in oceanic regions gas hydrate accumulations are located in unconsolidated sediment along the outer continental margin, where cold water is present. Gas hydrate has been recovered from the ocean by the Ocean Drilling Program and in piston cores from the Black and Caspian Seas.

Gas hydrate exists within ocean-floor sediments because the hydrate is trapped in intergranular pores and because gas is available, either biogenic gas produced by bacteria or thermogenic gas rising from deeper strata. Temperature increases downward through the sediment piles along a geothermal gradient, and although pressure also increases (which tends to make the hydrate more stable), the conditions eventually become too warm for hydrate to exist. The geothermal gradient is about the same within a given region; therefore, a zone of hydrate-cemented sediment extends down from the seafloor and is commonly several hundred meters thick.

Most gas hydrate along continental margins is generated microbially, associated with rapid sedimentation and an abundant supply of organic carbon, which in turn is related either to high biologic productivity under a zone of oceanic upwelling or to organic-carbon-rich river sources. Off the east coast of the United States, gas hydrate is concentrated both in areas of rapid sediment deposition and along a linear group of diapirs and associated faults. The sources of natural gas at these locations are mostly bacterial (microbial), but possibly some comes from a deep thermogenic source that uses faults as channelways. Bering Sea deep-sea sediment contains abundant gas hydrate. Estimates suggest that as much as 33 trillion cubic meters [1160 trillion cubic feet] occurs in the Bering Sea. However, a large percent of the hydrate is considered to be of thermogenic origin rather than microbial.

Gas Hydrate and Global Economics

It is extremely difficult to measure the amount of methane in gas hydrate. First of all, knowledge about its occurrence is very incomplete, thereby contributing to a wide range of estimates. There is some agreement among scientists that a total of 10 to 11×10^{18} grams (0.35 to 0.39×10^{18} ounces) of methane occurs in gas hydrate accumulations worldwide. This is equal to about 20×10^{15} cubic meters (706×10^{15} cubic feet) of methane gas. It is a prodigious amount. If their estimates are correct, the amount of methane carbon in gas hydrate deposits is a factor of two larger than the carbon present in known fossil-fuel deposits (natural gas, oil, and coal). Even small areas contain large amounts of methane. For example, the estimated amount of methane in gas hydrate for an area of about 3000 square kilometers (1060 square miles) on Blake Ridge, off the east coast of the United States, is 1.13×10^{11} cubic meters (40×10^{11} cubic feet).

Gas traps can occur where a seal is formed by the gas-hydrated-cemented layer. They are observed (1) where the seafloor forms a dome, (2) above diapirs, and (3) at locations where strata dip relative to the ocean floor and the updip regions of porous strata are sealed by the cemented layer to form a trap. Production of gas from such traps would result in extraction of both the free gas and the gas derived from the breakdown of the hydrate seal by depressurization.

The economic (profitable) recovery of natural gases from gas hydrates has not yet happened and probably won't occur until a critical need for energy arises. Thus far, the use of the fossil fuels from conventional drilling and coal mining is profitable and there is still an abundant, although diminishing, supply of fossil fuels available in the world.

Global Warming

Another factor to consider, however, is the effect that a sudden (few years to a century) release of methane might have on global warming. If the ocean water heats up, as it seems to be doing as ice sheets melt, can the methane from gas hydrates be released into the ocean and thence into the atmosphere? If so, will it become a greenhouse gas and trap solar radiation, like other gases (e.g., CO_2)?

The importance of global warming potential for a particular greenhouse gas depends on its abundance, the wavelength of solar radiation that it absorbs, and its atmospheric lifetime. Carbon dioxide is an important greenhouse gas because it is abundant and very effective in absorbing certain wavelengths of infrared energy, mostly between 1 and 7 micrometers (0.00004 and 0.00027 inch) and above 14 micrometers (0.00055 inch). Methane, chlorofluorocarbons, and ozone are relatively rare in the atmosphere and absorb infrared energy in the 7- to 14-micrometer wavelength window, where the other gases are ineffective. Presently, the atmosphere allows 80 percent of the energy in this window to escape into space. Therefore, an increase in the amount of methane can play a significant role in trapping solar radiation.

The atmospheric lifetime, or residence time, of greenhouse gases is also very important. Methane, for example, has a short residence time (about 10 years) because it reacts with atmospheric oxidants to form carbon dioxide and water vapor. Therefore, if we shut off all human-related contributions of methane to the atmosphere, the concentrations would return to natural levels in about 10 years. Carbon dioxide, however, has a much longer residence time (200 to 500 years), because its removal from the atmosphere depends on rates of transfer to and from the oceans and the biosphere. Therefore, methane is a potent greenhouse gas in the short term and a potential source of carbon dioxide and water vapor in the long term. Methane also has a potential influence on the ozone layer as a contributor to ice cloud formation, where catalytic conversion of ozone to oxygen takes place. This lessens the amount of ozone. Some scientists, however, suggest that methane may combine with chlorine and thereby reduce the effects of chlorofluorocarbons on the ozone layer. Clearly, more studies are needed.

Therefore, if the volume of methane were rapidly increased by the release of methane from gas hydrates, the long-term effect would be an increase in the amount of trapped solar radiation because of the conversion of methane to carbon dioxide and water vapor. This could lead to an increase in the rate of global warming.

Tracy L. Vallier

FURTHER READING
Claypool, George E., and Isaac R. Kaplan. "The Origin and Distribution of Methane in Marine Sediments." In Isaac R. Kaplan, ed., *Natural Gases in Marine Sediments.* New York: Plenum Press, 1974.
Cole, Frances. "Environmental Consequences of Increased Natural-Gas Usage." In David G. Howell, ed., *The Future of Energy Gases.* U.S. Geological Survey Professional Paper 1570. Washington, D.C.: U.S. Government Printing Office, 1993.
Dillon, William P., Lee W. Myung, Kristen Fehlhaber, and Dwight F. Coleman. "Gas Hydrates on the Atlantic Continental Margin of the United States: Controls on Concentration." In David G. Howell, ed., *The Future of Energy Gases.* U.S. Geological Survey Professional Paper 1570. Washington, D.C.: U.S. Government Printing Office, 1993.
Howell, David G., Francis Cole, Michael Fanelli, and Katryn Wiese. "An Introduction to the Future of Natural Gas." In David G. Howell, ed., *The Future of Energy Gases.* U.S. Geological Survey Professional Paper 1570. Washington, D.C.: U.S. Government Printing Office, 1993.
Kvenvolden, Keith A. "Methane Hydrate: A Major Reservoir of Carbon in the Shallow Geosphere?" *Chemical Geology,* Vol. 71 (1988), pp. 41–51.
———. "A Primer on Gas Hydrates." In David G. Howell, ed., *The Future of Energy Gases.* U.S. Geological Survey Professional Paper 1570. Washington, D.C.: U.S. Government Printing Office, 1993.
———. "Gas Hydrates: Geological Perspective and Global Change." *Reviews of Geophysics,* Vol. 31 (1993) pp. 173–187.
Scholl, David W., and Patrick Hart. "Velocity and Amplitude Structures on Seismic-Reflection Profiles: Possible Massive Gas-Hydrate Deposits and Underlying Gas Accumulations in the Bering Sea Basin." In David G. Howell, ed., *The Future of Energy Gases.* U.S. Geological Survey Professional Paper 1570. Washington, D.C.: U.S. Government Printing Office, 1993.

RELATED ARTICLES
Continental Margin; Deep-Sea Sediment; Diapir; Upwelling

Gastropoda

As a group, gastropods are probably the most familiar members of the phylum Mollusca: the snails, slugs, and their relatives. With approximately 40,000 or more living species and 15,000 fossil forms, gastropods comprise the largest, most diverse, and most successful molluscan class. The gastropod fossil record extends unbroken from the early Cambrian Period to the present, and during this interval gastropods have exhibited extensive adaptive radiation. Gastropods inhabit fresh water and the oceans (where representatives can be found both on the seafloor and in the water column and from the intertidal to great depth). In addition, gastropods are the only terrestrial mollusks.

General Features

The class Gastropoda comprises an extremely diverse group of organisms, and it is important to note that most generalizations about the class have many exceptions. Nevertheless, there are some "typical" gastropod features. In general, gastropods have a distinct head, simple eyes, and one or two pairs of sensory tentacles. Most species have a flat muscular foot for creeping along the substrate, but the foot is modified in species that swim or burrow. Gastropods have at most one pair of gills; in some species one or both gills are lost. The majority of gastropods also have a single unchambered shell, which may be uncoiled and symmetrical or symmetrically or asymmetrically coiled, although many species exist in which the shell is reduced (e.g., heteropods) or completely absent (e.g., nudibranchs). Usually consisting of a thin organic outer layer (the periostracum) and two to three calcareous layers, the gastropod shell evolved from being merely a shield to becoming a protective space into which the animal can withdraw. Some species can close the shell's opening with a structure called an *operculum*. The most familiar gastropod shell shape is that of a single conical clockwise spiral (dextral coiling). The shells of some species, however, coil counterclockwise (sinistral coiling). Gastropod shells range in size from microscopic to longer than 70 centimeters (27.6 inches). Shells can be long and slender, short and squat, or flattened. Some shells have a low conical shape with no visible coiling (e.g., limpets). Other gastropods produce a shell that resembles a wormlike tube (e.g., vermetids), and in still others the shell is not visible, because the mantle (the fleshy, outer dorsal body wall) covers it.

The most unique characteristic of gastropods is that they undergo torsion during embryonic development. Torsion is the process in which the visceral mass and mantle rotate counterclockwise by as much as 180 degrees relative to the head–foot. Torsion usually occurs during the late veliger larval stage, and it is not synonymous with coiling of the shell (they are two separate events). Torsion results in a twisted body sitting atop an untwisted foot, and it allows the head to be withdrawn into the shell before the foot. Generally, the process places the anus and mantle cavity above the head, forces the gut into a U-shape, and twists the nerve cords into a figure eight. All gastropods undergo torsion during development, but as adults some groups (e.g., the opisthobranchs) untwist (detort) to various degrees. As a result of torsion, most gastropods are asymmetrical and have a single mantle cavity on the left side of the body; usually, the gill (for respiration), atrium (heart), and nephridium (for excretion) on the right side are reduced or lost.

Gastropods have only one gonad that is usually at the upper end of the visceral mass. Some gastropods have separate sexes, whereas others are hermaphroditic (either simultaneous or sequential). Often, copulation (internal fertilization) is required to fertilize eggs. Some species produce egg capsules or egg cases, whereas others spawn into the seawater. Development can be direct (no larval stage), mixed, or indirect. Species with indirect development produce a free-swimming trochophore larva that in many species is followed by a more highly developed veliger larval stage.

Most gastropod species have a well-developed radula for feeding (a radula is a rasping tongue-like ribbon of chitinous teeth). The exact structure of the radula varies among groups depending on diet (e.g., members of the three Prosobranch orders have different types of radulae). As a group, gastropods display an enormous diversity in feeding strategies. Although many gastropods are herbivores (e.g., garden snails eat plants and many marine snails eat algae), many others are carnivores, scavengers, parasites, suspension feeders, and deposit feeders. For example, some species are carnivores and bore into the shells of other invertebrates using mechanical and chemical action. Cone snails use poison-injecting teeth (a modified radula) at the end of a long proboscis to kill fish and invertebrates; the poison of some species can kill a human. Some sacoglossans suck the chloroplasts out of algal cells, transport them to their dorsal surface, and benefit from the products of photosynthesis. Some nudibranch species eat cnidarians and then store and use unfired nematocysts (stinging cells) for defense. Of the few pelagic gastropods, the heteropods are planktonic predators, whereas the shelled pteropods suspension feed using a mucous net and the shell-less pteropods are carnivores. Several prosobranch snails and vermetids (tube builders) also suspension feed.

Taxonomic Diversity

The class Gastropoda is extremely diverse and comprises numerous orders, families, genera, and species. The most common classification scheme groups gastropods into three subclasses: the Prosobranchia (e.g., shelled marine snails), the Opisthobranchia (e.g., sea hares and nudibranchs), and the Pulmonata (e.g., land snails and slugs). The latter two groups evolved from the prosobranchs.

Subclass Prosobranchia

The subclass Prosobranchia comprises the majority of gastropods. Many prosobranchs are marine, but freshwater and terrestrial representatives are known. Prosobranchs generally have a flat foot, respire via one or two gills, display obvious torsion, and have tentacles and eyes. The prosobranch nervous system is shaped like a figure eight. The prosobranch shell in most species is spirally coiled, although some species have cap-shaped (e.g., limpets) or tubular shells. Typically, prosobranchs have an operculum. Most prosobranchs have a radula and it varies in structure from order to order.

Prosobranchs are subdivided into three orders. The most primitive group, the Archaeogastropoda, contains approximately 3000, mainly marine species in 26 families and includes abalones, keyhole limpets, true limpets, top shells, and turban snails. Archaeogastropods are found primarily in rocky marine habitats. The order Mesogastropoda includes approximately 10,000 species in about 100 families. Mesogastropods inhabit marine, freshwater, and terrestrial environments. This group includes cap limpets, conchs, cowries, horn shells, horse hoof limpets, moon snails, periwinkles, slipper shells, turret shells, and worm gastropods (vermetids). Mesogastropoda also includes some groups modified for pelagic life such as the heteropods and the janthinids, and some modified for parasitic life such as eulimids. Approximately 24 families comprise the order Neogastropoda, most of which are carnivores. Auger shells, cone shells, dove shells, harp shells, olive shells, tulip shells, and whelks are all Neogastropods.

Subclass Opisthobranchia

Most opisthobranchs are marine and benthic, although a few freshwater species are known. The Opisthobranchs include the bottom-dwelling sea hares and nudibranchs and the pelagic pteropods and planktonic sea slugs. Opisthobranchs exhibit detorsion, and many species display secondary bilateral symmetry as adults. They often have a reduced or absent shell and usually lack an operculum. Gills and mantle cavity are often reduced or absent as well. Most opisthobranchs also have two pairs of tentacles. Opisthobranchs are hermaphroditic. Some opisthobranch are brightly colored and highly ornamented, and many produce bad-tasting chemicals as a defense against predation. Opisthobranchs encompass at least nine orders and more than 100 families.

Subclass Pulmonata

The last gastropod subclass, Pulmonata, includes terrestrial snails and slugs as well as some freshwater forms and a few marine species. Pulmonates lack gills, and their mantle cavity is modified into a lung. Most species produce a coiled shell (although a shell is reduced or absent in some groups) and all pulmonates lack an operculum. The pulmonate body is detorted to various degrees. Pulmonates are hermaphroditic and exhibit direct development (except for marine species). Three orders comprise the subclass Pulmonata. Members of the Archaeopulmonata have a spirally coiled shell, lack an operculum, and are found mainly in littoral habitats. The Basommatophora usually have a spirally coiled shell without an operculum; they inhabit fresh water and the intertidal. Over 15,000 described terrestrial species comprise the order Stylommatophora; when a shell is present, it usually is spirally coiled.

Lynn L. Lauerman

FURTHER READING

Brusca, Richard C., and Gary J. Brusca. *Invertebrates.* Sunderland, Mass.: Sinauer, 1990.

Barnes, Robert. *Invertebrate Zoology.* Philadelphia: Saunders, 1963; 6th ed., by Edward Ruppert, Fort Worth, Texas: Saunders, 1994.

Hughes, Roger N. A. *Functional Biology of Marine Gastropods.* Baltimore: Johns Hopkins University Press, 1986.

Lalli, Carol M., and Ronald W. Gilmer. *Pelagic Snails: The Biology of Holoplanktonic Gastropod Mollusks.* Stanford, Calif.: Stanford University Press, 1989.

Solem, George Alan. *The Shell Makers: Introducing Mollusks.* New York: Wiley, 1974.

RELATED ARTICLES
Heteropoda; Mollusca; Pteropoda

Gastrotricha

Gastrotricha is a small phylum of multicellular animals, most of which range in size from 0.1 to 2.0 millimeters (less than 0.08 inch), with a mean length of perhaps 0.5 millimeter (0.02 inch), and a few species reaching 3 or 4 millimeters (less than 0.2 inch) in length. They may be bottle-shaped, rectangular, or strap-shaped. Gastrotrichs can live wherever there is sufficient moisture and a food supply of bacteria, flagellates, or small diatoms. They are fed upon, in turn, by larger protozoans, rotifers, nematodes, copepods, and whichever immature macrofauna may temporarily live in their habitat. Typically, gastrotrichs glide in close contact with their substratum by means of cilia that are located in ventral tracts or patches, although a few can move freely in the water column using elongate lateral spines for a kind of jerky swimming motion. All have a digestive tract that consists of a mouth, a triradiate sucking pharynx, an intestine that serves for both digestion and absorption of food into the body, and a ventral anus. Primitively, each individual has both sexes, although they cross-fertilize among individuals; many species, especially the freshwater dwellers, have also taken to parthenogenesis, a form of asexual reproduction. Their life span may be several months for the marine dwellers or at most a month for the freshwater forms. Their substratum is beach sand, stream gravel, or surface detritus lying on the bottom of a lake or pond; thus they can be marine, estuarine, or freshwater, with different species having their own salinity, oxygen, and temperature preferences. Depth in the lake or sea is not as important as these other factors. Indeed, some live in ghost-crab burrows, on barnacles, in tree holes, on air plants, or amid mosses moistened by waterfalls, and some inhabit aquarium filters.

There are about 600 described species, more or less evenly divided between the marine and freshwater realms, although both the greatest

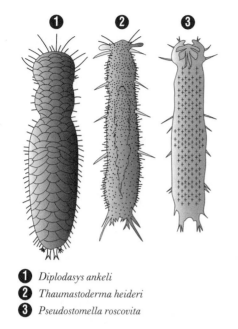

1 *Diplodasys ankeli*
2 *Thaumastoderma heideri*
3 *Pseudostomella roscovita*

Three examples of gastrotrichs.

morphological diversity and the area of research activity is in the marine realm. The phylum is divided into two orders, the Macrodasyida, which is mainly marine–estuarine, and the Chaetonotida, which is marine, estuarine, and freshwater. Although there is no fossil record for this group, its fine-structural anatomy suggests that stem gastrotrichs are among the most primitive of metazoans, probably dating back to the Cambrian Epoch, some 600 million years ago. Ecologically, where they show a high species diversity, we can infer a healthy environment; where diversity is reduced, we look for possible causes: a stressful natural environment, an environment that is eutrophic (too rich in organics), or one that is permeated with toxic pollutants (petrochemicals, pesticides, or mine acids).

William D. Hummon

FURTHER READING

Barnes, Robert. *Invertebrate Zoology.* Philadelphia: W. B. Saunders, 1963; 6th ed., by Edward Ruppert, Fort Worth, Texas: Saunders College Publishing, 1994.

Hummon, W. D. "Gastrotricha." In Sybil P. Parker, ed., *Synopsis and Classification of Living Organisms.* New York: McGraw-Hill, 1982; pp. 857–863.

Ruppert, E. E. "Gastrotricha." In Robert P. Higgins and Hjalmar Thiel, eds., *Introduction to the Study of Meiofauna.* Washington, D.C.: Smithsonian Institution Press, 1988; pp. 302–311.

Schwank, P. "Gastrotricha." In Jurgen Schwoerbel and Peter Zwick, eds., *Süsswasserfauna von Mitteleuropa,* Band 3. Stuttgart: Gustav Fischer Verlag, 1990; pp. 1–152.

Strayer, D., and W. D. Hummon "Gastrotricha." In James H. Thorp and Alan B. Covich, eds., *Ecology and Classification of North American Invertebrates.* San Diego: Academic Press, 1991; 2nd ed., 2001; pp. 181–194.

RELATED ARTICLES
Meiofauna; Nematoda; Rotifera

Geochronology

Geochronology is the study of time relationships in Earth's history. Geochronology places events either in a relative framework (one event occurred after another) or in an absolute framework, denominated in years before the present. Relative dating is accomplished primarily through stratigraphic methods, whereas absolute dating methods are based principally on the transformation of one substance into another at a known rate.

Relative Dating

Several principles guide interpretation of the relative order of events, including: superposition, cross-cutting relationships, inclusion, and correlation of time-varying features. The principle of superposition posits that undisturbed rock strata have been deposited successively, one on top of the other. Therefore, older strata must be on the bottom of the pile. There are many examples where older rocks actually lie above younger rocks. In these cases, some disturbance, for example, faulting or folding, has cut across the originally undisturbed strata. Thus, in a cross-cutting relationship, a feature that cuts across a rock unit, like a fault, or a dike, or an erosional surface, must have been created after the formation of the rock unit that is cut. With inclusion, if one rock unit has been encased in another (e.g., xenoliths engulfed by an intruding magma, or rock fragments deposited in a debris flow) the event of encasement must postdate the included material. The relative succession of several kinds of time-denominated features can be used to establish the time equivalence of rock units. These include fossils of short-lived taxa, remnant magnetization from polarity changes in Earth's magnetic field, and the oxygen-isotopic composition of fossils or chemical sedimentary rocks that reflect changing seawater composition as ice caps grow and shrink due to periodic variations in Earth's orbit around the Sun. These features are the basis for biostratigraphic, magnetostratigraphic, and climatostratigraphic correlation, respectively. If one rock unit contains the same fossil association, displays the same pattern of magnetic polarity reversal, or exhibits the same sequence of isotopic-composition variation as another, the two units may each be considered to have formed during the same interval of Earth's history when the relevant events were occurring, and thus be the same age.

Absolute Dating

CONCEPTUAL MODEL

Many methods for determining the time of events in Earth's history rely on the transformation of one substance to another. Conceptually, all these methods are analogous to an hourglass. There is a parent material, which is equivalent to the sand in the upper chamber of the hourglass. There is a daughter product, which is equivalent to the sand in the lower chamber of the hourglass. The process of transformation is equivalent to the sand falling through the hole between the two chambers. The material to be dated, (e.g., a mineral grain or piece of organic material) is the equivalent of the glass vessel. The event to be dated is the moment when the hourglass became closed with the parent inside the upper chamber

(e.g., when a mineral grain crystallized from a magma) so that the parent-element atoms were locked into the crystal lattice. This point is known as the *blocking temperature* of the mineral with respect to the particular element.

RADIOMETRIC DATING

Radiometric dating is based on the transformation of an unstable parent isotope into a stable daughter isotope. Isotopes are different species of an element that differ only in the number of neutrons in the nucleus. Because neutrons do not affect the number of electrons in the atom, different isotopes of the same element behave exactly the same chemically. However, the differing number of neutrons makes some isotopes radioactive; they fall apart spontaneously to form a new element, plus energy, plus or minus free subatomic particles. The transformation takes place at a known rate, so that the ratio of parent to daughter, or the ratio of parent and/or daughter to some invariant component of the system, is proportional to the time since the system became closed. The fraction of parent remaining at time t is expressed as $A_t/A_0 = e^{-\lambda t}$, where A_t is the amount of parent remaining at time t, A_0 is the amount of parent originally present, and ? is the decay constant. The amount of time needed to reduce the amount of parent to one-half its original value is known as the *half-life*; this amount of time is constant no matter what the starting quantity of parent. Some common systems of parent/daughter isotopes used in radiometric dating, their half-lives, and their decay constants are summarized in the accompanying table. As a practical matter, an isotopic system is not useful for dating events that are more than 10 or 11 half-lives old (2^{10} or 2^{11}), because not enough of the parent is left to detect. For this reason, carbon-14 dating is not useful for material older than about 70,000 years. On the other hand, an isotopic system is also not useful to date events that occurred less than 0.5 percent of the half-life (2^{-8} or 2^{-9}), because not enough of the parent has decayed for the difference to be noticeable. For this reason, potassium–argon dating is not used for very recent material.

In most cases it is not possible to determine the original amount of parent (the amount of sand in the upper chamber of the hourglass), nor to know if some daughter product was initially incorporated into the material (starting the hourglass with some sand already in the lower chamber). It is also rarely known if some parent or daughter product has been removed from the system (a leaky hourglass)—for example, by heating the mineral to a temperature at which the crystal lattice does not bind either the parent or the daughter. These difficulties are overcome by the isochron method, which determines ratios of the parent and daughter to a third isotope. The third isotope is a stable isotope of the daughter element not produced by radioactive decay. For example, age determinations using the rubium–strontium system are based on the ratios $^{87}Sr/^{86}Sr$ and $^{87}Rb/^{86}Sr$.

The isochron method is equivalent to having two different colors of sand in the hourglass: one color that can pass between the chambers and one that cannot. In this case the amount of sand in each chamber is unimportant. Parent material will become less abundant with respect to the stable component over time, and daughter material will become more abundant; these relationships are expressed in the ratios rather than in absolute amounts. The algebraic characteristics of the three-component system allow inferences about the initial content of daughter material in the system and about the "leakiness" of the system.

Other Dating Methods

Although radioactive decay is the basis for many age-dating techniques and for the techniques that reach farthest back into Earth's history, there are many other techniques that fit the same hourglass conceptual model. Three of these methods are accumulation of cosmogenic nuclides in surface materials, accumulation of

ISOTOPIC SYSTEMS USED IN GEOCHRONOLOGY

Parent isotope (radioactive)	Daughter isotope (stable)	Half-life (billions of years)	Decay constant (10^{-11} per year)
^{14}C	^{14}N	5.37×10^{-6} (5370 years)	
^{40}K	^{40}Ar	1.25	5.81
^{87}Rb	^{87}Sr	48.8	1.42
^{147}Sm	^{143}Nd	106.0	0.654
^{176}Lu	^{176}Hf	35.9	1.93
^{187}Re	^{187}Os	43.0	1.612
^{232}Th	^{208}Pb	14.0	4.948
^{235}U	^{207}Pb	0.704	98.485
^{238}U	^{206}Pb	4.47	15.5125

(Adapted from Dalrymple, 1991, Table 3.1)

fission tracks in uranium-bearing minerals and glasses, and racemization of amino acids in fossilized organic material. These methods are most useful for geologically young materials, typically less than 1 million years old.

Cosmogenic nuclides are created when cosmic rays strike atoms in Earth-surface materials and cause them to spall off some subatomic particles. The new elements produced by spallation are typical for Earth materials, but the particular isotopes are produced only by cosmogenesis. Cosmogenic nuclides that are useful in geochronology include ^{36}Cl (from ^{39}K and ^{40}Ca), ^{10}Be (from ^{16}O), ^{26}Al (from ^{28}Si), and ^{3}He (from ^{40}Ca, ^{7}Li, ^{58}Ni, ^{64}Zn, ^{40}K). The concentration of cosmogenic nuclides depends on the concentration of the target atom and on the intensity and duration of bombardment by cosmic rays. Intensity and duration of bombardment are determined by how close the material is to Earth's surface and for how long.

Fission tracks are produced in uranium-bearing minerals when ^{238}U splits into two highly charged nuclei of subequal atomic mass. This reaction occurs with a fixed probability and thus at a fixed rate. The two nuclei repel each other and plow through the crystal lattice of the host mineral, shattering atomic bonds as they go. The fission tracks are less than 20 micrometers (about 0.8 thousandth of an inch) long and less than 10 nanometers (0.4 millionth of an inch) in diameter, but the damaged crystal lattice around them can easily be dissolved (e.g., by hydrofluoric acid) to a dimension that can be seen with a standard light microscope. The damage to the crystal lattice caused by the fission tracks can be "healed" if the mineral is heated above a certain level, known as the *annealing temperature*. The number of fission tracks per volume of mineral increases steadily as a function of the time that has passed since the mineral last cooled below the annealing temperature.

Most of the amino acids in animal proteins occur as asymmetric molecules, in which four different side chains are bonded to a central carbon. The same side chains can be arranged in two geometrical configurations that are mirror images of each other. The mirror images are arbitrarily named "left" (L) and "right" (D for dextral). In living material, most amino acids are virtually 100 percent L (D:L = 0). After death, the amino acids gradually alter to a mixture of D and L forms with an equilibrium D:L ~ 1. The amount of time needed to reach equilibrium depends strongly on temperature and varies from one biological material to another; the time may range from thousands to millions of years.

W. A. Heins

FURTHER READING

Condie, K. C., and R. E. Sloan. *Origin and Evolution of Earth: Principles of Historical Geology.* Upper Saddle River, N.J.: Prentice Hall, 1998; chapt. 1.

Dalrymple, G. B. *The Age of the Earth.* Stanford, Calif.: Stanford University Press, 1991.

Faul, H. *Ages of Rocks, Planets, and Stars.* New York: McGraw-Hill, 1966.

Gradstein, F. M., and G. J. van der Zwaan, eds. "Ordering the Fossil Record; Challenges in Stratigraphy and Paleontology; Selected Papers from a Symposium Held in Honour of the 75th Birthday of Cor Drooger." *Earth-Science Reviews,* Vol. 46, No. 1/4 (1999).

Noller, J. S., J. M. Sowers, and W. R. Lettis, eds. "Quaternary Geochronology, Methods and Applications." *American Geophysical Union Reference Shelf,* Vol. 4 (2000).

York, D., and R. M. Farquhar. *The Earth's Age and Geochronology.* Oxford: Pergamon Press, 1972.

RELATED ARTICLES
Geologic Time; Radiometric Dating

Geologic Time

Geologic time begins with the formation of Earth. Earth coalesced from a cloud of dust and gas during the formation of our solar system, over a period of about 300 million years. This time is bracketed by 4.54 billion years, when the radiogenic lead isotopes ^{206}Pb and ^{207}Pb began to accumulate in an Earth system isolated from the rest of the solar system, and about 4.2 billion years, when Earth was sufficiently cool and stable to block the escape of heavy noble gases such as xenon from the solid Earth. During this span of time, Earth heated up, due to the decay of radioactive elements and from the conversion of kinetic energy in the constituent dust particles to thermal energy as they collided. Earth evolved from an undifferentiated mass of cosmic dust to a structured planet with a core, mantle, and crust as this heat partially melted Earth, allowing denser materials to migrate to the center of gravity and lighter materials to float to the surface. The isolation of Earth from the common lead reservoir, the segregation of the core, or the closure of Earth to loss of heavy noble gases could all be considered appropriate events for the start of geologic time. Most geologists consider the oldest date, when Earth and primitive meteorites were physically isolated from the rest of the solar system with respect to transfers of lead, as the beginning of geologic time.

Subdivisions of Geologic Time

The vast span of geologic time is broken into smaller units for convenience (see figure). The geologic time scale is based on three ideas. First, Earth has changed over time as a function of time-dependent processes. Second, the processes have left evidence of their operation within Earth materials that are visible today. Third, we can work out a discrete sequence of events based on the evidence preserved. Each of the units of geologic time, at every scale, is delineated by significant events in Earth history of short duration but widespread geographic effect. Boundaries between units that span a lot of time are defined by profound events, whereas successively shorter time divisions are marked by progressively more subtle events.

The units that cover the most time are eons. There are two eons, the Cryptozoic and the Phanerozoic. The names refer to "hidden life" and "visible life," respectively; the time boundary between them at 570 million years before the present coincides approximately with the evolution of macroscopic, complex organisms with hard body parts. The Cryptozoic traditionally is called the Precambrian, because it comes before the Cambrian Period.

Eons are divided into eras. The eras of the Phanerozoic are the Paleozoic, the Mesozoic, and the Cenozoic, referring respectively to "early," "middle," and "recent" life; the time boundaries between these eras coincide approximately with mass extinctions that dramatically altered the ecological balance of the planet and opened up environments for dramatically different kinds and associations of organisms. Precambrian era names are not well disseminated among the geologic community. Most geologists who do not work on questions related to the Precambrian recognize two sub-eons, the Archean and the Proterozoic, with the time boundary between them at approximately 2.5 billion years before the present, at about the time that the crust of Earth had accumulated to a sufficient thickness and composition to exhibit plate-tectonic motions similar to those observed today. Precambrian time-unit names generally receive less publicity than their

Phanerozoic counterparts because the direct evidence of events during the Precambrian is quite sparse compared to evidence for Phanerozoic events. Furthermore, the evidence that does exist often has been modified extensively by subsequent events, so that unraveling the sequence of Precambrian events is a daunting task.

Eras are divided into periods. Period names typically are based on the name of the region where rocks of the appropriate age were first studied. For example, the Permian Period is the time when rocks that are exposed around the town of Perm, in the Ural Mountains of Russia, were formed, whereas the Jurassic Period is the time when rocks that are exposed in the Jura Mountains on the border between France and Switzerland were formed.

Periods are divided into epochs. Epochs may be named for places (e.g., Ludlow, which is a town in England as well as an epoch of the Silurian Period), for rock types that are typical of the period (e.g., the Zechstein of the Permian Period), or for biologic phenomena (e.g., the Paleocene, Eocene, Oligocene, and Miocene epochs of the Tertiary Period, which originally denoted strata in Italy that contained marine fossils progressively more similar to modern forms). Geologists from all over the world almost universally agree about period names in the Phanerozoic, generally agree about the epoch names within those periods, and subscribe to a common process for determining the time points associated with boundaries among them.

Epochs are divided into stages. Most stages are named after places, but there are many competing stage names and competing definitions of stage boundaries. Many regions have their own local names and definitions. Although some international consensus may occasionally be reached for different parts of the time scale, as in the figure, local workers often use stages that are well defined and agreed upon only within a specific geographic context.

GEOLOGIC TIME

Eon	Era	Period	Epoch	Stage	Stage Start (Ma*)
Phanerozoic	Cenozoic (Cz)	Quaternary *Note 1*	Holocene		0.01
			Pleistocene		1.64
	Tertiary	Neogene (Ng)	Pliocene (Pli)	Piacenzian	3.4
				Zanclian	5.2
			Miocene (Mio)	Messinian	6.7
				Tortonian	10.4
				Serravallian	14.2
				Langhian	16.3
				Burdigalian	21.5
				Aquitanian	23.3
		Paleogene (Pg)	Oligocene (Oli)	Chattian	29.3
				Rupelian	35.4
			Eocene (Eoc)	Priabonian	38.6
				Bartonian	42.1
				Lutetian	50.0
				Ypresian	56.5
			Paleocene (Pal)	Thanetian	60.5
				Danian	65.0
	Mesozoic (Mz)	Cretaceous	Gulf (Gul) / Sennonian (Sen)	Maastrichtian	71.3
				Campanian	83.5
				Santonian	85.8
				Coniacian	89.9
			Gallic (Gal)	Turonian	93.5
				Cenomanian	98.9
				Albian	112.2
				Aptian	121.0
			K_1 / Neocomian (Neo)	Barremian	127.0
				Hauterivian	132.0
				Valanginian	137.0
				Berriasian	144.2
		Jurassic	Malm	Tithonian	150.7
				Kimmeridgian	154.1
				Oxfordian	159.4
			Dogger	Callovian	164.4
				Bathonian	169.2
				Bajocian	176.5
				Aalenian	180.1
			Lias	Toarcian	189.6
				Pliensbachian	195.3
				Sinemurian	201.9
				Hettangian	205.7
		Triassic	Late	Rhaetian	209.6
				Norian	220.7
				Carnian	227.4
			Middle	Ladinian	234.3
				Anisian	241.7
			Scythian (or Early)	Spathian	241.9
				Nammalian	243.4
				Griesbachian	247.5

Eon	Era	Period	Epoch	Stage	Stage Start (Ma*)
Phanerozoic	Paleozoic (Pz)	Permian	Zechstein / Loping-ian	Changxingian	248.2
				Longtanian	250.0
			Guadelupian	Capitanian	252.5
				Wordian	255.0
				Ufimian	256.1
			Rotliegendes	Kingurian	259.7
				Artinskian	268.8
				Sakmarian	281.5
				Asselian	290.0
		Carboniferous / Pennsylvanian	Gzelian	Noginskian	293.6
				Klazminskian	295.1
			Kasimovian	Dorogomilovskian	298.3
				Chamovnicheskian	299.9
				Krevyakinskian	303.0
			Moscovian	Myachkovskian	305.0
				Podolskian	307.1
				Kashirskian	309.2
				Vereiskian	311.3
			Bashkirian	Melekesskian	313.4
				Cheremshanskian	318.3
				Yeadonian	320.6
				Marsdenian	321.5
				Kinderscoutian	322.8
		Mississippian	Sherpukov-ian	Alportian	325.6
				Chokierian	328.3
				Arnsbergian	331.1
				Pendleian	332.9
			Visean	Brigantian	336.0
				Asbian	339.4
				Holkerian	342.8
				Arundian	345.0
				Chadian	349.5
			Tournais-ian	Ivorian	353.8
				Hastarian	362.5
		Devonian	Late	Famennian	367.0
				Frasnian	377.4
			Middle	Givetian	380.8
				Eifelian	386.0
			Early	Emsian	390.4
				Pragian	396.3
				Lochkovian	408.5
		Silurian	Pridoli	*Note 2*	410.7
			Ludlow	Ludfordian	415.1
				Gorstian	424.0
			Wenlock	Gleedonian	425.4
				Whitwellian	426.1
				Sheinwoodian	430.4
			Llandovery	Telychian	432.6
				Aeronian	436.9
				Rhuddanian	439.0

GEOLOGIC TIME

Eon	Era	Period	Epoch	Stage	Stage Start (Ma*)
Phanerozoic	Paleozoic (Pz)	Ordovician	Ashgill	Hirnantian	439.9
				Rawtheyan	440.1
				Cautleyan	440.6
				Pusgillian	443.1
			Bala / Caradoc	Onnian	444.0
				Actonian	444.5
				Marshbrookian	447.1
				Longvillian	449.7
				Soudleyan	457.5
				Harnagian	462.3
				Costonian	463.9
			Dyfed / Llandeilo	Late	465.4
				Mid	467.0
				Early	468.6
			Llanvirn	Late	472.7
				Early	476.1
			Canadian / Arenig	Late (boundary defined, but not dated) Early	493.0
			Tremadoc	Note 2	510.0
		Cambrian	Merioneth	Dolgellian	514.1
				Maentwrogian	517.2
			St. David's	Menevian	530.2
				Solvan	536.0
			Caerfi	Lenian	554.0
				Atdabanian	560.0
				Tommotian	570.0
Cryptozoic	Proterozoic	Sinian	Vendian / Ediacara	Poundian	580
				Wonokan	590
			Varanger	Mortensnes	600
				Smalfjord	610
		Sturtian			800
		Riphean	Kudash + Karatau (Late Riphean)		1050
			Yurmatin (Middle Riphean)		1350
			Burzyan (Early Riphean)		1650
		Animikean			2200
		Huronian			2450
		Randian			2800
		Swazian			3500
	Archean	Isuan			3800
		Hadean	Early Imbrian		3850
			Nectarian		3950
			Basin Groups 1-9		4150
			Cryptic		4560

Note 1: There is no generally accepted Period name for the most recent part of the Cenozoic. "Anthrogene" is commonly used in the former Soviet sphere; "Pleistogene" has also been proposed. "Quaternary" and "Tertiary" are archaic, although still widely used, names. They are subdivisions of the Cenozoic Era, and so are reported here as "sub-eras"; they are not Periods. The Quaternary traditionally encompasses the Holocene and Pleistocene epochs, whereas the Tertiary includes the Pliocene through Paleocene epochs.

Note 2: There are no widely accepted stage names within the Pridoli and Tremadoc epochs.

*Ma, million years ago.

SOURCES: *Geologic Ages of Earth History*. Jeff Poling. 1995; 1997. <http://www.dinosauria.com/dml/dmlf.htm>.

Gradstein, F. M., F. P. Agterberg, J. G. Ogg, J. Hardenbol, P. van Veen, J. Thierry, and Z. Huang. *A Triassic, Jurassic and Cretaceous Time Scale*. In W. A. Berggren, D. V. Kent, M.-P. Aubry, and J. Hardenbol, eds., *Geochronology, Time Scales, and Global Stratigraphic Correlation*. SEPM Special Publication No. 54., c. 1995, pp. 95–126.

Harland, W. Brian, Richard Armstrong, Allan Cox, Craig Lorraine, Alan Smith, and David Smith. *A Geologic Time Scale, 1989*. New York: Cambridge University Press, 1990.

Establishing and Dating Time-Unit Boundaries

HISTORICAL DEVELOPMENT

From the late eighteenth through the nineteenth century, when most of the era and period names of the Phanerozoic were coined, geologists were concerned primarily with *lithostratigraphy*, the sequence in which layered rocks were formed. Their focus was on defining, classifying, and ordering the rocks, which were described as a system, rather than explicitly dividing up geologic time into periods. For example, the Triassic System was first named by Friedrich von Alberti (1795–1878) in 1834, based on three formations of sedimentary rocks found in central Europe, which contained a consistent group of fossils that were different from fossils in Permian strata below and from fossils in Jurassic strata above. Although the change in fossil content from the Permian to the Triassic to the Jurassic implied time-dependent processes, the actual definition of the system was based on the rocks that

19

contained the evidence rather than on the processes that created the evidence.

Those early geologists recognized that often the packages of rocks they described as belonging to the same system were bounded by profound *unconformities*, erosional surfaces representing rocks that have been removed, and thus missing as evidence for geologic time. They explicitly placed their boundaries into parts of geologic time that could not be precisely defined. This was a useful practice for local work, but it provided a problematic framework for global comparison, since erosion at one place (that produces an unconformity) delivers sediment for deposition somewhere else, so that a boundary that falls into a prominent gap in the lithostratigraphic column in one part of the world may correspond to an unremarkable level in the column of another part of the world where evidence of distinctive events is indiscernible. This fundamental problem hampered the development of a globally applicable lithostratigraphic column and led to a plethora of competing system names, many of which fell into disuse. The pioneering geologists had no clear idea about the absolute age of Earth nor of the length of time represented by the rocks of their various systems, because they lacked the tools of modern geochronology. They were, however, very concerned with and very able to discriminate the relative order of events in geologic time and to place all the rocks of the world into sequential order.

MODERN PRACTICE

Today, the names and relative order of the eras, periods, and epochs have largely been handed down from the pioneering geologists of the eighteenth and nineteenth centuries, but the practice for defining the boundaries among them has been regularized under the auspices of the International Commission on Stratigraphy (ICS) and the International Geologic Correlation Programme (IGCP). These bodies establish working groups for each boundary. Working

groups review and select candidates for a Global Stratotype Section and Point (GSSP) for each boundary. They look for a succession of strata somewhere in the world that is continuous across the boundary, which contains clear evidence of a change at the boundary, and which contains features that are datable by as many techniques of geochronology as possible to aid in recognition of the time point in other sequences around the world. Each GSSP is a kind of "golden spike" against which other sequences can be judged. Not all boundaries have an agreed-upon GSSP, and GSSPs are subject to revision as more evidence accumulates. Thus, there will never be a "final" geologic time scale but, rather, one that is constantly refined.

W. A. Heins

FURTHER READING
Dalrymple, G. Brent. *The Age of the Earth*. Stanford, Calif.: Stanford University Press, 1991.
Faul, Henry, and Carol Faul. *It Began with a Stone: A History of Geology from the Stone Age to the Age of Plate Tectonics*. New York: Wiley, 1983.
Gradstein, F. M., and G. J. van der Zwaan, eds. "Ordering the Fossil Record: Challenges in Stratigraphy and Paleontology; Selected Papers from a Symposium Held in Honour of the 75th Birthday of Cor Drooger." *Earth-Science Reviews*, Vol. 46, No. 1/4 (1999).
Harland, W. B., Richard L. Armstrong, Allan V. Cox, Lorraine E. Craig, Alan G. Smith, and David G. Smith. *A Geologic Time Scale, 1989*. Cambridge and New York: Cambridge University Press, 1990.

RELATED ARTICLES
Geochronology; Mass Extinction

Geostationary Operational Environmental Satellite

The geostationary operational environmental satellites (GOES) are a series of U.S. meteorological and remote sensing satellites that orbit and monitor Earth from a height of nearly 36,000 kilometers (22,370 miles).

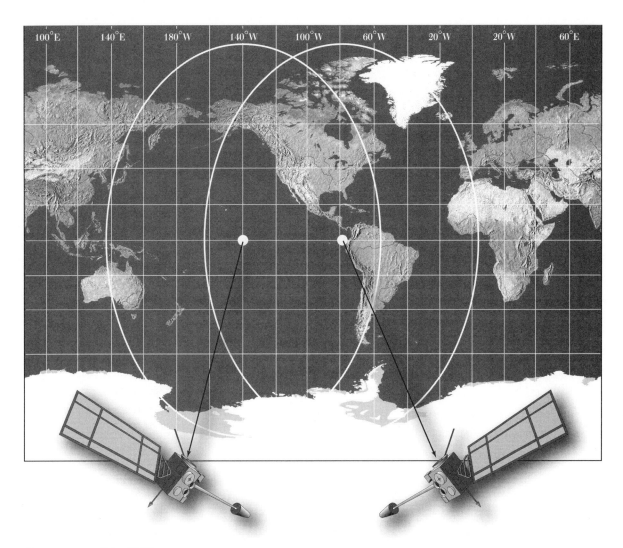

Coverage area of the GOES system.

The GOES program was launched by the U.S. National Aeronautics and Space Administration in the 1970s after a test program in the late 1960s. The satellites occupy a special geostationary or synchronous orbit. The further the distance at which a satellite orbits Earth, the longer it takes to circle the planet. At around 35,800 kilometers (22,245 miles) up, it takes precisely 23 hours 56 minutes. A satellite above the equator will therefore orbit Earth at precisely the same rate as the ground below it spins, so it "hangs" permanently above the same spot on the surface and has a permanent view of one hemisphere of the planet.

The first satellites in the program were designed as meteorological satellites, but from 1975 onward, GOES missions were equipped to collect a far wider range of data. Two GOES satellites can monitor the entire North American continent and its surrounding waters (Earth's curvature distorts a single satellite's view of the planet so that it cannot monitor a complete hemisphere), but seven GOES missions were launched in total between 1975 and 1987 in order to keep at least two fully operational satellites in orbit. From 1990 onward, a new generation of GOES-I-M satellites have replaced the earlier design.

The GOES-I-M satellites are designed to fulfill a wide range of functions. As well as acquiring data from their unique vantage point in orbit, the satellites also act as fixed communication platforms carrying out some tasks similar to a dedicated communications satellite. These include data collected by remote weather stations, or weather buoys far out at sea, which are broadcast as signals to Earth. Also included are data broadcasts relaying incoming data to a ground station and transmissions of weather forecasts and other important information for use by anyone with a suitable receiver.

The main role of GOES-I-M satellites is still acquiring environmental data from space. To this end, each satellite is equipped with an array of instruments. A multispectral imager observes strips of Earth's surface in visible light and at four different infrared wavelengths simultaneously. Imaging at five wavelengths allows the satellite to detect various types of clouds, measure the size of the water droplets within them (and therefore whether the clouds are likely to produce rain), and monitor air and ocean surface temperatures. While the imager is a passive instrument, the sounder is an active one; it fires beams of radiation at 19 different wavelengths into Earth's atmosphere and detects the returning echoes from the surface. The sounder operates in visible light and at 18 radio wavelengths: seven long-wave, five medium-wave, and six short-wave. Normally, all these wavelengths of radiation travel through space at the same speed—the speed of light—but conditions in Earth's atmosphere slow down different wavelengths by different amounts. By emitting these beams simultaneously along the same path through the atmosphere and measuring the delay and intensity of the returning signals, the sounder can reconstruct a wide variety of data including temperature and moisture profiles at different depths in the air and stability or movement of air masses.

Both the imager and sounder use a movable mirror to direct toward the instruments light collected by a telescope. This provides flexible scan control so that the field of view can be adjusted

and the instruments can focus on small areas for long periods of time: for example, monitoring the development of a single storm system.

The final role of the GOES-I-M satellites is to collect data about the "weather" in near-Earth space. Changes in Earth's magnetic field and the solar wind of electrically charged particles from the Sun can affect conditions in the upper atmosphere, creating auroral storms of polar lights and altering the properties of Earth's ionosphere.

Giles Sparrow

FURTHER READING

Burroughs, William James. *Watching the World's Weather.* New York and Cambridge: Cambridge University Press, 1991.
Hill, Janice. *Weather from Above: America's Meteorological Satellites.* Washington, D.C.: Smithsonian Institute Press, 1991.
Kidder, Stanley O., and Thomas H. Vonder Haar. *Satellite Meteorology: An Introduction.* San Diego: Academic Press, 1995.

RELATED ARTICLES
Infrared Radiation

Gibbs, William Francis
1886–1967
Naval Architect and Marine Engineer

As an American naval architect and marine engineer, Gibbs is best known for his creation, the SS *United States*, a liner that broke the transatlantic speed record in 1952. Gibbs designed fast, elegant ships with improved safety features and pioneered efficient ship production methods.

William Francis Gibbs was born in Philadelphia, Pennsylvania, in 1886, son of a financier. Educated at Delancey School, Philadelphia, as a child and teenager Gibbs was fascinated by ships and firefighting. His father was determined that Gibbs have a career in economics, although William harbored the ambition to become an engineer. He gained a degree in economics at Harvard in 1910 and then entered Columbia University to study law; he left in 1913 with both bachelor and master's degrees. Gibbs joined a law firm in 1913, but in 1914 the collision and sinking of a luxury passenger liner, the *Empress of Ireland,* convinced him to follow his true vocation, to become a ship designer and manufacturer.

Gibbs began his career as a self-taught designer and engineer by spending a year researching the shipbuilding industry. Among his conclusions was the belief that the implementation of correctly designed bulkheads and watertight compartments could have prevented the *Empress of Ireland* tragedy, which claimed 1000 lives. William and his brother Frederick, convincing others of their ideas, joined the International Mercantile Marine Company in 1915. By 1919, William Gibbs was chief of construction.

In 1922, the Gibbs brothers received their first commission as a newly established company, Gibbs Brothers, Inc. They converted the captured German liner SS *Vaterland,* used by the United States as a troop carrier in World War I, into an Atlantic luxury passenger liner, the SS *Leviathan.* The quality of the overhaul impressed many potential clients. In terms of appearance, safety, and efficiency, the refurbished vessel was a great improvement on the original. Without the original plans for the ship, the brothers had to make a painstaking analysis of the ship's design, construction, fixtures, and fittings—an exercise that was to yield great dividends later.

Between 1923 and 1927, Gibbs Brothers developed a growing reputation for vessels—new or refurbished—that were safer, faster, and more luxurious than those of their rivals. In 1927 they completed the SS *Malolo,* the fastest liner of its time. A collision during its maiden voyage made a 5-meter (16-foot) gash in its port side but did not sink the ship. This potently demonstrated the effectiveness of the Gibbs multiple-compartment approach. This innovation was to become standard practice within the industry.

In 1929, yacht maker Daniel H. Cox joined Gibbs Brothers to form Gibbs and Cox, Inc. The company diversified to produce a wide range of sea vessels, including small luxury craft as well as freighters, hospital ships, and liners. Incorporating the latest technology and advanced safety features continued to be hallmarks of the Gibbs approach to shipbuilding.

By 1933, William Gibbs was drawn increasingly into work modernizing the U.S. Navy. In the mid-1930s he convinced the navy to adopt high-pressure, high-temperature steam turbines for the propulsion of its destroyers. So efficient were these engines that turbines of similar design were later employed in all larger naval craft, including cruisers, battleships, and aircraft carriers.

In 1941, when the United States entered World War II, William Gibbs was designing many of the navy's vessels. By the end of the war, between 5000 and 6000 ships had been built using working plans drawn up under Gibbs's leadership. These vessels included the Liberty ships, used to carry cargo between North America and Europe. Gibbs spearheaded a manufacturing revolution by having different stages in ship production taking place at different locations. Prior to this, ships were built from start to finish at a single shipyard. Gibbs's streamlining of production, along with design innovations, enabled a Liberty-type ship to be assembled in as short a period as four days. Gibbs served first as controller of shipbuilding for the War Production Board and later as chair of the Combined Shipbuilding Committee of the Combined Chiefs of Staff. By the end of World War II, more than 2000 Liberty ships were in service.

After the war, Gibbs and Cox continued to design and prepare working plans for naval vessels, but the company also returned to the manufacture of commercial passenger and cargo ships. In 1937, Gibbs had designed the SS *America,* of record-breaking size and speed for a U.S.-built merchant ship. Gibbs's long-held ambition was to produce a transatlantic passenger liner of even greater stature.

In 1952, William Gibbs's crowning achievement, the SS *United States,* was launched. This luxury passenger liner was designed over a five-year period and took slightly more than 28 months to build. It incorporated many of the best features that the Gibbs brothers had been developing over 25 years. The vessel was built to naval specifications (enabling its use as a troop transport in wartime if necessary). Welded joints and the use of aluminum alloys reduced its weight to a minimum. Fireproof fabrics and furniture were used in its decoration and fitting. Its propulsion system was the most efficient and high performance of its type. On one 1952 trip across the Atlantic, the SS *United States* averaged 35.05 knots [64.9 kilometers (40.3 miles) per hour], breaking the transatlantic speed record set by the *Queen Mary* 17 years before.

In 1946, William Gibbs was awarded the Society of Naval Architects and Marine Engineers' gold medal for both naval architecture and engineering, the only person ever to have done so. In 1953, Gibbs received the prestigious Franklin Medal of the Franklin Institute. He died in 1967—a man who had shunned publicity but had achieved remarkable breakthroughs in modernizing naval, merchant, and passenger shipbuilding.

Trevor Day

BIOGRAPHY
- William Francis Gibbs.
- Born 24 August 1886 in Philadelphia, Pennsylvania.
- Educated at Delancey School, Philadelphia; Yale University (graduating in economics in 1910); and Columbia University (obtaining M.A. and LL.B. law degrees by 1913).
- In 1913, he began work in a law firm but left in 1914 to become a ship designer and manufacturer.
- Worked with his brother for the International Mercantile Marine Company until 1922, when they began their own shipbuilding business.
- Gibbs Brothers, Inc. (later Gibbs and Cox, Inc.) gained a reputation for building fast, safe, and

efficient ships incorporating the latest technology, and in 1937 built the SS *America,* the biggest and fastest U.S. merchant ship of the period.
- Gibbs was responsible for organizing the rapid construction of Liberty cargo ships during World War II.
- In 1952, his SS *United States* broke the transatlantic speed record for a passenger liner.
- Gibbs died 6 September 1967 in New York.

FURTHER READING
Fabry, J. *Swing Shift: Building the Liberty Ships.* San Francisco: Strawberry Hill Press, 1982.
McMurray, Emily J., ed. *Notable Twentieth-Century Scientists.* Detroit: Gale Research, 1995.
Munro-Smith, R. *Ships and Naval Architecture.* London: Institute of Marine Engineers, 1973.
Paine, L. *Ships of the World: An Historical Encyclopedia.* Boston: Houghton Mifflin, 1997.

RELATED ARTICLES
Shipbuilding

Gills

Gills enable aquatic organisms to take oxygen out of the water when water is either passed over the gills or the gills are moved. Oxygen is removed by diffusion across the gill filaments into the blood or body fluids. Gills have a large surface area, allowing a greater amount of water to move across the membranes, thereby increasing the amount of oxygen that is available to enter the blood or body fluids. In addition to aquatic organisms, other organisms, such as amphibians and vertebrates, may also possess gills in the early stages of development.

Gills of most bony fishes comprise gill arches containing gill rakers and gill filaments. The gill rakers face toward the mouth and protect the gill filaments from harmful particles within the water. They can also be used to strain food organisms from the water (as with typically long, thin gill rakers such as those found in anchovy) or to function as another set of "teeth" (as with typically short, sharp gill rakers in larger, predatory fishes such as tuna or groupers) in breaking down food items. Lamellae present on the filaments help facilitate gas exchange. Fishes employ various methods of passing water over the gills. In buccal pumping, water is passed over the gills by coordinated opening and closing of the mouth and gill covering (operculum). Some species respire by means of *ram ventilation*, in which the mouth is held open to force water in the mouth and over the gills. However, because there are no mechanisms to pass water continually over the gills, the animal must constantly swim to force water over the gills.

In fishes, gills may or may not have an operculum. The agnathans, or jawless fishes, and the chondrichthyans (sharks, skates, and rays) do not have an operculum. Agnathans have 1 to 14 tiny pores located laterally along the anterior portion of the body for gas exchange; chondrichthyans have five to seven gill slits. Most chondrichthyans also have a *spiracle*, or external opening to the gill chamber, which can be used to take in water, especially in bottom-dwelling species where the mouth is occluded by the substrate.

Invertebrates, such as crabs and lobsters, house gills within the protective exoskeleton in structures called *branchial chambers*, which are found between the carapace and the sides of the body. Gill bailers are used to facilitate the movement of water currents across these chambers. The gill chambers keep gills moist and allow some organisms to live in intertidal zones, where frequent exposure to air occurs. Dermal gills protrude from the bodies of sea stars and sea urchins, where ciliated epidermal cells pass water over the gills.

Gills also function in *osmoregulation*, which is the regulation of ion and water concentrations in the body. Marine fishes can lose water from their bodies through the epithelium of the gills. To counteract this, they drink salt water and secrete ingested salt back into the environment. The opposite case is true in freshwater fishes, whose body fluids are saltier than the water they live in and therefore can gain water from their environment. To counteract this tendency, freshwater fishes excrete excess water by producing large quantities of dilute urine. Lost internal solutes are replaced with those absorbed into the body with food or by the gills, using active transport mechanisms. Gills also enable organisms to excrete carbon dioxide and other gaseous wastes.

Gill efficiency and oxygen uptake are increased in some organisms by a mechanism known as *countercurrent exchange*, where oxygen diffuses from higher to lower concentrations across a thin membrane. This is accomplished by directing the flow of blood opposite that of water. Blood with low oxygen content then comes into contact with water containing high concentrations of oxygen, resulting in increased amounts and rates of oxygen taken in by the organism. This process is more efficient than if blood and water flowed in the same direction, because countercurrent exchange maximizes the difference in oxygen content between the water and blood.

Erin O'Donnell

FURTHER READING
Eckert, Roger, and David Randall. *Animal Physiology*. San Francisco: W. H. Freeman, 1978; 4th ed. by Roger Eckert, David Randall, and George Augustine, *Eckert Animal Physiology: Mechanisms and Adaptations*, New York: W. H. Freeman, 1997.
Moyle, Peter B., and Joseph J. Cech. *Fishes: An Introduction to Ichthyology*. Englewood Cliffs, N.J.: Prentice Hall, 1982; 4th ed., Upper Saddle River, N.J.: Prentice Hall, 2000.
Nybakken, James W. *Marine Biology: An Ecological Approach*, 5th ed. San Francisco: Benjamin Cummings, 2001.
Raven, Peter H., and George B. Johnson. *Biology*. St. Louis, Mo.: Times Mirror/Mosby, 1986; 5th ed., Boston: WCB/McGraw-Hill, 1999.

RELATED ARTICLES
Agnatha; Chondrichthyes; Osmoregulator

Glacial Marine Processes

Numerous glaciations have been recorded throughout the geologic past, with major events occurring during the Late Precambrian (2450 million to 570 million years ago), Late Ordovician (463 million to 439 million years ago), Carboniferous/Permian (362.5 million to 248 million years ago), and Quaternary (1.64 million years ago to the present) Periods. However, according to scientific evidence, the glacial cycles became much more frequent and intense during the Pleistocene Epoch (1.64 million to 0.01 million years ago). Processes associated with moving ice (glaciers) that comes in contact with the marine environment are referred to as *glacial marine processes.* These processes occur on different spatial and temporal scales and are often influenced by other climatic and oceanic conditions. As a glacier comes in contact with the marine environment, there is a transition between terrestrial and marine glacial processes, the boundaries of which are often hard to distinguish. Scientists have divided the glacial marine environment into various zones or subenvironments in order to examine and compare the similarities and differences of the unique physical, chemical, and biological systems that exist; however, no universally accepted classification exists today.

Types of Marine-Ending Glaciers

Glaciers that enter the ocean can do so in one of two ways. One involves a floating terminus and the other involves a grounded tidewater cliff. Ice masses that terminate while floating, such as ice shelves or ice tongues, must be cold (polar or dry base), which means that the ice must be freezing at its base rather than melting. A warm (wet base) ice mass is melting at its base and therefore cannot support a floating platform. In this case, the glacier forms a vertical cliff at sea level because the ice calves, or breaks loose, faster than it melts.

Each of these two types of marine-ending glaciers has associated glacial marine processes.

Erosional Processes

Glaciers have amazing erosive power that more than doubles the erosion by major river systems. Hence glacial landscapes often contain large erosional landforms. In the marine environment, icebergs play an important role in scouring and reworking shelf sediments. On land, ice generally erodes by *plucking* (debris entrainment) and abrasion. These processes are somewhat indirectly related to the glacial marine environment, in that the eroded terrestrial material can be deposited as glacial erratics, or *dropstones*, in the marine environment.

High-latitude continental shelves commonly have plough and furrow marks that are the result of iceberg scouring. When icebergs float into water that is shallower than the thickness of the iceberg, the base or keel of the ice carves elongate features into the seafloor as the ice continues to move. At some point the iceberg may become grounded or drift into deeper water that is out of reach of the iceberg keel. Furrows cut by iceberg keels are typically a few meters deep and tens of meters wide. These erosional features have been found in water depths as great as 500 meters (1640 feet) on the Antarctic continental shelf. As a result of iceberg scouring, primary stratigraphy and biotic communities may be destroyed, producing a characteristic deposit termed *ice-keel turbate.*

Plucking occurs when weakness exists in the substrate over which the glacier is moving. Large blocks of rock (up to kilometers across) can be dislodged, or plucked, by plastic flow around an object and carried within the glacial ice and deposited in the marine environment. Plucking can also occur in association with a twofold process known as *regelation.* This process involves both melting of ice under pressure and refreezing of ice associated with the release of that pressure. For example, debris can be frozen to the base of

26

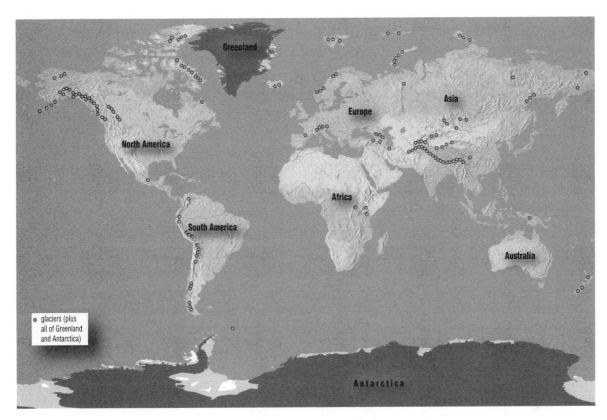

Distribution of glacial ice throughout the world, including most of Greenland and Antarctica.

the glacier in the lee of a bedrock outcrop. This same debris may melt when in contact with the next outcrop, forming a cycle of freezing and melting that produces a debris-rich zone along the base of the glacier.

Glacial abrasion is the mechanical wearing or grinding away of a rock surface by friction. Below wet-based glaciers, basal debris abrades the bedrock and produces rock flour, which is composed of small [often less than 1 millimeter (0.04 inch)] mineral and rock fragments. Abrasion also produces striations, gouges, and polished rock surfaces. Stress from the overlying ice can cause fracturing in the bedrock, which is revealed by crescentic fractures and gouges in the rock surface. These features can also indicate the direction of ice flow across the rock surface.

Transport of Glacial Material

One of the most diagnostic features of glacial marine sediment is the existence of glacial erratics, or dropstones, in otherwise fine-grained sediment. In fact, the concept of glaciers originated during the 1830s in Europe in response to a need for explaining the existence of similar onland erratics. Such out-of-the-ordinary clasts are transported via rafting by icebergs, sea ice, and ice shelves. Icebergs are parts of glaciers that have calved off the marine terminus. Icebergs, as well as ice shelves, transport material eroded from onland outcrops. For example, icebergs that calve off glaciers in Greenland between 60 and 70°N latitude float as far south as 40°N latitude and deposit Greenland rocks and sediment in the form of dropstones and drop sands. Most sea ice, on the other hand, forms at sea and therefore transports only windblown, or eolian, terrestrial debris. In all cases, as the floating ice melts, the debris contained in the ice drops out and settles to the seafloor, becoming incorporated into the existing marine sediment.

In many cases, large volumes of sediment are transported to the marine environment by meltwater in the form of freshwater streams that enter the ocean as meltwater plumes or high-speed jets below sea level. Terrestrial material is carried through subglacial, englacial, or supraglacial meltwater conduits until reaching the glacial terminus, where the sediment load is deposited. A majority of the sediment is deposited at the *grounding line,* which is the contact between the glacier terminus and the seafloor. However, fine-grained material may be retained in the freshwater plume as it rises to the surface and be deposited as fallout over large areas.

Other forms of transport involve reworking of previously deposited glacial marine sediments. Because sediment that comes in contact with marine-ending glaciers is often water-saturated,

Landsat 1 *MSS image of the Byrd Glacier, Antarctica, on 16 January 1974. The image shows the Byrd Glacier, which originates in the East Antarctic ice sheet, passing through the Transantarctic Mountains into the eastern margin of the Ross Ice Shelf, West Antarctica (toward the top of the image). Bedrock outcrops are visible in the left center of the image. (Landsat image from the U.S. Geological Survey's EROS Data Center, Sioux Falls, South Dakota; Courtesy, Richard S. Williams, Jr., U.S. Geological Survey, Woods Hole, Massachusetts)*

it is easily pushed and squeezed at the grounding line by the moving ice margin. This process has been termed *glacial push/squeeze.* Currents also play a major role in transporting and reworking glacial marine sediments. The currents that are most effective at moving sediment in the glacial marine environment are *tidal currents* and those that flow parallel to the ice margins, known as *contour currents.* A phenomenon called *ice shelf pumping* occurs in the Antarctic, involving periodic uplift and setdown of the grounding line due to tidal current activity. This causes a flushing of subglacial sediments on the ebbing tide. Contour currents erode and transport large amounts of sediment along specific depth contours. Studies in Antarctica have identified these currents flowing around much of the continent. Extensive glacial deposits are present where these currents are diverted offshore.

Mass-wasting events such as slumps, slides, debris flows, and turbidity flows also play a role in redistributing glacial sediments. For instance, sediment deposited at the grounding line continually slumps and slides in response to high rates of sedimentation. Also, large volumes of unsorted sediment that are transported to the shelf break by ice sheets are then carried down the continental slope in gravity flows and deposited on the continental rise.

Depositional Processes

Many of the processes that deposit sediment in a terrestrial glacial environment operate in the marine environment as well. However, deposition within the marine environment is greatly affected by the constantly shifting temperature and salinity regimes associated with the dynamics of marine ice margins. G. T. Philippi first defined glacial marine sediments in 1910, and over the years numerous definitions and classifications have been proposed. Glacial marine sediments can be distinguished from other "normal" marine deposits based on some of the following physical characteristics: poor sorting; lack of stratification; striated, angular erratic clasts; invertebrates preserved in growth position; presence of foraminifera and diatoms; and irregular ice gouge surfaces. Names of a few lithologies described as glacial marine include diamictons, glaciomarine drift, and dropstone laminite.

Glaciers that enter the ocean are characterized according to where and how the ice is in contact with the seafloor (the grounding line). Sediments deposited at the grounding line, termed *ice-contact deposits*, are often chaotic, due to reworking. Scientists have studied ancient (pre-Holocene) and modern grounding line depositional patterns to determine the sedimentary environments in which these deposits formed. As a result, some scientists have associated grounding lines with specific depositional systems, such as grounding line fans and glacier-contact deltas, morainal banks, and grounding line wedges. Each of these systems has characteristic processes of formation, geometry, and stratigraphy.

Beyond the grounding line, glacial marine sediments tend to be less chaotic than those nearest the grounding line, with little reworking. Basal melting at the ice–seawater interface under a floating terminus contributes a small amount of glacial debris to the seafloor seaward of the grounding line. Most deposition takes place beyond the calving line, where ice-rafted debris is deposited over a broad range and becomes incorporated into fine-grained sediments, often forming dropstone laminite deposits. Tidewater glaciers contribute little to no material due to basal melting because the ice is grounded at sea level. Instead, most of the sediment comes from icebergs that are shed from the tidewater cliffs. Icebergs at tidewater termini usually contain much greater quantities of glacial debris than those at floating termini. As a result, rockfall from tidewater icebergs often forms moraines.

Deposition of ice-rafted debris in the deep sea is also typical during glaciation. For instance, in the North Atlantic and elsewhere, large influxes of glacial meltwater have been suggested as the mechanism for deposition of *Heinrich layers*, characterized by a chaotic fabric of dropstones and mud clasts within a matrix of sandy to silty mud. These distinctive layers have been used in attempts to correlate the retreat of the Laurentide Ice Sheet with other documented climatic and oceanic events.

Glaciotectonic Processes

Tectonic processes such as uplift and subsidence can occur as a direct result of the formation and ablation of glaciers. As a glacier forms, the resulting isostatic imbalance causes local subsidence of the crust. The weight of the ice induces subcrustal flow of hot, semiplastic rock away from the ice-loaded zone. As this ice melts, the crust is uplifted as the subcrustal flow reverses. These two related processes are often termed glacial loading and glacial rebound. As an ice sheet expands across the continental shelf, *glacial loading* causes compaction of the underlying sediments, resulting in local subsidence, or shelf overdeepening. During interglacial periods, *glacial rebound* occurs as the ice sheet retreats toward the grounding line. The magnitude of glacial loading and rebound is directly related to the thickness of the ice.

The subsidence and uplift due to glacial loading and unloading often coincides with sea-level fluctuations. For instance, during glaciations the grounded ice sheet depresses the continental shelf, while concurrently sea level is lowered as water evaporates from the ocean and is stored in the form of glacial ice on land and at sea. As a result of deglaciation, glacial rebound occurs at the same time as sea level is rising from the addition of water due to melting. Therefore, it is difficult to measure the resultant magnitude of crustal subsidence and uplift precisely because these measurements are made based on a shifting sea-level datum. The combined rates of crustal and sea-level change result in the appearance of either sinking or rising landmasses.

Another form of glaciotectonism involves deformation of the substrate due to ice movement and/or static ice loading. Deformation occurs when the stress applied by the overriding glacier exceeds that of the stressed material. Ice exerts both drag and shear stresses during lateral movement. The weight of a glacier also applies a vertical stress on the underlying surface. For instance, ice push/squeeze at the glacier terminus and shearing along the glacier margins exert lateral stresses, which can produce folded and faulted substrate. Large slabs of rock that are plucked by the glacier, and are often transported long distances, can undergo deformation if carried up into the ice as the result of compressive flow.

Global Importance

Because of recent concern over the theory of global warming, many questions have been raised concerning the relationships between fluctuating polar ice volumes and both climatic and oceanic processes. An important part of answering these questions has been, and continues to be, further investigation of the processes in question, including glacial marine processes. In particular, glaciers that come in contact with the ocean have a reciprocal relationship with both the ocean and the atmosphere. For instance, thermohaline circulation, which allows vertical mixing in the world's oceans, depends on the formation of deep water by sea ice. In the past, when deepwater formation ceased, the oceans became stratified, surface temperatures increased, upwelling terminated, and the biologic pump that is active today did not exist. In addition, warming temperatures and/or decreased precipitation accelerate ice sheet melting, which in turn destabilizes ice shelves, possibly causing large-scale calving events. Eustatic, or global, sea level is closely tied to such fluctuating ice volumes. Therefore, rapid

melting of polar ice sheets due to warming temperatures and the corresponding rise in sea level would have direct consequences for coastal communities around the world. Glacial marine processes play a pivotal role in local as well as global climatic and oceanic systems, and comprehensive understanding is necessary.

Janet E. Tilden

FURTHER READING

Dowdeswell, J. A., and J. D. Scourse, eds. *Glacimarine Environments: Processes and Sediments.* Geological Society Special Publication 53. London: Geological Society, 1990.

Elverhøi, A., and R. Henrich. "Glaciomarine Environments 'Ancient Glaciomarine Sediments.'" In John Menzies, ed., *Past Glacial Environments: Sediments, Forms, and Techniques,* Vol. 2. Oxford and Boston: Butterworth-Heinemann, 1996.

Kennett, James. *Marine Geology.* Englewood Cliffs, N.J.: Prentice Hall, 1982.

Miller, J. M. G. "Glacial Sediments." In H. G. Reading, ed., *Sedimentary Environments: Processes, Facies and Stratigraphy,* 3rd ed. Oxford: Blackwell Science, 1996.

Powell, R., and E. Domack. "Modern Glaciomarine Environments." In John Menzies, ed., *Modern Glacial Environments: Processes, Dynamics, and Sediments,* Vol. 1. Boston: Butterworth-Heinemann, 1995.

Shipboard Scientific Party. "Antarctic Glacial History and Sea-Level Change." In *Proceedings of the Ocean Drilling Program, Initial Reports,* Vol. 178, College Station, Texas, 1999.

RELATED ARTICLES

Continental Shelf; Deep-Sea Sediment; Eustatic Sea Level; Submarine Mass Wasting; Thermohaline Circulation

Global Positioning System

The global positioning system (GPS) uses a system of satellites in orbit around Earth to provide accurate navigational information to ships, aircraft, and individual users. Introduced in the 1970s, it was not fully functional until the mid-1990s, but since then it has revolutionized the art of navigation, making calculations of position, direction, and speed simpler and faster with the aid of computers.

Radio and Satellite Navigation

The GPS system uses measurements from three separate satellites to *triangulate* the position of a receiver. Because radio signals from each satellite take a measurable amount of time to reach the user, a computer in the receiver can calculate the distance of the three satellites and therefore find its own position. The system can allow a user to find his or her location anywhere on Earth to within just a few meters.

GPS evolved from earlier radio navigation systems. The first of these was Loran, a system developed during World War II and used by civilians from the 1950s onward. Loran used a network of radio antennae positioned along the Atlantic coast of Europe and the eastern seaboard of the United States. Each antenna broadcast a time signal on a unique identifying radio frequency. By measuring the tiny time delay between two signals arriving from opposite sides of the Atlantic, the navigator could place a ship or aircraft somewhere on a line between them. Signals from a third antenna allowed the position to be pinpointed.

The first navigation satellites were launched early in the Space Age. Military systems such as the U.S. Transit and the Soviet Union's Tsyklon used satellites in low orbits sending out simple radio beeps at different frequencies. The systems relied on the Doppler effect, which causes a change in the frequency of a radio wave depending on its speed toward or away from a receiver. The same effect causes police sirens to change their pitch as the siren moves toward or away from you.

By measuring the frequency of the signal from a Transit or Tsyklon satellite, an operator who knew the satellite's exact orbit could work out its precise position and speed and use the Doppler shift to work out his or her own position and speed on Earth's surface. Once again, the system relied on triangulation from several satellite signals to get an accurate position.

Both these early radio navigation systems, however, have limitations. Loran can be used only in regions where a network of transmitters is established, while the Doppler shifts caused by satellite movements are very small and cannot be measured accurately enough to get a really precise position. In 1973 the United States decided to develop the GPS system for military use, which would get around both these problems. The first satellite was launched in 1979, but by the time the system was operational in the late 1980s, the changing political situation meant that GPS was also made available for civilian use.

How GPS Works

The GPS system is divided into three segments: the space segment, the control segment, and the user segment. The *space segment* consists of 24 Navstar satellites in orbit around Earth in a pattern or constellation, hence between five and eight satellites are above the horizon at any time and at any place on Earth. The *user segment* is the receiver unit, which can range from a small handheld unit to a complex computer linked into a ship or aircraft autopilot. The *control segment* is a network of ground stations around the world that constantly monitors and updates information about the position of the satellites.

The GPS Navstar satellites are each 5 meters (16 feet) long and equipped with solar panels, an atomic clock, an onboard computer, and a radio transmitter. The satellites orbit at an altitude of 17,700 kilometers (11,000 miles), and at this altitude they circle Earth exactly twice each day. Each satellite broadcasts time signals from its atomic clock to Earth at two frequencies, 1575 megahertz (MHz) and 1228 MHz. The time signal is carried by modulating the frequency of the radio waves in the same way that an FM (frequency modulation) radio signal carries audio information.

The time signal reaches Earth's surface about one-twentieth of a second after it leaves the satellite. Points directly below the satellite receive the signal first, and a point 161 kilometers (100 miles) away on the surface will receive the signal a fraction of a second later. The GPS receiver unit consists of a radio receiver, an accurate electronic clock, and another computer. As it picks up the 1575-MHz signal, it compares the satellite time with its own internal clock and calculates the satellite's exact position at the moment the signal was sent. The time delay places the receiver somewhere on a circle around the point directly below the satellite.

The receiver now locks onto a second satellite and repeats the process, placing itself on a second circle. The receiver must be at one of the two points where the circles cross, and a reading from a third satellite establishes which one. Shipboard GPS can establish its position from just three satellites, because the receiver is, by definition, at sea level. The calculations are more complicated for aircraft, but a fourth signal can provide an altitude measurement and allow an aircraft's position to be calculated.

Refining GPS

Using GPS in the way described above allows positions to be calculated to within approximately 100 meters (330 feet), and until recently this was the limit of accuracy for civilian users. Military GPS units, however, carried decoding software that enabled them to unscramble the second, 1228-MHz, GPS signal, which allowed them to calculate positions within just 10 meters (30 feet). Since May 2000, however, the scrambling of the 1228-MHz signal has been removed and all GPS units can access it.

The second signal boosts the accuracy of GPS because it allows the receiver to take account of Earth's atmosphere. The GPS signal travels more slowly inside the atmosphere than in the vacuum of space and is particularly affected by conditions in the electrically charged region called the

ionosphere. Low-resolution GPS simply uses a standard formula to estimate the delaying effect of the ionosphere, but using a second signal allows the effect to be measured directly. This is possible because the ionosphere slows down the different signals by different amounts, and measuring this delay allows the receiver to calculate the overall delay to both signals.

The accuracy of GPS measurement is only as good as the data held in the receiver unit's computer, so the data have to be updated regularly. This is the role of the GPS control segment. A global network of tracking stations monitors changes in the satellite orbits constantly, and these are collected at Schriever Air Force Base, Colorado. They are used to create an almanac with precise details of the satellite orbits at the time. Once a day the almanac is transmitted to the GPS satellites, which relay the information to GPS receiver units wherever they are in the world, in a 12.5-minute transmission. At the same time, the satellites' onboard clocks can be corrected, and these corrections are also broadcast to the receivers. This allows GPS to maintain its peak accuracy at all times.

GPS Applications

The major application of GPS is, of course, in navigation. GPS units are routinely linked to autopilots and carried by rescue teams or individual travelers in remote environments. Ocean research buoys, submersibles, and autonomous underwater vehicles (AUVs) are fitted with GPS coupled with radio beacons, enabling them to broadcast their precise positions.

GPS can also be used in surveying. By comparing the radio signals arriving at two separate receiver units, it is possible to find positions to within just a few inches. This method has limits, however, and the position of one of the two units must already be accurately known, and the receivers have to be kept within about 30 kilometers (18.5 miles) of each other.

Giles Sparrow

FURTHER READING

French, Gregory T. *Understanding the GPS: An Introduction to the Global Positioning System.* Santa Fe, N.Mex.: OnWord Press, 1997.

GPS World. Eugene, Oreg.: Advanstar Communications, 1990.

Grubbs, Bruce. *Using GPS: Finding Your Way with the Global Positioning System.* Helena, Mont.: Falcon Publishing, 1999.

Hofmann-Wellenhof, B. *Global Positioning System: Theory and Practice.* New York: Springer-Verlag, 1992; 4th ed., 1997.

Luther, Arch C., and Andrew Inglis. *Satellite Technology: An Introduction.* Boston: Focal Press, 1991; 2nd ed., 1997.

RELATED ARTICLES

Loran; Navigation

Global Warming, see Climate Change

Glomar Challenger

Glomar Challenger was the first ship built exclusively for scientific ocean drilling. Launched in 1968, she was owned and operated by Global Marine Inc. for the Deep Sea Drilling Project until retired from service in 1983. *Glomar Challenger* proudly carried the name of her forebear, HMS *Challenger*, the world's first dedicated oceanographic exploration vessel. She was a sister ship to Global Marine's *Glomar Grand Isle* and *Glomar Conception* drilling ships, but incorporated a number of significant innovations.

Glomar Challenger had a length of 122 meters (400 feet), a beam of 20 meters (65 feet), and a draft of 6 meters (20 feet). She displaced 9450 tonnes (10,400 tons) when loaded. She was diesel-electric powered with a power plant capable of 8800 continuous or 10,000 intermittent horsepower. Amidships was a 43-meter (141-foot)-high derrick with a hook load capacity of 454,000 kilograms (1,000,000 pounds). Forward of the derrick an automatic pipe racker carried

7315 meters (24,000 feet) of drill pipe, with additional pipe stored in the hold below decks. Aft of the derrick was the core laboratory, the most advanced seagoing geological laboratory of the time, and the superstructure housing the living quarters. The ship was a self-sustaining unit, with berthing, meal service, laundry, recreation, and medical facilities for the ship's crew, rig crew, and scientists and technical staff. She carried sufficient supplies to remain at sea for 90 days, although most voyages lasted only 55 to 60 days.

Advanced features of *Glomar Challenger* included: (1) dynamic positioning, employing transverse thrusters in bow and stern, which in combination with the ship's main screws enabled the ship to move in any direction and thus to remain on station in midocean, where the water depth precludes anchoring; (2) automatic stationkeeping, whereby computers calculated the ship's position (using signals from hydrophones on the bottom of the ship) relative to a seafloor sonar beacon, and then controlled the thrusters and main screws to maintain the ship's heading and position within 12 meters (40 feet) of the desired location; (3) a gyroscopically controlled tank stabilizing system, which increased safety and performance of the drilling operation; and (4) satellite navigation to determine the ship's position within 180 meters (0.1 nautical mile). *Glomar Challenger* was the first nonmilitary vessel to carry satellite navigation.

Innovation did not stop after the ship was launched. Although drilling operations were successful beyond expectations, two problems quickly became apparent. First, *Glomar Challenger* drilled with open circulation; that is, there was no riser (conductor pipe) between the ship and the drill hole in the seafloor. To allow for changing wornout drill bits, a deepwater reentry system was developed. This consisted of a 5-meter (16-foot)-diameter funnel placed on the seafloor in the mouth of the drill hole. This could be relocated with a scanning sonar (lowered through the drill pipe) and be used to guide the drill string back into the hole after the bit had been replaced. The first operational reentry was achieved on Christmas Day in 1970. Second, successful coring requires that the drill string and tools be protected from the motion of the ship. Bending stresses caused by the pitch and roll of the ship are hazardous to the pipe, while the pumping action and pounding of the bit on the bottom of the hole resulting from the heave greatly reduces core quality. A trumpet-shaped cone (guidehorn) located between the rig floor and the keel of the ship moderated bending of the drill pipe. The effects of heave were reduced by a hydraulic heave compensator, designed to isolate the drill string from the vertical motion of the ship. *Glomar Challenger* had the first deep-sea passive heave compensator, essentially a giant shock absorber. The system was never completely successful, but it paved the way for the development of active heave compensators (where the system anticipates ship motion) in use today.

Glomar Challenger was retired in 1983, after having steamed more than 600,000 kilometers (324,000 nautical miles) in service to the international science community. Although she was eventually broken up, she will be remembered as a historic pioneer whose unique capabilities made possible major advances in our understanding of Earth beneath the sea.

Thomas A. Davies

FURTHER READING

Davies, T. A. "Deep Ocean Drilling." *Ocean Science and Engineering,* Vol. 9, No. 4 (1985), pp. 381–446.

Edgar, N. T. "Drilling into the Ocean Floor." In *Science Year: the World Book Science Annual.* Chicago: Field Enterprises Educational Corporation, 1972; pp. 121–135.

Peterson, M. N. A., and N. T. Edgar. "Deep Ocean Drilling with Glomar Challenger." *Oceans,* Vol. 1, No. 5 (1969), pp. 17–32.

Taylor, D. M. "The Challenger's Adventure Begins." *Ocean Industry,* Vol. 3, No. 10 (1968), pp. 35–50.

RELATED ARTICLES

Deep Sea Drilling Project; Oceanographic Research Vessel

Gnathostomata

The development of jaws marks one of the most significant advancements in vertebrate evolution. Members of the superclass Gnathostomata (from the Greek *gnathos,* jaw, and *stoma,* mouth) are distinguished from other vertebrates (craniates) based on the presence of jaws. The jawless fishes (Agnatha) comprise the second vertebrate superclass. The innovation of a vertical biting structure supported the transition to predatory and more active lifestyles. The ability to crush or dismember prey items with the aid of closable jaws greatly diversified the range of available prey. The Gnathostomata, also known as gnathostomes, are the most abundant vertebrate taxa known today. Recent gnathostomes include sharks, rays, and chimaeras (class Chondrichthyes), ray-finned fishes (class Actinopterygii), lobe-finned fishes (Sarcopterygii), and the terrestrial vertebrates.

Taxonomy

Distinct relationships among jawed vertebrates and their possible connection to the Agnatha are unclear, the result of differing approaches to the study of these relationships and a limited fossil record. Currently, gnathostomes are divided into three grades: Chondrichthiomorphi, Placodermiomorphi, and Teleostomi. Chondrichthiomorphi is represented by the cartilaginous fishes of the class Chondrichthyes. Once a diverse class of armored fishes, the extinct Placodermi make up the Placodermiomorphi. The lobe-finned Sarcopterygii, ray-finned Actinopterygii, and the extinct Acanthodii ("spiny sharks") are the three classes that comprise the grade Teleostomi. Terrestrial gnathostomes (Stegocephalians) evolved from the Sarcopterygii.

General Features

In addition to the presence of jaws, gnathostomes are characterized by a variety of shared features: paired, internally supported appendages, internally supported gill arches, three semicircular canals in the inner ear, and paired nasal sacs. Other common anatomical and physiological features, such as myelinized nerve fibers and sperm ducts linked to the urinary tract, have been found to be unique to living gnathostomes. However, the presence of these soft tissues among the remains of extinct jawed vertebrates cannot be detected in the fossil record.

The jaw of the earliest recognized gnathostomes was relatively simple, consisting of two cartilaginous elements: the upper jaw (palatoquadrate) and the lower jaw (Meckel's cartilage). The upper jaw was attached by ligaments to the skull and the lower jaw was supported by a cartilaginous chain known as the *hyoid arch*. The early jaw structure of gnathostomes has undergone dramatic changes in shape, size, and position during the course of evolution from ancestral fishes to modern ray-finned fishes and to the terrestrial gnathostomes. One of the major advances among recent fishes is the change from a firm biting jaw to a more flexible jaw. The upper jaw of modern sharks, skates, and rays, although still relatively simple in organization, is clearly separated from the braincase (hyostylic suspension), allowing free movement and protrusability. Among modern bony fishes, modifications in the function of the principal bones of the upper jaw and the teeth-bearing bones have resulted in complex jaw morphology. These adaptations resulted in varying degrees of jaw protrusion and suction capabilities. Combined with a rapid expansion of the mouth, jaw protrusion creates water flow that carries food items directly into a fish's mouth. This modification to the jaw extends the range at which prey can be captured and further expands potential foraging options.

In addition to advancements in feeding, the ability to close the jaws is theorized to improve respiration by preventing the backflow of water over the gills. Closable jaws also created a means by which objects can be manipulated. The use of jaws as a defense mechanism may also have led to a general evolutionary deemphasis on armor, which in turn resulted in greater mobility and flexibility. Mobility and maneuverability were also enhanced by modifications to the paired appendages (pelvic and pectoral fins). These shared characteristics introduced new possibilities for gnathostome adaptation and evolutionary advancement, resulting in the rapid and highly successful radiation of the superclass.

Origin and Evolution

Jaws evolved in fishes, but the ancestors of the first gnathostomes are unknown. No fossil evidence of a direct link between jawed and jawless vertebrates has been found. Structural differences between the braincases, gill supports, and gill filaments indicate that the two groups evolved separately. The origins of jaws and the features that characterized the early gnathostomes are lost in the fossil record, probably belonging to an unknown, extinct group.

Although the ancestors of the gnathostomes remain a mystery, the evolutionary modifications that led to the development of jaws are widely accepted. Jaws are believed to have derived originally from the modification of the first (anterior) pair of gill arches. The second gill arch was probably modified to serve as a gill support and link the braincase with the jaws. Gill arches and jaws originate from the neural crest cells of the early-stage brain and spinal cord during embryonic development. The embryological origin of the jaws and gill arches is distinct from that of the rest of the head. The muscles of the jaws and gill arches also develop from a different source than the rest of the gnathosome body musculature. The distinct origins of jaw, gill arches, and their associated musculature strongly support the evolution of the first jaw from gill arches.

Debate over the relationships among gnathostomes has been extensive and continues to be dynamic. The earliest gnathostomes have been

35

presumed by many to be the sharks (grade Chondrichthiomorphi), based in part on their relatively basic jaw structure and on scales that have been dated to the Late Ordovician and Early Silurian more than 438 million years ago. Although scales have been found in deposits from this period, shark teeth have been dated no later than the early Devonian, approximately 400 million years ago. Based on the dating of these early shark teeth, the Chondrichthiomorphi are the most recent grade of gnathostomes to emerge. Whether the earlier scales belonged to sharks that possessed teeth and jaws has not yet been resolved.

Controversy over the relationship of the two extinct gnathostome classes, Acanthodii and Placodermi, exists as well. The Acanthodii are often considered to be the first advanced jawed fishes. Incomplete fossil forms first appeared some 425 million years ago. The similarity of these "spiny sharks" to true sharks (Chondrichthyes: Elasmobranchii) is largely superficial. The presence of a bony gill cover, the shape of the braincase, and the presence of three otoliths suggest that they are a sister group to the extant bony Teleostomi, not the Chondrichthiomorphi. The Placodermi arose 20 million years after the first acanthodians and died out in the early Carboniferous approximately 350 million years ago. Although this unique group has been considered to be ancestral to some modern fishes, the validity of such a relationship has been heavily debated for many years. Placoderm tooth and jaw structure differ from that of other gnathostomes. Instead of teeth, most placoderms have large bony plates attached to the margins of the jaws. These differences suggest that placoderms evolved from a lineage of primitive jawed vertebrates other than those that gave rise to the Teleostomi and Chondrichthyes; however, it has been suggested that sharks and placoderms evolved from a common stock.

Although evidence for the first presence of Chondrichthyes, Acanthodii, and Placodermi appear in the Silurian more than 420 million years

ago, the ancestral lineages of these classes and their relationships to each other and to the Teleostomi are unclear. Numerous characteristics support common ancestry between each of the groups, and researchers continue to investigate these relationships. The challenges of interpreting interrelationships, independent lineages, and possible ancestors of modern groups from the fossil record are well exemplified by the gnathostomes.

By the early Carboniferous, approximately 340 million years ago, the majority of the many families of jawless fishes had become extinct. During the Silurian (439 to 408.5 million years ago), agnathans were the dominant fish type, and the early jawed fishes were comparatively rare. By the beginning of the Devonian (408.5 million years ago), all major groups of jawed fishes had evolved, reaching their peak diversity by the middle and late Devonian (386 to 362.5 million years ago). By the end of this period, only the unarmored, jawless lampreys and the hagfishes remained. It is likely that jawless fishes were limited in their feeding modes to planktivory, detritivory, parasitism, and microcarnivory. With the development of jaws, both carnivory and herbivory became possible on a large scale. This innovation and the rapid increase in the diversity of gnathostomes may have conferred significant advantages over the once diverse and abundant jawless fishes, contributing directly to their extinction.

Wade D. Smith

FURTHER READING
Carroll, R. L. *Vertebrate Paleontology and Evolution.* New York: W. H. Freeman, 1988.
Colbert, Edwin H. *Evolution of Vertebrates: A History of Backboned Animals through Time,* 3rd ed. New York: Wiley, 1980; 4th ed., 1991.
Helfman, Gene S., Bruce B. Collette, and Douglas E. Facey. *The Diversity of Fishes.* Malden, Mass.: Blackwell Science, 1997.
Long, John A. *The Rise of Fishes: 500 Million Years of Evolution.* Baltimore: Johns Hopkins University Press, 1995.

Nelson, Joseph S. *Fishes of the World*. Upper Saddle River, N.J.: Prentice Hall, 1982; 4th ed., 2000.

Radinsky, Leonard B. *The Evolution of Vertebrate Design*. Chicago: University of Chicago Press, 1987.

RELATED ARTICLES
Acanthodii; Actinopterygii; Agnatha; Cephalaspidomorphi; Chondrichthyes; Elasmobranchii; Holocephali; Placodermi; Ray; Sarcopterygii; Shark; Skate; Teleostei

Gnathostomulida

The phylum Gnathostomulida comprises more than 80 species of tiny, flattened, wormlike animals usually less than 1 millimeter in length that are confined to the interstitial spaces in fine marine sediments. Although the animals had been discovered in the 1950s, they were first thought to be turbellarian flatworms. The phylum was formally described in 1969, thus making it one of the most recent of the animal phyla to be discovered. One reason for their late discovery was the fact that they are most abundant in anoxic sediments, a habitat that was thought to be unsuitable for metazoan animals.

Gnathostomulids are characterized by an epidermis that lacks a cuticle and in which each cell has a single cilium. They also lack any connective tissue or an internal body cavity, with the result that the internal organs are sandwiched between the epidermal layers. They have a blind digestive tract with a ventral mouth that bears a complex set of jaws. They apparently feed on bacteria and fungi scraped up by the jaw apparatus. Gnathostomulids are usually hermaphroditic, with the female system consisting of an ovary and associated bursa for storing sperm. The male system consists of one or two testes located posteriorly and usually, a copulatory organ that may or may not bear a stylet. Copulation has never been observed but is assumed to be hypodermic. Fertilized eggs are laid via rupture of the body wall. Development of the egg is direct, with no larval form. Gnathostomulids are thought to be related to both the phylum Platyhelminthes and the phylum Cnidaria, perhaps forming an evolutionary bridge between the two phyla.

James W. Nybakken

FURTHER READING
Barnes, Robert. *Invertebrate Zoology*. Philadelphia: W. B. Saunders, 1963; 6th ed., by Edward Ruppert, Fort Worth, Texas: Saunders College Publishing, 1994.

Brusca, Richard C., and Gary J. Brusca. *Invertebrates*. Sunderland, Mass.: Sinauer, 1990.

Lammert, V. "Gnathostomulida." In F. W. Harrison and E. E. Ruppert, eds., *Microscopic Anatomy of Invertebrates*, Vol. 4, *Aschelminthes*. New York: Wiley-Liss, 1991; pp. 19–39.

RELATED ARTICLES
Cnidaria; Platyhelminthes

Gorda Plate

The Gorda Plate is a small oceanic plate located off the coast of northern California that is subducting underneath the West Coast of North America at a rate of approximately 30 to 50 millimeters (1.2 to 2.0 inches) per year. Measuring about 270 kilometers (168 miles) from north to south and between 150 and 200 kilometers (93 to 124 miles) from east to west, it is the smallest tectonic plate of the Pacific region. The Gorda Plate was once part of the larger Juan de Fuca Plate to the north but broke away sometime between 18 and 5 million years ago. It is generated at a spreading center called the Gorda Ridge, which is 200 to 300 kilometers (124 to 186 miles) west of the subduction zone.

Both the northern and southern edges of the Gorda Plate border on transform faults. The southern transform fault separates the Gorda Plate from the Pacific Plate and is known as the Mendocino Fracture Zone. The northern boundary is an extension of the Blanco Fracture Zone, the transform fault that separates the Gorda Plate from the Juan de Fuca Plate. At its eastern boundary the Gorda Plate meets the Cascadia Subduction Zone, which stretches from British Columbia to northern California. The Gorda Ridge forms the western boundary of the Gorda Plate. In addition, the southeastern corner of the Gorda Plate marks the area where three plates—the Gorda Plate, the North American Plate, and the Pacific Plate—are in contact, forming the Mendocino Triple Junction. Within this area the Mendocino Fracture Zone, the San Andreas Fault, and the Cascadia Subduction Zone converge, creating an extremely complex and seismically active region.

Subduction of the Gorda and Juan de Fuca Plates underneath the North American Plate has produced the mountain range known as the Cascade Range, a chain of volcanoes that includes Mount Saint Helens and Mount Rainier. One of the most recent large volcanic eruptions caused by the subduction of the Gorda Plate was a series of explosive eruptions at Mount Lassen between 1914 and 1917, which sent a plume of ashes more than 9 kilometers (5.6 miles) above the summit and produced debris flows that extended more than 15 kilometers (9 miles) from the volcano. Subduction of the Gorda and Juan de Fuca Plates has also caused extensive earthquake activity along the west coast of the United States and Canada, including a series of very large earthquakes (magnitude > 8) that have occurred on average every 500 years. The last of these large earthquakes took place in 1700, and apparently caused rupturing along the entire length of the Cascadia subduction zone.

Earthquakes, some as large as magnitude 7, occur frequently in the middle of the Gorda Plate, along the transform faults on the northern and southern edge, and in the spreading center. Geologists are currently trying to determine why there are so many earthquakes along the transform faults and in the interior of the plate and relatively few in the subduction zone. Another

unusual feature of the Gorda Plate is the large number of faults that cross the plate, mostly along a northeasterly trend. It is generally believed that the young, brittle crust of the Gorda Plate cracks in response to the pressure exerted on it as it approaches the North American Plate. Due to the proximity of the Gorda Ridge to the subduction zone, the oldest section of the Gorda Plate is only about 9 million years old. Some researchers believe that the southeastern corner of the Gorda Plate is also being squeezed under the Pacific Plate, causing frequent earthquakes along the Mendocino Fracture Zone.

The Gorda and Juan de Fuca Plates are believed to be remnants of a much larger plate, the Farallon Plate, which was subducted underneath the North American Plate. The Cocos and Nazca Plates, west of Central America and South America, respectively, are also thought to be remnants of the Farallon Plate. Subduction of this ancient plate started about 200 million years ago when the supercontinent Pangea began to rift apart. Rifting of the land created the Atlantic Ocean and caused the North American Plate to move west and collide with the Farallon Plate.

Sonya Wainwright

FURTHER READING

Fox, Chris, and Robert Dziak. "Internal Deformation of the Gorda Plate Observed by Hydroacoustic Monitoring." *Journal of Geophysical Research, Solid Earth*, Vol. 10 (August 1999), pp. 17,603–17,615.

Hyndman, Roy D. "Giant Earthquakes of the Pacific Northwest." *Scientific American*, December 1995.

Kilbourne, Richard, and George Saucedo. "Gorda Basin Earthquake, Northwestern California." *California Geology*, Vol. 34, No. 3 (March 1981).

McCaffrey, Robert, and Chris Goldfinger. "Forearc Deformation and Great Subduction Earthquakes: Implications for Cascadia Offshore Earthquake Potential." *Science*, Vol. 267, pp. 856–858.

Orr, Elizabeth L., and William N. Orr. *Geology of the Pacific Northwest*. New York: McGraw-Hill, 1996.

Velasco, Aaron, Charles Ammon, and Thorne Lay. "Recent Large Earthquakes near Cape Mendocino and in the Gorda Plate: Broadband Source Time

Functions, Fault Orientations, and Rupture Complexities." *Journal of Geophysical Research, Solid Earth*, 10 January 1994, pp. 711–728.

RELATED ARTICLES
Cascadia; Cocos Plate; Convergent Plate Boundary; Explorer Plate; Farallon Plate; Gorda Ridge; Juan de Fuca Plate; Mendocino Triple Junction; Nazca Plate; Pacific Plate; Plate Tectonics; Subduction Zone; Transform Fault

Gorda Ridge

Gorda Ridge is an active mid-ocean ridge spreading center located 170 to 270 kilometers (106 to 168 miles) offshore of northern California between Cape Blanco and Cape Mendocino. At approximately 310 kilometers (190 miles) in length, it is the southernmost part of the Juan de Fuca Ridge, a spreading ridge separating the Juan de Fuca and Pacific Plates. Rising 1400 to 1600 meters (4590 to 5250 feet) above the surrounding seafloor, the ridge has segments as shallow as 1400 meters (4590 feet), significantly shallower than the 2500-meter (8200-foot) average for mid-ocean ridge crests. At its northern end, the ridge terminates at the Blanco Fracture Zone, whereas the southern end abuts the Medocino Fracture Zone. Gorda Ridge appears bent because it consists of two segments of roughly equal length but with slightly different trends. The northern segment trends approximately 20° east of north, whereas the southern segment trends almost due north. These two segments also differ slightly in morphology: The southern has a well-developed axial rift valley but the northern does not. Seafloor spreading across the ridge is moderate, with the plates on either side of the ridge moving 5.4 centimeters (2.1 inches) apart each year. Gorda Ridge is notable for its unusually shallow crestal depths and bent trend, which probably result from deformation of the Juan de Fuca Plate, whose southernmost piece, bounded by the Gorda Ridge, acts as a separate plate (the Gorda).

William W. Sager

FURTHER READING
Moores, Eldridge M., and Robert J. Twiss. *Tectonics*. New York: W. H. Freeman, 1995.
Stoddard, Paul R. "A Kinematic Model for the Evolution of the Gorda Plate." *Journal of Geophysical Research*, Vol. 92 (1987), pp. 11,524–11,532.
Wilson, Douglas S. "A Kinematic Model for the Gorda Deformation Zone as a Diffuse Southern Boundary of the Juan de Fuca Plate." *Journal of Geophysical Research*, Vol. 91 (1986), pp. 10,259–10,269.

RELATED ARTICLES
Cascadia; Gorda Plate; Juan de Fuca Plate; Mid-Ocean Ridge; Plate Tectonics

Gorgonian

Sea fans and sea whips (collectively called *horny corals*) are gorgonians. Gorgonians are arborescent (branching tree-like) colonial cnidarians, are abundant on tropical and subtropical reefs, and are exclusively marine. Often, they are brilliantly colored in yellow, red, orange, and lavender, and some species can grow to several meters across. Depending on the nature of their internal skeleton, gorgonians can be rigid or flexible.

Gorgonians come in many sizes, shapes, and colors; they are a diverse group comprising 18 families. Taxonomically, gorgonians belong in the order Gorgonacea of the subclass Octocorallia (= Alcyonaria) within the class Anthozoa. As is true for all anthozoans, gorgonians lack the medusoid generation that is typically found in other cnidarian classes. Like their octocorallian relatives (e.g., sea pens, sea pansies, and soft corals), gorgonians are composed of colonies of small polyps connected to one another with tissue called *coenenchyme*. The colony is usually supported by an internal axial skeleton. Polyps bear eight pinnate tentacles, have eight complete *mesenteries* (or walls of tissue), and each polyp has a single siphonoglyph (a ciliated groove that pumps water into the animal's body) running down the pharynx (the tubular area just inside the mouth).

The entire surface of the colony is covered by epidermis. Little is known about the reproductive biology of gorgonians except that they often produce new polyps asexually by budding and that the product of sexual reproduction is a polyp-producing planula larva.

Unique to gorgonians is the composition of the internal skeleton: it is made of a horny protein and mucopolysaccharide mixture called *gorgonin* (from which the order gets its name). The coenenchyme and polyps are wrapped around the central gorgonin axis. Embedded in the coenenchyme are calcareous ossicles or *spicules* (also called *sclerites*); in some species the spicules are fused.

Ecologically, gorgonians can interact with many other organisms and can be important members of coral reef communities. Like some of their true coral relatives, some gorgonians get nutrients from internal photosynthetic symbionts called *zooxanthellea*. Horny corals are carnivores, and like all cnidarians, use tentacles to catch prey and nematocysts (stinging cells) to subdue them. In turn, because they are sessile (permanently attached to the substrate), gorgonians can be easy prey for motile predators. For example, in the Caribbean, snails, fireworms, and file fish are known to prey on gorgonians. Some gorgonian species have developed chemical defenses to help protect them from predators and from other sessile species that are competing for space. The branching nature of gorgonians results in a large surface area for feeding and also in space to be occupied by other animals. Organisms such as tunicates, barnacles, bivalves, snails, and fish may live in a symbiotic relationship (the relationship is beneficial to both partners) with gorgonians.

Lynn L. Lauerman

FURTHER READING
Barnes, Robert. *Invertebrate Zoology*. Philadelphia: Saunders, 1963; 6th ed., by Edward Ruppert, Fort Worth, Texas: Saunders, 1994.

Muscatine, Leonard, and Howard M. Lenhoff, eds. *Coelenterate Biology: Reviews and New Perspectives*. New York: Academic Press, 1974.
Romashko, Sandra. *The Coral Book: A Guide to Collecting and Identifying the Corals of the World*. Miami: Windward, 1975.

RELATED ARTICLES
Cnidaria

Grab Sampler

A grab sampler is a mechanical device that collects samples of bottom sediment, loose debris, and associated fauna by enclosing the sample with movable jaws triggered by contact with the water bottom. Grab samplers are used commonly by marine scientists to obtain bottom samples in shallow water. A common design is the Van Veen grab, which consists of hinged halves reminiscent of a clam shell. Each half has the shape of a quarter cylinder, and the two sides are fixed open by latches above the hinge for launching. Upon striking the bottom, the latches release, allowing the halves to fall and close as the grab is raised. In soft sediments, the weight of the grab allows it to sink so that it "bites" into the sediments. Once closed, the halves form an enclosure that prevents water from flushing the sample away as the grab is raised. Grab samplers range in size from hand-held devices approximately 15 centimeters (6 inches) square to large, winch-deployed tools nearly 1 meter (39.4 inches) on a side. Although many grabs rely solely on gravity to close the jaws, others, such as the Smith–MacIntyre grab, use springs to force the jaws deeper into more resistive sediment. Other common names for grab samplers are *snappers*, *clamshell snappers*, and *Shipek samplers*.

William W. Sager

FURTHER READING
Bates, Robert L., and Julia A. Jackson, eds. *Glossary of Geology*, 4th ed. Alexandria, Va.: American Geological Institute, 1997.

Garrison, Tom. *Oceanography*. Belmont, Calif.: Wadsworth, 1993; 3rd ed., 1998.

Holme, N. A., and D. M. MacIntyre, eds. *Methods for the Study of Marine Benthos*. London: Blackwell Science, 1971; 2nd ed., Oxford and Boston: Blackwell Scientific, 1984.

Kennett, James. *Marine Geology*. Englewood Cliffs, N.J.: Prentice Hall, 1982.

RELATED ARTICLES
Deep-Sea Sediment, Dredge

Grand Banks

The Grand Banks region lies south and southeast of Newfoundland, Canada. It is an irregular series of low-relief ridges, troughs, and knolls that range in depth from 18 to 200 meters (60 to 655 feet). This irregular bathymetry (seafloor topography) is mostly the result of glacial processes that left behind moraines and other debris as the glaciers melted and receded. Extending for 560 kilometers (350 miles) north to south and 675 kilometers (420 miles) east to west, the Grand Banks are part of the North American continental shelf. They are located where the cold Labrador Current from the north and the warm Gulf Stream from the south are in contact, thereby creating an ideal mixing area that leads to high biologic productivity. However, the banks are also a perilous region that contains occasional icebergs and experiences severe storms.

The mixing of the warm and cold currents and the irregular relief and coarse-grained sediments makes the Grand Banks region one of the richest fishing grounds in the world. In fact, when John Cabot (1450–99), an Italian explorer who sailed for the English, first "discovered" the Grand Banks in 1498, he found cod so plentiful that his crew could harvest fish in baskets. Since that time until the demise of the Grand Banks groundfish fishery in the 1990s, the banks were exploited prolifically by fishing fleets. By the 1600s, western European nations such as England, France, Spain,

and Portugal were fishing the banks for groundfish such as cod and flounder; this was followed by participation from Canadian and U.S. fishing fleets. As the number of fleets increased throughout the twentieth century, along with technological advances (such as large factory ships), Canada began to impose stricter fishery conservation measures. In 1977, Canada declared a 320-kilometer (200-mile) exclusive economic zone, leaving only 10 percent of the banks (called the "nose" and "tail" of the Grand Banks) beyond its jurisdictional limit. However, the conservation measures did not prevent the famed collapse of the Grand Banks groundfish fishery.

In 1968, Newfoundland had 40,000 people involved in fishing and fish-processing activities, yielding 735, 000 tonnes (810,000 tons) of cod annually. Over a decade later, in 1981, the fishery employed 62,000 people (20 percent of all jobs in Newfoundland). The fishery collapsed in 1992, and the Canadian government closed the Grand Banks to cod and flounder. Certain fisheries in the Grand Banks have since recovered, and fishermen have found success in switching to animals such as crabs and shrimp. However, the famed

Grand Banks.

groundfish fishery reported by Cabot and others when first exploited has not rebounded.

The Grand Banks are also rich in oil and natural gas. By the late 1960s, Canadian geologists had recognized the region's potential for petroleum production. In 1979, the Hibernia oil field was discovered in the northeast portion of the Grand Banks. It contains 3 billion barrels of oil and 3.5 trillion gallons of natural gas, making it the fifth-largest field ever discovered in Canada. Located in 80 meters (262 feet) of water, commercial production has been approximately 150,000 barrels per day since 1997.

Manoj Shivlani

FURTHER READING

Harris, M. *Lament for an Ocean: The Collapse of the Atlantic Cod Fishery: A True Crime Story.* Toronto: McClelland and Stewart, 1998.

Woodward, C. "A Run on the Banks: How High Technology, Willful Ignorance and Basic Ecology Decimated One of the World's Greatest Fisheries–The Supposedly Inexhaustible Cod of Newfoundland's Grand Banks." *E: The Environmental Magazine*, Vol. 12, Pt. 2 (2001), pp. 34–39.

RELATED ARTICLES

Continental Shelf; Exclusive Economic Zone; Fisheries; Gulf Stream; Labrador Current

Gravity Anomaly

Earth, like all other objects in the Universe, responds to the force of gravity, which is directed toward the center of the planet. The force of gravity is proportional to the mass of objects and is inversely proportional to the square of their distance. If Earth were perfectly homogeneous and spherical, the gravitational forces on an object would be the same everywhere. However, Earth is not homogeneous or spherical, and its physical irregularities give rise to small lateral variations in the force of gravity that are called *gravity anomalies*. A gravity anomaly is the difference between the actual measured value of gravity and the theoretical or calculated value at that measured site. Understanding gravity anomalies allows scientists to determine the density of materials that are present in the subsurface of Earth.

P. Bouguer discovered that measurements of gravity are affected by latitude, altitude, density of rocks in the area, and rotation of Earth. To correct differences in values of gravity due to elevation and distance, measurements are changed to values at sea level, which is called the *free-air correction*. Any anomalous value remaining after this correction is termed the *free-air anomaly*. An additional correction is applied to compensate for the difference in density between the actual measured material and the hypothetical gravity model. This is the *Bouguer correction* and any anomalous value remaining after this correction is termed the *Bouguer anomaly*.

In the nineteenth century, scientists J. H. Pratt (1809–71) and G. B. Airy (1801–92) found that mountains create negative gravity anomalies that require corrections. The corrections, however, were smaller values than anticipated. This discovery led Pratt to the concept of *isostasy*, in which the crust is in gravitational equilibrium through a buoyancy mechanism. A negative gravity anomaly means that there is an excess of low-density rocks below the surface, whereas a positive gravity anomaly means that there is an excess of high-density rocks below the surface. In general, the continents are characterized by negative Bouguer anomalies and the ocean basins are characterized by positive Bouguer anomalies. The continents are composed primarily of lithospheric material and are less dense than the ocean basins, which are composed of heavier material from the asthenosphere.

Within the ocean basins, trenches and island arcs are marked by negative gravity anomalies. These anomalies may be explained by subduction (one lithospheric plate overriding another lithospheric plate), loss of mass along a Benioff zone (a narrow zone that dips under the overriding continent), and the presence of light-density material in the trenches. Surprisingly, there is no gravity anomaly at spreading ridges (where new oceanic crust is formed). With the emplacement of heavier, denser material from the mantle, one would expect a positive anomaly at these sites. However, the emplaced material is much hotter than the surrounding oceanic crust, and as a result, the mantle material expands. As it expands the volume increases and the density decreases. Thus the thermal expansion of asthenospheric material at spreading centers accounts for the absence of a gravity anomaly.

David L. White

FURTHER READING

Condie, Kent C. *Plate Tectonics and Crustal Evolution.* New York: Pergamon Press, 1976; 4th ed., Oxford and Boston: Butterworth-Heinemann, 1997.

Kennett, James. *Marine Geology.* Englewood Cliffs, N.J.: Prentice Hall, 1982.

Levin, Harold L. *The Earth Through Time,* 3rd ed. Philadelphia: W. B. Saunders, 1988.

Montgomery, Carla W. *Physical Geology,* 3rd ed. Dubuque, Iowa: Wm. C. Brown, 1993.

RELATED ARTICLES

Island Arc; Isostasy

Gravity Wave

Gravity waves are ocean waves—surface or internal—for which the principal restoring force (the force that tends to restore wave crests and troughs to an "average" smooth level) is gravity. Gravity waves are often considered to be wind-driven surface waves with a wavelength (distance between one wave crest and the next) in the range 1.73 centimeters (0.68 inch) to a few kilometers. Surface waves of wavelength 1.73 centimeters and less are called *capillary waves* or *ripples*. For these, the main restoring force is the water's surface tension.

In addition to the larger wind-driven surface waves, stationary waves (seiches), internal waves, seismic sea waves (tsunamis), and storm surges are also types of gravity waves. Tides—waves of long wavelength generated by lunar-solar gravitational forces—are not classified as gravity waves. For them, the Coriolis effect (an apparent deflection caused by Earth's rotation) is an important restoring force. Wind-driven surface waves are the focus of this article.

Generally, as winds increase in power and duration, they generate higher waves with longer wavelengths and higher speeds (up to a maximum of about 80 percent of wind speed). As a wave begins to form, it adopts a classical sine-wave shape, but as it builds progressively under continued wind action, it becomes trochoidal (with pointed crests and rounded troughs). Eventually, a wind-generated wave will reach a maximum height, speed, and wavelength for a given wind speed. This state is called a *fully conditioned* or *fully developed sea.* Away from its area of creation, where wind speeds are lower, the gravity wave reverts more nearly to its original sine-wave shape.

Once formed, gravity waves dissipate their energy slowly, losing it by internal friction, air resistance, and divergence (fanning out from the area of origin). Wind-driven waves can travel many hundreds of kilometers before they hit an obstacle, usually a shoreline. Here, much of their energy is dissipated as heat or is used to erode the shoreline, transport sediment, or create longshore currents.

When a wind-generated gravity wave progresses across the ocean surface in deep water, the waveform and the energy associated with the wave move with it, but the water molecules within the wave do not. Instead, they move in an orbital fashion in a vertical plane without major net movement in a horizontal direction.

Deepwater waves are wind-driven waves for which water depth is greater than 50 percent of the wave's wavelength. For these waves, wave speed or celerity (C) is independent of water depth but is related to wavelength (L) by the following equation, with g as the acceleration due to gravity [9.8 meters (32.2 feet) per second per second]:

$$C^2 = \frac{gL}{2\pi}$$

For shallow-water waves, for which water depth is less than 5 percent of the wave's wavelength, wave speed is a function of water depth (d). Waves travel faster in deeper water, as given by

$$C^2 = gd$$

For waves in water of depth 5 to 50 percent that of their wavelength, the speed of travel is given by an equation that combines the elements of the two equations above.

When waves enter shallow water, they build and slow, but their *period* (the time taken for one wave form to pass by) remains the same. Eventually, in very shallow water, the wave crest builds to a height where it can no longer support itself and the wave collapses (breaks) to become surf. Commonly, this happens when water depth is 1.3 times wave height.

Trevor Day

FURTHER READING

Ikeda, Motoyoshi, and Frederic W. Dobson. *Oceanographic Applications of Remote Sensing.* Boca Raton, Fla.: CRC Press, 1995.

Kampion, Drew. *The Book of Waves: Form and Beauty on the Oceans.* Niwot, Colo.: Arpel, 1989.

Open University Course Team. *Waves, Tides and Shallow Water Processes.* Oxford and New York: Pergamon Press, in association with the Open University, Milton Keynes, England, 1989; 2nd ed., Boston: Butterworth-Heinemann, in association with the Open University, 1999.

Young, Ian R., and Greg J. Holland. *Atlas of the Oceans: Wind and Wave Climate.* Oxford and Tarrytown, N.Y.: Pergamon Press, 1996.

RELATED ARTICLES

Internal Wave; Seiche; Seismic Sea Wave (Tsunami); Storm Surge; Wave

Grazing

Grazing in the marine environment is generally defined as feeding on sessile autotrophic organisms or sessile colonial animals by cropping all or part of the surface growth or alternatively, by removing entire autotrophic organisms from the water column. Grazers play an essential role in all marine environments, as they are responsible for transferring energy from autotrophs (or lower-level consumers) to higher trophic levels in the food chain. Moreover, some grazers may also create large amounts of detritus, thereby facilitating nutrient recycling in their environments. Finally, grazers may maintain a dynamic balance in marine ecosystems by limiting levels and spatial distributions of their prey (which may, in turn, affect total grazer populations).

It is important to contrast marine grazing from its terrestrial counterpart, as both systems are often very different. First, unlike in terrestrial systems, where herbivores graze only part of the standing biomass, marine grazers, especially planktonic ones, can effectively remove a majority of standing biomass (with certain exceptions). Second, very small organisms generally dominate productivity in the marine environment, and these marine organisms do not have woody structures present in terrestrial plants and are easily consumed whole. Finally, there is a greater turnover in marine ecosystems than there is in terrestrial ones. Apart from these general differences, there are other ecosystem-specific variations in marine grazing, in terms of grazer diversity and effects, which are described in greater detail for each of the following marine and coastal regions: estuaries, intertidal, subtidal, and pelagic ecosystems.

Estuarine Ecosystems

Estuaries are often described as the interface between freshwater and marine environments, receiving input from both sources.

Mudflats are large expanses composed primarily of mud sediments. Major producers on mudflats are diatoms, macroalgae, and seagrasses (described in greater detail below). Grazers that feed on these algae include crustaceans such as amphipods and crabs, polychaetes and other worms, snails, and other deposit and suspension feeders. Other grazers invade the mudflats only at higher tides, including fish such as mullet and other crustaceans. Grazers generally combine herbivory with detritus feeding on mudflats, as they tend to ingest either floating material or deposit mud.

Mangroves, which are tropical estuarine ecosystems composed of vascular plants and associates, have few direct grazers. Terrestrial insects can remove 10 to 25 percent of primary production, leading to changes in understory seedling growth rates, changes in leaf form and chemistry, and the alteration of branch architecture of trees and forests. Larger terrestrial grazers include monkeys. Marine grazers are limited to some crustaceans, especially grapsid crabs, that can feed on fallen leaf litter, flowers, and fruits on mangroves. With their burrowing activities, some isopod crustaceans can reduce mangrove root growth rates by 50 percent.

As in mangroves, a majority of salt marsh biomass is consumed by detritivores. However, grazers do affect plant biomass and community structure. Typical estimates suggest that between 5 and 10 percent of salt marsh plant biomass is grazed. However, marine grazers (zooplankton, mollusks, and others) consume most of microalgal production in the aquatic portion of salt marshes, which can account for one-fourth of total vascular plant production. The dominant terrestrial grazers are insects, and they feed on various parts of marsh plants. Larger grazers include birds and mammals, including waterfowl (e.g., brent and snow geese) and rodents. Certain marine invertebrates, such as crabs and snails, also graze on the above-water portions of marsh plants.

Intertidal Ecosystems

The intertidal region is a highly stratified environment that has discrete zones shaped by a combination of physical and biological factors. This zonation is more pronounced in rocky intertidal areas than in sandy or muddy intertidal ones. A temperate rocky intertidal ecosystem is described below to illustrate the zonation scheme.

The highest zone is wetted infrequently by the highest tides and by splash. Lichen and cyanobacteria mark the uppermost producer layer as well as filamentous green algae. Grazers in this zone include snails, limpets, and occasional crustaceans. Both algal and grazer vertical limits in the upper intertidal are determined by their abilities to withstand physical conditions and exposure. The middle intertidal is occupied by more species, as it is a more benign environment. The growing algae provide a food source for grazers, which consists mainly of limpets and snails. Grazers also affect the spatial distribution and dominance of algae that compete with attached barnacles and other animals for space. Algae are more abundant in the lower intertidal than in the higher intertidal areas.

Subtidal Ecosystems

Subtidal areas are represented by a variety of ecosystems, including sandy, unvegetated areas, rocky subtidal communities, kelp forests, seagrass meadows, and coral reefs.

Plants and sessile organisms cover rocky subtidal areas, where both autotrophs and grazers exhibit high levels of diversity. Distribution of algal species is determined by a combination of grazing and physical factors. Grazers include snails, limpets, fishes, and most important, sea urchins. In fact, sea urchins play a key role in the determination of algal composition in many rocky subtidal ecosystems, where their activities can lead to a shift in dominance from foliose algae to crustose coralline forms. However, foliose algae can also recolonize disturbed areas and in the absence, or in a lower abundance, of sea urchins (due to predation).

Kelp forests consist mainly of large, macrophytic algae that dominate primary production in such ecosystems. Production in kelp forests is complemented by an understory of smaller algae. Few herbivores graze directly on the algae, and only approximately 10 percent of the algal biomass is transferred via grazing. Prominent grazers include sea urchins, snails, sea slugs, limpets, and fishes. These animals feed mostly on drift algae, or algae that break apart. As in rocky subtidal ecosystems, sea urchin grazing can lead to the depletion of kelp forests. Overgrazing occurs when the amount of drift algae present is not sufficient or with an increase in sea urchin abundance. Although some have assumed that urchin populations are kept in check by predators, the evidence supporting that control is conflicting. In certain areas, predators such as sea otters do control the sea urchin densities; however, in other areas, assumed predators such as lobster have been shown to prey mainly on other organisms. Perhaps other, nonpredatory effects have led to changes in kelp and sea urchin populations.

Seagrass ecosystems are among the few vascular plant communities present in the marine environment. Distributed along shallow coastal zones of continents, seagrass communities often grow expansive, luxurious beds that contain a variety of algal and epiphytic counterparts. Seagrass ecosystems can be very productive regions, but only about 10 percent of the biomass is grazed. The associated benthic algae and epiphytic algae (such as diatoms and other microalgae, as well as bryozoans and other colonial organisms) also represent an important food source for grazers. Sea urchins and birds are among the most prolific grazers on the seagrass plants themselves, and in tropical climates, sirenians (dugongs and manatees) and sea turtles are important herbivores as well.

Coral polyps and a variety of algal forms serve as primary food sources for marine grazers in coral reef ecosystems. Grazers include gastropods, nudibranchs, barnacles, crabs, polychaetes, corallivorous fish, starfish, and sea urchins. Corallivores consist of starfish, sea urchins, snails, polychaetes, and some species of fish (including butterflyfish, parrotfish, pufferfish, and some triggerfishes). Most corallivores feed on the rapidly growing species of coral, thereby assisting in maintaining a diverse assemblage of coral species.

Among the most prolific grazers on coral reefs is the well-studied crown-of-thorns starfish (*Acanthaster planci*). An Indo-Pacific species, the starfish can devastate reefs by digesting the living tissues of corals. On some reefs, the starfish have been responsible for killing nearly 90 percent of corals. Other corallivores are smaller and have fewer effects, but snail and fish predation can have significant local impacts.

Grazers also play an important role in controlling the competitive balance between algae and corals in coral reef ecosystems. Since algae generally grow faster than coral, grazers actually assist in the dominance of coral by feeding on the algae. The two most important grazing groups on reefs are sea urchins and herbivorous fish, which can both graze nearly 100 percent of algal production. Other, less studied grazers include polychaetes, mollusks, and crustaceans, many of which also feed on algae.

Pelagic Ecosystems

Primary productivity in pelagic ecosystems is dominated by phytoplankton. It is estimated that almost half of the world's entire photosynthetic production is performed by phytoplankton. These, in turn, provide an enormous food base for the food chain, and the predominant herbivores, or grazers, are zooplankton.

Phytoplankton production in pelagic ecosystems depends on a number of physical, chemical, and biological factors. These include sunlight, temperature, nutrient availability, and grazing, among others. In tropical latitudes, phytoplankton production is constant, but standing crops remain low, due to continuous grazing (and nutrient limitation). The same is true at many higher latitudes, where grazing keeps up with production, maintaining a very low (dipping to 0.5 percent) standing crop. However, in some regions at higher latitudes, where the breeding cycles of dominant grazers lag behind phytoplankton growth, there is a seasonal spurt of production, called a *phytoplankton bloom*. This is followed by an increase in zooplankton populations, which graze on the phytoplankton in the spring and summer months. Dominant phytoplankton and grazer species may shift during the season.

Microbial Loop

The study into the importance of very small [less than 20 micrometers (0.008 inch)] organisms to marine food chains and webs has developed only recently. Scientists have discovered that there is a parallel but coupled microbial loop that is at times and places more important than the larger grazing food chains described above.

The microbial loop begins with bacteria that either feed on the organic matter in the water or are responsible for assimilating dissolved organic matter from the water column. The organic matter is supplied by a number of sources, including zooplankton and phytoplankton waste products and parts. There is also considerable leakage of dissolved organic matter from autotrophs that is resorbed into the food chain by bacteria. It is estimated that 20 percent of phytoplankton weight is lost as detritus during capture and handling by grazers. All this material is then brought back into the food chain via bacterial ingestion. Microalgae also add production at the microbial level. The microbial loop then extends to micrograzers

that feed on both bacteria and microalgae. The loop is coupled with the classic food chain when the micrograzers are themselves grazed by larger zooplankton. Together, the two food webs—the classic food chain and microbial loop—function as a single system that recycles nutrients and in which grazers play an essential role in transferring energy toward higher consumer levels.

Manoj Shivlani

FURTHER READING
Barnabe, G., and R. Barnabe-Quet. *Ecology and Management of Coastal Waters: The Aquatic Environment.* New York: Springer-Verlag, 2000.
Barnes, R. S. K., and R. N. Hughes. *An Introduction to Marine Ecology.* Boston: Blackwell Scientific, 1982; 3rd ed., Malden, Mass.: Blackwell Science 1999.
Bertness, M. D., S. D. Gaines, and M. E. Hays, eds. *Marine Community Ecology.* Sunderland, Mass.: Sinauer, 2001.
Graham, L. E., and L. W. Wilcox. *Algae.* Upper Saddle River, N.J.: Prentice Hall, 2000.
Harris, G. P. *Phytoplankton Ecology: Structure, Function, and Fluctuation.* New York: Chapman and Hall, 1986.
Little, C. *The Biology of Soft Shores and Estuaries.* New York: Oxford University Press, 2000.
Nybakken, James W. *Marine Biology: An Ecological Approach,* 5th ed. San Francisco: Benjamin Cummings, 2001.
Pomeroy, L. R. "The Ocean's Food Web: A Changing Paradigm." *BioScience,* Vol. 24 (1974).
Sumich, J. L. *An Introduction to the Biology of Marine Life.* Boston: WCB/McGraw-Hill, 1976; 7th ed., 1999.
Valiela, I. *Marine Ecological Processes.* New York: Springer-Verlag, 1984; 2nd ed., 1995.

RELATED ARTICLES
Autotrophic; Food Chain; Food Web; Herbivore; Intertidal; Kelp Forest; Microbial Loop; Pelagic; Primary Productivity; Seagrass; Standing Crop; Zooplankton

Great Barrier Reef

Australia's Great Barrier Reef is truly one of the wonders of the natural world. Recognized as a

World Heritage Site because of its remarkable biodiversity and cultural importance, the world's largest coral reef also contributes an estimated AU$2.3 billion to the Australian economy. Conflicts between economic activities and environmental protection, and natural threats such as coral bleaching and outbreaks of the coral-destroying crown-of-thorns starfish, continue to threaten the reef.

Geography

The Great Barrier Reef extends 2300 kilometers (1400 miles) along the length of the Queensland (northeastern) coast of Australia, from just south of the Tropic of Capricorn almost to Papua New Guinea over roughly 14° of latitude. The "reef" is actually around 3400

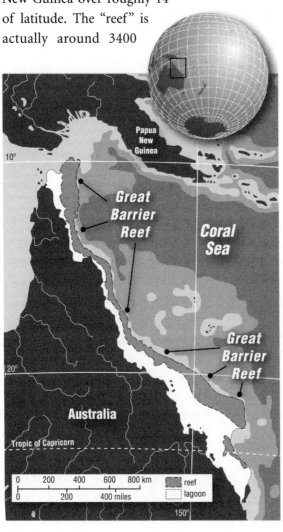

Great Barrier Reef.

separate reefs and associated components, including 760 fringing reefs, 300 coral cays (213 unvegetated, 43 vegetated, and 44 wooded), and 618 continental islands. The width of the reef varies considerably along its length, from around 23 kilometers (14 miles) at Cape Melville (14°S) near Cooktown, to 270 kilometers (168 miles) near Swain Reefs (22°S). The Great Barrier Reef World Heritage Site includes an area of some 34,870,000 hectares (86,163,800 acres), and the Great Barrier Reef Marine Park Area represents 33,126,500 hectares (81,855,600 acres) within that. Almost 9 percent of this area is occupied either by reefs or submerged shoals.

From north to south, some notable areas of the reef include the wreck of the HMS *Pandora*; Raine Island (a seabird resting and roosting site and a turtle nesting habitat); the Great Detached Reef (habitat of sharks and whales); Tijou Reef (a remarkable series of caves in the wall of a ribbon reef); Lizard Island (a resort and research station); the *Yongala* shipwreck; the Whitsunday islands (a group of 100 continental islands noted for sailing and water sports); the Pompey Complex (a wilderness area featuring very diverse reefs and fast-moving currents); Swain Reefs (an important seabird habitat); the Keppel Islands (habitat of loggerhead turtles and snakes); and the Capricorn and Bunker Groups (home to humpback whales during winter).

Estimates of the reef's age vary considerably, but the world's largest coral reef system is also one of its youngest. Little of it is more than 1 million years old and most is less than 500,000 years old. This explains why much of the reef is relatively thin.

Biodiversity

Because of television documentaries and underwater photography, the reef's biodiversity is probably its best known feature, and it is certainly one of the main attractions for the region's 1.6 million annual visitors. Given the reef's vast size (and also, given Australia's relatively small community of native marine scientists), considerable areas remain unexplored and the estimated numbers of species are therefore necessarily vague. However, the Great Barrier Reef Marine Park Area is home to an estimated 400 species of coral (including over a third of the world's soft coral species); 1500 fish species; 4000 mollusk species; 500 seaweed species; 242 bird species; 16 sea snake species; plus a variety of other species, including six of the seven species of marine turtles, whales (humpback, minke, and killer), and dolphins (bottlenose, Irrawaddy, Indo-Pacific humpback, and spinner). The reef is also home to one of the world's largest populations of dugongs (*Dugong dugon*, also known as sea cows).

Common vertebrates include sharks (such as whale, leopard, whitetip, and hammerhead), rays, flounder, trumpetfish, goatfish, angelfish, puffer fish, and flatfish. Common invertebrates include many species of worms, anemones, sponges, and crustaceans. Algae, important in the reef-building process, also provide food for many species, including fish, turtles, and mollusks.

The reef includes diverse habitats as well as diverse species. Apart from the corals themselves, these include continental and low-wooded islands, coral cays, mangrove estuaries, algal and sponge gardens, and over 3000 square kilometers (1160 square miles) of sea grass beds. The reef's 14 species of sea grass provide grazing for various animals, including the dugongs. The Great Barrier Reef Marine Park Area is also noted as a turtle breeding habitat and includes breeding areas of international importance for the endangered green turtle (*Chelonia mydas*) and loggerhead turtle (*Caretta caretta*).

Cultural Heritage

The reef's designation as a United Nations Educational, Scientific, and Cultural Organization (UNESCO) World Heritage Site reflects not just its extraordinary biodiversity, but also the importance of its archaeology and cultural heritage. The northern section of the reef includes sites on various islands that are of great cultural importance to the indigenous Aboriginal and Torres Strait Island peoples. Culturally significant items include sacred sites and extraordinary galleries of rock paintings on some of the reef's islands, species such as turtles and dugongs, and, of course, the ocean itself.

The reef's more recent history is also of archaeological importance. The difficulty of navigating a ship through the reef has produced more than 30 shipwrecks of historic interest, some of which are protected sites that attract divers from around the world. One of the oldest wrecks, HMS *Pandora*, sank toward the north of the reef in 1791 and is well known as the vessel sent by the Royal Navy in pursuit of the armed transport ship *Bounty* and its mutineers. Another wreck, the *Yongala*, which sank in a cyclone in 1911, has become one of the reef's most popular diving sites. Now liberally covered with numerous coral species, it is home to a rich diversity of marine life and is strictly protected by law against damage and disturbance. Some believe it is one of the best shipwreck dive sites in the world.

Economy and Environment

The reef's biodiversity makes it Australia's single biggest tourist attraction, contributing an estimated AU$1.8 billion to the nation's economy. Popular tourist activities include scuba diving, reef walking (carefully treading over exposed reefs at low tide), turtle and whale watching, and seabird watching. Tourism has grown by a factor of approximately 40 since the 1940s, and by the late 1990s, roughly 1.6 million people were visiting the reef each year.

However, the reef also comes under pressure from a number of other economic and human activities. Commercial fishing in the area contributes another AU$0.5 billion to the Australian economy, and both foreign and recreational fishing boats operate in the area. Fishing practices such as overfishing or the use of explosives, poison, or trawling have long been recognized as a threat to biodiversity in the area; a single pass of a trawl can remove a quarter of the marine life in a given area, including turtles and other species that are of no commercial value to the fishing vessels. Illegal trawling in the area now carries a fine of AU$1 million. Other threats to the reef come from coastal development, oil prospecting, and mining. A proposal to mine Ellison Reef in 1967 was defeated after major publicity through a well-coordinated environmental campaign. Pollution also poses a threat, not only through the addition of chemicals such as pesticides but also by introducing nutrients (typically through sewage) that disrupt the coral reef ecosystem; runoff is responsible for 39 percent of the nitrogen and 52 percent of the phosphorus that enters the Great Barrier Reef. The reef is also prone to environmental problems that threaten coral reefs around the world, including cyclones and floods, global warming, coral bleaching, and outbreaks of the coral-eating crown-of-thorns starfish (*Ancanthaster planci*), which has killed up to 95 percent of corals in affected areas.

Important measures have been taken in the last 25 years to safeguard the future of the Great Barrier Reef. The Great Barrier Reef Marine Park Authority (GBRMPA) was established in 1975 to manage the area and reconcile the conflicting needs of economic activity and environmental protection. The designation of the area as a World Heritage Site in 1981 underlined the international importance and fragile nature of the reef but offered little in the way of protection. More pragmatic measures have included various acts of legislation, zoning of the reef to prohibit certain activities in certain areas, and a 25-year strategic management plan published in 1994 by the GBRMPA. This plan, and a comprehensive review of the state of the reef published in 1998 by the GBRMPA, suggested that the reef was generally in good shape.

Still, conservation and marine scientists continue to highlight the dangers faced by the reef and its ecosystem. In November 2000, an environmental catastrophe was narrowly averted when a large container ship carrying oil and dangerous chemicals ran aground on the reef close to the city of Cairns in Queensland. Some believe that economic activities such as commercial shipping should be regulated more strictly. Others have called on UNESCO to reflect the fragility of the Great Barrier Reef by placing it on its World Heritage in Danger list.

Chris Woodford

FURTHER READING

Bennett, Isobel. *The Great Barrier Reef.* Melbourne, Australia: Lansdowne, 1971; London: Frederick Warne, 1973; New York: Scribner's, 1973.

Cannon, Lester, and Mark Goyen. *Exploring Australia's Great Barrier Reef: A World Heritage Site.* Surrey Hills, Australia: Watermark Press, 1989.

Connell, D. W. "The Great Barrier Reef Conservation Issue: A Case History." *Biological Conservation*, Vol. 3, No. 4 (1971), p. 249.

Great Barrier Reef Marine Park Authority. *The Great Barrier Reef, Keeping It Great: A 25-Year Strategic Plan for the Great Barrier Reef World Heritage Area.* Townsville, Australia: Great Barrier Reef Marine Park Authority, 1994.

Hopley, D. "Continental Shelf Reef Systems." In R. W. G. Carter and C. D. Woodroffe, eds., *Coastal Evolution.* Cambridge and New York: Cambridge University Press, 1994.

Wachenfeld, D. R., J. K. Oliver, and J. I. Morrissey. *State of the Great Barrier Reef World Heritage Area.* Townsville, Australia: Great Barrier Reef Marine Park Authority, 1998.

Zell, Len. *Diving and Snorkeling: Australia's Great Barrier Reef.* Melbourne, Australia, and Oakland, Calif.: Lonely Planet, 1999.

USEFUL WEB SITES

"Reef HQ: The Reef Up Close" <http://www.reefhq.org.au>.

Barrier Reef; Coral Bleaching; Coral Reef; Ecotourism; Fringing Reef; Pollution, Ocean

Green Algae, see Chlorophyta

Greenland Sea

Greenland Sea is shaped like an elongated rhomb that trends northeast–southwest. It is bounded approximately by 67 and 78°N latitude and 0 and 20°W longitude. The south boundary is the Denmark Strait, which lies between southern Greenland and Iceland. Denmark Strait also divides the Greenland and Irminger Seas. The north boundary is Fram Strait, which lies between northern Greenland and West Spitsbergen. The east boundary is the mid-ocean ridge. Seafloor spreading between Europe and North America began forming basins of the Greenland Sea about 60 million years ago.

The area of Greenland Sea is 1,205,000 square kilometers (465,250 square miles) with an average depth of 1444 meters (4738 feet). It is divided into two basins by the Jan Mayen Fracture Zone, which extends east–west at about 72°N latitude, with Iceland Basin to the south and Greenland Basin to the north. Ocean floor sediments are dominated by glacial marine deposits. Silty sands, gravels, and boulders cover large parts of the Greenland continental shelf, and the deep-sea sediments consist of turbidites and ice-rafted materials with small amounts of foraminiferal and diatom oozes.

Arctic pack ice, sea ice, and icebergs cover a large part of Greenland Sea from October to August. Icebergs calve off glaciers along the east coast and drift south. Some enter the main shipping route between Europe and North America. In 1912, the cruise liner *Titanic* collided with a Greenland-spawned iceberg and sank, killing 1490 passengers.

The wind system is influenced by the Icelandic Low, which generates cyclonic (counterclockwise) winds. Surface currents are dominated by the East Greenland Current, which flows south along the coast of Greenland. A deeper countercurrent moves northward under the East Greenland Current. Surface water temperatures range from 6°C (43°F) in the south, in August, to -1°C (30°F) in the north, in February.

Susan Morrell

FURTHER READING

Larsen, Hans C., and Andrew D. Saunders. "Tectonism and Volcanism at the Southeast Greenland Rifted Margin: A Record of Plume Impact and Later Continental Rupture." In Andrew D. Saunders, Hans C. Larsen, and Sherwood W. Wise, Jr., eds., *Proceedings of the Ocean Drilling Program, Scientific Results*, Vol. 152. Washington, D.C.: U.S. Government Printing Office, 1998.

Talwani, Manik, and Olav Eldholm. "Evolution of the Norwegian–Greenland Sea." *Geological Society of America Bulletin*, Vol. 88 (1977), pp. 969–999.

Tomczak, Matthias, and J. Stuart Godfrey. *Regional Oceanography: An Introduction*. Oxford and New York: Pergamon Press, 1994.

Arctic Ocean; Deep-Sea Sediment; Diatom; Foraminifera; Mid-Ocean Ridge; Oceanic Microfossil; Pack Ice; Turbidite

Gross Primary Production

Productivity is defined as the rate at which organic material is produced by an organism. *Gross primary production* is defined as the rate at which organic matter is produced by the process of photosynthesis before the costs of respiration are subtracted.

Plants require the Sun's energy to combine carbon dioxide and water to produce organic compounds in a process called *photosynthesis*. Respiration involves breaking down the high-energy bonds of organic compounds, which in turn release energy for the animal's metabolic requirements. Although both plants and animals perform the respiration process continuously, plants can carry out photosynthesis only when there is sufficient sunlight available.

Microscopic organisms called *phytoplankton* conduct photosynthesis in the ocean and form the base of most marine food chains. Primary production in the ocean is limited by environmental variables such as light, temperature, and nutrient availability. The amount of light diminishes from the equator to the poles as the angle of the sun changes. Therefore, as variations in day length and light increase and decrease seasonally with higher latitudes, primary production rates tend to show a seasonal pattern as well. The tropics generally have low rates of plankton production due to nutrients being limited in those regions.

Anne Beesley

FURTHER READING
Burchett, Michael, Marc Dando, and Geoffrey Waller. *Sealife: A Complete Guide to the Marine Environment.* Washington, D.C.: Smithsonian Institution Press, 1996.
Dawes, Clinton. *Marine Botany.* New York: Wiley, 1981; 2nd ed., 1998.
Nybakken, James W. *Marine Biology: An Ecological Approach,* 5th ed. San Francisco: Benjamin Cummings, 2001.

RELATED ARTICLES
Photosynthesis; Phytoplankton; Primary Productivity

Guano

Guano is a phosphatic deposit derived from the waste products of seabirds. It can be found on the rocky coasts and islets of the Pacific and other rainless regions, such as the island of Nauru and small islands off Peru and the northern coast of Chile, notably Baker, Howland, Lobos, and Chincha. Fish-eating birds with large rookeries, such as the Peruvian guanays

(cormorants), terns, boobies, shearwaters, petrels, frigates, and tropic birds, resort to islands to breed in safety. Over millennia their droppings build up and, because of the hot, dry climate, are not eroded but are compacted. The uric acid is intermingled with birds' skeletons and eggs, decomposed fish, seals, sea lions, and any other marine creatures frequenting the area. The thick accumulation is grayish brown and is compact or friable. Considering the immense thicknesses, up to 30 meters (90 feet), and their necessarily slow accumulation, the lower beds must be of vast antiquity, possibly even back to Pleistocene (1.6 to 0.01 million years ago).

A large guanay may consume 30 million anchovies per year. The birds funnel nutrition from the ocean fish chain to guano in dry atolls. But El Niño–La Niña controls the anchovy stocks along the South American coastline, and guano production decreases when plankton disappear, followed by fish and then seabirds, in a relentless cycle.

The term guano is also applied to the droppings of bats (usually as deposits in caves). Guano is primarily a Holocene (Recent; 0.01 million years ago to present) soft rock formed of calcium phosphate or apatite rich in ammonia, ammoniacal salts, with various nitrates and carbonates. These chemicals constitute its principal value and define its main use as a high-quality fertilizer and manure.

Susan Turner

FURTHER READING
Durward, L. Allen, ed. *The Fascinating World of Oceans and Islands.* Sydney, Australia: Reader's Digest, 1972.
Notholt, Arthur J. G., S. Highley, D. E. Highley, and P. M. Green. *Phosphate: A World Monograph.* Keyworth, England: British Geological Survey, 1999.

RELATED ARTICLES
Anchoveta; El Niño; La Niña

Gulf of Alaska

The Gulf of Alaska is an embayment of the eastern Pacific Ocean. The Gulf of Alaska is located off the southern coast of Alaska and is bordered on the west and northwest by the Alaskan Peninsula and Kodiak Island, and on the east by Cape Spencer, slightly to the west and south of the border between Canada's Yukon and British Columbia provinces. The gulf covers some 1,533,000 square kilometers (592,000 square miles) and lies between 58 and 61°N latitude and 137 and 155°W longitude.

A continental shelf about 200 meters (650 feet) deep underlies much of the gulf, ranging in width from 50 to 250 kilometers (30 to 155 miles). A number of undersea canyons and valleys cut the shelf to depths as great as 1000 meters (3300 feet), and to the east, a group of seamounts rise up to as high as 20 meters (65 feet) below sea level. At the edge of the shelf, the ocean dives to about 4000 meters (13,000 feet) in depth. To the extreme west of the gulf, just south of Kodiak Island, the Aleutian Trench begins; here ocean depths plunge to more than 6000 meters (19,000 feet).

The Gulf of Alaska features many fjords and other inlets, including the Cook Inlet and Prince William Sound, and the Copper and Susitna Rivers empty into the gulf. The waters of the gulf travel from east to west as part of the Alaska Current, the northern split of the North Pacific Current, which carries water from Japan to the west coast of North America. The coast of the gulf is very rugged, with high mountains and scenic glaciers, and to the east the coast lies atop two major earthquake faults, the Chugach–St. Elias Fault and the Fairweather Fault. The Gulf of Alaska is also home to a great number and diversity of wildlife, including beluga whales, killer whales, sea lions, and many different types of fish. The gulf remains an important commercial fishing ground for pollack and cod.

The Gulf of Alaska is an important oil-shipping lane because the trans-Alaskan oil pipeline ends at the city of Valdez, located on Prince William Sound. The sound is the location of the worst oil spill in the history of the United States. In 1989, the *Exxon Valdez* oil tanker ran aground, spilling nearly 11 million gallons of crude oil into the Gulf of Alaska. The oil fouled 2400 kilometers (1500 miles) of coast along the gulf, killing thousands of sea and shore animals. Despite a $2.3 billion cleanup and the recovery of bald eagle and river otter populations, studies conducted 12 years later found that populations of killer whales, harbor seals, and some species of birds were still severely depleted. Some of the difficulties these animals face in regaining population may be due to warmer-than-normal temperatures found in the gulf during the 1990s.

Mary Sisson

FURTHER READING

Alaska Oil Spill Commission. *Spill: The Wreck of the* Exxon Valdez. Anchorage: State of Alaska, 1990.

Hood, Donald W., and Steven T. Zimmerman, eds. *The Gulf of Alaska: Physical Environment and Biological Resources*. Washington, D.C.: U.S. Government Printing Office, 1987.

Keeble, John. *Out of the Channel: The* Exxon Valdez *Oil Spill in Prince William Sound*. New York: HarperCollins, 1991; 2nd ed., Cheney: Eastern Washington University Press, 1999.

Loughlin, Thomas R., ed. *Marine Mammals and the* Exxon Valdez. San Diego: Academic Press, 1994.

RELATED ARTICLES
Alaska Current; Bering Sea; Seamount

Gulf of California

The Gulf of California, also known as the Sea of Cortez, is a long, narrow finger of the Pacific Ocean located between the Baja California peninsula and the mainland of Mexico. It ranges in width from about 100 to 150 kilometers (62 to

93 miles) and is approximately 1200 kilometers (750 miles) in length. Seafloor topography within the gulf consists of eight depressions separated by shallower regions. These basins have depths ranging from about 1 to 2 kilometers (3300 to 6600 feet). Basin depths decrease northward from the mouth of the gulf because of the accumulation of sediments, mainly from the Colorado River (Rio Colorado), which empties into the northwest tip at 32.8°N latitude. Two large islands, Isla Angel de la Guardia and Isla Tiburon, and several smaller islets constrict the sea at 29 to 30°N, north of the port of Guaymas. Other islands in the gulf are small and near shore (except for Isla Tortuga, a small island at the edge of the Guaymas Basin).

Geologic and geophysical data indicate that the Gulf of California formed as Baja California was ripped off the Mexican mainland. The event that initiated the rifting was the collision of a spreading ridge, the East Pacific Rise, with North America. Beginning about 30 million years ago, this collision metamorphosed western North America subduction zones into a transform fault system, whose best-known component is the San Andreas Fault. As a result, slivers of continent have been rifted from North America and transported northward with the Pacific Plate. Baja California is one such sliver. Rifting of the Gulf of California began about 12 million years ago, but most of the basin has opened since about 5 million to 6 million years ago, when the rifting intensified. The boundary between the Pacific and North American Plates runs along the center of the gulf. Along most of its length, this boundary is a transform fault; however, fault segments are interrupted and offset by short spreading ridge segments that occur within the basins inside the gulf.

The Gulf of California has unusual oceanographic characteristics, owing to its shape and location. Mountain ranges in Baja California isolate the gulf from the subtropical Pacific climate, giving the northern reaches an arid, temperate environment, whereas the mouth of the gulf is wet and subtropical. As a result of the warm, generally arid environment, the gulf is the only evaporative basin of the Pacific, with evaporation 1 to 2 meters (3.3 to 6.6 feet) per year greater than precipitation in its northern extreme. This situation leads to the formation of warm, salty surface waters. The gulf also shows a net gain in atmospheric warming, so it exports heat into the Pacific. These conditions lead to a two- to three-layer system of thermohaline (heat and salinity driven) currents, with colder water flowing into the gulf at depth and warmer water flowing out near the surface (and sometimes a third, shallow, warm surface layer). Because this circulation leads to extensive upwelling of nutrient-rich subsurface waters, the gulf has high primary productivity in surface waters (i.e., phytoplankton multiply rapidly). The narrow shape of the gulf also causes the surface currents to be complex and generally desultory. In general, the surface circulation is cyclonic in summer and anticyclonic in spring, fall, and early winter, with the main transport directions following the axis of the gulf. The narrow shape of the gulf causes tides to be focused, resulting in spring tides of nearly 10 meters (33 feet) in its northern reaches. Tidal waves travel up the gulf in 5.5 to 6.0 hours, and as a result, semidiurnal tides may be low on one end of the gulf while high at the other.

The Gulf of California also claims another distinction. It is one of the rare places on the planet where chemosynthetic organisms have been discovered at hydrothermal vents along a spreading ridge, in this case located in Guaymas Basin. The Guaymas hydrothermal vent system is also unusual because its heat has distilled petroleum from the organic-rich sediments deposited atop the hot spreading ridge, leading to seepage of hydrocarbons near the vent.

William W. Sager

FURTHER READING

Alvarez-Borrego, Saul. "Gulf of California." In Bostwick H. Ketchum, ed., *Estuaries and Enclosed Seas.* Amsterdam and New York: Elsevier Scientific, 1983.

Atwater, Tanya. "Implications of Plate Tectonics for the Cenozoic Evolution of Western North America." *Geological Society of America Bulletin,* Vol. 81 (1970), pp. 3513–3636.

Bray, Norman A. "Thermohaline Circulation in the Gulf of California." *Journal of Geophysical Research,* Vol. 93 (1988), pp. 4993–5020.

Lonsdale, Peter. "Geology and Tectonic History of the Gulf of California." In E. L. Winterer, D. M. Hussong, and R. W. Decker, eds., *The Eastern Pacific Ocean and Hawaii,* Vol. N, *The Geology of North America.* Boulder, Colo.: Geological Society of America, 1989.

Moores, Eldridge M., and Robert J. Twiss. *Tectonics.* New York: W. H. Freeman, 1995.

Oskin, Michael, Joann Stock, and Arturo Martin-Barajas. "Rapid Localization of Pacific-North America Plate Motion in the Gulf of California." *Geology,* Vol. 29 (May 2001), pp. 459-462.

RELATED ARTICLES

Hydrothermal Vent; Primary Productivity; Seafloor Spreading; Subduction Zone; Transform Fault

Gulf of Mexico

The Gulf of Mexico is a relatively shallow oceanic-type body of water located at the southeastern border of the North American continent. The Yucatán Channel connects it to the Atlantic Ocean, by the Straits of Florida, and to the Caribbean Sea. To the west and southwest it is bounded by the east coast of Mexico, while to the north it is bounded by the southern coast of the United States. Cuba forms a partial boundary to the southeast. The gulf covers an area of about 1,550,000 square kilometers (600,000 square miles). The greatest depth recorded in the gulf is 5203 meters (17,070 feet).

Geology

The Gulf of Mexico formed during the early part of the Jurassic Period, approximately 200 million years ago, as North America tore away from Africa and South America

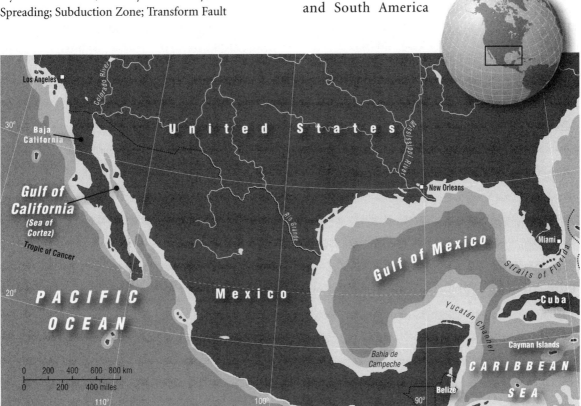

Gulf of California and Gulf of Mexico.

during early phases of the opening of the Atlantic Ocean. Over a long period of time, thousands of feet of sediment were deposited in the gulf. Organic matter, deposited along with the sediments, was subjected to heat and pressure of burial to become petroleum and natural gas. During early stages of formation, the gulf was an evaporation basin of the proto-Atlantic, and thick layers of salt were formed. Sigsbee Knolls, salt domes that presently intrude into the thick clastic sediment deposits of the gulf, are diapirs and an expression of these buried salt deposits. Sigsbee Knolls rises as many as 430 meters (1400 feet) above the floor of the Sigsbee Abyssal Plain in the central gulf.

Geologic features include the coastal zone, the continental shelf, the continental slope, Mississippi Delta and Mississippi Fan, fault scarps, and an abyssal plain. The coastal zone consists of sandy beaches, tidal marshes, lagoons, estuaries, mangroves, and numerous bays. Coral reefs form where clastic sediments are rare. The continental shelf is continuous around the basin. The Campeche Shelf off the coast of the Yucatán Peninsula and the Florida Shelf off the western Florida coast form the southern and northwestern boundaries of the gulf basin. Maximum width of the continental shelf is 520 kilometers (323 miles) where the Mississippi Delta forms the seafloor off the states of Texas, Louisiana, and Mississippi, and the narrowest point extends only 40 kilometers (25 miles) off the coast of Mexico. Topography varies along the continental shelf. North and northwestern areas contain knolls, mounds, ridges, and domes. The Yucatán (Campeche) shelf is relatively smooth, although broken by terraces corresponding to former stands of sea level. Coral reefs are present on the Yucatán shelf and on the western Florida Shelf.

The continental slope for the most part is continuous around the border of the basin. The Florida Escarpment is one of the world's largest cliffs, rising as much as 1800 meters (6000 feet) high, and supports many erosional features that mimic those on land. The continental slope is gentler on the northern continental slope and an extremely hummocky relief distinguishes the northwestern Gulf of Mexico. This topography is due to salt domes and submarine slumping within deposits of the Mississippi Delta.

The abyssal plain is bounded to the east and south by steep fault scarps toward Florida and the Yucatán Peninsula and by more gentle slopes to the north and west where the Mississippi Fan covers the seafloor. The deep abyssal plain is one of the flattest places on Earth, with a rise of only 0.3 meter (1 foot) for every 2440 meters (8000 feet). The floor of the basin is dominated by the Mississippi Fan or Cone, which is the result of millions of years of sedimentation supplied primarily by the Mississippi River system and covers an area of 77,000 square kilometers (30,000 square miles).

Water and Climate

Water from the Caribbean Sea enters through the Yucatán Channel, which has a sill depth of about 1600 meters (5250 feet), and exits through the Straits of Florida. This clockwise-flowing current is known as the *Gulf Stream* and is accompanied by many sinuous loop currents that break off and also move clockwise into the northeastern part of the gulf. Seasonal and annual variations occur in these loop currents as well as weaker currents present in the western gulf. Waters of the continental shelves and along the coastal regions experience seasonal variations as well as pattern changes caused by prevailing wind directions.

The climate of the gulf region ranges from tropical to subtropical. During hurricane season, meteorological and oceanographic conditions are favorable for the formation of hurricanes anywhere in the gulf. Hurricanes generated in the South Atlantic may also travel through the gulf at this time.

Wind waves generated within the gulf seldom exceed 5 meters (16 feet) in height except during long-lasting hurricanes, when experienced sailors stay in port. Storm surges caused by the intense atmospheric lows associated with hurricanes pose a threat to coastal inhabitants, as low-lying areas are flooded.

The salinity of the gulf varies according to location. Over the central gulf basin, the salinity of the surface waters is comparable to that of the North Atlantic at about 36.0 practical salinity units (psu), whereas the salinity of nearshore water is greatly influenced by evaporation, local runoff, river discharge, and infusion of water from the Caribbean. The Mississippi River greatly influences the salinity of the gulf. When the volume of the Mississippi's flow is greatest, salinities as low as 14 to 20 psu occur as far as 32 to 48 kilometers (20 to 30 miles) offshore.

Sea-surface temperatures in February vary between 18°C (64°F) in the northern gulf and 24°C (75°F) off the Yucatán coast. In summer, surface temperatures of about 32°C (90°F) have been measured. Bottom-water temperatures of about 6°C (43°F) have been recorded near the Yucatán Channel. The thickness of the isothermal layer (a surface layer of water of constant temperature) varies from a few meters to more than 150 meters (490 feet), depending on seasonal and local conditions. The tidal range is small, averaging less than 0.6 meter (2 feet) in most places; in general, only diurnal tides occur (one period of high water and one of low water during a lunar day).

Animals and Resources

The shores of the Gulf of Mexico provide a major haven for waterfowl and shorebirds. Migratory birds, including pelicans, boobies, notties, and other seabirds, winter along the coast of the gulf and offshore islands. Fish are bountiful in the gulf waters, especially along the continental shelf, and supply approximately one-fifth of the total U.S. commercial catch. Shrimp, shellfish, flounder, grouper, red snapper, mullet, oysters, and crab are the most important commercial harvests. Oyster shells are gathered from the shallow waters of the

Texas Gulf Coastal Plain and from bays and estuaries. They provide a source of calcium carbonate as well as material for building roads. Offshore wells have been drilled principally in the waters off the coasts of Texas, Louisiana, and in the Bay of Campeche off the coast of Mexico. Important reserves of natural gas and petroleum supply a substantial proportion of domestic needs in the United States and Mexico.

Deanna Madison

FURTHER READING

Berberian, George A., and Adrianna Y. Cantillo. "Oceanographic Conditions in the Gulf of Mexico and Straits of Florida, Fall 1976." Miami, Fla.: U.S. Department of Commerce, National Oceanic and Atmospheric Administration, Oceanic and Atmospheric Research Laboratories, Atlantic Oceanographic and Meteorological Laboratory/Springfield, Va.: National Technical Information Service, distributor, 1999.

Jochens, Ann E., and Worth D. Nowlin, Jr., eds. *Northeastern Gulf of Mexico Chemical Oceanography and Hydrography Study between the Mississippi Delta and Tampa Bay: Annual Report: Year One.* New Orleans, La.: U. S. Department of the Interior, Minerals Management Service, Gulf of Mexico OCS Region, 1998.

————. *Northeastern Gulf of Mexico Chemical Oceanography and Hydrography: Annual Report: Year Two.* New Orleans, La.: U.S. Department of the Interior, Minerals Management Service, Gulf of Mexico OCS Region, 1999.

Murray, Grover E. *Geology of the Atlantic and Gulf Coastal Province of North America.* New York: Harper and Brothers, 1976.

RELATED ARTICLES

Abyssal Plain; Caribbean Sea; Continental Shelf; Coral Reef; Florida Escarpment; Gulf Stream; Mississippi Fan; Ocean Current; Plate Tectonics; Submarine Mass Wasting

Gulf of Thailand

An inlet of the South China Sea, the Gulf of Thailand is bordered on the west and north by

Thailand and on the east by Cambodia and Vietnam. The gulf, formerly known as the Gulf of Siam, is about 725 kilometers (450 miles) long and 500 kilometers (310 miles) wide. It is located between 6 and 14°N latitude and 99 and 105°E longitude. The Chao Phraya and Nakhon Chai Si Rivers flow into the gulf from the north. The gulf, which lies atop the Sunda continental shelf, is quite shallow, generally less than 100 meters (330 feet) deep. Currents in the Gulf of Thailand are weak and change with the seasons, flowing out of the gulf toward the north in winter and toward the south in summer.

The gulf's coastal areas are important fishing grounds for the nations that surround it. Prawns, mackerel, and anchovies are all commercially important species, both for domestic consumption and for export, but overfishing and habitat degradation have threatened fish populations. Advances in commercial-fishing technology have made fishermen more effective at finding and catching fish, while pollution, warming temperatures, and destructive fishing practices such as the use of cyanide have damaged the coral reefs and mangrove forests that provide fish with breeding grounds and habitats.

As a result, the government of Thailand routinely bans fishing in the gulf for certain periods of time and limits the type of equipment that fishermen can use. Such bans have helped some fish populations regain strength, but the bans are unpopular among fishermen and difficult to enforce. Since the late 1960s, the Gulf of Thailand has become an increasingly important source of natural gas, which is found in undersea deposits.

Mary Sisson

FURTHER READING
Bunge, Frederica M., ed. *Thailand: A Country Study*, 5th ed. Washington, D.C.: U.S. Government Printing Office, 1981.
Pluvier, Jan M. *Historical Atlas of South-East Asia.* Leiden, the Netherlands, and New York: E. J. Brill, 1995.
Siddayao, Corazón Morales. *The Off-Shore Petroleum Resources of South-East Asia: Potential Conflict Situations and Related Economic Considerations.* Kuala Lumpur, Malaysia, and New York: Oxford University Press, 1978.

RELATED ARTICLES
Fisheries

Gulf Stream

The Gulf Stream is the most famous of the ocean currents of the North Atlantic. It begins as a recognizable current within the Straits of Florida and disperses at around 45°N, 45°W, off the Grand Banks of Newfoundland. Off Cape Hatteras, North Carolina, the Gulf Stream's flow averages some 3 kilometers (1.9 miles) per hour, but elsewhere its flow reaches 9 kilometers (5.6 miles) per hour. It is one of the world's fastest major surface currents and has a volume flow several times that of all the world's rivers. Like most major surface currents, the Gulf Stream is primarily wind-driven but modified by Earth's rotation. It is also influenced by *thermohaline circulation*, which is driven by salinity and temperature differences in seawater.

The Gulf Stream is the western boundary current of the North Atlantic gyre. This gyre turns clockwise, as do other gyres in the northern hemisphere. The eastward rotation of Earth deflects wind-driven surface currents to the right in the northern hemisphere, thus creating the tendency toward a clockwise circulation. The Gulf Stream is fed primarily by warm water emerging from the Gulf of Mexico. It is supplemented by water deflected northward from the westward-flowing North Equatorial Current and from the Sargasso Sea. Much of the water entering the Caribbean Sea from the North Equatorial Current reaches the Gulf of Mexico through the Yucatán Channel, where it circulates and is further warmed before leaving through the Straits of Florida to join the Gulf Stream.

From about 40°N, the Gulf Stream's eastward flow of water is assisted by westerly winds. Beyond this, after meeting the Newfoundland Rise, the current becomes the Gulf Stream Extension. It splits into the northeasterly North Atlantic Drift and the southeasterly Azores Current that joins the Canary Current to the south. The Canary Current feeds the North Equatorial Current, which itself is driven westward by trade winds, so completing the gyre. Today, the Gulf Stream is perhaps the most heavily investigated of any of the ocean's major currents. The behavior of the Gulf Stream has climatic effects that resonate across eastern North America, Western Europe, and deep into the Arctic Circle.

A River in the Sea

The Gulf Stream is commonly depicted as a well-defined surface current, "a river in the sea." In fact, the Gulf Stream extends to the ocean floor. From its westerly extent, near 79 to 65°W, the Gulf Stream shifts north–south by as much as 40 kilometers (25 miles) from one year to the next. The limit of the Gulf Stream to the east is less clearly defined because it breaks up into meandering water masses. A substantial part of the Gulf Stream's volume has disappeared by this point, in part through the formation of eddies that break off from the main flow. Using infrared satellite imagery and satellite-tracked, free-drifting buoys, these eddies have been the subject of intensive study since the 1970s. In fact, the flow within the Gulf Stream system, particularly at deep levels, is more complex than the foregoing description suggests.

Eddies

One of the most striking features of the Gulf Stream is its interaction with the cold, relatively low-salinity Labrador Current. When the

Gulf Stream.

Labrador Current meets the Gulf Stream, the interaction of the two currents creates eddies, which spawn rings of water that detach from the main current. These rings may be 50 to 500 kilometers (31 to 310 miles) across. North of the Gulf Stream these rings tend to be at the smaller end of this range, and they rotate clockwise and enclose warm water. South of the main current, the rings tend to be larger and to rotate counterclockwise and enclose cold water. The northern warm core rings contain captured Gulf Stream or Sargasso seawater. The southern cold core rings enclose Labrador Current water. Both kinds of rings may survive for many months and often retain a flora and fauna distinct from that of the surrounding water. For example, in warm core rings, phytoplankton blooms may be characteristic of Sargasso Sea flora. The water within rings is sometimes associated with increased productivity.

Influence of the Gulf Stream

The climatic impact of the Gulf Stream on the U.S. east coast and northwestern Europe is profound. In both regions, the Gulf Stream warms coastal areas and moderates winter temperatures, raising air temperatures by as much as 5°C (41°F). The Gulf Stream's great influence on the climate of Europe is due in large part to the presence of two oceanic pumps, one in the southern Labrador Sea and the other, more particularly, east of Greenland. These pumps, which draw down warm surface water to the cool depths, help pull Gulf Stream water northeastward across the Atlantic. The Gulf Stream and North Atlantic Drift waters release heat into the cold northern atmosphere at an estimated rate of a trillion kilowatts (10^{15} watts), equivalent to about 100 times humanity's current energy consumption.

The Gulf Stream acts as a wall that prevents the cold, nutrient-rich waters of the Labrador Current from reaching the central Atlantic Ocean. The interaction between the two currents causes nutrient-rich water to remain off the coast of Nova Scotia and Newfoundland, where it is warmed, fueling phytoplankton blooms, which are harvested by zooplankton, which in turn support populations of larger predators. Important fisheries for cod, haddock, and other demersal (bottom-living) fish were located here. Overfishing has heavily depleted these stocks.

Icebergs calved off Greenland's glaciers drift into Baffin Bay and the Labrador Sea, and many are carried south on the Labrador Current. When the Labrador Current interacts with the Gulf Stream, remnant icebergs normally melt rapidly—the temperature differential between the two currents is sometimes in excess of 20°C (68°F). The Gulf Stream undoubtedly provides a great service in keeping the central Atlantic Ocean free of most traffic-endangering icebergs. However, not all icebergs melt before reaching major shipping lanes. In April 1912, one such iceberg sank the RMS *Titanic*.

Many marine species take advantage of the Gulf Stream's powerful flow and its warming influence. The larvae of the European freshwater eel, *Anguilla anguilla*, hatch in the Sargasso Sea. They drift on the Gulf Stream and North Atlantic Drift to reach the rivers of northwestern Europe. As far north as the Barents Sea, the interaction of warm Gulf Stream water and cold Arctic water creates comparatively warm, nutrient-rich conditions to support phytoplankton production.

Here, bowhead whales feed, and more than 60 large seabird colonies thrive on Franz Josef Land.

The Future

The North Atlantic pumps and the Gulf Stream are parts of the global ocean circulation system (dubbed the "conveyer belt" by oceanographers). Warm surface water is drawn northward throughout the Atlantic. On reaching the Greenland and Labrador seas, the water sinks. This water, the North Atlantic Deep Water, then travels southward at a depth of about 2 kilometers (1.24 miles) and eventually reaches the Southern Ocean. The pumps are driven by water density differences, which are determined primarily by salinity and temperature. Cold temperatures and high salinities increase density and cause water to sink relative to warmer or less saline water. At North Atlantic pumps, warm surface water arriving from the south is cooled by subarctic air and sinks, so driving the pumps. The temperature of the arriving water and its salinity are crucial in maintaining the pumps' activity. If the arriving surface water is too warm, and it is diluted excessively by rain, rivers, and melting snow, its density might fall sufficiently to keep the pumps from working.

Since the early 1980s, concern has been expressed that global warming—the result of increased levels of carbon dioxide and other greenhouse gases in the atmosphere—might affect the pump's efficiencies. Meteorologists and oceanographers are studying this possibility using climate-modeling experiments. Paleoclimatologists are also searching the Greenland Ice Sheet and accumulated Atlantic seafloor sediment for evidence of climatic shifts in the last few tens of thousands of years. These might be linked to the shutdown of the global conveyor belt system in the North Atlantic. Climate models are being refined, and the evidence for past climatic shifts is still equivocal. The possibility of a southward shift in the Gulf Stream's influence, plunging northwest Europe into temperatures 5 to 10°C (41 to 50°F) lower than those at present, is a very worrying prospect. Such a shift would also have a major impact on marine life in the North Atlantic and parts of the Arctic.

Trevor Day

FURTHER READING

Duplessy, Jean-Claude. "Oceanography: Climate and the Gulf Stream." *Nature*, 9 December 1999, pp. 593–595.

Rahmstorf, Stefan. "Ice-Cold in Paris." *New Scientist*, 8 February 1997, pp. 26–30.

Richardson, P. L. "Tracking Ocean Eddies," *American Scientist*, Vol. 81, No. 3 (1993), pp. 261–271.

Stommel, Henry. *Gulf Stream*. Berkeley: University of California Press, 1958; 2nd ed., 1965.

Thurman, H. *Essentials of Oceanography*. Columbus, Ohio: Merrill, 1983; 6th ed., with Al Trujillo, Upper Saddle River, N.J.: Prentice Hall, 1999.

RELATED ARTICLES

Gulf Stream Meander; Gyre; Ocean Circulation; Ocean Current; Western Boundary Current

Gulf Stream Meander

The Gulf Stream is part of a major ocean current located off the Atlantic coast of North America that lies between Cape Hatteras and the Grand Banks. South of Cape Hatteras this current is called the Florida Current, and beyond the Grand Banks it is called the North Atlantic Current. The Gulf Stream is made up of multiple currents, countercurrents, undercurrents, filaments, eddies, and meanders. South of Cape Hatteras, the Florida Current is tightly bound to the continental slope. Near Cape Hatteras, the Gulf Stream leaves the coast and moves offshore, where its path is no longer fixed. At this point the Gulf Stream becomes an ocean current rather than a coastal current. The character of the Gulf Stream changes dramatically after it leaves the coast. It becomes much deeper and transports far greater quantities of water, which become entrained along its path. It is bounded on the right (looking downstream) by the Sargasso Sea and on the left by the Slope Water, a circulation cell located between the Gulf Stream and the continental shelf along the U.S. east coast.

The Gulf Stream transports relatively warm high-salinity water from lower to higher latitudes. Velocities along the axis of the Gulf Stream are as high as 200 centimeters per second (4 knots). Because the Gulf Stream is relatively narrow [on the order of 100 kilometers (62 miles) wide] and is fast moving, it is jetlike in its behavior and so is often referred to as a jet. The position and shape of the Gulf Stream vary over time.

One of the most interesting characteristics of the Gulf Stream is that it develops north–south oscillations or "meanders" along its path. These meanders begin to develop and grow beyond about 65°W. They have typical amplitudes of 80 kilometers (50 miles) and the distances between successive bulges are roughly 400 kilometers (250 miles). They evolve slowly, taking a month or longer to develop fully. As these meanders grow in amplitude in the downstream direction, they eventually pinch off to become eddies that are separate from the Gulf Stream itself. Meanders can form on either side of the Gulf Stream. Meanders to the left capture waters from the Sargasso Sea and eventually pinch off to become eddies in the Slope Water region, called *warm core rings*. Meanders to the right capture waters from the Slope Water and eventually separate to become eddies in the Sargasso Sea called *cold core rings*. Thus, meanders provide a means of exchanging water back and forth between the Slope Water and the Sargasso Sea.

The development of meanders may be related to several factors. Based on theoretical considerations, the Gulf Stream is known to be a dynamically unstable or unpredictable system. Because the Gulf Stream is inherently unstable, as it passes over variable bottom topography along its path, the bottom itself may initiate the development of small meanders that grow to become large meanders that eventually separate to become independent eddies.

Laurence C. Breaker

FURTHER READING
Fairbridge, Rhodes W., ed. *The Encyclopedia of Oceanography,* Vol. 1 of *Encyclopedia of Earth Sciences.* New York: Reinhold, 1966.
Warren, Bruce A., and Carl Wunsch, eds. *Evolution in Physical Oceanography.* Cambridge, Mass.: MIT Press, 1981.

RELATED ARTICLES
Eddy; Gulf Stream

Guyot

A guyot (pronounced *ghee-oh*), sometimes called a *tablemount*, is a flat-topped submarine volcano (seamount). Guyots represent a particular stage in the evolution of seamounts and islands, from a subaerial volcano, to a wave-cut platform, to an atoll, and finally, to a guyot. Guyots are abundant in all oceans but are especially numerous in the Pacific Ocean. Many guyots have shallow-water sediment and fossils on their flat tops.

Volcanism on the ocean floor results in volcanic ridges or seamounts. If volcanism lasts a long time, the seamount will break the water surface and form an island. When volcanism ceases, the island stops growing. When this occurs, the island slowly starts to sink. During the sinking process, waves continue to batter and erode the island and eventually plane the top of the island. Continued sinking of the planed island creates a flat-topped seamount or guyot. If the island is in a tropical environment and conditions are optimum, corals will grow around the volcano. Once the volcano is submerged, the coral will continue to grow upward toward the light and around the circumference of the submerged volcano, thereby forming an atoll. When corals stop growing and the volcano continues to subside, a guyot is formed.

Guyots are thought to develop in one of two tectonic settings. First, seamounts that form along or near spreading centers are related to thermal contraction of the seafloor as it moves away from the spreading ridge. The seafloor cools and contracts; contraction leads to an increased density and causes the seafloor and seamount to sink. The second method is based on isostatic compensation. The mass of the guyot loads the lithosphere and this leads to sinking in local areas. Hotspot volcanoes may evolve into guyots as they move away from the thermal source. Many guyots in the Emperor Seamount chain formed by this mechanism.

David L. White

FURTHER READING
Kennett, James. *Marine Geology.* Englewood Cliffs, N.J.: Prentice Hall, 1982.
Montgomery, Carla W. *Physical Geology,* 3rd ed. Dubuque, Iowa: Wm. C. Brown, 1993.
Thurman, Harold V. *Essentials of Oceanography.* Columbus, Ohio: Charles E. Merrill, 1983; 6th ed., with Alan P. Trujillo, Upper Saddle River, N.J.: Prentice Hall, 1999.

RELATED ARTICLES
Emperor Seamounts; Hotspot; Seamount; Volcanic Ridge

Gyre

The atmosphere is free to flow around Earth but the continents interrupt the east–west flow of ocean currents except between 56 and 62°S, where the Southern Ocean circles the globe. The blocking effect of the continents, combined with forcing by winds, causes the surface waters of the ocean to flow in semiclosed circular or elliptical patterns called *gyres.* These are the largest-scale features of the ocean circulation and span thousands of kilometers.

The large-scale oceanic gyres are either subtropical or subpolar. They typically consist of four currents, which because of their permanent nature, have been given distinct names. Each current transports water in one direction: eastward, northward, westward, or southward. The flows along the western boundary of the ocean basins are the strongest currents in the gyre; they are narrow and may extend to the bottom. In contrast, the eastern boundary currents are broad, shallow currents. Where the western boundary currents of the subpolar and subtropical gyres come together, strong gradients of temperature exist, which are called *fronts* or *convergence zones*.

Subtropical Gyres

Subtropical gyres occur between about 10 and 40° latitude. Their flow is anticyclonic (e.g., clockwise in the northern hemisphere and anticlockwise in the southern hemisphere). Although the pattern of eastward and westward currents is similar to the direction of the easterly trades and prevailing westerlies that lay above them, the currents are not driven by the wind stress directly. The current transport caused by the easterly trades is poleward and that due to the westerlies is equatorward. This convergent flow, called *Ekman pumping*, forces the thermocline down in the center of the subtropical gyre. The deep thermocline results in a dome of warm water that can readily be identified with satellite altimeter measurements or by computing the steric height of the sea surface from hydrographic measurements. Horizontal pressure gradients are directed away from large steric heights and are balanced by the rotation of Earth; this results in an anticyclonic flow.

There are three anticyclonic gyres that have well-developed western boundary currents: in the North Pacific, the North Atlantic, and the Southern Indian Ocean. The North Pacific Gyre consists of the Kuroshio (poleward-flowing western boundary current), the eastward-flowing North Pacific Drift Current, the equatorward-flowing California Current, and the westward-flowing North Equatorial Current. The North Atlantic Gyre includes the Gulf Stream, the eastward-flowing North Atlantic Drift Current, the southward-flowing Canary Current, and the westward-flowing North Equatorial Counter Current. The South Indian Ocean Gyre consists of the poleward (southward)-flowing Agulhas Current, eastward in the Antarctic Circumpolar Current, northward in the West Australian Current, and westward in the South Atlantic Current.

The other two southern hemisphere subtropical gyres have weak western boundary currents. The South Pacific Subtropical Gyre consists of the southward-flowing East Australian Current, the eastward-flowing Antarctic Circumpolar Current, the northward-flowing Peru–Chile Current, and the westward-flowing South Equatorial Current. The reason the East Australian Current is weak is that the boundary between Australia and Asia is not continuous, and this allows a portion of the Pacific South Equatorial Current to flow into the Indian Ocean through the Indonesian Archipelago. The South Atlantic Subtropical Gyre includes the southward-flowing Brazil Current, the eastward-flowing Antarctic Circumpolar Current, the northward-flowing Benguela Current, and the westward-flowing South Equatorial Current.

The other northern hemisphere subtropical gyre in the Indian Ocean is strongly affected by the monsoons. During the period of the southwest monsoon (June–October), a strong northward-flowing western boundary current develops along the coast of Somali, which is called the Somali Current. During the period of the Northeast Monsoon (December–April), the currents in the northern Indian Ocean reverse and circulation along the western boundary consists of weak equatorward flow.

Subpolar Gyres

The subpolar gyres are located poleward of the subtropical gyres between 40 and 60° latitude. The pattern of flow in the subpolar gyres is cyclonic (e.g., anticlockwise in the northern hemisphere and clockwise in the southern hemisphere). The gyres are a result of the midlatitude westerly and polar easterly winds. These winds cause Ekman pumping in the center of the gyre to be upward, so that the thermocline is shallow at the center of the subpolar gyres. The resulting horizontal pressure gradients are directed toward the center of the gyre, and the circulation is anticlockwise in the northern hemisphere. In general, the circulation is weaker in subpolar gyres than in subtropical gyres.

Two subpolar gyres are located in the northern hemisphere. These subpolar gyres have smaller horizontal scales than the subtropical gyres and a more complicated geometry because Greenland and the Aleutian Islands almost subdivide the subpolar regions and result in a more complicated pattern of ocean currents. In the Atlantic, the eastern portion of the subpolar gyre is made up of the southward-flowing East Greenland Current, the eastward-flowing North Atlantic Current, the northward flowing Norwegian Current, and the westward-flowing Irminger current. The western portion of the subpolar gyre is located in the Labrador Sea and includes the southward-flowing Labrador Current, the eastward-flowing North Atlantic Current, and the northward-flowing East Greenland Current. In the eastern North Pacific, the gyre in the Gulf of Alaska consists of the northward-flowing Alaska current, the westward-flowing Alaska Stream, and the eastward-flowing North Pacific Current. The subpolar gyre in the western North Pacific includes the southward-flowing Kamchatka and Oyashio currents and the eastward-flowing North Pacific Drift.

In the southern hemisphere, the Antarctic Circumpolar Current bounds the subtropical gyres, and subpolar gyres similar to those that exist in the northern hemisphere do not exit. A pattern of cyclonic flow exists off the southern coast of Argentina, where the northward-flowing Falkland (or Malvinas) Current is found. To the south of the Circumpolar Current, a cyclonic gyre is also found within the Weddell Sea.

Other Gyres

Although *gyre scale* usually refers to the large-scale circulation discussed above, the semiclosed circular circulations that are found within an ocean basin may also be called a gyre. For example, the circulation in the Beaufort Sea, called the Beaufort gyre, consists of an anticyclonic circulation around the Canadian basin of the western Arctic Ocean. The circulation around even smaller basins, such as the Adriatic Sea or the Black Sea, may also be referred to as a gyre. Finally, features that might more properly be called eddies but occur at a fixed location on a regular basis have also been called gyres (e.g., the Socotra Gyre).

Future Research Problems

There are many things that we don't understand about gyres. For example, gyres wobble and appear to change their intensity. Satellite altimeters do a good job of mapping these changes so that oceanographers can concentrate on finding out what causes the wobble. Another important question is determining how gyres exchange water with one another. Finally, oceanographers are working to determine the role of eddies in maintaining or damping the gyre-scale circulation.

Curtis A. Collins

FURTHER READING

Pickard, G. L., and W. J. Emery. *Descriptive Physical Oceanography: An Introduction,* 5th ed. Elmsford, N.Y.: Pergamon Press, 1990.
Tomczak, M., and J. S. Godfrey. *Regional Oceanography: An Introduction.* Tarrytown, N.Y.: Pergamon Press, 1994.

RELATED ARTICLES
Anticyclonic Flow; Cyclonic Flow; Eastern Boundary Current; Thermocline

Hadalpelagic Zone

The hadalpelagic zone refers to the pelagic (open water) environment of the deep ocean trenches, notionally at depths between 6000 and 11,000 meters (19,700 and 36,100 feet). The fauna of the hadalpelagic zone has been poorly investigated because of the difficulties in obtaining open water samples from such extreme depths and pressures (6000 to 1100 atmospheres) and bringing the samples to the surface intact. Trends observed at shallower depths—in the bathypelagic [1000 to 4000 meters (3280 to 13,120 feet depth)] and in the abyssopelagic [4000 to 6000 meters (13,120 to 19,685 feet depth)]—suggest that the species diversity and population density of pelagic fauna become sparser with depth.

Net plankton samples from the Kuril–Kamchatka trench system in the Pacific, described by Russian biologist M. E. Vinogradov (1927–), show chaetognaths, polychaetes, octracods, and some crustaceans (copepods, mysids, and amphipods) present in the upper hadalpelagic, but of similar or smaller biomass than those found in the lower abyssopelagic. Euphausids were found in the abyssopelagic but were entirely absent from hadalpelagic samples.

Fishes of the upper hadalpelagic, like those of the lower abyssopelagic, have reduced skeletons and musculature. At the boundaries of the upper hadalpelagic and the hadal (deep seafloor) zones are benthopelagic fishes and crustaceans that take advantage of the comparatively high concentration of food that accumulates there.

Traditionally, animals of the hadalpelagic have been sampled by trawl net, with acoustical "pingers" to help ascertain depth. Large and fast-swimming animals are likely to be poorly represented in such samples. In the future, the use of cameras mounted on remote-operated vehicles (ROVs) or autonomous underwater vehicles (AUVs), and large, suspended acoustic and optical sensory arrays, may greatly improve our currently meager knowledge of the life of this zone.

Trevor Day

FURTHER READING
Broad, William J. *The Universe Below.* New York: Simon and Schuster, 1997.
Gage, John D., and Paul A. Tyler. *Deep-Sea Biology: A Natural History of Organisms at the Deep-Sea Floor.* Cambridge and New York: Cambridge University Press, 1991.
Nybakken, James W. *Marine Biology: An Ecological Approach,* 5th ed. San Francisco: Benjamin Cummings, 2001.
Vinogradov, M. E. "Some Problems of Vertical Distribution of Meso- and Macroplankton in the Ocean." *Advances in Marine Biology,* Vol. 32 (1997), pp. 1–92.

RELATED ARTICLES
Abyssopelagic Zone; Bathypelagic Zone; Benthos; Copepod; Crustacea; Hadal Zone; Net Plankton

Hadal Zone

The hadal zone is the benthic (seafloor) realm below about 6000 meters (19,400 feet). It encompasses the deep seabed of ocean trenches. The fauna of the hadal zone has been little studied because the extreme depths and high pressures involved make the zone difficult to access.

Danish expeditions by the research vessel *Galathea* between 1950 and 1952 trawled samples from five trenches in the western Pacific and Indian Oceans. Between 1953 and 1962 the Soviet research vessel *Vityaz* systematically explored several Pacific trenches. These expeditions confirmed that the hadal fauna is distinct from that found at shallower depths. The hadal animal community comprises mostly sediment feeders, especially holothurians (sea cucumbers), polychaetes (bristle worms), and bivalve mollusks (clams). Later investigations by U.S. scientists Bob Hessler and Art Yayanos showed that bait lowered into the Philippine Trench would soon attract the attention of swarms of scavenging amphipod crustaceans. They would consume the bulk of a fish carcass within a matter of hours.

The biomass of animals per unit area on the trench seafloor can be as high as that on the adjacent abyssal plain at about 2000 to 6000 meters (6560 to 19,700 feet) depth. This can be explained by the comparatively rich food supply that finds its way into trenches. Most trench systems are found near land where oceanic crust is being subducted below continental crust at a destructive plate boundary. The trench is supplied by food sources from land and by the "snowfall" of dead plankton and animal feces descending from the productive surface waters.

As in the abyssal zone, seawater temperature and salinity are almost uniform, at about 2°C (36°F) and 35 practical salinity units (psu), respectively. Pressures range from about 600 atmospheres at 6000 meters (19,700 feet) to 1100 atmospheres at 11,000 meters (36,090 feet).

Hadal animals and microbes are adapted to these extreme pressures. Cell function is disrupted when they are raised to shallower depths.

Trevor Day

FURTHER READING

Broad, William J. *The Universe Below: Discovering the Secrets of the Deep Sea.* New York: Simon and Schuster, 1998.

Gage, John D., and Paul A. Tyler, eds. *Deep-Sea Biology.* Cambridge: Cambridge University Press, 1991.

Kunzig, Robert. *The Restless Sea: Exploring the World Beneath the Waves.* New York: W. W. Norton, 1999.

Nybakken, James W. *Marine Biology: An Ecological Approach*, 5th ed. San Francisco: Benjamin Cummings, 2001.

RELATED ARTICLES
Benthos; Trench

Hadley Cell

English physicist George Hadley (1685–1768) proposed the Hadley cell, in its original incarnation, in 1735. It is a simple model describing Earth's atmospheric circulation. Hadley's original conception describing atmospheric circulation has long since been superseded by a series of better models. However, the term *Hadley cell* is still used today to describe the major vertical air circulations that occur between the equator and latitudes 30°N and 30°S.

The Hadley cell circulations of tropical and subtropical latitudes extend over more than half of Earth's surface. They are major components of the general atmospheric circulation and the heat energy transfer between low and high latitudes. The Hadley cell circulation is driven by the differential heating of Earth's surface by solar radiation. The tropics, being closer to the Sun and facing it directly, receive more solar radiation than do the North and South Poles, which are farther away from the Sun and are at an oblique angle to it. Since warm air rises and cool air sinks, it is easy to envisage how warm air rising near the equator, and cool air sinking toward the poles, could generate a vertical circulation pattern.

Historical Development

The first well-documented model seeking to explain Earth's atmospheric circulation was put forward by English physicist Edmund Halley (1656–1742) in 1686. He envisaged a simple equatorward flow of air near Earth's surface—accounting for the trade winds—and a poleward flow at high altitudes. George Hadley refined this model to take into account the influence of Earth's rotation—the Coriolis effect that deflects airflows to the right in the northern hemisphere (producing northeasterly trade winds) and to the left in the southern hemisphere (southeasterly trades). Hadley's model did not attempt to account for, or explain, westerly winds found at middle latitudes. It assumed compensatory winds at high altitudes moving opposite to the trade winds.

A simple circulation, with warm air rising at the equator and sinking at the poles, should result in low pressures at the equator and high pressures at the poles. Nineteenth-century observations of surface pressures revealed a more complex pressure pattern. To explain this, American meteorologist William Ferrel (1817–91) proposed a three-cell (tricellular) model to explain major surface winds. According to this scheme, Hadley-type cells are found at tropical and polar latitudes in each hemisphere, with an opposing circulation, the Ferrel cell, at middle latitudes. Many modifications of the tricellular model have been integrated since that time, but in generalities, if not in details, the tricellular model works quite well as a simple description of Earth's major wind systems. Meteorologists and climatologists have retained the term *Hadley cell* to describe the dominant atmospheric circulation in tropical latitudes.

Components of the Hadley Cell Circulation

There are essentially four components of the tropical Hadley cell circulation:

1. *Subtropical anticyclones* (high-pressure systems) at about 30°N and 30°S provide the descending (subsiding) limb of the cell. As the air descends, it typically spreads out above a cooler layer of surface area, thus creating a temperature inversion and stable atmospheric conditions. As a result, extensive cloud cover is prevented from forming. These climatic regions are almost rainless, and in central regions of continents give rise to desert biomes, as in the Sahara and Kalahari Deserts of Africa. At sea, the skies are generally clear and conditions are calm, with high evaporation rates. The surface water in these regions is of higher-than-normal salinity. These are the "horse latitudes," where in bygone eras, becalmed sailors would kill their cargo of horses to conserve food and water.

2. The *trade-wind system* blows across the sea surface from the subtropical anticyclones toward the equator. The trade winds drive northeasterly in the northern hemisphere and southeasterly in the southern hemisphere. They are strongest in winter and weakest in summer, but often blow steadily in speed and

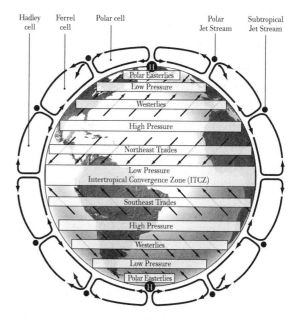

Hadley cell and other related components in Earth's atmospheric circulation.

direction for weeks at a time. Seafarers named them the trade winds and rode on them when heading in a westerly direction. The trade-wind system extends over latitudes 10 to 25°N and 5 to 20°S. Here, rainfall and cloud cover are variable, punctuated by periodic tropical storms. The trade-wind system is modified in the Indian Ocean and in the western Pacific, where monsoon winds predominate.

3. The *Intertropical Convergence Zone* (ITCZ) is a region between 10°N and 5°S where the two trade-wind systems meet in an equatorial trough of low pressure. Here convective upcurrents power the entire Hadley circulation. Towering cumulonimbus clouds form, releasing heat into the atmosphere and triggering heavy precipitation. The heat energy in the rising warm air is exported to higher latitudes. Surface winds are light and variable. Seafarers called this region of equatorial calm the *doldrums*, from an old English word meaning "dull."

4. The *high-altitude return flow* of the Hadley circulation arises from the top of the ITCZ as weak upper easterlies. These winds become westerlies and increase in velocity as they move poleward. They eventually form part of the core of the westerly subtropical jet stream at latitudes 30 to 40° that subsides to feed the subtropical anticyclones.

This simple overview is made complicated because in some places, components of the Hadley circulation pass over land, and in other parts, over sea. Sea and land have very different heat exchange characteristics; for example, land warms and cools more rapidly than sea. There are seasonal changes, too, with Hadley cell components in the relevant hemisphere shifting slightly toward higher latitudes in summer and lower latitudes in winter. Longer-term oscillations in ocean–atmosphere interactions, such as the Southern Oscillation and the El Niño phenomenon, introduce further complications.

Monsoons as a Hadley Cell Anomaly

The monsoon winds of the Indian and western Pacific Oceans are a significant variation on the Hadley cell trade-wind theme. During summer in the northern hemisphere, the warm African and Indian continents deflect the ITCZ northward, with the result that the southern hemisphere trade winds (southeasterlies) extend into the northern hemisphere, where the influence of the Coriolis force is in the opposite direction (to the right). In the northern Indian Ocean, this establishes southwesterly monsoon winds that deliver storms and torrential rain to India and Southeast Asia in the summer. However, the delivery system is highly variable, with some years yielding severe floods, and other years, droughts.

Rapid cooling of the Eurasian continent in the northern winter deflects the ITCZ and the northern subtropical anticyclone southward. The net effect is to reverse the direction of the Indian Ocean monsoon winds, which become northeasterlies. Similar but more complex wind reversals occur elsewhere across the Indian Ocean and western Pacific region, extending from Africa to Australia and Japan. For centuries, coastal traders from India and Southeast Asia have sailed southwest on the northeasterly monsoons in winter to reach east Africa and Madagascar. They returned on the southwesterly monsoons in summer.

Significance of the Hadley Circulation

In the tropics, geographic location within the Hadley cell circulation sets the predominant wind direction and its endurance, the general pattern of cloud cover, and the average rainfall. Thus the workings of the Hadley circulation largely determine the surface temperatures, salinities, and major surface currents of tropical and subtropical ocean bodies. For example, the oceanic gyres in the Pacific and Atlantic Oceans and in the southern Indian Ocean, and the equatorial surface currents, can be explained in terms of northeasterly and southeasterly trade winds.

The Hadley circulation, by its interaction with the mid-latitude Ferrel cells and its transfer of heat energy to polar cell circulations, profoundly influences the climate of the entire globe.

Trevor Day

FURTHER READING

Barry, Roger C., and Richard J. Chorley. *Atmosphere, Weather and Climate.* New York: Holt, Rinehart and Winston, 1970; 7th ed., London and New York: Routledge, 1998.

Burroughs, Wiiliam J. *Watching the World's Weather.* Cambridge and New York: Cambridge University Press, 1991.

Burroughs, William J., Bob Crowder, Ted Robertson, Eleanor Vallier-Talbot, and Richard Whitaker. *Weather.* London: HarperCollins, 1996.

Charnock, H. "The Atmosphere and the Ocean." In C. P. Summerhayes and S. A. Thorpe, eds., *Oceanography: An Illustrated Guide.* London: Manson, 1996; pp. 27–40.

Musk, Leslie F. *Weather Systems.* Cambridge and New York: Cambridge University Press, 1988.

RELATED ARTICLES

Coriolis Effect; Doldrums; El Niño; Intertropical Convergence Zone; Monsoon; Ocean Wind System; Trade Winds

Halocline

A depth interval (usually near the ocean surface) where salinity changes markedly is called a halocline. Most haloclines are found in areas near river discharge or in areas of high precipitation. In these areas salinity increases through the halocline. The reverse situation, where high-salinity water overlies low-salinity water, is not common in the oceans because high-salinity water has high density, so that for waters of equal temperature, high-salinity waters sink beneath low-salinity waters. Haloclines where salinity decreases with depth are always accompanied by a thermocline in which temperature decreases with depth.

In surface waters salinity can be increased by evaporation and decreased by the input of rain, snow, and river water. A salinity profile in areas in which high rainfall dilutes surface water will show a rapid progression from low to high salinity with increasing depth. Surface waters influenced by river runoff and melting ice also exhibit low surface salinity. Conversely, surface water in areas that experience high rates of evaporation may exhibit a halocline that progresses from high to low salinity. Because salinity affects density, haloclines sometimes coincide with pycnoclines (density gradients). For example, the two gradients occur together in the Black Sea and in surface waters of coastal areas affected by the influx of fresh water from rivers. However, the range of temperatures found in the ocean is much larger than the range of salinities; thus temperature usually has more of an effect on water density.

The range of salinities in the ocean is greatest in surface waters where air–sea interactions affect dilution or concentration of salts, but haloclines are found throughout the oceans. For example, haloclines are common in surface waters and at low and midlatitudes from the bottom of the mixed layer to about 1000 meters (3280 feet). Density stratification in the North Pacific Ocean is caused by an excess of precipitation over evaporation, and surface waters there are the lowest in the world's open ocean. In fact, due to the strong halocline, oceanographers have made the analogy that the circulation in the North Pacific acts like an estuary. A strong halocline in the Arctic Ocean is caused by the many rivers that discharge into that basin.

Haloclines can also occur in estuaries, where salt and fresh water mix, and the type and strength of the halocline helps determine how water circulates in estuaries. The halocline in estuaries separates the seaward-flowing surface waters from the landward-flowing bottom waters. The strongest haloclines [where salinity may increase by 10 practical salinity units in 10 meters (32.8 feet)] can be found in fjord estuaries and in salt-wedge estuaries, where river discharge is large but tidal mixing is small.

Lynn L. Lauerman

FURTHER READING

Knauss, John A. *Introduction to Physical Oceanography.* Englewood Cliffs, N.J.: Prentice Hall, 1978; 2nd ed. rev., Upper Saddle River, N.J.: Prentice Hall, 2000.

Lalli, Carol M., and Timothy R. Parsons. *Biological Oceanography: An Introduction.* Oxford and New York: Pergamon Press, 1993; 2nd ed., Oxford: Butterworth-Heinemann, 1997.

Pickard, George L. *Descriptive Physical Oceanography.* Oxford and New York: Pergamon Press, 1964; 5th enl. ed., Oxford and Boston: Butterworth-Heinemann, 1995.

RELATED ARTICLES

Estuary; Pycnocline; Thermocline

Haptophyta

Haptophytes (phylum or division Haptophyta) are tiny, single-celled algae. They are one of the chief components of the ocean phytoplankton (plantlike plankton), which forms the base of the marine food chain. Many haptophytes are free-swimming, solitary organisms, but some species also produce colonies at some stage in the life cycle. The taxonomy of haptophytes is unresolved, and some authorities consider these organisms too diverse to be grouped together in a single phylum or division.

Haptophytes are usually less than 20 micrometers (0.0008 inch) wide. They are distinguished by the possession of a coiled, threadlike structure called a *haptoneme*, which is located at the front end of the cell, and/or by the possession of organic or mineralized scales on the cell surface. The haptoneme is sometimes used as a holdfast to anchor the cell to a solid object. Two long, hairlike flagella, used for swimming, lie on either side of the haptoneme in free-swimming forms.

Haptophyte colonies, produced by species such as *Phaeocystis poucheti*, consist of nonmotile cells that lack flagella and are grouped together in a gelatinous mass or in filaments. In temperate waters during spring, *P. poucheti* produces blooms of glutinous colonies, each several millimeters wide, that can clog plankton nets. Like plants, haptophytes obtain their food by photosynthesis. Their photosynthetic pigments are typically golden brown in color and are concentrated in one or two structures called *chromatophores*. The products of photosynthesis are stored as leucosin (a carbohydrate) and fat.

The most numerous and widespread haptophytes are the coccolithophorids. These are less than 10 micrometers (0.0004 inch) wide and possess, at some point in their life cycle, tiny, disk-shaped scales of minerals such as calcium carbonate (chalk) on the cell surface. The scales, known as *coccoliths*, bear intricate patterns that vary from one species to another and can be identified by electron microscopy. Fossilized coccoliths are abundant in some forms of limestone, such as that found in the white cliffs of Dover in England, and provide an important means of dating rock strata.

Haptophytes have complex life cycles with several modes of reproduction. They may divide by binary fission into two daughter cells or by multiple division into many daughter cells, and the products of division may be motile or nonmotile and may possess or lack scales. As well as reproducing asexually, haptophytes sometimes swarm together in an amoeboid form before division occurs. In some species there are distinct generations that alternate. Members of the coccolithophorid genus *Cricosphaera*, for example, exist in two alternating forms: solitary planktonic cells that possess coccoliths and benthic colonies that lack coccoliths. The complex life cycles of haptophytes have made them difficult to classify, and for this reason coccolith-bearing forms were once thought to be a distinct class of organism.

Ben Morgan

FURTHER READING

Margulis, Lynn. *Five Kingdoms: An Illustrated Guide to the Phyla of Life on Earth.* San Francisco: W. H. Freeman, 1982; 3rd ed., New York, 1998.

Parker, Sybil P., ed. *Synopsis and Classification of Living Organisms.* New York: McGraw-Hill, 1982.

Sieburth, John McNeill. *Sea Microbes.* New York: Oxford University Press, 1979.

RELATED ARTICLES

Phytoplankton

Hardy, Alister Clavering

1896–1985

Marine Biologist and Designer of the Hardy Continuous Plankton Recorder

British marine biologist Sir Alister Hardy designed a continuous plankton recorder that enabled an assessment of marine plankton diversity and abundance from a sample taken continuously from a moving vessel at sea. Systematic sampling with modern versions of this device provides invaluable data on phytoplankton stocks. Hardy's two-volume work, *The Open Sea*, was highly influential in the late 1950s and 1960s.

Alister Clavering Hardy was born in an outlying area of the English midland city of Nottingham in 1896. His father, Richard Clavering Hardy, was an architect with a love of the countryside. From an early age, Alister was encouraged by his parents to study and appreciate the beauty of nature. As a schoolchild, Alister soon assembled a collection of insects gathered from the woods and fields near his home. He was educated at Oundle School, Northamptonshire, where an eye disorder exempted him from sports. While his classmates engaged in athletics, he was allowed out on country walks and soon became a proficient natural history artist, first in pencil and then watercolor. In 1915, during World War I, his observational and drawing skills were employed when he enlisted in the Royal Engineers and, as assistant camouflage officer, was flown over enemy territory to locate concealed gun emplacements from the air. He rose to the rank of captain, and after the war he enrolled at Exeter College, Oxford University, to study zoology. During his undergraduate years he was awarded two notable fellowships: the Christopher Welch Biological Scholarship and a scholarship to travel to study at the Stazione Zoologica in Naples. He returned to England and graduated in 1921. In that year, Hardy joined the Department of Agriculture and Fisheries as an assistant naturalist in the Fisheries Laboratory in Lowestoft, Suffolk.

Hardy's initial studies were on the feeding habits of North Atlantic herring (*Clupea harengus*). Hardy soon designed a net that could be towed at relatively high speeds to sample plankton. Hitherto, the standard plankton net, developed by German zoologist Johannes Müller in the nineteenth century, was towed behind a slow-moving vessel [speed less than about 4 kilometers per hour (2 knots; 2.5 miles per hour)], or pulled along at various depths from a stationary vessel. Fast towing created turbulence ahead of the net, hampering sampling. Hardy's innovative device, incorporating a tube and fins, allowed sampling to take place at higher speeds, so a much greater area could be sampled in a single voyage. Its simple, yet elegant design also enabled herring boats to take plankton samples while on their fishing grounds. High concentrations of the herring's food plankton usually preceded a good catch.

In 1924, when Hardy applied to join the *Discovery* expedition to Antarctica, his achievements earned him the position of chief zoologist. During his four years with the expedition, he studied Antarctic marine life and wrote extensive journals that were published four decades later under the title *Great Waters*. In 1928, one year after his return, he was appointed professor of zoology and oceanography at University College, Hull, where he founded the Department of Oceanography in 1931. There, he was to develop the Hardy continuous plankton recorder, probably his greatest contribution to oceanography.

Hardy's continuous plankton recorder incorporates a propeller, gearbox, and winding mechanism that draws silk mesh across the flow of incoming water. The mesh collects plankton and is then wound together with another mesh, trapping the plankton in the manner of a sandwich filling. The mesh is graduated along its length, enabling a specific sample to be cross-referenced to its location of capture. The mesh roll is stored in preservative solution for later detailed examination in the laboratory.

Hardy's instrument can be deployed at sea by nonscientific personnel and towed at a depth of 10 meters (33 feet) and at cruising speeds, 15 to 30 kilometers (9 to 18 miles) per hour, behind a seagoing vessel. Since the 1930s, annual surveys covering thousands of kilometers have yielded a seven-decade time series for plankton distribution and abundance in the Atlantic Ocean and North Sea. The work continues today under the aegis of the Sir Alister Hardy Foundation for Ocean Science based in Plymouth, England. The data, originally of great importance to the pelagic fishing industry, has more recently proved to be an invaluable indicator of climate change.

In 1942, Hardy was appointed Regius Professor of Natural History at the University of Aberdeen, Scotland. Four years later he returned to Oxford University as Linacre Professor of Zoology and Comparative Anatomy and held this post for 15 years, until 1961. Alister Hardy was knighted in 1957 in recognition of his achievements in marine biology.

During the 1960s, Hardy publicly joined the scientific debate on the evolutionary origin of human beings from apes. Hardy suggested that the lack of hair in humans was suggestive of an aquatic or partially aquatic phase in human evolution. Perhaps humans evolved on two legs not so much to enable them to walk and run on the African savanna but to wade in shallow water.

This hypothesis, almost entirely ignored at the time, has been revisited by a few scientists who have grown frustrated with lack of progress in resolving the savanna-origin hypothesis.

Throughout his adult life, Hardy held an unusual view on the relationship between science and religion. A convinced Darwinist, he also believed that religious experience was amenable to scientific investigation. In 1963, Hardy returned to the University of Aberdeen as Gifford Lecturer and used his position to investigate psychic and spiritual phenomena using scientific methodology. In 1968, he founded the Religious Experience Research Unit at Oxford University's Manchester College. During the 1960s and 1970s, Hardy wrote several books on the scientific investigation of religion. More than one fisheries department librarian has been duped when ordering Hardy's book, *The Biology of God*, assuming the fourth word to be a misprint of the name of a fish.

Hardy's lasting legacy to oceanography has been the continuous plankton recorder surveys, which provide an internationally recognized time series for registering environmental change, and his technical, yet highly readable popular books, which have inspired a generation of marine biologists.

Trevor Day

BIOGRAPHY
- Alister Clavering Hardy.
- Born 10 February 1896 near Nottingham, England.
- Educated at Oundle School, Northamptonshire, and Exeter College, Oxford University.
- Undergraduate studies interrupted by World War I.
- Returned to Oxford in 1919 to complete studies in zoology.
- Graduated from Oxford in 1921, having studied overseas at the Stazione Zoologica, Naples.
- First employed at the Fisheries Laboratory, Lowestoft, beginning long-term interest in phytoplankton and fisheries.
- In 1924, appointed chief zoologist on *Discovery* expedition (1925–27) to Antarctica.

- Appointed professor of zoology and oceanography at University College, Hull, in 1928, where he developed the Hardy continuous plankton recorder.
- Regius Professor in Natural History at Aberdeen University, 1942–46.
- Linacre Professor in Zoology, Oxford University, 1946–60.
- Knighted in 1957 for services to marine biology.
- In 1960s, his interests turned to science and religion, and he founded the Religious Experience Research Unit at Manchester College, Oxford University, in 1968.
- Died 23 May 1985, in Oxford.

SELECTED WRITINGS

Hardy, A. C. "A New Method of Plankton Research." *Nature*, Vol. 118 (1926), pp. 630–632.
———. *The Open Sea*, Vol. 1, *The World of Plankton*. London: Collins, 1956.
———. *The Open Sea*, Vol. 2, *Fish and Fisheries*. London: Collins, 1959.
———. "Studying the Ever-Changing Sea." *Nature*, Vol. 196 (1962), pp. 207–210.
———. *Great Waters*. London: Collins, 1967.

FURTHER READING

Reid, P. C., M. Edwards, H. G. Hunt, and A. J. Warner. "Phytoplankton Change in the North Atlantic." *Nature*, Vol. 391 (1998), p. 546.
Schlee, S. *The Edge of an Unfamiliar World: A History of Oceanography*. New York: Dutton, 1973.

USEFUL WEB SITES

Sir Alister Hardy Foundation for Ocean Science home page. <http://www.sahfos.org>.

RELATED ARTICLES

Pelagic; Phytoplankton; Plankton Net

Harmful Algal Bloom

Phytoplankton, a dominant form of plant life in aquatic ecosystems, is comprised primarily of drifting, single-celled photosynthetic organisms called *algae*. When conditions are favorable, these cells are capable of increasing their numbers rapidly by asexual reproduction. In this way they create a locally dense concentration of algal cells or phytoplankton bloom. Phytoplankton blooms are an important food source for animals ranging from the smallest zooplankton to the great whales. However, some phytoplankton species are toxic or can affect the environment adversely. A bloom of these nuisance species is called a *harmful algal bloom* (HAB). Commonly, although erroneously, referred to as "red tides," not all HABs discolor the water, and they are unrelated to tides. They are, however, a phenomenon that is occurring with increasing frequency, plaguing fisheries, fouling beaches, and endangering marine animals and humans.

The economic, environmental, and aesthetic tolls incurred by HABs result from a variety of physical, biological, and chemical mechanisms. At high cell concentrations, light may no longer penetrate the depth of the bloom, resulting in a massive mortality of phytoplankton, which in the absence of light is unable to photosynthesize. The process of decomposition rapidly depletes the water of oxygen, resulting in the death of fish and other animals due to anoxia. Other phytoplankton species possess armor of siliceous spines, which pierce the gills of fish that feed on them. An effective deterrent to grazing pressure, the fish then die as a result of fatal hemorrhaging or subsequent bacterial infections.

HABs, which receive the most attention and have some of the greatest impacts, are caused by toxic phytoplankton species. Although more than 5000 species of phytoplankton are recognized worldwide, fewer than 50 are known to produce toxins. These phycotoxins are diverse and often complex chemical compounds that cause illness and mortality in animals, including humans. Toxicity occurs through ingestion, exposure to secreted toxins, or via toxin transfer through food webs. Some of the best known toxin-producing phytoplankton are dinoflagellates. Members of this group are responsible for numerous poisoning syndromes affecting humans: paralytic shellfish poisoning (PSP), neurotoxic shellfish poisoning (NSP), diarrhetic shellfish poisoning (DSP), and ciguatera poisoning (tropical fish poisoning). PSP occurs when sufficient levels of saxotoxins, produced by the dinoflagellate genus *Alexandrium*, accumulate in filter-feeding fish and mollusks that are then consumed by humans. At concentrations of 7 to 17 micrograms of toxin per kilogram of shellfish meat, these potent neurotoxins cause death by respiratory paralysis in humans. Furthermore, due to the bioaccumulation of the toxins by filter-feeding organisms, PSP can occur when *Alexandrium* concentrations in the water are quite low. In 1990, butter clams harvested from the Aleutian Peninsula, Alaska, were reported to contain 77,500 micrograms of toxin per kilogram of tissue, or 5000 to 11,000 lethal human doses.

Gymnodinium breve is a dinoflagellate associated with NSP and brevetoxins. This class of phycotoxins binds to sodium channels on nerve and muscle cell membranes, causing an excessive influx of sodium ions across the membranes, leading to cell death. Like PSP toxins, they accumulate in filter-feeding organisms, including commercially important shellfish. Additionally, inhalation of brevetoxins aerosolized by sea spray leads to respiratory irritation in humans and other marine animals.

Dinoflagellates of the genus *Dinophysis* rarely occur in large numbers; however, they have been shown to cause DSP at concentrations of only a few hundred cells per liter. Diarrhetic shellfish poisoning results from a suite of toxins, the best known of which is okadaic acid. When humans ingest shellfish contaminated with these toxins, they are likely to experience extreme gastrointestinal distress, including severe abdominal pain, diarrhea, and vomiting. Long-term exposure to some of the other *Dinophysis* toxins is now a suspected cause of certain types of gastrointestinal cancer.

Several species of the diatom genus *Pseudonitzschia* produce domoic acid, a potent neurotoxin, responsible for amnesiac shellfish poisoning (ASP). In humans, birds, and marine mammals symptoms of domoic acid include short-term memory loss, disorientation, and gastrointestinal distress and can result in death. Because *Pseudonitzschia* often dominate phytoplankton blooms, attaining cell densities of over 1 million per liter, domoic acid readily permeates local food webs. Anchovy and sardines filter-feed exclusively on phytoplankton and are among the most important prey for many marine birds and mammals. A well-publicized event in 1998 left more than 400 California sea lions dead, victims of toxin transferred via consumption of these fish. Many historical accounts of unexplained seabird deaths are now attributed to ASP events. In 1961, tens of sooty shearwaters, disoriented after gorging on what is now suspected to have been domoic-acid contaminated sardines, fell from the sky in Capitola, California. This event is said to have inspired Alfred Hitchcock's famous 1963 movie *The Birds*.

Although few would argue that toxic bloom events have increased over the last several decades, there are many differing opinions about the causes. Ever-increasing human populations on our coasts and growing demand for fish and shellfish have stimulated scientific awareness. These factors, coupled with new surveillance techniques and more observers, may result in better detection of phenomena that have always occurred. There is also much speculation that global climate change, already linked to a host of emerging diseases affecting marine organisms, may play a role. It is not difficult to imagine how increases in storms or changes in circulation patterns might alter the transport and distribution of HAB species. Nutrient enrichment of coastal marine environments as a result of human activities including industrial and agricultural runoff is implicated in many HABs. In shallow, coastal marine waters with restricted circulation, nutrient enrichment leads to excessive production of organic matter in a process known as *eutrophication*. Such environments are prime sites for

HABs. Humans have also contributed to the global expansion of HABs by transporting toxic and nuisance species in ship ballast water. Indeed, the practice of taking on ballast water to stabilize cargo ships has been responsible for introduction of nonindigenous and invasive species to marine ecosystems worldwide.

A recent government sponsored study on the economic impacts from HABs in the United States estimates an average cost of U.S.$49 million per year during the period 1987–92. Major economic impacts are on public health, commercial fisheries, and recreation and tourism. Although the economic effects are measurable, mechanisms that trigger, sustain, and terminate HABs are only beginning to be understood. Our increasing reliance on coastal zones for aquaculture, commerce, and recreation warrants further research on HABs. It is only through better understanding of the causes (e.g., by improving predictive capabilities and preventing practices that exacerbate HABs) that we will be able mitigate their potentially disastrous effects.

Susan Coale

FURTHER READING

Anderson, D. M. "Red Tides." *Scientific American,* Vol. 271, No. 2 (Aug. 1994), pp. 53–58.

Anderson, D. M., and Alan W. White. "Marine Biotoxins at the Top of the Food Chain." *Oceanus,* Vol. 32, No. 3 (Fall 1992).

Anderson, D. M., Porter Hoagland, Yoshi Kaoru, and Alan W. White. "Estimated Annual Economic Impacts from Harmful Algal Blooms (HABs) in the United States." *Sea Grant Tech. Rep. WHOI-2000-11.* Woods Hole, Mass.: Woods Hole Oceanographic Institution, 2000.

CENR. *National Assessment of Harmful Algal Blooms in U.S. Waters.* Washington, D.C.: National Science and Technology Council Committee on Environment and Natural Resources, October 2000.

USEFUL WEB SITES

"Marine Biotoxins and Harmful Algal Blooms." Northwest Fisheries Science Center. <http://www.nwfsc.noaa.gov/hab>.

RELATED ARTICLES

Anoxia; Ciguatera; Dinoflagellate; Eutrophic; Phytoplankton; Pollution, Ocean; Red Tide

Hawaiian–Emperor Bend

The Hawaiian–Emperor Volcanic Chain stretches across about 6125 kilometers (3806 miles) of the North Pacific Ocean and has a pronounced bend in the middle, separating the older Emperor Seamounts from the younger Hawaiian Volcanic Chain. The chain is age progressive, with volcanoes at the northwestern end about 85 million years old and the active volcanoes Mauna Loa, Kilauea, and Loihi at the southeastern end.

The chain is the best example of an age-progressive linear volcanic chain on Earth and thus the type locale of a hotspot-generated volcanic chain in which the volcanoes form sequentially from the same region of the mantle, only to be carried away on the moving, overlying lithospheric plate. Paleomagnetic data indicate that the Hawaiian hotspot has remained fixed since the bend but may have been located at more northerly latitudes prior to that. The chain has been proposed to map the rate and direction of motion of the overlying Pacific Plate and has played a prominent role in plate tectonic reconstructions. It has also been important in the development of models of mantle convection since hotspots are widely viewed as mantle plumes, rising either from the core–mantle boundary or from a shallower seismic discontinuity in Earth's mantle at about 675 kilometers (419 miles) depth.

The dramatic change in orientation of the chain that is called the Hawaiian–Emperor Bend has been dated using K–Ar and Ar–Ar techniques at 43.1 ± 1.4 million years, although more recent dating suggests that this age may be too young by several million years. This change in orientation has been widely interpreted to reflect a change in the rate and direction of motion of the Pacific

Plate, perhaps ultimately caused by collision of the Indian subcontinent with Eurasia. In these models, the collision resulted in reorganization of oceanic spreading centers, the initiation of subduction zones in the western Pacific Ocean, and eventually in the change in rotation of the Pacific Plate recorded as the Hawaiian–Emperor Bend. In recent years, several studies have concluded that the Hawaiian–Emperor Bend is not related to motion of the Pacific Plate, mostly because the timing of the bend and of changes in spreading rates and directions do not appear to coincide. Evaluation of these models, however, must await more precise age determinations of the volcanoes in the Hawaiian–Emperor Volcanic Chain and of the magnetic polarity timescale.

The islands, banks, atolls, submarine volcanoes, and guyots that make up the chain have a combined volume above the seafloor of about 1 million cubic kilometers (0.24 million cubic miles) and probably a similar volume below the seafloor. Nearly the entire chain consists of guyots and submarine volcanoes, with islands only in the younger Hawaiian chain. Nearly all the volcanoes have a pronounced break in slope that is interpreted to mark the shoreline when voluminous eruptive activity ceased. These shorelines have been used to identify which of the volcanoes reached sea level and to quantify the size and height of the former islands. Of the 129 volcanoes that comprise the chain, 104 reached sea level to become islands. The smaller volcanoes were islands for less than 1 million years, but the largest probably persisted for up to 16 million years before finally subsiding beneath sea level.

David A. Clague

FURTHER READING

Clague, D. A. "The Growth and Subsidence of the Hawaiian-Emperor Volcanic Chain." In A. Keast and S. C. Miller, eds., *The Origin and Evolution of Pacific Island Biotas, New Guinea to Eastern Polynesia: Patterns and Processes.* Amsterdam: SPB Academic Publishing, 1996; pp. 35–50.

Clague, David Alan, and G. B. Dalrymple. *The Hawaiian–Emperor Volcanic Chain*, Part 1, *Geologic Evolution.* U.S. Geological Survey Professional Paper 1350. Washington, D.C.: U.S. Government Printing Office, 1987; pp. 5–54.

Dalrymple, G. B., and D. A. Clague. "The Age of the Hawaiian–Emperor Bend." *Earth and Planetary Science Letters*, Vol. 31 (1976), pp. 313–319.

Norton, I. O. "Plate Motions in the North Pacific: The 43 Ma Nonevent." *Tectonics*, Vol. 14 (1995), pp. 1080–1094.

RELATED ARTICLES

Emperor Seamounts; Hawaiian Islands; Hotspot; Mantle Plume; Pacific Plate; Plate Tectonics; Subduction Zone

Hawaiian Islands

Recent study of the submarine flanks of the Hawaiian Islands has revealed important new information about the geologic history of the islands. The Hawaiian Islands are the youngest portion of the linear Hawaiian–Emperor Volcanic Chain and consist of the eight principal islands of Kauai, Niihau, Oahu, Molokai, Lanai, Maui, Kahoolawe, and Hawaii. Loihi Seamount, Kilauea, and Mauna Loa are active volcanoes. Hualalai volcano on Hawaii and Haleakala volcano on Maui, each active in the past few hundred years, and Mauna Kea, last active about 4500 years ago, are considered dormant.

Side-scan mapping with the GLORIA system in the 1980s revealed that flanks of nearly all the islands had been modified by numerous giant landslides, evidenced by the distribution of blocks scattered on the seafloor adjacent to the islands. Some of these landslides, such as the Nuuanu Slide northeast of Oahu, are truly gargantuan, with blocks as large as 30 kilometers (19 miles) long by 5 kilometers (3 miles) wide by 2 kilometers (1.2 miles) tall, and a combined volume of the larger [greater than 1 cubic kilometer (0.24 cubic miles)] blocks exceeding 1400 cubic kilometers (335 cubic miles). There are at least 17 such landslide deposits on the seafloor adjacent to the principal Hawaiian Islands, indicating a recurrence interval of 340,000 years. Since many of the deposits may well be from more than one landslide and other slides probably buried beneath the next volcano that formed, this recurrence interval is clearly a minimum. Study of these older landslides has provided insight into the active processes in the Kilauea and Mauna Loa volcanoes, where the flanks slide seaward along a nearly horizontal fault and thrust the flanks of the volcanoes over the ocean crust. Study of the landslide blocks and flanks of the volcanoes has also shown that a large part of the flanks of the volcanoes consist of fragmental volcanic rocks that form when subaerial lava flows enter the sea and fragment. As the volcano grows, subaerial lava flows extend seaward on top of the core of fragmental rock.

The evidence that the islands subside rapidly during and after they form is also recorded on their submarine flanks as a series of old shoreline deposits. Off the west coast of Kohala volcano on Hawaii, a series of terraces formed as the island subsided and sea level fluctuated during Pleistocene glacial and interglacial periods. Each time that sea level rose quickly at the beginning of an interglacial period, the coral reef that was growing drowned. By

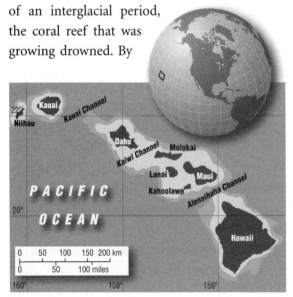

Hawaiian Islands.

the time sea level fell at the start of the next glacial period, the previously formed reef had subsided too far and was too deep to grow again. The final result is a series of stairstep reefs ranging from 150 to 1325 meters (490 to 4350 feet) deep, each marking the rapid rise in sea level that accompanied the change from glacial to interglacial climate. The depths of these terraces provide a direct measure of the amount of subsidence since that particular reef drowned. For the island of Hawaii, this amounts to a rate of 2.6 millimeters (0.1 inch) each year.

David A. Clague

FURTHER READING

Clague, D. A. "Geology." In S. P. Juvik and J. O. Juvik, eds., *Atlas of Hawai'i*, 3rd ed. Honolulu, Hawaii: University of Hawaii Press, 1998; pp. 37–46.

Decker, R. W., T. L. Wright, and P. H. Stauffer, eds. *Volcanism in Hawaii*, 2 vols. U.S. Geological Survey Professional Paper 1350. Washington, D.C.: U.S. Government Printing Office/Denver, Colo.: U.S. Geological Survey, 1987.

Macdonald, Gordon A., and Agatin T. Abbott. *Volcanoes in the Sea: The Geology of Hawaii*. Honolulu, Hawaii: University of Hawaii Press, 1970; 2nd ed., with Frank L. Peterson, 1983.

Stearns, Harold T. *Geology of the State of Hawaii*, 2nd ed. Palo Alto, Calif.: Pacific Books, 1985.

RELATED ARTICLES

Emperor Seamounts; Hawaiian–Emperor Bend, Hotspot; Pacific Plate; Submarine Mass Wasting; Submarine Volcanism

Headland, see Coastal Morphology

Heat Capacity

The heat capacity of a material is a thermal property of matter that expresses the temperature rise when a given amount of heat is absorbed by a material. For distilled water this is 4217 joules per kilogram per degree Celsius (about 1 kilocalorie per kilogram per degree Celsius). As with other thermal properties, the heat capacity of water is anomalously high compared with other materials. The heat capacity of rock is about 1500 joules per kilogram per degree Celsius (0.4 kilocalorie per kilogram per degree Celsius). The difference between thermal properties of water and other materials is due to hydrogen bonding between water molecules. The larger the heat capacity, the smaller is the temperature rise, due to the absorption of heat. For example, adding 4000 joules of heat to 1 kilogram of water raises water temperature about 1°C (1.8°F), while that same amount of heat raises the temperature of 1 kilogram of copper cookware by about 5°C (9°F).

Water's high heat capacity and heat of vaporization are important, because the presence of water on Earth regulates temperature. This can be seen by comparing summertime air temperatures along a temperate coast with those inland: Where the daytime coastal air temperature may be 15°C (59°F), temperatures only a few miles inland may rise to 35°C (95°F). While the heat capacity of soil or rock is less than half that of water, the difference between the coastal and inland air temperature depends largely on turbulent mixing at the sea surface. Thus, ocean waters are heated over tens of meters while soils and rocks are heated only to centimeters.

The heat capacity of water varies only slightly in the oceans, depending on temperature (T), salinity (S), and depth (Z). The heat capacity of fresh water ($S = 0$) is higher than that of salt water ($S = 35$) by 5 percent. Over the oceanic salinity range of $S = 33$ to 38, the difference is only 0.7 percent. Temperature has a small effect on heat capacity: Heat capacity increases with temperature by only 0.3 percent for the oceanic temperature range −2 to 37°C (28.4 to 98.6°F). At average oceanic depth of 4000 meters (about 13,100 feet) the heat capacity is 3 percent less than that at the surface. A typical value of heat capacity for surface water in the oceans ($S = 35$, $T = 10°C$) is 3986 joules per kilogram per degree Celsius.

William W. Broenkow

FURTHER READING
Berner, Elizabeth Kay, and Robert A. Berner. *The Global Water Cycle: Geochemistry and Environment.* Englewood Cliffs, N.J.: Prentice Hall, 1987.
UNESCO. *Calculation of the Fundamental Properties in Seawater.* Technical Papers in Marine Science 44. Rome: UNESCO, 1983.

RELATED ARTICLES
Temperature, Distribution of

Heezen, Bruce Charles
1924–1977
Marine Geologist

Bruce C. Heezen is best known for his leading contribution to the identification and characterization of the mid-ocean ridge system. He was also an expert on turbidity currents and other sediment-transporting phenomena in the deep ocean. An influential map, "The Floor of the Oceans" (1959; compiled with Marie Tharp), is found in most college-level marine science books published between the 1980s and mid-1990s.

Born in Vinton, Iowa, in 1924, Bruce Charles Heezen spent his childhood on a turkey farm close to the banks of the Mississippi River. While studying for his B.S. degree in geology at the University of Iowa, Bruce attended an inspiring lecture given by leading marine geologist Maurice Ewing (1906–74). In a discussion after the lecture, Ewing invited Heezen to take part in a forthcoming expedition to plot the then-uncharted Mid-Atlantic Ridge. Heezen accepted and, without any seagoing experience, was surprised to find himself booked on the cruise as chief scientist. Undaunted, the mission was a success and launched Heezen on his lifetime career in marine geology.

Heezen joined the Lamont (later Lamont–Doherty) Geological Observatory of Columbia University as a postgraduate in 1949, the year the observatory was founded by Maurice Ewing. Heezen was to remain with the Lamont Observatory his entire working life, becoming assistant professor in 1960 and associate professor in 1964.

Back in 1949, on a meager postgraduate fellowship, Heezen had the choice of buying a car or renting a room. Characteristic of Heezen's love of social life and travel, he chose the car and slept under his desk at night.

By 1952, Heezen had compiled convincing evidence for the existence of turbidity currents—mass flows of seawater and suspended sediment. Using precise historical records for the 1929 Grand Banks earthquake, Heezen was able to show how underwater communication cables in the Grand Banks region were severed in sequence as an underwater disturbance passed over them. He reconstructed the movement of 100 cubic kilometers (about 25 cubic miles) of sediment as it raced along at speeds approaching 85 kilometers (53 miles) per hour, snapping cables in its path. These turbidity currents, as previous researcher Reginald Daly (1871–1957) had predicted, contributed to the carving of submarine canyons. The currents carried suspended sediment long distances, adding to the sediment cover of the abyssal plains. For many years, Heezen was to advise both the navy and the cable industry of the potential hazards to deep-sea cables from geological events.

The 1950s were an immensely fertile decade in marine geology. Improvements in seabed mapping techniques, spurred on by technological developments from World War II, meant that a wealth of geological and geophysical data on the ocean floor was being collected. For the first time, the deep-ocean floor was being mapped in detail. Under the guidance of his mentor Maurice Ewing, Bruce Heezen recognized the potential benefits in collating and plotting these

data to produce charts showing the morphology of the seabed. Working with geologist and cartographer Marie Tharp (1920–), they set about devising a physiographic method of presentation, presenting the contours of the seabed as a three-dimensional representation on flat paper. These maps—with their vertical scale exaggerated—gave the impression of an ocean drained of water and used color coding or shading to represent different provinces. The maps could be readily interpreted, even by geological nonspecialists. The first Heezen-Tharp physiographic diagram, which mapped the North Atlantic, was published in 1956.

Arguably, Heezen's greatest contribution to marine geology was his identification of the mid-ocean ridge system as a 65,000-kilometer (40,400-mile)-long mountain range. Its axis was associated with shallow seismicity, and Heezen was able to predict where as-yet-unidentified parts of the system—for example, ridges southeast of Africa and across the Arctic Ocean—were to be found. Heezen, Tharp, and Ewing noted

Bruce Heezen. (Courtesy, Lamont-Doherty Earth Observatory)

that features such as the Red Sea, the East African rifts, and the cracks of the central Icelandic graben were continuous with the mid-ocean ridge system. Along the axis of this system the crust was split and under tension. Initially, Heezen thought this was evidence for an expanding Earth but dropped this idea once ocean trenches were recognized as subduction zones that could assimilate excess crust. Heezen went on to show how an embryonic rift valley could evolve into a fully developed ocean, with the African Rift Valley, the Red Sea, the Labrador Sea, and the North Atlantic as examples of different stages in that sequence. This insight was an important conceptual step leading to the discovery of seafloor spreading.

Heezen was an enthusiastic if unconventional teacher who encouraged his students to be independent learners. His scientific papers demonstrate the breadth of his reading. His articles encompassed whales caught up in submarine cables and the volcanic destruction of the Mediterranean island of Thera, with its possible link to the collapse of the Minoan civilization. In 1971, Heezen collaborated with former student Charles Hollister (1936–99) to publish *The Face of the Deep,* a photographic collection with accompanying text. This popular book summarized much of Heezen's work observing the seafloor from submersibles.

During his career Heezen conducted research from a wide variety of vessels, including oceanographic ships, cable ships, drilling ships, and submersibles and submarines. On 21 June 1977, Heezen was about to dive in the U.S. nuclear research submarine *NR-1* to study the Mid-Atlantic Ridge south of Iceland when he suffered a heart attack and died. In that same year, Bruce Heezen and Marie Tharp's epic achievement—their map of the ocean floor, "The Floor of the Oceans"—was published. This map has been reproduced in most college-level marine science textbooks since, and has informed and excited many thousands of aspiring and professional oceanographers.

Trevor Day

Biography

- Bruce Charles Heezen.
- Born 11 April 1924 in Vinton, Iowa.
- Graduated in geology at the University of Iowa (1948).
- Gained his M.A. (1952) and Ph.D. (1957) at the Lamont–Doherty Geological Observatory, Columbia University, where he spend his entire career, becoming assistant professor in 1960 and associate professor in 1964.
- Author or coauthor of more than 300 scientific articles, he published (with Charles Hollister) *The Face of the Deep* (1971) and with Marie Tharp (1977) the famous seafloor map "The Floor of the Oceans."
- Heezen died at sea on 21 June 1977, aged 53.

Selected Writings

Heezen, B. C. "Turbidity Currents." In M. N. Hill, ed., *The Sea,* Vol. 3. New York: Wiley-Interscience, 1963; pp. 742–775.

Heezen, B. C., and M. Ewing. "The Mid-Oceanic Ridge." In M. N. Hill, ed., *The Sea,* Vol. 3. New York: Wiley-Interscience, 1963; pp. 388–410.

Heezen, B. C., and C. D. Hollister. *The Face of the Deep.* New York: Oxford University Press, 1971.

Heezen, B. C., and H. W. Menard. "Topography of the Deep-Sea Floor." In M. N. Hill, ed., *The Sea,* Vol. 3. New York: Wiley-Interscience, 1963; pp. 233–280.

Heezen, B. C., M. Tharp, and M. Ewing. "The Floors of the Oceans: I. The North Atlantic." *Geological Society of America Special Paper 65,* 1959.

Further Reading

Anderson, Roger N. *Marine Geology.* New York: Wiley, 1986; 2nd ed., 1988.

Menard, H. W. *The Ocean of Truth: A Personal History of Global Tectonics.* Princeton, N.J.: Princeton University Press, 1986.

Schlee, Susan. *The Edge of an Unfamiliar World: A History of Oceanography.* New York: Dutton, 1973; London: Hale, 1975.

Related Articles

Ewing, William Maurice; India Plate; Mid-Atlantic Ridge; Mid-Ocean Ridge; Seafloor Spreading; Submarine Canyon; Turbidity Current

Heinrich Layer

Heinrich layers may mark catastrophic climate change. They are distinct sediment layers in the North Atlantic, which were probably deposited from armadas of melting ice. The origin of the layers and the cause of the catastrophic calving of large continental ice sheets is one of the most exciting and controversial discoveries of paleoceanography during the late 1980s and 1990s.

Marine sediments are excellent recorders of changes in the ocean and climate. For example, many of the major discoveries about the glacial cycles of the last few million years, called the Ice Ages, came from studying the composition of marine sediments. This information comes in a variety of forms. Probably most important are the tiny plant and animal-like organisms called *plankton* that live in the ocean. When they die, their shells fall to the seafloor and become sediment. Just as organisms on land live where the climate is suited to their needs, so do marine organisms. Some, such as coral, live only in warm, clear tropical waters. Others seek out cold, nutrient-rich areas for their home. One of the most important plankton used in these studies are foraminifera, animal-like creatures that build their shells from calcium carbonate. Some live near the ocean bottom and others near the ocean surface. They are important because in addition to species preference for a specific environment, their shells are used for oxygen and carbon isotopic analyses. This allows us to determine the temperature of the past ocean.

Other marine sediment comes from land. Very fine-grained particles are blown by the wind. Particles of a variety of sizes are transported in high-density currents off the continental shelf and onto the ocean floor. In polar and northern temperate regions, icebergs, which have broken off continental ice sheets, carry a variety of sizes of land sediment long distances into the ocean.

To examine the changes in the ocean, paleoceanographers and marine geologists collect cores, which are long tubes of sediment. The top layer contains the most recent sediment and the bottom layer the oldest sediment. To see what changes have occurred, sediment samples are taken from a core and examined. For example, in the late 1970s, William Ruddiman (1943–), studying sediment cores from the North Atlantic, showed that during past glacial times, sand-sized particles from melting ice were more likely to occur in a band across the Atlantic north of 46°N latitude. He had discovered the track of ancient icebergs.

Description of Heinrich Layers

Sediments deposited in the North Atlantic between about 14,500 and 70,000 radiocarbon years ago contain six layers whose composition is distinct from the surrounding sediment. Called *Heinrich layers* after Hartmut Heinrich (1953–), who first described them in 1988, they are designated as H-1 (youngest) through H-6 (oldest). These layers can be over 0.35 meter (1 foot) thick in Hudson Bay and only a fraction of an inch thick in the eastern North Atlantic. The variation in thickness is one of the indicators that the sediment originated in North America.

In all six layers, the sand-sized particles contain few foraminifera. This suggests that there was either a decrease in productivity or that the layers were deposited so rapidly that there wasn't time for foraminifera to grow. The foraminifera that are present are primarily left-coiling *Neogloboquadrina pachyderma*, a species that grows only in polar waters. These foraminifera have about 2 parts per thousand lower d ^{18}O values than those found in surrounding layers. This suggests that they grew in low-salinity water. The salinity of the ocean surface could be lowered if large amounts of ice were to melt and not mix with the deeper water.

A second distinctive feature of Heinrich layers is the composition of the land-derived sand particles. Most sand in glacial-marine sediments is transported by icebergs that break off from large, land-based ice sheets and melt. The sand is usually about 80 percent quartz with a wide variety of other minerals and small rock fragments, reflecting the composition of the continents. This is not the case in four of the six Heinrich layers. These layers also contain about 80 percent quartz, but the rest is limestone. Sediments above and below the Heinrich layers have almost no limestone. The abundance of limestone decreases from west to east. Two of the layers, H-3 (about 27,000 years) and H-6 (about 70,000), have only limestone particles in cores collected from the Labrador Sea. This suggests that the source of the ice was Canada, in particular the Laurentide Ice Sheet.

The fine sediment in the Heinrich layers is also distinct. It lacks smectite, a clay mineral that is derived from the weathering of basalt and thus is not likely to have come from Iceland and the ocean-spreading centers. In addition, the cumulative radiometric age of the Heinrich clays is much greater than that of the surrounding clays, roughly 0.9 billion years versus 0.44 billion years. More convincing information comes from isotopic age determinations on single mineral grains. Unlike grains in the surrounding, non-Heinrich layers, which show a wide range of ages, these ages are tightly clustered around 1.7 and 2.7 billion years, again indicative of a northern Canadian source, in this case the Churchill Province.

Significance

The significance of these events extends beyond the North Atlantic. Heinrich layers occur at times of worldwide climatic and atmospheric changes. Remarkably, Heinrich layers were deposited in the coldest part of Dansgaard–Oeschger (D-O) cycles, just before the most dramatic warmings where Earth's atmospheric temperature rose 6 to 7°C (10.8 to 12.6°F) in as little as 50 years. The close association of these two phenomena suggests that they are related.

D-O cycles were originally identified from oxygen isotope measurements in the Greenland ice cores. They were first described in the late 1960s and 1970s, but in part because the very rapid temperature change they imply was so difficult to accept, people were skeptical. It wasn't until the 1980s, when additional ice cores showed similar features, that they were accepted as a real record of climate. In each D-O cycle, which takes roughly 2000 years to complete, there is a gradual cooling followed by rapid warming. These cycles are bundled together, so that each successive cycle gets colder, much as each stair in a staircase gets lower. Then, for reasons that are still not clear, there is a dramatic warming and the atmospheric temperature returns to the much warmer levels (the top of the staircase). The stepwise cooling cycles start all over again. The bundles of D-O cycles are called *Bond cycles*. In the mid- to late 1990s, Gerard Bond (1940–) and his colleagues, working at Lamont–Doherty Earth Observatory, identified the bundling and correlated the Heinrich layers with the cold interval before the rapid warming.

Beginning in the 1990s, D-O cycles have been recognized in ocean and land sediment around the world. Therefore, whatever causes them is connected to worldwide atmospheric and oceanic changes and thus makes the cause of Heinrich layer deposition that much more intriguing.

Theories of Origin

The origin of these layers is controversial. However, most scientists agree that instabilities in the ice-stream flow within the North American Laurentide Ice Sheet led to the periodic release of armadas of icebergs into the Atlantic Ocean. As the ice melted it created a freshwater lid, which decreased productivity and probably decreased ocean circulation. Currently under debate is the cause of the instability, the exact source of the ice, and the timing of ice flow from different areas surrounding the North Atlantic Ocean. This is especially true for Heinrich layers H-3 and H-6.

Several models have been proposed to explain the origin of the ice instability. One of the most popular models proposes binge/purge oscillations of ice sheet buildup and collapse. This model suggests that as ice thickened around Hudson Bay, it flowed from the highlands into the bay. There it froze to the mud and rocks and continued to grow through several D-O cycles. Weight of the ice and heat from Earth eventually caused the base of the ice sheet to become unstable. It collapsed catastrophically, purging itself and sending huge armadas of ice and sediment through the Hudson Strait, into the Gulf of St. Lawrence, and into the North Atlantic. Another model attributes the instability to earthquakes, due, in part, to the additional weight caused by ice loading. Still others have proposed changes in the amount of energy that Earth receives from the Sun (insolation) and sea-level fluctuations.

Although these models may in part be true, it is likely that the model that finely explains Heinrich layers will be part of a model that also explains D-O and Bond cycles. Because of the worldwide connections, such a model will probably look to a mechanism that has a strong atmospheric component.

Suzanne O'Connell

FURTHER READING

Alley, Richard. *The Two-Mile Time Machine.* Princeton, N.J.: Princeton University Press, 2000.

Ruddiman, William F. *Earth's Climate, Past and Future.* San Francisco: W. H. Freeman, 2000.

University Corporation for Atmospheric Research. *Our Nation's Climate.* Reports to the Nation. Oxford, Md.: NOAA, 1997.

RELATED ARTICLES

Climate Change; Deep-Sea Sediment; Glacial Marine Processes; Oxygen Isotopes; Paleoceanography

Helium

Helium (He) is an inert (unreactive) noble gas. It is the seventh most abundant gas in seawater, after nitrogen (N_2), oxygen (O_2), carbon dioxide (CO_2), argon (Ar), hydrogen (H), and neon (Ne). Oceanographers use helium measurements to study different oceanographic processes, such as abyssal circulation.

Helium exists as two isotopes (atoms that have the same atomic number but different mass number, i.e., an equal number of protons but a different number of neutrons): ^{3}He and ^{4}He. The isotope ^{4}He exists in the ocean due to gas exchange from the atmosphere and as a result of radiogenic decay from sediments containing uranium (U) and thorium (Th). The isotope ^{3}He exists in the ocean due to the beta decay of tritium (^{3}H) in the upper layer of the oceans and primordial input from the interior of Earth (primarily, outgasing through mid-ocean ridge hydrothermal vent systems).

Oceanographers use the ^{3}He/^{4}He ratio when measuring helium to determine its source and to better understand oceanographic processes. For example, in the east Pacific, the flux of ^{3}He emanating from hydrothermal vents is greatly enriched. This enrichment causes the ^{3}He/^{4}He ratio in hydrothermal plume water to be over 10 times the atmospheric value. The helium-enriched plume is transported thousands of kilometers by deep-sea currents before it is so diluted by mixing that the plume is no longer distinguishable. This dramatic increase in the deepwater helium ratio can therefore be used as a tracer of deep water and hydrothermal vent fluid circulation.

Daniel Schuller

FURTHER READING

Broecker, Wallace S., and Tsung-hung Peng. *Tracers in the Sea.* Palisades, N.Y.: Lamont–Doherty Geological Observatory, Columbia University, 1982.

Millero, Frank J. *Chemical Oceanography.* Boca Raton, Fla.: CRC Press, 1992; 2nd ed., 1996.

Pinet, Paul R. *Invitation to Oceanography.* Minneapolis/St. Paul, Minn.: West, 1996; 2nd ed., Sudbury, Mass.: Jones and Bartlett, 1998.

RELATED ARTICLES

Hydrothermal Vent; Radiometric Dating; Trace Gas; Tritium

Helland-Hansen, Bjørn

1877–1957

Physical Oceanographer

Norwegian scientist Bjørn Helland-Hansen, probably more than any other early twentieth-century oceanographer, helped transform oceanography from a descriptive science to one based on physical and chemical principles.

Bjørn Helland-Hansen was born in Christiania (now Oslo), Norway, in 1877. An incident while he was a medical student at Christiania helped steer his subsequent career. In 1898, as a member of the *Aurora Borealis* expedition, he had the misfortune to lose fingers on each hand to frostbite. He turned from medicine to the natural sciences, studying first at Christiania, then at Stockholm, Sweden, and finally at Copenhagen, Denmark. His interests and ability took him in the direction of physical oceanography.

At Stockholm, Helland-Hansen studied under the world-renowned meteorologist and hydrographer Vilhelm Bjerknes (1862–1951) and met the man who was to be his lifelong colleague, Vagn Walfrid Ekman (1874–1954). At Copenhagen, Helland-Hansen worked with the internationally famous Danish oceanographer Martin Knudsen (1871– 1949) before being appointed, in 1900, as assistant at the Fishery Directorate in Bergen. By this time he had met Fridtjof Nansen (1861–1930), the famous Norwegian explorer and oceanographer based at Christiania. Nansen and Helland-Hansen were to develop a long-standing friendship and collaboration that was to yield two notable treatises: one on the Norwegian Sea (1909) and the other on the eastern North Atlantic (1927). Another noted collaboration was to be with the fisheries biologist Johan Hjort (1869–1948), for whom Helland-Hansen undertook mathematical computations of growth and survival patterns in fish populations.

Over a 10-year period, Helland-Hansen participated in, and often led, cruises of the research vessel *Michael Sars,* first in the seas of northwest Europe, and then, in 1910, in a major expedition traversing a large proportion of the North Atlantic. The advances in oceanographic knowledge accruing from these expeditions were highlighted in the 1912 oceanographic classic, *The Depths of the Ocean,* for which Helland-Hansen wrote the "Physical Oceanography" section.

In 1903, Helland-Hansen collaborated with Johan W. Sandstrom to derive a dynamical method for computing ocean currents. First, they had concluded that the massive current gyres in ocean basins revolve around a mid-ocean bulge of water. Other factors being equal, in the open ocean, water will move under gravity to seek its own level, and seawater of low density (as determined by temperature and salinity) will tend to rise above—and therefore flow toward—seawater that is more dense. Away from the equator there will be a turning force on the moving water as a result of Earth's rotation (the Coriolis effect). The resulting currents were later called *geostrophic* (from the Greek *geo*, Earth, and *strophe*, turning).

Sandstrom and Helland-Hansen devised an equation that related current speed and direction based on the height of the central mound, which in turn can be calculated from the density of water. This enabled oceanographers to compute theoretical current flows based on latitude, plus water topography (derived from precise measurements of temperature, salinity, and depth), without the need for extensive current measuring in situ. Sandstrom and Helland-Hansen's equations were later called *geostrophic equations.* In the 1960s, altimeter measurements from the Seasat satellite revealed the existence of the central mounds of gyres for the first time, a feature that for six decades had been a theoretical presumption.

As early as 1903, Helland-Hansen was placed in charge of the International Courses in Ocean Researches administered by the Fishery Directorate in Bergen and later by the Bergen

Museum. A special feature of these courses was their emphasis on the interdependence of physical and biological oceanography. These courses continued under Helland-Hansen's leadership until 1914 and helped establish Scandinavia's importance on the international oceanographic scene.

Aged less than 30, Helland-Hansen had already achieved an international reputation as a leading oceanographer. In 1906, despite being primarily a physicist, he was appointed director of the Marine Biological Station in Bergen. This reflected his proven qualities of leadership and seamanship, his ability as an administrator, and his wide-ranging skills in oceanographic research. In 1910, the University of Christiania sought to entice Helland-Hansen with the offer of a special professorship. Helland-Hansen chose to stay in Bergen. He was rewarded with having a research vessel built to his own design, and he finally received Bergen Museum's own, newly established professorship in 1914. Helland-Hansen's vessel, the *Armauer Hansen*, barely 23 meters (75 feet) long, was purchased with funds subscribed by the citizens of Bergen. It was to undertake many cruises in the Norwegian Sea and Atlantic Ocean, achieving remarkable successes for such a small vessel. It was well equipped for research vessels of the time, containing a panoply of physical and chemical oceanographic sampling devices, plus nets that could be lowered to 2000 meters (6560 feet) and more. The ship's use helped convince other oceanographic institutions that midsized vessels were a cost-effective approach to research. The *Armauer Hansen* served for more than 40 years before being replaced by the appropriately named *Helland-Hansen* in 1957.

In 1917, Helland-Hansen founded the Geophysical Institute of Bergen, and at his instigation, new buildings were completed in 1928, again financed by monies raised from the local populace. In 1930, Helland-Hansen became chair of the board of administrators for the Christian Michelsen Institute of Science and Intellectual Freedom, a fund bequeathed by the former prime minister of Norway. From about this time, Helland-Hansen became increasingly active in international scientific matters. In 1936 he was elected president of the International Association of Physical Oceanography, and in 1945 he became president of the International Union of Geodesy and Geophysics. A leading scientist, manager, and administrator, Helland-Hansen died in Bergen in 1957, leaving a wife, five sons, and a daughter.

Trevor Day

BIOGRAPHY

- Bjørn Helland-Hansen.
- Born 16 October 1877 at Christiania (now Oslo), Norway.
- He lost several fingers to frostbite in the *Aurora Borealis* expedition of 1898.
- Joined Bergen's Fishery Directorate in 1900, and led several *Michael Sars* expeditions up to 1910.
- In 1903, with Johan W. Sandstrom, he published geostrophic equations for computing ocean currents.
- In 1909, with Fridtjof Nansen, he released a comprehensive and influential treatise on the Norwegian Sea.
- He became professor at Bergen Museum in 1914.
- The construction and use of his vessel *Armauer Hansen* proved the effectiveness of mid-sized research vessels.
- Founded the Geophysical Institute of Bergen (1917) and elected president of the International Association of Physical Oceanography (1936) and International Union of Geodesy and Geophysics (1945).
- Died 7 September 1957 at Bergen.

SELECTED WRITINGS

Helland-Hansen, B. "Physical Oceanography." In J. Murray, and J. Hjort, eds., *The Depths of the Ocean*. London: Macmillan, 1912; pp. 210–306.

Helland-Hansen, B., and F. Nansen. "The Norwegian Sea: Its Physical Oceanography Based upon the Norwegian Researches, 1900–1904." *Report on Norwegian Fishery and Marine Investigations*, Vol. 2 (1909).

Sandstrom, J. W., and B. Helland-Hansen. "On the Mathematical Investigation of Ocean Currents." Translated by D'Arcy W. Thompson. In *Report of the North Sea Fisheries Investigation Commission (Northern Area), 1902–1903. Parliamentary Papers.* London: HMSO, 1905; pp. 136–163.

FURTHER READING

Schlee, Susan. *The Edge of an Unfamiliar World: A History of Oceanography.* New York: Dutton, 1973; London: Hale, 1975.

Sears, M., and Merriman, D., eds. *Oceanography: The Past.* New York: Springer-Verlag, 1980.

Tait, J. B. "Professor Bjorn Helland-Hansen." *Nature*, Vol. 181, No. 4607 (1958), pp. 453–454.

RELATED ARTICLES

Atlantic Ocean; Ekman, Vagn Walfrid; Gyre; Nansen, Fridtjof; Norwegian Sea

Hemichordata

Hemichordates (phylum Hemichordata) are soft-bodied animals; one group lives in burrows in marine sediments and the other is colonial and inhabits tubes. There are some 90 species, divided unequally into two main classes: Enteropneusta (acorn worms or tongue worms) with 75 species and Pterobranchia with perhaps 10 species. A third class, Plancosphaeroidea, contains only one known species.

Enteropneusts are solitary and typically live in mucus-lined burrows in shallow water. They have long, cylindrical bodies divided into three regions: a flexible, muscular proboscis (snout), which is used for burrowing; a collar at the base of the proboscis, where the mouth is located; and a long trunk, which forms the main part of the body. The conical shape of the proboscis has earned them the common name *acorn worms*. Most species are 8 to 45 centimeters (3 to 18 inches) long as adults, although one species is known to reach up to 2.5 meters (8 feet) long. They obtain food either by swallowing sediment and extracting the organic matter or by catching waterborne plankton on the sticky, mucus-covered proboscis. Sexes are separate, and fertilization takes place in the open water. Embryos

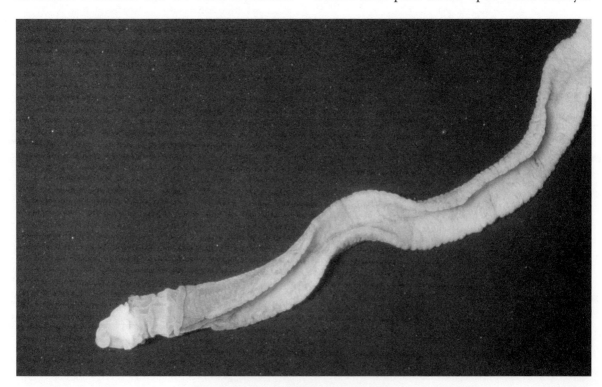

An acorn worm, Glossobalanus samiensis. (© Frank Lane Picture Agency/Corbis)

may develop into free-swimming planktonic larvae or directly into adults.

Pterobranchs were first discovered in deep-sea sediments, but they have recently been found in shallow waters, too. Most species are less than 7 millimeters (0.3 inch) long, and many live in colonies produced by asexual budding. Each individual secretes a rigid tube into which it can withdraw quickly to escape danger. Food is caught from the water with cilia-covered tentacles, and digestion takes place inside a U-shaped intestine. The anus is close to the mouth, unlike that of enteropneusts, which is at the base of the trunk. Pterobranchs reproduce sexually as well as asexually. Their ciliated larvae disperse in the plankton and eventually mature into adults.

Planctosphaeroidea (*Planctosphaera*) are known only as free-swimming larvae. They are classified as hemichordates because they resemble the larvae of pterobranchs.

Zoologists once classified hemichordates as members of the phylum Chordata, which includes all the vertebrates, such as mammals, reptiles, and fish. However, careful study has revealed that hemichordates lack one of the three defining features of chordates—namely, a notochord (a rod of supportive tissue running along the back)—and they are now placed in their own phylum. DNA studies suggest that the hemichordates' closest living relatives might be echinoderms (phylum Echinodermata).

Ben Morgan

FURTHER READING

Brusca, Richard C., and Gary J. Brusca. *Invertebrates*. Sunderland, Mass.: Sinauer, 1990.
Margulis, Lynn. *Five Kingdoms: An Illustrated Guide to the Phyla of Life on Earth*. San Francisco: W. H. Freeman, 1982; 3rd ed., New York, 1998.
Pechenik, Jan A. *Biology of the Invertebrates*. Boston: Prindle, Weber and Schmidt, 1985; 4th ed., Boston: McGraw-Hill, 2000.

RELATED ARTICLES

Chordata; Echinodermata; Meroplankton

Hensen, (Christian Andreas) Victor

1835–1924
Physiologist and Marine Biologist

In the field of marine biology, German scientist Victor Hensen is best known for his coining of the term *plankton* and his pioneering quantitative studies of plankton abundance that showed, among other discoveries, that most open-ocean tropical waters are less productive than temperate ones.

Victor Hensen was born in the Danish duchy of Schleswig, now a part of Germany, in 1835. His father was Hans Hensen, director of Schleswig's deaf and dumb school, and his mother, Henriette Caroline Amalie Suadicani, was daughter of the court physician Carl Ferdinand Suadicani. Victor was one of seven boys and eight girls, the children of his father's two marriages.

Hensen attended Schleswig's cathedral grammar school between 1845 and 1850, achieving, by the reports of his contemporaries, only mediocre results, and not passing the final examinations until 1854. From 1854 to 1856 he studied medicine at Würzburg and then transferred to Berlin and then to Kiel, where he passed his final examinations in 1858. At Kiel in 1859, Hensen became lecturer in anatomy and histology at the Institute of Anatomy, rising to associate professor of physiology in 1864 and to full professor in 1868. He remained at Kiel in various roles, such as dean of medicine and rector of the university, until 1911.

In his work on physiology, Hensen often used histology (staining of tissues and their examination under the microscope) in conjunction with experimental physiology (e.g., altering structures to see what effect it had on function). Between 1863 and 1902, Hensen published notable studies on sensory physiology in a variety of animals, including humans, such as his coauthored 1868 publication with J. C. Voelckers (1836–1914) on accommodation in the mammalian eye, and a key paper in 1893 on touch. In the human inner ear the cells of Hensen and the canal of Hensen are named after him. Hensen's facility with the microscope was to have particularly beneficial application in another area of research—marine biology.

From 1863, Hensen developed an amateur interest in marine biology, which soon turned to a professional one. Hensen began developing ways of assessing the abundance of local marine fish stocks. By the late 1860s, Hensen had been elected as a political representative for Schleswig-Holstein and used his academic and political position to influence the Prussian government in Berlin to further a government fisheries research program. This led to setting up the fisheries research commission at Kiel in 1870.

Hensen's original aim in marine biology was pragmatic and economic: to study the ocean's productivity with a view to maintaining or improving the fisheries that depended on natural food availability. From the 1870s, Hensen's major research focus was microscopic plankton. Plankton was a term he coined in 1887 to mean all forms of life—animal and plant—that drift or float in the ocean. His definition included larger forms such as fish and squid that can actively swim against a current, but Ernst Haeckel (1834–1919) and others have since revised the plankton definition to exclude these larger, swimming forms—nowadays called *nekton*.

Hensen came to believe that the population sizes of some spawning fishes could be estimated from the abundance of their eggs in plankton samples. Since planktonic fish larvae eat other forms of plankton, plankton abundance could be used as a measure of potential fisheries productivity. Further, Hensen believed that plankton abundance could be reliably estimated by hauling a fine-meshed net vertically through the top 200 meters (660 feet) of water.

In 1885, Hensen successfully tested suitable sampling equipment—the Hensen net—in the North Sea and Baltic. In 1889, Hensen led a high-profile expedition in the steamer *National*, a voyage that was to be dubbed the Plankton Expedition. The cruise

Victor Hensen. (*Courtesy, State Library of Schleswig-Holstein*)

covered more than 25,000 kilometers (15,500 miles) of the Atlantic Ocean in a figure-eight route that extended westward from Kiel to the cold currents of Greenland, then southward through the Gulf Stream and Sargasso Sea, eastward to Ascension, and then back via the mouth of the Amazon and the Azores. The expedition's primary aim was to determine the richness and spatial distribution of plankton in the surface waters to 200 meters (660 feet) depth. The expedition sampled more than 100 stations using a vertically towed plankton net with mesh sizes down to approximately 50 micrometers (0.002 inch). Hensen computed the number of organisms per unit volume using mouth diameter, distance of haul, and an experimentally determined filtering coefficient for each net. Additional samples were taken using a coarser-meshed net and a special closing net. The expedition's most important findings were as follows:

- Above all, the cruise demonstrated that quantitative assessments of plankton abundance were possible.

- At all locations, the biomass of microscopic plants and animals exceeded that of larger organisms.
- In general, the open ocean had lower plankton abundance than that in bays and river mouths.
- In contradiction to theory and expectation, there was a greater concentration of plankton in temperate waters than in tropical waters.

The expedition's initial findings, when published in 1891, came under criticism from Ernst Haeckel (1834–1919), the influential and outspoken German biologist. Haeckel and his land-oriented colleagues believed that productivity in the sea should follow the pattern on land, with greater biomass in the tropics and less at high latitudes. Haeckel also doubted that Hensen's colleagues could spend hours per day counting plankton under the microscope: "How such work [plankton counting] can be carried through without the ruin of mind and body I cannot conceive."

Hensen and his colleagues, such as Karl Brandt (1854–1931), countered many of the criticisms of Haeckel and others in a series of articles and books that explained the expedition's methods and findings in detail. One concern was that tiny plankton could pass through the mesh of the plankton nets and would not be sampled, so skewing the results. By the 1920s, one of Hensen's own researchers had established that the pattern of nanoplankton abundance (collected by centrifuging water samples) followed that of the net plankton samples. In all, some 36 scientists over a period of more than 30 years analyzed the material from the *National* expedition. The final monograph in the *Plankton-Expedition Results* series was published in 1926, completing a dozen large volumes that contained, among other treasures, plankton illustrations of outstanding beauty.

The findings of the *National* expedition have since been largely vindicated. Other scientists, including Hensen's colleague Brandt, were to show later that nutrient limitation accounted for the relative scarcity of plankton in tropical waters. Hensen pioneered quantitative marine biology and he helped establish the link between plankton abundance and total productivity—the vital importance of microscopic plankton at the base of most marine food webs.

Trevor Day

BIOGRAPHY
- Christian Andreas Victor Hensen.
- Born 10 February 1835 in duchy of Schleswig.
- In 1858, graduated in medicine at the University of Kiel.
- In 1859, he joined the Kiel staff as lecturer, then associate professor in 1864 and full professor in 1868.
- Retired in 1911.
- Achieved advances in animal and human physiology.
- In marine biology, his major achievements were associated with the introduction of quantitative methods for estimating plankton abundance.
- Led the famous Plankton Expedition of 1889.
- Died 5 April 1924 in Kiel, Germany.

SELECTED WRITINGS
Hensen, V. "Über die Bestimmung des Planktons oder des im Meere treibenden Materials an Pflanzen und Thieren." *Jahresbericht der Kommission zur Wissenschaftlichen Untersuchung der Deutschen Meere in Kiel für die Jahre 1882–1886,* 1887, pp. 1–107.

———. "Das Plankton der östlichen Ostee und des Stettiner Haffs." *Bericht der Kommission zur Wissenschaftlichen Untersuchung der Deutschen Meere in Kiel für die Jahre 1887–1891,* 1893, pp. 103–137.

———. "Über die quantitative Bestimmung der kleineren Plankton-oganismen." *Wissenschaftliche Meeresuntersuchungen,* Vol. 5, 1901, pp. 67–81.

FURTHER READING
Gillispie, C. C., ed. *Dictionary of Scientific Biography,* Vol. 4. New York: Scribner's, 1971; pp. 287–288.

Mills, E. L. *Biological Oceanography: An Early History, 1870–1900.* Ithaca, N.Y.: Cornell University Press, 1989.

Schlee, Susan. *The Edge of an Unfamiliar World: A History of Oceanography.* New York: Dutton, 1973; London: Hale, 1975.

Sears, M., and D. Merriman, eds. *Oceanography: The Past.* New York: Springer-Verlag, 1980.

RELATED ARTICLES
Fisheries; Food Web; Nutrient Limitation; Plankton; Plankton Net

Herbivore

A herbivore is an animal that consumes plants or plantlike protists (i.e., organisms that are capable of photosynthesis). Photosynthetic organisms, which are also called *primary producers* or *autotrophs*, use energy from sunlight to convert inorganic building blocks and carbon dioxide into energy-rich organic compounds. Primary producers capture and store energy and represent the first trophic level in a given food web. Herbivores, which graze on these primary producers, comprise the second trophic level. Herbivores are consumed by predators at the third trophic level, which in turn are eaten by higher-level carnivores. Thus herbivores play a crucial role in marine and terrestrial food webs because they are the first link in energy transfer between primary producers and higher trophic levels. Herbivores can also play an important role in structuring communities through biological interactions such as predation and competition. For example, predation on a herbivore population can protect plant populations from being depleted, and herbivores can reduce competition among plant species by feeding on dominant forms.

Because herbivores eat only plant material and to survive require this food source, they are limited to environments where their plants coexist. In the oceans, photosynthetic organisms are limited to lit areas such as the intertidal zone, coastal areas where light penetrates to the seafloor, and the euphotic zone of the open ocean [200 meters (660 feet) deep or shallower]. Herbivores also inhabit unlit areas where plant debris commonly collects, such as parts of submarine canyons. Marine herbivores feed on photosynthetic organisms such as kelp, algae, phytoplankton, and sea grass. Marine invertebrate herbivores include crustaceans, echinoids, and gastropods. Vertebrate herbivores include fish, sea turtles, and manatees. The assemblage of herbivores and their role in the community varies with each habitat.

In the rocky intertidal zone, grazing by gastropods, crustaceans, sea urchins, and fishes helps set upper and lower limits of growth of particular algal species. Fish and sea urchin grazers also limit algal growth on coral reefs so that competition for space between algae and coral is reduced. The rocky subtidal zone in many areas of the world harbors low-growing plants that are grazed by sea urchins, gastropods, and fishes. In this environment, many photosynthetic organisms and animals compete for space and grazers can affect such competition directly. Sea urchins are often the dominant grazer in these environments and herbivory by urchins can affect both the abundance of algae and its vertical and horizontal zonation. Sea urchins are also the major grazers in kelp beds, which are common in the rocky subtidal zone of many cold and temperate coastal areas of the world. Despite being an abundant source of food for herbivores, few animals consume kelp directly. Only about 10 percent of the net production by kelp is introduced to the food web by grazing; the remainder is used by other organisms once it has been broken down into detritus. Seagrasses are also major primary producers in some areas of the world, yet few grazers feed on them directly. Seagrass grazers include manatees, sea urchins, and certain species of birds, fishes, and sea turtles. In the euphotic zone, copepods comprise 70 to 90 percent of the net zooplankton biomass and are the most important grazers of large phytoplankton cells such as diatoms and dinoflagellates; their grazing pressure can regulate phytoplankton population dynamics. Other grazers of net phytoplankton include crustaceans such as euphausiids and shrimp, and mollusks such as pteropods. Flagellates and ciliates graze the smaller phytoplankton and bacterioplankton.

Lynn L. Lauerman

FURTHER READING

Harrold, C., and D. Reed. "Food Availability, Sea Urchin Grazing and Kelp Forest Community Structure." *Ecology*, Vol. 66, No. 4, 1985, pp. 1160–1169.

Nybakken, James W. *Marine Biology: An Ecological Approach*, 5th ed. San Francisco: Benjamin Cummings, 2001.

Ogden, J. C. "Faunal Relationships in Caribbean Seagrass Beds." In R. C. Phillips and C. P. McRoy eds., *Handbook of Seagrass Biology: An Ecosystem Perspective*. New York: Garland STPM Press, 1980; pp. 173–198.

RELATED ARTICLES

Copepod; Kelp Forest; Manatee; Phytoplankton; Seagrass

Hermatypic Coral

Hermatypic corals are small marine animals whose skeletons build up to form coral reefs. All hermatypic corals are members of the order Scleractinia (true or stony corals) within the phylum Cnidaria.

Coral organisms are like tiny sea anemones. Some are solitary, but most hermatypic (reef-building) species grow in large colonies formed by asexual reproduction (*budding*) of one sexually produced individual. The individuals in a colony are called *polyps*. Each polyp secretes a cup-shaped external skeleton of calcium carbonate (limestone) within which it sits, attached by the base of the body. The skeletons of neighboring polyps are continuous and form a combined mass that gives the colony a distinctive shape. Some coral colonies form delicate leaflike shapes, for example, while others form rounded domes or elaborate branches. Coral of the genus *Acropora*—the most important reef-building corals—form colonies that look like antlers and therefore are known as *staghorn* or *elkhorn coral*. When corals die, their skeletons remain, providing the foundations for future generations to build on. As a result, coral reefs gradually spread and rise up, and may even turn into land.

Corals feed on planktonic organisms in seawater, using stinging tentacles to capture and immobilize prey. Food is then transferred to a central mouth at the center of the ring of tentacles and into a blind-ended gastrovascular cavity that serves both as a digestive system and for brooding larvae. Corals have no respiratory or circulatory organs and obtain oxygen simply by diffusion from seawater. Sensory cells are linked to muscles via a simple nerve network that allows them to move their tentacles and withdraw from danger, but they have no brains.

Paradoxically, hermatypic corals flourish only in relatively clear waters where there is little plankton. They are able to survive this apparent lack of food because of the symbiotic algae that live within their bodies. There may be up to 30,000 of these microscopic algae, called *zooxanthellae*, within each cubic millimeter of coral tissue. The algae give hermatypic corals their color, ranging from green to bluish green and golden brown.

Zooxanthellae are photosynthetic: They harness sunlight to make their own food, just as plants do on land. Some of the food is passed on to the corals as glycerol, glucose, and the amino acid alanine. In return, the corals provide protection from predators and a source of nitrogenous compounds and carbon dioxide, both of which are needed for photosynthesis. As well as providing their coral hosts with a supply of food, the zooxanthellae are thought to increase the rate at which corals deposit calcium carbonate in their skeletons, although the chemical mechanism underlying this effect remains unknown.

Zooxanthellae require sunlight to survive, so hermatypic corals grow only in shallow sunlit water up to a depth of 90 meters (300 feet) or so. They also require warm water, so coral reefs are found only in tropical seas. However, if the water temperature rises too high, corals lose their symbiotic algae and turn white, a phenomenon known as *bleaching*. When bleaching occurs, the diversity of life supported by the reef may decline sharply. Bleaching has become a major problem in many of the world's coral reefs in recent years. Some scientists believe that the underlying cause may be a rise in global sea temperature caused by the greenhouse effect.

As well as reproducing asexually to form colonies, hermatypic corals reproduce sexually. Fertilization may take place within the coral's bodies or in the open water, depending on the species. In some reefs all the corals spawn together at the same time. Such mass spawnings usually involve just one species at a time, but in Australia's Great Barrier Reef, hundreds of different species have been seen to spawn together. The sperm and egg cells fuse to form embryos, and these develop into tiny larvae called *planulae*, which are coated with microscopic beating hairs (cilia) that enable them to swim. The planulae swim away in the plankton to colonize new habitats. Eventually, they settle on the seafloor and metamorphose into polyps, thus starting a new coral colony.

Ben Morgan

FURTHER READING

Brusca, Richard C., and Gary J. Brusca. *Invertebrates.* Sunderland, Mass.: Sinauer, 1990.

Davidson, Osha Gray. *The Enchanted Braid: Coming to Terms with Nature on the Coral Reef.* New York: Wiley, 1998.

Pechenik, Jan A. *Biology of the Invertebrates.* Boston: Prindle, Weber and Schmidt, 1985; 4th ed., Boston: McGraw-Hill, 2000.

Steene, Roger. *Coral Seas.* Willowdale, Canada, and New York: Firefly Books, 1998.

Sumich, James L., and Collard Sneed. *An Introduction to the Biology of Marine Life.* Dubuque, Iowa: Wm. C. Brown, 1976; 7th ed., Boston: WCB/McGraw-Hill, 1999.

RELATED ARTICLES

Ahermatypic Coral; Cnidaria; Coral Reef; Scleractinia; Zooxanthellae

Hess, Harry Hammond

1906–1969

Originator of Theory of Plate Tectonics

Harry Hammond Hess helped develop the theory of plate tectonics, which revolutionized the study of geology in the later part of the twentieth century. Hess was born in New York City on 24 May 1906 and received his undergraduate degree in geology from Yale University in 1927. Hess completed his Ph.D. in geology in 1932 and began teaching at Princeton University in 1934. In 1948, he obtained a professorship at Princeton, a post he held until 1966.

Hess served in the U.S. Navy during World War II. His first tour of duty, in the North Atlantic, led him to develop a method of detecting German submarines. While captain of a transport vessel in the Pacific, Hess did extensive echo soundings for studies of flat-topped underwater seamounts, which he termed *guyots*. These early investigations helped Hess to formulate his hypothesis on the formation and structure of the seafloor. He came to think of ocean floors as qualitatively different from continents. In 1959, in an informal paper, he suggested that undersea mountain ranges, called *mantle ridges*, extruded over areas where hot rock material, or magma, oozed up through the ocean floor. Therefore, unlike mountains on land, which are formed by folding and compression, seamounts resulted from mantle processes, that is, the spreading of the ocean floor and rising of hot fluid materials above cooler ones. Hess's essay on this revolutionary theory—"History of Ocean Basins"—was published in 1962.

Hess proposed that the surface of Earth was an integrated system in which continents passively move across ocean floors rather than driving through them. He suggested that in the process of this passive traveling across the seafloor, continents collided with each other, sometimes fusing together, driving up mountain and/or splintering apart. Hess's theory on the formation and development of ocean basins provided the first comprehensive explanation of mountain building and continental drift, the latter hypothesis being first proposed by Alfred Wegener (1880–1930) half a century earlier. The movement of the ocean floor was a critical component in the plate tectonics model, which provided an answer to many geological questions puzzling scientists.

Robert Dietz (1914–95), another American geologist, took up Hess's work. In 1961, he called Hess's model of Earth's history *seafloor spreading.* Other scientists substantiated the theory with new evidence in the years that followed. In 1963, F. J. Vine (1939–) and D. H. Matthews cited magnetic anomalies along the North Atlantic Ridge as evidence supporting the idea of seafloor spreading.

Hess's other scientific achievements included work in space science, particularly the 1968 development of a method of analyzing lunar rocks using x-ray technology.

Harry Hammond Hess. (Courtesy, Geosciences Department of Princeton University)

Hess was the recipient of many scientific awards and honors. Among them was President John F. Kennedy's 1962 appointment of Hess as the chairman of the Space Science Board of the National Academy of Science. Although his major contributions were in foundations of plate tectonic theory in geology, he also contributed to space science at a critical period in U.S. history. Hess died on 25 August 1969, in Falmouth, Massachusetts.

Doris G. Simonis

BIOGRAPHY
- Harry Hammond Hess.
- Born 24 May 1906 in New York City.
- Hess earned a degree in geology at Yale, 1927, and began research on oceans in 1931.
- He finished his Ph.D. in geology at Princeton in 1932 and began teaching there in 1934.
- He served in the U.S. Navy during World War II, 1941–45.
- His revolutionary essay "History of Ocean Basins" was shared with colleagues in 1960 and published in 1962.
- Hess was appointed by President John F. Kennedy to chair the Space Science Board of the National Academy of Science in 1962 and developed an x-ray method of analyzing lunar rocks in 1968.
- Died 25 August 1969, in Falmouth, Massachusetts.

SELECTED WRITINGS
Hess, H. H. "History of Ocean Basins." In A. E. J. Engel, H. L. James, and B. F. Leonard, eds., *Petrologic Studies: A Volume in Honor of A.F. Buddington.* New York: Geological Society of America, 1962; pp. 599–620.

FURTHER READING
Anderson, A. H. *The Drifting Continents.* New York: Putnam, 1971.
Martin, Ursula. *Continental Drift: Evolution of a Concept.* Washington, D.C.: Smithsonian Institution Press, 1973.
Miller, Russell. *Continents in Collision.* Alexandria, Va.: Time-Life Books, 1983.

RELATED ARTICLES
Dietz, Robert Sinclair; Guyot; Plate Tectonics; Seafloor Spreading; Wegener, Alfred Lothar

Hess Rise

Hess Rise, a submerged mountain range in the north-central Pacific Ocean, is one of the largest oceanic plateaus in the world's oceans. The geology of Hess Rise is similar to that of several other oceanic plateaus, particularly those in the Pacific and Indian Oceans. This entirely submerged feature was named for Harry Hess (1909–69), a prominent geologist who discovered many seafloor features during World War II while he served as an officer on U.S. Navy ships in the Pacific Ocean. Hess studied echo sounder records and became interested in the vast array of seafloor features that appeared on those records.

Location and Description

Hess Rise is a spectacular submerged mountain range. The plateau has an anchor, or inverted T, shape with the shank of the anchor, nearly 1000 kilometers (620 miles) long, elongated to the north northwest at about 327°, and the arms, over 1000 kilometers (620 miles) long, trend nearly east–west. It is bounded by latitudes 33°N to 42°N and longitudes 174°W to 173°E and has a surface area of about 400,000 square kilometers (154,400 square miles). Less than 100 kilometers (60 miles) west of the plateau's northwestern ridge, the Emperor Seamounts leave a mountainous trail as they trek northward with Hess Rise on the Pacific Plate. The plateau is truncated along its south side by the longest fracture zone (scar of an ancient transform fault) in the North Pacific Ocean, the Mendocino Fracture Zone. The east end of this fracture zone is colliding with northern California at Cape Mendocino.

Bathymetric charts of Hess Rise show that the plateau rises from an ocean floor depth of about 5200 meters (17,000 feet) to only 119 meters (390 feet) below sea level at Mellish Bank. Mellish Bank, previously thought to be a high point on the southern edge of the plateau, has been searched for by ships during the past two decades, but its existence has not been confirmed. One pinnacle on the southern part of the plateau, however, does rise to a depth of only 1400 meters (4580 feet). If Mellish Bank is not included because of the premise that it may not exist, the relief of the plateau, from its lowest to highest point, is still about 3800 meters (approximately 12,500 feet). For comparison purposes, if Hess Rise were on land, it would occupy most of the area that is included in the states of Washington and Oregon. Its relief is similar to that of the Cascade Mountains in Oregon and Washington. For example, Mt. Adams, one of the Cascade volcanoes located in south-central Washington, rises to a height of about 3750 meters (12,300 feet) above sea level.

Composition

Hess Rise is a sediment-covered plateau with a volcanic base. It is buoyed up by a much thicker crust than most other crust of the ocean basins. Hess Rise was born about 100 to 110 million years ago along an ancient oceanic spreading center that formed a boundary between the Pacific and Farallon lithospheric plates. It originated near the equator in the South Pacific and subsequently traveled northward on the Pacific Plate to its present position. The plateau cooled and subsided while it traveled northward. Pelagic sediments rained down on the feature and draped over it like a blanket. These sediments consisted mostly of calcareous nannoplankton, such as coccolithophores, and foraminifera, radiolaria, and clay.

Marine geophysical surveys, completed on the oceanic plateau in the middle 1970s, collected bathymetric, stratigraphic, magnetic, and gravity data. Basically, these geophysical studies established that Hess Rise is a large feature and that it has a sediment section overlying a volcanic pedestal. Based in part on the results from these geophysical surveys, four sites were drilled and cored in the middle to late 1970s by the

Glomar Challenger as part of the Deep Sea Drilling Project. One site, 464, was located on the northern part, site 310 was located on the central part, and two sites, 465 and 466, were drilled and cored on the southern arm. Igneous

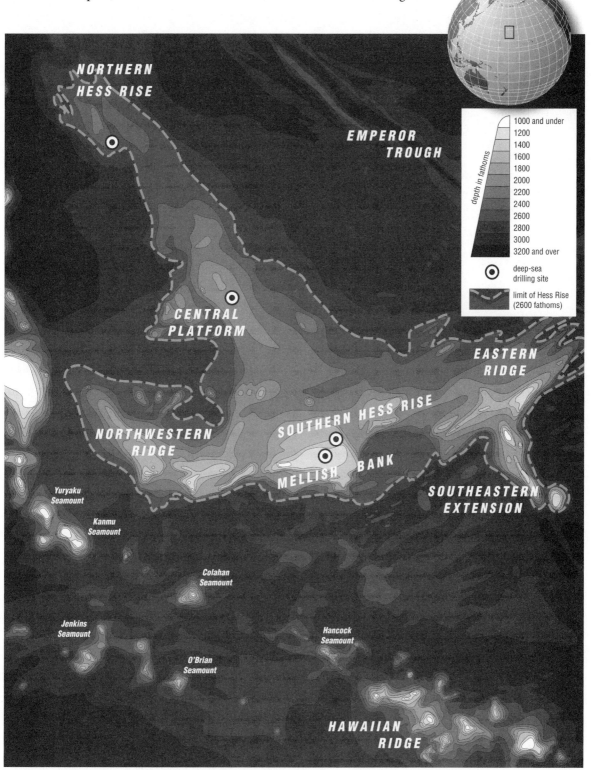

Hess Rise. (Adapted from Vallier et al, 1983. Courtesy, The Geological Society of America.)

rocks of the volcanic pedestal, recovered beneath sedimentary rocks at sites 464 and 465, consisted of basalt and trachyte, respectively.

Geologic History

From oldest to youngest, and lowest to highest, the rock and sediment section on Hess Rise records a simple and intriguing geologic history. The stratigraphic, or layered, succession has volcanic rocks 110 to 100 million years old overlain by Cretaceous and Cenozoic (100 million years ago to present) limestone, chert, chalk, calcareous ooze, and brown clay. The volcanic rocks were erupted onto the seafloor, in places building large volcanic cones that grew upward through the column of seawater to become islands. Subsequently, erosion occurred as the plateau began its long northward trip on the back of the Pacific Plate, from near the equator to its present position. The islands subsided until all of Hess Rise was below sea level. As the plateau passed slowly through the equatorial zone, where the divergence of ocean currents created zones of upwelling with attendant high biologic productivity, pelagic sediments were deposited. These pelagic sediments included thick successions of foraminifera and calcareous nannoplankton that formed calcareous ooze, chalk, and ultimately, limestone. Siliceous radiolaria became porcellanite and chert. Those parts of the plateau that subsided below the calcium carbonate compensation depth, a level in the ocean below which calcareous materials dissolve, are now covered by pelagic brown clay. The brown clay, here and elsewhere in most parts of the oceans, is derived from the constant deluge of very fine-grained sediments that are dropped into the ocean from winds. Most of these fine-grained particles were eroded from the world's great deserts, and some were blasted into Earth's jet streams by far-off volcanic eruptions.

The Cretaceous–Tertiary boundary (65 million years ago) was recovered in a Deep Sea Drilling Project core from Hess Rise. Studies of the boundary indicate that a significant decrease in both surface temperature and biologic productivity occurred at the end of the Cretaceous Period. Many species became extinct. Furthermore, an abrupt increase in transition metals and iridium suggests that an extraterrestrial source was responsible for these characteristics. Although Hess Rise is far removed from the great meteor impact that closed the Cretaceous Period, the existence of this small layer of debris at the boundary does indicate that dust from the impact site in Mexico reached most, and perhaps all, of the world through its winds.

Future Possibilities

If the Pacific Plate continues to move northwestward, as it has for the past approximately 42 million years, Hess Rise will someday reach the Kuril Trench and its adjacent subduction zone. The plateau will break apart and most of it will probably be subducted into Earth's mantle to be recycled. Perhaps the high parts will not be subducted but will be zippered to the front of the Kuril Islands. When Hess Rise reaches the Kuril Trench, its rocks and sediments will have passively recorded about 150 million years of Earth's history.

Tracy L. Vallier

FURTHER READING

Larson, Roger, et al. *Initial Reports of the Deep Sea Drilling Project*, Vol. 32. Washington, D.C.: U.S. Government Printing Office, 1975.

Nemoto, Kenji, and Loren Kroenke. "Marine Geology of Hess Rise: Bathymetry, Surface Sediment Distribution, and Environment of Deposition." *Journal of Geophysical Research*, Vol. 86 (1981), pp. 10,734–10,752.

Pringle, Malcolm, William Sager, William Sliter, and Seth Stein, eds. *The Mesozoic Pacific: Geology, Tectonics, and Volcanism.* Geophysical Monograph 79. Washington, D.C.: American Geophysical Union, 1993.

Thiede, Jörn, et al. *Initial Reports of the Deep Sea Drilling Project*, Vol. 62. Washington, D.C.: U. S. Government Printing Office, 1981.

Vallier, Tracy, Walter Dean, David Rea, and Jörn Thiede. "Geologic Evolution of Hess Rise, Central North Pacific Ocean." *Geological Society of America Bulletin*, Vol. 94 (1983), pp. 1289–1307.

RELATED ARTICLES

Calcium Carbonate Compensation Depth; Emperor Seamounts; Fracture Zone; Manihiki Plateau; Ocean Plateau; Ontong Java Plateau; Subduction Zone; Shatsky Rise; Transform Fault

Heterokontophyta, see Ochrophyta

Heteropoda

Heteropods comprise a small group (34 species) of gastropod snails that live out their entire life in the open ocean. Most species are cosmopolitan at tropical to subtropical latitudes in the Atlantic, Pacific, and Indian Oceans.

Three distinctive families are recognized; the microscopic Atlantidae [less than 10 millimeters (0.39 inch) shell diameter; 21 species], the macroscopic Carinariidae [to 220 millimeters (9 inches); nine species], and the macroscopic Pterotracheidae [to 330 millimeters (13 inches); four species]. In the atlantids the body can be retracted into the thin-walled, laterally flattened shell, and the shell opening can be closed off with the operculum (as in many bottom-dwelling snails). The bodies of the animals in the Carinariidae and Pterotracheidae are greatly enlarged and elongated and are capable of much greater swimming speeds than the atlantids. Also, buoyancy is achieved by exchanging light for heavy ions in the body fluids. In the carinarids the shell is limited to the stalked visceral mass, either as a thin, caplike covering or a microscopic remnant at the top of the visceral mass. However, in the pterotracheids the shell has been lost altogether, and the visceral mass is compressed into a teardrop-shaped structure that is partially embedded in the body.

The heteropods show striking differences from their bottom-dwelling (benthic) relatives in locomotion, vision, feeding, reduction and loss of the shell (as noted above), and reproduction. The foot of benthic gastropods is flattened and sole-like, producing slow, crawling movements along the seafloor. In the heteropods the ventral foot is laterally flattened to form a large, muscular swimming fin. While swimming in their normal upside-down body orientation, the fin propels the animal forward. When present, the eyes in benthic snails are developed as simple, multi-celled photoreceptors that are used to discriminate light-intensity differences. The heteropods, on the other hand, have paired image-forming eyes. Each eye is complete with a distal spherical lens, a proximal retina, and an intermediate pigmented shielding layer. However, the retina is most unusual in that it is ribbonlike, with the result that the formed image is a very narrow rectangular area. Several species of heteropods have been observed to rock their eyes repeatedly through a dorsal-to-ventral arc, described as *scanning eye movements*, which presumably creates a composite image. All heteropods capture their prey with their radula, which has elongate, terminally hooked teeth that unfold when the radula is protruded from the mouth. In the macroscopic heteropods, prey are ingested whole, but in the microscopic atlantids, the prey usually are held by the large sucker on the ventral side of the foot and pieces of prey tissue are removed by the radula and ingested. They feed on a variety of zooplanktonic prey, specifically shelled pteropods; other atlantids; copepods and chaetognaths in the atlantids; and salps, doliolids, chaetognaths, siphonophores, and crustaceans in the carinarids. The feeding habits of pterotracheids are poorly known.

All heteropods are dioecious (separate sexes) and show sexual dimorphism. Males have a penis and penial appendage on the right side of the body. In female pterotracheids the fin sucker is absent (implying that the fin sucker in males is used to hold the females during copulation), and cuticular spines develop anterior to the eyes in some species. Internal fertilization follows sperm transfer by spermatophores during copulation. Fertilized eggs are normally laid in egg strings that either are free floating or remain attached to the female. Larval development leads to a free-swimming, shelled veliger larva that is planktotrophic (feeds on phytoplankton and small zooplankton). In pterotracheids, the larval shell is lost at metamorphosis, whereas in the other two families the shell is retained as the protoconch of the adult shell. The larvae can be quite beautiful, with the ciliated velum drawn out into four or six velar lobes.

Roger R. Seapy

FURTHER READING
Lalli, Carol M., and Ronald W. Gilmer. "Pelagic Snails." In *The Biology of Holoplanktonic Gastropod Mollusks.* Stanford, Calif.: Stanford University Press, 1989.
Spoel, Siebrecht van der, Leslie Newman, and Kenneth W. Estep. "Pelagic Molluscs of the World." *World Biodiversity Database CD-ROM Series.* Expert Center for Taxonomic Identification (ETI), Amsterdam, The Netherlands. Paris: UNESCO, 1997.
Thiriot-Quiévreux, Catherine. "Heteropoda." In Harold Barnes, ed., *Oceanography and Marine Biology: An Annual Review,* Vol. 11. London: Allen and Unwin, 1973; pp. 237–261.

RELATED ARTICLES
Gastropoda; Mollusca; Zooplankton

Heterotrophic

Heterotrophic describes the type of nutrition by which organic compounds are used for food. For example, a phytoplankton species that obtains the nutrients it needs (carbon, nitrogen, phosphorus, sulfur, etc.) from organic sources would be called a heterotroph. Because heterotrophs are unable to manufacture food from non-carbon-based, inorganic compounds, they must rely on consuming the bodies or products of other organisms.

In a typical ecosystem, a series of energy transfer levels exist called *food chains* or *feeding levels.* The first feeding level (also called a *trophic level*) is composed of the primary producers or autotrophs, which are plants and bacteria. These organisms are self-supporting and photosynthetic, which means that they are capable of using the Sun's energy to produce organic compounds for nutrition. Heterotrophs depend on the autotrophic organisms' production of energy. Heterotrophs have two main forms: primary consumers (called *herbivores*), which are animals that eat plants as their main source of nutrition, and secondary consumers (called *carnivores*), which are animals that feed exclusively on other animal tissue. Two other groups of heterotrophic organisms also play a significant role in the development of trophic levels: detritivores, which feed on decomposing plant or animal material, and decomposers (fungi and bacteria), which break down organic compounds into inorganic components.

Anne Beesley

FURTHER READING
Barnes, Robert. *Invertebrate Zoology.* Philadelphia: W. B. Saunders, 1963; 6th ed., by Edward Ruppert, Fort Worth, Texas: Saunders College Publishing, 1994.
Burchett, Michael, Marc Dando, and Geoffrey Waller. *Sealife: A Complete Guide to the Marine Environment.* Washington, D.C.: Smithsonian Institution Press, 1996.
Dawes, Clinton. *Marine Botany.* New York: Wiley, 1981; 2nd ed., 1998.

RELATED ARTICLES
Food Chain

HMS *Beagle*

The HMS *Beagle* was the British naval survey ship that, under the command of Captain Robert

Fitzroy, undertook a round-the-world survey, from 27 December 1831 to 2 October 1836, with Charles Darwin on board. Built at Woolwich Dockyard on the Thames in 1820, the *Beagle* had already completed an arduous survey cruise around South America, so arduous that halfway through the cruise, her captain had committed suicide. Fitzroy was appointed to complete the first survey and retained command for the second. The *Beagle* had originally been built as a class of vessel known as "coffin brigs" because so many sank. But she was almost immediately modified into a bark (i.e., with three masts rather than two). Fitzroy supervised her refit before the 1831–36 cruise, increasing her headroom below decks to 1.83 meters (6 feet) and fitting her masts with lightning conductors. This refit increased her displacement to 219 tonnes (242 tons). She was just 27.4 meters (90 feet) long (the distance between two bases on a baseball field) and had a crew of 72, so conditions were extremely cramped.

The objectives of the cruise were to continue charting the South American coastline and to improve the accuracy of longitudinal fixes by carrying out a chain of chronological reckonings around the world. She carried 22 chronometers used to fix longitude. Britain, as a naval and trading nation, had a long tradition of charting the seas and improving the technology of navigation. The ship arrived off Bahia in South America in March 1832 and worked around South America visiting Rio de Janeiro, Montevideo, Port Desire, the Falklands, Tierra del Fuego, Valparaiso, and Concepción until September 1835.

It was three and a half years into the voyage when the *Beagle* visited the Galápagos in September 1835. It was this visit that has traditionally been considered to have stimulated Darwin's ideas about natural selection, but from his letters sent back during the voyage it is clear that the idea had been evolving throughout the voyage. For example, between successive visits to Concepción, Chile, they saw that a massive earthquake had uplifted the island of Santa María by nearly 3 meters (9.8 feet). In the Andes, Darwin had already found clear evidence of recent marine sediments at altitudes of 396 meters (1300 feet). Early in the voyage he had found fossils of giant sloths that were far bigger than modern sloths, which posed critical questions about the veracity of the biblical story of Noah's flood. Such observations contributed to his developing ideas about the origins of coral reefs and atolls, as well as his theory of evolution by natural selection. The return voyage was relatively uneventful. It took them across the Pacific to New Zealand and Australia. Then she sailed across the Indian Ocean to round the Cape of Good Hope, then across the Atlantic again and back to Britain via the Azores.

The five-year voyage is now remembered solely because of its impact on Darwin's thinking and his subsequent work. However, at the time it made massive contributions to the safety of navigation around South America, producing 82 coastal charts, 80 plans of harbors, and 40 views, some of which remained in use for over a hundred years. Fitzroy pioneered the use of the barometer at sea for forecasting the weather. He also was among the first to use the Beaufort scale of wind speed, an innovation introduced by the Royal Navy's hydrographer.

This voyage was not the *Beagle*'s last. She undertook another six-year surveying cruise to Australia from 1837 to 1843. Then in 1845, having covered perhaps a quarter of a million miles, she became a watch vessel for smugglers off the southeast coast of Britain. She was renamed *W.V.7*, and after a further 25 years of neglect and decay was finally broken up in 1870, an inglorious end to a ship on which the observations were made that were to lay the foundations of a revolution in biological, geological, and religious concepts and beliefs.

Martin Angel

FURTHER READING

Keynes, Richard Darwin. *The Beagle Record: Selections from the Original Pictorial Records and Written Accounts of the Voyage of HMS* Beagle. Cambridge and New York: Cambridge University Press, 1979.

Mellersh, H. E. L. *Fitzroy of the* Beagle. London: Hart-Davis, 1968.

Moorehead, Alan. *Darwin and the* Beagle. New York: Penguin Books, 1971.

Ritchie, G. S. *The Admiralty Chart.* New York: Elsevier, 1967; new ed., Edinburgh, and Durham, N.C.: The Pentland Press, 1995.

Thomson, Keith. *HMS Beagle: The Story of Darwin's Ship.* New York and London: W. W. Norton, 1995.

RELATED ARTICLES

Darwin, Charles Robert

HMS *Challenger*

The HMS *Challenger* undertook one of the most influential expeditions in the history of oceanography, circumnavigating the globe from 1872 to 1876. The expedition, one of the first lengthy government-sponsored expeditions dedicated solely to the scientific exploration of the sea, produced a wealth of data about the ocean's biological and physical characteristics. The *Challenger* expedition, underwritten by the British government, followed a number of short expeditions that had dredged the ocean floor and made some intriguing discoveries about the bottom of the sea. Several scientists had put forth conflicting (and often quite colorful) theories regarding sea life at extreme depths and the mechanisms that created ocean currents. Data were badly needed to test these imaginative theories.

Other countries were also funding oceanic research, and the idea of a British expedition circumnavigating the globe had a definite nationalist appeal for a country that prided itself on its maritime prowess. The British government was hardly an enthusiastic backer of oceanographic research, but an appeal of the expedition was that it was to be a one-time-only project, which backers claimed would not require many years of funding and would yield priceless information about the sea. Although the first claim turned out to be false, the second proved more true than even the most optimistic backers had hoped.

The *Challenger* was a 2090-tonne (2306-ton) naval warship that was refitted with what was at the time cutting-edge and experimental oceanographic devices such as deep-sea thermometers, sampling bottles, and dredges. (The performance of these devices was publicized in scientific periodicals during the course of the expedition, so one near-immediate result of the expedition was their rapid improvement.) The director of the ship's scientific staff was Charles Wyville Thomson (1830–82), and the scientists included naturalists John Murray (1841–1914), Rudolf

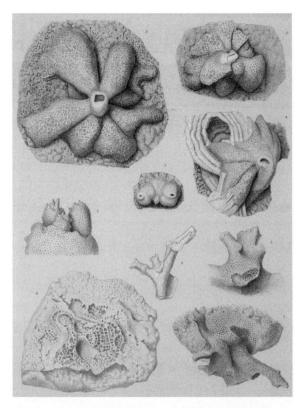

Carpenteria–Polytrema Plate from Report on the Scientific Results of the Voyage of HMS *Challenger, published between 1850 and 1895 by C. Wyville Thomson. (© The Natural History Museum, London)*

von Willemoës-Suhm (who became one of the expedition's few casualties when he died of disease in the Pacific), and Henry Nottidge Moseley (1844–91). James John Wild served as the staff's artist (an essential job before the introduction of durable, portable photographic equipment) and secretary. The scientific staff included only one physical scientist, the chemist John Young Buchanan (1844–1925), and most of the physical measurement of the ocean was performed by the ship's regular crew, which was led by Captain George Strong Nares (1831–1915) until 1875, then by Captain Frank Tourle Thomson.

The *Challenger* set out from Portsmouth, England, on 7 December 1872, and for three-and-a-half years the ship slowly wound a circuitous route around the world, traveling almost 111,000 kilometers (69,000 miles). The crew sampled ocean floor and ocean water and took temperature measurements (used to determine currents) across the Atlantic and Pacific Oceans and near Antarctica. The expedition immediately paid off, helping to settle some scientific questions before the *Challenger* even returned home. For example, many scientists believed that it was impossible for life to exist in the ocean past a certain depth, while others theorized that any life that did exist in such a remote environment would be of some ancient species, utterly unlike life found in the shallows or on land. The *Challenger*'s dredging demonstrated that life could exist at extreme depths, and furthermore, that the creatures that lived there were closely related to those found in shallow water nearer the shore.

Another theory that the *Challenger* expedition helped lay to rest was that of spontaneous generation, or the theory that certain nonliving material could suddenly give rise to life. The ooze that was found in many places on the ocean floor was believed by some to have that property. Indeed, in the years before the *Challenger* expedition, the respected oceanographer Thomas Henry Huxley

(1825–95) "discovered" a jellylike substance on the ocean floor he called *Bathybius haeckelii*, which was believed to be an extremely primitive type of life from which all other life had evolved. The hundreds of ocean-floor samples dredged up by the *Challenger* proved that the ooze was made up of the skeletons of dead plankton that had sunk down to the ocean floor, and that it had no life-generating capabilities. *Bathybius haeckelii* could not be found, and Buchanan inadvertently debunked the substance during the course of the expedition when he accidentally manufactured it by mixing alcohol and seawater.

The *Challenger*'s temperature studies settled few debates about the workings of ocean currents, indicating instead that the forces behind the currents were more complex than imagined. But the scientific staff did reach one important conclusion: that the ocean basins were cut off from each other by underwater ridges that prevented a complete mixture of water.

Another startling discovery of the *Challenger* was that the Pacific Ocean was considerably deeper than the Atlantic, and that it contained trenches that were deeper still. The Pacific had been studied even less than the Atlantic, and the unique properties of that ocean created great excitement in scientific circles. The presence in the Pacific of large numbers of manganese nodules, which formed around the fossil teeth and bones of ancient sharks and whales, as well as quartz and pumice in the clay of the ocean floor suggested extensive volcanic activity undersea.

The *Challenger* returned to England on 24 May 1876, but the saga of the *Challenger* expedition was far from over. The expedition had gathered more than 13,000 specimens of animals and plants, more than 1400 samples of ocean water, and vast quantities of data on the ocean's physical properties. Responsibility for organizing the small army of scientists needed to analyze these samples and publish the results fell to Thomson, who made the controversial decision

Specimens collected during the voyage of the HMS Challenger. (© The Natural History Museum, London)

to parcel out the samples to scientists who were leaders in the appropriate field, regardless of nationality. In addition, it became evident that the results of the expedition would not be published quickly, but instead, the project would require several more years of funding. Thomson spent most of his final years convincing the British government that the project was neither a waste of money nor a swindle conducted by foreigners, a task that overwhelmed his already fragile health. He died in 1882, and Murray took over the project.

The product of their efforts, the *Report on the Scientific Results of the Voyage of H.M.S. Challenger*, was published in 50 volumes from 1880 to 1895. The sheer volume of samples and data the expedition gathered meant that many of the volumes became the authoritative source of information in the field for decades to come. Although most of the volumes were descriptive, one volume, written on the chemical composition of seawater and published in 1884, contained its own discovery. Written by William

Dittmar, who was not a member of the expedition, the analysis demonstrated that about a dozen chemicals in seawater were in near-perfect balance with each other. For example, if one sample contained twice as much chloride as another, it almost always contained twice as much of every other common chemical. This meant that the total salinity of seawater could be determined by testing for only one element, a discovery that made life much easier for marine chemists.

The influence of the *Challenger* expedition, however, went beyond its discoveries. The success of the expedition inspired other governments and institutions to fund oceanographic studies. Thomson's international outlook brought together like-minded scientists from Europe and the United States, and once the *Challenger* project was over, they sought to work together on other projects. The evolution of oceanography from a hobby or a commercial venture into a robust science that encompassed many disciplines owed a great deal to the *Challenger* expedition and its aftermath.

Mary Sisson

FURTHER READING

Deacon, Margaret. *Scientists and the Sea, 1650–1900: A Study of Marine Science.* London and New York: Academic Press, 1971.

Great Britain, Challenger Office. *Report on the Scientific Results of the Voyage of H.M.S.* Challenger *During the Years 1873–76.* 50 vols. London: Her Majesty's Stationery Office, 1880–1895.

Idyll, C. P., ed. *Exploring the Ocean World: A History of Oceanography.* New York: Crowell, 1966.

Jones, R. W. "The Challenger Expedition (1872–1876): Henry Bowman Brady (1835–1891) and the *Challenger* Foraminifera." *Bulletin of the British Museum of Natural History,* Historical Series 18, No. 2 (1990), pp. 115–143.

Schlee, Susan. *The Edge of an Unfamiliar World: A History of Oceanography.* New York: Dutton, 1973.

RELATED ARTICLES

Murray, John; Thomson, Charles Wyville

Holdfast

Organisms that live in turbulent waters are in constant danger of being washed away, particularly where wave action is strong. Yet such waters are often rich in oxygen, nutrients, and planktonic food. Many plants and animals have colonized such habitats by evolving structures called holdfasts, which anchor them to the seafloor.

The term *holdfast* is most often used to refer to the rootlike structures used by seaweeds to cling to the seafloor. Holdfasts are most conspicuous in large seaweeds, such as kelps (order Laminariales). The body, or thallus, of a kelp is highly flexible to tolerate constant battering by waves. Gas-filled bladders called *pneumatocysts* help to support the organism in the water, and the long, flexible stalk, or *stipe*, is anchored to the seafloor by the holdfast. The holdfast of many kelps resembles a tight knot of roots, but unlike the roots of land plants, they are not specialized to absorb nutrients or water, merely to provide anchorage. In other brown algae the holdfasts are often disklike structures. In some species the holdfast also provides a means of surviving from one growing season to the next. At the end of the growing season the main body of such seaweeds is lost, and a new thallus develops from the holdfast at the start of the next season.

The term *holdfast* is also sometimes used to refer to the anchorage organ of stalked marine animals such as the stalked sea lilies (class Crinoidea). Stalked sea lilies live attached to the deep-sea floor by a stalk.

Ben Morgan

FURTHER READING

Brusca, Richard C., and Gary J. Brusca. *Invertebrates.* Sunderland, Mass.: Sinauer, 1990.

Hoek, C. Van den, D. G. Mann, and Hans Jahns. *Algae: An Introduction to Phycology.* Cambridge and New York: Cambridge University Press, 1995.

Sze, Philip. *A Biology of the Algae,* 3rd ed. Boston: Wm. C. Brown/McGraw-Hill, 1998.

RELATED ARTICLES
Crinoidea; Haptophyta; Ochrophyta; Pneumatocyst

Holocephali

The Holocephali (chimaeras) are one of two subclasses of chondrichthyan (cartilaginous) fishes, the other being the Elasmobranchii (sharks, skates, and rays). Holocephalans are linked with the elasmobranchs mainly due to their cartilaginous skeleton, internal fertilization, spiral valve intestine, the use of an oil-filled liver rather than a gas bladder for buoyancy, and copulatory organs in males (claspers). "Whole heads," the translation of their Greek name, refers to the fusion of the cranium and upper jaw, a primitive condition called *autostylic suspension.* The taxonomic relationships of holocephalans are not well known, mainly because their anatomical parts indicate affinities with a variety of groups and include many unique features. Accordingly, their common name refers to the chimaera of Greek mythology, a monster composed of many incongruous parts. Some scientists favor an ancestry from early elasmobranchs, while others link holocephalans to placoderms, an extinct class of heavily plated, benthic-oriented fishes that arose in the late Silurian Period and disappeared in the early Carboniferous Period (between about 420 million and 350 million years ago). Anatomical differences between holocephalans and elasmobranchs are many and include, respectively, the presence of a fleshy operculumlike gill covering rather than gill slits, autostylic rather than hyostylic suspension (a protrusible upper jaw connected to the cranium by ligaments), tooth plates that continue to grow during development rather than being replaced continuously, separate urogenital openings rather than a single opening, or cloaca, as well as differences in the position and structure of the gill chamber.

Fossil evidence suggests that the first holocephalans arose in the late Devonian Period (about 370 million years ago). Extant species represent a small fraction of a previously successful and diverse group, and eight fossil orders, represented by perhaps 20 families, lived during the Paleozoic (570 million to 248.2 million years ago) and Mesozoic (248.2 million to 65 million years ago) Eras. Early holocephalans exhibited varied morphologies, and many were diminutive in size, not exceeding 10 centimeters (about 4 inches). Modern chimaeras have fossil records dating to the Jurassic (205.7 million to 114.2 million years ago) and Cretaceous (114.2 million to 65.0 million years ago) Periods. There are currently only three families in a single order (Chimaeriformes), with six genera and about 31 species. Most species are contained within the family Chimaeridae (21 species).

Chimaeras are oviparous, laying approximately 10-centimeter (about 4-inch)-long eggs with horny shells like those of some sharks and skates. Adult sizes range from 60 to 200 centimeters (approximately 2 to 6.6 feet), with females often larger than males, as is common in elasmobranchs. Males in modern species have an extra clasper (tentaculum) located on the head whose function is unknown. Chimaeras are cool-water marine fishes. Although geographically widespread, low-latitude species occur in deeper waters (tropical submergence). As a group they are mainly found between 80 and 2600 meters (about 260 and 8500 feet) and are usually captured close to the seafloor. All apparently feed on bottom-dwelling crustaceans and mollusks, which they crush with their pavementlike teeth. They have an erectable spine preceding the dorsal fin with an associated venom gland for defense against predators. The chimaeras are also commonly known as ratfish because of their long, slender tail and large, pointed head. This body shape is convergent with that of teleosts (e.g., Macrouridae), which also live on the bottom in deep water.

Joseph J. Bizzarro

FURTHER READING

Bond, Carl E. *Biology of Fishes*. Philadelphia: W. B. Saunders, 1979; 2nd ed., Fort Worth, Texas: Saunders College Publishing, 1996.

Carroll, R. L. *Vertebrate Paleontology and Evolution*. New York: W. H. Freeman, 1988.

Helfman, Gene S., Bruce B. Collette, and Douglas E. Facey. *The Diversity of Fishes*. Malden, Mass.: Blackwell Science, 1997.

Lund, R., and E. D. Grogan. "Relationships of the Chimaeriformes and the Basal Radiation of the Chondrichthyes." *Reviews in Fish Biology and Fisheries*, Vol. 7, No. 1 (1997), pp. 65–123.

Moyle, Peter B., and Joseph J. Cech. *Fishes: An Introduction to Ichthyology*. Englewood Cliffs, N.J.: Prentice Hall, 1982; 4th ed., Upper Saddle River, N.J.: Prentice Hall, 2000.

Nelson, Joseph S. *Fishes of the World*. Englewood Cliffs, N.J.: Prentice Hall, 1982; 4th ed., Upper Saddle River, N.J.: Prentice Hall, 2000.

RELATED ARTICLES

Chondrichthyes; Crustacea; Elasmobranchii; Gnathostomata; Ray; Skate

Holoplankton

Planktonic organisms are the drifters of the ocean; the word *plankton* comes from the Greek word for "wandering." An extremely diverse assemblage of minute plants and animals comprises the plankton, and generally these organisms are categorized based on their size and life history characteristics. The term *holoplankton* describes the free-floating or weakly swimming organisms that spend their entire lives drifting in the currents of the ocean. This lifestyle is in contrast to that of the meroplankton, which spend only a short part of their life in the plankton.

Holoplanktonic organisms include the phytoplankton, bacterioplankton, viroplankton, and many members of the zooplankton. The phytoplankton are the larger [approximately 2.0 micrometers to 2 centimeters (0.000079 to 0.79 inch)] chlorophyll-bearing organisms that perform much of the photosynthesis in the sea. Throughout the world's oceans, two protistan groups (diatoms and dinoflagellates) dominate the assemblage of phytoplankton that can be caught in nets (net phytoplankton). The diatoms can be found alone or in chains and are distinguishable by their glass houses and lack of locomotory structures. The dinoflagellates usually are solitary, have a cell wall made of cellulose, and have two flagella that allow weak locomotion. Diatoms are extremely abundant in many locales; they can be as dense as 10 million cells per liter (0.22 gallon) of seawater. Dinoflagellates also are common and abundant; massive blooms of some toxin-producing species are responsible for the red tides that sometimes kill localized populations of fish and invertebrates.

Other much smaller holoplanktonic photosynthesizers include the prochlorophytes, haptophytes, and cyanobacteria. These minute photosynthetic organisms, which are part of the nanoplankton (2 to 20 μm) and picoplankton (0.2 to 2.0 μm), also make a significant contribution to oceanic primary production (i.e., photosynthesis). Picoplanktonic prochlorophytes are probably the most abundant photosynthesizers in the open ocean; in some locales they can be found at a concentration of 1 million cells per milliliter (0.04 ounce) of water. Haptophytes, which include the coccolithophores, are also important primary producers in many areas of the ocean. Cyanobacteria (blue-green bacteria), which comprise part of the bacterioplankton, are photosynthetic and abundant in the tropics.

Bacterioplankton also include the numerous bacteria that inhabit the seas. Marine bacteria are most abundant near the sea surface, and their biomass may be greater than that of the phytoplankton. Although not photosynthetic, bacteria play an important role in recycling organic compounds. Together with the viroplankton (marine viruses), these tiny organisms play an enormous role in the oceanic food web.

Many nonphotosynthetic members of the plankton are holoplanktonic as well. The most common and abundant holoplanktonic animal-like protists are the foraminiferans, the radiolarians, and certain types of ciliates and flagellates. Among the animals that can be caught in nets (net zooplankton), the most important are the free-living copepods. Copepods are crustaceans (phylum Arthropoda), usually one to several millimeters long, and they dominate the zooplankton assemblage throughout the world's oceans. Copepods provide a major trophic link in the oceanic food web; by grazing on phytoplankton and then getting eaten by larger animals, copepods transfer energy to higher trophic levels. Other abundant holoplanktonic crustaceans include cladocerans, ostracods, amphipods, euphausiids, and decapods. Many other animal phyla, including Cnidaria, Ctenophora, Nemertea, Annelida, Mollusca, Chaetognatha, and Chordata, contain holoplanktonic representatives.

Lynn L. Lauerman

FURTHER READING
Fraser, James. *Nature Adrift: The Story of Marine Plankton.* London: Foulis, 1962.
Nybakken, James W. *Marine Biology: An Ecological Approach,* 5th ed. San Francisco: Benjamin Cummings, 2001.
Smith, DeBoyd L., and Kevin B. Johnson. *A Guide to Marine Coastal Plankton and Marine Invertebrate Larvae.* Dubuque, Iowa: Kendall/Hunt, 1977; 2nd ed., 1996.

RELATED ARTICLES
Copepod; Meroplankton; Pteropoda; Zooplankton

Holothuroidea

Holothuroidea is one of the six classes into which scientists divide the echinoderms (sea stars, sea urchins, and their relatives). There are more than 1000 species of holothurians. Better known as *sea cucumbers,* they are soft, sausage-shaped animals that live on the seafloor and typically use their muscular bodies to wriggle through mud, earthworm-style. Although many live in shallow waters, sea cucumbers are found at all depths and are among the dominant animals in the deep sea. Like other members of the phylum Echinodermata, they are headless and brainless as adults.

Evolution has made the sea cucumbers very different from the other echinoderms. Whereas sea stars and sea urchins have a tough and brittle skeleton below the skin to protect them, sea cucumbers have developed much softer bodies by a reduction in the size of their skeletal plates. Most echinoderms are radially symmetrical, but some are secondarily bilaterally symmetrical: The mouth is located at one end of the body, surrounded by a ring of tentacles (usually, a multiple of five). Sea cucumbers lost their arms during evolution, their bodies became stretched out, and they now lie on one side, with the mouth at one end of the body and the anus at the other. The body wall is often dark and warty, and in some species it bears a close resemblance to the skin of a cucumber. Some sea cucumbers can grow up to 2 meters (6.6 feet) long.

Echinoderms possess a distinctive network of fluid-filled tubes running through the body, known as the *water vascular system.* The liquid inside the water vascular system is similar to seawater and helps to distribute oxygen and nutrients around the body as well as to carry away waste chemicals. In some sea stars and sea urchins the tubes of the water vascular system end in tiny, suckerlike extensions on the body's underside, which serve as feet. In sea cucumbers some of these "feet" form large tentacles surrounding the mouth. Filter-feeding species have feathery tentacles covered with sticky mucus to

A large sunflower star attempts to prey upon a sea cucumber, which manages to wiggle out of its captor's arms. (© Stuart Westmorland/Corbis)

capture fragments of food drifting through the water, but most sea cucumbers use their tentacles to shovel mud into their mouths as they wriggle through fine sediment on the seafloor. Edible matter in the mud is digested; the rest of the mud passes out of the anus. Scientists have estimated that some sea cucumbers pass over 130 kilograms (287 pounds) of mud through their intestines every year.

Unlike most echinoderms, sea cucumbers have well-developed muscles to suit their burrowing lifestyle. The high protein content of their bodies has made some a delicacy in Pacific countries. The flesh, known as *bêche-de-mer*, is boiled, dried, or smoked, and then made into soup.

Certain sea cucumbers have a very unusual form of self-defense. When attacked, they eject certain internal organs out through the anus. In some species it is their intestines, but others eject a mass of tangled tubes that may be sticky or poisonous. Once the sea cucumber has shaken off its attacker, it must slowly regrow the lost organs.

Ben Morgan

FURTHER READING
Barnes, Robert. *Invertebrate Zoology.* Philadelphia: W. B. Saunders, 1963; 6th ed., by Edward Ruppert, Fort Worth, Texas: Saunders College Publishing, 1994.
Brusca, Richard C., and Gary J. Brusca. *Invertebrates.* Sunderland, Mass.: Sinauer, 1990.
Pechenik, Jan A. *Biology of the Invertebrates.* Boston: Prindle, Weber and Schmidt, 1985; 4th ed, Boston: McGraw-Hill, 2000.

RELATED ARTICLES
Echinodermata

Horseshoe Crab

Horseshoe crabs are classified in the class Chelicerata of the phylum Arthropoda and have remained unchanged for millions of years. Although some of their relatives have become extinct, five species have survived and the best known species is the Atlantic horseshoe crab. The horseshoe crabs inhabit shallow-water areas with sandy or muddy shores, where they feed on worms, mollusks, and other benthic or bottom-dwelling invertebrates.

The body of horseshoe crabs is divided into a prosoma (cephalothorax) and an opisthosoma (abdomen). A pair of chelicerae, which are feeding structures, are followed by one pair of pedipalps and four pairs of walking legs. Blood is oxygenated by means of book gills, thin plates carried on the abdomen. The circulatory system is well developed, and the animals have a separate mouth and anus. Horseshoe crabs move primarily by walking and use the telson, the tail-like structure, to right the body if they are flipped over.

The sexes are separate and reproduction occurs when masses of the crabs converge in shallow water. Females are larger than males and can be found with several males attached to them. Females dig a nest in the sand to deposit their eggs, which the males then fertilize. When the larvae hatch, they dig their way up to the surface of the sand.

In the nineteenth and twentieth centuries, horseshoe crabs were used for fertilizer and animal feed. Today, they are harvested as bait for fishing conch and eel. Horseshoe crabs are also harvested by the medical industry for their blood, which contains an important component used in pharmaceuticals and for medical testing.

Erin O'Donnell

FURTHER READING
Barnes, Robert. *Invertebrate Zoology.* Philadelphia: W. B. Saunders, 1963; 6th ed., by Edward Ruppert, Fort Worth, Texas: Saunders College Publishing, 1994.
Brusca, Richard C., and Gary J. Brusca. *Invertebrates.* Sunderland, Mass.: Sinauer, 1990.
Buchsbaum, Ralph. *Animals Without Backbones.* Chicago: University of Chicago Press, 1938; 2nd ed., 1976.

RELATED ARTICLES
Arthropoda; Chelicerata

Hotspot

A hotspot is an area roughly 100 to 300 kilometers (60 to 185 miles) in diameter with high heat flow, copious quantities of rising magma, and persistent volcanic activity. Oceanic hotspot activity typically dominates volcanism within intraplate oceanic settings, forming constructional highs of igneous origin. Overlooking volcanic ridges and island arcs (which by definition lie on or adjacent to plate margins), the majority of volcanically derived oceanic islands probably are the result of hotspots. Many of the submerged conical bathymetric highs, called *seamounts*, are often inferred to be hotspot volcanoes. Even after volcanism has stopped, islands and submarine volcanic highs are still termed *hotspot volcanoes* or simply *hotspots*.

Mantle Plumes and the Origin of Hotspots

A molten hot (expanded and mobile) rising plume ascending within Earth's mantle has sufficient positive buoyancy (compared to its surroundings) to rise into the upper mantle and crust. It thus ascends through progressively colder, denser surrounding materials, somewhat analogous to warmed fluids in a pot on the stove or in the multicolored fluids rising in "lava lamps." In the case shown, the plume spreads greatly in its upper reaches. Many models show the flaring bulbous upper part of the plume, now thought to be on the order of 100 to 300 kilometers (60 to 185 miles) in diameter. Such a process of flaring and expansion is thought to promote large-scale crustal doming associated with a mantle plume. Once the magma reaches shallow depths, small quantities leak through the upper crust and escape onto the seafloor.

Geoscientists infer that hotspots come from plumes of magma ascending for a period of tens of millions of years. These plumes also appear quasistationary compared to Earth's more mobile, uppermost mantle and crust of the tectonic plates. Thus, as a mobile plate passes over the plume, a series of volcanoes develops on the seafloor, often forming a relatively linear chain in which radiometrically determined ages of seamounts and islands appear in chronological order. In other words, these island and seamount chains are thought to represent hotspot tracks, whereby the mobile plates move over a comparatively stationary hotspot.

An Analogy

For a simple analogy, this process appears like a sheet of steel (the crust) moving over a hot, stationary cutting torch (the mantle plume), leaving a trail of melted steel (a chain of hotspot volcanoes). Once the sheet has passed some distance away from the torch, it cools. In the case of hotspot dynamics, at some distance away from a mantle plume the hotspot volcano becomes cut off from its source of new magma. Here, off and away from the mantle plume, the volcano leaves the zone of upwelled and swollen crust. The crust cools and the older hotspot volcanoes gradually subside.

Evolution

In figure 1, which shows an inferred evolution of a hotspot volcano, the topographic descent of the initial volcanic island (on the right) as it passes off the updomed area above the mantle plume and moves to the left with the indicated age progression is purposely emphasized and exaggerated. Charles Darwin (1809–82) suggested that atolls may stem from sinking volcanic edifices, with the growth of coral keeping pace with the descent, an idea that prevails today. As the volcanic edifice sinks, its summit erodes, but simultaneously, it develops an increasingly large fringing reef, eventually an atoll, and finally becomes a guyot. The seamount ultimately collides with the inner wall of the trench at the plate margin, both enduring and causing large structural perturbations there.

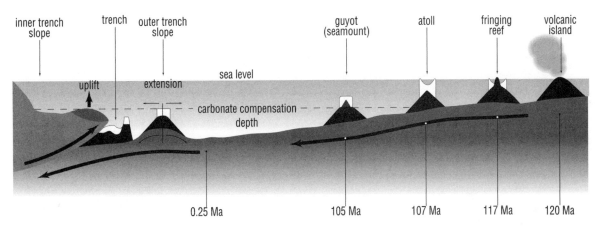

Figure 1. Schematic mid- to late-stage evolution of a hotspot volcano large enough to form an island. The progressive evolution starts with the hotspot volcano (on the right). With submergence, it subsequently develops into a guyot with a fringing reef. As the oceanic plate brings it into contact with a trench, subduction begins along with the onset of burial in deformed and uplifted accretionary-wedge sediments. The age dates apply to a specific case, the Daiichi Kashima Seamount, which currently sits in the Japan Trench. Ma indicates million years ago. (Adapted from Schmidt and Schminke, 2000, with permission from Elsevier Science.)

Hawaiian–Emperor Chain

For a good example of consistent age, and spatial and topographic progression, consider the Hawaiian–Emperor chain. The chain is an alignment of over 100 oceanic volcanoes, stretching some 6000 kilometers (3728 miles) across the Pacific. Erupted lavas occupy a volume of approximately 750,000 cubic kilometers (about 180,000 cubic miles). At the southeastern end lie the eight main Hawaiian islands. At the extreme southeastern end, on the island of Hawaii, we find Kilauea volcano (historically, the most active volcano and erupting at the time of this writing). Loihi, the youngest volcano in the Hawaiian Islands area, is a submarine vent lying 35 kilometers (22 miles) southeast of the island of Hawaii, residing at 1 kilometer (0.6 mile) depth. In the northwesterly direction, the various islands' radiometrically determined ages increase.

Progressing farther northwest to the youngest volcanoes of the Emperor Seamounts, the alignment of the volcanoes shifts directions, they no longer emerge from the sea to form islands, and they ultimately stretch far across the North Pacific to end off the westernmost islands of the

Aleutian Arc. Emperor volcanoes also continue to progress in age toward the northwest. The oldest Emperor volcano yields an age date of approximately 70 million years. Few other hotspot chains portray such a well-ordered age progression. Anomalous reversals in age progression are common elsewhere, perhaps due to dating inconsistencies or peculiarities in the lava delivery process.

How Many, and What Impact?

Older studies cited the worldwide number of oceanic hotspots in the hundreds. More recent studies, with more advanced and diverse technologies that can better detect submerged seamounts, have found upward of several thousand large seamounts within chains in the Pacific Ocean alone, mainly interpreted as due to hotspots. The seamounts occur as chains, isolated individuals, or in clusters.

Many current definitions of seamounts require that they rise at least 1 kilometer above the surrounding seafloor to be counted, a rather arbitrary requirement since volcanoes can be much smaller. Even with this definition, there could be many more, yet unidentified seamounts.

109

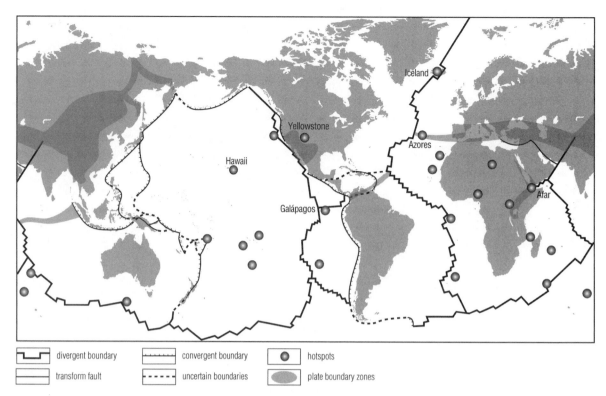

Figure 2. Selected hotspots around the world. (Adapted from U.S. Geological Survey, USG/Denver, Colorado.)

The behavior of seamounts as they enter trenches is exciting new areas of research. There are suggestions that the roughness of the seafloor brought on by topographic irregularities due to seamount size may slow the rate of subduction and plate motion. Recent seafloor imagery off western Costa Rica suggests that subducted seamounts can dramatically influence the shape of the trench.

Conflicting Ideas on Shallow versus Deep "Roots"

Although many geoscientists subscribe to the idea of mantle plumes generating hotspot volcanism, the depth, genesis, and evolution of plumes remain controversial. There may be more than one kind; for example, some may be associated with meteorite impacts, others with sources perhaps as deep as Earth's fluid outer core, approximately 3000 to 5000 kilometers (1865 to 3100 miles) below the surface.

Rick Wunderman

FURTHER READING

Burke, Kevin, and J. Tuzo Wilson. "Hot Spots on the Earth's Surface." In *Volcanoes and the Earth's Interior.* Readings from *Scientific American.* San Francisco: W. H. Freeman, 1982; p. 31.

Schmidt, Ralf, and Hans-Ulrich Schminke. "Seamounts and Island Building." In Haraldur Sigurdsson, ed., *Encyclopedia of Volcanology.* London: Academic Press, 2000; pp. 383–402.

Seyfert, Carl K., ed. "The Encyclopedia of Structural Geology and Plate Tectonics." In *Encyclopedia of Earth Sciences Series,* Vol. X. New York: Van Nostrand Reinhold, 1987.

Simkin, T. S., et al. *This Dynamic Planet: A World Map of Volcanoes, Earthquakes, and Plate Tectonics.* Denver, Colo.: U.S. Geological Survey, 1994.

Smith, David G., ed. *The Cambridge Encyclopedia of Earth Sciences.* Cambridge and New York: Cambridge University Press, 1982.

RELATED ARTICLES

Coral Atoll; Emperor Seamounts; Fringing Reef; Guyot; Hawaiian–Emperor Bend; Hawaiian Islands; Island Arc; Mantle Plume; Plate Tectonics; Seamount; Volcanic Ridge

Hudson Bay

Hudson Bay is a large, shallow, inland sea that is located entirely within Canada. It was named after Henry Hudson, the first European to explore the region, in 1610. The bay connects with the Arctic Ocean through Foxe Channel and with the Atlantic Ocean through Hudson Strait. It is bounded by latitudes 51°30′ to 63° 30′N and longitudes 78° to 95°W. The Hudson Bay, including James Bay on the south, is about 1450 kilometers (900 miles) long and 1050 kilometers (650 miles) wide and covers an area of approximately 1,230,000 square kilometers (475,000 square miles).

Hudson Bay has an average depth of about 100 meters (330 feet). The greatest depth is near the northern end at about 867 meters (2844 feet). Pleistocene (last 1.64 million years) continental glaciers were important factors in Hudson Bay's history. They not only gouged out the bay but also left sediments on the seafloor during their retreat. The climate is severe. January air temperatures average about -29°C (–20°F), and July temperatures average about 8°C (46°F). Much of the bay is covered with ice from October to mid-July. Surface-water temperature is as high as 9°C (48°F) in early September.

Three major rivers enter Hudson Bay: the Churchill, Severn, and Nelson. The large volume of fresh water from these rivers dilutes the bay, which keeps salinity low. Surface currents move in a counterclockwise direction, driven by the rivers' outflow and by ocean water inflow from the north.

The Inuit are the primary inhabitants in the north, and Cree Indians are the aboriginal people in the south. They live mostly by fishing and hunting. The bay contains abundant commercial fish (cod, halibut, and salmon). Seals, walruses, dolphins, whales, and polar bears are common, particularly in the northern areas.

Susan Morrell

FURTHER READING
Carter, Herbert Dyson. *Sea of Destiny: The Story of Hudson Bay—Our Undefended Back Door.* New York: Greenberg, 1940.
Okrainetz, Glen. "Towards a Sustainable Future in Hudson Bay; and the Inception of the Hudson Bay Program." *Northern Perspectives,* Vol. 20 (Fall/Winter 1992), pp. 12–16.
Rosenberg-Herman, Yvonne. *Marine Geology and Oceanography of the Arctic Seas.* New York: Springer-Verlag, 1974.

RELATED ARTICLES
Arctic Ocean; Atlantic Ocean

Hurricane

A hurricane, or tropical cyclone, is a violent tropical maritime storm. This weather system is characterized by an approximately circular shape, wind speeds in excess of 119 kilometers per hour (kph) [74 miles per hour (mph)], and very low sea-level pressures at the core (commonly 950 millibars or less). Tropical cyclones in the Atlantic and eastern North Pacific that impinge on North and Central American or Caribbean coastlines are called *hurricanes.* In the western North Pacific tropical cyclones are called *typhoons,* and in the Bay of Bengal and around Australia, they are called *cyclones.* In the following account, the emphasis is largely but not entirely on Atlantic hurricanes.

The more powerful tropical cyclones rank among the most destructive of meteorological phenomena. Forecasting their development and movement is one of the most essential services in meteorology. Beginning in 1953, the U.S. National Weather Service gave tropical cyclones individual female names (in alphabetical sequence through the season). In the late 1970s, male names were added.

Hurricane Features

Hurricanes and tropical cyclones in general share the following features:

- They are rotating tropical storm systems that have attained surface wind speeds in excess of 119 kph (74 mph).
- They average some 650 kilometers (405 miles) in diameter and have a central, calm, almost cloud-free core, the eye, that is about 15 to 25 kilometers (9 to 15 miles) across.
- They are strictly tropical oceanic phenomena, being generated in specific regions where sea temperatures in the top 60 meters (196 feet) of the water column are at least 27°C (80°F).
- They form mainly in late summer and early autumn (July–September in the northern hemisphere and January–March in the southern hemisphere).
- The requirement for warm water and a sufficient Coriolis effect (the deflecting force on a moving body generated by Earth's rotation) to generate a rotating storm system means that 80 to 85 percent of tropical cyclones originate between latitudes 5 and 15°.
- More than two-thirds of tropical cyclones occur in the northern hemisphere. None occur in the South Atlantic or in the southeastern Pacific Ocean because of the presence of cooling currents.

Hurricane Structure

A mature hurricane consists of bands of rain clouds spiraling around the eye. The bands contain helical rising winds that gradually increase in intensity toward the eye. The strongest thunderstorms are usually found immediately outside the eye, in the eye wall. Here, the bank of clouds can extend 15 kilometers (9 miles) above sea level. The entire weather system may contain hundreds of thunderstorms and measure up to 1000 kilometers (about 620 miles) across. The Coriolis effect determines that hurricanes turn counterclockwise in the northern hemisphere and clockwise in the southern hemisphere.

Hurricane Formation and Decline

The source of energy that fuels a tropical cyclone is the latent heat absorbed when water evaporates from the sea surface and is later released when clouds form. (Latent heat is the heat energy absorbed or released when a substance changes state.) The released heat energy warms the airmass,

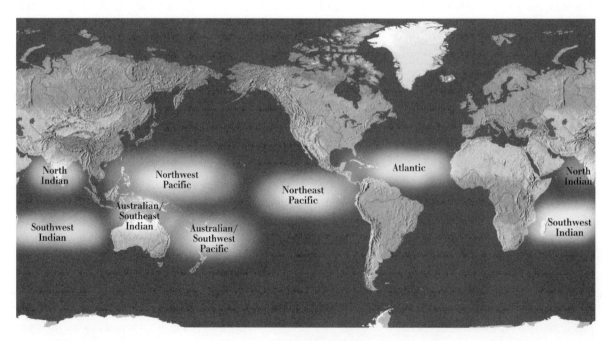

Figue 1. Hurricane basins.

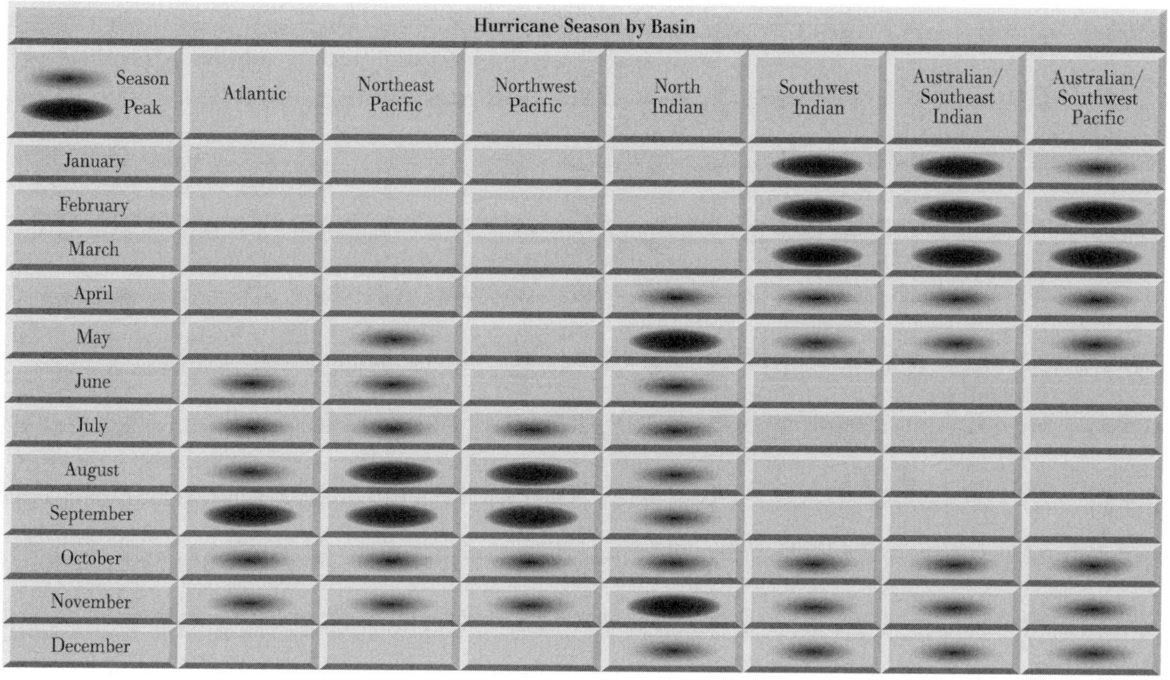

Figure 2. Hurricane seasons by basin.

latent heat energy is cut off. Even so, hurricanes become low-pressure systems that may unload vast quantities of rain and cause widespread inland flooding. A hurricane that makes landfall can spawn tornadoes.

Destructive Effects of Hurricanes

In popular terminology, the three main causes of hurricane damage are the three Ws: winds, waves (storm surges), and water (flooding from storm surges and precipitation). Hurricane winds can reach over 180 kph (about 112 mph) with gusts in excess of 240 kph (about 150 mph). Damage results from the wind force itself, from objects propelled by the wind, and from pressure differentials between the upwind and downwind sides of buildings, which cause oscillations that collapse the structures.

A storm surge is, strictly, not a wave but a mound of sea piled up ahead of the approaching hurricane or generated by the low-pressure zone in the center of the storm. A surge can reach 7 meters (23 feet) tall, extend more than 160 kilometers (100 miles) across, and when superimposed on a

lowers its density, and causes it to rise, generating updrafts and strong surface winds.

Atlantic hurricanes typically originate from storms off the coast of western Africa. Clusters of thunderstorms progressing over the Atlantic, encouraged by instabilities, may produce a rotating storm system as they move to higher latitudes and are influenced by the Coriolis effect. The latent heat of evaporation, later released as the latent heat of condensation, fuels the storm. When the disturbance has a well-defined circulation and has surface wind speeds of less than 62 kph (39 mph), it is classed as a *tropical depression*; if sea surface wind speeds increase to 62 kph, it becomes a *tropical storm*; and at 119 kph (74 mph), it is called a *tropical cyclone*. For the storm to become a cyclone, diverging upper-level winds must be present to draw air upward through the storm system.

Once spinning, a storm system tends to move away from the equator. If the storm moves toward the equator, it usually begins to weaken because of the lessening Coriolis effect.

A hurricane gradually subsides when it moves over colder water or onto land and the supply of

Destruction caused by Hurricane Mitch in Tegucigalpa, Honduras, in the fall of 1998. (© AFP/Corbis)

local high tide, can cause widespread and devastating coastal flooding. In November 1970, the storm surge generated by a tropical cyclone in the Bay of Bengal caused flooding that killed 300,000 people in Bangladesh.

Flooding does not result just from the storm surge. The torrential rain associated with a tropical cyclone, even after the storm has largely subsided, can cause coastal and inland flash flooding. Rainfall of 300 to 600 millimeters (12 to 24 inches) in a 24-hour period is not unknown. In 1998, rainfall from Hurricane Mitch set off mudslides in El Salvador, Honduras, and Nicaragua, killing at least 9000 people. In 1999, the most damaging effects of Hurricane Floyd on the southeastern and eastern U.S. states were caused by inland flooding after torrential rain.

Loss of life is greatest in those countries where disaster preparedness—storm warnings, evacuation procedures, reinforced buildings, and so on—are least developed. In the United States, hurricane warning systems (utilizing satellite, aircraft, and radar observation) coupled with hurricane preparedness, have casued the annual death toll from tropical cyclones to decline in the past 100 years. However, building construction has greatly increased in that time and storm damage to property has grown.

Hurricane Surveillance and Prediction

During the local tropical cyclone season, meteorologists study hourly satellite images while looking for signs of embryonic hurricanes over tropical oceans. Satellite photography is complemented by radar scatterometry, where the strength of backscattered satellite radar signals is used to infer the velocity of surface winds. If a storm system becomes rotational, moves into higher latitudes, develops an eye, and has surface wind speeds breaking the 119-kph (74-mph) barrier, it is declared a hurricane and assigned a name. As long as the storm persists, warnings are issued to shipping and aircraft traffic and to the general public. Within 240 kilometers (150 miles) of the coastline, hurricanes are tracked by radar.

A hurricane's path is difficult to predict since it veers erratically in response to surface and upper atmospheric winds. Computer forecasting uses several approaches. The hurricane's path can be projected based on existing speed and direction. Predictions can be based on past histories of similar storms in the area, and plotting falling air pressures ahead of the hurricane's arrival (a hurricane tends to follow a path through low air pressures) is a feasible approach. However, predicting the path of a hurricane to within ±80 kilometers (50 miles), 24 hours ahead of time, typically has a success rate no better than about 50 percent. To err on the side of caution, hurricane conditions are declared to allow time for preparation and evacuation. In many cases the hurricane's predicted arrival at a destination does not materialize.

The Future

In 1995, the Intergovernmental Panel on Climate Change (IPCC) made certain best-estimate

projections based on contemporary understanding of global warming and the greenhouse
effect. If these projections are broadly correct,
global sea levels can be expected to rise over the
next century and the warm-water area over
which hurricanes can form and develop is likely
to increase. This raises the specter of larger and
more frequent hurricanes, with greater likeli-
hood of severe floods.

Trevor Day

FURTHER READING
Burroughs, William J., et al. *Weather*. Alexandria, Va.:
Time Life Books, 1996.
Cobb, C. E., Jr. "Bangladesh: When the Water Comes."
National Geographic, Vol. 183, No. 6 (1993), pp.
118–134.
Dokken, David J., et al., eds. *Climate Change, 1995:
Impacts, Adaptations, and Mitigation of Climate
Change.* Cambridge and New York: Cambridge
University Press, 1996.
Musk, Leslie F. *Weather Systems.* New York: Cambridge
University Press, 1988.
Smith, F. G. W. "Hurricane Special: An Inside Look at
Planet's Powerhouse." *Sea Frontiers,* Vol. 38, No. 6
(1992), pp. 28–31.

USEFUL WEB SITES
Hurricane Floyd Reports.
<http://www.disastercenter.com/hurricf9.htm>.
U.S. National Hurricane Center.
<http://www.nhc.noaa.gov/index.shtml>.

RELATED ARTICLES
Coriolis Effect; Equator; Latent Heat, Fusion and
Evaporation; Storm Surge

Hydrocarbon Seep

A hydrocarbon seep is a site on the seafloor where
hydrocarbon gases and/or petroleum oil escape
from the sediment. Petroleum is a variable mixture of mostly hydrocarbons (organic compounds
composed solely of carbon and hydrogen atoms)
with carbon-chain lengths in the range of 18 to
40. Sulfur, nitrogen, oxygen, and heavy metals are
often present as impurities. Natural gas contains
predominantly methane (CH_4), with variable
amounts of ethane (C_2H_6), propane (C_3H_8),
butane (C_4H_{10}), and larger hydrocarbons. Since
the 1980s, hydrocarbon seeps have been discovered along many continental margins. Seeps of
various kinds, including those releasing fluids
from which hydrocarbons are sparse or absent, are
now known to be a general feature of the geology
and hydrology of continental margins.

Hydrocarbon seeps reflect geological processes
taking place deep in the sediment. Their compositions and physical properties alter the rocks
through which they flow, and as their products
rise through the water and reach the sea surface,
they affect the chemistry of the ocean and atmosphere. At their points of discharge, the seeps support unusual biological communities. The base of
the food chain for these communities consists of
bacteria that manufacture organic material by
harnessing chemical energy gained from the oxidation of reduced compounds, such as hydrogen
sulfide and methane, in a process called
chemosynthesis. These cold seep biological communities, like hydrothermal vent communities,
are unusual because they depend on geochemical
energy rather than sunlight.

Hydrocarbon seeps are associated with
deposits of petroleum or natural gas below the
seabed, some of which may migrate upward to
the seabed through faults in otherwise impermeable strata. Oil and gas deposits are formed from
rapidly buried organic material. Along continental margins, plankton may be rapidly smothered
by sediment, leading to the exclusion of oxygen
and preventing normal processes of biological
decomposition. When undecomposed organic
material is buried at depths of 2 to 4 kilometers
(1.25 to 2.5 miles) and subjected to high pressures and temperatures [50 to 150°C (122 to
302°F)], short-chain hydrocarbons are "cracked"
from much larger parent molecules over millions
of years. The consistency of the petroleum

deposit gradually thickens and then changes to a thinner liquid as maturation progresses. Methane can form early or late in this process and is also added by microbial activity in the surface layers of sediment. Deposits generally yield a characteristic mix of hydrocarbons and other compounds that reflect the specific organic source material and the unique history of the deposit and its discharge. The best oil and gas deposits for commercial extraction are found where the fuels migrate and collect in porous rock overlaid by impermeable strata. Hydrocarbon seeps in the locality can betray the presence of these deposits.

Seeps locally alter water and sediment chemistries. For example, where methane, carbon dioxide (CO_2), and hydrogen sulfide (H_2S) are components of the discharge, dissolved oxygen levels tend to fall, dissolved inorganic carbon concentrations rise, and pH is altered, encouraging deposition of carbonates. Sulfides, tar, and gas hydrates (clathrates) may deposit at seeps. Gas hydrates are icelike substances that contain methane or other hydrocarbons caged in a lattice of water molecules. They form under great pressure and at low temperatures (but above the freezing point of seawater). Estimates made in the early 1990s suggest that global gas hydrate reserves contain more fuel energy than is present in conventional coal, oil, and natural gas deposits.

In 1985, natural releases of petroleum from seeps were estimated to amount to about 8 percent of oil that was released into the sea by human activity. This is probably an underestimate. In some localities, such as Coal Oil Point near Santa Barbara, California, and in parts of the western Gulf of Mexico, natural oil discharges are regarded as significant pollutants. Vast stores of gas hydrates could, theoretically, release disturbingly large volumes of the greenhouse gas methane should temperatures rise above 6°C (43°F) at several hundred meters depth. The importance of hydrocarbon seeps is being actively investigated by many international teams of marine geophysicists, geochemists, and biologists.

Trevor Day

FURTHER READING
Libes, Susan M. *An Introduction to Marine Biogeochemistry.* New York: Wiley, 1992.
MacDonald, Ian R. "Natural Oil Spills." *Scientific American*, November 1998, pp. 30–35.
Spies, R. B. "Natural Submarine Petroleum Seeps." *Oceanus*, Vol. 26, No. 3 (1983), pp. 24–29.

USEFUL WEB SITES
Lorenson, T. D., K. A. Kvenvolden, F. D. Hostettler, R. J. Rosenbauer, J. B. Martin, and D. L. Orange. "Hydrocarbons Associated with Fluid Venting Process in Monterey Bay, California." <http://walrus.wr.usgs.gov/hydrocarbons/index.html>.
Sassen, Roger. "Gas Hydrate Gardens of the Gulf of Mexico." *Quarterdeck*, Vol. 5, No. 3 (1997). <http://ocean.tamu.edu/Quarterdeck/QD5.3/sassen.html>.

RELATED ARTICLES
Chemosynthesis; Cold Seep; Continental Margin

Hydrogen Bond

Hydrogen bonds are weak chemical bonds that are ubiquitous in nature; they are responsible for linking adjacent water molecules together. Two hydrogen (H) atoms, and one oxygen (O) atom, form an individual water molecule (H_2O). Each H is linked to the O with a *covalent bond* (a bond in which each atom donates an electron to a shared pair); the two H atoms sit at one end of the molecule and the O atom sits at the other. The O atom tends to pull the shared electrons closer to its nucleus and this scenario creates polarity. The O atom attains a slight negative charge and the H atoms become slightly positive. Hydrogen bonds result from the attraction of oppositely charged O and H atoms from adjacent water molecules. Because hydrogen bonds are weak (they are only about 6 percent as strong as the covalent bonds linking atoms in an individual water molecule), they can be broken and formed easily.

Hydrogen bonds and the polarity of water molecules are responsible for some of the unique properties of water that make life on Earth possible. For example, without these properties, water would have a freezing point lower than ambient temperatures over much of Earth's surface. Water also has a high boiling point, which allows it to remain in the liquid (rather than the gas) phase despite relatively warm temperatures on Earth. Hydrogen bonding means that water, unlike other liquids, becomes less dense upon freezing and therefore ice floats. Hydrogen bonding is responsible for surface tension at the air–water interface that allows organisms to skim over the top or rest just below the surface. Hydrogen bonding and polarity also make water an almost universal *solvent* (a liquid with the ability to dissolve substances). For example, in water, salts dissolve into their individual ions, thus making them available to other chemical processes.

Lynn L. Lauerman

FURTHER READING

Millero, Frank J. *Chemical Oceanography.* Boca Raton, Fla.: CRC Press, 1992; 2nd ed., 1996.

Nybakken, James W. *Marine Biology: An Ecological Approach,* 5th ed. San Francisco: Benjamin Cummings, 2001.

RELATED ARTICLES

Heat Capacity; Latent Heat, Fusion and Evaporation; Water Molecule

Hydrogen Sulfide

Hydrogen sulfide (H_2S) is a naturally occurring compound and a by-product of anaerobic (i.e., oxygen-deficient) metabolism. The foul odor of hydrogen sulfide is commonly detected in the smell of rotten eggs. Hydrogen sulfide is more toxic than hydrogen cyanide. H_2S is found in chemically reducing environments such as hydrothermal springs, volcanic gases, marine anoxic basins, and anoxic sediments. Hydrogen sulfide is not found generally throughout the ocean, nor in the atmosphere, because it reacts quickly with molecular oxygen to form oxidized sulfur compounds such as sulfur dioxide, thiosulfate, and sulfate.

Hydrothermal vent waters boiling out of *smokers* discovered along seafloor spreading centers in the eastern Pacific contain high (millimolar) concentrations of hydrogen sulfide. Near the plumes, H_2S-bearing waters are mixed rapidly with oxygenated waters. Special chemical probes manipulated by remote-operated vehicles (ROVs) have detected measurable H_2S concentrations only very close [< 1 meter (3.3 feet)] to the hydrothermal vents. In this environment, hydrogen sulfide plays an important role in chemosynthesis, by which sulfur-oxidizing bacteria synthesize organic matter using the energy from oxygen sulfide oxidation rather than the solar radiant energy that drives photosynthesis near the ocean surface. Highly specialized and highly localized communities of vent organisms (unknown to oceanographers 20 years ago) have evolved to live in this environment.

In some deep fjords (in Norway and British Columbia), the Black Sea, and Cariaco Trench, hydrogen sulfide is found in deep waters where the deep circulation is limited by strong pycnoclines. Here sulfur-reducing bacteria chemically oxidize organic matter using sulfate (a major constituent of sea salt) in place of molecular oxygen. The Black Sea is a land-locked basin overlain by a layer of oxygenated, brackish water that forms a strong halocline. Its deep waters, from 200 to 2000 meters (656 to 6560 feet), contain diluted seawater (i.e., salinity of about 22 practical salinity units [psu]), no dissolved oxygen, and 0.3 millimolar H_2S concentrations.

In anoxic sediments H_2S is also formed by bacterial oxidation of organic matter using sulfate as the electron donor. In anoxic sediments the vertical scale is very small: Oxygenated interstitial waters extend to depths of only millimeters or centimeters. Below that, in the sulfide-rich reducing environment, many metals in their reduced state are solubilized, and their geochemistry differs considerably from that in the oxygenated water column.

William W. Broenkow

FURTHER READING

Berner, Elizabeth Kay, and Robert A. Berner. *The Global Water Cycle: Geochemistry and Environment.* Englewood Cliffs, N.J.: Prentice Hall, 1987.

Grasshoff, K. "The Hydrochemistry of Landlocked Basins and Fjords." In J. P. Riley and G. Skirrow, eds., *Chemical Oceanography.* London and New York: Academic Press, 1965; 2nd ed., 1975.

Horne, Ralph. *Marine Chemistry.* New York: Wiley-Interscience, 1969.

Millero, F. J. "Redox Processes in Anoxic Basins." In Antonio Gianguzza, Ezio Pelizzetti, and Silvio Sammartano, eds., *Chemical Processes in Marine Environments.* Berlin and New York: Springer-Verlag, 2000.

Thompson, G. "Hydrothermal Fluxes in the Ocean." In J. P. Riley and G. Skirrow, eds., *Chemical Oceanography.* London and New York: Academic Press, 1965; 2nd ed., 1975; pp. 43–171.

RELATED ARTICLES
Anoxic Basin; Hydrothermal Vent

Hydrography

Hydrography is an applied science that deals with measurement and description of the physical features of surface waters and adjoining coastal areas, with special reference to their use for the purpose of navigation. Hydrography has two branches. One, based in civil engineering, is responsible for surveying, measuring, describing, and charting the physical features of oceans, seas, rivers, and lakes. These data are used to produce navigational charts, tide and current tables, and sailing directions for mariners. The second branch, based in physical oceanography, produces charts of water properties (temperature, salinity, dissolved oxygen, and nutrients) used to understand ocean processes.

The process of collecting the data needed for making charts is called *surveying*. The quality of the data collection effort depends critically on accurate navigation and measurements of water depth. Accurate navigation involves precise determination and marking of positions on land and measurements of reference directions and distance and must take into account the curvature of Earth. In addition to the delineation of coastlines and the location and measurement of submerged features, a hydrographic survey also includes measurements of magnetic declination and dip, currents, water levels, and weather conditions.

The practice of hydrography has changed dramatically in the past century. In the nineteenth century, surveys depended on astronomical observations and point measurements of water depth. Lead lines consisting of suitably marked lines having a weight attached to one end were lowered to the bottom by sailors or machines until early in the 20th century. Echo sounding equipment was developed subsequently to provide accurate measurements of the depth of water beneath a ship. Modern survey vessels have an array of hull-mounted acoustic transducers that effectively image a swath of the ocean as the ship moves through the water. Aircraft can also conduct rapid surveys of shallow waters using airborne lasers to measure the depth of water.

Modern sounding techniques require continuous and accurate navigation. This is made possible by the global positioning system (GPS). Users can find their position at any time, in any weather, with an accuracy of 4 meters (13 feet) in the horizontal and 8 meters (26 feet) in the vertical. Surveyors have GPS systems that can achieve higher accuracy, 10 centimeters (4 inches) or less.

The capabilities of modern computers may make printed charts obsolete. Larger ships have electronic charts that are interfaced with a GPS so that the position of the ship is displayed continuously. A second advantage of electronic charts is that other kinds of information can easily be overlaid on the chart. These systems are called *geographical information systems* and are important tools for regional planning and environmental assessment.

Curtis A. Collins

FURTHER READING

Abbott, V. J., and A. E. Ingham. *Hydrography for the Surveyor and Engineer,* 3rd ed. Malden, Mass.: Blackwell Science, 1994.

Defense Mapping Agency. "Hydrography and Hydrographic Reports." In *The American Practical Navigator,* Publ. 9. Bethesda, Md.: DMA Hydrographic/Topographic Center, 1995; pp. 411–426.

International Hydrographic Bureau. *Hydrographic Dictionary.* Monaco: International Hydrographic Organization, 1990.

Ritchie, G. S. *No Day Too Long: An Hydrographer's Tale.* Durham, England: Pentland Press, 1992.

RELATED ARTICLES
Global Positioning System

Hydrologic Cycle

Hydrology is a field of Earth science devoted to the study of waters, including their occurrence, distribution, circulation, physical and chemical properties, interactions with the environment, and relationship to plants and animals. In accordance with this definition, hydrology includes the complete life history of water on Earth. Hydrology is concerned with measuring the amount and intensity of precipitation; how much water is stored as snow or in glaciers; how fast glaciers are advancing or retreating; how much water various rivers discharge into larger bodies of water; rates at which water is being gained or lost in various storage areas; soil moisture and its rates of change; and the gain or

loss and movement of water located under Earth's surface.

The central concept in hydrology is the hydrologic cycle, which describes the circulation or transfer of water in its various forms from the ocean to the atmosphere, to the land, and back to the ocean (see figure). Its primary source of energy is the Sun. Approximately 97 percent of Earth's water is in the oceans, about 2 percent occurs in glaciers and the polar ice caps, and less that 1 percent is found in the atmosphere. Water evaporates from the ocean surface into the atmosphere in the form of water vapor. This is by far the largest contribution of water to the atmosphere. Water also evaporates from other surfaces, including rivers, lakes, reservoirs, and snow. Water molecules are also emitted from ice surfaces into the atmosphere directly without becoming a liquid. This process is called *sublimation*. Rain partially evaporates as it falls, and finally, moisture in the soil provides yet another source of moisture that evaporates into the atmosphere. In the atmosphere, water vapor condenses into clouds. Humid air masses that have received moisture from the ocean move over land due to the prevailing atmospheric circulation. When moisture-laden air masses rise over other air masses, or over mountainous terrain, they are cooled, and often this cooling produces precipitation. This precipitation can take the form of rain, snow, hail, or sleet.

The distribution of precipitation over Earth is very uneven, with some areas, such as rainforests, receiving up to several hundred inches of rain a year, whereas other regions, such as deserts, may receive less than 2.5 centimeters (1 inch) of rain within a given year. Although most precipitation occurs over the ocean, approximately 20 percent of Earth's total precipitation occurs over land. Of the precipitation that reaches the ground, some evaporates almost immediately, some penetrates the soil, and some runs over land surfaces into ponds, lakes, rivers, and oceans. The absorption of water into the soil is called *infiltration*. Water that does not evaporate from the soil may

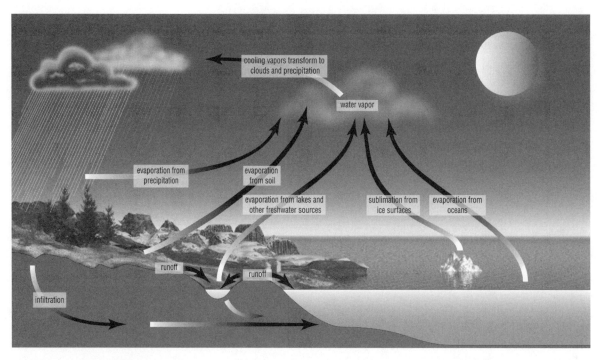

Hydrologic cycle, showing the transfer of water from the oceans and other water sources to the atmosphere and continents and back to the oceans again.

infiltrate to deeper levels. Gravity, in turn, carries water to still deeper levels below the surface, where it becomes groundwater. Groundwater accumulates over long periods. Areas where surface waters infiltrate the groundwater reserves are known as *recharge zones*. However, due to the increasing demands of agriculture, groundwater reserves in some areas are now being depleted more rapidly than they can be replaced. Groundwater from the Ogallala aquifer, for example, which covers a region from South Dakota to Texas, is being used in some areas at a rate up to 20 times higher than the rate at which it is being naturally replaced. Groundwater moves slowly, but it provides a source of water for lakes and rivers through seepage. Groundwater also enters the ocean through underground pathways. When rain falls too rapidly, much of the water becomes surface runoff or overland flow that can enter rivers and lakes directly without ever penetrating the soil. Surface runoff provides a path for pollutants to enter local waterways. Water in the soil is also used by plants; it is drawn into their

systems through extensive networks of tiny roots. This water is carried upward through the trunk and branches to the leaves, where it is discharged back into the atmosphere in the form of water vapor. This process is called *transpiration*.

Example and Formulation of the Hydrologic Cycle

The following example illustrates the various elements of the hydrologic cycle for a specific area. Lake effect snowfall around the U.S. Great Lakes begins in the late fall as cold winds blow across the Great Lakes. Evaporation of warm surface lake waters increases the amount of moisture in the cold dry air that flows just above the lake surfaces. As evaporation continues, the increased water vapor in the overlying atmosphere condenses and forms clouds containing ice crystals. These clouds are transported toward the shore by the prevailing winds. When these clouds reach the shore they contain enough moisture to produce snowflakes that fall along the shoreline as precipitation. When the fallen snow begins to melt, part of the water is absorbed by the soil and becomes groundwater through infiltration. The remaining water flows back to the lakes as runoff, thus completing the cycle.

A convenient way to combine the major elements of the hydrologic cycle that has been described above is to form a global water balance. This balance can be stated as follows: $P = E + R + G$, where P represents precipitation, E represents evaporation, R represents the runoff from land into the oceans, and G is a storage term comprising the net gain or loss of water. When applied over the period of a year and averaged over many years, the storage term is essentially zero, because no water is ultimately created or destroyed: thus, $P = E + R$. If we separate the continents from the oceans, precipitation exceeds evaporation over land, whereas evaporation exceeds precipitation over the ocean. When we consider the entire Earth, the runoff terms cancel out and we achieve a global balance.

Laurence C. Breaker

FURTHER READING
Maidment, David R., ed. *Handbook of Hydrology.* New York: McGraw-Hill, 1993.
Parker, Sybil P., ed. *McGraw Hill Encyclopedia of Ocean and Atmospheric Sciences.* New York: McGraw-Hill, 1980.

USEFUL WEB SITES
"Hydrological Sciences Branch Code 974." November 2000. <http://hsb.gsfc.nasa.gov/hsb.html>.

RELATED ARTICLES
Hydrology; Ice Cap

Hydrology

Hydrology deals with the cycling of continental water (solid, liquid, and vapor) at all scales as well as with the physical, chemical, and biological processes that are driven by that cycling. The interface between marine science and hydrology occurs where continental water and ocean water meet: in estuaries and in the coastal ocean at river mouths. An interface between fresh continental waters and ocean waters can also occur subsurface where the geological formations that contain continental water are exposed on the continental shelf and slope. Biological species that live in these zones between fresh continental and salty ocean water or that pass through them are a concern to both hydrologists and oceanographers. Hydrologists and oceanographers also share an interest in processes that are common to the two disciplines, such as evaporation and precipitation, since they are important for the cycling of water through both the ocean and the continents.

The study of hydrology is traditionally broken into five broad areas: precipitation, evaporation, surface water, groundwater, and water resource development. Precipitation and evaporation are discussed in the "Hydrologic Cycle" article, but unlike oceanographers, hydrologists must consider how plants affect both precipitation and evaporation. Plants withdraw water from the soil and are also able to absorb some water directly when it falls. Water is either stored in plant tissue or converted to water vapor by the plant and discharged into the atmosphere. This process is called *evapotranspiration*. It varies for different types of plants, their stage of growth, and for the amount of light and wind to which the plant is exposed. The amount of moisture in the soil also affects the rate of evapotranspiration.

Surface Water

Hydrologists are concerned with surface waters, including lakes and streams as well as snow, ice, and glaciers. Hydrologists gauge streams and lakes, measure snow pack, and study the mineralization of water and the factors that influence runoff. Nature controls runoff principally through the geology and topography of the drainage basin. Geological factors include the physical character of the underlying rocks, their ability to absorb and retain water, and the degree to which they dissolve. For given geological conditions, steeper and more rugged topography will shorten the amount of time it takes water to run off. Given a shorter runoff time, peak flows and water levels will increase downstream.

Groundwater

Groundwater includes all waters that are found beneath Earth's surface. A geological formation that contains water and yields water to wells is called an *aquifer*. Water can move very slowly within an aquifer due to spatial differences in water elevation. Movement can also be caused by capillary forces and is controlled by the physical properties of rock formations. Basic properties of aquifers are classified as either microproperites or macroproperties.

Microproperties can be measured in a laboratory and include porosity, permeability, and specific yield. Porosity is a measure of the open spaces or voids that exist in rocks and is expressed as the percent of the total volume not occupied by solid material. Permeability is the capacity to transmit water through the interstices of the material and is measured by determining the rate of flow though a given cross-sectional area of material under a given pressure. Specific yield is the total quantity of water drained after a very long time, divided by the original volume of the material.

Macroproperties are those that are possessed by the aquifer acting as a unit. They include transmissibility and the coefficient of storage. Transmissibility is similar to permeability, but it is measured in the field and differs from laboratory measurements because the structure of the aquifer is not homogeneous. The coefficient of storage is the volume of water that an aquifer releases from (or takes into) storage per unit horizontal surface area of aquifer per unit change in water height. It is determined by the elasticity of the aquifer, the confining geological formations, and water. The coefficient of storage varies from 5×10^{-5} to 5×10^{-3}, so substantial

pressure changes are required to produce a significant amount of water.

Aquifers are classified by their ability to yield water and their source of replenishment. Sandstones have the best water yield. Sources of replenishment are rain or seepage from lakes or streams. In coastal regions, aquifers extend under the seabed so that they are exposed to seawater some distance from shore. In these cases, if too much fresh water is pumped out of an aquifer over land, seawater may move into the aquifer, making wells that are located near the coast unusable. Alternatively, fresh water may be discharged directly into the ocean, and in some cases, this freshwater discharge supports unique biological populations.

Data and Water Usage

In the United States, an extensive database for continental water is maintained by the U.S. Geological Survey (USGS). These data include daily streamflow data, reservoir and lake levels, well levels, surface- and groundwater quality, and rainfall. At selected surface- and groundwater sites, instruments continuously record physical and chemical characteristics of the water, including pH, specific conductance, temperature, dissolved oxygen, and percent dissolved oxygen saturation. Many of these data are available nearly in real time from the USGS Web site. These data are essential for managing water, and they are also needed by coastal oceanographers to determine estuarine water budgets.

Globally, the supply of fresh water is under considerable stress. This is due to increasing human populations, political and economic instability, and possibly, climate change. Only 35 percent of the global population have access to safe drinking water, and only 32 percent have proper sanitation. During the past 50 years, global use of continental water has quadrupled.

The United States does not face a water crisis of this magnitude. In 1995, the United States used about 341 billion gallons of fresh water each day, with 77 percent coming from surface-water supplies and 23 percent from groundwater. The two principal uses of fresh water in the United States are power generation and irrigation (39 percent each), followed by the use of water for homes and businesses at 12 percent, and industrial uses at 7 percent. Important trends in the United States include increasing use of ground water and increasing use of water for power generation. When conflicts over water supply develop in the United States, either over irrigation, domestic supply, or wildlife support, there are usually good alternatives available to us, often at small cost, such as building additional reservoirs.

Curtis A. Collins

FURTHER READING

Burnett, W., J. Chanton, J. Christoff, E. Kontar, S. Drupa, M. Lambert, W. Moore, D. O'Rourke, R. Paulsen, C. Smith, L. Smith, and M. Taniguchi. "Assessing Methodologies for Measuring Groundwater Discharge to the Ocean." *EOS: Transactions American Geophysical Union*, Vol. 83, No. 11 (2002), p. 117.

Hornsberger, G. M., J. P. Raffensperger, P. L. Widberg, and K. N. Eshleman. *Elements of Physical Hydrology.* Baltimore: Johns Hopkins University Press, 1995.

Maidment, David R., ed. *Handbook of Hydrology.* New York: McGraw-Hill, 1992.

National Research Council. *Opportunities in the Hydrologic Sciences.* Washington, D.C.: NRC, 1991.

Parker, Sybil P., ed. *McGraw Hill Encyclopedia of Ocean and Atmospheric Sciences.* New York: McGraw-Hill, 1980.

RELATED ARTICLES
Hydrologic Cycle

Hydrophone

A hydrophone is an acoustic–electrical transducer that converts sound waves into equivalent electric waves. It is the underwater equivalent of a microphone, which receives and converts sound waves in the air. Hydrophones normally consist of a piezoelectric sensing element such as barium titanate, lead zirconate, tourmaline, or quartz that converts changes in pressure into electrical impulses. These electrical signals may be passed through preamplifiers before being transmitted to a recording unit. Hydrophones are used extensively in seismic exploration of Earth beneath the sea. Whereas geophones used in land exploration usually respond to vertical particle motion, hydrophones are sensitive to pressure changes in the water coming from any direction. In seismic surveying, hydrophones are towed 150 to 300 meters (490 to 980 feet) or greater behind a ship at speeds of 1.5 to 5.1 meters per second (3 to 10 knots). Different array configurations and towing techniques are employed. The most simple single-channel array is to place several hydrophones in a 15- to 30-meter (49- to 98-foot) length of flexible oil-filled plastic tubing with the hydrophones connected electrically. Some detector cables used in petroleum exploration consist of 48, 96, 200, or more groups usually arrayed over lengths of 2400 or 3200 meters (7874 to 10,499 feet). These arrays are designed to be approximately neutrally buoyant so as to remain at a constant towing depth.

In addition to seismic exploration, hydrophones are used in the marine environment for military purposes, such as in sonar apparatus and in certain underwater weapons. They are also used by marine biologists for listening to dolphins and whales, as well as for listening to all forms of sea life for recreational and educational purposes.

Philip Rabinowitz

FURTHER READING

Nelson, H. Roice, Jr. *New Technologies in Exploration Geophysics.* Houston, Texas: Gulf Publishing, 1983.

Verma, Rajni K. *Offshore Seismic Exploration.* Houston, Texas: Gulf Publishing, 1986.

RELATED ARTICLES
Acoustic Oceanography; Seismic Profiling; Seismic Stratigraphy; Sonar

Hydrosphere

The hydrosphere includes all the water on Earth—gas, liquid, and solid. This includes inland seas, lakes, rivers, streams, snow and ice, groundwater, water vapor, and the oceans. The distribution of water in the oceans is discussed in the article "Oceans, Water Budget of." Here other elements of the hydrosphere are discussed, with emphasis on their interaction with the sea.

Water Vapor

Water vapor is water in the gaseous phase. The process by which water changes from liquid to gas is called *evaporation*. The latent heat required to evaporate 1 kilogram (2.2 pounds) of seawater averages 2400 kilojoules but decreases with increasing temperature and decreasing salinity. The process of evaporation is the largest source of heat loss for the ocean, averaging 90 watts per square meter. Evaporation results in the loss of 1.2 meters (about 4 feet) of water from the ocean each year.

Meteorologists use different terms to express the amount of water vapor in air. Some refer to the actual amount, or concentration, of water vapor in the air, and others relate to the amount that would saturate the air. Air is said to be saturated when it contains the maximum possible amount of water vapor without causing any condensation. At that point, the rate at which water molecules enter the air by evaporation must exactly balance the rate at which they leave by condensation.

The partial pressure of a given sample of moist air that is attributable to water vapor is called the *vapor pressure*. *Relative humidity* is the most commonly used term to quantify the amount of water vapor. Relative humidity is the ratio of the existing vapor pressure to the vapor pressure corresponding to saturation at the prevailing temperature and pressure. Specific humidity is the ratio of the mass of water vapor in a sample to the total mass of the moist air, including both the dry air and the water vapor. Mixing ratio is the ratio of the mass of water vapor to the mass of only the dry air in the sample. As ratios, relative humidity, specific humidity, and mixing ratio are dimensionless. However, because atmospheric concentrations of water vapor are at most only a few percent of the amount of air, specific humidity and mixing ratio are often expressed in units of grams of water vapor per kilogram of (moist or dry) air. Absolute humidity is the water vapor density and is defined as the mass of water vapor divided by the volume of associated moist air and has units of grams per cubic meter.

Evaporation increases with increasing wind speed and decreasing humidity and is greatest in the subtropics due to low humidity and steady winds. In these latitudes the largest evaporation is found over the oceans at their western boundaries in winter. This is due to the interaction of cold dry air from continents with warm western boundary currents.

The weight of the atmosphere's water vapor contributes only about 0.25 percent of the total sea-level pressure. If all the water vapor in the air at a particular time were to condense and fall as rain, it would amount to a depth of only about 2.5 centimeters (less than 1 inch). This is called *precipitable water*. Because water vapor is not evenly distributed globally, there would be about 5 centimeters (about 2 inches) near the equator and less than one-tenth as much at the poles. The average water molecule spends about 10 days in the air before returning to the surface of Earth.

Water vapor is a greenhouse gas and has about twice the effect of all other gases combined. Warm air can hold more water vapor than cold air without becoming saturated. To the extent that global warming increases the temperature of Earth, more evaporation may take place and the amount of water vapor would rise. The increased concentration of water vapor would, in turn, lead to higher temperatures. This is called *positive feedback* and is a feature of climate models that are used to estimate the effect of greenhouse gases.

Water vapor plays an important role in Earth's heat budget. The heat from the Sun that is used to evaporate water is returned to the air when condensation occurs. The evaporation–condensation cycle moves heat from Earth's surface to the atmosphere. The atmosphere can then move the heat (and water vapor) around Earth.

Precipitation

Clouds and fog form when water vapor condenses upon minute particles of dust and salt in the air. Further condensation causes the particles to fall. Precipitation is any kind of condensed water vapor (liquid, freezing, or frozen) that falls on Earth. On land and at sea, precipitation rates are measured by determining how much water falls in a given time period. This is complicated somewhat at sea by the motion of the rain gauge and the fact that spray from the ocean occasionally finds its way into the rain gauge.

The average precipitation over the globe is about 1 meter (about 3.3 feet) annually. Highest rainfall over the ocean occurs under the Intertropical Convergence Zone (ITCZ), especially in the western tropical Pacific where rainfall rates can exceed 10 millimeters (about 0.4 inch) per day. The ITCZ, called the *doldrums* by mariners, separates the northeast trades of the northern hemisphere from the southeast trades of the southern hemisphere. It is generally located between 3 and 10°N and can be thought of as the climatic equator. The ITCZ is readily identified on satellite images as a band of clouds that often circle Earth. Because of the precipitation, the salinity of the sea surface is lower under the ITCZ than it is at latitudes immediately poleward. Very high rainfall rates also occur in the Bay of Bengal during the period of the Southwest Monsoon (June through August). Here rainfall can exceed 15 millimeters (about 0.6 inch) per day. As under the ITCZ, this results in a freshening of the surface waters.

Groundwater

Water is stored within aquifers under land. The water within an aquifer can be either fresh or salty. Along coasts, aquifers are bounded at their seaward margins by ocean waters. Under natural conditions, the seaward movement of water in aquifers will prevent ocean water from encroaching into coastal aquifers, and the interface between continental and ocean waters is maintained near the coast or far below the land surface. The interface between the waters is a diffuse zone in which continental and ocean waters mix. When the water in the aquifer is fresh water and is withdrawn for agricultural or other use, the freshwater flow toward the ocean is reduced and this causes salty ocean waters to be drawn farther into the freshwater zone of the aquifer. These saltwater intrusions decrease freshwater storage in the aquifer and in some cases result in abandonment of wells.

Substantial discharge of brackish groundwaters occurs along the southeastern coast of the United States, rivaling river inputs to the ocean in this area. A similar situation occurs near the mouths of the Ganges–Brahmaputra and Mississippi–Atchafalaya Rivers. In other areas, such as Monterey Bay, smaller seeps occur. These groundwaters can have large concentrations of nutrients, metals, organic compounds, and inorganic carbon and may be capable of sustaining unique biological communities.

Ice

Ice, the solid form of water, is formed by freezing. Ice in the sea comes from two sources. The most important source is freezing of seawater, which produces sea ice. The second source is breaking of ice from glaciers, which results in icebergs.

SEA ICE

Sea ice covers from 6 to 8 percent of the ocean's surface. The formation of sea ice has important climatic consequences. It prevents solar radiation from warming the waters but also prevents the waters from losing their heat directly to the atmosphere. Ice reflects incoming radiation to a much greater extent than water does. The reflectivity of ice is 30 to 40 percent and can increase to as much as 95 percent when it is covered by fresh snow. In addition to reflecting much of the incoming radiation, sea ice serves to insulate the ocean and prevent the transfer of heat directly from the water to the atmosphere.

Salinity (*S*) affects the freezing point of water and the temperature of maximum density. The freezing point of fresh water is 0°C (32°F). The addition of salt to water depresses the temperature at which sea ice forms, so when $S = 35$ practical salinity units (psu) the freezing point is -1.91°C (about 30.9°F). The maximum density of fresh water occurs at 3.94°C (34.2°F). As salt is added, the temperature of maximum density decreases. At $S = 24.7$ psu, the temperature of maximum density is -1.33°C (31.3°F), which coincides with the freezing point.

For waters fresher than 24.7 psu, water reaches its maximum density before freezing and sinks. This overturning continues until all water reaches the temperature of maximum density. With further cooling, surface water is lighter, so ice freezes from the top down. When the salinity is above 24.7 psu, this situation changes and the entire water column must be cooled to the freezing point, delaying the formation of ice.

The stratification of sea-ice formation areas in the Arctic is marked by a strong halocline between 50 and 200 meters (164 and 656 feet). This halocline is a consequence of the seasonal melting and freezing of sea ice and outflow from Siberian and North American rivers. It also means that the fresher surface waters can be cooled to their freezing point without becoming denser than the saltier water below the halocline.

The rate of ice formation depends on environmental conditions. Ice forms most rapidly when the salinity is low, winds are calm, and the water depth is shallow. At -30°C (-22°F), 3 centimeters (about 1.2 inches) of ice can form in 1 hour and 30 centimeters (about 12 inches) in three days. The rate of increase of thickness decreases with thickness. Each winter, 2 to 3 meters (6.6 to 9.8 feet) may form, melting by July.

Ice formation occurs in well-defined stages in the open ocean. The appearance of the sea surface first becomes greasy or oily with a gray or leaden tint, due to the presence of ice crystals. Next, individual spicules of ice develop and become visible. These aggregate, forming frazil ice, which aggregates in turn to form slush ice. Next, the slush forms flat rounded sheets 0.5 meter (1.6 feet) or more in diameter called *pancake ice*. Finally, the individual pancakes freeze together to form sheet ice or ice floes. When one floe encounters another, individual pieces may be forced together into a thickly compacted ice mass. Bending, tenting, and rafting may take place. A line of ice piled along the edge of two floes that have collided is called a *pressure ridge*. The surface of older sea ice has numerous mounds called *hummocks*.

Arctic ice is further classified as polar cap ice, pack ice, or shelf ice. Polar cap ice is most extensive. It is present year round and covers about 70 percent of the Arctic. It has many hummocks and averages several years old. Maximum thickness, under ice ridges, is 50 meters (164 feet). During summer, melting produces enclosed water bodies called *polynyas*, but even in winter, 5 to 15 percent of the polar ice cap may be ice-free, due to differential movement of ice floes. The average thickness of the polar cap ice is 2 meters (6.6 feet) in summer. The polar cap ice circles clockwise around the Arctic Ocean and about one-third is carried into the Greenland Sea by the East Greenland Current and replaced by new pack ice.

Pack ice lies outside the polar cap and covers about 25 percent of the Arctic. At winter's peak, it extends into the Pacific through the Bering Strait to the Bering Sea and Sea of Okhotsk, and in the North Atlantic, it extends as far south as

Newfoundland and Nova Scotia. Some pack ice melts in summer and the rest is added to polar cap ice by rafting. In the Southern Ocean, the seasonal changes of pack ice cover 16 million square kilometers (6.18 million square miles), much greater than the Arctic, with ice reaching as far north as 60 to 65°S.

Shelf ice forms from the shore and extends out to the pack. It is firmly attached to the shore and its thickness in winter exceeds 2 meters (6.6 feet). Shelf ice melts completely in summer. When shelf ice breaks away from shore, it may have some sediments frozen into it that may be carried some distance before being dropped into the sea.

PHYSICAL PROPERTIES OF SEA ICE
The density of pure ice is 916.8 kilograms per cubic meter. The density of sea ice may be greater if brine is trapped or less if gas bubbles are present. The density ranges from 924 to 857 kilograms per cubic meter. The latent heat of melting for fresh water is 335 kilojoules per kilogram at 0°C (32°F) and this decreases to 63 kilojoules per kilogram at -1°C (30.2°F) and S = 15 psu. When sea ice forms, brine is trapped in pockets within the ice. The salinity of newly formed sea ice is 5 to 15 psu. The faster the ice forms, the more saline it is. If the ice is above sea level, the brine will drain out, so that older ice is fresher. The strength of sea ice is only about one-third that of freshwater ice.

ICEBERGS
Icebergs are a menace to ships in North Atlantic and Antarctic waters. The most common sources of icebergs in the North Atlantic are the west coast of Greenland and the east coast of Ellesmere Island. About 7500 icebergs are formed each year, and about 400 reach 48°N. Icebergs have a much greater vertical extent than that of sea ice, frequently extending to 70 meters (about 230 feet) above sea level. The ratio of volume above sea level to volume below sea level is 7, but the ratio of maximum depth to height above sea level

depends on the shape of the iceberg and is less. Water currents determine the drift of icebergs.

In the Antarctic, glaciers extend onto the continental shelf, forming a shelf of ice that is 200 to 300 meters (660 to 980 feet) thick. At the outer edges, large pieces break away, forming tabular icebergs. Dimensions of these bergs are very large, on the order of 100 kilometers (62 miles) long and tens of kilometers wide.

Curtis A. Collins

FURTHER READING
Chahine, M. T. "The Hydrological Cycle and Its Influence on Climate." *Nature*, Vol. 359 (1992), p. 373.
Webster, P. J. "The Role of Hydrological Processes in Ocean–Atmosphere Interactions." *Reviews of Geophysics*, Vol. 32, No. 4 (1994), pp. 427–476.

RELATED ARTICLES
Coastal Aquifer; Intertropical Convergence Zone; Pack Ice; Salinity; Sea Ice Sediment

Hydrothermal Vent

Hydrothermal vents are places near mid-ocean ridges (and submarine volcanoes) where volcanic activity causes energy to transfer from inside Earth to the ocean above in a plume of heated seawater and mineral particles. Apart from providing a new understanding of the chemistry and geology of the oceans, studies of vents have also led to the discovery of over 300 new species of benthic marine life. These vent communities live not by photosynthesis (making biomass from sunlight) but by chemosynthesis (making biomass from chemicals—in this case, those present in the hydrothermal plumes). The bacteria on which food webs in these communities are based are thought to have been among the earliest forms of life on Earth.

The first hydrothermal vent was discovered in the spring of 1977 during a deep-sea dive by the manned submersible *Alvin* about 280 kilometers (174 miles) northeast of the Galápagos Islands. At a depth of around 2500 meters (8200 feet), the scientists aboard, John B. Corliss and John M. Edmond (1944–2001), noticed that the water was significantly warmer than they had anticipated. They observed an entire marine community of mussels, giant clams, crabs, anemones, and large pink fish. They had discovered the first hydrothermal vent and the extraordinary community of life it supported.

Geochemistry

The geological theory of plate tectonics supports the idea that there must be places where new ocean floor (new basaltic crust) is being formed as hot molten magma rises to the surface and then cools (associated with seafloor spreading). At these spreading centers, which generally are along mid-ocean ridges, seawater can trickle down perhaps a mile or more through cracks in Earth's crust. Heated up, it returns to the surface, interacting with the rock it passes through at high temperature and pressure. In the course of its journey, seawater scavenges metals from the rocks and becomes a substance called *hydrothermal fluid,* a mixture of seawater and minerals that eventually spews back into the ocean as a hydrothermal plume.

A plume differs from the surrounding seawater because of its heat and chemical and mineral contents. The chemical and physical characteristics of a plume vary from place to place, but crucially for the marine life they support, plumes usually feature a high concentration of hydrogen sulfide (H_2S). The heat of a plume derives ultimately from radioactive decay of isotopes such as those of uranium, thorium, and potassium, which melts magma and drives its convection inside Earth's crust. The hydrogen sulfide is produced when seawater (containing sulfate) reacts with iron-containing rock, producing iron oxides as a by-product.

The temperature of a plume depends on the extent to which the seawater cools on its return to the surface. Substantial cooling produces a warm-water vent, with a temperature of perhaps 30°C (86°F) or lower. Less cooling produces vents called white smokers typically at temperatures of 30 to 350°C (86 to 662°F). When there is little or no cooling, hot plumes spew out a black-colored mixture of seawater and minerals at temperatures over 350°C (662°F) from chimneylike vents 30 meters (100 feet) or more high; these are called, appropriately, *black smokers.* When the hot water from the plume mixes with the cold surrounding water, the metals in the plume precipitate (come out of solution). It is this process that builds up the chimney of a black smoker and carpets the seafloor around it with metals such as zinc, iron, and copper.

Vast amounts of water flow through hydrothermal vents. According to some estimates, each year a volume of water equivalent to the annual discharge of the Amazon River flows through all the vents combined.

Chemosynthesis and Archaea

Far from light and with apparently little in the way of nutrients, the ocean floor might be a desolate and barren place. The discovery of hydrothermal vent biocommunities was particularly surprising because rich marine life had never been expected to develop under such conditions. Chemosynthesis at hydrothermal vents on the ocean floor serves as an analogous process to photosynthesis near the ocean surface. Whereas photosynthesis in green plants uses light to convert water and carbon dioxide into carbohydrate and oxygen, chemosynthesis at hydrothermal vents turns oxygen, hydrogen sulfide, and carbon dioxide into carbohydrate, sulfur, and water.

Chemosynthesis takes place in microscopic sulfur-eating bacteria called *Archaea,* which are located at the bottom of the vent food web. Some of these bacteria live freely in hydrothermal plumes or nearby and provide grazing for the animals of the vent communities. Higher organisms, including the thick clumps of red-headed giant tube worms (*Riftia pachyptila*) often seen in photographs of hydrothermal vents, contain sulfur-eating bacteria inside their bodies. The relationship is symbiotic: The bacteria grow inside the worms and provide food for them. The *Riftia* extract hydrogen sulfide from the vent water using the red hemoglobin in their "heads," and the bacteria inside them chemosynthesize these chemicals to form organic carbon. In the more sophisticated giant clam, *Calyptogena magnifica*, the sulfur-eating bacteria are incorporated into the creature's gills. Other species, such as the vent mussel *Bathymodiolus thermophilus*, can obtain their food either from their internal sulfur-eating bacteria or from filter-feeding other organisms.

Not all seafloor communities are based on hydrogen sulfide-eating bacteria; some bacteria oxidize methane and thrive in seafloor regions where that gas is produced by geological processes, such as the cold seeps in the Gulf of Mexico.

Vent Biocommunities

Chemosynthetic, symbiotic bacteria form the crux of the hydrothermal vent biocommunities, which consist of a variety of exotic and never previously encountered species. Because hydrogen sulfide is highly toxic to most marine creatures (and dissolved metals are harmful, too), they do not live near hydrothermal vents. Vent organisms, by contrast, have evolved defenses and are therefore specialized to live in precisely this environment; for example, in *Riftia*, hemoglobin carries the toxic hydrogen sulfide gas and the symbiotic bacteria break this down into other harmless compounds. Apart from the giant tube worms, clams, and mussels, vent communities include species such as 30-centimeter (1-foot)-long Jericho worms (*Tevnia jerichonana*) and 60-centimeter (2-foot)-long bottom-feeding *Bathysaurus* fish. All told, marine scientists estimate that they have discovered at least 300 new species in vent communities.

Life around a hydrothermal vent is a much more precarious affair than in other parts of the ocean. A vent may flow for only a few decades, and the community of life it supports will then die unless it can find an alternative vent or an alternative source of food. It has been proposed that vent communities might travel from one vent to another using an intermediate food source, such as the hydrogen sulfide bacteria produced by a decaying animal; this theory is sometimes called the *dead whale hypothesis*. It is not just the disappearance of a vent that can endanger the life of the vent community. In April 1991, scientists visiting a vent community on the East Pacific Rise arrived just after a seafloor volcanic eruption and found that the community had been largely wiped out, with dead tube worms looking like "spent firecrackers." Yet when they revisited the scene (dubbed the "tube-worm barbecue") 21 months later, a new vent community, including 1.2-meter (4-foot)-long tube worms, had already evolved.

This rapid regeneration illustrates another important feature of life in vent communities: the rapid rate at which biomass is accumulated. It has been estimated that vent clams grow 300 times more quickly than comparable deep-sea clams, for example. Other features of the vent system also develop quickly. During one dive in 1991, *Alvin* accidentally demolished a 10-meter (33-foot)-long black smoker. Three months later, during a return dive, scientists found that 6 meters (20 feet) of the smoker had already grown back.

Origins of Life

Hydrothermal vents are of interest not just for their biocommunities living on Earth's geothermal energy rather than energy from the Sun; some scientists (including vent discoverer John B. Corliss) believe that life on Earth may have evolved from the sulfur-eating bacteria in a vent community. A copious supply of ammonia has long been considered a prerequisite for the production of amino acids and the formation of life on the early (prebiotic) Earth. The minerals produced in abundance at hydrothermal vents can act as catalysts in the conversion of nitrogen to abundant quantities of ammonia at high temperatures and pressures. According to some researchers, this suggests that hydrothermal vents may have been the "crucibles" of life on Earth; others believe that life began in cold conditions and later adapted to suit hot conditions. Fossil records and genetic analysis of Archaea are currently being used to test and further develop various theories.

Chris Woodford

FURTHER READING

Ballard, Robert D., and J. Frederick Grassle. "Incredible World of Deep-Sea Rifts." *National Geographic,* November 1979, p. 680.

Balter, Michael. "Did Life Begin in Hot Water?" *Science,* Vol. 280, No. 5360 (3 April 1998), p. 31.

Corliss, John B., et al. "Submarine Thermal Springs on the Galápagos Rift." *Science,* 16 March 1979, p. 1073.

Crabtree, Robert. "Where Smokers Rule." *Science,* Vol. 276, No. 5310 (11 April 1997), p. 222.

Edmond, John, and Karen Von Damm. "Hot Springs on the Ocean Floor." *Scientific American,* April 1983, p. 78.

Hessler, Robert, Peter Lonsdale, and James Hawkins. "Patterns on the Ocean Floor." *New Scientist,* 24 March 1988, p. 47.

Kunzig, Robert. *Mapping the Deep: The Extraordinary Story of Ocean Science.* London: Sort of Books/New York: W. W. Norton, 2000.

Lutz, Richard, and Rachel Haymon. "Rebirth of a Deep-Sea Vent." *National Geographic,* November 1994, p. 114.

Rona, Peter. "Deep-Sea Geysers of the Atlantic." *National Geographic,* October 1992, p. 105.

Service, Robert. "A Biomolecule Building Block from Vents." *Science,* Vol. 281, No. 5385 (25 September 1998), p. 1936.

Van Dover, Cindy Lee. *The Ecology of Deep-Sea Hydrothermal Vents.* Princeton, N.J.: Princeton University Press, 2000.

USEFUL WEB SITES

NOAA PMEL Vents Program. <http://www.pmel.noaa.gov/vents/home.html>.

RELATED ARTICLES

Chemoautotrophic Bacteria; Chemosynthesis; Deep-Sea Exploration; Hydrogen Sulfide; Mid-Ocean Ridge; Seafloor Spreading; Tube Worm

I

Ice Cap

There is some disagreement among scientists as to the definition of *ice cap*. Some feel that the term can be applied to masses of ice that form over water as well as over landmasses, whereas others feel that the term should be reserved for ice masses overlying land. If the first definition is accepted, the only ice cap in the marine environment would be that over the Arctic Ocean (sometimes referred to as the *polar cap ice*). Currently, the majority opinion probably favors the latter definition.

Ice caps are vast dome-shaped areas of permanent ice that cover up to 50,000 square kilometers (19,300 square miles); larger areas of permanent ice are called *ice sheets*. The ice in an ice cap is so thick that it covers the underlying topography. The dome shape is formed and maintained by ice and snow that accumulate over mountain ranges, fill in valleys, and become compacted. This process can occur over hundreds of thousands of years or more; for example, the layers of ice at the bottom of Greenland's ice cap are up to 2 million years old. The ice in an ice cap is not static; it flows very slowly outward from the center of the dome.

Only 3 percent of water on Earth is fresh, and most of it is frozen in the world's ice sheets and ice caps. Ice caps exist in various parts of the world (e.g., glaciers in Europe, China, Alaska), but the largest are found in Antarctica and Greenland. The largest mass of frozen fresh water lies in Antarctica; most of the continent is covered by ice

year round. The Antarctic ice cap is greater than 4.8 kilometers (3.0 miles) thick at its maximum depth; reports of average thickness range from 2 to 2.7 kilometers (1.2 to 1.7 miles). Earth's second largest repository of fresh water is in the ice that covers 90 percent of Greenland. The thickness of the Greenland ice cap ranges from 1.5 kilometers (0.9 mile) to over 3 kilometers (1.9 miles).

Ice caps and ice sheets are of great interest to climatologists. Some researchers believe that global warming is causing the world's ice sheets and caps to melt, which ultimately would lead to a rise in sea level and subsequent flooding. Others are skeptical, claiming that the ice is holding steady.

Lynn L. Lauerman

FURTHER READING
Hansen, Wallace R. *Greenland's Icy Fury*, 1st ed. College Station: Texas A&M University Press, 1994.
Mulvaney, Kieran. *At the Ends of the Earth: A History of the Polar Regions*. Washington, D.C.: Island Press/Shearwater Books, 2001.

RELATED ARTICLES
Antarctica; Hydrosphere; Southern Ocean

Ichthyology

The scientific study of fishes is known as ichthyology. There are estimated to be some 25,000 fish species, accounting for more than half the world's vertebrate species. Fishes are found in freshwater and marine habitats throughout the world, from the ocean depths to mountain torrents, and some have even adapted to spend most of their lives on land. Their highly muscular bodies are rich in protein and oil, making fishes by far the most important source of marine food consumed by humans.

Because fishes are incredibly diverse, numerous, and widespread, the science of ichthyology necessarily involves a wide range of disciplines, including taxonomy (classification), anatomy, physiology, animal behavior (ethology), and ecology. The most important practical aspects of ichthyology are those that relate to the commercial exploitation of fishes, in which an understanding of life cycles and population dynamics are of great significance both in maintaining sustainable fisheries and in designing artificial systems for maximizing yields in fish farms.

Fish Classification

Taxonomy is the science of classifying organisms into species and arranging species in higher groupings, such as genera (plural of *genus*) and families. Modern taxonomists try to construct classification systems that reflect evolutionary history, building up to form a family tree. One of the most common classification systems is cladistics, which involves placing species into groups called *clades*, defined by a single common ancestor. The clade to which a fish belongs also includes animals that evolved from fish, such as amphibians, reptiles, mammals, and birds.

Taxonomists divide fishes into two major groups: those with jaws (superclass Gnathostomata) and those without (superclass Agnatha). The jawless fishes are a small group of slimy, eel-like species with rasping, circular mouths. Known as hagfishes and lampreys, they exhibit a variety of feeding strategies. Agnathans may act as parasites (on fishes), scavengers (on animal remains that fall to the seafloor), and predators (on invertebrates in muddy benthic habitats). Although hagfishes and lampreys are grouped together,

recent studies suggest that their apparent similarity results from adaptation to a similar lifestyle, called *convergent evolution*, and the notion that they are closely related is starting to lose favor. Indeed, the hagfishes (Myxiniformes) are arguably not even vertebrates. As a consequence, some authorities divide fishes into the two subphyla Myxini (hagfishes) and Vertebrata (vertebrates). Hagfishes may represent the last surviving members of the evolutionary line that gave rise to the vertebrates.

The vast majority of fishes belong to the superclass Gnathostomata, the jawed vertebrates. Jawed fishes evolved from jawless ancestors more than 400 million year ago. The evolution of jaws enabled fishes to tackle larger prey and thus triggered a major diversification of species, leading to many forms known only as fossils, such as placoderms (armored fishes). Modern jawed fishes are split into two groups: cartilaginous fishes (class Chondrichthyes), such as sharks, rays, and ratfishes; and bony fishes (Osteichthyes).

Cartilaginous fishes are a fascinating and diverse group that share a number of distinctive features, such as a skeleton made of flexible cartilage rather than bone; skin containing rough, toothlike (placoid) scales; and no swim bladder. They are sometimes called primitive, although in some respects they are more advanced than bony fishes. Sharks, for instance, possess sophisticated electroreception systems (ampullae of Lorenzini) that can detect the muscle movements of prey and have exceptionally keen olfactory senses.

Bony fishes have a skeleton consisting of true bone rather than cartilage or ossified cartilage. Unlike cartilaginous fishes, their skin contains layered scales rather than toothlike projections (although many species lack scales entirely), and their gill slits are covered by a protective covering called an *operculum*. Bony fishes are divided into two extant groups: lobe-finned fishes (class Sarcopterygii) and ray-finned fishes (class Actinopterygii). There are only seven living species of lobe-finned fishes: six species of air-breathing lungfishes and one species of coelacanth, a "living fossil" once thought extinct but discovered alive in 1938 near East Africa. Biologists think that amphibians and all other tetrapods (including reptiles, mammals, and birds) originated from a now-extinct species of lobe-finned fish whose fins were modified by evolution to form weight-bearing limbs.

The vast majority of fishes belong to the subclass Actinopterygii. There are estimated to be more than 23,000 species in this group, and 100 to 200 new species are described each year. Most ray-finned fishes have movable fins, consisting of thin membranes stretched across bony spines, and a gas-filled organ called a swim bladder, which enables them to control buoyancy in water. As a result of these adaptations, the ray-finned fishes are often fast and agile swimmers and have colonized almost every habitat in both fresh and salt water. Also of crucial importance in their success was the evolution of more flexible and protrusible upper jaw bones, which allowed the group to exploit a greater diversity of foods. In the oceans they filter plankton from the water, scrape algae from rocks, grub through mud for invertebrates, and prey on all manner of other animals, including each other.

Aquatic Habitat

Oceans cover about 70 percent of Earth's surface and contain 97 percent of our planet's water, comprising a vast aquatic habitat. As fish are by far the most numerous vertebrates in this habitat, they are arguably the dominant form of vertebrate life on Earth. Yet surprisingly, freshwater habitats contain almost as many fish species as the oceans, although rivers and lakes cover only 1 percent of Earth's surface and contain a mere 0.0093 percent of our planet's water. Although oceans contain 58 percent of fish species, 41 percent of fish species occur in fresh water and 1 percent live in both environments. The great

diversity of freshwater fishes is probably a consequence of isolation. Freshwater fish populations that become isolated in rivers or lakes are more likely to evolve into new species, especially if such populations are small.

Within the oceans the distribution of fishes is far from even. The greatest diversity is found in tropical seas, where the temperature stays roughly constant throughout the year, providing less stressful physical conditions. The majority of marine fishes—about 44 percent of all fish species or 78 percent of marine species—live near the coast, where the sunlit, sediment-rich waters support the marine organisms on which fish depend. Fishes that live in well-lit water rely predominantly on sight to hunt, and most have excellent vision. The open ocean, where food is more scarce, is home to only 13 percent of fish species: 1 percent inhabit the open ocean surface; 5 percent live in deep, unlit water; and 7 percent live on the deep-sea floor. Those species that live in murky or dark waters often have special sense organs to find their way or locate prey, such as barbels or electric organs. Some deep-sea species even produce their own light to locate mates or lure prey toward them.

Living in water poses certain challenges that fishes have overcome in a limited range of ways. Water is much denser than air, so a fish must be highly streamlined to move through it efficiently. Unlike air, water is almost incompressible, so fish must push it out of the way in order to move. As a result, a large proportion of a fish's body consists of muscles devoted to forward movement. The increased density of water also reduces the effect of gravity on fishes. Through adaptations such as swim bladders or lipid storage, fishes can remain neutrally buoyant in their medium, unlike vertebrates on land.

The density and incompressibility of water also make it a much better transmitter of vibrations than air, and this is exploited by the sensory systems of fishes. Most fish have not only an excellent sense of hearing, with no need for external ears to concentrate sound waves, but also a lateral line organ running along each side of the body. This organ can detect the characteristic vibrations produced by prey, potential mates, or other members of the school.

Oxygen is more difficult to obtain for aquatic than for terrestrial animals because it is only partially soluble in water. As a result, fish must expose a large area of gill tissue to the water to maximize oxygen intake, and this has several important consequences. For instance, it increases the risk of absorbing pollutants from the water, and it makes fish highly sensitive to the water's salt concentration, which is why most species are unable to move easily between fresh and salt water. The gills also serve as organs of excretion, ridding the bloodstream of harmful wastes such as ammonia and carbon dioxide.

History of Ichthyology

Although the Greek philosopher Aristotle (384–322 B.C.) identified 117 species of fishes and recorded numerous observations about their natural history, the science of ichthyology did not really begin to develop until the sixteenth century. The first European to publish a natural history of fishes was Pierre Belon (1517–64). His work and that of later naturalists laid the foundations for the classification system devised by Peter Artedi (1705–34). Regarded as the father of ichthyology, Artedi invented standard measurements and counts that are still used. His classification was incorporated into *Systema Naturae* (1735), a book by Carl Linnaeus (1707–78), that established the modern system of giving every species a two-part Latin name.

Natural history and exploration were highly respected pursuits in Europe during the eighteenth and nineteenth centuries, and many naturalists contributed to the growing body of knowledge on fishes, among them Marc Elieser Bloch (1723–99), Georges Cuvier (1769–1832),

and B. G. E. Lacepède (1756–1826). Whereas many of the early naturalists concentrated on listing and categorizing species, Alexander Monro (1707–1817) examined anatomy and physiology in his book *The Structure and Physiology of Fishes Explained and Compared to that of Man and Other Animals* (1785).

Icthyologists of the nineteenth century expanded our knowledge of fishes by searching out undiscovered species in new parts of the world. For instance, *The Fishes of New York* (1815), by Samuel L. Mitchill (1764–1831), was the first major book on the fishes of North America. In 1829, Louis Agassiz (1807–73) published a book on fishes of the Amazon, based on specimens collected by Johann Baptiste von Spix (1781–1826). Agassiz subsequently became an expert on fossil fishes, and his studies could have been used to support Darwin's theory of evolution had Agassiz not been one of Darwin's chief opponents.

Agassiz's classification was later revised by prominent evolutionists, including Thomas Huxley (1825–95), but Agassiz was not the last ichthyologist to resist evolutionary theory. Albert Günther (1830–1914), one of the most important ichthyologists of the late nineteenth century, was also a staunch opponent of Darwin's ideas. His massive *Catalogue of the Fishes in the British Museum* (1866) was an attempt to list every fish species known based on collections housed in the British Museum.

Later ichthyologists realized that attempting to catalog every fish species in the world was a daunting task and instead concentrated their efforts on specific regions, as did George A. Boulenger (1858–1937) in his *Catalogue of the Freshwater Fishes of Africa* (1909) and David Starr Jordan (1851–1931) and B. W. Evermann (1853–1932) in their *Fishes of North and Middle America* (four volumes, 1896–1900). However, modern technology has made this vigorous task possible, and William Eschmeyer (1939–)

recently authored a new compilation of the world's fish species, *Catalog of Fishes* (three volumes, 1998). During the twentieth century the practice of cataloging species became less significant, and although classification remains important, ichthyology has diversified substantially and now incorporates aspects of ecology, physiology, animal behavior, and genetics.

Applications of Ichthyology

Fish is the second most important source of animal protein to people after beef, accounting for an estimated 25 percent of the world population's animal protein intake. The commercial exploitation of fishes is a massive international industry—commercial fisheries generate a large proportion of the export revenue of Canada, Iceland, and other countries. However, many of the world's most important fisheries have been overexploited, with the result that catches of traditional fish species have fallen worldwide, sometimes dramatically. It is not surprising, therefore, that the expertise of professional ichthyologists has become crucial to the fishing industry, both to help sustain wild fish populations and to devise more efficient means of rearing fishes in controlled conditions, such as through aquaculture or fish farming.

The role of the professional ichthyologist is diverse and varied. Management of commercial fisheries requires knowledge of the number of fish that can be caught without depleting stocks, and ichthyologists can estimate this figure based on studies of the life cycle and population dynamics of the species in question. In commercial fish farms ichthyologists design experiments to determine the ideal conditions for rearing fish intensively. Many factors influence the growth and life cycle of fishes, including temperature, day length (photoperiod), crowding, diet, and parasites. By regulating these factors in a controlled environment, ichthyologists can determine how to make fish spawn out of season,

grow rapidly, and flourish, and can figure out how best to minimize harmful effects of disease, parasites, or cannibalism.

Ben Morgan

FURTHER READING
Bond, Carl E. *Biology of Fishes.* Philadelphia: W. B. Saunders, 1979; 2nd ed., Fort Worth, Texas: Saunders College Publishing, 1996.
Helfman, Gene S., Bruce B. Collette, and Douglas E. Facey. *The Diversity of Fishes.* Malden, Mass.: Blackwell Science, 1997.
Moyle, Peter B., and Joseph J. Cech. *Fishes: An Introduction to Ichthyology.* Englewood Cliffs, N.J.: Prentice Hall, 1982; 4th ed., Upper Saddle River, N.J.: Prentice Hall, 2000.
Nelson, Joseph S. *Fishes of the World,* 3rd ed. New York: Wiley, 1994.
Nybakken, James W. *Marine Biology: An Ecological Approach,* 5th ed. San Francisco: Benjamin Cummings, 2001.
Paxton, John R., and William N. Eschmeyer, eds. *Encyclopedia of Fishes.* San Diego: Academic Press, 1994.

RELATED ARTICLES
Actinopterygii; Agassiz, Jean Louis Rodolphe; Agnatha; Buoyancy; Chondrichthyes; Coelacanth; Fins; Fisheries; Fish Propulsion; Gills; Gnathostomata; Lateral Line; Myxini; Osteichthyes; Parasitism; Placodermi; Sarcopterygii; Shark; Swim Bladder

Indian Ocean

The Indian Ocean is the smallest of the three major oceans. It extends from the shores of Antarctica to about 25°N in the Arabian Sea. On the west the Indian Ocean is bounded by Africa, on the north by the Arabian Peninsula, India, and southeast Asia, and to the east by Indonesia and Australia. To the south it merges with the circum-Antarctic Southern Ocean, connecting via wide seaways with the Atlantic south of Africa and with the Pacific south of Australia. The Gulf of Aden/Red Sea and Gulf of Oman/Persian Gulf extend north from the Arabian Sea (northwestern

Indian Ocean) to either side of the Arabian Peninsula. To the northeast and east the Andaman Sea/Malacca Strait and the shallow seas and straits of the Indonesian Archipelago provide shallow-water low-latitude connections to the Pacific, but there are no connections from the Indian Ocean to high northern latitudes. The Indian Ocean covers a total area of 73,600,000 square kilometers (28,400,000 square miles) and has an average depth of 3890 meters (12,760 feet).

Long known to Arab and Far Eastern traders, and later to venturesome European explorers, the Indian Ocean was the last of the major oceans to receive scientific attention. Although several scientific expeditions visited during the first half of the twentieth century, the first major study was the International Indian Ocean Expedition of 1959–66, during which 46 ships from 10 countries participated in a series of loosely coordinated scientific cruises. Since then, numerous expeditions have added to our knowledge of this complex region.

Geology and Sediments

Geologically, the Indian Ocean is the youngest of the major ocean basins, having been formed by the breakup of Gondwana (the supercontinent that subsequently broke apart to form the present southern continents) and separation of Africa, India, and Australia from Antarctica. Although the breakup of Gondwana began within the Late Jurassic (150 million years ago), most of the growth and development of the Indian Ocean has occurred during the last 80 million years with the rapid northward movement away from Antarctica of India, followed by Australia. Today the Indian Ocean floor is composed largely of parts of three tectonic plates, the African, India (which includes Australia), and Antarctic Plates, separated by a system of active, spreading mid-ocean ridges arranged in an inverted "Y." The northern branch of this ridge system rises in the Gulf of Aden, separating Africa from the Arabian

Peninsula, and extends southeast and south along the Carlsberg Ridge and the Central Indian Ridge, which separates Africa from India. At 25°S, 70°E the Central Indian Ridge joins the two other branches, the Southeast Indian Ridge, which extends toward the South Pacific between Antarctica and India and Australia, and the Southwest Indian Ridge, which extends between Africa and Antarctica, ultimately linking up with the Mid-Atlantic Ridge. The northward movement of the India Plate is absorbed in a zone of convergence between Southeast Asia and the India Plate, which extends from New Guinea to Myanmar. This zone is the site of frequent earthquakes and volcanic activity, and includes Tambora and Krakatao, each the site of massive eruptions within the past 200 years. Farther west the collision of India and Asia has resulted in the uplift of the Tibetan Plateau and the Himalayas.

A distinctive feature of the Indian Ocean is the large number of relatively shallow, aseismic ridges and plateaus. These include one of the world's largest igneous provinces, the Kerguelen Plateau. Important linear ridges are the Ninetyeast Ridge, extending along 90°E longitude, and the Chagos–Laccadive Ridge. Other significant plateaus and rises include the plateaus off Western Australia (Naturaliste, Cuvier, Wallaby, Exmouth), Broken Ridge, the Mascarene Plateau, the Madagascar Plateau, Del Cano Rise, Crozet Plateau, Conrad Rise, Mozambique Ridge, and Agulhas Plateau.

The Java Trench, extending along the northeastern margin of the Indian Ocean west of Sumatra, marks the subduction of the India Plate beneath Indonesia. Elsewhere, the Indian Ocean is surrounded by passive, tectonically quiet ocean margins, which preserve a sedimentary record of much of its history.

The broad pattern of present-day sediment distribution in the Indian Ocean is relatively simple. Carbonate-rich sediments are accumulating in the shallow areas along the African and Australian coasts, on the shallow ridges and plateaus of the western Indian Ocean, and on Ninetyeast and Broken Ridges in the east. The intervening deep basins are receiving deep-sea clays and siliceous sediments, except in the Central Indian, Wharton, and southern Mascarene Basins where it appears that little sediment is accumulating. Siliceous sediments are confined to the equatorial high-productivity regions and to the subpolar regions of the Crozet Basin. The Indus and Bengal Fans, lying west and east of India, respectively, are major features composed of enormous accumulations of terrigenous

Indian Ocean.

sediment eroded from the still-rising Himalayas. The Bengal Fan is the world's largest such feature, with a volume of about 5 million cubic kilometers (1.2 million cubic miles). Other areas of substantial terrigenous buildup are the Zambesi Fan, which receives sediment from a large area of southern Africa, and the western Somali Basin, where the prograding continental margin has built up a tremendous thickness of sediment. South and west of the Indonesian island arc is the major present-day accumulation of volcanogenic sediment. Volcanic ash from this region is distributed over a wide area of the northeastern Indian Ocean.

Circulation

The Indian Ocean differs from the Atlantic and Pacific primarily in being landlocked to the north. Thus the southern Indian Ocean exhibits features typical of other oceans, while the portion north of the equator is unique, being governed by seasonally reversing monsoonal circulation. Surface water circulation is dominated by three distinct circulation systems: a monsoonal gyre north of 10°S, a southern hemisphere subtropical gyre, and Antarctic circulation associated with the Circumpolar Current.

The monsoonal circulation is driven by seasonally changing winds associated with the development of strong high- and low-pressure systems over the Asian continent. During the Northeast Monsoon (northern hemisphere winter) the monsoonal gyre consists of the North Equatorial Current, a southward-flowing current off Somalia, and a countercurrent running north of 10°S. Thus there is a net counterclockwise flow, which brings dry conditions to western India and Southeast Asia and warm, moist air to Somalia. During the Southwest Monsoon (northern hemisphere summer) the flow is reversed, being driven by the South Equatorial Current, a strong northward-flowing Somali Current, and an easterly-flowing monsoon current. The Southwest

Monsoon produces strong upwelling off Somalia and the Arabian Peninsula and brings warm wet conditions to western India and Southeast Asia.

The subtropical gyre is similar in many respects to analogous areas in other oceans, although a strong eastern boundary current is lacking, thus there is no strong upwelling off western Australia. It consists of the Southern Equatorial Current, the Agulhas Current, an eastward flow north of the subtropical convergence, and a diffuse northward flow off Australia. The subtropical gyre is generally low in nutrients in comparison to the monsoonal gyre.

Circulation in the Indian Ocean sector of the Southern Ocean is similar to that associated with the Atlantic and Pacific Oceans. It is dominated by the polar front and the strong Antarctic Circumpolar Current. Major upwelling associated with the Antarctic divergence leads to high nutrient fluxes and primary productivity. The surface waters are generally low in salinity due to excess precipitation and ice melting.

Bottom water is probably not forming in the Indian Ocean sector of the Southern Ocean. The deep water of the Indian Ocean is dominated by inflow of North Atlantic deep water and Antarctic Bottom Water by way of the Atlantic sector of the Southern Ocean. These deep waters flow generally northward toward lower latitudes through fracture zones in the Southwest Indian Ridge, increasing slightly in temperature as they go. Although deepwater circulation in the Indian Ocean is generally less vigorous than in the Atlantic, it is active enough in places to erode sediment on the ocean floor.

Thomas A. Davies

FURTHER READING

Gross, M. G. *Oceanography: A View of the Earth.* Englewood Cliffs, N.J.: Prentice Hall, 1972; 7th ed., Upper Saddle River, N.J.: Prentice Hall, 1996.

Nairn, A. E. M., and F. G. Stehli, eds. *The Ocean Basins and Margins*, Vol. 6, *The Indian Ocean.* New York: Plenum Press, 1996.

Pernetta, J., ed. *Philip's Atlas of the Oceans.* London: George Philip, 1994.

Udintsev, G. G., R. L. Fisher, V. F. Kanaev, A. S. Laughton, E. S. W. Simpson, and D. I. Zhiv. *Geological–Geophysical Atlas of the Indian Ocean.* Moscow: Academy of Sciences of the U.S.S.R., 1975.

Wyrtki, K. *Oceanographic Atlas of the International Indian Ocean Expedition.* Washington, D.C.: National Science Foundation, 1971.

RELATED ARTICLES

Agulhas Current; Andaman Sea; Antarctic Circumpolar Current; Bay of Bengal; Bottom Water Formation; Boundary Current; Equatorial Currents, North and South; India Plate; Kerguelen Plateau and Broken Ridge; Monsoon; Ninetyeast Ridge; Persian Gulf; Red Sea

India Plate

Tectonic plates are shells on the surface of Earth that move with respect to adjacent plates. They are 100 kilometers (62 miles) thick, and they interact to cause earthquakes, volcanoes, and mountain building. The India Plate, one of the fastest moving, travels northward at 6 centimeters (2 inches) per year. It underlies the northeastern part of the Indian Ocean and carries India on its back.

The India Plate shares much of its motion with the Australia Plate to the southeast, from which it has only recently become partly decoupled. The India and Australia Plates are bounded on the west by the Central Indian Rift, on the south by the Southeast Indian Rift, on the east by the Java Thrust, and on the north by the Himalaya Thrust (see figure). They move together toward the north, colliding with the Eurasia Plate, and pushing up the Himalayas. India has jammed underneath the Tibet Plateau to produce Mount Everest, the world's highest prominence.

Plate Collision at the Himalayas

The oceanic crust of the India Plate under the Indian Ocean has a thickness of about 6 kilometers (4 miles), and the continental crust under India,

Pakistan, and Bangladesh has a thickness of 35 kilometers (22 miles). The India Plate rolls down under the Eurasia Plate in the northern part of India at the foothills of the Himalayas. A segment of continental crust on the India Plate equal to the area of Tibet has gone down ahead of India. The two thicknesses of crust there, one each from the India and Eurasia Plates, have stacked together. The total thickness of crust under Tibet averages 70 kilometers (43 miles). This double crustal thickness is easily measurable, because earthquake waves travel to seismographs more slowly through crustal rocks than through mantle rocks. India's

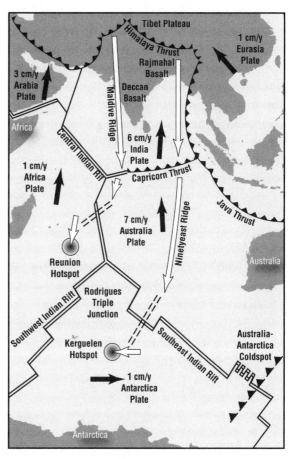

India Plate and adjoining plates showing the plate collision in the Himalayas along with related hotspots and coldspots. Filled arrows show the rate of plate movement with respect to the body of Earth in centimeters per year (1 centimeter equals 0.4 inch). Spreading axes are shown as double lines, transform faults as heavy single lines, and subduction zones as barbed lines with the barbs pointing in the direction of the movement of the downgoing plate.

light crust seems to have peeled off the top of the India Plate and inserted itself above the heavy mantle of the Eurasia Plate directly beneath Tibet's crust. The process is analogous to a collision between two rafts, where one of them ends up on top of the other. Because Earth's crust is less dense than the underlying mantle, it tends to "float" high, and the double-thick crust under the Tibet Plateau produces this "Top of the World," which has an average altitude of 5000 meters (16,400 feet).

Isostatic Balance of Tibet, India, and the Indian Ocean

Despite the great height of the Tibet Plateau, it balances on the surface of Earth with the plains of India and with the floor of the Indian Ocean. This gravitational balance is termed *isostasy*. Each Earth layer has a characteristic specific gravity, the ratio of its density to that of water. The specific gravities used in balancing the India Plate are as follows: Earth's mantle, 3.3; Earth's crust, 2.8; seawater, 1.0; and air, 0.0.

For each balanced column to the level of Tibet's deep crustal root, the sum of each layer's specific gravity times its thickness yields similar totals for Tibet, India, and the Indian Ocean. Following are the calculations in kilometers, using Tibet's 70-kilometer crustal thickness and starting from its 5-kilometer altitude for the length of all the columns. Specific gravity times thickness for the materials in each column is listed in the order of air + water + crust + mantle.

Tibet: $(0.0 \times 0) + (1.0 \times 0) + (2.8 \times 70) + (3.3 \times 0)$
= 196

India: $(0.0 \times 5) + (1.0 \times 0) + (2.8 \times 35) + (3.3 \times 30)$
= 197

Indian Ocean: $(0.0 \times 5) + (1.0 \times 5) + (2.8 \times 6) + (3.3 \times 54) = 200$

Why Is Mount Everest So Tall?

The collision of the India Plate with the Eurasia Plate made the Tibet Plateau. It also helped push up the great range of the Himalayas, which arcs as a high serrated rib along the plateau's south side. The world's highest peaks punctuate the Himalayas, and they culminate in Mount Everest (Chomolungma), which has an altitude of 8848 meters (29,029 feet). The Tibet Plateau is remarkably flat at an altitude of 5000 meters (16,400 feet). It is also very dry, and most of its drainage is internal into ephemeral lakes. By contrast, the Himalayas face the full brunt of the southwestern monsoon from the Indian Ocean. This has led to a sawtooth range with deep, glacially carved valleys between the peaks.

Lawrence Wager proposed in 1933 that the principal cause of the height is the erosion of the edge of the plateau. A profile along the range shows that its average altitude is almost the same as that of the plateau. The deep valleys lighten the crustal load along the Himalayas, and consequently, the deep crustal root buoyantly pushes the range up as a whole, making the peaks stand much taller than the plateau.

Discovery of the India Plate

Although Mount Everest was not conquered on foot until 1953, the great balustrade of the Himalaya had been well mapped by the middle of the nineteenth century. In 1900, the walls of most classrooms displayed a shaded-relief map of Asia on which the Himalayas and the mountains of flanking Pakistan and Myanmar festooned dynamically around India. At the International Geological Congress in 1924, geologist Emil Argand said that India had collided with Tibet. Alfred Wegener (1880–1930) made that idea a cornerstone of the 1924 edition of his book on continental drift, *The Origin of Continents and Ocean Basins*. The grand era of seafloor exploration that followed World War II was required before Wegener's thin continents, which he thought plowed through the ocean floors, could be replaced by the thick plates of plate tectonics, on which the continents ride piggyback.

In 1960, Bruce Heezen (1924–77) of Columbia University's Lamont–Doherty Earth Observatory laid the foundation for the next step toward a full understanding of Earth's dynamics when he mapped the great seafloor rift that encircles the globe like the seam on a baseball. In the middle of the Indian Ocean, he accurately depicted what is now called the Rodrigues Triple Junction. It is the prototype mid-ocean triple junction, where spreading between the Africa, Antarctica, and Australia Plates intersects along three rifts arrayed 120° apart.

The next step came in 1965, when Tuzo Wilson mapped all the world's major plates. He followed Argand and Heezen's borders for a combined India and Australia Plate. Finally, seafloor profiles from Lamont's ship RV *Vema* revealed the young Capricorn boundary thrust between the India and Australia Plates to complete the plate tectonic picture of the Indian Ocean.

Kerguelen and Reunion Hotspots

Two major hotspots have left volcanic tracks on the moving India and Australia Plates. Their present-day volcanic centers are at Reunion Island and Kerguelen Island in the southern part of the Indian Ocean. Hotspots are formed by slender plumes of mantle material that rise from directly above Earth's core. Oceanic plates that in the distant past entered subduction zones sank down toward the core. They sank because the overlying seawater had chilled them and made them denser than the hot adjacent mantle material. Upon reaching the core, an oceanic plate piles up there and begins to warm up. The plate contains a small fraction of low-density crustal material as well as a higher water content than that of the deep mantle material. Therefore, when the plate warms up, it becomes less dense than the adjacent deep mantle material, and it sends toward the surface a buoyant plume estimated to have a diameter of 50 kilometers (31 miles). This entire subduction plume circuit takes an estimated 1 billion years.

The Kerguelen and Reunion Plumes rose beneath the India Plate, where they broke through and produced volcanoes at the surface. The earliest evidence of the Reunion Hotspot is on the west side of India, where it produced a large tract of basaltic lava, the Deccan Basalt. The Deccan Basalt formed during the Cretaceous Period, approximately 100 million years ago. The Kerguelen Hotspot first appears at Bangladesh on the east side of India as the Rajmahal Basalt, also of Cretaceous age. In addition, some investigators believe that the Bunbury Basalt, near Perth, Western Australia, is another patch of volcanic rock from the Kerguelen Hotspot, because during the Cretaceous Period Australia lay adjacent to Bangladesh. The traces of both hotspot plumes disappear to the north into the subduction zone beneath the Himalayas.

On the east side of India, the Kerguelen Hotspot left a remarkably straight south-trending volcanic track on the floor of the Indian Ocean called the Ninetyeast Ridge. On the west side of India, the Reunion Hotspot left the shorter Maldive Ridge. Both hotspots first left their tracks on continental India. Then as the India Plate moved northward over the hotspots, which are fixed in the mantle, the tracks ran off the continent and onto the seafloor. The two tracks are useful in helping to define northward movement of the India Plate.

Approximately during the middle of the Tertiary Period (40 million years ago), the spreading axis trailing behind the India Plate overrode the two hotspots. This broke the continuity of the tracks. Now the Kerguelen Hotspot and its active volcanoes are on the Antarctica Plate, and the Reunion Hotspot is on the Africa Plate. Both hotspot tracks now contain ever-widening gaps, where the new and younger seafloor of the mid-ocean ridge has formed across their alignments.

Australia–Antarctica Coldspot

Australia broke away from Antarctica 100 million years ago. Today, Australia continues to move away from Antarctica along the Southeast Indian Ridge, a mid-ocean spreading axis between the two continents. Directly south of Australia, a segment of the ridge differs from all the world's other seafloor-spreading axes. It is deeper by about 1000 meters (3280 feet), and its offsetting transform faults are more closely spaced than usual. This segment is now called the Australia–Antarctica Coldspot. The coldspot has been puzzling ever since it was discovered, but a hypothesis now is in hand that seems to explain it satisfactorily. In 1998, Michael Gurnis and collaborators suggested that a fossil subduction zone underlies the anomalous area.

During part of the Cretaceous Period (144 million to 100 million years ago), before Australia and Antarctica began to separate, a north-trending subduction zone lay east of New Zealand, which was then next to Australia at a not-yet-opened Tasman Sea. The cold Pacific Plate moved down into the subduction zone and under Australia. That subduction zone was abandoned when Australia began to move northward, but its thick cold slab remained beneath the Australia Plate.

The continental rifting at what would become the Southeast Indian Ridge was a slow process. The buoyant continental crust slowly thinned and slid down from the two continents toward the spreading axis. Mid-ocean ridge basalt did not appear at the seafloor for 10 million to 20 million years. Finally, it broke through when the attenuating toes of crust from the separating continents had become thin enough to permit decompression melting of the mantle to produce basalt. The new seafloor basalt melted in part from the old subducted slab. Because Antarctica is nearly stationary, the spreading axis shifted northward behind Australia, and it continually exposed fresh cold slab material to the crosscutting ridge. Hence, the ridge acquired its unusual coldspot properties from the unusual mantle material beneath it.

Geologic History of the India Plate

Plate tectonic processes have operated since soon after Earth was formed 4.54 billion years ago. Australia contains the oldest, presently known mineral, zircon crystal from the Archean Era, 4.40 billion years ago. The oldest rocks of Antarctica and India have a similar age. During the late Proterozoic Era (700 million years ago), Australia, Antarctica, and India rifted away from the west coast of North America. By the Ordovician Period (500 million years ago), they had swung around Africa and collided with it to produce the continent of Gondwana. During the Permian Period (270 million years ago), Gondwana closed against Laurasia (North America and Asia) to produce Pangea ("All Earth"). The continent of Pangea extended from pole to pole and included most of Earth's continental crust. Pangea was surrounded by the Panthalassa Ocean.

Pangea began to break in half during the Triassic Period (220 million years ago), and by the middle Jurassic Period (180 million years ago) a widening sea extended across it through the Gulf of Mexico, the central Atlantic Ocean, and the Mediterranean Sea. This Tethys Ocean connected across Pangea from the shrinking two sides of Panthalassa, which evolved into the Pacific Basin.

During the Cretaceous Period (120 million years ago), a new continental rift extended through the South Atlantic Ocean, around Africa and India, along the northwestern side of Australia, and into the Tethys Ocean. This was the beginning of the Indian Ocean on the eastern side of still-joined India and Africa. Later in the Cretaceous Period (100 million years ago), new rifts around India organized into their present configuration, and the India Plate was born.

India then began its northward transect, closing up the Tethys Ocean and moving across the Kerguelen and Reunion Hotspots. The leading-edge subduction was at first beneath an offshore island arc south of Eurasia. During the Eocene

Epoch (40 million years ago), India collided with the island arc, swept it up, and continued moving toward a new subduction zone at the Himalaya Thrust. The Karakorum and Ladakh Batholiths of northern Pakistan and India are remnants of the volcanic roots of the island arc.

During the remainder of the Tertiary Period, India tightened against Eurasia, raised Tibet, and shoved central China northeastward to rift open the Sea of Japan (Miocene; 20 million years ago) and Russia's Lake Baikal (still opening).

The India Plate is now decelerating. During the Pliocene Epoch (5 million years ago), the Capricorn Thrust wrinkled up to form a new subduction zone across the Indian Ocean. Full activation of the Capricorn Thrust will eventually lead to the demise of a separate India Plate.

The Force That Drives the Plates

The path taken by the Australia Plate when it rolls down into the subduction zone beneath the Java Thrust has been tracked by seismic tomography. This process uses hundreds of deep crosscutting paths between earthquakes and seismographs to produce a three-dimensional image of sound velocity within Earth. A computer calculates a best-fit image from the individual path velocities in much the same way that a CAT-scan image uses multiple x-ray paths to produce a three-dimensional picture of the human body.

Sound velocity in Earth bears a direct relationship to rock density, and cool rocks have a faster sound velocity than hot rocks of the same composition. Hence, the Australia Plate, chilled by its long contact with the cold floor of the Indian Ocean, shows up clearly on tomographic images below the Java Thrust as a cool (high-sound-velocity) slab to a depth of at least 1600 kilometers (990 miles).

The moving plates, which are 100 kilometers (62 miles) thick, are integral parts of giant convection cells that involve the entire mantle of Earth, which is 2900 kilometers (1800 miles) thick. Dispersed radioactivity within the mantle and the underlying core heats the cells, and the atmosphere and hydrosphere at the surface of the plates cool them.

Most evidence suggests that subduction is the primary driving force of the convection cells. It follows narrow lines at the surface of Earth, such as at the Java and Himalaya Thrusts. On the other hand, the upward return flow of the convection cells is broad and diffuse. Whereas movement of the plates away from a spreading axis such as the Southeast Indian Rift causes local mantle upwelling, the right-angle offsets at that place and at the other spreading axes worldwide suggest that the rifting is passive. Forces from distant subduction transmitted through the rigid plates and the entrained subplate mantle seem to be the ultimate cause of plate movement.

The unusual situation at India, where a large continental mass enters a subduction zone, leads to special flow characteristics. The thick buoyant crust peels off to lift up the Tibet Plateau, and only the lower part of the plate moves downward—the heavy mantle part—which has a thickness of 65 kilometers (40 miles).

George W. Moore

FURTHER READING
Fielding, Eric J. "Morphotectonic Evolution of the Himalayas and Tibetan Plateau." In Michael A. Summerfield, ed., *Geomorphology and Global Tectonics*. New York: Wiley, 2000; pp. 202–222.
Gordon, Richard G. "Present Plate Motions and Plate Boundaries." *American Geophysical Union Global Earth Physics*, Vol. 1 (1995), pp. 66–87.
Gurnis, Michael, R. Dietmar Mueller, and Louis Moresi. "Cretaceous Vertical Motion of Australia and the Australian–Antarctic Discordance." *Science*, Vol. 279 (1998), pp. 1499–1504.
Heezen, Bruce C. "The Rift in the Ocean Floor." *Scientific American*, Vol. 203, No. 4 (1960), pp. 98–110.
Moore, George W. "Plate-Tectonic Map of the Circum-Pacific Region Explanatory Notes." U.S. Geological Survey Map CP-41, 1992, pp. 1–14.
Moore, George W., and Stephen L. Eittreim, "Mechanism of Extension and Rifting at the

Antarctica Continental Margin." *Circum-Pacific Earth Science Series*, Vol. 5A (1987), pp. 89–97.

Richards, Mark A., Richard G. Gordon, and Rob D. van der Hilst, eds. "The History and Dynamics of Global Plate Motions." *American Geophysical Union Geophysical Monograph*, Vol. 121 (2000), pp. 1–398.

Wager, Lawrence R. "Elevation of the Himalayas in Sikkim." *Nature*, Vol. 132 (1933), p.28.

Wilson, J. Tuzo. "A New Class of Faults and Their Bearing on Continental Drift." *Nature*, Vol. 207 (1963), pp. 536–538.

RELATED ARTICLES
Convergent Plate Boundary; Heezen, Bruce Charles; Hotspot; Indian Ocean; Mid-Ocean Ridge; Ninetyeast Ridge; Pacific Plate; Plate Tectonics; Wegener, Alfred Lothar

Infauna

Infauna are benthic organisms that live either buried in the substrate or within burrows in the sediment. Representing both transient and permanent residents, infauna are most abundant in soft substrates such as sand and mud. Harder substrates such as coral and rock generally contain fewer species of infauna, hosting more *epifauna* (or organisms that live on top of the benthic substrate). Most phyla are represented within infauna, but the most common species are invertebrates, such as mollusks, arthropods, and annelids, among others.

Infauna are categorized in a number of ways, including by their size, classification, and ecological role. There are three major size groups: macrofauna, meiofauna, and microfauna. *Macrofauna* are organisms larger than 1 millimeter (0.04 inch), and these include many different invertebrates. *Meiofauna*, between 62 micrometers and 0.5 millimeter (0.002 to 0.02 inch), are also known as *interstitial organisms*. They occupy the spaces between sediment particles. A number of the larger phyla are represented in the meiofauna, including Annelida, Echinodermata, Mollusca,

and Cnidaria, while phyla such as Gastrotricha, Loricifera, Tardigrada, and Rotifera are exclusively meiofaunal in distribution. More so than their larger counterparts, meiofauna have a variety of morphological adaptations to cope with their unstable environment. These include modified appendages or organs by which to hold on to sediment particles and hardened skeletons by which to avoid damage. Finally, *microfauna* are all organisms smaller than 62 micrometers (0.002 inch), and they include bacteria and protozoans. Anaerobic bacteria can live beyond the oxygen layer, past the depth known as the *redox discontinuity layer* (RDL), where they form a food web based on sulfate-reducing bacteria. Fine muds, which are rich in such bacteria, are characterized by their characteristic smell (of hydrogen sulfide) and dark color. Macrofauna can live beneath the RDL only if they can oxygenate their immediate surroundings, which several large organisms do by constructing burrows or using modified tubes for breathing.

The ecological role that infauna play is determined largely by their feeding style, burrowing, and movement through the sediments. Infaunal feeding styles are varied, as the organisms include carnivores, grazers, detritivores, and suspension feeders. Infauna that feed on organic material within the sediments play an important ecological role in turning over the substrate. It is estimated that a dense population of polychaetes can circulate the upper 10 centimeters (3.9 inches) of sediment through their guts in less than two years. Burrowing, or *bioturbation*, is another way that infauna affect their surrounding ecosystem. Burrowing for either feeding or movement in the sediment greatly destabilizes the substrate. Certain infauna, however, build durable burrows (used to facilitate circulation) and thus stabilize the sediments.

As do other benthic organisms, infauna interact with the overlying pelagic ecosystem. Many infauna serve as predators or prey of pelagic animals. Also, infaunal detritivores and suspension feeders assist in the recycling of organic material. Finally, a majority of infauna, with the exception of meiofauna, have planktonic larvae.

Manoj Shivlani

FURTHER READING

Barnes, R. S. K., and R. N. Hughes. *An Introduction to Marine Ecology.* London and Boston: Blackwell Scientific, 1982; 3rd ed., Oxford and Malden, Mass.: Blackwell Science, 1999.

Higgins, Robert P., and Hjalmar Thiel, eds. *Introduction to the Study of Meiofauna.* Washington, D.C.: Smithsonian Institution Press, 1988.

Little, Colin. *The Biology of Soft Shores and Estuaries.* New York: Oxford University Press, 2000.

Nybakken, James W. *Marine Biology: An Ecological Approach,* 5th ed. San Francisco: Benjamin Cummings, 2001.

RELATED ARTICLES
Benthos; Epifauna; Macrofauna; Meiofauna

Infralittoral Fringe

The infralittoral fringe is the lowermost portion of the ocean's rocky intertidal zone; the intertidal (or littoral) zone is the area of seashore that lies between the highest high and lowest low tides. The two other horizontal zones of the rocky intertidal, the midlittoral zone and the supralittoral fringe, lie landward of the infralittoral fringe.

The infralittoral fringe extends seaward from the uppermost distribution of the large laminarian kelps to the lowest low-tide mark. This portion of the intertidal is exposed to air only during extremely low tides; thus organisms that inhabit the infralittoral fringe experience fewer drastic environmental changes than do organisms that live higher up in the intertidal zone. Because the infralittoral fringe is almost always submerged, the organisms that live there are not adapted to survive extended exposure to air. Many types of algae and kelp grow in the infralittoral fringe. Plant life and

rocky substrate create a three-dimensional environment in which marine animals such as anemones, crabs, limpets, sea urchins, sea stars, shrimp, and small fish thrive.

Lynn L. Lauerman

FURTHER READING

Nybakken, James W. *Marine Biology: An Ecological Approach,* 5th ed. San Francisco: Benjamin Cummings, 2001.

Ricketts, Edward F., and Jack Calvin. *Between Pacific Tides,* 5th ed., rev. by Joel W. Hedgpeth. Stanford, Calif.: Stanford University Press, 1985.

RELATED ARTICLES
Intertidal; Littoral Zone; Midlittoral Zone; Supralittoral Fringe

Infrared Radiation

Like visible light, x-rays, and microwaves, infrared (IR) is a type of electromagnetic radiation. IR radiation is emitted by all warm objects, such as the Sun, the human body, and Earth and its oceans. The wavelength of IR radiation in the electromagnetic spectrum lies between those of visible light [shorter than 1 micrometer (0.000039inch)] and radio waves [longer than 1000 micrometers (0.039 inch)]. Humans detect invisible IR radiation as heat, the sensation you feel when you place your hand near a light bulb. Oceanographers use IR sensors primarily to map ocean surface temperatures.

Infrared radiation can be detected in two ways: by infrared photography and by thermal infrared imaging. Infrared photography works in a similar way to normal photography, but the photographic film is sensitive to infrared rather than visible wavelengths. Aerial photographs taken with color infrared film enhance the contrast between clear and silted-up water, provide better discrimination between land and water, and show clearly the difference between healthy and dying vegetation. Infrared photography has also proved useful for studying geothermal activity on the seabed. For example, equipped with a sophisticated camera system known as ALISS (Ambient Light Imaging Spectral System), the Woods Hole manned submersible *Alvin* has produced infrared images of hydrothermal vents.

Thermal imaging is the main method of IR sensing in the earth sciences. Object(s) with a temperature greater than absolute zero (-273°C or -459° F) emit a spectrum (from short to long wavelengths) of radiation, depending on their temperature. The intensity of IR radiation is a measure of the object's temperature. The most important oceanographic use of thermal imaging is to measure sea surface temperature remotely from Earth-orbiting satellites or aircraft. Two examples of IR imaging satellites are the GOES (Geostationary Operational Environmental Satellite) and the AVHRR (Advanced Very High Resolution Radiometer) satellites. The GOES satellite is positioned over the equator and gives a nearly full hemisphere view of the oceans. This satellite measures both ocean surface temperatures and cloud temperatures. GOES provides most of the imagery used on the nightly weather news. AVHRR satellites are in polar orbit, allowing them to map the entire Earth over a period of five days. GOES and AVHRR data are used to produce images of world ocean temperatures, which may be animated to show how temperatures vary over time. This technique has proved invaluable for studying phenomena such as El Niño, the climatic phenomenon in the Pacific that involves a dramatic reversal in normal ocean temperatures. Variations in surface temperature also provide an important method of studying ocean circulation and currents. A thermal image of the North Atlantic, for example, would pick out the warmer temperature of the Gulf Stream current against cooler surrounding waters.

One new application of IR sensing helps oceanographers understand how energy is dissipated when waves break on the surface of the ocean. IR radiation is strongly absorbed by water, thus IR imagery measures the temperature of only the upper 1 millimeter (0.039 inch). Because the temperature of the "skin layer" may be slightly warmer or cooler than the waters below, oceanographers can study the effects of breaking waves. This provides a new technique for studying how the oceans and atmosphere exchange heat and gases through wave processes.

Chris Woodford

FURTHER READING
Barrett, E. C., and L. F. Curtis. *Introduction to Environmental Remote Sensing.* London: Chapman and Hall, 1976; 4th ed., Cheltenham, England: Stanley Thornes, 1999.
Jessup, A. T., C. J. Zappa, M. R. Loewen, and V. Hesany. "Infrared Remote Sensing of Breaking Waves." *Nature,* 2 January 1997, p. 52.
Sabins, Floyd F. *Remote Sensing: Principles and Interpretation,* 3rd ed. New York: W. H. Freeman, 1997.

RELATED ARTICLES
Geostationary Operational Environmental Satellite; Satellite Remote Sensing

Insecta

Scientists have so far identified more than 1 million species of insects (class Insecta), and there are an estimated 20 to 50 million more still waiting to be named. An evolutionary success story, insects have colonized almost every imaginable habitat on land and in fresh water, and by evolving the power of flight have even conquered the air. Yet, mysteriously, one habitat remains almost completely untouched by them: the oceans.

Insecta is one of 10 classes that make up the phylum Arthropoda, the largest phylum in the animal kingdom. The other arthropod classes include such animals as spiders, centipedes, crabs, and lobsters. Although the insects are placed only in a class (a relatively low ranking in the biological hierarchy), they far outnumber not only all other arthropods but also all other animal species combined. To accommodate so many members, the class Insecta is divided into two subclasses: Apterygota, the wingless insects, and Pterygota, the winged insects, and these in turn are divided into 32 orders. The orders consist of more familiar groupings. For example, grasshoppers and crickets together make up the order Orthoptera (around 20,000 recognized species), cockroaches make up the order Blattodea (around 4000 recognized species), and beetles make up the order Coleoptera (at least 300,000 recognized species).

Like other arthropods, insects have a jointed body with an external skeleton, or cuticle, made of a complex organic substance called *chitin*. The insect body is divided into three distinct regions: the head, which bears sensitive antennae, compound eyes, and highly adaptable mouthparts; the thorax, which bears three pairs of legs and sometimes wings; and the abdomen, which contains intestines and reproductive organs.

Insects show many adaptations to life on land. The jointed exoskeleton is ideal for walking without the support of water, and tiny air holes in its surface lead to a network of tubes, or trachea, that run through the body and allow an insect to breathe. Insects reproduce by internal fertilization: The male puts his sperm directly into the female's abdomen, so there is no risk of sperm or egg cells drying out.

Despite being so well adapted to life on land, many insects have successfully colonized freshwater habitats. Diving beetles breathe from a bubble of air that surrounds them when they dive, for instance, and water scorpions breathe through a snorkel. The larvae of dragonflies and mayflies are completely aquatic, having evolved gills to extract oxygen from water. However, although thousands of insect species have adapted to life in fresh water, far fewer have made the transition to marine habitats.

The 300 or so insect species that spend part of their life in or on seawater are mostly flies whose aquatic larvae develop in marshes exposed to salt water from tides. These include mosquitoes, horse flies, deer flies, sand flies, and midges, many of which are blood-sucking. Marine water striders live on the open ocean, where they skate on top of the water's surface. Some species of rove beetles live in the intertidal zone of sandy beaches, where they dig air-filled burrows to survive immersion at high tide.

Scientists are not sure why insects have been so unsuccessful in the oceans, but a possible explanation is that they are unable to compete with their arthropod relatives, the crustaceans, who are better adapted to life underwater. Similarly, crustaceans have had little success on land, the one notable exception being the isopods (pill bugs, or woodlice).

Ben Morgan

FURTHER READING

Brusca, Richard C., and Gary J. Brusca. *Invertebrates.* Sunderland, Mass.: Sinauer, 1990.

Nybakken, James W. *Marine Biology: An Ecological Approach,* 5th ed. San Francisco: Benjamin Cummings, 2001.

Pechenik, Jan A. *Biology of the Invertebrates.* Boston: Prindle, Weber and Schmidt, 1985; 4th ed., Boston: McGraw-Hill, 2000.

USEFUL WEB SITES

Marine Insect Home page.
    <http://www.ianr.unl.edu/ianr/entomol/ marine_insects/marinehome.html>.

RELATED ARTICLES

Arthropoda; Crustacea

Internal Wave

Internal waves occur within the water column rather than at the water surface. Internal waves in the top few hundred meters of the water column often have *periods* (the time taken for a complete waveform to pass by) in the range 5 to 8 minutes. Their wavelengths are typically in the range 600 to 1000 meters (about 1970 to 3280 feet). In deep water, internal waves travel at about 12 percent of the speed of surface waves of similar period.

Internal waves can be generated wherever there are marked density discontinuities, such as those caused by temperature and/or salinity differences. A displacement at the density boundary generates internal wave motion. Common causes of internal waves are a rapid tidal flow, sharp atmospheric pressure differences over a small area of ocean, the fast flow of water over an irregular sea bottom, and displacement caused by a ship's propellers or its bow wave.

In the days of early steamships, internal wave generation—or rather, its effects—was particularly noticeable in places where fresh water from melting ice overlay seawater to produce a marked density discontinuity. The captains of slow-moving steamers would find their vessels "sticking" and behaving sluggishly. The thrust from the steamer's propellers was generating and maintaining internal waves rather than propelling the ship forward. Increasing the ship's speed would cause this "dead water" effect to disappear. Internal waves are common across the world's oceans because density discontinuities, such as thermoclines, are widespread within the top 1 kilometer of the water column. Other things being equal, internal waves have greater wave height where water density variation is large and abrupt.

Internal waves are sometimes observable as elongated moving slicks or glassy patches on the surface. The internal waves may be 7 to 15 meters (about 23 to 49 feet) high but barely register on the surface. In deep water, internal waves may reach heights of 30 to 150 meters (about 98 to 490 feet) and have periods in excess of 30 minutes. An important class of internal waves, called *internal tides,* has a period of about 12.5 hours. Internal waves of short period have

more power and have been implicated in displacing oil production platforms in the South China Sea and elsewhere.

When internal waves break on continental shelves they mix waters from above and below the thermocline. Locally, this may enhance biological productivity as cold, nutrient-rich water from below mixes with warm, nutrient-poor water from above, fueling phytoplankton growth.

Internal waves are of great interest to navies because of their influence on subsurface communication and underwater exploration. Internal waves can displace a submarine tens of meters vertically with potentially dangerous consequences. Internal waves can disrupt the transmission of sound waves, and their location must be pinpointed and their effects interpreted if naval underwater operations are not to be compromised.

Trevor Day

FURTHER READING
Ikeda, M., and F. Dobson, eds. *Oceanographic Applications of Remote Sensing.* Boca Raton, Fla.: CRC Press, 1995.
Open University Course Team. *Waves, Tides and Shallow Water Processes.* Oxford and New York: Pergamon Press, in association with the Open University, Milton Keynes, England, 1989; 2nd ed., Boston: Butterworth-Heinemann, in association with the Open University, 1999.
Smail, J. "Internal Waves: The Wake of Sea Monsters." *Sea Frontiers,* Vol. 28, No. 1 (1982), pp. 16–22.
Young, Ian R., and Greg J. Holland. *Atlas of the Oceans: Wind and Wave Climate.* Oxford and Tarrytown, N.Y.: Pergamon Press, 1996.

RELATED ARTICLES
Gravity Wave; Kelvin Wave; Wave

Interstitial Water, Chemistry of

Interstitial water is fluid contained between particles in both living and nonliving systems. Interstitial water in nonliving systems describes any water that resides in the spaces, or interstices, between particles.

In the physical environment, interstitial water includes water that exists in the soil, marine, and river sediments and in other areas where spaces between particles permit the collection of water. Even in very arid regions, such as high deserts, interstitial water exists between the particles of soil in Earth's strata. The interstitial water in soil and sediments is also known as *pore water,* and the interstices between the soil particles are called *pore spaces.*

In marine environments, the interstitial water of deep-sea sediments is a storehouse for dissolved organic matter (DOM). In fact, this fluid contains approximately 10 times the concentration of DOM as that found in the upper layers of the ocean. This DOM is a vital food source for many marine organisms, especially those of the deep-sea region.

In addition to DOM, the interstitial water of marine sediments is a reservoir for various minerals, nutrients, and gases. As the interstitial water contacts the surrounding sediments, movement of the water column, surge, and other mechanisms of water movement result in the dissolution of inorganic material from the sediment, especially in coastal sediments. Minerals such as calcium and magnesium are leached from the sediments and dissolved into the seawater in ionic form. Inorganic salts are also liberated and dissolved into the water column, contributing to the salinity of seawater.

In calm areas of the sea, with low water movement, the interstitial water maintains a relatively constant concentration of gases, nutrients, minerals, and dissolved substances. In areas of low water movement, equilibrium is maintained since the conditions are relatively constant, minimizing the concentration gradients and pressure gradients. Less exchange between the interstitial water and the water column reduces the availability of new nutrients for growing bacterial populations.

Therefore, the deeper into the sedimentary bed one explores, the more a relative state of stasis will be observed. Concurrently, fewer bacterial and algal species are likely to be observed, reflecting a condition of reduced biodiversity.

Alison Kelley

FURTHER READING
Gage, John D., and Paul A. Tyler. *Deep-Sea Biology: A Natural History of the Deep-Sea Floor.* Cambridge and New York: Cambridge University Press, 1991.
Mann, K. H., and J. R. N. Lazier. *Dynamics of Marine Ecosystems.* Boston: Blackwell Scientific, 1991; 2nd ed., 1996.
Pickard, George L. *Descriptive Physical Oceanography.* Oxford and New York: Pergamon Press, 1964; 5th enl. ed., Oxford and Boston: Butterworth-Heinemann, 1995.
Scanlon, Valerie C., and Tina Sanders. *Essentials of Anatomy and Physiology.* Philadelphia: F.A. Davis, 1991; 3rd ed., 1999.

RELATED ARTICLES
Deep-Sea Sediment; Dissolved Organic Matter

Intertidal

The term *intertidal* refers to the area of shoreline lying between the tides. This area, which marks the transition between land and sea, encompasses a great diversity of habitats, such as rocky cliffs and headlands, sandy beaches, mudflats, estuaries, mangrove forests, sloughs, and salt marshes. Intertidal animals and plants are subject to tremendous daily environmental extremes, including dehydration from sun and wind, exposure to freshwater rainfall, and pounding waves from the incoming tide. Despite such extreme environmental conditions, a great array of mainly marine organisms can be found, all of which possess specific adaptations to enable survival at the interface between land and sea.

The wide variation of intertidal habitats is dependent on physical parameters such as the type of underlying substrate and the level of exposure to wind and wave action. Freshwater damage from heavy land runoff or massive rainfall from storms such as hurricanes can be significant in estuarine, marsh, and wetland habitats. However, it is the tides that define the margins of this environment.

Tides

The physical aspects associated with tides are an essential component in the characterization of various intertidal habitats. Tides are caused by the gravitational force of the Moon and, to a lesser extent, the Sun. During both full and new Moon phases, the Moon and Sun are aligned, and their combined gravitational pull results in more extreme spring tides. This explains the extreme high and low tides during these times of the month. Conversely, during the half-Moon phases, the Sun and Moon are at right angles with respect to Earth, lessening the gravitational pull and resulting in less extreme neap tides.

Tidal range and patterns differ greatly from one geographic location to another. Whereas in some places high tide may differ from low tide by only a few feet, in others, such as parts of Alaska, the tidal range can exceed 15 meters (50 feet). The North American Pacific coast has a semidiurnal tidal pattern, represented by two high and two low tides of unequal heights each day. In contrast, the daily high and low tides on the Atlantic coast are almost equal in height.

Another important factor is the steepness of the shoreline, which defines the horizontal range of the intertidal zone. Tidal change appears less dramatic at shores with steep cliffs than at locations with low gradient mud or sand flats. In places where large bodies of water must pass through a narrow channel, the turning of the tide can cause dramatic currents of great speed and strength.

Zonation

Biologists have observed patterns or *zones* within the intertidal habitat. Each zone can be defined by

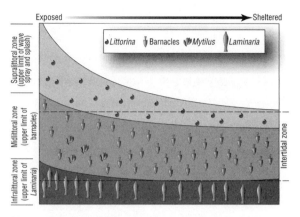

Zones of the intertidal region.

a group of organisms (see figure). For example, in rocky intertidal habitats, the highest zone is dominated primarily by littorine snails and lichens, which are capable of remaining far from the water's edge and withstanding extreme temperatures and exposure to fresh water from rainfall. This high zone, often referred to as the *supralittoral* or *splash zone*, gets wet only at the highest tides. In contrast, the infralittoral, or lowest, zone is uncovered only at the lowest tides. The infralittoral is inhabited by organisms less resistant to dehydration. The area between the high and low zones, the midlittoral, is the most diverse, with many species of algae and invertebrates, which may form additional bands or zones.

Zonation patterns are most easily observed on vertical hard substrates such as boulders, cliffs, and wharf pilings, where well-defined bands of organisms are visible as the tide drops. In areas of soft substrate, such as mudflats, zonation is not apparent because animals live in burrows and tunnels.

These patterns of zonation are caused by both physical and biological factors. Many organisms possess adaptations to survive at specific tidal levels. However, biologists have discovered that several species, when transplanted, are capable of growing in different zones but are absent due to biological factors such as grazing, competition, and/or predation. Animals and plants are thus limited both by the physical parameters of tidal range, and by biological pressures from other species.

Biological Adaptation to Physical Stresses

The intertidal is a region of dynamic transition, in perpetual flux from exposure to the changing tides and breaking waves. Special conditions prevail in the intertidal, demanding specialized physical and biological adaptations to enable survival of the life forms that colonize the shores.

Organisms must survive dehydration as the tide recedes. This poses a threat to creatures that are largely dependent on salt water for basic life functions such as respiration, feeding, and reproduction. Delicate soft-bodied animals and plants are particularly susceptible to dehydration from wind and sun and have evolved various adaptations to overcome this problem. Anemones retract tentacles at low tide, reducing overall surface area and minimizing exposure. Some species of anemones and tubeworms exude mucus, encouraging a coating of sand and shell fragments for protection against exposure.

Ultraviolet radiation is an additional challenge posed by exposure to the Sun. Ultraviolet radiation can cause considerable damage to the external tissues. Algae overcome this hazard with cell walls of cellulose and algin, a gelatinous, protective substance.

Dramatic changes in salinity present another challenging feature to intertidal organisms. Tide pool fish and crabs must withstand elevated temperatures and high salinity on warm days. Heavy rainfall and freshwater runoff can lower the salinity of intertidal habitats substantially.

Impact from wave action on exposed shorelines limits survival in these habitats to species with mechanisms for anchorage and protection. Algae cling to rocky substrates using specialized holdfasts. Abalone, snails, and other mollusks have a muscular foot to hold them in place. Mussels fasten to rocks and to each other with byssus threads of great mechanical strength.

Mobile invertebrates, such as crabs, find protection in crevices and under rocks. In soft-substrate habitats, organisms dig burrows and tunnels to shelter from surf. Although sand scouring from wave action often prevents settlement of algae and invertebrates, some species can withstand burial under sand for temporary periods.

Substrate

The intertidal environment encompasses a broad range of habitats. The rocky intertidal features cliffs, caves, wave-cut platforms, tide pools, and channels. Rocky shores, although often exposed to the forces of wind and surf, provide ideal substrate for hundreds of species of algae and invertebrates. Seals and sea lions rest on isolated rocky shores, and numerous shorebirds, including cormorants, pelicans, and gulls, occupy nearshore rocks and outcroppings.

Rocky coasts are often interspersed with areas of sedimentation and stretches of sand. Longshore currents carry and deposit sand from one place to another, resulting in a highly dynamic and ever-changing system. Sandy beaches are home to many invertebrates, such as sand crabs, clams, sand dollars, and the shorebirds that feed on them. Remote beaches provide vital nesting habitat for seabirds and turtles and breeding grounds for seals.

Wharf pilings, jetties, and other human-made structures present interesting habitats for exploring intertidal organisms. Vertical pilings offer an especially good view of zonation patterns: From high to low, bands of barnacles and limpets, anemones and mussels, sea stars, sponges, and tunicates, as well as various types of algae are clearly delineated.

At river mouths and in sloughs, the estuarine habitat is often characterized by tidal mudflats, which provide substrate for algae, clams, worms, echiurans, mussels, snails, juvenile fish, sponges, and tunicates. In more tropical latitudes, mangrove trees colonize estuaries, providing sheltered habitat and breeding grounds for fish and birds. Sponges, tunicates, and algae can be found clinging to mangrove roots in the absence of other hard substrate.

Salt marshes and wetlands are additional habitats of the intertidal. Halophytes, salt-tolerant plants, of many different types live in saline soils of marine marshes along with burrowing invertebrates and assorted populations of fish. Marshes and wetlands offer important seasonal habitat for migratory birds.

At the interface of two different worlds, seashores represent the dramatic transition between land and sea. Physical forces and biological interactions continually shape the appearance and composition of community structure. Among the dynamic, ever-changing habitats of the intertidal, the only constant feature is the daily ebb and flow of the tides.

Miranda L. Sanders

FURTHER READING

Hedgpeth, J. W. *Introduction to Seashore Life of the San Francisco Bay Region and the Coast of Northern California.* Berkeley: University of California Press, 1962; 2nd ed., 1975.

Karleskint, George, Jr. *Introduction to Marine Biology.* Philadelphia: W. B. Saunders, 1998.

Nybakken, James W. *Marine Biology: An Ecological Approach,* 5th ed. San Francisco: Benjamin Cummings, 2001.

Ricketts, Edward F., and Jack Calvin. *Between Pacific Tides,* 5th ed., rev. by Joel W. Hedgpeth. Stanford, Calif.: Stanford University Press, 1985.

Schwartz, Maurice L., ed. "Beaches and Coastal Environments." In *Encyclopedia of Earth Sciences.* Stroudsburg, Pa.: Hutchinson Ross, 1982.

Stephenson, Thomas A., and Anne Stephenson. *Life between Tidemarks on Rocky Shores.* San Francisco: W. H. Freeman, 1972.

Sumich, James L., and Collard Sneed. *An Introduction to the Biology of Marine Life.* Dubuque, Iowa: Wm. C. Brown, 1976; 7th ed., Boston: WCB/McGraw-Hill, 1999.

RELATED ARTICLES

Critical Tide Level; Littoral Zone; Midlittoral Zone; Neap Tide; Spring Tide; Supralittoral Fringe; Tide Pool; Wave-Cut Platform

Intertropical Convergence Zone

The Intertropical Convergence Zone (ITCZ) is a belt that surrounds Earth and lies close to the equator (i.e., it is intertropical). Regions or phenomena such as winds that are aligned east to west are said to be zonal, so this belt is properly called a zone. It is the region where the northeasterly trade winds of the northern hemisphere and the southeasterly trade winds of the southern hemisphere converge.

Although the ITCZ lies close to the equator, its precise position corresponds to the region of the surface that is heated most strongly by the Sun. Since this region moves with the seasons, so does the ITCZ. In July it lies to the north of the equator, at about 25°N latitude over the interior of continental Asia and between 5 and 10°N over the oceans. In January it straddles the equator over the oceans and is at about 15°S over South America, Africa, and Australia. The ITCZ is never very far from the equator, and its influence is felt there throughout the year.

The strong solar heating of the surface produces vigorous convection in the air in the ITCZ. Because the ITCZ lies mainly over the ocean, the rising air is very moist and unstable. Its moisture condenses as it rises, producing towering cumulonimbus clouds and heavy precipitation. The ITCZ can be identified in satellite images by the belt of clouds associated with it.

When the air that rises over the ITCZ reaches the tropopause, at an altitude of 12 to 15 kilometers (7.5 to 9.3 miles), it flows away from the equator and sinks back to the surface in the latitude of the tropics. The subsiding air divides near the surface, but most returns toward the equator as the trade winds. The English physicist and meteorologist George Hadley (1685–1768) was the first person to describe this circulation accurately, in 1735; it is known as a *Hadley cell.* There is not just one Hadley cell, however (as Hadley supposed), but several.

Air on the subsiding side of the Hadley cells approaches the equator from the northeast in the northern hemisphere and from the southeast in the southern hemisphere. This flow comprises the trade winds, and the trade winds drive surface ocean currents known as the North and South Equatorial Currents. The Equatorial Currents form part of the gyres in the Atlantic, Pacific, and Indian Oceans.

Converging air produces low atmospheric pressure at the surface and high pressure in the upper troposphere. The ITCZ therefore marks a belt of permanently low surface air pressure known as the *equatorial trough*. The converging air begins to rise some distance from the center of the equatorial trough and between the winds of the two hemispheres there is a region containing the doldrums, where winds are usually light and variable and where often there is no wind at all.

Weather conditions within the ITCZ are fairly constant. Disturbances in the circulation do occur, in the form of troughs of low pressure that move slowly from east to west. They are quite weak at the surface but extend to a considerable height, sloping to the east. Winds converge as they approach the waves from the east and diverge as they blow away from waves on the western side. Cumulonimbus clouds form behind the troughs, bringing heavy rain and thunderstorms. These disturbances, called *easterly waves*, appear to be linked to the formation of tropical depressions, tropical storms, and tropical cyclones (hurricanes, cyclones, and typhoons). Many originate over the Caribbean at times when the trade wind inversion is weak.

Rainfall within the ITCZ is heavy. Fanning Island, a Pacific island at 3.85°N latitude and 3 meters (10 feet) above sea level, lies within the ITCZ throughout the year. Its annual rainfall averages 2104 millimeters (83 inches). Places the ITCZ reaches for only part of the year have a seasonal climate marked by a pronounced rainy season during the summer, when the ITCZ covers them, and a dry season in winter, when the ITCZ is in the other hemisphere.

Michael Allaby

FURTHER READING
Henderson-Sellers, Ann, and Peter J. Robinson. *Contemporary Climatology.* London: Longman Scientific/New York: Wiley, 1986; 2nd ed., Harlow, England: Addison-Wesley, 1999.
McIlveen, J. F. Robin. *Fundamentals of Weather and Climate.* London and New York: Chapman and Hall, 1992.
Schneider, Stephen H., ed. *Encyclopedia of Climate and Weather,* 2 vols. New York: Oxford University Press, 1996.

RELATED ARTICLES
Equatorial Countercurrent; Equatorial Currents, North and South; Gyre; Trade Winds

Invertebrate

An invertebrate is an animal without a backbone. The term *invertebrate* encompasses well-known animals such as sponges, jellyfish, earthworms, snails, insects, and sea stars and less familiar animals such as ctenophores, flatworms, roundworms, and sipunculans. Together the approximately 34 invertebrate phyla comprise about 95 percent of the animal kingdom. Invertebrates have characteristics common to all animals: They are multicellular, have plasma membranes around their cells, and are nonphotosynthetic. Otherwise, however, only the lack of a backbone ties them together; invertebrates are an incredibly diverse assemblage of animals that range in size from microscopic to giant and show every possible permutation of structural diversity, adaptation to different environments, and survival techniques in general.

An examination of the characteristics of the major invertebrate phyla illustrates a gradual increase in complexity and the emergence of evolutionary novelties that ultimately resulted in evolution of the backbone. Members of the phylum Porifera, the sponges, are grouped on their own in a separate subkingdom (Parazoa) because they do not have true tissues, are asymmetrical, and lack the complexity of other animal groups. All other animals are classified within the subkingdom Eumetazoa. Radial symmetry, in which the body is arranged around a central axis, is an evolutionary novelty found in two phyla: the Cnidaria (jellies, anemones, corals) and the Ctenophora (comb jellies). Cnidarians have an incomplete digestive tract (one opening serves for both ingestion and egestion); egestion in ctenophores is through anal pores and the mouth.

With the evolution of bilateral symmetry came the development of a distinct head (*cephalization*). The flatworms (phylum Platyhelminthes) were the first to show these traits. This phylum contains the free-living planarians and the parasitic flukes and tapeworms. These animals are acoelomates because they lack a *coelom* (the fluid-filled body cavity between the body wall and digestive tube). Flatworms have an incomplete digestive system. The phylum Nemertea (ribbon worms) is another acoelomate group, but members have a complete digestive system (mouth and anus) and a true coelomic space surrounding the *proboscis* (a muscular eversible organ used for feeding and defense).

Evolutionary novelties found in the remaining animal phyla include a complete digestive tract and a body cavity. A fluid-filled body cavity provides many advantages, including a hydrostatic skeleton, against which muscles can work to create locomotion, a cushion for internal organs, a place to transport materials, and a repository for gametes. Phyla with a body cavity are divided into two groups, representing different evolutionary lineages: the body cavity in pseudocoelomate phyla is not lined completely with mesoderm, whereas the cavity in coelomates is lined completely. The Nematoda (roundworms), the Rotifera (wheel animals), and a variety of phyla

that include parasitic forms and tiny forms living between sand grains (e.g., the Gastrotricha) are pseudocoelomate phyla.

The coelomate phyla are subdivided based on characteristics of embryonic development that suggest two separate evolutionary lineages. Protostomes exhibit spiral and determinate cleavage, whereas deuterostomes have radial indeterminate cleavage. Protostome phyla include the Mollusca (bivalves, snails, and octopus), the Annelida (segmented worms), and the Arthropoda (spiders, insects, and crustaceans). The arthropods, of which there are more than 1 million species, are the most diverse and successful animal group. The phyla Echinodermata (sea stars, brittlestars, crinoids, sea urchins, and sea cucumbers), Hemichordata (acorn worms), and Chaetognatha (arrowworms) are deuterostomes. The phylum Chordata includes the subphyla Urochordata (tunicates), Cephalochordata (lancelets), and Vertebrata (animals with backbones).

A number of other phyla are difficult to place in an evolutionary tree. For example, the Onychophora appear to be intermediate between annelids and arthropods because they have characteristics of both. The lophophorate phyla, Phoronida, Ectoprocta, and Brachiopoda, are often considered deuterostomes, but their evolutionary place remains controversial.

Lynn L. Lauerman

FURTHER READING
Barnes, Robert. *Invertebrate Zoology.* Philadelphia: Saunders, 1963; 6th ed., by Edward Ruppert, Fort Worth, Texas: Saunders, 1994.
Brusca, Richard C., and Gary J. Brusca. *Invertebrates.* Sunderland, Mass.: Sinauer, 1990.
Solomon, Eldra P., Linda R. Berg, Diana W. Martin, and Claude Ville. *Biology.* Philadelphia: Saunders, 1985; 5th ed., Fort Worth, Texas: Saunders, 1999.

RELATED ARTICLES
Annelida; Arthropoda; Cnidaria; Ctenophora; Echinodermata; Mollusca; Nematoda; Nemertea; Platyhelminthes; Porifera; Rotifera

Irish Moss

Irish moss is the common name of *Chondrus crispus* Stackhouse, an economically important red alga that is abundant in the lower littoral and upper sublittoral zones of rocky shores of the North Atlantic Ocean. The red color comes from the dominant photosynthetic pigment, phycoerythrin. Other pigments are present, and plants can range from yellow-green in strong sunlight to almost black near their lower depth limit. The upper limit depends on exposure to drying and freezing, and the lower limit is determined by light availability. The life cycle of Irish moss includes two conspicuous phases, the diploid tetrasporophyte and haploid male and female gametophytes. A third, microscopic phase in the life cycle results from fusion of the gametes. It develops within the tissue of the female gametophyte after fertilization. The conspicuous forms occur as bushy plants up to 15 centimeters (6 inches) tall, consisting of flattened, repeatedly dichotomously branched fronds. Individual fronds may survive up to four years and grow out of a slender basal portion attached to a holdfast. New fronds arise vegetatively from the long-lived holdfast. Irish moss is a major source of the gelling agent carrageenan, a sulfated polysaccharide extracted from the cell walls and used widely in the dairy and cosmetics industries. Irish moss is harvested commercially using rakes. In Atlantic Canada (Nova Scotia), it has also been cultivated in a land-based tank farm, by selecting the best strains and determining optimal conditions for growth and carrageenan production. Irish moss has been used in research on marine plant tissue culture. Portions of its DNA have been sequenced to study species relationships.

Gene Rosenberg

FURTHER READING

Bold, H. C., and M. J. Wynne. *Introduction to the Algae,* 2nd ed. Englewood Cliffs, N.J.: Prentice Hall, 1985.
Lobban, Christopher S., and Paul J. Harrison. *Seaweed Ecology and Physiology.* New York: Cambridge University Press, 1994.

RELATED ARTICLES

Algae; Carrageenan

Irish Sea

The Irish Sea is a shallow semienclosed coastal sea that lies between mainland Britain and Ireland, stretching from the north Channel (approximately 56°N; 7°W) between northern Ireland and the Scottish islands, and St. Georges Channel between southwestern Wales and southern Ireland (approximately 52°N; 6°W), covering just over 100,000 square kilometers (38,600 square miles). Its depth is mostly shallower than 91 meters (296 feet), apart from a few troughs where depths are about 183 meters (600 feet). There is a large island in the center of the sea, called the Isle of Man.

During the glaciations (the last began melting about 20,000 years ago), the Irish Sea was completely covered by ice, which gouged out several deep basins. Today, much of it is subject to strong tidal currents with a residual current drift to the north. Its water is exchanged every few weeks, entering via the St. Georges Channel and exiting via the North Channel. The radioactive contaminants from the nuclear reprocessing plant at Sellarfield can be used as chemical tracers to track the water as it disperses northward up the Scottish coast, around the North Sea, and eventually into the Norwegian Sea.

The seabed is composed of a great variety of sediments and bare rock. The rock was laid bare by glacial erosion and the gravel originated as moraines. The sand and mud reflect the contemporary sedimentary regime. The incidence of mud increases in the north, particularly in the area between the Isle of Man and Ireland, where tidal flows are small, so the water stratifies and is relatively stagnant.

Tidal fronts develop each summer. Their positions are predictable, based on the ratio between the depth and the cube root of the maximum tidal velocity. They form at the boundary between the stratified and fully mixed water. Vertical mixing occurs along these fronts, so locally the primary production is increased. Since they develop in the same locality each year, the seabed beneath them is inhabited by an unusually rich and varied fauna, including many suspension feeding species.

Even though the Irish Sea's primary productivity per unit area is similar to that of the North Sea, its production of fish is only about half; the reasons for this disparity are not known.

Martin Angel

FURTHER READING

Oslo and Paris Commission. *Quality Status Report for Region III: The Irish and Celtic Seas.* London: OSPAR, 2000.

USEFUL WEB SITES

Irish Marine Institute Home page.
    <http://www.marine.ie>.

RELATED ARTICLES

Primary Productivity; Radioactive Contamination

Iron

Iron is the second most abundant metal on Earth's crust and has one of the most complex biogeochemical roles in seawater, despite being a trace metal in the World Ocean. Iron's oceanographic behavior revolves around its solubility, which depends on its oxidation state. In our current reducing atmosphere, iron is largely oxidized and therefore insoluble. Its distribution is variable in time, concentration, depth, and location. The biological demand for iron can often result in the removal of all measurable amounts of the element from the water.

Iron has a variable patchy distribution throughout the World Ocean. This is due to a brief residence time in the ocean; the average

iron molecule spends only 54 years in the ocean (a water molecule has a residence time of 38,000 years). Iron exhibits a nutrientlike depth profile because organisms absorb it actively. High concentrations can be found near shore, due to inputs from terrestrial sources. Offshore iron concentrations can be very low; the main inputs are from windblown dusts in the atmosphere, advection of iron-rich water, and extraterrestrial particles. Removal of iron from the ocean is caused by the sinking of particles and organisms that contain iron.

Iron is a transition metal with a *d*-orbital configuration. It exists in seawater mainly as Fe(III), $Fe(OH)_3$, and $Fe(OH)_3^-$. Iron is used in proteins and molecules within cells, assisting in many functions, the most important of which is respiration. It can change its redox state with the addition or removal of electrons, allowing molecules associated with it to carry energy from one location to another within a cell membrane. This allows cells to transfer the energy from food molecules or photosynthetic-derived sources to other molecules for use within the cell. All organisms on Earth use iron as an electron carrier, which makes it a necessity in the existence of both plants and animals.

Iron occurs naturally in two states, Fe(II) and Fe(III), the first being the reduced state and the second, the oxidized state. Due to the large amount of oxygen in the atmosphere and in seawater, iron is quickly oxidized to the Fe(III) state. This oxidized state is very insoluble in water and quickly precipitates out of solution, whereas the reduced state is soluble in seawater. This is demonstrated by looking back at Earth's early biological development. The primordial atmosphere was composed largely of carbon dioxide, with very little oxygen gas. This reducing atmosphere thoroughly mixed into the seas and allowed soluble Fe(II) to accumulate to relatively high concentrations. Some believe that life evolved in these iron-rich waters and that as a result, iron is an integral part of organic life. Conversely, today's atmosphere has high oxygen concentrations and iron is oxidized back to Fe(III), rendering it nearly insoluble. Thus the oceans currently have very low concentrations of iron.

The biological need for iron is apparent in the oceans. Without iron all photosynthesis and most forms of respiration could not take place. Several key functions for iron in cells take advantage of its oxidation and reduction capabilities. Iron-containing compounds such as hemoglobin, cytochrome c, and ubiquone are electron-carrying proteins that have iron at the heart of their functional structure. Furthermore, iron is used in anoxic regions as a terminal electron acceptor. Oxidixed Fe(III) can be reduced to Fe(II), allowing bacteria to use it as a respirative substrate.

Measuring iron can be challenging. Coastal, oligotrophic, and deepwater concentrations of iron vary from 0 to 50, 0 to 1.4, and about 1.5 nanomolar, respectively. This wide range of dilution means that seawater has to be specially sampled with clean techniques to avoid contamination with unwanted iron. Contamination and the use of many different measuring techniques makes agreement among scientists as to the true concentrations of iron in seawater very difficult.

In 1934, T. J. Heart recognized that iron might be a limiting factor in phytoplankton growth. That hypothesis was not acted upon until toward the end of the century, when improved analytical techniques aided John Martin's (1935–93) studies on iron as a limiting nutrient. Martin found that iron was the last necessary "ingredient" for phytoplankton to grow in areas of high nutrients and low chlorophyll (HNLC). Since then it has been found that competition for iron in the HNLC areas has caused organisms not only to seek iron actively but also to send out chelators called *siderophores*, which bind iron and make it available only to a particular species.

Matthew P. Huber

FURTHER READING

Bruland, K. W. "Trace Elements in Sea-Water." In *Chemical Oceanography.* London: Academic Press, 1983.
Coale, K., et al. "A Massive Phytoplankton Bloom Induced by an Ecosystem-Scale Iron Fertilization Experiment in the Equatorial Pacific Ocean." *Nature,* Vol. 383 (1996), pp. 495–501.

RELATED ARTICLES
Biogeochemical Cycle; Nutrient; Photosynthesis and Iron Limitation

Iron Limitation, see Photosynthesis and Iron Limitation

Iselin, Columbus O'Donnell
1904–1971
Physical Oceanographer

Columbus O. Iselin was a key figure in the development of modern oceanography in the United States between the late 1920s and 1960s. An expert on the physical oceanography of the western North Atlantic, especially the Gulf Stream, Iselin was the captain of the Woods Hole Oceanographic Institution's first research vessel. He later became the director of Woods Hole and played an influential role in the development of national and international programs in marine research. He was also a pioneer in the use of small submarines, buoy systems, and heavily-instrumented aircraft as observational platforms for research.

Columbus O'Donnell Iselin was born in New Rochelle, New York, in 1904, the son of a banker. His well-to-do family was passionate about sailing, and Iselin built his first, rather leaky full-sized boat at the age of 11. In 1922, Columbus entered Harvard University to study mathematics, but partly under the influence of renowned marine biologist Henry B. Bigelow (1879–1967), turned his attention to marine science. While still an undergraduate, Iselin bought a 23-meter (75.5-foot) schooner that he renamed *Chance*. In 1926, when he graduated with a bachelor's degree, he immediately organized and led an oceanographic expedition in the *Chance* to study the Labrador Current, a voyage that Iselin was later able to claim "produced at least one professor for Harvard." His expedition confirmed that the actual movement of icebergs matched closely the data computed from theoretical equations developed by Norwegian oceanographers. Henceforth, the International Ice Patrol used these equations to predict the movements of icebergs. Based on data gathered on the expedition, Iselin was to publish four papers that gained him wide attention in the physical oceanographic community.

In 1928, Iselin gained his master's degree at Harvard, and from 1929 through to 1948 he was assistant curator of oceanography at the university's Museum of Comparative Zoology. When the Woods Hole Oceanographic Institution (WHOI) was founded in 1930, Iselin was made general assistant to the director and captain of WHOI's research vessel *Atlantis*. On the ketch's maiden voyage from Plymouth, England, to Boston, Massachusetts, he was in charge of 25 shipmates, many of them his senior. At the tender age of 25, he was also responsible for organizing that trip's oceanographic program.

In the 1930s, Iselin became WHOI's physical oceanographer, and his studies of the Gulf Stream led to several classic papers such as "The Development of Our Conception of the Gulf Stream System" (1933) and "Problems in the Oceanography of the North Atlantic" (1938). It was not until 1947 that Iselin gained his doctorate, an honorary D.Sc., from Brown University based on his publication record and his overall contribution to oceanographic research.

In 1940, when Iselin's former Harvard professor Henry Bigelow retired as director of WHOI, Iselin replaced him. Between 1940 and 1950 Iselin

guided WHOI through a tenfold expansion in size and budget. He left Woods Hole in 1950 to devote himself full time to scientific research, and returned as WHOI's director in 1956, for the International Geophysical Year. He resigned again in 1958 to devote more time to scientific research and teaching, first as lecturer and then as professor at Massachusetts Institute of Technology and finally, in 1960, as Henry Bryant Bigelow Professor of Oceanography at Harvard.

In the 1930s, Iselin was among the first oceanographers to recognize that rivers were an overriding influence on currents in continental shelf areas fed by significant freshwater runoff. In contrast, in waters beyond the continental shelf, prevailing winds were usually the key energy source driving surface currents. Iselin was also an early promoter of the view that the sea and air should be studied as an integrated ocean–atmosphere system, since the transfer of heat energy and water between the two are so fundamental to the circulation of both. From the late 1950s, Iselin was to give great thought to the rational use of ocean resources—physical, chemical, and biological—laying some of the groundwork that was to inform international legal developments following the first United Nations Conference on the Law of the Sea (UNCLOS-I) in 1958.

During the early part of World War II, under Iselin's direction, WHOI became a research and development laboratory investigating a wide variety of marine phenomena, including underwater sound transmission and the development of underwater explosives. One example serves to illustrate WHOI's great contribution to the war effort. Iselin, together with Athelstan Spilhaus (1911–98), inventor of the bathythermograph (a device for measuring the temperature gradient of the ocean's upper layers), were convinced that German U-boats were escaping detection by hiding in the thermocline. The temperature gradient in surface layers was acting like a series of lenses or prisms, bending sonar rays away from the object to which they were directed. Iselin was instrumental in convincing the Admiralty in London to install bathythermographs on their destroyers, so improving submarine detection. Thousands of Allied lives were probably saved by this expedient.

Among his many honors, Iselin received the Medal of Merit (1948) for his contribution to warfare research, the Agassiz Medal (1943), and the Henry Bryant Bigelow Medal (1966). Iselin's colorful life and his achievements have been documented widely, even extending to an article in *Time* magazine's Atlantic edition. With his quiet, yet direct and disarming manner, penetrating insight into the crux of a problem, and his masterly management of investigations at sea, he was an inspiration to hundreds of oceanographers. When he died in 1971, an entire volume of *Oceanus* was given over to warm tributes by dozens of scientists who had worked with him in the United States and Europe.

Trevor Day

BIOGRAPHY
- Columbus O'Donnell Iselin.
- Born 25 September 1904 at New Rochelle, New York.
- Gained bachelor's (1926) and master's (1928) degrees from Harvard University.
- Awarded Honorary D.Sc. from Brown University in 1947.
- In 1926 he led an oceanographic expedition to the Labrador Current.
- From 1929 to 1948, he was assistant curator of oceanography at Harvard's Museum of Comparative Zoology.
- Joined Woods Hole Oceanographic Institution (WHOI) when it was founded in 1930.
- Initially, he served as assistant to the director and first captain of the research vessel *Atlantis*.
- He was WHOI's physical oceanographer (1932–40), then director (1940–50 and 1956–58), overseeing enormous expansion of the institution and important involvement in marine warfare research during World War II.
- 1950–56, he served as senior physical oceanographer at WHOI, and from 1958, as lecturer

and then professor at Massachusetts Institute of Technology.
- From 1960 on he was Henry Bryant Bigelow Professor at Harvard.
- He died on 5 January 1971, at Vineyard Haven, Massachusetts.

SELECTED WRITINGS

Emery, K. O., and C. O. Iselin. "Human Food from the Ocean." *Science*, Vol. 157, No. 3894 (1969), pp. 1279–1281.
Iselin, C. O. "The Development of Our Conception of the Gulf Stream System." *Transactions of the American Geophysical Union*, 14th Annual Meeting, 1933, pp. 226–231
———. "A Study of the Circulation of the Western North Atlantic." *Papers in Physical Oceanography and Meteorology*, Vol. 4, No. 4 (1936), pp. 1–101.
———. "Problems in the Oceanography of the North Atlantic." *Nature*, Vol. 14 (1938), pp. 772–776.
———. "The Gulf Stream System." *Proceedings of the American Philosophical Society*, Vol. 96, No. 6 (1952), pp. 660–662.
———. "Synoptic Studies in Oceanography." *Oceanus*, Vol. 5, No. 3/4 (1957), pp. 3–12.
———. "Improving World Fisheries: 2. The Oceanographer's Viewpoint." *AIBS Bulletin*, Vol. 13, No. 5 (1963), pp. 69–70.
———. "The Loss of the *Thresher*." *Oceanus*, Vol. 10, No. 1 (1963), pp. 4–6.
———. "Oceanographic Forecasts." *Oceanus*, Vol. 10, No. 4 (1964), pp. 8–13.

FURTHER READING

"Oceanographer: Columbus Iselin." *Time*, Atlantic ed., 6 July 1959, pp. 34–35.
Oceanus, Vol. 16, No. 2 (1971).
Schlee, Susan. *The Edge of an Unfamiliar World: A History of Oceanography*. New York: Dutton, 1973; London: Hale, 1975.

RELATED ARTICLES
Gulf Stream; Labrador Current

Island Arc

Volcanic arcs may form where two or more oceanic crustal plates converge. Curved (arcuate), and sometimes linear, chains of islands are built that are referred to as island arcs. Island arcs have distinctive topography (and bathymetry), earthquake zones, structure, and igneous (crystallized from molten magma) rocks. When two oceanic plates collide the older plate, which is the more dense and deeper plate, sinks below the younger and more buoyant upper plate. The upper plate is composed of fragments and pieces of oceanic crust and mantle that have been greatly modified by younger sedimentary and igneous processes (volcanism and plutonism).

Shape of Island Arcs

All island arcs are not arcuate in shape. In fact, many are distinctly linear. The more arcuate are the Izu-Bonin, Mariana, New Britain, Indonesian, Kuril, Lesser Antilles, and Aleutian Island Arcs. Most of these island arcs are bounded on one or both ends by an obstruction, either a continental landmass, oceanic plateau, or another type of ridge or island chain. These obstructions have noticeably affected the curvature of the island chains by compressing the ends and allowing extension to occur elsewhere. For example, the Bonin and Mariana Island Arcs have obstructions at each end and are extending seaward by a process of back-arc spreading in which new ocean crust is being formed behind the magmatic (volcanic) axis. In contrast, some of the linear island arcs are the Tonga, Kermadec, New Hebrides, and Solomon Island Arcs.

Earthquakes

Island arcs have the deepest earthquake foci (places within Earth where the ruptures occur) in the world and many of the earthquakes have very large magnitudes (greater than 8.0). The deepest earthquakes are as much as 670 kilometers (415 miles) beneath Earth's surface and their epicenters (places on Earth's surface directly above the foci) can be up to 400 kilometers (250 miles) from the trench. Most earthquakes parallel the subducting slab (Wadati–Benioff zone). However, other earthquakes occur within the upper plate of the island arc and in the oceanic crust as it bends downward into the trench.

Topography, Bathymetry, and Structure

Island arcs have a surface topography (referred to as *bathymetry* below sea level) that is related directly to the tectonic and igneous processes that form and modify them. But the topography and bathymetry of every island arc is different because each has a unique geologic history. Gravity profiles reflect the structure and composition of island arcs. For example, a strong negative gravity anomaly is evident over the upper part of the subduction zone (where two or more plates converge), reflecting the less dense material in the trench, upper part of the subduction zone, and accretionary prism. A strong positive gravity anomaly occurs over the magmatic axis where rocks are relatively denser.

Starting at a point seaward of the trench and then proceeding perpendicular to the trench and across the upper plate, the major topographic and structural features are as follows (see figure): (1) deep ocean floor, (2) trench, (3) accretionary prism and inner trench wall, (4) fore-arc region with an outer high and a sedimentary basin, (5) magmatic (volcanic and plutonic) axis where islands protrude above the ocean surface, (6) back-arc basin with a spreading center and very young crust, and (7) remnant arc.

1. *Deep ocean floor.* The deep ocean floor is the surface of the older (and denser) oceanic plate. As the plates converge, the older plate is bowed up into a swell by the collision and the resultant compressional forces. The landward side of this swell forms the outer wall of a trench. Extensional earthquakes are common as the subducting plate cracks and begins its journey into the mantle.
2. *Trench.* Trenches are typical of island arcs and form between the bent subducting plate and either an accretionary prism or an inner trench

wall composed of an arc's igneous and sedimentary pedestal. Trench floors are the deepest parts of the oceans. Depending on the size, relief, and climate of the sediment source region(s) and erosional and transportation processes, trenches can be either completely filled with sediments (eastern Aleutian and northern Indonesian Island Arcs), partially filled (western Aleutian and central Kuril Island Arcs), or almost barren (Tonga and Mariana Island Arcs). Large oceanic plateaus and volcanic ridges impinge upon and fill some parts of trenches (Solomon, New Hebrides, and southern Tonga Island Arcs). Collision of the massive Ontong Java Plateau with the Solomon Island Arc, beginning about 20 million years ago and continuing today, not only filled the old trench but also choked the subduction zone, causing a change in subduction direction.

3. *Accretionary prism.* Landward of the trench an accretionary prism can form. It generally is composed of thrust-bounded packages of trench sediments and pieces of the underlying basalt of the subducting oceanic plate. Slices of serpentinized mantle are often caught up along faults. These packages are stacked sequentially during the subduction process, with the youngest nearest the trench. Most sediments are swallowed during the subduction process, but if the throat of the subduction zone is full, the excess will be shoved onto the leading edge of the island arc. In some places the top of an accretionary prism surfaces and becomes islands, as with the Andaman and Nicobar islands off Sumatra and the island of Barbados.

4. *Fore-arc region.* The fore-arc region of an island arc can be either simple and composed almost

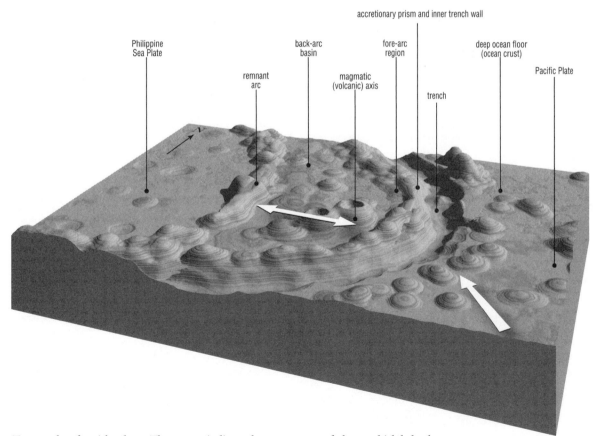

Topography of an island arc. The arrows indicate the convergence of plates, which helped to create the arc's structure. Example is taken from the Philippine Sea.

entirely of island arc igneous crust (Tonga Island Arc), or extremely complex and composed of an accretionary prism and a fore-arc basin filled with sediments, both stacked against and built on top of the arc's igneous crust, respectively, as reported in the Aleutian Island Arc. The accretionary prism can be thick (eastern Aleutian Island Arc) or thin (western Aleutian Island Arc) and the fore-arc basin can be either extensive and filled with several kilometers of sediment (Aleutian Island Arc) or small with only a thin layer of sediment (New Britain Island Arc). Some rocks and sediments that are traveling down the subduction chute can be peeled off and piled against the upper plate through a process called *underplating*. This process is not well understood and remains one of the mysteries in island arc evolution.

5. *Magmatic (volcanic) axis.* Melting occurs above the subducting slab at depths between 200 kilometers (124 miles), such as in the New Hebrides and Solomon Island Arcs, and 110 kilometers (68 miles) in the Aleutian Island Arc. Volcanic and plutonic rocks, along with some of their detritus, occupy the magmatic axis. In part because of the depleted nature of the magma's source regions under the arcs, certain characteristics make the igneous rocks of island arcs distinct from igneous rocks that form in other tectonic settings, such as hotspots and mid-ocean ridges. Petrologists can distinguish a suite of island arc rocks by their chemical compositions and relate them to melting and differentiation processes. For example, most island arc igneous rocks have low potassium contents. Titanium and its related high-field-strength (charge/ionic radius) elements zirconium, tantalum, hafnium, and niobium also have contents that are low relative to rocks from other tectonic settings. Furthermore, certain ratios of radiogenic/stable isotopes (neodymium, strontium, and lead) are characteristic of island arc

rocks. Most petrologists conclude that igneous rocks of island arcs have a source region (where melting occurs) in the mantle wedge above the subducting slab, but that fluids derived from subducted sediments and the crust of the downgoing plate have important influences on chemical characteristics.

6. *Back-arc basin.* The magmatic axis is a zone of weakness, and as arcs extend over the downgoing slab, the magmatic axis often splits apart, which initiates a new phase of seafloor spreading. As crust is formed along the new spreading axis, it moves laterally and subsides, forming a new ocean basin. Good examples of back-arc basins formed by seafloor spreading are Lau Basin behind (west of) the Tonga Island Arc and Mariana Basin behind the Mariana Island Arc.

7. *Remnant arc.* Part of the former magmatic axis becomes a ridge that moves away from its sibling as the back-arc basin grows. The ridge subsides because it is separated from a more buoyant magmatic axis. Good examples of remnant arcs are the Kyushu–Palau Ridge west of the Mariana Basin and Lau Ridge west of Lau Basin.

Tracy L. Vallier

FURTHER READING

Condie, Kent C. *Plate Tectonics and Crustal Evolution.* New York: Pergamon Press, 1976; 4th ed., Oxford and Boston: Butterworth-Heinemann, 1997.

Davidson, Jon P., Walter E. Reed, and Paul M. Davis. *Exploring Earth: An Introduction to Physical Geology.* Upper Saddle River, N.J.: Prentice Hall, 1997.

Gill, James B. *Orogenic Andesites and Plate Tectonics.* Berlin and New York: Springer-Verlag, 1981.

Kennett, James. *Marine Geology.* Englewood Cliffs, N.J.: Prentice Hall, 1982.

Seibold, Eugene, and Wolfgang H. Berger. *The Sea Floor: An Introduction to Marine Geology,* 2nd rev. and updated ed. Berlin and New York: Springer-Verlag, 1993.

Vallier, Tracy, et al. "Geologic Framework of the Aleutian Arc, Alaska." In George Plafker and Henry C. Berg, eds., *The Geology of Alaska.* Boulder, Colo.: Geological Society of America, 1994; pp. 367–388.

Isohaline

The term *isohaline* refers to water masses of equal salinity. *Iso* comes from the Greek *isos* and means "equal" or "similar." *Haline* is derived from the Greek *halos*, meaning "sea," and refers to the salt content. These masses may be isolated from each other geographically or spatially but have equal concentrations of salt. Thus on maps of the world's oceans, you may see lines that join points at which salinity measurements have been taken and found to be similar.

Salinity is of considerable importance to organisms in the oceans of the world because it has a significant effect on the physiology of the organism. Marine organisms vary in their ability to tolerate differences in salinity, and most animals, microorganisms, and plants of the open ocean have limited or little ability to tolerate changes in salt content. These organisms are osmoconformers, meaning that their internal salt concentrations vary with the salt content of the surrounding water in which they live. Osmoregulators, on the other hand, are those organisms that have the ability to control their internal salt concentrations independent of the salt content of the medium in which they live. Such organisms usually live in habitats such as estuaries in which the salt content varies over various periods of time.

James W. Nybakken

FURTHER READING
Nybakken, James W. *Marine Biology: An Ecological Approach*, 5th ed. San Francisco: Benjamin Cummings, 2001.

Isostasy

Isostasy is a condition of equilibrium in which continental crustal blocks float on a denser mantle and are in gravitational balance. Mountain belts stand higher above the surface and have roots that extend deep beneath the mountain range. The crust beneath mountains is thicker and lighter and extends as roots into the mantle.

During a topographic survey of India, scientists J. H. Pratt (1809–71) and G. B. Airy (1801–92) discovered that a negative gravity anomaly occurred in the area of the Himalaya Mountains. The amount of correction needed was less than anticipated and led Pratt to the concept of isostasy, in which the crust is in gravitational equilibrium through a buoyancy mechanism.

The contact between the crust and the mantle varies. The shape of the Moho (the Mohorovicic discontinuity, the boundary between the mantle and crust) mimics the shape of the continent above it. The base of the root zone will change its shape in response to changes in the exposed mass. A ratio of exposed continent to root zone is established and is similar to an iceberg. The continents have a depth to the Moho of about 30 kilometers (18.6 miles), and the ocean has a depth to the Moho of about 11 kilometers (6.8 miles).

Isostasy is often compared with blocks of wood that are floating in water. In this analogy, the wood represents the continents and the water represents the underlying mantle. The wood will float in the water to a height equal to the amount of water it displaces. As more blocks are stacked on top of each other, they displace more water and consequently, ride higher in the water. The terms *isostatic adjustment* or *isostatic rebound* are used to describe rocks that achieve equilibrium by vertical movement. The blocks that rise and fall are not bounded by vertical faults but rather are broad flexures, or curves, of the crust. As the crust rises or sinks, plastic flow from the mantle accommodates the changes of motion. When the root zone balances the continental block, it is in equilibrium and is said to be *compensated*. When the root zone beneath a mountain is too small for the mountain, it is said to be *undercompensated* and the mountain will sink. When the root is too large, it is overcompensated and the mountain will rise.

Older mountain ranges are thought to be in isostatic equilibrium and their height is attributed to the most recent adjustment. The height of most areas is related to the thickness of the crust at that location. For example, the crust under the Tibetan Plateau is 75 kilometers (46.6 miles) thick, whereas under Kansas, the crust is 44 kilometers (27.3 miles) thick. The crust beneath the city of Denver is 50 kilometers (31 miles) thick. But just west of Denver the Rocky Mountains are over 2 kilometers (1.2 miles) higher than the city, but the crust is the same thickness. Similar anomalies have been reported for the southern Sierra Nevada. These crustal root discrepancies have been explained by the fact that the mantle is hot and the asthenosphere is shallow in these areas. This causes the rocks to be less dense and thus they appear to be undercompensated. Clearly, there is much more to learn about these phenomena.

David L. White

FURTHER READING

Plummer, Charles, David McGeary, and Diane Carlson. *Physical Geology.* Dubuque, Iowa: Wm. C. Brown, 1979; 8th ed., Boston: Wm. C. Brown/McGraw-Hill, 1999.
Tarbuck, Edward J., and Frederick K. Lutgens. *The Earth: An Introduction to Physical Geology.* Columbus, Ohio: Charles E. Merrill, 1984; 6th ed., Upper Saddle River, N.J.: Prentice Hall, 1999.

RELATED ARTICLES
Gravity Anomaly; Isostatic Rebound

Isostatic Rebound

Isostatic rebound or *isostatic adjustment* refers to the vertical movement of the lithosphere (Earth's crust and uppermost mantle) to regain equilib-

rium. Isostatic rebound is caused by the buoyant tendency of the lithosphere as it floats on the denser, thicker asthenosphere (mantle below the lithosphere that is weak and where the adjustments occur). The continental crust is thicker than the oceanic crust but both float on the denser mantle. The continental crust is less dense than the oceanic crust and therefore floats higher and has deeper roots in the mantle. The denser oceanic crust has smaller mantle roots, but because of its greater density, still depresses the mantle to form low areas (basins) that the oceans occupy.

Isostatic rebound occurs when a weight has been removed from the crust. When the crust is laden (such as thickening during mountain building, sedimentary loading, and continental glaciation), it will sink into the mantle. Mantle material that is displaced causes the crust to rise until it reaches equilibrium. Once the weight has been removed (e.g., by the erosion of mountain ranges and melting of glaciers), the crust will rise buoyantly until the mantle and the crust again regain equilibrium.

During the Pleistocene Epoch (from 1.6 million to 10,000 years ago) large areas of North America and Europe were covered by continental ice sheets as thick as 5 kilometers (3 miles). The weight of the ice and included sediments depressed the crust and caused a reequilibration deeper in the mantle. Melting of the ice and the lessened load on the crust caused the crust to rebound upward as the mantle adjusted to the weight change. This uplift is common today in areas where ice has recently melted. Isostatic rebound (from glacier melting) occurs today in the Hudson Bay area; in Norway, Denmark, and Sweden; and in the Great Lakes region.

Erosion also lowers mountaintops and the crust will rise in response to the lessened load. Each succeeding rise is slightly less than the amount of elevation lost. This process will continue until the continental block reaches "normal" crustal thickness, where the mountains have eroded nearly to sea level and the deformed, metamorphosed roots are exposed at the surface. Eroded material from the mountain is deposited in continental margins and causes crustal sagging and subsidence. This initiates crustal imbalance with the mantle and the cycle begins again.

David L. White

FURTHER READING
Kennett, James. *Marine Geology.* Englewood Cliffs, N.J.: Prentice Hall, 1982.
Montgomery, Carla W. *Physical Geology*, 3rd ed. Dubuque, Iowa: Wm. C. Brown, 1993.
Plummer, Charles, David McGeary, and Diane Carlson. *Physical Geology.* Dubuque, Iowa: Wm. C. Brown, 1979; 8th ed., Boston: Wm. C. Brown/McGraw-Hill, 1999.
Thurman, Harold V. *Essentials of Oceanography.* Columbus, Ohio: Charles E. Merrill, 1983; 6th ed., with Alan P. Trujillo, Upper Saddle River, N.J.: Prentice Hall, 1999.

RELATED ARTICLES
Isostasy; Unconformity

Isothermal

The term *isothermal* refers to a water mass that is the same temperature throughout. *Iso* comes from the Greek *isos,* meaning "similar" or "equal." *Thermal* comes from the Greek *therme,* meaning "heat." In marine science, an isothermal line is a line on a map that connects points of similar water temperature. Isothermal water masses may be separated horizontally or vertically in the world's oceans. In physical geography, an isotherm is a line on a map that joins points having the same temperature.

Temperature varies in the oceans and is a significant factor in the distribution of marine organisms in the oceans of the world. Temperatures in the marine waters may fluctuate from below the freezing point of fresh water in Antarctic seas to around 30°C (86°F) in the tropics. Such a wide variation in temperature is not seen with most other physical factors in the open oceans of the world, except for the variation in pressure with

depth. Most biogeographical distribution patterns of surface-dwelling ocean organisms are strongly influenced by temperature.

James W. Nybakken

FURTHER READING
Nybakken, James W. *Marine Biology: An Ecological Approach*, 5th ed. San Francisco: Benjamin Cummings, 2001.

RELATED ARTICLES
Temperature, Distribution of

Izu–Bonin Island Arc

The active volcanic arc of the Izu–Bonin region is a nearly linear chain of volcanoes that stretches 1220 kilometers (758 miles) from Tokyo to Iwo Jima. The volcanic islands make up the Izu Arc and lie about 200 kilometers (120 miles) west from the Izu–Bonin Trench. The trench is a deep trough that has formed where subduction of the Pacific Ocean lithospheric plate (the ocean crust and the upper part of Earth's mantle) occurs beneath the eastern edge of the Philippine Sea Plate. The 11 main islands of the Izu Arc lie atop a submarine ridge that is nearly 400 kilometers (250 miles) wide over the northern half. The ridge deepens southward and narrows to about 100 kilometers (62 miles) wide. The southern half of the ridge is split along its length by east–west extension. A fault-bounded trough formed by the extension occurs between 100 and 190 kilometers (62 to 118 miles) west of the trench. The edge of the fault block immediately east of the trough rises above sea level to form the Bonin Islands, which are not active volcanoes but were formed by ancient submarine eruptions.

The magmas (molten rock) of the active Izu volcanic island arc form when fluids driven out of the subducting plate infuse the mantle deep beneath the arc. These fluids derive from chemical reactions involving dehydration of minerals in

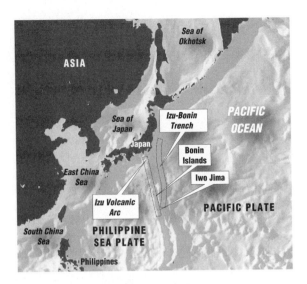

Components of the Izu–Bonin Island Arc.

the subducting oceanic lithosphere. The fluids reduce the melting point of the already hot overlying mantle. The mantle melts at depths of about 100 kilometers (62 miles) and the composition of the magmas reflects the infusion of the magma source region with components derived from the subducted oceanic plate. The magmas are more buoyant than the surrounding mantle and rise from their source region toward the surface. They erupt on the seafloor and form the arc volcanoes.

The arc volcanoes are steep-sided, cone-shaped stratovolcanoes, with alternating layers of lava flows and explosive eruptive products such as ash and cinder. Some have significant summit calderas [a summit depression with a diameter larger than 1.6 kilometers (1 mile) that formed either by violent explosions or by collapse caused by the withdrawal of magma from a subterranean chamber]. The Izu Islands lie in a relatively narrow band up to a few tens of kilometers wide. There are, however, far more submarine volcanoes in the Izu Arc than there are islands. They are spread across a width of up to 250 kilometers (155 miles) and are distributed along cross chains that follow fault lineaments trending southwest from the band of active arc volcanoes into the Shikoku Basin. These cross-chain volcanoes are not currently active. The

structures that control their distribution are inherited from older fault trends associated with rifting of the arc as long ago as 30 million years. Cross-chain volcanoes also form in other island arcs, but the Izu Arc has the longest in the world.

The band of active volcanism is split in the northern half by relatively narrow [up to 24 kilometers (15 miles) wide] fault-bounded extensional troughs. These troughs represent the beginning of a back-arc basin. Active volcanoes are forming within these troughs. Some of them erupt lavas that are compositionally similar to the Izu Arc volcanoes, but some of the lavas have a different source region. The faulting of the arc probably causes decompression melting at shallower levels in the arc lithosphere. These shallow magmas have compositions different from the deep-sourced arc magmas. The volcanism of the Izu Arc demonstrates that the tectonic deformation processes in an island arc influence not only volcano distribution but also the composition of lavas erupted in them.

Patricia Fryer

FURTHER READING

Fryer, P., et al. "Petrology and Geochemistry of Lavas from the Sumisu and Torishima Backarc Rifts." *Earth and Planetary Science Letters*, Vol. 100 (1990), pp. 161–178.

Hochstaedter, Alfred G., James B. Gill, Brian Taylor, Osamu Ishizuka, Makato Yuasa, and Sumito Morita. "Across-Arc Geochemical Trends in the Izu–Bonin Arc: Constraints on Source Composition and Mantle Melting." *Journal of Geophysical Research, Series B, Solid Earth and Planets*, Vol. 105, No. 1 (2000), pp. 495–512.

Taylor, B. "Rifting and the Volcanic–Tectonic Evolution of the Izu–Bonin–Mariana Arc." *Proceedings of the Ocean Drilling Program Scientific Results*, Vol. 126. College Station, Texas: Ocean Drilling Program, 1991; pp. 627–651.

RELATED ARTICLES

Convergent Plate Boundary; Island Arc; Mariana Island Arc; Pacific Plate; Plate Tectonics; Subduction Zone; Tonga Island Arc

Janthinidae

The Janthinidae is a family of gastropod snails that live attached to a bubble raft that floats on the ocean surface. Among the four groups of oceanic snails (the others being the heteropods, pteropods, and nudibranchs), the janthinids are the least modified for an open-ocean existence. They have a coiled shell [maximal height of about 4 to 5 centimeters (1.6 to 2.0 inches)] and a flat, solelike foot (such as is seen in bottom-dwelling snails). The animals are normally oriented in an upside-down position with the foot attached to the underside of the float. To build or enlarge the float, the foot is extended above the water surface and a bubble of air is trapped and encased in mucus (secreted by the foot). The mucus dries and the air bubble is added to the float. With the addition of air bubbles, the float becomes elongated, attaining a size upward of 13 centimeters (5 inches) in length and 2 centimeters (0.8 inch) in width. Because janthinids are incapable of swimming, they will sink if they become detached from their float or the prey upon which they are feeding. Wind-driven surface currents can carry janthinids great distances, and they are occasionally washed up on shores where their distinctive blue to violet color and clear bubble raft make them conspicuous to beachcombers.

Janthinids feed on species of hydrozoan jellyfish that also float on the ocean surface. Their prey include the by-the-wind sailor (*Velella*), a relative (*Porpita*) that lacks the "sail" of *Velella*, and the Portuguese man-of-war (*Physalia*). The janthinids feed by rasping off pieces of tissue with their radula, which has elongate, terminally hook-shaped teeth. The blue to violet color of the janthinids and of their prey approximates that of the clear tropical waters and presumably serves as camouflage against potential predators both from above and below the ocean surface.

Reproduction in the janthinids is unusual. Both *hermaphroditism* (each individual contains both male and female systems) and *protrandry* (small individuals are males and become females as large animals) have been described. Both hermaphrodites and protrandrous males lack a penis or other type of copulatory organ. Instead, they produce two different kinds of sperm: small ones that fertilize eggs and large ones that carry the small sperm to the female gonopore. Planktivorous (plankton-feeding) larvae develop from the fertilized eggs. Except for one species (which releases free-swimming veliger larva directly into the plankton), janthinids produce egg capsules that they attach to the underside of their bubble rafts and from which the veligers hatch out.

Despite the fact that this group is distributed throughout the world's oceans at tropical to subtropical latitudes, only seven or eight species are currently recognized. A large number (about 70 species) have been described, although only five in the genus *Janthina* and two or three in the genus

Recluzia are probably valid. Our knowledge about the biology of janthinids is based almost entirely on studies of species in the genus *Janthina*; the biology of *Recluzia* is virtually unknown.

Roger R. Seapy

FURTHER READING
Lalli, Carol M., and Ronald W. Gilmer. *Pelagic Snails: The Biology of Holoplanktonic Gastropod Mollusks.* Stanford, Calif.: Stanford University Press, 1989.
Laursen, Dan. *The Genus* Janthina: *A Monograph.* Copenhagen, Denmark: C. A. Reitzels, 1953.

RELATED ARTICLES
Gastropoda

Jellyfish

Jellyfish is the common name given to many different marine organisms classified in the phylum Cnidaria. Most jellyfish belong to the class Scyphozoa. Some are quite large, growing to over 2 meters (over 6.5 feet) across with tentacles trailing many meters behind. The class Hydrozoa contains jellyfish and siphonophores, which are colonial organisms containing many different individuals, the most common example of which is the Portuguese man-of-war. The sea wasps and box jellyfish are classified under the class Cuboza.

The familiar body form of the jellyfish is the umbrella-shaped or bell-shaped medusa. Jellyfish typically float on the surface of the water. The bell contains a large layer of gelatinous material between two layers of tissue, the epidermis and the inner gastrodermis, and can function as a flotation mechanism. In floating jellyfish, tentacles hang from the margin of the bell and are used to capture food. Limited movement forward is achieved by contracting muscles in the bell and forcing water out of the bottom of the bell. Muscular movement and other actions are controlled by a simple nervous system called the *nerve net*. Jellyfish have no brain; information is collected by nerve cells and receptors. Jellyfish are radially symmetrical and can be divided in half to create a mirror image.

Jellyfish have a central mouth surrounded by elongated margins of the mouth called *oral arms*. The marginal tentacles and the oral arms are equipped with nematocysts, which lie within cells called *cnidocytes*. Nematocysts are stinging cells that contain toxins. When potential prey brush against the tentacles, they are injected with toxins by the nematocysts. After the prey is paralyzed by the toxin, it is directed into the mouth by the oral arms and tentacles. Food enters the blind gastrovascular cavity, where enzymes begin to digest the food. Digestion is finished within food vacuoles and waste is excreted through the same opening as that through which food enters.

Most jellyfish exhibit alternation of generations, generally spending the earlier part of their lives in an asexual polyp stage and the remainder of their lives in the sexual medusoid stage. Asexual reproduction is achieved by budding, and sexual reproduction produces planula larvae. Besides causing painful and occasionally fatal stings to humans, jellyfish can be a nuisance to the fishing industry. Large aggregations of jellyfish clog fishing nets and can cause considerable damage. Jellyfish also prey on the larvae of commercial fishes, in addition to competing with other fishes for food.

Erin O'Donnell

FURTHER READING
Brusca, Richard C., and Gary J. Brusca. *Invertebrates.* Sunderland, Mass.: Sinauer, 1990.
Buchsbaum, Ralph. *Animals Without Backbones.* Chicago: University of Chicago Press, 1938; 3rd ed., with Mildred Buchsbaum, John Pearse, and Vicki Pearse, 1987.
Nybakken, James W. *Marine Biology: An Ecological Approach,* 5th ed. San Francisco: Benjamin Cummings, 2001.

RELATED ARTICLES
Cnidaria

Juan de Fuca Plate

The Juan de Fuca Plate is a small tectonic plate located off the western edge of North America. It is bound by the Pacific Plate to the west, the Explorer Plate to the north, the North American Plate to the east, the Gorda Plate to the south, and runs from Cape Blanco in Oregon to the northern tip of Vancouver Island, British Columbia, Canada. The Juan de Fuca Plate, at its widest point, spans less than 485 kilometers (300 miles) from its divergent boundary with the Pacific Plate to its convergent boundary with the North American Plate. The Juan de Fuca Ridge, the active spreading center separating the Pacific and Juan de Fuca Plates, has hydrothermal vent fields with thriving biological communities, and the convergent plate boundary between the Juan de Fuca and North American Plates is responsible for formation of the Cascade Mountain Range and the 1980 eruption of Mount Saint Helens volcano in Washington State.

Geologic History

Over 10 million years ago the Explorer, Juan de Fuca, and Gorda Plates were all one plate, a remnant of the northern portion of the ancient Farallon Plate. Geological processes involving the slowing of subduction (when two tectonic plates collide) rates caused the breaking apart of the Juan de Fuca and Gorda Plates about 10 million years ago. Approximately 4 million years ago, the Explorer Plate broke away, rotated, and stopped subducting. As a result, there are no geological features associated with subduction zones (such as volcanoes) in southern Canada.

Juan de Fuca Ridge

Although the Juan de Fuca Ridge comprises only 1 percent of the world's mid-ocean ridge system, it has been studied extensively due to its close proximity to land and major oceanographic institutions. In the last two decades several submarine volcanic eruptions and earthquakes have been detected along the Juan de Fuca Ridge. Additionally, scientists in the deep submersible vehicle, *Alvin*, found hydrothermal vent fields and associated chemosynthetic biological communities along the ridge axis in the late 1980s. In the 1990s, scientists retrieved a black smoker chimney for the American Museum of Natural History in Washington, D.C. Not only was this a great achievement for underwater engineering, but it also allowed geologists to study closely the chemical and physical composition of rocks and minerals that make up hydrothermal vent chimneys. Moreover, the display of this chimney has enabled vast members of the public to view a unique structure found only at great depths along the seafloor.

In 1996 and 1999, legs 168 and 169 of the Ocean Drilling Program (ODP) studied the region of the Juan de Fuca Ridge spreading center. Basalt is the primary lava type being produced and the ages of volcanic rocks studied ranged from 0.8 to 3.6 million years old. Furthermore, the middle valley of the Juan de Fuca Ridge contains vast sediment and mineral deposits, which are of interest to scientists. Scientists study these sediments and minerals in order to learn about past ocean climates and geological processes that occurred many thousands, even millions of years ago. These mineral deposits may have economic implications for the United States. Large sulfide deposits located on this portion of the ridge are within the U.S. Exclusive Economic Zone and have the potential to be mined for sulfide minerals such as galena (lead) and sphalerite (zinc).

Currently, there are instruments on the seafloor along the ridge axis that send data back to scientists on land. These instruments have allowed rapid response to seismic and volcanic activity on the plate in an effort to better understand this region. Hydrothermal fields, submarine volcanism, and seafloor spreading are interconnected activities that must be studied in context with each other.

Cascadia Subduction Zone

The Juan de Fuca Ridge is spreading at a rate of 56 to 60 millimeters (2.2 to 2.4 inches) per year, which pushes the Juan de Fuca Plate to the northeast. Because of this movement, the Juan de Fuca Plate is colliding with the western edge of the North American Plate, where it forms a convergent plate boundary and attendant subduction zone. Upon convergence with the North American Plate, the denser oceanic crust of the Juan de Fuca Plate is thrust beneath the less dense continental crust of the North American Plate. As the Juan de Fuca Plate plunges deep into the mantle, parts of it and the overlying plate melt to form magma, which works its way back to the surface to form volcanoes. Starting with the Farallon Plate and continuing over geologic time, this process has resulted in the formation of the Cascade Mountain Range, and this subduction zone is called the Cascadia Subduction Zone. Thus, the volcanic Cascade Mountains are an expression of the subduction of the Juan de Fuca Plate beneath the North American Plate. The Juan de Fuca Plate is young and warm, which does not allow the seafloor much time to cool before subduction. As a result, it is very buoyant and does not slide smoothly underneath the continental plate. Consequently, other processes such as accretion, underplating, and overthrusting occur. Violent earthquakes and volcanoes are also associated with this (and other) subduction zones. In 1700 an earthquake estimated at 9.0 on the Richter scale is believed to have occurred along the Cascadia Subduction Zone. There have been approximately 20 "notable" earthquakes in the Pacific Northwest since 1993.

Earthquakes can cause seismic sea waves (tsunamis), which may have devastating effects on both sides of the Pacific (i.e., United States and Japan). Terrestrial volcanic activity caused by the Cascadia Subduction Zone is specifically of concern to residents of the Pacific Northwest. On 18 May 1980, Mount Saint Helens erupted explosively, depositing ash over a 320-kilometer (200-mile) distance. Other volcanoes of concern include Mount Hood in Oregon and Mount Rainier in Washington, both close to urban areas.

Future Possibilities

The Juan de Fuca Plate's small size and close proximity to land make it an ideal candidate to study extensively in order to gain a better picture of plate tectonics on a global scale. Scientists at the University of Washington and Woods Hole Oceanographic Institution in Massachusetts (in conjunction with Massachusetts Institute of Technology) have proposed the North East Pacific Time-Series Undersea Networked Experiments (NEPTUNE) in an effort to fully understand all the interconnected tectonic activities taking place on the Juan de Fuca Plate. NEPTUNE is a project intended to wire the entire plate with a system of high-speed fiber-optic submarine cables linking a series of seafloor instruments, video equipment, and robotic vehicles with real-time sea-to-shore data transmission capabilities. This is an essential step in understanding the various geological interactions that mold the seafloor, generate earthquakes and volcanoes, form mineral and sediment deposits, and support life in extreme environments.

Additionally, Juan de Fuca Plate dynamics have shaped and are continuing to shape the Pacific Northwest. Increased scientific understanding of Cascadia Subduction Zone processes such as volcanoes and earthquakes has led to a greater public awareness of these natural hazards. Volcanoes cause hazards such as volcanic ash in the air; landslides; volcanic gases; and debris, lava, and mud flows. Earthquakes can cause structural damage to buildings and highways as well as rupture gas and electrical lines, which can become a serious fire hazard. Various groups, such as CREW

(Cascadia Region Earthquake Workgroup) and RACE (Rapid Alerts for Cascadia Earthquakes), have been formed to study, understand, and react to these far-reaching tectonic consequences.

Daniel Schuller

FURTHER READING

Davis, E. E., and R. G. Currie. "Geophysical Observations of the Northern Juan de Fuca Ridge System: Lessons on Sea-Floor Spreading." *Canadian Journal of Earth Science,* Vol. 30 (1993), pp. 278–300.

Delaney, J. R., and A. D. Chave. "NEPTUNE: A Fiber-Optic Telescope to Inner Space." *Oceanus,* Vol. 42 (2000), pp. 10–11.

Embeley, R. W., R. A. Feely, J. E. Lupton. "Introduction to Special Section on Volcanic and Hydrothermal Processes on the Southern Juan de Fuca Ridge." *Journal of Geophysical Research,* Vol. 99 (1995), pp. 4735–4740.

Vine, F. J., and J. T. Wilson. "Magnetic Anomalies over a Young Oceanic Ridge off Vancouver Island." *Science,* Vol. 150 (1965), pp. 485–489.

Wright, John, and Dave Rothery. *The Ocean Basins: Their Structure and Evolution.* Oxford and New York: Pergamon Press/Milton Keynes, England: Open University Press, 1989; 2nd ed., Oxford: Butterworth-Heinemann in association with the Open University, 1998.

RELATED ARTICLES

Convergent Plate Boundary; Divergent Plate Boundary; Exclusive Economic Zone; Explorer Plate; Farallon Plate; Gorda Plate; Gorda Ridge; Hydrothermal Vent; Juan de Fuca Ridge; Pacific Plate; Plate Tectonics; Seafloor Spreading; Subduction Zone

Juan de Fuca Ridge

The Juan de Fuca Ridge (JDFR) is a medium-rate oceanic spreading center located off the west coast of the United States and Canada. Traversing a north–northeast direction, it separates the Juan de Fuca and Pacific Plates. The ridge extends for 500 kilometers (310 miles), running from 44 to 48°N and 130°W. The JDFR was discovered and identified via magnetic anomalies in the early 1960s. Volcanically active hydrothermal vents and associated benthic chemosynthetic biological communities (bacterial mats, tube worms, spider crabs, etc.) are common along the ridge axis.

Large-scale scientific investigations of this spreading center have taken place since the discovery of hydrothermal activity on the ridge and perhaps due in part to its close proximity to major oceanographic institutions. The JDFR spreads symmetrically at a rate of about 6 centimeters (2.4 inches) per year. Over 30 kilometers (19 miles) of the ridge crest is volcanically active. This ridge is an extremely important location for plate tectonics research. Magnetic data collected on and near the JDFR were the bases for many fundamental papers on seafloor spreading and transform faults. In 1991, the highly active southern segment was designated as the site of the Ridge Interdisciplinary Global Experiment (RIDGE). Currently, there are a series of scientific instruments on the seafloor to monitor physical parameters such as temperature, seismicity, hydrothermal vent fluid chemistry, and biological activity.

The Juan de Fuca Ridge is extremely important for developing techniques to understand Earth's large volcanic systems and heat budget. Moreover, ridge axis hydrothermal vents are a significant source of dissolved elements such as iron and manganese in the ocean. Vent studies also yield important insights into the biology of fascinating deep-sea creatures. These creatures live at extremely high pressures and use chemicals from the vent effluent in order to live and thrive. It is thought that primitive life formed in the depths of the ocean around hydrothermal vents.

Daniel Schuller

FURTHER READING

Davis, E. E., and R. G. Currie, "Geophysical Observations of the Northern Juan de Fuca Ridge System: Lessons on Sea-Floor Spreading." *Canadian Journal of Earth Science,* Vol. 30 (1993), pp. 278–300.

Vine, F. J., and J. T. Wilson. "Magnetic Anomalies over a Young Oceanic Ridge off Vancouver Island." *Science*, Vol. 150 (1965), pp. 485–489.

Wright, John, and Dave Rothery. *The Ocean Basins: Their Structure and Evolution.* Oxford and New York: Pergamon Press/Milton Keynes, England: Open University Press, 1989; 2nd ed., Oxford: Butterworth-Heinemann, in association with Open University, 1998.

RELATED ARTICLES

Chemosynthesis; Hydrothermal Vent; Juan de Fuca Plate; Magnetic Anomaly; Mid-Ocean Ridge; Plate Tectonics; Seafloor Spreading

K

Kara Sea

The Kara Sea, with an area of 800,000 square kilometers (309,000 square miles), is located on the continental shelf off northwestern Siberia. It is bounded by Vaygach Island across Kara Strait to Novaya Zemla in the west with its connection to the Barents Sea, the eastern limit of Franz Josef Land to the northwest with its connection to the Arctic basin, and the Severnaya Zemlya Islands to the east with their connection to the Laptev Sea. The chief ports of the Kara Sea are Dickson, located at the mouth of the Yenisei River, and Novyy Port, located in the Gulf of Ob. The Kara Sea receives the Ob, the Yenisei, the Pyasina, and the Taimyra Rivers, which are important fishing grounds for cod, salmon, and sturgeon and provide approximately one-third of the fresh water to the Arctic Ocean. The sea has relatively shallow depths; 40 percent of the Kara Sea lies in water depths of less than 50 meters (164 feet), with an average depth of only 125 meters (410 feet). Several troughs are present, with depths reaching up to 620 meters (2030 feet). The sea is covered by ice during most of the year and is navigable for fishing only during August and September. Midwinter surface temperatures of the water average from -28 to -20°C (-18 to -4°F); midsummer temperatures average -1 to 6°C (30 to 43°F). The bottom sediments consist of silty clays or muds and terrigenous silt of glacial marine type in all the deeper regions. Shallow deposits near the mouths of the rivers consist of sands and silty sands.

Philip Rabinowitz

FURTHER READING

Lisitsyn, A. P., and M. E. Vinogradov. "International High Latitude Expedition in the Kara Sea (the 49th Cruise of the R/V *Dmitriy Mendeleev*)." *Oceanology*, Vol. 34, No. 5 (1995), pp. 583–590.

National Geographic Society. *National Geographic Atlas of the World*. Washington, D.C.: National Geographic Society, 1963; 7th ed., 1999, p. 133.

RELATED ARTICLES
Arctic Ocean; Barents Sea; Continental Shelf

Kelp, see Kelp Forest

Kelp Forest

The nearshore subtidal habitats in most of the world's temperate and subarctic latitudes are dominated largely by large brown algae (Phaeophyta) in the order Laminariales. These seaweeds, commonly referred to as *kelps*, form dense stands on rocky substrates from the low intertidal to deeper than 30 meters (100 feet). Their inordinately high productivity, large vertical structure, and ability to produce thick canopies have earned them the title of marine forests. Although the physical structure of a kelp forest depends highly on the species of kelp that are present, they all tend to support extremely diverse biological communities and are some of the world's most productive ecosystems.

Distribution

Kelp forests tend to be concentrated in or near areas of coastal upwelling or at least in areas where ocean waters are cool and nutrient rich, with the dominant species varying greatly among geographic locations. In general, species of the genus *Laminaria* dominate kelp forest communities throughout the Atlantic Ocean and along the coasts of Japan and China, whereas species of *Ecklonia* dominate many southern hemisphere coastlines, including South Africa, New Zealand, and Australia. Species of the genus *Macrocystis*, also called *giant kelp*, dominate kelp forest communities along southern parts of the west coast of South America, several southern hemisphere ocean islands, and parts of the northeast Pacific Ocean from central Baja California, Mexico, to central California, United States. Species of the genera *Nereocystis*, *Alaria*, *Pterygophora*, and *Laminaria* dominate much of the rest of the northeast Pacific Ocean from California to the western Aleutian Archipelago, a range characterized by the greatest diversity of kelp species.

Kelp Life Cycle

Kelps exhibit a complex life cycle that alternates between a large diploid sporophyte (i.e., a life stage that possesses two copies of each chromosome and produces spores) and a microscopic haploid gametophyte (i.e., a life stage that possesses only one copy of each chromosome and produces sperm or eggs). Reproduction, which can take a few weeks to several months to complete, begins when cells in the sporophyte undergo a reduction division and produce haploid zoospores (i.e., mobile reproductive bodies that possess a single copy of each chromosome). These zoospores, which can number in the billions, are released into the surrounding water

where they remain for a few minutes to several hours, during which they disperse away from the parent sporophyte. The zoospores then settle on the bottom and germinate into male and female gametophytes that when sexually mature will produce antheridia and oogonia (male and female sex organs), respectively. The male gametophytes release sperm into the surrounding water that are chemically attracted to and swim toward the female gametophytes. Upon contact with the oogonia, the sperm fuse with the eggs (syngamy), producing zygotes that will grow into new sporophytes. When fully grown, the sporophytes of some kelp species reach a maximum size of less than 1 meter (3.3 feet) in length (e.g., *Polstelsia*), whereas the sporophytes of other species attain lengths greater than 40 meters (130 feet) (e.g., *Macrocystis*).

Kelp Forest Community

Much like plants in terrestrial forests, kelps grow attached to the substrate by a rootlike holdfast, whereas the majority of their photosynthetic biomass occurs in the form of leaflike blades that are supported above the bottom. Depending on the species, these blades are supported either by a single, rigid, trunklike stalk (called a *stipe*) or by long flexible stipes that are buoyed by gas-filled bladders called *pneumatocysts*. When they occur in high enough densities, these blades can form thick canopies that are capable of blocking more than 99 percent of the available light reaching the bottom and, in turn, strongly influencing the distribution and abundance of associated kelp forest species. As a consequence, kelps tend to be their community's competitive dominant macroalgae and major habitat-forming structures, and in turn play an integral role in maintaining species diversity.

In general, kelp forests support a rich mosaic of demersal and pelagic organisms that utilize the three-dimensional structure provided by the dominant kelps. For example, a single holdfast of the giant kelp *Macrocystis pyrifera* may contain as many as 150 species of invertebrates, while the midwater and canopy portions of the kelp forests are utilized as habitat and feeding for numerous species of invertebrates, fin fish, marine mammals, and seabirds. One of the most conspicuous of these is the sea otter, *Enhydra lutris*, which is closely associated with the kelp forests of the northeast Pacific Ocean and Aleutian Archipelago. Furthermore, by modifying the physical environment (i.e., light and water motion), kelp forests provide a dynamic and heterogeneous habitat that fosters a rich mosaic of benthic algae, fin fish, and invertebrates. Upon their removal and ultimate decay, kelps may fuel other coastal ecosystems, such as sandy beach, rocky intertidal, and deep-sea benthic communities.

Ecology

The persistence of kelp forests depends largely on the presence of a hard substrate, cool nutrient-rich waters, and benthic light intensities equivalent to about 1 percent surface irradiance. As a consequence, kelp forests are generally limited to habitats shallower than 30 meters (100 feet), although areas of unusually high water clarity may allow some kelp forests (e.g., *Pleurophycus* forests along central California) to persist deeper than 45 meters (150 feet). Within their geographic ranges, exposure to ocean waves plays an important role in regulating the distribution and abundance of many kelp forest species. Because large ocean waves can dislodge kelps at their holdfasts or break their stipes midwater, they often result in significant canopy loss. Also, because the hydrodynamic forces associated with ocean waves increase with decreasing water depth, they may be important in regulating the shallow limit of some kelp species. Finally, hydrodynamic forces may also be important in setting the latitudinal range limits of some kelp forest species. For example, along the west coast of North America, the northern limit of the giant kelp, *Macrocystis*, is set near Santa Cruz, California [97 kilometers (60 miles) south of San Francisco] by unfavorable hydrodynamic forces.

A scuba diver swims in a giant kelp forest off the coast of southern California. (© Jeffrey L. Rotman/Corbis)

North of this point, the more resistant bull kelp, *Nereocystis*, becomes the dominant forest-forming kelp species. In contrast, the southern limit of *Macrocystis* appears to be set near Bahía Asuncion, Baja California, Mexico, by unfavorable temperature-nutrient conditions and poor substrate quality. South of this point, the subsurface kelp, *Eisenia*, which is more tolerant to poor nutrient conditions, becomes the dominant kelp species along the Baja Peninsula.

Kelp forest communities are also affected periodically by biological and physical disturbances. For example, intense grazing by sea urchins can have a devastating impact on kelp forest communities by stripping areas completely of all macroalgae, creating "urchin barrens." These are commonly observed after severe storms remove all of the sea urchins' primary food—unattached drift algae—from an area, resulting in the urchins actively grazing on attached algae. Also, the reduction or loss of the urchin's primary predator, the sea otter, from many of the Aleutian Islands in the northern Pacific Ocean and Bering Sea has resulted in staggering increases in urchin densities and a subsequent loss of nearly all the kelp from many of the islands. But perhaps the most significant disturbance to kelp forests occurs in the *Macrocystis* forests in the northeastern Pacific Ocean during El Niño-Southern Oscillation (ENSO) events. The El Niño event of 1997–98 resulted in a an almost complete loss of all giant kelp throughout nearly half its range and caused wide-ranging changes in the associated kelp forest communities, while the El Niño of 1982–83, which also caused wide-ranging loss of giant kelp, also resulted in about 50-kilometer (31-mile) northward migration of the species' southern limit in the northeast Pacific Ocean. Recovery from these disturbances can be facilitated by the presence of cool, nutrient-rich oceanographic conditions characteristic of La Niña events and by the removal of the primary grazers by storms, disease, or predation.

Economic and Social Value

In addition to their ecological importance, kelp forests are an important economic resource. The canopies of some kelp species are harvested commercially for the extraction of algin, an emulsifying agent used in cosmetics, pharmaceuticals, and food products and for feeding cultured abalone, which are sold to restaurants. Along the west coast of the United States, where giant kelp canopies were initially harvested for the extraction of potash and acetone for making explosives during World War I, and for use as livestock and poultry feed in the 1920s, these canopies are currently harvested for algin in an industry that grosses tens of millions of dollars annually. In addition to their direct commercial value, kelp forests provide an important resource for numerous sport fishery,

recreational scuba diving, and tourism industries, as well as some commercial fishery-based economies. In fact, some local economies along much of the Pacific coast of Baja California, Mexico, are based almost exclusively on fisheries that rely on kelp forest ecosystems.

Given their worldwide distribution, kelp forests are of tremendous economic, social, and ecological value. As a consequence, a considerable amount of information has been collected on their ecology. However, comparatively little is known about the factors that set their range limits, the ecology of the microscopic life stages in nature, or the effects of long-term changes in ocean conditions due to fishing, urban development, and global warming. Clearly, more information is needed in these areas to better manage and protect these important resources.

Matthew S. Edwards

FURTHER READING

Kennelly, Steven J., and Anthony W. D. Larkum. "A Preliminary Study of Temporal Variation in the Colonization of Subtidal Algae in an *Ecklonia radiata* Community." *Aquatic Botany*, Vol. 17 (1983), pp. 275–282.

McPeak, Ronald H., Dale A. Glantz, and Carole R. Shaw. *The Amber Forest: Beauty and Biology of California's Submarine Forests.* San Diego: Watersport Publishing, 1988.

North, Wheeler J. *The Ecology of Giant Kelp Beds (Macrocystis) in California.* Lehre, Germany: J. Cramer, 1971.

North, Wheeler J., George A. Jackson, and Steven L. Manley. "Macrocystis and Its Environment, Knowns and Unknowns." *Aquatic Botany*, Vol. 26 (1986), pp. 9–26.

RELATED ARTICLES

Algin; Demersal; El Niño; Grazing; La Niña; Pelagic; Upwelling

Kelvin Wave

Kelvin waves are boundary waves with very long periods within the range of hours to many days (a period is the time taken for one waveform to pass by). A boundary or trapped wave is a surface and/or internal wave that exists due to the presence of a physical or dynamical boundary. The shoreline is a physical boundary and the equator is a dynamical boundary—both trap Kelvin waves.

Kelvin waves propagate as shallow-water waves for which water depth is less than 5 percent of the wave's wavelength. For such waves, speed or celerity (C) is related to water depth (d) and acceleration due to gravity [g, at 9.8 meters (32.2 feet) per second per second] according to the equation

$$C^2 = gd$$

Kelvin waves affect sea surface height and the depth of the *thermocline* (a steep vertical temperature gradient). Kelvin waves appear to play a key role in the initiation and termination of El Niño events.

Since the 1980s, Kelvin waves in the equatorial Pacific have been monitored by moored buoys that measure sea surface temperature (SST), depth, and zonal winds. The *TOPEX/Poseidon* satellite, launched in August 1992, uses high-resolution radar altimetry that can reveal the movements of Kelvin waves in the equatorial Pacific. Analysis of data from the first two years of *TOPEX/Poseidon*'s operation revealed eight downwelling Kelvin wave impulses moving eastward, the majority of them being associated with strong eastward wind stresses in the western Pacific.

In an El Niño year, a wind anomaly (weakening winds in the western Pacific associated with the Southern Oscillation) causes a change in Ekman transport in the western Pacific equatorial region. Water flows toward the equator rather than away from it. Warm surface water accumulates along the equator and depresses the thermocline. This causes oscillations at the thermocline, which propagate eastward as Kelvin waves. When the Kelvin waves first arrive in the eastern Pacific and depress the thermocline there, they help precipitate an El Niño event. The prominent easterly

Kelvin waves that are associated with the onset of an El Niño event are bulges that travel at about 2.4 to 2.8 meters (7.9 to 9.2 feet) per second or about 250 kilometers (155 miles) per day. They have an amplitude (half of wave height) at the thermocline of several tens of meters and at the sea surface of several centimeters. The lengths of these waves are thousands of kilometers. The waves take about two months to travel from west to east across the equatorial Pacific. When the waves strike the coastline of South America, those in the northern hemisphere propagate northwestward, with the coastline acting as a wave guide.

The elements from the Tropical Ocean Global Atmosphere (TOGA) program (1985–94) and the Tropical Atmosphere Ocean (TAO) array of moored buoys were in place to capture the unfolding drama of the 1997–98 El Niño—for some parameters, the strongest El Niño on record. From January to late summer 1997, westerly winds generated downwelling equatorial Kelvin waves that moved eastward and depressed the thermocline in the eastern Pacific by more than 90 meters (295 feet), thus reducing the eastern Pacific upwelling, a symptom of an El Niño event. In late 1997 and early 1998, upwelling Kelvin waves, apparently produced by Rossby waves reflecting off the western Pacific boundary but also generated by easterly wind anomalies, caused cooling of equatorial western Pacific surface water, preconditioning the ocean for the demise of the El Niño event. Kelvin waves probably play a key role in other far-reaching oceanic–atmospheric interactions, which have yet to be subject to such close scrutiny.

Trevor Day

FURTHER READING

Ikeda, M., and F. Dobson, eds. *Oceanographic Applications of Remote Sensing*. Boca Raton, Fla.: CRC Press, 1995.

McPhaden, Michael J. "Genesis and Evolution of the 1997–1998 El Niño." *Science*, Vol. 283, No. 5403 (12 February 1999), pp. 950–954.

Open University Course Team. *Waves, Tides and Shallow Water Processes.* Oxford and New York: Pergamon Press, in association with the Open University, Milton Keynes, England, 1989; 2nd ed., Boston: Butterworth-Heinemann, in association with the Open University, 1999.

Young, Ian R., and Greg J. Holland. *Atlas of the Oceans: Wind and Wave Climate.* Oxford, and Tarrytown, N.Y.: Pergamon Press, 1996.

Useful Web Sites
"Tropical Atmosphere Ocean Project Real-Time Data." <http://www.pmel.noaa.gov/tao/jsdisplay/>.

Related Articles
Ekman Transport; El Niño; Internal Wave; *TOPEX/Poseidon*

Kerguelen Plateau and Broken Ridge

The Kerguelen Plateau is a mostly undersea, yet elevated region of the seafloor in the southern Indian Ocean between 45 and 65°S latitude and 60 and 90°E longitude. Named after Yves-Joseph de Kerguelen-Trémarec (1734–97), who in 1772 discovered the eponymous archipelago surmounting the feature, the northwest–southeast elongated plateau is commonly less than 2000 meters (6560 feet) below sea level, whereas the surrounding ocean basins are generally greater than 4000 meters (13,125 feet) deep. The Kerguelen Plateau and Broken Ridge, the latter oriented east–west in the eastern Indian Ocean between 25 and 35°S latitude and 85 and 105°E longitude, formed a contiguous plateau until about 43 million years ago, when they were separated by seafloor spreading. Together, the two features encompass approximately 2 million square kilometers (772,200 square miles) of the seafloor, an area roughly one-third the size of Australia. Under the U.N. Convention on the Law of the Sea, France claims the northern third of the Kerguelen Plateau and Australia the southern two-thirds. Broken Ridge lies entirely in international waters.

Although mostly covered by pelagic sediment, igneous and metamorphic rocks of the Kerguelen Plateau and Broken Ridge have been recovered by drilling at 11 sites and dredging. According to radiometric dating of volcanic rocks, construction of the Kerguelen Plateau began about 120 million years ago in the young but growing ocean basin formed by the separation of Antarctica and India. Most of the plateau and Broken Ridge had been built by about 85 million years ago, although northern reaches of the former have formed since about 70 million years ago, and mostly since about 40 million years ago. Volcanism attributed to the same long-lived mantle magma source, or hotspot, continues today on Heard and McDonald Islands, the only islands on the plateau other than those in the Kerguelen archipelago.

Although the dominant igneous rock type of the Kerguelen Plateau and Broken Ridge is oceanic-type basalt, more silica-rich rocks were erupted in the final stages of magmatism. Nearly all of the igneous rocks heretofore sampled were erupted in a subaerial environment; the lavas and overlying, deepening sediment facies indicate that the features have gradually subsided by as much as several thousand meters since construction. Such subsidence is probably attributable to contractional cooling. Furthermore, petrological, geochemical, and geophysical evidence suggest that at least part of the Kerguelen Plateau is of continental origin. Notably, garnet-bearing gneiss, a metamorphic rock typically found only on the continents, was recovered from Elan Bank on the western portion of the plateau by Ocean Drilling Program scientists in 1999. This rock is petrologically and geochronologically similar to rocks found on India and Antarctica, confirming that parts of these continents were isolated in the growing Indian Ocean basin by northward jumps of seafloor spreading, or mid-ocean ridge axes.

Structurally complex, the Kerguelen Plateau and Broken Ridge have experienced several episodes of faulting, differential subsidence, volcanism, and plutonism since they formed. Relatively strong intraplate earthquakes occur on the Kerguelen Plateau today, indicating that deformation is ongoing. Two large basins containing up to several kilometers of sediment have formed on the Kerguelen Plateau, one between the Kerguelen archipelago and Heard and McDonald Islands, and the Raggatt Basin on the southern plateau. Since about 30 million years ago, the Antarctic Circumpolar Current has swept across the Kerguelen Plateau, eroding and redepositing sediment.

Millard F. Coffin

FURTHER READING

Coffin, Millard F., and Olav Eldholm. "Large Igneous Provinces." *Scientific American,* Vol. 269, No. 4 (1993), pp. 42–49.

Coffin, Millard F., Fred A. Frey, Paul J. Wallace, et al. *Proceedings of the Ocean Drilling Program, Initial Reports,* Vol. 183. College Station: Texas A&M University, 1998. CD-ROM.

RELATED ARTICLES

Antarctic Circumpolar Current; Indian Ocean; India Plate; Ocean Basin; Ocean Drilling Program; Ontong Java Plateau; Radiometric Dating; Seafloor Spreading

Keystone Species

The marine environment is home to a wide variety of plant and animal communities, each of which is characterized by a host of factors, including location, number, and types of species present. Each organism contributes to the overall integrity or structure of its community environment and food web, be it predator, prey, or habitat modifier. Marine ecologists have found that some species, called *keystone species,* have more of an impact on their communities than do others. The name stemmed from an analogy: If the keystone is removed from a stone archway, the archway would change at the very least, and could collapse at the very worst. Removing keystone species from their particular environment leads to changes in the overall community structure. More often than not, the "new" community is less efficient and not as stable. Keystone species play an important role in the diversity of an ecosystem. It is important to note, however, that a keystone species is not necessarily the most abundant in its community. Keystone species are species whose impact on the community or ecosystem is large compared to their abundance; removing them from the environment alters the overall community makeup.

Development of the Keystone Species Theory

The field of ecology is ripe with theories that attempt to explain the development of various ecosystems. For example, communities are more diverse (i.e., a greater number of species is present) in tropical communities than in temperate regions. Ecologically speaking, a diverse community is a healthy community. One of these theories, called the *predation theory,* was proposed by Robert Paine (1933–) in 1966. The theory suggests that predators keep their prey species at population sizes that are below the environment's *carrying capacity* (the number of prey the habitat can accommodate). Diversity is greater in the tropics because the greater number of predators keep prey populations in check; therefore, competition is reduced so that a greater number of resources (food and space) are available and more species can coexist. Other ecological factors at work in determining community biodiversity include competition between species (survival of the fittest), the amount of time that a community has existed (the longer its history, the more diverse an ecosystem becomes), the stability of the climate (stable climates such as the tropics are more diverse), the degree of productivity (the tropics are more productive and have more energy cycling through ecosystems), and the size of the area (the greater the area, the more diverse an ecosystem will be).

Paine's Field Experiment

Paine studied rocky intertidal communities in the state of Washington. One particular community consisted of about 15 species, including the sea star *Pisaster*, which was the top predator, as well as mussels, whelks, chitons, limpets, gooseneck barnacles, and acorn barnacles. Mussels typically dominate rocky intertidal areas (i.e., they have the greatest abundance). Paine hypothesized that the sea star was a keystone species. He monitored diversity and the abundance of prey species in experimental plots, from which he removed the sea stars, and in control areas, which he left alone. When Paine removed the sea stars, the community diversity decreased from 15 to eight species, and the number of mussels (*Mytilus*) and barnacles increased relative to the control plots. Mussels ended up dominating the new community. Paine found that removing any of the other species did not affect the diversity of the community as much as when he removed the sea stars. He therefore called the sea stars a keystone predator, and the concept of the keystone species was born. The sea stars effectively reduced competition among the prey species; in other words, when the mussels were preyed upon by the sea stars, they could not outcompete and exclude other species from the community at large. Paine's experiment helped solidify the definition of a keystone species: one whose large effect on a community is out of proportion with its relatively low biomass (i.e., it is not necessarily the most abundant species).

Problems with the Term Keystone Species

The concept of a keystone species is loosely defined. The term should be used to define species that are essentially responsible for the structure of the community; they have a significant impact on the environment that is surprising given their relatively low abundance. However, in recent years species that may play a "key" role in their environment have been referred to as keystone species, when in fact they may not qualify as such according to the technical definition. It is also important to recognize that a dominant species, or one that is most abundant in a community, is not necessarily a keystone species. Furthermore, a keystone species is not always a predator; it can define any organism whose removal causes the community to change.

Other Examples of Keystone Species

The sea star in the Pacific Northwest is the most commonly cited example of a keystone marine species. Another frequently cited example of a keystone species is the sea otter, also found in Pacific marine communities. In a properly functioning food web, sea otters prey on sea urchins, which graze on the kelp that form the matrix of kelp communities. Therefore, the otters effectively keep the sea urchin population in check. However, if sea otter populations decline as they did in the twentieth century because of the fur trapping industry, the number of sea urchins increases and kelp beds disappear. This causes the overall biodiversity of the community to plummet, weakening the ecosystem.

Sharks are another example of a keystone predator. As top predator, sharks play a significant role in maintaining the overall integrity and equilibrium of the environment. Removing large sharks from the environment means that a greater number of smaller sharks roam the waters, resulting in fewer prey fish species in the ecosystem. Sharks may not be the most abundant marine species in an ecosystem, but their presence is critical to the overall ecosystem structure.

Significance of Keystone Species

The concept of a keystone species is significant in terms of restoration ecology, the science of restoring altered habitats to their natural state. Not all species in a particular community contribute to the overall integrity or structure of the community equally, or in the same way. Because keystone species affect an ecosystem significantly—much more than expected by their abundance—they warrant special attention when it comes to ecosystem management strategies. Declining keystone populations should raise concerns because losing them means losing a much greater number of other species as well.

Kristen M. Kusek

FURTHER READING

Ehrlich, Paul R., and Jonathan Roughgarden. *The Science of Ecology.* New York: Macmillan/London: Collier Macmillan, 1987.

Ormond, Rupert F. G., John D. Gage, and Martin V. Angel. *Marine Biodiversity: Patterns and Processes.* Cambridge and New York: Cambridge University Press, 1997.

Paine, R. T. "Food Web Complexity and Species Diversity." *American Naturalist,* Vol. 100 (1966), pp. 65–75.

———. "A Note on Trophic Complexity and Species Diversity." *American Naturalist,* Vol. 103 (1969), pp. 91–93.

RELATED ARTICLES
Biodiversity; Food Web

Kinorhyncha

The Kinorhyncha constitute a phylum of multicellular, bilaterally symmetrical, exclusively free-living marine invertebrate animals. They are very small, all less than 1 millimeter (0.039 inch) long, and always associated with a substrate and thus are categorized as meiofauna (= meiobenthos). Some kinorhynchs, along with similarly small invertebrates, live in the interstices formed

Echinoderes kozloffi (Kinorhyncha).

by sediment particles, especially marine sand. Kinorhynchs often burrow through fine particulate material such as mud, making their own space as they move through the oxygenated upper few centimeters of mud, where they feed primarily on microalgae, especially diatoms. A few are associated with the surface of a substrate, especially surfaces of rooted aquatic plants. Occasionally, they venture into the seawater but remain close to the substrate itself. Rarely, kinorhynchs are found in association with bryozoans, clams, and sponges either because they have been accidentally ingested or find the surface a suitable habitat. Kinorhynchs occur throughout the world, from tropical to polar waters and from intertidal beaches to depths exceeding 5000 meters (16,400 feet).

Kinorhynchs are segmented and often mistaken for small shrimplike copepods or even immature insects. Their segmentation is evidenced by the organization of their nervous system, their muscular system, a system of subcuticular glands, sequential rings of scalids on the head (segment one) and variously divided cuticular rings on the neck (segment two), and an 11-segmented trunk, thereby comprising a total of 13 segments. Their body cavity is a sac filled with amoebocytic tissue. The excretory system consists of a single pair of protonephridia, primitive osmoregulatory organs situated on either side of the gut in segments 10 and 11; sexes are separate, and saccate gonads lie on either side of the gut and open at segment 12. Growth is by molting of a series of six juvenile stages. About 150 species have been described.

Robert P. Higgins

FURTHER READING

Higgins, Robert P. "Kinorhyncha." In Robert P. Higgins and Hjalmar Thiel, eds., *Introduction to the Study of Meiofauna.* Washington, D.C.: Smithsonian Institution Press, 1988; pp. 1–487.

Kristensen, Reinhardt M., and Robert P. Higgins. "Kinorhyncha." In Frederick W. Harrison and Edward E. Ruppert, eds., *Microscopic Anatomy of Invertebrates,* Vol. 4, *Aschelminthes.* New York: Wiley-Liss, 1991; pp. 328–331.

Margulis, Lynn, and Karlene V. Schwartz. "Kinorhyncha." In Lynn Margulis, ed., *Five Kingdoms: An Illustrated Guide to the Phyla of Life on Earth.* San Francisco: W. H. Freeman, 1982; 3rd ed., New York, 1998; pp. 206.

RELATED ARTICLES
Meiofauna

Krill

The name *krill* was first used by Norwegian whalers to describe the stomach contents that spewed out of the guts of whales as they were cut up (flensed). The right whales that were the initial targets of the whalers feed predominantly on euphausiids. These are malacostracan arthropods, which are shrimplike in appearance. The term *krill* has become the common name for any of the 86 species of euphausiids, which are often the dominant group of animals in the macroplankton. In the Southern Ocean the name is more specifically applied to the dominant large species, *Euphausia superba*, which grows to a length of nearly 5 centimeters (2 inches), and in the North Atlantic, another large species, *Megancyiphanes norvegica*, is known as the northern krill.

In the Southern Ocean, *E. superba* accumulates in massive swarms especially near the edge of the pack ice and near some islands, where they are readily exploited by a wide range of vertebrate predators, including whales, crabeater and fur seals, penguins, and albatrosses. Swarms can reach densities of tens of kilograms per square meter of sea surface. It is considered to be an important species in the Southern Ocean ecosystem since it occupies a central position in the food web, with many other species being heavily dependent on it as a major food source. In the austral spring the krill graze on the dense diatom blooms that develop particularly in the transition zone between pack ice and open sea, but at other times of year they feed omnivorously. In winter they migrate down into deeper water and often shrink in size because of starvation. In the spring they migrate back up to the surface, where the adult females, after putting on weight, lay yolky eggs that are heavier than water. These sink to depths of 2000 meters (6560 feet) and hatch into nonfeeding larvae. These larvae start the long swim back toward the surface, living off rich reserves of yolk and developing as they travel. They arrive back near the surface just as they run out of reserves and reach the stage at which they start to feed. This is presumably a strategy that maximizes the ability of the larvae to survive their earliest stages when they are most vulnerable to predation. The entire life cycle takes two to five years to complete. Estimates of the quantities of krill that occur in the Southern Ocean, which are based on the abundances of the vast

Krill swim in a tank on Palmer Station in Antarctica. (© Peter Johnson/Corbis)

populations of predators they support, are in the region of 500 million tonnes (550 tons). Some fishermen and governments consider krill to be a resource that the burgeoning human population needs to exploit; others, including many scientists and conservationists, perceive krill as integral to the entire Southern Ocean ecosystem, making this species too vulnerable to the risks of overexploitation even to contemplate any exploitation.

The northern krill, *M. norvegica*, can also be very abundant. At night in calm conditions its swarms can be seen at the surface as patches of blue-green light (bioluminescence) more than 30 meters (100 feet) across. However, it does not achieve "keystone" status in the northern oceans, a role that tends to be taken up by copepods, particularly *Calanus finmarchicus*. In tropical oceans, there is a much greater variety of krill species, but they occur in very low abundances. Several of these are predators

rather than herbivores; carnivorous species of *Stylocheiron* are remarkable for their bilobed eyes. Only one species, *Bentheuphausia amblyops*, has a fully bathypelagic distribution. In the upwelling region of the Benguela Current off South Africa, *Euphausia hanseni* has a life cycle similar to that of krill, which enables it to seed deeper water with its eggs and developing larvae so that some are upwelled and are the first to exploit the abundant bloom of phytoplankton.

Martin Angel

FURTHER READING

Knox, George A. *The Biology of the Southern Ocean.* Cambridge and New York: Cambridge University Press, 1994

Mauchline, John. "The Biology of Euphausiids." *Advances in Marine Biology,* Vol. 18 (1980), pp. 375–623.

USEFUL WEB SITES

Alfred Wegener Institute: Krill
  <http://e-net.awi-bremerhaven.de/Eistour/krill-e.html>.

Cousteau Krill Library.
   <http://www.ecoscope.com/krill4u.htm>.

RELATED ARTICLES
Food Chain; Food Web; Macroplankton; Photophore;
Southern Ocean

Kula Plate

The Kula Plate is an ancient oceanic plate. About 120 to 90 million years ago, the Kula Plate occupied almost all of the North Pacific Ocean (see figure) and has since been mostly destroyed. As such, it is a model for the geologic histories of other consumed plates in the Pacific Ocean. The major premise of the plate tectonic paradigm is that oceanic plates grow from spreading centers and are consumed in subduction zones where the plates ultimately mix with Earth's upper mantle. Lithospheric plates have shuffled Earth's surface for most of its history, but only continental plates have survived. What happened to the ancient oceanic plates? No part of an existing oceanic plate is older than about 165 million years; it is obvious that older oceanic plates and parts of present-day plates have been consumed.

The present-day Pacific Ocean is floored by several plates. The Pacific Plate is by far the largest, encompassing about 22 percent of Earth's surface and most of the Pacific Ocean floor. Other active plates in the Pacific Ocean include the Antarctic Plate on the south; the Nazca and Cocos Plates off South America; the Gorda, Juan de Fuca, and Explorer Plates off western North America; and the Australian-Indian and Philippine Plates of the western Pacific. The ancient Pacific Ocean also was floored by several crustal plates, including the Kula Plate, which is one of these older plates. Two other major ancient plates in the Pacific Ocean basin were the Phoenix and Farallon Plates.

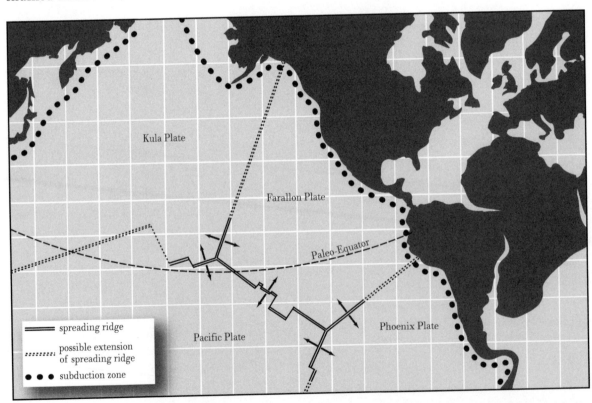

Possible arrangement of the Pacific Ocean plate structure, including the Kula Plate, 110 million years ago. (Adapted from Geological Society of America Bulletin, vol. 83, p. 3654, 1972. Courtesy, The Geological Society of America.)

Kula means "all gone" in a North American Indian Athabaskan dialect, and during the early stages of plate tectonic studies it was thought that the entire plate had been consumed. However, later studies have shown that part of the Bering Sea, specifically the Aleutian Basin, is probably floored by part of the late Mesozoic Kula Plate. Furthermore, a small remnant of the Kula Plate and a short segment of the extinct Kula–Pacific spreading ridge still exist south of the islands of Attu and Agattu in the western Aleutian Islands. The small remnant, about the size of the state of Delaware, is bounded on the south by Stalemate Ridge, an ancient fracture zone. This remnant is about 47 to 41 million years old and is slowly being consumed in the Aleutian subduction zone.

The interpreted geologic history of the Kula Plate suggests that between about 200 and 150 million years ago, it was being subducted beneath eastern Asia as the Pacific Plate grew rapidly on the southeast flank of the Kula–Pacific Ridge. The Kula Plate subsequently split from the Farallon Plate and almost all of the crust accreted along the Kula–Farallon spreading center has been subducted beneath North America. Most of the ocean floor in the present North Pacific Ocean is crust that had formed along the southern flank of the Kula–Pacific Ridge, a large part of which has been subducted beneath the Aleutian Arc.

The small remnant of the Kula Plate, now south of the western Aleutian Islands, has been part of the Pacific Plate ever since the Kula–Pacific spreading ridge died about 41 million years ago. In a few million years this small remnant will be gone, entirely consumed beneath the Aleutian Arc.

Tracy L. Vallier

FURTHER READING
Condie, Kent C. *Plate Tectonics and Crustal Evolution.* New York: Pergamon Press, 1976; 4th ed., Oxford and Boston: Butterworth-Heinemann, 1997.
Grow, John A., and Tanya Atwater. "Mid-Tertiary Tectonic Transition in the Aleutian Arc." *Geological Society of America Bulletin*, Vol. 81 (1970), pp. 3715–3722.
Lonsdale, Peter. "Paleogene History of the Kula Plate: Offshore Evidence and Onshore Implications." *Geological Society of America Bulletin*, Vol. 100 (1988), pp. 733–754.
Vallier, Tracy L., Carlos A. Mortera-Gutierrez, Herman A. Karl, Douglas C. Masson, Libby Prueher, and Thomas E. Chase. "Geology of the Kula Paleo-Plate, North Pacific Ocean." In James V. Gardner, Michael E. Field, and David C. Twichell, eds., *Geology of the United States' Seafloor: The View from GLORIA*. Cambridge: Cambridge University Press, 1996.

RELATED ARTICLES
Aleutian Arc; Aleutian Islands; Farallon Plate; Pacific Plate; Plate Tectonics; Subduction Zone

Kuroshio

The Kuroshio, or Japan Current, is an ocean current that flows northward from the Philippines, past Taiwan and the Ryukyu Islands, and along the coast of Japan. The name *Kuroshio* means *black current*, referring to the color of its water, which is darker than the adjacent ocean.

In summer, a branch from the Kuroshio flows through the Korea Strait, along the western coast of Japan, and into the Sea of Japan. This branch is known as the *Tsushima Current*. The main part of the Kuroshio skirts the eastern coast of the Japanese island of Kyushu and at about 35°N latitude, level with central Honshu, the largest of the Japanese islands, it turns to the east and meets the cold Oyashio. The combined currents continue eastward into the North Pacific Ocean as the *Kuroshio Extension*, which finally joins the North Pacific Current. At about 170°W longitude, a large part of the Kuroshio water flows southward in a large eddy, called the *Kuroshio Countercurrent*, which joins the North Equatorial Current.

A typical western boundary current, the Kuroshio is less than 80 kilometers (50 miles) wide, only about 400 meters (1310 feet) deep, and fast, flowing at speeds ranging from 2 to 11 kilometers (1.2 to 6.8 miles) per hour. The current is strongest in summer. It carries warm water, with an average temperature of about 20°C (68°F). Its salinity, of about 34 practical salinity units (psu), is a little below the average for seawater (35 psu).

The warm water of the Kuroshio has a marked effect on the Japanese climate. South of 38°N water evaporating from it adds to the high humidity and heavy rain of the summer monsoon. Its influence is felt as far away as British Columbia, which has a milder climate than its latitude (49 to 60°N) would suggest. Dense sea fogs are common where the Kuroshio and Oyashio meet.

Michael Allaby

FURTHER READING

Kendrew, W. G. *The Climates of the Continents,* 5th ed. Oxford: Clarendon Press, 1961.

King, Cuchlaine A. M. *Introduction to Physical and Biological Oceanography.* London: Edward Arnold; New York: Crane, Russak, 1975.

Sellers, William D. *Physical Climatology.* Chicago: University of Chicago Press, 1965.

RELATED ARTICLES

Boundary Current; Monsoon; Oyashio; Salinity; Sea of Japan

Labrador Current

The Labrador Current forms part of the circulatory gyre of the North Atlantic Ocean. The current originates in Davis Strait, at the southern end of Baffin Bay between northwestern Greenland (Kalaallit Nunaat) and Baffin Island, Canada, where three currents meet. The West Greenland Current flows northward along the eastern side of Baffin Bay. It turns at the northern end of Baffin Bay and flows south along the western side of the bay. At the southern end of Baffin Island, this current is joined by the Baffin Island Current, flowing south from Baffin Island, and by water flowing out of Hudson Bay through the Hudson Strait. These currents merge to form the Labrador Current.

The water of the Labrador Current is cold, with an average temperature of −1.7°C (29°F), and because of the fresh water entering it from the surrounding land, especially Greenland, its salinity is low, averaging 30 to 34 practical salinity units (psu). It is a deep current, but it flows above the continental shelf, which limits its depth to a maximum of about 600 meters (2000 feet). The current transports between 3.5 million and 5.4 million cubic meters (124 million to 190 million cubic feet) of water per second.

In the region of the Grand Banks, to the southwest of Newfoundland, the cold water of the Labrador Current meets the warm water of the Gulf Stream. Relatively warm, moist air

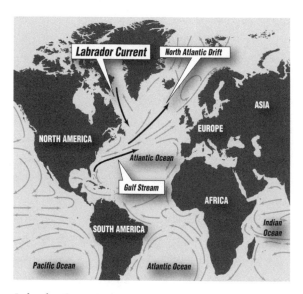

Labrador Current.

above the Gulf Stream moves over the much colder surface water of the Labrador Current. This reduces the air temperature to below the dewpoint, causing water vapor to condense, forming advection fog and making this one of the foggiest areas in the world, with fog occurring about 180 days in the year.

Contact with the Labrador Current also chills air that moves westward, toward the coast of Newfoundland, Labrador, and northern Québec. Southern Labrador is at about the same latitude as Liverpool, but frost is common in every month except July, and the 15°C (59°F) isotherm, marking the average July temperature, passes well to the south of the island of Newfoundland.

The Labrador Current meanders as it flows southward, collecting many icebergs. Icebergs that enter the sea from glaciers along the southern third of the eastern coast of Greenland are carried southward by the East Greenland Current, around the southern tip of Greenland, and northward along the western coast, carried by the West Greenland Current. They are then carried southward, parallel to the coast of Baffin Island, and finally join the Labrador Current. Once they are moving southward, the icebergs travel between 20 and 40 kilometers (12 to 25 miles) per day. Most icebergs melt when they enter the warmer water of the Gulf Stream, but some drift farther south. In 1926, an iceberg reached the latitude of Bermuda.

Greenland glaciers release up to about 50,000 icebergs every year. About 800 of these are carried into the open ocean by the Labrador Current, and an average of 375 enter the North Atlantic to the south of Newfoundland, at latitude 48°N. Glaciers on the western coast produce more than those on the eastern coast. The Illulissat (Jakobshavn) Glacier is the most productive. It moves at about 20 meters (66 feet) per day and releases about 1350 icebergs every year. It was an iceberg from this glacier that drifted into the North Atlantic in 1912 and sank the *Titanic*.

Michael Allaby

FURTHER READING

Kendrew, W. G. *The Climates of the Continents*, 5th ed. Oxford: Clarendon Press, 1961.

Schneider, Stephen H., ed. *Encyclopedia of Climate and Weather*, 2 vols. New York: Oxford University Press, 1996.

USEFUL WEB SITES

"How Do the Labrador and Gulf Stream Currents Affect Icebergs in the North Atlantic Ocean?" <http://www.uscg.mil/lantarea/iip/faq/faq12.html>.

RELATED ARTICLES

Grand Banks; Gulf Stream; Gyre; Labrador Sea; Salinity

Labrador Sea

The Labrador Sea is a northern extension of the Atlantic Ocean. It is bounded to the west by the coast of Labrador and to the east by Greenland. The southern boundary is a line from the southern tip of Greenland to Cape St. Charles on the northern side of Belle Isle Strait. The northern boundary is the 66°N latitude line that joins Greenland and Baffin Island north of the Arctic Circle.

Seafloor topography includes a linear trough that is open to the southeast but is cut off to the north by a submarine ridge across Davis Strait. Depth increases from 800 meters (2625 feet) in the north to about 3700 meters (12,140 feet) in the southeastern part of the sea. Bottom sediments are mostly glacial marine sands and silts with abundant dropstones. The continental shelf is relatively narrow off the coast of Greenland, where the distance to the 200-meter (656-foot) contour is about 50 kilometers (30 miles). In contrast, the continental shelf off the coast of Labrador extends to about 100 kilometers (62 miles).

Circulation features include the West Greenland Current and the Labrador Current, which flow counterclockwise. Labrador Sea is part of the passageway through which low-salinity water flows out of the Arctic Ocean and into the Atlantic Ocean. This low-salinity Arctic Ocean water either is incorporated into subpolar gyre circulation and eventually, subtropical circulation, or is moved offshore into the Labrador and Irminger Seas. The resulting nearly homogeneous water mass, the Labrador Sea Water, has water temperatures of 3.0 to 3.6°C (37.4 to 38.5°F), salinities of 34.86 to 34.96 practical salinity units (psu), and high dissolved oxygen content.

Most of the eastern one-third of the Labrador Sea is ice-free the entire year except for a region along the coast of southwest Greenland. Because the Labrador Current carries many icebergs, the main shipping lanes are in the eastern part of the sea, where waters are navigable from midsummer to late fall.

Deanna Madison

FURTHER READING
Kennett, James P. *Marine Geology*. Englewood Cliffs, N.J.: Prentice Hall, 1982.
Rosenberg-Herman, Yvonne, ed. *Marine Geology and Oceanography of the Arctic Seas*. New York: Springer-Verlag, 1974.

RELATED ARTICLES
Gyre; Labrador Current; Salinity; Sea Fog; Water Mass

Lagoon

Lagoons are shallow coastal environments that are separated from the ocean by barrier islands or coral reefs. They usually have at least limited connection to the ocean by inlets, and most lagoons are oriented parallel to the shoreline with depths that are seldom more than a few meters (approximately 10 feet). Their waters can be highly saline or completely fresh. Lagoons differ from estuaries in that the latter usually form in the lower courses of drowned river valleys, where mixing of fresh and saline waters creates distinct patterns of estuarine circulation. Nearly 15 percent of the world's shoreline, including arid, humid, high-latitude, and low-latitude regions, is covered by lagoons; in the United States more than 75 percent of the shoreline along the east and Gulf coasts is fronted by barrier islands and backed by lagoons.

Lagoons are formed by rising sea level. They are best developed on gently sloping coastal plains that have been submerged by the late Quaternary sea-level rise (last 15,000 to 20,000 years) and are virtually absent on steep or rocky coasts, or along shorelines where the tide range is greater than about 4 meters (13 feet). Lagoon formation is tied intimately to barrier island processes since lagoons and barrier islands are two components of a coupled system. The extent to which lagoons are enclosed by barrier islands allows them to be classified as choked, restricted, or leaky. Choked lagoons, such as Lake St. Lucia, South Africa, have a single connection to the ocean and can become temporarily or permanently hypersaline (abnormally high salinity). Restricted lagoons, such as Lake Pontchartrain, Louisiana, have two or more connections and are influenced by tides as well as winds. Leaky lagoons, such as Wadden Zee, the Netherlands, have many wide tidal openings, strong tidal currents, and salinities that are similar to those in the adjacent ocean.

An especially interesting type of lagoon forms within circular coral reefs called *atolls*. These lagoons begin forming behind the reefs that grow upward as barriers around volcanic islands. As the islands become old and gradually sink beneath the sea, the reefs of coral remain, forming atolls that encircle the lagoons. Lagoons of this type, such as those on the islands of Bikini and Eniwetok, are most common in the Pacific Ocean.

Lagoons are dynamic and complicated. Wind-driven flow is important because they are so shallow, and tidal currents can be strong. Storms can quickly modify coastal lagoons by erosion and deposition of sediments, and benthic organisms can stabilize sediment by secreting mucus and destabilize sediments by creating tracks and burrows. Lagoons are also modified by human activities, especially those that affect water quality, such as high nutrient inputs that lead to hypoxia (low oxygen content of waters).

Most lagoons are gradually filling with sediments derived from small tributary rivers, the surrounding shoreline, overwash processes (washed across barrier islands by storms), tidal delta deposition (washed in through inlets by tidal processes), and in some cases, from wind-blown materials. As sedimentary deposits reach the intertidal level, they can be colonized by marsh or mangrove vegetation, thereby more efficiently trapping sediments and accelerating the rate of infilling. Because they are so shallow, lagoons are sensitive to fluctuations in sea level, and the rate of infilling is dependent primarily on the balance between sea-level change and sediment supply. Thus lagoons are not only geologically young, but also have the potential to be short-lived on geologic time scales.

John T. Wells

FURTHER READING

Barnes, R. S. K. *Coastal Lagoons: The Natural History of a Neglected Habitat.* Cambridge and New York: Cambridge University Press, 1980.

Bird, E. "Physical Setting and Geomorphology of Coastal Lagoons." In Bjorn Kjerfve, ed., *Coastal Lagoon Processes.* Amsterdam and New York: Elsevier Science, 1994.

Cooper, J. A. G. "Lagoons and Microtidal Coasts." In R. W. G. Carter and C. D. Woodroffe, eds., *Coastal Evolution: Late Quaternary Shoreline Morphodynamics.* Cambridge and New York: Cambridge University Press, 1994.

Isla, F. I. "Coastal Lagoons." In G. M. E. Perillo, ed., *Geomorphology and Sedimentology of Estuaries.* Amsterdam and New York: Elsevier Science, 1995.

Nichols, M. M. "Sediment Accumulation Rates and Relative Sea-Level Rise in Lagoons." *Marine Geology,* Vol. 88 (1989), pp. 201–219.

RELATED ARTICLES
Bay; Coastal Morphology; Shoreline Morphology

Land Breeze, see Sea Breeze, Land Breeze

Langmuir Circulation

Occasionally, streaks, called *windrows*, form on the surface of the sea when the wind speed exceeds about 6 knots [11 kilometers (7 miles) per hour]. These streaks are caused by Langmuir circulations and consist of air bubbles, plankton, organic films, or other flotsam that floats at the sea surface. They were discovered in 1938 by Irving Langmuir (1881–1957), who noticed long regular bands of *Sargassum* weed while crossing the Sargasso Sea. In addition to affecting the dispersal of surface particles, Langmuir circulations can deepen the surface mixed layer.

Langmuir circulations consist of counter-rotating vortices. These vortices have a horizontal axis that is aligned approximately in the direction of the wind. Neutrally buoyant particles follow a helical pattern along this vortex, alternately sinking and rising as they move downwind. Since adjoining vortices rotate in opposite directions, at the surface (and bottom), convergence and divergence regions alternate between pairs of vortices. If a surface particle has enough buoyancy so that it cannot sink, it is trapped at the surface in a convergence zone.

The surface streaks are aligned within 20° of the wind direction. If the wind shifts suddenly, the streaks can respond and change their direction within 10 minutes. The spacing of the convergence lines has a range of scales, and the mean spacing increases with the wind speed. The mean distance in meters between the convergence lines is about five times the wind speed in meters per second. The length of the windrows increases with wind speed and can range from meters to kilometers. At high wind speeds, "Y" branches can form downwind, with the arms of the "Y" at 30° to the upwind windrow. The circulation cells typically do not extend more than 3.6 meters (11.8 feet) in depth. They persist from several minutes to hours.

Langmuir cells are created by an instability that is forced through an interaction between the wind and the surface waves. The surface currents have greater downwind velocities in convergence zones. The downwelling velocity is approximately 0.85 percent of the wind speed.

Curtis A. Collins

FURTHER READING
Leibovich, S. "The Form and Dynamics of Langmuir Circulations." *Annual Review Fluid Mechanics,* Vol. 73 (1983), pp. 715–743.

Li, M., K. Zahariev, and C. Garrett. "The Role of Langmuir Circulation in the Deepening of the Ocean Surface Mixed Layer." *Science*, Vol. 270 (1995), pp. 1955–1957.

Weller, R. A., and J. F. Price. "Lagrangian Circulation within the Oceanic Mixed Layer." *Deep-Sea Research*, Vol. 35 (1988), pp. 711–747.

RELATED ARTICLES
Convergence; Divergence

La Niña

Often referred to as the cold phase of El Niño warming events, both El Niño and La Niña are part of the broader El Niño–Southern Oscillation (ENSO) cycle; ENSO is a major climatic event propagated by atmospheric pressure changes across the Pacific Ocean. In normal years a pattern of high atmospheric pressure over the eastern tropical Pacific Ocean and low atmospheric pressure over Indonesia and northern Australia causes the trade winds to blow from the eastern to western Pacific Ocean (or from high to low pressure). This difference in pressure is often measured in terms of a Southern Oscillation Index (SOI) by comparing the surface pressure in Tahiti (French Polynesia) to that in Darwin, Australia. El Niño years are associated with a low SOI value, when the difference in pressure between the two parts of the Pacific is lower than normal, resulting in weaker trade winds, increased sea surface temperatures, and other El Niño–related events. However, when the SOI value is high, such that the pressure is lower than normal over Indonesia and northern Australia, this results in stronger trade winds and the development of La Niña [also known as an *anti–El Niño* or *El Viejo* (meaning "the old one" in Spanish)].

During La Niña years, the eastern Pacific sea surface temperatures (SSTs) are colder than normal and extend farther west. SSTs can drop as much as 4°C (7°F) along the equatorial Pacific Ocean during a strong La Niña. Also, La Niña episodes disrupt normal patterns of rainfall and atmospheric circulation. Rainfall increases over Indonesia, Malaysia, and northern Australia. Wetter-than-normal conditions are also observed over northern South America (near Brazil) and southeastern Africa. The Indian monsoon is typically stronger during a La Niña year as well. Other regions, such as the west coast of South America and Gulf coast of North America, are drier then usual. Within the United States, northern states experience colder winters, the Pacific Northwest is colder and rainier, and midwestern and southeastern states become warmer and drier than normal. Whereas during El Niño years the jet stream over the United States is oriented west to east over northern Florida and the Gulf of Mexico, La Niña episodes result in the jet stream extending farther north. As a result, there is the potential for severe storms farther north and west during La Niña. Also, during La Niña years, scientists predict that hurricane activity increases substantially in the eastern United States and Caribbean.

La Niña episodes can persist for several (9 to 12) months, sometimes lasting for as long as two years. They do not always follow an El Niño event, and they are less frequent than their warmer counterparts; La Niñas occur only half as frequently as El Niños. The average ENSO cycle is between 3 and 5 years, although the interval in the historical record has varied between 2 and 7 years. The most recent La Niña episodes occurred in 1988, 1995, and 1998.

ENSO events are monitored via a variety of direct and indirect methods. Scientists monitor SSTs in the tropical, equatorial Pacific with a network of data buoys, research vessels, and satellites. The information obtained via monitoring is fed into a number of models and used to predict ENSO events. ENSO prediction of both warm and cold episodes is important not only to understand how this global system operates but also to provide affected nations with an advanced warning notice on how to prepare for and mitigate against the impending event.

Manoj Shivlani

Further Reading

Bigg, G. R. *The Oceans and Climate.* New York: Cambridge University Press, 1996.

Glantz, M. H. *Currents of Change: El Niño's Impact on Climate and Society.* New York: Cambridge University Press, 1996; 2nd ed., 2001.

Philander, S. G. *El Niño, La Niña, and the Southern Oscillation.* San Diego: Academic Press, 1990.

Pielke, R. A., and C. W. Landsea. "La Niña, El Niño, and Atlantic Hurricane Damages in the United States." *Bulletin of the American Meteorological Society,* Vol. 80 (1999), pp. 2027–2033.

Useful Web Sites

Climate Prediction Center. El Niño/La Niña home page. <http://www.cpc.ncep.noaa.gov/products/ analysis_monitoring/lanina/index.html>

National Oceanic and Atmospheric Administration. NOAA La Niña home page. <http://www.elnino.noaa.gov/lanina.html>.

Related Articles
El Niño

Laptev Sea

The Laptev Sea, with an area of 700,000 square kilometers (about 270,270 square miles), is primarily a continental shelf sea north of Siberia whose bottom topography breaks rather sharply toward the Arctic Ocean. It has an average depth of 578 meters (1896 feet) and greatest depth of 3385 meters (11,106 feet). Approximately 60 percent of the area is less than 100 meters (328 feet) deep. It stretches from the eastern coast of the islands of Severnaya Zemlya (North Land) and the Taymyr Peninsula at 95°E to the New Siberian Islands at 140°E, where it is connected to the East Siberian Sea by means of the Dmitri Laptev,

Eterikan, and Sannikov Straits. Its main port is at Tiksi, located close to where the Lena River flows into the sea, forming the extensive Lena River delta. The continental shelf of the Laptev Sea is characterized by fine-grained terriginous sediment derived from the geologically complex mainland Siberia and reflects the harsh continental climate, fluvial transport history, and current patterns of the area. The bottom topography of the shallow part of the sea is highly irregular, owing in large part to erosion from ancient rivers and glaciers. Most of the year the sea is covered with ice, with mean annual temperatures below about –13°C (9°F); during the months of August and September, large areas are ice free, due to melting that is partially induced by the inflow of warmer waters from the Olenek, Lena, and Yana Rivers. Significant river runoff into the Laptev Sea makes it an important freshwater source for the Arctic Ocean. During winter months the Laptev Sea is also known as the ice factory of the Arctic since large amounts of sea ice are formed on its continental shelf. In the wintertime, the water temperature just below the ice ranges from –1.8 to –0.8°C (28.8 to 30.6°F); in the ice-free regions in the summer, the surface water temperatures are just above freezing.

Philip Rabinowitz

Further Reading

Kassens, H., ed. *Laptev Sea System: Expeditions in 1994.* Bremerhaven, Germany: Alfred-Wegener-Institut Für Polar- und Meeresforschung, 1995; p. 195.

National Geographic Society. *National Geographic Atlas of the World.* Washington, D.C.: National Geographic Society, 1963; 7th ed., 1999, p.133.

Related Articles
Arctic Ocean; Kara Sea

Larvacean

Larvaceans (phylum Chordata, class Larvacea, also known as Appendicularia) are tadpolelike animals that live among the ocean plankton. They are closely related to sea squirts (subphylum Urochordata), but unlike sea squirts they retain the larval body form throughout life and do not metamorphose into a distinct adult form. Whereas sea squirts live on the seafloor as adults, larvaceans spend their entire lives among the plankton. Biologists think that larvaceans may have evolved from sea squirts by a process called *neoteny*, the acceleration of sexual development to such an extent that larvae become sexually mature.

Most larvaceans are about 6 millimeters (0.24 inch) in length and have transparent bodies. The heart, stomach, digestive system, and reproductive organs are located in the head. The long, muscular tail is used for movement. Unlike a sea squirt larva, a larvacean secretes and lives inside a large gelatinous structure called the *larvacean house* within which the animal can move freely. By beating its tail inside the house, the larvacean drives a current of water through the structure and out of a narrow exit hole, driving the house weakly through the water by jet propulsion. Filters in the house strain planktonic organisms from the water current, providing the larvacean with a supply of food. When the house becomes littered with feces or the filters clogged with detritus, the larvacean abandons the house and secretes a new one.

Larvaceans reproduce only sexually and are hermaphroditic. Sperm and egg cells are released into the open water, where fertilization takes place. The resulting embryos then grow into the characteristic, larvalike adults.

Larvaceans belong to the phylum Chordata, which also includes vertebrates such as mammals, reptiles, and fish. Like all chordates, larvaceans possess a distinctive rod of strengthening tissue (notochord) that runs along the back, pharyngeal gill slits, and a dorsal hollow nerve cord.

Ben Morgan

FURTHER READING

Brusca, Richard C., and Gary J. Brusca. *Invertebrates.* Sunderland, Mass.: Sinauer, 1990.

Postlethwait, John. *The Nature of Life.* New York: McGraw-Hill, 1989; 3rd ed., 1995.

RELATED ARTICLES

Chordata; Tunicate

Larvae

Larvae are immature forms of organisms that change in body structure (metamorphosis) before becoming adults. They are part of the life cycle of many marine organisms and are extremely important in the ocean environment, particularly in the benthos, which is the collective name for organisms living on or attached to the bottom of the ocean. Larvae of benthic organisms are part of the meroplankton, organisms that are plankton for only a portion of their life cycle and are carried by water currents. Species that have a larval stage benefit from water currents dispersing the larvae to areas where the species is not found. This also helps to reduce crowding in the larvae birth area. Larval settlement can determine the distribution and abundance of benthic invertebrates, and the larvae may be an important food source for other organisms. Where larvae settle is a key component of the community structure, since the adults will become part of the community. Some larvae will settle only where other adults are present, and others will not settle in areas where there are similar organisms.

There are several types of larvae. Planktotrophic larvae depend on feeding on other organisms in the plankton to provide energy. With this strategy, many eggs are produced and the larvae swim freely in the plankton. Planktotrophic larvae are typically found where the food source is reliable. The advantage of this strategy is that many young can be produced rather quickly; however, they are subjected to predation because by spending time in the plankton, they may be consumed. If there is not an adequate supply of food, they may not survive. Lecithotrophic larvae are born with an energy store known as *yolk*, and fewer are produced than planktotrophic larvae. Because they have their own energy store, they do not need to feed in the plankton. This strategy is common where food resources are limited and reduces the risk of predation. They do not, however, have as great a dispersal range as do planktotrophic larvae, because they are not present in the water column for any length of time. The nonpelagic larvae, or juveniles, do not have a free-swimming phase. Few individuals are produced, but they are equipped with large energy stores. There is a lower risk of predation and a shorter range of dispersal. This is a beneficial strategy where nutrients are limited.

Larval settlement is determined by many environmental factors. Larvae are able to delay settling until a favorable habitat is found. Chemicals, light, and water movements all play a role in where and when larvae settle. The presence of other adults of the same species also indicates a suitable habitat, and larvae will tend to settle where the species can survive.

Erin O'Donnell

FURTHER READING
Duxbury, Alison B., and Alyn C. Duxbury. *Fundamentals of Oceanography.* Dubuque, Iowa: Brown, 1993; 2nd ed., 1996.
Hall, Brian K., and Marvalee H. Wake, eds. *The Origin and Evolution of Larval Forms.* San Diego: Academic Press, 1999.
McEdward, Larry. *Ecology of Marine Invertebrate Larvae.* Boca Raton, Fla.: CRC Press, 1995.
Nybakken, James W. *Marine Biology: An Ecological Approach*, 5th ed. San Francisco: Benjamin Cummings, 2001.

RELATED ARTICLES
Benthos; Lecithotrophic Larvae; Meroplankton; Planktotrophic Larvae

Latent Heat, Fusion and Evaporation

The latent heat of evaporation and latent heat of fusion of water are of great importance in energy exchange processes between the ocean and atmosphere. The latent heat of evaporation (LHE) is the energy absorbed during the evaporation of a mass of liquid water or the energy released during the condensation of water vapor to a liquid. The LHE for seawater is 2490 kilojoules per kilogram (596 calories per gram) at 0°C (32°F); it decreases by 2.2 kilojoules per kilogram per degree Celsius (0.52 calorie per gram per degree Celsius) between 0 and 30°C (32 and 86°F). The value of 540 (calories per gram) usually given in textbooks is that at the boiling point (100°C or 212°F). In the ocean, evaporation occurs at temperatures in the range above. The LHE of water is the highest of all substances.

The latent heat of fusion (LHF) for pure water at 0°C (32°F) is 333 kilojoules per kilogram (79.7 calories per gram). The LHF for sea ice, which contains some salt, cannot be expressed as energy per mass of water and does not occur at a fixed temperature. The LHF of sea ice decreases to about 155 kilojoules per kilogram (37 calories per gram) for sea ice with a salinity of 10 practical salinity units (psu). The LHF for pure water is higher than that of any other liquid except ammonia.

These anomalously high thermal properties of water are caused by hydrogen bonding between the polar water molecules. This results in water structure consisting of clusters of water molecules in which the hydrogen bonds between molecules are made and broken millions of times a second. Thus water behaves as though its molecular weight is 20 times larger than its actual molecular weight of 18.

Without the anomalous thermal behavior of water, Earth's climate would be much different. Temperatures on the waterless Moon vary from

135°C (275°F) during the lunar day to −155°C (−247°F) during the lunar night. Temperature variations on Earth depend strongly on proximity to the ocean. Air temperatures along the California coast vary seasonally by only 10°C (18°F), while temperatures a few hundred miles inland in the desert vary from 0°C (32°F) in winter to 43°C (109°F) in summer.

The LHE is a quantity whose effects may affect us directly. The 540 calories per gram absorbed upon evaporation is used to great effect in evaporative air conditioners. The same effect may be felt in nature during meteorological microbursts, where rain falls into lower dry air, such as in afternoon rain showers in the desert in the southwestern United States. One gram of evaporating rainwater cools 54 grams (about 50 liters) of air by 10°C. This increases the air density to form pleasantly cool, sometimes strong, and potentially dangerous downdrafts.

The opposite effect occurs in hurricanes. North of the equator during late summer, where the upper ocean has been warmed to temperatures of 27°C (80.6°F) or greater, the high ocean temperatures result in humid surface-level airmasses. As tropical storms evolve, some become strong enough that rising air in their center expands, cools, and loses water vapor as rain. This adds the LHE back into the atmosphere, however, where the air again warms, ascends, and causes more water vapor to condense, releasing more LHE. This process continues until the excess water vapor is removed at high altitudes [10,000 meters (32,800 feet)]. In these situations hurricanes result. Hurricanes are perhaps the most powerful consequence of the anomalously high thermal properties of water, which are important in the global heat balance. Hurricanes and tropical storms are thought to be more important than warm ocean currents in transferring heat from the tropics to temperate latitudes.

William W. Broenkow

FURTHER READING

Gross, M. Grant. *Oceanography: A View of the Earth,* 6th ed. Upper Saddle River, N.J.: Prentice Hall, 1999.

Open University Course Team. *Seawater: Its Composition, Properties and Behavior.* Oxford: Pergamon Press, 1989.

Sverdrup, H. U., M. W. Johnson, and R. H. Fleming. *The Oceans, Their Physics, Chemistry and General Biology.* Englewood Cliffs, N.J.: Prentice Hall, 1942.

RELATED ARTICLES

Hurricane; Hydrosphere

Lateral Line

The lateral line is a sophisticated sensory system present in the skin of fishes. It detects vibrations produced by animals or objects in the vicinity, and thus gives a sense of touch at a distance. Fishes can detect predators, prey, or potential mates through their lateral line system without seeing, smelling, or touching them. A lateral line runs along both sides of a fish's body, often marked by a conspicuous dark or pale stripe in the skin. The lines are often continuous with a network of similar lines on the face and head. Water vibrations pass into a fluid-filled canal in the lateral line via a row of open pores in the skin. The vibrations cause tiny blobs of jelly, which are set into the walls of the canal, to wobble. These blobs of jelly, or *cupulas,* are the tips of sensory structures known as *neuromasts* or *lateral line organs.* Enclosed in each blob of jelly is a cluster of minute hairs linked to sensory cells in the base of the neuromast, and these sensory cells are in turn linked to the lateral line nerve, which runs along the fish's body. When a neuromast wobbles, the sensory cells send impulses along the lateral line nerve to the brain. Neuromasts are not only found inside lateral lines; some also exist freely on the body surface, although they are usually contained in shallow pits or canals.

All fishes have at least some neuromasts on the body. The lateral line system differs between fishes and is related to their mode of life. For example, fishes living in turbid environments (i.e., stream fishes) tend to have neuromasts located in canals. Those in still water may have no canals at all or minor pores. This is to maximize detection in the quiescent environment and minimize external stimulus in the turbid one. The lateral line provides fish with a sense that humans and other land animals do not possess. Due to its high density, water is an excellent conductor of vibrations, so the ability to detect these vibrations creates an extension of the sense of touch. The lateral line sense should not be confused with hearing—fish also possess inner ears, but these respond to vibrations of a different frequency.

Many fish can identify other animals from the pattern of vibrations they produce. Sharks, for example, respond to the pattern of vibrations caused by animals in distress. Scientists have found that depriving fishes of their lateral line sense causes them to bump into solid objects. It seems likely, therefore, that fish can feel solid objects at a distance by sensing changes in the water currents around them. Fish that swim in tight-knit schools probably depend in part on their lateral line sense to synchronize their movements and avoid collisions.

The human sense of balance is created by sensory cells within our inner ears that work in a similar way to lateral line organs. Indeed, some scientists have suggested our balance detectors originally evolved from the lateral line system of a distant aquatic ancestor, although evidence for this remains uncertain. Lateral lines are also found in the larvae of amphibians (tadpoles), but they usually disappear during metamorphosis into the adult form.

Ben Morgan

FURTHER READING

Banister, Keith, and Andrew Campbell. *The Encyclopaedia of Underwater Life*. London: Allen and Unwin, 1985.

Moyle, Peter B., and Joseph J. Cech. *Fishes: An Introduction to Ichthyology*. Englewood Cliffs, N.J.: Prentice Hall, 1982; 4th ed., Upper Saddle River, N.J.: Prentice Hall, 2000.

Nelson, Joseph S. *Fishes of the World*, 3rd ed. New York: Wiley, 1994.

Paxton, John R., and William N. Eschmeyer, eds. *Encyclopedia of Fishes*. San Diego: Academic Press, 1994.

RELATED ARTICLES
Ichthyology; Shark

Lau Basin

Rimming the western Pacific Ocean are many of the world's convergent plate boundaries and their island arcs, trenches, and marginal seas. Behind several island arcs are actively widening back-arc basins, including Lau Basin, where new ocean crust and lithosphere are being formed in a process similar to that at mid-ocean ridge spreading centers. It is thought that western Pacific back-arc basins form because of stretching at the trailing edge of the Asian and Indo-Australian Plates, which are moving generally westward, away from the western Pacific trenches. The trenches, formed where the Pacific Plate slides downward into the mantle, are immense troughs in which the island arcs of the retreating plates are stuck, causing those plates to be in tension. As a result, the island arcs are split apart into a volcanically active frontal arc ridge and a dormant remnant arc ridge left behind. In between, magma rises into the void to form new crust, typically with symmetric spreading centers much like those at mid-ocean ridges.

Lau Basin sits like a giant "V" north of New Zealand and east of the islands of Fiji. The left (or west) side is the Lau Ridge, whose top is crowned by the Lau Islands, a string of extinct volcano summits. Forming the right (or east) arm is the Tonga Ridge, which contains the Tofua Arc, a chain of active volcanoes fed by the

196

sinking Pacific Plate in the mantle below. Lau Basin sits between the two ridges. From its base near 25°S to its top near 15°S, the "V" stretches nearly 1100 kilometers (685 miles). The top is approximately 720 kilometers across (447 miles), whereas the bottom is 330 kilometers (205 miles) in width. Depths in the Lau Basin generally descend toward the basin center because of sediment aprons that cover the ridges on either side. Maximum depths are approximately 2500 meters (8200 feet). This is considerably shallower than depths of the abyssal Pacific Plate [approximately 5600 meters (18,370 feet)] and the Tonga Trench [9000 to 10,800 meters (29,530 to 35,430 feet)] immediately east of the basin.

During the last approximately 6 million years, Lau Basin formed by the splitting of an ancestral ridge into the Lau and Tonga Ridges. The two ridges opened like the blades of a pair of scissors, pivoting around a point near the confluence of the ridges south of the basin. At first, the splitting was taken up by stretching of the crust and lithosphere, but by about 4 million years ago, new crust was being formed in the basin at a spreading ridge. This opening continues today. The pace seems to have increased in the past million years and recent geodetic measurements give opening rates of approximately 16 centimeters (6 inches) per year at 16°S (the top of the basin).

William W. Sager

FURTHER READING

Hawkins, James W. "Evolution of the Lau Basin: Insights from ODP Leg 135." In Brian Taylor and James Natland, eds., *Active Marginal Basins of the Western Pacific.* Washington, D.C.: American Geophysical Union, 1995.

Hawkins, James W., et al. *Proceedings of the Ocean Drilling Program, Initial Reports,* Vol. 135. College Station, Texas: Ocean Drilling Program, 1992.

Taylor, Brian, Kirsten Zellmer, Fernando Martinez, and Andrew Goodliffe, "Sea-Floor Spreading in the Lau Back-Arc Basin." *Earth and Planetary Science Letters,* Vol. 144 (1996), pp. 35–40.

RELATED ARTICLES
Convergent Plate Boundary; Island Arc; Pacific Plate; Tonga Island Arc

Lecithotrophic Larvae

The production of lecithotrophic larvae represents one of many reproductive strategies used by marine invertebrates. Lecithotrophic larvae are free-swimming nonfeeding aquatic larvae that live in the water column and use egg yolk as an energy source; this nutritional mode distinguishes them from planktotrophic larvae, which are free-swimming forms that feed in the plankton during development. The production of lecithotrophic or planktotrophic larvae is called *indirect* development because the larval form is distinctly different from that of the adult; both types of larvae undergo metamorphosis to become an adult. In contrast, embryos that undergo direct development develop into adultlike juveniles without passing through a free-swimming larval stage. Some organisms brood embryos before releasing them as larvae, thereby exhibiting a mixture of the two developmental patterns. These descriptive terms are generally used in reference to benthic invertebrates, although midwater invertebrates exhibit similar strategies.

In general, organisms that produce lecithotrophic larvae release a relatively small number of yolk-rich eggs, and the eggs hatch into larvae that derive their energy from yolk. Lecithotrophic larvae spend a relatively short amount of time in the plankton and this pelagic phase is used mainly for dispersal. In contrast, organisms that produce planktotrophic larvae produce numerous tiny eggs with very little yolk. The eggs hatch rapidly into free-swimming larvae that spend a long time living and feeding in the plankton. Each strategy has advantages and disadvantages. Lecithotrophic larvae have a constant and dependable food supply (yolk) and are exposed to predators for a limited time. However, they require a large energy investment per egg, which limits the number of eggs that can be produced for a given amount of energy. In addition, the short time spent in the plankton limits dispersal. Planktotrophic larvae experience the disadvantages of depending on a patchy and unpredictable food source (the plankton) and being exposed to predators for a relatively longer time. However, the sheer numbers of energetically cheap eggs released may offset a higher relative plankton mortality, and a long time spent in the plankton results in wide dispersal.

Lecithotrophic and planktotrophic larvae comprise the meroplankton, which are the organisms that spend only a part of their life in the plankton. All major and most minor phyla have representatives that produce lecithotrophic and planktotrophic larvae. Although organisms that produce lecithotrophic larvae are found in all areas of the ocean, they are particularly common in cold-temperate waters and in the deep sea.

Lynn L. Lauerman

FURTHER READING
Nybakken, James W. *Marine Biology: An Ecological Approach*, 5th ed. San Francisco: Benjamin Cummings, 2001.
Smith, DeBoyd L., and Kevin B. Johnson. *A Guide to Marine Coastal Plankton and Marine Invertebrate Larvae*. Dubuque, Iowa: Kendall/Hunt, 1977; 2nd ed., 1996.

RELATED ARTICLES
Meroplankton; Planktotrophic Larvae

Leeward

Leeward is the direction toward which wind and waves travel, and *windward* (i.e., upwind) is the opposite direction (i.e., downwind). The term can refer to the sheltered sides of islands, peninsulas, and bays. The Leeward Islands of the Lesser Antilles derive their name from the prevailing east-to-west direction of the winds, which places the islands' location leeward, or downwind, of the Windward Islands.

Wave and weather differences on leeward shores strongly influence coastal morphology. The protected leeward shores of islands are sites of sediment deposition, while wind and wave erosion can dominate windward shores. Leeward shores are more likely to be where beaches are composed of fine-grained sediments and where salt marshes or mangrove forests develop. Large, mountainous islands that interrupt prevailing wind patterns can have distinctive windward (wetter) and leeward (dryer) climates. As a result, the vegetation and weathering of land on the leeward sides of these islands can differ significantly from that on their windward coasts.

On coral reefs, leeward areas may be termed *back reef environments*. These areas are sites of reef lagoons and protected waters. A coral reef dissipates wave energy from windward to leeward. This water movement results in characteristic zonation patterns over the shallow-water areas of a reef. Leeward from the windward reef margin is the algal ridge, the reef flat, and a shallow coral zone that grades into sand deposits as water deepens. On the leeward margin of atolls, this zonation pattern may be less distinct, due to lower wave energy. The sheltered leeward areas and lagoons of reefs are often habitats for large fish populations and prolific coral growth. The calm conditions on leeward reef flats often accumulate reef sediments into intertidal sand banks and islands.

William E. Kiene

FURTHER READING
Fairbridge, Rhodes W., ed. *Encyclopedia of Earth Sciences*, Vol. 3, *The Encyclopedia of Geomorphology*. New York: Reinhold, 1968.
Hopley, David. *The Geomorphology of the Great Barrier Reef: Quaternary Development of Coral Reefs*. New York: Wiley, 1982.

RELATED ARTICLES
Coral Reef

Lichen

Lichens are slow-growing and mutualistic symbiotic associations and can be found in the upper intertidal zone in marine ecosystems. They are also abundant in terrestrial, or land, ecosystems. Lichens are actually comprised of two organisms, a fungus and a green alga or a cyanobacterium, with the fungal portion comprising the majority of the lichen. Lichens represent one of the many symbiotic relationships present in the marine environment. In a symbiotic association known as *mutualism*, both organisms benefit from each other, although some researchers suggest that the alga is parasitized by the fungus. In the case of the lichen, the fungus provides water, minerals, and protection from intense light to the alga or cyanobacterium, while the alga photosynthesizes and provides food in the form of sugars to the fungus. The fungus absorbs the sugars from the algal cells with specialized structures called *haustoria*.

The genus *Verrucaria* encrusts rocks on shores and forms a black tarlike crust. It is olive-brown to black in color and conspicuous on temperate rocky shores. Marine lichens may be completely out of the water for weeks but are able to survive because fungal cells store water and keep the photosynthetic cells moist. Because lichens can *desiccate*, or dry out, and then rehydrate, they are able to live for a long time. In some conditions the photosynthetic cell is able to survive without the fungus, but the fungus can never survive alone.

Lichens can exist in three forms. *Crustose forms* resemble crusts that cover rocks and other hard surfaces; *fruticose lichens* are branching forms that resemble shrubs; and *foliose forms* are shaped like leaves. The body of the lichen is composed of the *hyphae*, threadlike structures that make up the fungus. Photosynthetic cells are located near the hyphae. Lichens reproduce by *soredia*, which are clumps of hyphae and photosynthetic cells. The soredia are very small and are located on the surface of the lichen. They disperse by wind or rain. Lichens will then form from the soredia if environmental conditions are favorable.

Lichens are important in the primary succession of plants. They are able to survive on surfaces on which plants cannot survive, by growing on barren surfaces such as rocks, and can provide a suitable surface on which other plants can grow. They release acids that break down rocks and produce soil that is enriched by other decaying lichens, thereby enabling plants to grow. Lichens are extremely sensitive to air pollution, probably because they are not able to excrete toxins. They will not grow in polluted areas and therefore have become indicators of toxic elements in the environment.

Erin O'Donnell

FURTHER READING
Ahmadjian, Vernon. *The Lichen Symbiosis.* Waltham, Mass.: Blaisdell, 1967.
Gosner, Kenneth L. *A Field Guide to the Atlantic Seashore: Invertebrates and Seaweeds of the Atlantic Coast From the Bay of Fundy to Cape Hatteras.* Boston: Houghton Mifflin, 1978.
Muller, Walter H. *Botany: A Functional Approach.* New York: Macmillan, 1963; 4th ed., 1979.
Solomon, Eldra P., Linda R. Berg, Diana W. Martin, and Claude Ville. *Biology.* Philadelphia: Saunders, 1985; 5th ed., Fort Worth, Texas: Saunders, 1999.
Wilson, Carl L. *Botany.* New York: Dryden Press, 1952; 5th ed., with Walter E. Loomis, and Taylor A. Steeves, New York and London: Holt, Rinehart and Winston, 1971.

RELATED ARTICLES
Algae; Cyanobacteria; Marine Fungi; Mutualism

Light Attenuation

Attenuation is a measure of the reduction in light energy with distance from the light source. The portion of solar energy that reaches the ocean's surface as visible light is very important in the ocean. It provides the energy to heat the upper layers of the ocean as well as that needed for plants to grow. An understanding of how light is attenuated in the ocean will allow prediction of rates of heating and plant growth with depth.

Visible light is bounded by wavelengths from 400 to about 700 nanometers (a nanometer is 10^{-9} meter) that correspond to blue and red light, respectively. The light that reaches the ocean's surface passes through the atmosphere, where it is attenuated so that much of it becomes diffuse sky radiation and does not have a point source. In the ocean, light energy decreases exponentially with depth, z. Irradiance, E, is defined as the flux of light energy normal to the horizontal. Units of irradiance are watts per square meter. The attenuation, α, is the rate at which the irradiance decreases, $E_2/E_1 = e^{\alpha(z_2 - z_1)}$, where the subscripts refer to different depths.

Light is attenuated in the ocean due to spreading, scattering, and absorption. Spreading can be ignored for solar radiation, and it is assumed that the sea surface is evenly illuminated. Light is absorbed and scattered by both molecules and particulate matter. In the open ocean, absorption and scattering increases with decreasing wavelength. Molecular scattering is inversely proportional to the fourth power of the wavelength, so that blue light is scattered much more than red light, and this is partly responsible for the deep blue of the open ocean. Absorption is significantly greater than scattering.

Since absorption and scattering depend on wavelength, so does the attenuation, but it is strongly modified by increased biological activity and particulate matter. In the open ocean, the attenuation coefficients for blue and green light are about 0.02 per meter (about 0.07 per foot) compared to 0.2 per meter (about 0.7 per foot) for red light. This means that 82 percent of the blue-green light incident at the sea surface would still be present at 10 meters (about 33 feet), whereas only 14 percent of the red light would be present. The rapid disappearance of red light in the upper

ocean means that at depth, red objects appear to be black. Compared to sound, the attenuation for light is very high; for example, blue light in clear water is attenuated about 10^5 more than a 1000-hertz acoustic pulse.

In coastal waters, organic material in the water absorbs the blue light so that yellow and green light is able to penetrate to greater depth than the blue light. For turbid coastal waters, a typical minimum attenuation is 0.4 per meter (about 1.3 per foot) for yellow light and 0.7 per meter (about 2.3 per foot) for blue light. Note that both of these attenuation coefficients are greater than those for the open ocean, so that light is absorbed much more rapidly in coastal waters.

The attenuation of light with depth is measured with a radiometer that is lowered by wire into the ocean. To ensure that attenuation is measured in a meaningful and reproducible way, radiometers must be equipped with filters so that they measure only one color of light. An even simpler measurement of the extinction of light with depth can be made with a Secchi disk. A Secchi disk is a 30-centimeter (1-foot)-diameter white plate that is lowered horizontally into the ocean, whose depth where the disk first disappears from view is recorded.

Curtis A. Collins

FURTHER READING
Mobley, C. D. *Light and Water: Radiative Transfer in Natural Waters*. San Diego: Academic Press, 1994.
Williams, J. "Optical Properties of the Sea." *United States Naval Institute Series in Oceanography*, 1970.

RELATED ARTICLES
Radiometer; Secchi Disk

Light–Dark Bottle Method

The rate of primary production is usually reported in grams of organic carbon fixed by photosynthesis in a square meter of sea surface water per day or per year. Developed in the 1920s, the first method designed to measure productivity in the oceans was the light–dark bottle method, also called the *Gran method*. Water samples were collected from specific depths, poured into pairs of light (transparent) and dark (opaque) bottles, and replaced at depth for an incubation period. Before incubation, the sample water was measured and assumed to be equal to that in the incubation bottles. After incubation, the samples were brought back to the surface and the oxygen content was measured. Photosynthesis occurred in the light bottles but not in the dark bottles (because there was no light). Therefore, increased oxygen content in the light bottles represented the growth of photosynthetic organisms inside the bottle. Net production was calculated by subtracting the initial oxygen content from the final oxygen content. In the dark bottles, the decreases in the initial dissolved oxygen corresponded to respiration (calculated by subtracting the final oxygen content from the initial amount). Gross production, the total amount of photosynthesis that occurred during incubation, was calculated by adding the respiration to net production.

This method suffers from limitations. For example, photosynthetic organisms do not live in bottles, so the bottle method fails to account for water mixing and other phenomena that usually occur in the natural environment. Another problem is that the zooplankton (which are not primary producers) in the water samples trapped in the bottles also consume oxygen, which distorts the final calculation of net production. A more modern way of measuring primary production is to use radioactive carbon (^{14}C) in the *^{14}C method*. Known quantities of radioactive-labeled bicarbonate are injected into paired light and dark bottles. After an incubation period, the amount of radioactive carbon incorporated into the phytoplankton is measured, and the net production is calculated using a conversion factor. Satellites that use color to measure chlorophyll are also used to measure production on

a global scale. Ocean color satellites can now map global distributions of near-surface phytoplankton pigments. Because primary production is correlated to pigment concentration, primary productivity rates can also be inferred.

Kristen M. Kusek

FURTHER READING
Castro, P., and M. E. Huber. *Marine Biology,* 3rd ed. Boston: McGraw-Hill, 2000.
Falkowski, P. G., ed. *Primary Productivity in the Sea.* New York: Plenum Press, 1980.
Nybakken, James W. *Marine Biology: An Ecological Approach,* 5th ed. San Francisco: Benjamin Cummings, 2001.
Thurman, Harold V., and E. A. Burton. *Introductory Oceanography,* 9th ed. Upper Saddle River, N.J. Prentice Hall, 2001.

RELATED ARTICLES
Primary Productivity

Light Transmission

Light is transmitted relatively short distances in seawater. In the clearest ocean waters, only about 20 percent of blue-green light [500 nanometers (nm), a nanometer being one billionth of a meter] penetrates to 100 meters (328 feet). At this depth virtually all of the blue-violet light (400 nanometers) and red light (>600 nanometers) has been absorbed. Infrared wavelengths (>700 nanometers) are absorbed in the upper meter, as are ultraviolet (<400 nanometers) rays.

The transmission properties of light in the sea are important in phytoplankton ecology, underwater visibility, and as a tracer of suspended sediments. In the past 20 years the field of optical oceanography has developed quickly, due to satellite remote sensing of ocean-wide phytoplankton distributions and to biological oceanographers' efforts to better understand phytoplankton production from shipboard measurements. The photic zone is limited to the

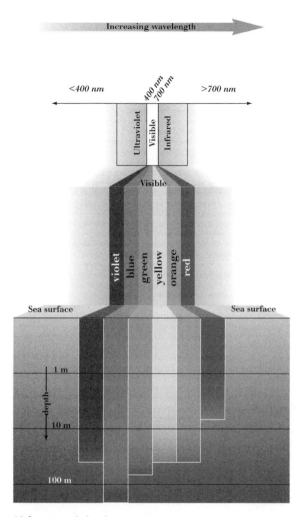

Light transmission in seawater.

upper 100 meters or so (about 328 feet) in the open ocean to a few meters in the coastal ocean. In sediment-laden estuaries and rivers, the photic zone may be restricted to a meter or two. Most oceanographic light transmission studies are limited to these depths.

Photons in the visible wavelengths of light between 400 nanometers (violet) and 700 nanometers (red) are absorbed and scattered by water molecules, phytoplankton, and suspended sediments. The remaining photons that are transmitted through a water layer give pure seawater its beautiful purple-blue color. This can be seen only in the center of ocean gyres, where the water contains only small amounts of particulate and dissolved matter. Water strongly absorbs red light

(above 600 nanometers), causing the deep blue coloration. In most near-shore waters, seawater takes on a greenish or brownish tinge. The green coloration is due to the presence of phytoplankton containing chlorophyll and other pigments that absorb blue light (450 nanometers), allowing green light (520 nanometers) to be scattered back to the viewer (again, water molecules absorb red wavelengths). The brown coloration is caused by suspended sediments that reflect light of all visible wavelengths. In nearshore areas, especially near rivers, suspended sediments block the transmission past a depth of a few centimeters or meters. These waters usually contain phytoplankton, with their blue-absorbing pigments. Thus green and red wavelengths are scattered back to the viewer, who observes a brown color.

Oceanographers use several instruments to measure light transmission with the purpose of understanding the distribution of materials (phytoplankton and suspended sediments) that decrease water clarity. The simplest device is the *Secchi disk,* a weighted white disk suspended from a line. The depth at which the disk disappears from the shipboard observer gives a measure of light transmission. In sediment-free waters Secchi measurements give an approximate estimate of phytoplankton abundance.

Because light transmission depends strongly on wavelength, light-measuring instruments use filters or diffraction grating spectrographs to measure at specific wavelengths. Light transmission may be measured precisely using an irradiance meter. This contains a photocell or an array of photocells that measure the intensity of sunlight. As the meter is lowered from the surface to depths as great as 100 meters (328 feet), light levels decrease exponentially with increasing depth. If we call the surface irradiance or intensity 100 percent, the intensity might be 10 percent at 20 meters (66 feet), 1 percent at 40 meters (131 feet), and 0.1 percent at 60 meters (197 feet). From these changes oceanographers through complex calculations can determine concentrations of plankton pigments and suspended sediments that attenuate the light.

The beam transmissometer gives a more direct method to determine the vertical structure of light-attenuating materials. The beam transmissometer has its own light source. Historically, an incandescent lamp was used, but current transmissometers use a light-emitting diode (LED). Since the instrument does not depend on sunlight, the transmissometer can be used at all depths. The light source is directed toward a photo diode detector over a short path usually 1 to 0.1 meter (3.3 feet to 0.33 foot). As the transmissometer is lowered over the side of a ship, turbid layers are indicated by low light transmission values, and particle-free water is indicated by high light transmission. In nearshore waters light transmission may be affected by high concentrations of dissolved organic matter that give water a tea coloration.

William W. Broenkow

FURTHER READING

Gross, M. Grant. *Oceanography: A View of the Earth.* Englewood Cliffs, N.J.: Prentice Hall, 1987.

Mobley, Curtis D. *Light and Water: Radiative Transfer in Natural Waters.* San Diego: Academic Press, 1994.

Open University Course Team. *Seawater: Its Composition, Properties, and Behaviour,* Vol. 2. Oxford: Pergamon Press, 1991.

RELATED ARTICLES

Chlorophyll; Dissolved Organic Matter; Phytoplankton; Secchi Disk

Lithospheric Plate, see Plate Tectonics

Lithothamnion Ridge

Lithothamnion ridge is an old term for what is commonly referred to as the *algal ridge* or *algal pavement* of a coral reef. The term *Lithothamnion* was often used as a generic term for all coralline algae. The observation that many intertidal areas of coral reefs were dominated by coralline algae led to the use of the term *Lithothamnion Ridge* for the hard, wave-resistant pavements on the windward intertidal margins of many Pacific and some western Atlantic coral reefs. In fact, these pavements are composed of a mixture of algal genera, which can include *Neogonolithon, Porolithon,* and *Lithophyllum,* among others. The genus *Lithothamnion* (*Lithothamnium*) is a minor component on algal ridges and can be found in cryptic habitats as well as deep reef environments [30 to 80 meters (100 to 260 feet) water depth].

Exposed to strong water movement, calcareous coralline algae exhibit rapid growth, and together with extensive calcium carbonate lithification they cement the intertidal surfaces of coral reefs into hard limestone conglomerates and pavements. In intertidal areas of the windward margin (sometimes called the *reef crest*), the algal ridge is up to 0.6 meter (2 feet) above the level of low tide. It often forms a series of stepped terraces, a few centimeters to tens of centimeters high, gently sloping seaward. Exposed to heavy surf, algal ridges are subjected to intricate cycles of construction and destruction by physical and biological forces that create buttresses and surge channels. Coralline algal encrustations grow as thick veneers on the heavily cemented surfaces of the ridge, while borers, grazing sea urchins, and chitons bioerode the limestone. The grazers not only cause bioerosion, but along with gastropods and fishes (feeding during high tides) they also can enhance the growth of the coralline algae by keeping their surfaces free of epiphytes.

The algal ridge is an important site of nutrient addition and sediment production on coral reefs. Cyanobacteria, algae, and other organisms in these windward environments acquire carbon, nitrogen, and other nutrients. These organisms are eroded by waves or are consumed by grazers. The nutrients, in particulate and dissolved forms, are then transported by water movement into lee-ward environments, where they are used by other organisms. Calcium carbonate sediments are also produced on the algal ridge by wave erosion and by the proliferation of large numbers of benthic foraminifera. These sediments are transported off the algal ridge by water movement and can make a significant contribution to the sediments that accumulate on reef flats, in lagoons, and in lee-ward environments of a reef.

William E. Kiene

FURTHER READING
Birkeland, C., ed. *Life and Death of Coral Reefs.* New York: Chapman and Hall, 1997.
Hopley, David. *The Geomorphology of the Great Barrier Reef: Quaternary Development of Coral Reefs.* New York: Wiley, 1982.
Jones, O. A., and R. Endean, eds. *Biology and Geology of Coral Reefs,* 4 vols. New York: Academic Press, 1973–77.
Karlson, R. H. *Dynamics of Coral Communities.* Boston: Kluwer Academic, 1999.

RELATED ARTICLES
Coralline Algae; Coral Reef; Surge Channel

Littoral Zone

The littoral zone can be described broadly as the region where ocean and land meet. However, scientists from different disciplines have defined the boundaries of the littoral zone differently depending on their interests. Biologists limit the littoral zone to the area between the lowest and highest tide levels: that is, all areas that are sometimes under water and sometimes in the air. This is also called the *intertidal zone* and describes the transition between terrestrial and oceanic habitats. For the biologist, the littoral zone includes rocky coastlines, sandy beaches, and muddy shores, and is generally characterized by high nutrient levels, plentiful sunlight, and often, extreme variation in physical parameters such as temperature, oxygen,

and air exposure. The resulting variety of microenvironments has led to a wonderful diversity of plant and animal forms. These include the organisms of the rocky shore, which are adapted to survive the onslaught of waves and are often firmly attached to the substrate, as well as the sandy shore, which is characterized by a lack of sessile animals and plants. Protected muddy shores are home to seagrasses and act as nurseries for many marine animals. The littoral zone is one of the richest habitats in the world, where variation in the physical environment has allowed species from many different phyla to coexist.

In contrast to biologists, geologists and physical scientists (who study the rocks, sand, waves, and water currents) define the littoral zone as including the beach and part of the continental shelf, where sediments are moved by waves. This is also referred to as the *nearshore zone* and includes the biologists' littoral and part of the biologists' *sublittoral zones*. To physical scientists, the littoral zone is characterized by breaking waves, which generate currents and turbulence. Waves, which are formed by wind blowing across the ocean surface, can travel thousands of miles across the deep ocean without losing energy. However, in water depths less than about 10 to 20 meters (33 to 66 feet), waves on the surface begin to drag on the seafloor, and energy is expended through friction, changing wave shape, moving sediment, and breaking. As a result, almost all wave energy is dissipated in the littoral zone, and this constant attack by waves shapes the physical environment at the seashore. Features of the littoral zone include sandbars, bar troughs, berms, and the beach face, or *swash zone*. Important littoral zone processes include shore-parallel or alongshore currents, undertow and rip currents, erosion of beaches and sea cliffs, and the development of barrier islands.

People have always been attracted to the seashore as a source of food, recreation, and commerce, and as our population has grown (more than half the U.S. population lives within 80 kilometers (50 miles) of the coast), human impacts on the littoral zone have increased. Because of the high energy and variability of the littoral zone, humans have attempted to control erosion and deposition using, for example, seawalls, jetties, and dredging. The biological richness of the littoral zone has been affected by runoff of pollutants, including sewage, agricultural fertilizers, and pesticides, and the draining of coastal wetlands for development and flood control.

Edith Gallagher

FURTHER READING

Bascom, Willard. *Waves and Beaches: The Dynamics of the Ocean Surface.* Garden City, N.Y.: Anchor Books, 1964.

Denny, Mark W. *Biology and Mechanics of the Wave Swept Environment.* Princeton, N.J.: Princeton University Press, 1988.

Komar, Paul D. *Beach Processes and Sedimentation.* Englewood Cliffs, N.J.: Prentice Hall, 1976.

Pinet, Paul R. *Invitation to Oceanography.* Minneapolis/St. Paul, Minn.: West Publishing, 1996; 2nd ed., Sudbury, Mass.: Jones and Bartlett, 1998.

Ricketts, Edward F., and Jack Calvin. *Between Pacific Tides,* 4th ed., rev. by Joel W. Hedgpeth. Stanford, Calif.: Stanford University Press, 1968.

RELATED ARTICLES

Littoral Zone Processes; Surf Zone; Swash Zone

Littoral Zone Processes

Littoral zone processes—the changing of waves as they approach shore, the back-and-forth flow under waves, the generation of currents, the movement of sediment—all affect the beach environment in many ways. It is these processes that determine whether a beach will erode or build up, whether a cliff will retreat from attack by waves, and whether a harbor will silt in. Littoral zone processes also affect the form of a beach, where we are able to build structures on the coast, and where and how we use the beach

for recreation. The littoral zone is the region from the highest part of the beach to depths where the movement of sediment by waves is less vigorous [usually, 10 to 20 meters (33 to 66 feet), although it can be deeper during large storms]. The littoral zone includes the beach, the beach face, longshore troughs, sandbars if present, and the offshore. Wave processes are the primary processes in the littoral zone.

Wave Processes in the Littoral Zone

As waves generated offshore move toward the coast, they are affected by the seafloor. Waves begin to "feel" bottom when the water depth is about equal to one-half the wavelength (the distance between two successive wave crests), and their form and movement are altered by the presence of the bottom. The bottom causes the wave to refract (bend), shoal (get larger), and eventually, to break.

Wave refraction occurs when waves approach the coast at an angle. Because the depth contours (lines of equal depth) offshore tend to parallel the shoreline, the part of the wave crest that is farthest from shore is in deeper water than the part closer to shore. Waves in the littoral zone move faster in deeper water. Different parts of the wave crest move at different speeds because they are in different water depths. The difference in speed causes the part farther out to catch up with the part closer to shore. The wave crest bends, or refracts, as the part in deeper water catches up to the part in shallower water. Waves tend to refract to bring the crests parallel to the depth contours (usually, shore parallel). When traveling toward a headland or point of land, wave refraction will cause the waves to bend toward the headland or point. Refraction creates a wave geometry that produces good surfing conditions in these areas (point breaks). Another characteristic of refraction is that it affects waves with longer wavelengths more than those with shorter wavelengths because refraction, for longer wavelengths, begins in deeper water, which is farther offshore. Because the wavelength is longer for longer-period (the time for two wave crests to pass a point) waves, they refract more than shorter-period waves.

Wave shoaling—the increase in the height of a wave as it moves into shallower water—is also greater for waves with longer wavelengths. This increase is caused by a rearrangement of energy. The energy of the wave is the same in both deeper and shallower water; it is just distributed differently. Moving into shallower water, the speed of the wave decreases and its wavelength decreases. To keep the energy flow constant, the wave height increases.

The height of the wave will continue to increase for as long as it is stable. When the wave becomes unstable, the top of the crest begins to collapse, and it breaks. Breaking is caused either by the shape becoming too steep or by the top part of the wave moving faster toward the shore than the bottom part. Breaking that is gentle is called *spilling*. Breaking may be violent, as it is in plunging breakers. This type of breaker is affected by the form of the wave offshore (steeper waves tend to plunge) and by the slope of the offshore (gentler slopes tend to create spilling breakers that lose their energy over a long distance as they break). The height of the breaking wave decreases as it moves inshore and loses energy. The region of wave breaking is called the *surf zone*. The process of breaking is important not only to surfers, but also to the generation of currents.

Wave-Generated Currents and Flows

Breaking waves pile water up onto the beach; this is called *setup*. Water leaving the beach generates offshore currents. The two primary types of offshore currents are undertow and rip currents. Undertow occurs when the setup returns offshore near the seabed. In an undertow system, water is moving onshore in the upper water column and offshore near the bed. The water piled up on the beach can also be concentrated into rip currents. Rip currents form where setup varies along the shore. Instead of moving offshore everywhere like undertow, the water first moves alongshore to an area where setup is less and then offshore in a concentrated region. Rip current velocities may exceed 3 meters (10 feet) per second. This is faster than a person can swim, and many people are killed needlessly by rip currents each year. People die by trying to fight the rip current and swim to shore against it. Rip currents are narrow, however, so if a person is caught in a rip current, simply swimming alongshore until out of it is advised. Once out of the rip current, waves push a swimmer toward shore.

Waves breaking at an angle to the shore generate longshore currents. The greater the height of the breaking waves and the greater the angle between the shore and the wave crests (up to 45°), the stronger the longshore current.

Both breaking and nonbreaking waves generate flow that changes direction from onshore to offshore during each wave. These currents, termed *wave oscillatory currents*, may be greater than 2 meters (6.6 feet) per second under large waves. Flow in oscillatory currents is onshore under the wave crest and offshore under the wave trough.

At the shore, waves also create flow that moves onshore and offshore. Water moves up the beach (*runup*) during each wave crest and down (*backwash* or *rundown*) during each trough. The combination of runup and backwash is called *swash*. The elevation of runup changes with the tide. At high tide, the swash zone is higher up the beach and runup is higher. Tides also create currents in the littoral zone. Interactions among waves may create large swash at long periods with runup elevations that vary alongshore. One type of long-period wave that affects swash is an edge wave.

Sediment Movement in the Littoral Zone

Currents generated by waves move sediment in the littoral zone. Swash moves sediment on beaches. Swash can either move sediment off-shore, causing the beach to erode, or move it landward, creating a berm. Swash approaching the beach at an angle moves sediment alongshore. During runup sediment moves both up the beach and alongshore; during backwash it moves down the beach. Swash moves sediment alongshore in zigzag pattern along the beach.

Sediment also moves alongshore in the surf zone when waves approach at an angle. Longshore currents generated by breaking waves work in concert with oscillatory currents to move sediment alongshore. The oscillatory currents lift the sediment into the water, and the longshore current moves it along the coast. The combination of longshore movement in the surf and swash zones is termed *littoral drift*. The direction of littoral drift is readily apparent when a barrier such as a groin or jetty interrupts the movement of sediment alongshore. The updrift side of the barrier will have a wider beach where sediment is trapped. The downdrift side of the barrier will have narrower beaches because its supply of sediment is interrupted.

Sediment movement across the littoral zone is also driven by wave-generated currents. Undertow moves sediment offshore from the beach and may create sandbars, shallow areas offshore, where it is deposited. Rip currents move sediment off the beach and deposit it outside the surf zone. As the waves shoal, their oscillatory currents have stronger onshore flow than offshore flow. The difference between onshore and offshore flow causes sediment to return to the beach. During calm periods (typically, summer), the beach grows as oscillatory currents under shoaling waves become the dominant mover of sediment.

Bruce E. Jaffe

FURTHER READING
Bascom, Willard. *Waves and Beaches: The Dynamics of the Ocean Surface.* Garden City, N.Y.: Anchor Books, 1964; rev. and updated, 1980.
Dean, Cornelia. *Against the Tide: The Battle for America's Beaches.* New York: Columbia University Press, 1999.
Komar, Paul D. *Beach Processes and Sedimentation.* Englewood Cliffs, N.J.: Prentice Hall, 1976.
———. ed. *CRC Handbook of Coastal Processes and Erosion.* Boca Raton, Fla.: CRC Press, 1983.
Short, Andrew, ed. *Handbook of Beach and Shoreface Morphodynamics.* New York: Wiley, 1999.

RELATED ARTICLES
Edge Wave; Littoral Zone; Rip Current; Swash Zone

Lobster

Lobsters belong to the crustacean order Decapoda, along with their close relatives crabs, crayfish, and shrimps. The most familiar species in the North Atlantic are members of the family Nephropidae, also known as true lobsters. These include the American lobster (*Homarus americanus*) and the Norwegian lobster (*Nephrops norvegicus*), both of which are edible and often sold alive. True lobsters vary in color from dark green to a striking blue, and turn red only when dropped in boiling water. In warm temperate and tropical waters, spiny lobsters of the family Palinuridae are abundant.

Lobsters have a segmented body protected by an external skeleton, which must be shed periodically for a lobster to grow. The head and thorax are fused together to form the *cephalothorax*, a structure covered by the *carapace*, a hard shield similar to the shell of a crab. The head bears a pair of movable eyes on stalks and two pairs of sensitive antennae (feelers), one pair of which may grow to a great length.

Running along a lobster's body are pairs of appendages (limbs) that serve a variety of functions. The small head appendages around the mouth are used for feeding and wafting water over the gills, which are situated between the carapace and the sides of the body. The thorax bears five pairs of large appendages, most of which serve as legs for walking on the seafloor. In true lobsters the three front pairs of legs are clawed, and the first pair of claws are enlarged (one claw usually being bigger than the other). Palinurid, spiny, and Spanish lobsters (all members of the infraorder Palinura) lack large front pincers, although some species have small claws.

The rear part of a lobster's body is the *abdomen*. Crabs have a small abdomen that folds tightly under the body, but lobsters have a long, flat, muscular abdomen that extends behind the thorax and ends in a wide tail fan. A sharp flex of the abdomen and fan gives a sudden burst of speed, enabling lobsters to dart quickly through the water to escape danger. The abdomen bears paired appendages called *swimmerets*, which are used for swimming and for brooding eggs.

Lobsters live on the seafloor, emerging at night to scavenge for dead fish and other organic detritus. Some species also prey on live animals or eat seaweed. The American lobster can grow up to 1 meter (3.3 feet) long and can weigh up to 18 kilograms (40 pounds), although most specimens that are harvested are much smaller than this. Shallow-water lobsters are caught in cagelike traps called lobster pots, which are baited with dead fish. Deepwater lobsters are caught by trawling. The edible parts are the fleshy claws and the muscular abdomen.

Ben Morgan

FURTHER READING

Brusca, Richard C., and Gary J. Brusca. *Invertebrates.* Sunderland, Mass.: Sinauer, 1990.

Fish, J. *A Student's Guide to the Seashore.* London and Boston: Unwin Hyman, 1989; 2nd ed., Cambridge and New York: Cambridge University Press, 1996.

Nybakken, James W. *Marine Biology: An Ecological Approach,* 5th ed. San Francisco: Benjamin Cummings, 2001.

Pechenik, Jan A. *Biology of the Invertebrates.* Boston: Prindle, Weber and Schmidt, 1985; 4th ed., Boston: McGraw-Hill, 2000.

RELATED ARTICLES

Arthropoda; Crustacea; Malacostraca

Lomonosov Ridge

Like some primordial seam left over from Earth's creation, the straight and narrow Lomonosov Ridge transects the Arctic Ocean basin from Siberia to North America, missing the North Pole by less than 100 kilometers (62 miles). This aseismic submarine ridge begins on the North American margin, in the Lincoln Sea, at the juncture of Greenland and Ellesmere Island (85°N, 60°W). After a short bend, it trends 1700 kilometers (1056 miles) straight across the Arctic Ocean, approximately along the 45°W–135°E meridian, ending on the Siberian margin north of Kotel'nyi Island (80°N, 145°E). The ridge rises approximately 3 kilometers (9843 feet) from the seafloor, separating the Makarov Abyssal Plain (also known as the Pole Abyssal Plain) on the European side from the Amundsen Abyssal Plain (also known as the Siberia Abyssal Plain) on the Alaska-Siberia side. Peaks along the ridge rise to summit depths of 837 to 1100 meters (2746 to 3609 feet) along the central region; the shallowest depths, slightly less than 500 meters (1640 feet), occur where the ridge meets the North American margin. The ridge varies from approximately 65 to 120 kilometers (40 to 75 miles) in width.

Discovered in 1948 by Soviet scientists making echo soundings, the Lomonosov Ridge is poorly mapped, as are most Arctic Ocean seafloor features, because the ice pack that covers that ocean makes geophysical surveys difficult. Nevertheless, geologic and geophysical data imply that the ridge is a continental sliver. Magnetic anomalies, used to reconstruct the history of the Arctic basin, suggest that the sliver was torn off northern Asia by seafloor spreading at a mid-ocean ridge, probably from the Kara and Barents Seas region. This separation is thought to have occurred early in the Cenozoic period, approximately 65 million to 56 million years ago.

William W. Sager

FURTHER READING

"Arctic Ocean Floor" (chart). Washington, D.C.:
    National Geographic Society, 1971.

Deitz, R. S., and G. Shumway. "Arctic Basin
    Geomorphology." *Geological Society of America
    Bulletin*, Vol. 72 (1961), pp. 1319–1329.

Herron, E. M., J. F. Dewey, and W. C. Pitman. "Plate
    Tectonics Model for the Evolution of the Arctic."
    Geology, Vol. 2 (1974), pp. 377–380.

Lawver, L. A., and C. R. Scotese. "A Review of Tectonic
    Models for the Evolution of the Canada Basin." In A.
    Grantz, L. Johnson, and J. F. Sweeney, eds., *The Arctic
    Ocean Region, Decade of North American Geology*,
    Vol. L. Boulder, Colo.: Geological Society of America,
    1990; pp. 593–618.

Perry, R. K., and H. S. Fleming. "Bathymetry of the
    Arctic Ocean" (chart). In A. Grantz, L. Johnson, and
    J. F. Sweeney, eds., *The Arctic Ocean Region, Decade of
    North American Geology*, Vol. L. Boulder, Colo.:
    Geological Society of America, 1990.

Wheeler, J. R., and J. F. Sweeney. "Ridges and Basins in
    the Central Arctic Ocean." In A. Grantz, L. Johnson,
    and J. F. Sweeney, eds., *The Arctic Ocean Region,
    Decade of North American Geology*, Vol. L. Boulder,
    Colo.: Geological Society of America, 1990;
    pp. 305–336.

RELATED ARTICLES

Arctic Ocean; Kara Sea; Magnetic Anomaly; Mid-Ocean
Ridge; Ocean Plateau; Seafloor Spreading

Longshore Current

The longshore current (also called the *littoral current*) is the flow of water parallel to the beach
within the surf zone. Most commonly, longshore
currents are caused by waves that break at an
angle relative to the beach. In the surf zone (the
region of breaking waves) water is pushed in the
direction of wave motion. If waves are coming
straight at the beach, this can cause an elevation in
the sea surface at the shoreline, called *setup*, and
this pile of water will escape the beach via narrow
rip currents. Longshore currents will often form
to feed rip currents, creating circulation cells. If
the waves are coming at the beach from an angle,

the water is pushed along the shoreline, causing a
longshore current. Longshore currents can also be
created by small changes in breaker height along a
stretch of coast. If waves are smaller in one area
(as in the shadow of an island or breakwater), they
will cause less setup than will larger waves some
distance away. This slight difference can cause
currents to flow from the area of higher waves to
lower waves. Similarly, tides and strong winds can
cause longshore currents.

Strong longshore currents can be 1 to 1.5
meters (3.3 to 5 feet) per second and can carry
swimmers long distances. Longshore currents are
very important to the movement of sediment
along the beach, called *littoral drift*. For example,
on the east coast of the United States, the littoral
drift is generally from north to south [with an
average rate of about 200,000 cubic meters
(7,100,000 cubic feet) per year], and the barrier
islands along this coast (and many others) are
particularly sensitive to interruptions in the littoral drift (e.g., jetties and dredged inlets).

Edith Gallagher

FURTHER READING

Bascom, Willard. *Waves and Beaches: The Dynamics of
    the Ocean Surface*. Garden City, N.Y.: Anchor Books,
    1964.

Komar, Paul D. *Beach Processes and Sedimentation*.
    Englewood Cliffs, N.J.: Prentice Hall, 1976.

Pinet, Paul R. *Invitation to Oceanography*.
    Minneapolis/St. Paul, Minn.: West, 1996; 2nd ed.,
    Sudbury, Mass.: Jones and Bartlett, 1998.

RELATED ARTICLES

Beach; Coastal Erosion; Littoral Zone Processes;
Rip Current; Surf Zone

Loran

Until about the middle of the twentieth century,
finding the location of a ship at sea was no easy
task. Prior to this, celestial navigation was
typically used, with a navigator laboriously

calculating a ship's whereabouts using a sextant to determine position relative to the Sun, planets, and stars. An obvious drawback is that position fixes are infrequent, especially if weather is inclement. With the rise of modern electronics, it became possible to develop navigation devices capable of more accurate and continuous fixes, and Loran is one such system that uses radio waves to triangulate a location.

Loran (long-range navigation) was developed to assist warships during and after World War II. Its operating principle is that a position fix can be determined from the time delays of radio signals sent from stations on shore. If two transmitters emit signals simultaneously or with a known delay, the time delay between signals will be constant on a line of position (LOP) that describes a hyperbola on Earth's surface. By adding another transmitter, another unique LOP can be determined, with a ship's position being at the intersection of the two hyperbolas. Early Loran systems required an operator to match two radio signal pulses on an oscilloscope manually to determine the required time delays. With improvements in electronics, compact receivers were designed to detect the radio pulses and calculate the offsets and position automatically.

Loran-C, a modern version of Loran, has been operated by the U.S. Coast Guard since 1958. It uses chains of radio stations operating near 100 kilohertz with transmission times controlled by atomic clocks. Typically, each Loran-C chain consists of a master station and up to four slave stations separated by distances of as much as 2000 kilometers (1240 miles). The master transmits a signal of nine pulses and then waits 40 to100 milliseconds before repeating. Slave stations emit eight pulses, the multiple pulses allowing for redundancy in the determination of time delays. Each station chain transmits with its own unique pulse repetition pattern to allow overlapping chains to operate simultaneously without interference. Loran-C station coverage includes the U.S. east and west coasts, the Gulf of Mexico and Caribbean Sea, the Gulf of Alaska and Aleutian Islands, the Hawaiian Islands, the North Atlantic Ocean, the Mediterranean Sea, the Red Sea, and the western Pacific Ocean.

Within about 1500 kilometers (930 miles) of a Loran-C station chain, positional accuracy is normally about 500 meters (1640 feet), depending on a number of factors, including LOP geometry, distance to the transmitters, and interference caused by radio-wave propagation anomalies. Greater accuracy can be achieved by operating Loran-C in a "differential" mode, using a station near the vessel's working location to make position corrections or by making calibration fixes at known locations to determine position offsets. Loran-C can be used at distances beyond 1500 kilometers (930 miles), but with less accuracy, owing to difficulty with separating signals that bounce off the ionosphere (sky waves) from those that travel directly to the receiver (ground waves). At long distances, fixes are often no more accurate than several kilometers.

Loran-C was widely used until recently when it was supplanted by the use of the global positioning system (GPS), a constellation of satellites orbiting Earth. GPS offers worldwide coverage and greater accuracy with small, inexpensive receivers. Nevertheless, Loran-C continues to operate and many ships retain Loran receivers as a backup navigation system.

William W. Sager

FURTHER READING
Dobrin, M. B., and C. H. Savit. *Introduction to Geophysical Prospecting.* New York: McGraw-Hill, 1952; 4th ed., 1988.
Jones, E. J. W. *Marine Geophysics.* Chichester, England, and New York: Wiley, 1999.
Spradley, L. H. *Surveying and Navigation for Geophysical Exploration.* Upper Saddle River, N.J.: Prentice Hall, 1988.

RELATED ARTICLES
Global Positioning System; Navigation

Loricifera

The Loricifera were first seen in 1974 and published as a phylum in 1983, although some recent discoveries and ongoing research suggests that reclassification may be necessary. The Loricifera are microscopic, less than 0.5 millimeter (0.0197 inch) in length, and always associated with a substrate, mostly ocean sediment from very shallow depths to waters of great depths. They are multicellular, bilaterally symmetrical marine invertebrates that are mostly free-living, although some may be symbiotic. They appear to be widely distributed in the oceans throughout a wide range of depths. Although researchers are aware of nearly 100 species, only 12 have been described thus far.

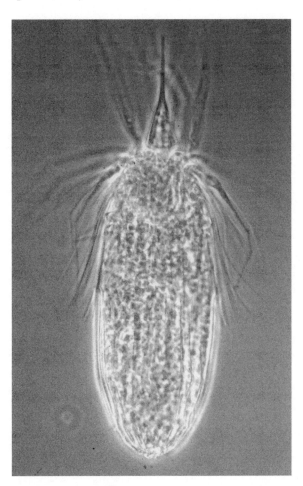

Phylum Loricifera, Pliciloricus enigmaticus. *(Courtesy, Robert P. Higgins)*

One of the principal characters of the Loricifera is the *lorica,* a thick region of cuticle protecting the trunk or lower half of the body. Loriciferans fall into two principal orders, the Nanaloricida and the Pliciloricida. The lorica of the former has a series of six vertical plates; the latter has a series of 24 vertical folds. In the center of the spherical head there is a telescopic mouth cone that is surrounded by external rings of complicated appendages called *scalids.* The former regions, together with a small thoracic region, can be withdrawn into the lorica and closed off by neck plates for protection. In this manner, it is similar to priapulids, kinorhynchs, and rotifers. Sexes are separate, and the female produces a single large fertilized egg at a time. The series of several larval stages, called Higgins larvae, are similar to the adult but most often have a prominent toe on either side of the terminal anus. The toes are thought to be adhesive organs, attaching the animal to the substrate. Several molts occur before the adult stage is reached.

Robert P. Higgins

FURTHER READING

Higgins, Robert P., and Reinhardt M. Kristensen. "New Loricifera from Southeastern United States Coastal Waters." *Smithsonian Contributions to Zoology,* No. 438, 1986.

Kristensen, Reinhardt M. "Loricifera: A New Phylum with Aschelminthes Characters from the Meiobenthos." *Zeitschrift fuer Zoologische Systematik und Evolutionsforschung,* Vol. 21, No. 3 (1983); pp.161–180.

———. "Loricifera." In Frederick W. Harrison and Edward E. Ruppert, eds., *Microscopic Anatomy of Invertebrates,* Vol. 4, *Ashelminthes.* New York: Wiley-Liss, 1991; pp. 351–375.

Margulus, Lynn, and Karlene V. Schwartz. "Loricifera." In Lynn Margulis, ed., *Five Kingdoms: An Illustrated Guide to the Phyla of Life on Earth.* San Francisco: W. H. Freeman, 1982; 3rd ed., New York, 1998; chap. A-17.

RELATED ARTICLES
Meiofauna

Macrobenthos

Macrobenthos are bottom-living animals that are retained on 1-millimeter (0.04-inch) sieves when the sediment is sieved. The macrobenthos includes members of most phyla and both the adults and juveniles of larger species. Although the species composition changes with depth, the more abundant taxa include mollusks, annelid worms, echinoderms, and a great variety of crustaceans. Some of the animals, the epifauna, live on the surface of the bottom, while others are infaunal, living buried within the sediment. All feeding types occur. The types and abundance of macrobenthic species are strongly influenced by the character of the sediment. Many species construct tubes that project above the surface of the sediment. These provide a measure of protection against predators but also enable the animal to feed in water above the viscous sublayer of water that is kept almost motionless by friction. The tubes themselves often acquire their own specialized community of small attached species.

The biomass of the macrobenthos can be large where there are large inputs of organic material. But at greater and greater depths, its biomass declines and becomes smaller relative to that of the meiobenthos.

Martin Angel

FURTHER READING

Gage, John D., and Paul A. Tyler. *Deep-Sea Biology: A Natural History of the Deep-Sea Floor.* Cambridge and New York: Cambridge University Press, 1991.

Ormond, Rupert F. G., John D. Gage, and Martin V. Angel. *Marine Biodiversity: Patterns and Processes.* Cambridge and New York: Cambridge University Press, 1997.

Smith, Craig, Loren Mullineaux, and Lisa Levin, eds. "Deep-Sea Biodiversity: A Compilation of Recent Advances in Honor of Robert R. Hessler." *Deep-Sea Research II,* Vol. 45 (1998), pp. 1–567.

RELATED ARTICLES
Epifauna; Infauna; Meiobenthos

Macrofauna

Macrofauna is a term used to describe a size class of benthic organisms. In shallow water and continental slope habitats, organisms larger than 0.5 millimeter (0.0197 inch) compose the macrofauna. In the deep sea, where many organisms are smaller than their shallow-water counterparts, scientists consider organisms as small as 0.3 millimeter (0.0118 inch) to be macrofauna. In many locales a few species constitute the bulk of individuals and biomass, and researchers have found recurrent assemblages of ecologically and taxonomically similar macrofaunal species in similar depths and substrate types throughout the world's oceans.

Macrofaunal organisms can live in the sediments (infauna) or they can live on the surface of the seafloor (epibenthic fauna). They can be mobile (e.g., burrowers) or sessile (e.g., tube builders). Macrofaunal species also live on or in hard substrates, such as coral reefs, canyon walls, and intertidal rocks. Polychaetes can compose up to 75 percent of the total macrofaunal abundance in both coastal and deep-sea sediments. Crustaceans (e.g., amphipods, isopods, ostracods, and tanaids), echinoderms (e.g., echinoids, holothuroids, and ophiuroids), and mollusks (e.g., bivalves and gastropods) are also dominant macrofaunal taxa. Macrofaunal assemblages in deep-sea sediments are particularly diverse and contain many undescribed species.

In ocean waters within diving depths, researchers can observe and collect macrofauna using scuba. In deeper water, scientists collect macrofauna by taking quantitative samples of the seafloor. Researchers lower various types of grabs and coring devices from a research vessel. The instrument slices into the seafloor and encloses a known volume of sediment [e.g., 0.1 square meter (1.0764 square feet)]. Upon recovery, researchers sieve the sample to remove sediment and retain macrofauna. Once macrofaunal organisms have been identified and counted, the data can be used to calculate such parameters as density, species richness, and diversity.

Lynn L. Lauerman

FURTHER READING
Gage, John D., and Paul A. Tyler. *Deep-Sea Biology: A Natural History of Organisms at the Deep-Sea Floor.* Cambridge and New York: Cambridge University Press, 1991.
Nybakken, James W. *Marine Biology: An Ecological Approach,* 5th ed. San Francisco: Benjamin Cummings, 2001.
Rumohr, H. *Soft Bottom Macrofauna: Collection, Treatment, and Quality Assurance of Samples.* Copenhagen: International Council for the Exploration of the Sea, 1999.

RELATED ARTICLES
Benthos; Crustacea; Echinodermata; Epibenthic; Infauna; Mollusca

Macroplankton

Macroplankton are free-floating organisms ranging in size from 2 to 20 centimeters (0.79 to 7.9 inches). They are part of the *net plankton,* those organisms that can be captured in a plankton net. Krill, mysids, and ctenophores belong to this size class of plankton and are also classified as *zooplankton* or animal-like plankton.

Erin O'Donnell

FURTHER READING
Brusca, Richard C., and Gary J. Brusca. *Invertebrates.* Sunderland, Mass.: Sinauer Associates, 1990.
Nybakken, James W. *Marine Biology: An Ecological Approach,* 5th ed. San Francisco: Benjamin Cummings, 2001.
Raymont, John E. G. *Plankton and Productivity in the Oceans,* Vol. 2, *Zooplankton.* New York and Oxford: Pergamon Press, 1963; 2nd ed., 1980.

RELATED ARTICLES
Ctenophora; Krill; Plankton; Zooplankton

Madrid Environmental Protocol

Negotiated by the member countries to the Antarctic Treaty in 1991, the Madrid Protocol represents a significant step forward in the conservation of Antarctica's natural resources and environment. The protocol effectively creates a "natural reserve" by banning mining extraction in Antarctica for a period of 50 years and setting up a framework for environmental regulation and the monitoring of human activities that may affect the Antarctic environment.

The Madrid Protocol is the culmination of conservation-based management and international cooperation that has taken place in the Antarctic region since the formation of the Antarctic Treaty (AT) in 1959. Although the AT did not replace the previous territorial claims of seven countries, it did create a legal system under which nations could conduct peaceful, scientific research in the region. The treaty was originally signed by 12 nations; as of 2000, there were 43 member countries. In 1964, AT member countries adopted the Agreed Measures for the Conservation of Antarctic Fauna and Flora, the first measure to protect the Antarctic ecosystem and its unique species. Two related conventions negotiated by AT member nations—the 1972 Convention for the Conservation of Antarctic Seals and the 1980 Convention for the Conservation of Antarctic Marine Living Resources—built upon the conservation framework, setting catch limits and protection measures for Antarctic coastal species such as seals, birds, fish, and invertebrates.

In 1988, AT member nations negotiated the controversial Convention for the Regulation of Antarctic Mineral Resource Activities (CRAMRA), which would regulate mineral mining activities on the continent. But in 1989, both Australia and France announced that they would not sign the convention; instead, these nations called for a stronger environmental regime that would ban mining altogether, leading to the development of the 1991 Madrid Protocol. The protocol not only bans mining in Antarctica until 2041, but also creates strong guidelines for environmental protection on the continent. Included in the protocol is a set of environmental principles that calls for the minimization of adverse effects on the Antarctic environment, planning of activities to reduce environmental impacts, the development of environmental impact assessments (EIAs) on proposed activities, and regular monitoring. The protocol creates a committee for environmental protection that will provide advice and recommendations to AT members on the status of the implementation and effectiveness of the protocol as well as on related matters. Finally, the protocol

contains five annexes, which elaborate on issues such as EIA procedures, conservation, waste disposal, marine pollution, and area protection.

The Protocol on Environmental Protection to the Antarctic Treaty (the official title of the Madrid Protocol) was negotiated on 4 October 1991, in Madrid, Spain, and it came into force on 14 January 1998.

Manoj Shivlani

FURTHER READING
Cornonnery, L. "Environmental Protection in Antarctica: Drawing Lessons from the CCAMLR Model for the Implementation of the Madrid Protocol." *Ocean Development and International Law,* Vol. 29, No. 2 (1998), pp. 125–146.
Myhre, Jeffery D. *The Antarctic Treaty System: Politics, Law, and Diplomacy.* Boulder, Colo.: Westview Press, 1986.
Richardson, M. G. "The Protocol on Environmental Protection Enters into Force." *Polar Record,* Vol. 34, No. 189 (April 1998), pp. 147–148.
Rothwell, D. R. *The Madrid Protocol and Its Relationship with the Antarctic Treaty System.* Antarctic and Southern Ocean Law and Policy Occasional Papers, No. 5. Hobart: Law School, University of Tasmania, 1992.
———. " UNEP and the Antarctic Treaty System." *Environmental Policy and Law,* Vol. 29, No. 1 (1999), pp. 17–24.

USEFUL WEB SITES
Full text of the Protocol on Environmental Protection to the Antarctic Treaty, 4 Oct. 1991. <http:sedac.ciesin.org/pidb/texts/ antarctic.treaty.protocol.1991.html>.

RELATED ARTICLES
Antarctica; Marine Sanctuary

Magnesium

Magnesium (Mg) is a silvery-white metal that is a member of the alkaline earth metals of group IIa in the periodic table. Alkaline earth metals are characterized by high melting points, low water solubility, and high reactivity. All elements in this group occur naturally in compounds.

In nature, magnesium is the eighth most abundant element in Earth's crust but does not occur uncombined, due to its reactivity. It combines readily with most acids and with many nonmetals and can act as a powerful reducing agent. It is found in abundance in the minerals brucite, magnesite, dolomite, and carnalite. Magnesium is a constituent of chlorophyll in plants and is an important nutrient for plants and animals. It can also be substituted for calcium in the skeletons of marine organisms.

Magnesium is the third most abundant element in seawater, where it is found in concentrations of 0.05 molar. It generally has a conservative distribution, which means that its concentration varies only as a function of salinity. Higher magnesium concentrations exist in the Atlantic Ocean than in the Pacific Ocean. Whereas rivers supply most of the magnesium to the oceans, hydrothermal circulation in Earth's crust is believed to be a major removal mechanism. Magnesium has an overall residence time of 13,000 years in the oceans.

Magnesium is recovered from seawater primarily by the process of electrolysis. Magnesium oxide plants also remove magnesium from seawater. This process involves increasing the pH of the seawater, which causes magnesium hydroxide to precipitate out. This precipitate is then baked to form magnesium oxide, which can then be used as firebricks in furnaces.

Magnesium and its alloys are used in manufacturing many products, due to their light weight and great strength. In the marine environment, plates of magnesium are laid next to buried steel pipelines or attached to ship bottoms to prevent corrosion of iron or steel.

Joanna M. Grebel

FURTHER READING
Libes, Susan M. *Marine Biogeochemistry.* New York: Wiley, 1992.

Millero, Frank J. *Chemical Oceanography.* Boca Raton, Fla.: CRC Press, 1992; 2nd ed., 1996.

RELATED ARTICLES
Residence Time; Seawater, Composition of; Trace Element

Magnetic Anomaly

Magnetic anomalies are one of the keystones in the theories of seafloor spreading and plate tectonics. These small magnetic fields are generated by permanently magnetized rocks in Earth's crust that result from the interaction of seafloor spreading and magnetic field reversals at divergent plate boundaries. In the mid-1960s, marine magnetic anomalies were cited as the initial evidence supporting the hypothesis of seafloor spreading. They are still the primary data used to determine the age of the oceanic crust throughout the ocean basins and the present and past rates of relative plate tectonic motion. Only these kinds of magnetic anomalies are described here, not those formed by other processes.

Magnetic Anomalies as a Record of Seafloor Spreading

In 1961, Harry Hammond Hess (1906–69) proposed the hypothesis that became known as *seafloor spreading*. This states that new oceanic crust is constantly forming at the crests of mid-oceanic ridges. As the flanks of the ridges diverge or spread apart, molten magma wells up and freezes in the rift at the spreading center. This forms a pattern of oceanic crust on the ridges that is elongate parallel to the ridge crest axis and becomes symmetrically older going down the flanks of both ridges.

Hess called his idea "an essay in geopoetry" because he could not think of a quantitative way to test it. However, in 1963, Frederick J. Vine (1939–) and Drummond Matthews proposed that Hess's process is recorded by magnetization of the newly formed oceanic crust and displayed as variations in magnetic field strength called magnetic anomalies. Oceanic crust becomes magnetized when magma freezes at the spreading center. As the flanks of the ridge diverge, this newly frozen crust is rifted in half and each half is rafted away on one of the ridge flanks. A distinctive and symmetric pattern of alternating magnetization is created because Earth's magnetic field occasionally reverses its polarity during the seafloor spreading process (see figure). When a field reversal occurs, the north and south magnetic poles effectively change places over a period of several thousand years. Each magnetic anomaly is the record of half of one of the constant-polarity intervals between field reversals present when the oceanic crust was forming at the spreading center. Constant-polarity intervals vary greatly in length from about 30,000 years to nearly 40 million years.

Magnetization of the Oceanic Crust

The uppermost oceanic crust consists of black igneous rock called *basalt*. Basalt contains about 5 percent iron-rich minerals that take on a strong, permanent magnetization when cooled below about 580°C (about 1076°F) in the presence of a magnetic field. The principal magnetic mineral is titanium-rich magnetite with a chemical formula of $(Fe_{3-x}Ti_x)O_4$. The permanent magnetization acquires a direction parallel to the magnetizing field. This permanent magnetization produces a field of its own that is superimposed on Earth's regional field and is called a magnetic anomaly. At high latitudes and at all north/south-trending spreading centers, oceanic crust with the same direction of magnetization as the regional field produces a positive anomaly. Conversely, if the magnetization was acquired during an opposite or reversed polarity interval,

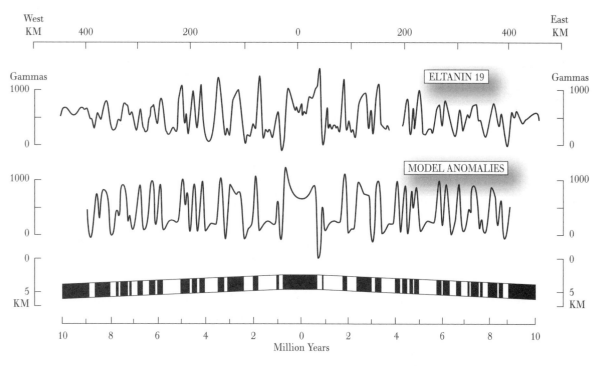

Marine magnetic anomalies across the spreading center between the Pacific and Antarctic Plates. The Eltanin 19 profile is the magnetic anomaly data recorded with a proton precession magnetometer, and the model anomalies are based on the magnetic reversal time scale illustrated at the bottom with a whole spreading rate of 90 kilometers (about 56 miles) per million years. Black blocks are normally magnetized and white blocks are reversely magnetized. The time scale of reversals is in millions of years and the spreading center is at zero million years. Note the close correspondence between the observations and the model. (Adapted from Roger L. Larson, "Le Géomagnétism Marin," La Research, May 1979, p. 460, Figure 4.)

a negative magnetic anomaly is produced when added to the present-day field.

Measuring Magnetic Anomalies at Sea

The total intensity of Earth's magnetic field is measured with a proton precession magnetometer. The sensor is towed on an electrical conducting cable far behind the research vessel so that the ship's permanent field will not interfere with the measurement. The sensor contains one to three coils of electrical conducting wire immersed in a source of free protons, also known as hydrogen ions, H^+. The proton source can be pure water, jet fuel, or paint thinner. Every few seconds the coils are polarized with several amperes of direct current sent from the ship through the conducting cable. The H^+ ions are naturally and individually spinning and the polarizing current tends to align their spin axes parallel to the magnetic field in the coils, which in general is not parallel to Earth's field. The direct current is then shut off and the aligned protons now are exposed only to the Earth's magnetic field. They begin to turn their axes of rotation toward that direction, which causes them to precess or wobble on their axes, similar to the wobble of a child's top if it is bumped slightly on the side when it is spinning. This precession induces an alternating current into the magnetometer coils, and that signal is transmitted up the cable and back to the ship. The frequency of this precession is proportional to the total intensity of Earth's magnetic field with a constant called the *gyromagnetic ratio,* which is approximately 23.49 nanotesla per hertz (cycles per second). The following formula relates total field intensity in nanotesla to precession frequency in hertz:

total field intensity = 23.49 × precession frequency

The total field intensity is a combination of the regional and anomalous fields. The regional field is well known and can be subtracted easily from the total field value. The remainder is the magnetic anomaly value at that location. Typical regional field values range from 35,000 to 70,000 nanotesla from the equator to the north and south magnetic poles. Typical magnetic anomalies measured at the sea surface that are symptomatic of a seafloor-spreading magnetization pattern 3 to 6 kilometers (about 1.9 to 3.7 miles) below the ship range from 100 to 1500 nanotesla (see figure).

Implications of Magnetic Anomaly Measurements

The patterns of magnetic anomalies can be compared to a time scale of magnetic reversals using modeling techniques (see figure). The time scale is essentially a calendar of magnetic field reversals going back millions of years. Identification of a distinctive pattern of magnetic anomalies is similar to identifying fingerprints or tree rings. When a pattern is identified, this determines two very important things. First, it provides an estimate of the age of the oceanic crust at that location. In this way it has been determined that the ocean basins range in age from the present on the spreading ridges back to about 175 million years at the edges of the North Atlantic and in the far western Pacific Ocean. Second, the spacing or widths of the magnetic anomalies combined with the time scale ages allow the calculation of present or past seafloor spreading rates for that area. It has been determined that seafloor spreading rates today vary from 10 to 160 kilometers (about 6 to 100 miles) per million years (see figure). The fastest rates are in the Pacific Ocean and the slowest are in the Atlantic, for reasons described in the "Plate Tectonics" article.

Roger L. Larson

FURTHER READING

Davies, Geoffrey. *Dynamic Earth: Plates, Plumes and Mantle Convection.* Cambridge and New York: Cambridge University Press, 1999.

Kearey, Philip, and Frederick J. Vine. *Global Tectonics.* Oxford and Boston: Blackwell Scientific, 1990.

Larson, Roger L. "Le Géomagnétisme Marin." *La Research*, May 1979, p. 456.

Plummer, Charles C., David McGeary, and Diane H. Carlson. *Physical Geology.* Dubuque, Iowa: Wm. C. Brown, 1992; 8th ed., Burr Ridge, Ill.: McGraw-Hill Higher Education, 1998.

Vine, Frederick J. "Spreading of the Ocean Floor: New Evidence." *Science*, 16 December 1966, p. 1405.

Vine, Frederick J., and Drummond R. Matthews. "Magnetic Anomalies over Oceanic Ridges." *Nature*, 7 September 1963, p. 947.

USEFUL WEB SITES

Blakely, Richard J., and Carol A. Raymond. "Crustal Magnetic Anomolies." U.S. National Report to IUGG, 1991–1994. *Review of Geophysics, American Geophysical Union*, Vol. 33 (1995). <http://earth.agu.org/revgeophys/blakel01/blakel01.html>.

RELATED ARTICLES

Deep Sea Drilling Project; Hess, Harry Hammond; Mantle Plume; Ocean Drilling Program; Oceanic Crust; Plate Tectonics; Seafloor Spreading

Magnetic Declination

Why doesn't a compass needle point to the North Pole? The answer is that force lines of the magnetic field, which the needle follows, are not aligned north–south in most places on Earth. Magnetic declination, defined as the angle between geographic north and the direction that a compass needle points (positive eastward), is therefore an important quantity when using a compass to navigate. For this reason, magnetic declination is printed on most topographic and marine navigation charts. Mariners also know this quantity by the name *magnetic variation.*

Magnetic declination exists because Earth's magnetic field is neither perfectly symmetric nor aligned precisely with the rotation axis. The field can be explained to within about 10 percent by a magnetic dipole, whose field geometry is the same as that of a bar magnet. The dipole that best approximates the magnetic field is located near Earth's center but with an axis inclined to Earth's rotation axis by 11°. Because of this tilt, the axis intersects Earth's surface in northwestern Greenland and eastern Antarctica at locations called *geomagnetic poles.* The part of the field not explained by the dipole also contributes to the magnetic declination, adding irregularities to the isogons, the name for lines of equal declination. Current values of magnetic declination range from 0 to 25° in latitudes less than about 45°. In high latitudes, large declinations are measured. Near the magnetic poles the compass needle can point away from the geographic pole, and large changes in declination occur over short distances.

Even at a fixed location, magnetic declination is not constant. Because it arises mostly from electric currents in the convecting outer core, the magnetic field evolves slowly with time, changing the magnetic isogons. Smaller, more rapid variations also occur because of electrical currents in the upper atmosphere. Typical rates of change in declination are several minutes of arc per year, but at some locations this can be as high as 14 to 15 minutes per year.

The first known record of magnetic declination comes from the Chinese astronomer Yi-Xing about A.D. 720. In Europe, Georg Hartman, a vicar of Nuremberg, made the first recorded declination measurement in Rome in about 1510. Declination appears to have been known to European mariners as much as a century earlier and was noted by Columbus (1451–1506) on his first voyage to the West Indies in 1492. The time variation of magnetic declination was discovered in 1634 by Henry Gellibrand (1597–1636), a professor of astronomy at Gresham College in London.

William W. Sager

FURTHER READING

Chapman, Sydney, and Julius Bartels. *Geomagnetism.* Vols. I and II. Oxford: Clarendon Press, 1940; 2nd ed., 1951.

Malin, S. "Historical Introduction to Geomagnetism." In
J. A. Jacobs, ed., *Geomagnetism*. Vol. 1. London, and
Orlando, Fla.: Academic Press, 1987.

Merrill, Ronald T., Michael W. McElhinny, and Phillip L.
McFadden. *The Magnetic Field of the Earth:
Paleomagnetism, the Core, and the Deep Mantle.*
San Diego: Academic Press, 1998.

Parkinson, Wilfred D. *Introduction to Geomagnetism*.
New York: Elsevier Science, 1983.

Press, Frank, and Raymond Siever. *Earth*. San Francisco:
W. H. Freeman, 1974; 4th ed., New York, 1986.

RELATED ARTICLES
Navigation

Malacostraca

The Malacostraca is one of five classes within the
Arthropod subphylum Crustacea. Almost three-
fourths of all crustacean species are malacostracans. The class is extremely diverse; the familiar
crabs, lobsters, crayfish, and shrimp are but a
few of the more than 20,000 known species.
Malacostracans inhabit both fresh and salt water,
and some species can be found on land.

General Features

Like all arthropods, malacostracans have a segmented body, paired jointed appendages, and a
hard exoskeleton that is shed and re-formed
(molting or ecdysis) as the animal grows. The
malacostracan body consists of 19 or 20 segments
(five cephalic, eight thoracic, and six or seven
abdominal segments) plus the telson (a flattened
tail fin that is used for swimming). A chitinous
cephalic shield may cover the head. In many
species the head and thorax are fused into a
cephalothorax that is covered by a chitinous carapace. A rostrum (an extension of the carapace
beyond the head) also is common among malacostracans. In many species, the abdomen is elongated; crabs, which have a reduced abdomen that
folds under the cephalothorax, are the notable
exception to this condition.

Malacostracans have numerous appendages
that differ from one another in form and function. Appendages are often biramous (they consist of two branches), although they can be
uniramous or triramous. The head bears one set
of antennules and one set of antennae that are
used for touch and taste, one pair of hard
mandibles for crushing and grinding food, and
two pairs of maxillae for handling food. The thorax bears zero to three pairs of maxillipeds for
manipulating food and transferring it to the
mouth and a varying number of uniramous or
biramous thoracic appendages (pereopods) for
walking, swimming, gas exchange, feeding,
and/or defense. One pair of thoracic appendages
may be modified into large chelae (claws).
Usually, the abdomen bears five pairs of biramous pleopods (swimmerets) and one pair of
biramous uropods (on either side of the telson).
The telson and uropods comprise the tail fan.

Most malacostracans have stalked or sessile
compound eyes. Gas exchange occurs via gills.
Antennal glands or maxillary glands in the head
comprise the excretory organs; excretion occurs
through ducts at the base of the antennae or the
second maxillae, respectively. Most malacostracans have separate sexes, although a few are hermaphroditic. Many exhibit elaborate courtship
behaviors. Males and females of some species are
paired all the time; others use techniques such as
chemoreception and synchronized migrations to
find mates. The male gonopores are located on
thoracic segment eight and the female gonopores
on thoracic segment six. Most species copulate; in

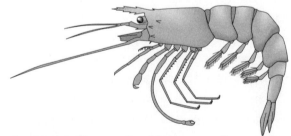

Sergestes similis, *a species of shrimp, part of
the class Malacostraca.*

males the first one or two pairs of swimmerets may be modified to transfer sperm to the female. Females may use the swimmerets to carry eggs. Species with indirect development produce a nauplius larva that often is followed by other larval stages. Many species, however, exhibit direct or mixed development and brood or deposit eggs until they hatch at a postnaupliar stage.

Taxonomic Diversity

Malacostracans are usually divided into two subclasses: Phyllocarida and Eumalacostraca. The division is based on the arrangement of body segments. Members of the Phyllocarida exhibit the primitive condition of five head segments, eight thoracic segments, and seven abdominal segments plus the telson (5–8–7). Eumalacostracans exhibit a 5–8–6 (plus telson) body plan.

SUBCLASS PHYLLOCARIDA

Phyllocarids typically have a head bearing a movable rostrum, stalked compound eyes, biramous antennules, uniramous antennae, a large folded carapace that covers the thorax, no maxillipeds, and paddlelike thoracic appendages. The elongated abdomen bears four biramous and two uniramous pleopods and lacks uropods. Direct development takes place in the female's brood pouch and young hatch as juveniles.

Phyllocarida comprises one order, the Leptostraca, and it contains only six genera and about 20 species. Most leptostracans are between 5 and 15 millimeters long (0.2 to 0.6 inch), although one species can reach 4 centimeters (cm; 1.6 inches). All species are marine, most are found on the seafloor from the intertidal to about 400 meters (m; 1312 feet) deep, and many inhabit low-oxygen habitats. Suspension feeding is the most common feeding strategy among leptostracans.

SUBCLASS EUMALACOSTRACA

Eumalacostraca encompasses the great diversity of the malacostracans; it is subdivided into four superorders and numerous orders, suborders, and so on. Typically, the head is fused with zero to three thoracic segments, the appendages of which are modified into maxillipeds. Antennules may be uni-, bi-, or triramous, and antennae are either uni- or biramous. Five pairs of pleopods are typical, and the telson and the uropods form a tail fan. Most eumalacostracans have a large well-developed carapace (although it is reduced or lost in some species) and a long muscular abdomen.

The superorder Hoplocaridae consists of one order, the Stomatopoda (mantis shrimp). The approximately 350 living species of stomatopods range in length from 2 to 30 cm (0.8 to 11.8 inches). These animals have a thick abdomen and a distinctive, large, raptorial, second thoracic appendage that they use to seize prey such as cnidarians, crustaceans, fishes, and mollusks. They also have abdominal rather than thoracic gills, which are rare among malacostracans. Stomatopods inhabit shallow subtropical and tropical marine environments, where they burrow in soft sediment or live in cracks and crevices or amongst rubble. Fertilized eggs are brooded or deposited in a burrow and young hatch at a postnaupliar stage.

Syncarida contains about 150 exclusively freshwater malacostracan species that are divided into two orders (Anaspidacea and Bathynellacea). They may represent the most primitive eumalacostracan taxon. Syncarids are less than 5 cm long (2.0 inches). They lack eyes, and some pleopods and pereopods may be reduced or lost. Syncarids do not carry their eggs following copulation; instead, they deposit fertilized eggs onto the substrate or shed them into the water column, where direct development occurs.

The superorder Eucarida is an extremely diverse group in form and function, but all members have a complete carapace that is fused to the thoracic segments to form a cephalothorax. The order Euphausiacea contains approximately 90 species of krill. These 4- to 15-cm (1.6- to 5.9-

inch)-long pelagic shrimplike animals live from the sea surface to a depth of 5000 m (16,404 feet). They often form dense schools and are a major source of food for nekton such as baleen whales, squids, fishes, and birds. Krill produce a nauplius larva. The order Amphionidacea contains only one planktonic species, which can be found to a depth of 1700 m (5577 feet); this species also produces a nauplius larva. Most Eucarids belong to the order Decapoda, which comprises over 10,000 species of lobsters, crayfish, crabs, and shrimp. The suborder Dendrobranchiata contains the penaeid and sergestid shrimps. The suborder Pleocyemata includes caridean shrimps, mud and ghost shrimps, crabs, crayfish, clawed lobsters, spiny lobsters, slipper lobsters, hermit crabs, porcelain crabs, mole crabs, sand crabs, and true crabs. Decapods inhabit all depths of all aquatic habitats, and some are terrestrial for much of their lives. Aquatic species can be pelagic or benthic, and benthic groups can be free-moving, sedentary, or burrowing. Decapods can be suspension feeders, predators, herbivores, or scavengers. Some species are hermaphroditic. Dendrobranchs shed fertilized eggs into the water column, where they often hatch as nauplii; all other species brood embryos that hatch at a postnaupliar stage.

The last malacostracan superorder, Peracarida, includes over 11,000 species divided among nine orders. This group includes the mysid shrimps, lophogatrids, cumaceans, tanaids, spelaeogrophaceans, thermosbaenaceans, mitaceans, isopods, and amphipods. Most peracarids range in length from a few millimeters to greater than 12 cm (4.7 inches), but a few giant species can reach 35 cm (13.8 inches) and 44 cm (17.3 inches). Many species are marine, but some inhabit land, fresh water, or hotsprings. The carapace, when present, usually is reduced. Peracarids generally have abdominal gills; members of one order, the Isopoda, have abdominal gills. Fertilized eggs are brooded by the female and undergo direct development.

Lynn L. Lauerman

FURTHER READING

Bliss, D. E. *Shrimps, Lobsters and Crabs.* Piscataway, N.J.: New Century, 1982.

Brusca, Richard C., and Gary J. Brusca. *Invertebrates.* Sunderland, Mass.: Sinauer, 1990.

Burukovskii, R. N. *Key to Shrimps and Lobsters.* Rotterdam, the Netherlands: Balkema, 1985.

Fincham, A. A., and P. S. Rainbow, eds. *Aspects of Decapod Crustacean Biology.* Oxford: Clarendon Press, published for the Zoological Society of London, 1988.

Schram, Frederick R. *Crustacea.* New York: Oxford University Press, 1986.

Warner, G. F. *The Biology of Crabs.* New York: Van Nostrand Reinhold, 1977.

RELATED ARTICLES

Arthropoda; Crab; Crustacea; Lobster; Penaeid Prawn

Manatee

Manatees are large, plant-eating mammals that live in tropical coastal shallows and river estuaries. They are classified as members of the order Sirenia, so named because of their supposed resemblance to mermaids. There are three manatee species: the Caribbean manatee (*Trichechus manatus*), the West African manatee (*T. senegalensis*), and the Amazonian manatee (*T. inunguis*). Some authorities also recognize two subspecies of the Caribbean manatee: the Florida manatee (*T. manatus latirostris*) and the Antillean manatee (*T. manatus manatus*). The dugong (*Dugong dugong*), a close relative of the manatee, lives in warm coastal waters in the Indian Ocean and Southeast Asia.

Sirenians are stocky animals, with a thick layer of insulating blubber and a streamlined, tapered shape. Like whales and dolphins, they evolved from land mammals that became adapted to a life spent entirely underwater. Their front limbs evolved to form flippers, and their back limbs disappeared. They move through the water as whales and dolphins do, by swinging a paddlelike tail up and down.

Manatee under water. (© Brandon D. Cole/Corbis)

All sirenians are herbivores. They feed on sea grasses and other aquatic plants in shallow coastal waters, lagoons, and slow-flowing rivers, using their mobile lips to grasp vegetation and their sensitive, bristly snouts to locate and dig up nutritious roots. The Amazonian manatee lives only in fresh water, but the other manatees are equally at home in fresh water and salt water. The dugong is exclusively marine. Sirenians are sociable animals and often live in family groups or herds of up to 20. They maintain contact by making chirplike noises and greet each other by rubbing muzzles.

To conserve energy, manatees move very slowly. Their docile nature has made them easy targets for human hunters, and all living species are now in decline. A fifth species of sirenian, Steller's sea cow (*Hydrodamalis gigas*), once inhabited the cold waters of the Commander Islands in the Bering Sea. It was discovered in 1741, but by 1768 had been hunted to extinction.

Ben Morgan

FURTHER READING

Macdonald, David. *The Encyclopaedia of Mammals.* London: Greenwich, 1999.

Ripple, Jeff. *Manatees and Dugongs of the World.* Stillwater, Minn.: Voyageur Press, 1999.

Walker, Sally. *Manatees.* Minneapolis, Minn.: Lerner Publications, 1999.

RELATED ARTICLES

Herbivore; Sirenia

Mangal, see Mangrove Forest

Mangrove, see Mangrove Forest

Mangrove Forest

Mangrove is the common name for woody plants that grow in salt water in tropical and subtropical estuaries, lagoons, and coastal mud flats. Mangroves inhabit a harsh environment compared to that of other terrestrial plants: They are exposed to tidal fluctuations, live in salty water, and grow in muddy, waterlogged anoxic sediments. Although mangroves comprise a taxonomically diverse group of trees and shrubs, they are united in having adaptations that allow them to tolerate these conditions and occupy wetlands where other plants cannot survive. Mangroves are the dominant vegetation in mangrove forests (which are also called *mangrove swamps, tidal forests,* or *mangals*). A mangrove forest comprises a complex community composed of mangroves and a diverse assemblage of other plants and animals.

Mangroves require a protected coastline so that they are not exposed to wave action. Mangrove distribution is also related to sea temperature; mangroves are rarely found in waters cooler than 20°C (68°F). These conditions are abundant in the tropics and subtropics where mangrove forests cover approximately 22 million hectares (54 million acres). In the tropics, about 70 percent of coastlines are composed of mangals.

Ecological Role of Mangrove Forests

Mangrove forests are among the most important coastal ecosystems in the world. In many tropical areas mangrove forests are the interface between land, fresh water, and the sea, and they serve as an important focal point in the exchange of organic materials and energy. Mangals are extremely productive systems in terms of gross primary productivity. Production by mangroves and micro- and macroalgae is high because light

Mangrove forest on Sanibel Island, gulf coast of Florida. (Courtesy, Christos Moschovitis)

penetrates the shallow water. In addition, nutrients from terrestrial sources enter the habitat via freshwater rivers and streams, and tidal movement promotes their circulation. Mangrove litterfall (e.g., leaves, fruits, twigs, pollen, branches, bark, and flower parts) provides a huge source of organic detritus, and mangrove roots trap and retain organic debris; thus, mangroves make a major contribution to coastal food webs by providing organic matter that serves as the base of marine food webs. Mangals often serve as nursery grounds for commercially important marine fish and shellfish.

In addition to their importance in primary productivity and in structuring a complex living community, mangrove forests are ecologically important for other contributions. They protect inland areas from storms, stabilize sediment, and help prevent coastal erosion. They also trap organic material that in time becomes peat; eventually, this process builds new coastal land.

Mangrove Community: Flora

MANGROVES

Mangroves are flowering terrestrial plants that range in size from shrubs to trees 40 meters (131 feet) tall. Approximately 16 families, 20 genera, and 54 species of mangroves are known, but species within two families [Avicenniaceae (black) and Rhizophoaceae (red)] dominate mangals throughout the world. Mangroves are all halophytes (salt lovers) and although taxonomically diverse, they are united by their ability to tolerate high-salinity, low-oxygen environments that undergo temperature and tidal fluctuations.

Mangroves usually are exposed to water that is saltier than fresh water but more dilute than seawater, although occasionally they must tolerate extremely saline conditions. Depending on the species and the environmental conditions, mangroves deal with high salinity by exclusion, tolerance, and/or secretion. Some mangroves exclude salt so that it does not enter the roots,

whereas others simply tolerate high salt concentrations in their tissues. Still other species have salt glands that they use to excrete excess salt. Mangroves also have tough succulent leaves with internal water storage that help them tolerate high temperatures.

Mangroves grow in waterlogged mud that prevents gas exchange and results in anoxia. Special root adaptations allow mangroves to live in anoxic mud. Some species have prop roots, or stilt roots, which are aerial roots that grow downward from stems or branches. They contain small pores called *lenticels* that allow the roots to "breathe." Other types of mangroves have lenticel-bearing *pneumataphores*, roots that branch upward out of the sediment to be above the high-tide level.

All mangroves disperse their offspring by water. Most species produce large, tough, long-lived propagules that can withstand harsh conditions, although a few species reproduce and disperse using fruit and seeds. The production of propagules is referred to as *vivipary* because the propagules are actually seedlings; young plants germinate and begin growing while still living on the parent plant. Eventually, the seedlings drop off the parent, float upright in the water, are dispersed by water currents, sink, take root, and grow.

Mangrove forests often exhibit zonation in which various species are found in bands ranging from the seaward fringe of the forest to land. The species assemblage of mangroves from different areas of the world is highly variable, however, and no single scheme describes the pattern of zonation in every locale.

OTHER PLANTS

Marine photosynthesizers such as phytoplankton, cyanobacteria, and benthic algae live among the roots of mangroves. In addition, many terrestrial plants use the mangrove canopy as a substrate on which to grow. For example, epiphytes growing on mangrove branches include ant plants, bromeliads, creepers, ferns, lichens, mistletoes, palms, orchids, and vines.

Mangrove Community: Fauna

Mangrove forests represent a unique environment. The combination of high productivity, three-dimensional structure, and terrestrial and marine components allows mangroves to support a rich diversity of animal life, and mangals are sometimes called "rainforests by the sea." Bacteria and fungi abound and are crucial in breaking down organic detritus and making it available to other organisms. Terrestrial animals may live permanently in the mangrove canopy or may simply forage there. Some marine animals use mangrove roots as substrate or a refuge from predators, whereas others live in the organically rich mud.

TERRESTRIAL ANIMALS

Terrestrial animals that live or forage in mangrove forests include representatives from many different taxa, and the species assemblage depends on the geographic location of the mangrove forest. Herbivores, detritivores, general foragers, and predators can be found among the terrestrial fauna. Arthropods, particularly insects, are abundant and include ants, bees, biting midges, butterflies, caterpillars, cockroaches, fireflies, mosquitoes, moths, sandflies, spiders, and termites. Alligators, crocodiles, iguanas, lizards, sea turtles, and snakes represent the reptiles, and crab-eating frogs represent the amphibians. Hundreds of bird species use mangrove forests for breeding, nesting, and refuge. Depending on the locale, cormorants, egrets, fantails, flycatchers, herons, honeyeaters, ibis, kingfishers, ospreys, pelicans, robins, and storks may be found in mangrove forests. Mammals that forage, graze, or prey in mangrove forests include antelopes, bandicoots, bats, deer, fish cats, flying foxes, mongooses, monkeys, otters, raccoons, rodents, swamp deer, water buffalo, and wild pigs. In some areas of the world, domestic camels and buffalo also graze in mangrove forests.

MARINE ANIMALS

Vertebrates that come from the sea to make use of mangrove forests include sea snakes, marine mammals such as dolphins, dugongs, freshwater dolphins, manatees, and porpoises, and many species of fish. Mangrove forests serve as nursery grounds for fishes such as mullet. Mudskippers are also common inhabitants of mangals. These big-eyed fishes spend most of their time out of water; they can breathe air through vascularized sacs in the mouth and gill chambers, and their eyes sit high on their heads so that they focus in air.

Mollusks and crustaceans are the dominant marine invertebrates in mangrove forests. Mangrove roots provide three-dimensional space for colonization by mussels, oysters, snails, hermit crabs, tree-climbing crabs, and other crab species, shrimp, barnacles, tunicates, bryozoans, sponges, cnidarians, and tube-building polychaete worms. Shipworm mollusks and isopods also burrow into mangrove roots. Commercially important shrimp species, such as those in the family Penaeidae, also inhabit mangrove forests. Fiddler crabs, ghost crabs, mud lobsters, amphipods, isopods, and pistol shrimps typically live under the mud surface. Many mud dwellers build burrows for protection, breeding, and feeding, and these tunnels also help the mangrove community by oxygenating the mud. Meiofaunal species that inhabit the mud include ciliates, gastrotrichs, harpacticoid copepods, kinorhynchs, nematodes, oligochaetes, tardigrades, and turbellarians.

Threats to Mangrove Forests

Mangrove forests are naturally resilient, but drastic changes in the rate of sedimentation, water movement, tidal cycle, and salinity can negatively affect a community. If changes in the physical environment occur gradually, a mangal may cope by undergoing succession, in which the species assemblage slowly changes. If sudden alterations in the environment occur, however, large areas of a mangrove forest may be destroyed. Natural causes of mangrove mortality include violent storms such as hurricanes and typhoons. Parasites, such as the isopod *Sphaeroma terebrans* that bores into mangrove roots and topples trees, can also destroy parts of mangrove forests.

Human activities are responsible for the decimation of vast areas of mangrove forests throughout the world. Traditionally, local cultures have used mangals as sustainable sources of firewood, timber, medicine, and food. For most people, however, mangrove forests conjure up images of heat, foul-smelling mud, mosquitoes, and an impenetrable mass of roots, and these rich ecosystems have been viewed as useless swamps. Humans have looked for alternative uses of mangrove-dominated coastlines, and in so doing have killed mangrove communities with pollution, herbicide spraying, large-scale timber harvesting, clearing to make way for aquaculture ponds, filling to create construction sites, dredging, and digging of channels to alter water flow. The result of these activities is that mangrove forests are among the most threatened habitats in the world.

Lynn L. Lauerman

FURTHER READING

Hogarth, Peter J. *The Biology of Mangroves.* Oxford and New York: Oxford University Press, 1999.

Jaccarini, Victor, and Els Martens, eds. *The Ecology of Mangrove and Related Ecosystems: Proceedings of the International Symposium,* Mombasa, Kenya, September 24–30, 1990. Dordrecht, the Netherlands, and Boston: Kluwer Academic, 1992.

Lodge, Thomas E. *The Everglades Handbook: Understanding the Ecosystem.* Delray Beach, Fla.: St. Lucie Press, 1994.

Nybakken, James W. *Marine Biology: An Ecological Approach,* 5th ed. San Francisco: Benjamin Cummings, 2001.

Odum, William E., and Carole C. McIvor. "Mangroves." In Ronald L. Myers and John J. Ewel, eds., *Ecosystems of Florida.* Orlando, Fla.: University of Central Florida Press, 1990.

Tomlinson, P. B. *The Botany of Mangroves.* Cambridge and New York: Cambridge University Press, 1986.

Walsh, G. E. "Mangroves: A Review." In R. J. Reimold and W. J. Queen, eds., *Ecology of Halophytes.* New York: Academic Press, 1974; pp. 51–174.

RELATED ARTICLES
Anoxia; Anoxic Sediment; Food Web; Gross Primary Productivity; Pneumatophore

Manihiki Plateau

Shaped overall like a large diamond, Manihiki Plateau is located just south of the equator in the central Pacific Ocean. From its broad base at abyssal depths of about 5000 meters (16,400 feet), two teardrop-shaped mountain ranges reach shallower depths. The main edifice is the eastern range, centered at about 12.5°S, 162°W, whose nearly flat top extends slightly above 1400 meters (4593 feet) depth. Around the edges of this high plateau are several seamounts, three of which form islands: Suvarov Island, Rakahanga Island, and Manihiki Island. The plateau derives its name from the latter, a large coral atoll.

Manihiki Plateau apparently formed about 123 million years ago when its core was constructed by voluminous volcanic eruptions. The similarity in age to Ontong Java Plateau and other volcanic constructs in the western Pacific has led many scientists to believe that these plateaus formed during a remarkable basin-wide volcanic event. Magnetic anomalies in the adjacent deep-sea basins indicate that Manihiki Plateau was originally emplaced on the Phoenix Plate, located across a spreading ridge to the south of the Pacific Plate. Sometime shortly after Manihiki formed, the spreading ridge jumped to the south, accreting the crust with the plateau to the Pacific Plate, on which it resides today. After the volcanic eruptions ended, the plateau subsided and rode northward on the Pacific Plate, collecting pelagic sediments on its summit. Today, those sediments are nearly 1 kilometer (3281 feet) thick. In 1973, the *Glomar Challenger* drilled through the sedimentary cap to volcanic basement at Deep Sea Drilling Project Site 317.

William W. Sager

FURTHER READING

Larson, Roger L. "Superplumes and Ridge Interactions Between Ontong Java and Manihiki Plateaus and the Nova–Canton Trough." *Geology*, Vol. 25 (1997), pp. 779–782.

Schlanger, Seymour, et al. *Initial Reports of the Deep Sea Drilling Project.* Vol. 33. Washington, D.C.: U.S. Government Printing Office, 1976.

Winterer, Edward L., Peter F. Lonsdale, John L. Matthews, and Bruce R. Rosendahl. "Structure and Acoustic Stratigraphy of the Manihiki Plateau." *Deep Sea Research*, Vol. 21 (1974), pp. 793–814.

RELATED ARTICLES
Ontong Java Plateau; Pacific Plate; Seamount

Mantle Plume

Mantle plumes cause some of the most spectacular examples of present-day geological activity, which include volcanic eruptions on Hawaii and Iceland and hot springs at Yellowstone Park in Wyoming. A mantle plume is a large upwelling of material with the initial shape of a mushroom, which rises from a thermal boundary layer in Earth's mantle toward the surface due to its thermal buoyancy. When plumes reach the base of the lithosphere, the plume head flattens and begins to melt, leading to Earth's largest volcanic eruptions, called *large igneous provinces*. The largest is the Ontong Java Plateau in the western Pacific Ocean, whose area is equal to that of Alaska. After the plume head dissipates, thermally buoyant material continues to rise through the low-viscosity chimney or conduit that has been established in the mantle, leading to continued eruptions of less magnitude, such as are now occurring at Hawaii, Iceland, and Yellowstone

Park. Because many plumes rise from deep in the mantle, they probably have smaller horizontal velocities than those of the overlying tectonic plates. Thus, the trends and age gradients of island chains formed by the ongoing volcanism can be used to estimate the horizontal velocities of the plates onto which the eruptions occur. In this manner the Hawaiian island chain can be used to estimate the velocity of the Pacific Plate at about 80 kilometers (about 50 miles) per million years toward about 70° west of north.

Mantle Structure

The mantle is the largest of Earth's three main layers, comprising two-thirds of the planet's mass and 83 percent of its volume. Like the white of a partially boiled egg, it separates the overlying crust or shell from the underlying semiliquid core (see figure). The mantle–crust boundary ranges from 7 kilometers (about 4.3 miles) deep beneath the seafloor down to about 50 kilometers (about 31 miles) deep beneath the continents. The core–mantle boundary lies about 2900 kilometers (about 1802 miles) below Earth's surface. The mantle is composed of silicate rock with relatively large amounts of iron and magnesium. It is solid on short time scales and can transmit seismic shear waves that do not propagate in liquids. However, because its temperature is close to the melting point, this material can flow over longer time periods of years and more, somewhat like a slowed-down version of road asphalt deforming plastically on a hot summer day. The mantle temperature ranges between about 100 and 1000°C (about 212 to 1832°F) at the mantle–crust boundary up to about 4000°C (about 7232°F) at the core–mantle boundary. Much of this temperature increase is adiabatic with depth, which means that temperature increases simply because of increasing pressure and not because heat is added to the system. However, just above the core–mantle boundary is a huge, nonadiabatic temperature increase of about 1500°C (about

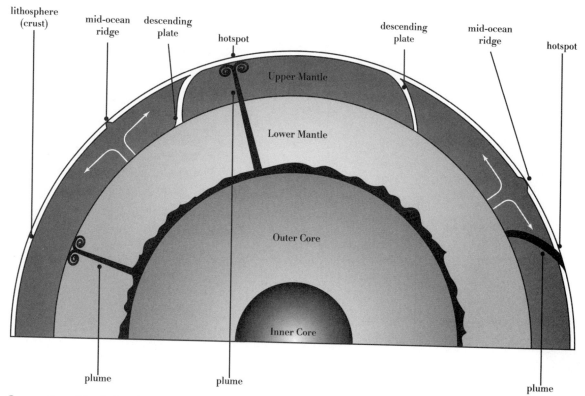

Cross section of Earth showing rising mantle plumes with associated features, including spreading mid-ocean ridges, subducting plates, and Earth's internal layers. (Adapted from Coffin and Eldholm, 1994.)

2732°F) over about 200 kilometers (about 120 miles) depth. There is probably another thermal boundary layer of much smaller magnitude at about 670 kilometers (about 416 miles) separating the upper and lower mantle (see figure). These thermal boundary layers, especially the core–mantle boundary, are the potential sources for mantle plumes.

Plume Structure

In 1971, W. Jason Morgan first proposed that hotspots such as Hawaii and Iceland were the surface manifestations of plumes of hot material rising from the lower mantle. He additionally proposed that the plumes were relatively fixed in place and thus could be used to determine the motions of overlying plates. Plumes rise from thermal boundary layers due to thermal buoyancy. The elevated temperature of the plume material reduces its density, leading to an upward-directed buoyant force. If this force is

sufficient to overcome the resisting force due to the viscosity (resistance to flow) by the overlying mantle material, the material begins to rise toward the surface as a plume. The process can be modeled by slowly heating a spot on the bottom of a transparent container of cold corn syrup or honey. The heated material at the bottom of the container eventually becomes sufficiently buoyant to overcome the resistance of the overlying material and a plume of syrup or honey results, which can be seen if colored dye has been initially placed in the container.

The sizes of large igneous provinces, especially in the ocean basins, suggest that plume heads can be very large, perhaps as much as 500 to 1000 kilometers (about 310 to 621 miles) in diameter. A plume head of this size has huge potential buoyancy and would probably rise even if the density contrast with the surrounding mantle is only 1 to 2 percent. However, because this density contrast and the viscosity of the lower mantle are both poorly known, the rate at which the initial plume heads rise from the thermal boundary layer is also poorly known. It is probably on the order of 1 to 10 centimeters (about 0.4 to 4 inches) per year. After a low-viscosity chimney or conduit is established from the thermal boundary layer to the surface, upward flow is almost certainly faster than the initial rise of the plume head. The dimensions of present-day plume conduits are only now being quantified by analysis of earthquake waves passing through them. The diameter of the plume conduit in the upper mantle beneath Iceland is estimated to be 150 to 200 kilometers (about 93 to 124 miles).

History of Mantle Plume Activity

For about the past 50 million years, mantle plumes have accounted for about 10 percent of the present-day volcanism in the ocean basins, with the other 90 percent due to seafloor spreading from mid-oceanic ridges. In the Cretaceous period about 80 to 120 million years ago, plumes appear to have been more active than they are today and accounted for up to 30 percent of ocean basin volcanism. This period, known as the *Cretaceous greenhouse* for its higher global temperatures and lack of glacial ice, may have resulted in part from the increased volcanic activity. Volcanism injects carbon dioxide into the atmosphere, and this may have led to a natural greenhouse effect.

Early in Earth's history its internal temperature was probably higher than today but also more uniform. Ironically, this suggests that mantle plume activity was less common several billion years ago than it has been in the more recent geological past because one of the requirements for plume initiation is a strong thermal boundary layer. Until Earth's outer layers cooled sufficiently for thermal boundary layers to be established, the mantle plume activity that we see today focused at specific locations was probably less common.

Roger L. Larson

FURTHER READING
Coffin, Millard F., and Olav Eldholm. "Large Igneous Provinces: Crustal Structure, Dimensions, and External Consequences." *Reviews of Geophysics,* February 1994, p. 1.

Davies, Geoffrey. *Dynamic Earth: Plates, Plumes and Mantle Convection.* Cambridge and New York: Cambridge University Press, 1999.

Larson, Roger L. "The Mid-Cretaceous Superplume Episode." *Scientific American,* February 1995, p. 66.

Morgan, W. Jason. "Convection Plumes in the Lower Mantle." *Nature,* 5 March 1971, p. 42.

Plummer, Charles C., David McGeary, and Diane H. Carlson. *Physical Geology.* Dubuque, Iowa: Wm. C. Brown, 1992; 8th ed., Burr Ridge, Ill.: McGraw-Hill Higher Education, 1998.

RELATED ARTICLES
Divergent Plate Boundary; Hotspot; Mid-Ocean Ridge; Ocean Drilling Program; Plate Tectonics; Seafloor Spreading; Volcanic Ridge

Mariana Island Arc

The Mariana Island Arc is a curving chain of volcanoes about 1670 kilometers (1035 miles) long that lies between 150 and 200 kilometers (93 to 124 miles) west from the deepest ocean trench in the world. The Mariana Trench marks the location where the lithospheric plate (the ocean crust and the upper part of the underlying mantle) of the Pacific Ocean is subducting beneath the Philippine Sea Plate.

The subducting plate is subjected to increasing temperatures and pressure as it descends. At depths between 80 and 100 kilometers (50 to 62 miles), these changing conditions dehydrate minerals in the subducting plate, releasing fluids (mainly water) that reduce the melting point of the already hot mantle overlying the subducting plate. The mantle starts to melt, and magmas form. The magma (molten rock) produced rises to form the arc volcanoes.

Island arc volcanoes can erupt explosively. The Mariana arc volcanoes are cone-shaped stratovolcanoes, with alternating layers of lava flows and volcanic ash or cinder. The composition of the volcanoes reflects the infusion of the magma source region with components derived from the subducted oceanic plate. Some of the volcanoes have significant summit calderas [a summit crater with a diameter larger than 1.6 kilometers (1 mile) that formed either by violent explosions or by collapse of the volcano summit in response to withdrawal of magma from a subterranean magma chamber]. Many have visible dikes (relatively thin sheets of solid rock formed by the intrusion of magma into fault planes that cut across other structures) protruding through the lava flows or ash deposits on the volcanoes. Mostly dikes are aligned parallel to regional fault trends.

Theoretical studies suggest that arc magmas may rise in batches spaced about 60 kilometers (about 37 miles) apart. However, seafloor mapping shows that fault patterns in the overriding lithospheric plate exert the strongest control over volcano distribution. Stretching and extension of the Mariana arc lithosphere in response to subduction dynamics has formed a fault-bounded back-arc basin starting at about 200 kilometers (124 miles) west of the trench. Magmas rise along portions of the bounding fault (an offset in the rock, in this case caused by extension) along the eastern side of the back-arc basin. The magmas erupt on the seafloor. Ten of the volcanoes grew large enough to reach sea level and become the islands we see today, but there are many more that remain below sea level.

Smaller volcanoes form along cross chains following faults trending southwest into the back-arc basin, which intersects the basin-bounding fault. These cross-chain volcanoes extend to the spreading center of the back-arc basin. Lavas with "arc" composition have been recovered from several areas along the back-arc basin spreading center. Small volcanoes also lie just trenchward of the basin-bounding fault in highly faulted near-arc regions. Submarine volcanoes

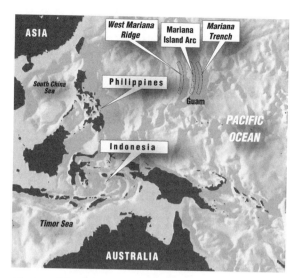

Mariana Island Arc.

extend northwest of the northernmost Mariana island (Maug) for 65 kilometers (40 miles) to the Volcano Islands (which include Iwo Jima), and extend southwest of Guam for over 500 kilometers (over 310 miles). The southern Mariana islands of Guam, Rota, Tinian, Saipan, and Farallon de Medinilla are not active volcanoes. They are uplifted fragments of the seafloor east of the basin-bounding fault and consist of older lavas and reefal limestone.

The Mariana Island Arc thus consists of a zone of volcanism that comprises the main arc volcanoes (along the basin-bounding fault), the cross-chain volcanoes (in the back-arc basin), and the much smaller volcanoes scattered trenchward of the back-arc basin bounding fault. Arc volcanism has probably been operating continuously along the Mariana arc system throughout three episodes of rifting and back-arc extension in the overriding plate starting about 50 million years ago.

Patricia Fryer

FURTHER READING

Fryer, P. "Tectonic Evolution of the Mariana Convergent Margin." *Review of Geophysics*, Vol. 34, No. 1 (1996), pp. 89–125.

Hussong, D. M., and S. Uyeda. "Tectonic Processes and the History of the Mariana Arc: A Synthesis of the Results of Deep Sea Drilling Leg 60." In D. M.

Hussong and S. Uyeda, eds., *Initial Reports of the Deep Sea Drilling Project.* Vol. 60. Washington, D.C.: U.S. Government Printing Office, 1981; pp. 909–929.

Stern, R. J., and S. H. Bloomer. "Subduction Zone Infancy." *Geological Society of America Bulletin,* Vol. 104 (1992), p. 1621.

RELATED ARTICLES
Island Arc; Plate Tectonics; Subduction Zone; Tonga Island Arc; Trench

Mariculture

Aquaculture is the name given to the practice of rearing plants and animals in water; *mariculture* is a more specialized form of aquaculture in which these species are cultivated either in coastal waters or in brackish (salt) water inshore. Although thought to have been practiced as long as 3000 years ago in Indonesia (where milkfish were reared in intertidal waters), mariculture has only recently attracted widespread interest in countries such as the United States.

Mariculture Industry

Mariculture already contributes substantially both to world food production and to the world's economy. Around a quarter of the seafood consumed (by weight) in the United States (which imports U.S.$14 billion of fish each year) is produced in this way. Mariculture currently represents around 10 percent of the global fish catch but constitutes about 20 percent of its economic value. Mariculture is one of the most important methods of producing salmon, and a fourth of the world's shrimp is produced in this way (between the early 1980s and the mid-1990s, shrimp aquaculture grew by 700 percent). Even with a maximum global fishing catch of around 91 million tonnes (100 million tons) (of which 70 percent is available for human consumption), the world's population was forecast to need up to 120 million tons of fish products for the year 2000, leaving a potential shortfall of up to 60 million tons that could be supplied by aquaculture (including mariculture).

Practice of Mariculture

Although mariculture is often thought of as a method of rearing fin fish (such as salmon, mullet, sea bass, and milkfish), three other types of marine organism are also commonly raised in this way: edible seaweeds (such as red, green, and brown algaes), mollusks (including oysters, scallops, mussels, and cockles), and crustaceans (notably shrimps and prawns).

Aquaculture (and therefore mariculture) can be a more efficient method of generating protein than, for example, cattle ranching. Fish are cold-blooded floating creatures and, unlike livestock, do not therefore need to waste energy supporting their body temperature or body weight. Fish also convert protein into body weight more efficiently than do land-reared animals such as pigs and sheep. Finally, unlike a grazing field, which is a two-dimensional rearing area, aquaculture uses a three-dimensional volume of water and so makes more efficient use of space.

There are at least three distinct types of mariculture. *Open mariculture* is the traditional method of rearing marine species in saltwater ponds or sheltered waters. *Closed mariculture* is a more intensive operation in which species are cultivated in tanks under carefully controlled conditions. *Ocean ranching* involves rearing young fish (notably salmon) in controlled conditions and then releasing them into places where they will thrive and grow and can later be caught as mature fish.

Each of these techniques can be practiced in different ways. In the case of shellfish, for example, open mariculture is used to place young bivalve mollusks called spat in large mesh containers or on long ropes attached to rafts. By filter-feeding plankton, they grow larger until they reach the size where they can be harvested (mussels typically take 18 months, while oysters take from 18 to 36 months). There is also a great deal of interest in using ocean thermal energy conversion (OTEC) plants with open mariculture. Because OTEC plants move cold, nutrient-rich waters from the ocean depths to the surface, they act as an artificial method of upwelling. This means that they can be used to replicate on a smaller scale the conditions that exist in places such as the Pacific coast of Peru, where upwelling produces abundant phytoplankton and, until the recent demise of the anchoveta, provided about a fifth of all the sea fish worldwide.

Benefits of Mariculture

With the world's population forecast to reach 10 billion by the year 2050, and with agricultural production facing increasing challenges, including land shortages, soil erosion, shortage of fresh water, and the uncertain impacts of global warming, governments around the world are turning to aquaculture as one method of feeding the world. The World Bank estimates that aquaculture might be used to meet 40 percent of world demand for fish by around 2010. The U.N. Food and Agriculture Organization (FAO) recently set a goal to double aquaculture production by the same year.

By providing an alternative source of food, aquaculture and mariculture theoretically also reduce pressure on natural fish stocks; indeed, supporters of techniques such as marine ranching and ocean fertilization believe that mariculture could even increase stocks. With countries such as the United States so heavily dependent on imported fish, mariculture also offers an attractive means for developing nations to earn foreign income. Some believe that it could also offer an alternative means of employment for people previously employed in the fishing industry but now prevented from earning a proper living by increasingly stringent fishing quotas.

Costs of Mariculture

Mariculture seems to offer important benefits, but in some countries the growth of the industry has been curtailed because of its environmental impacts. The concentration of cultivated species in a small area produces pollution (effluent, chemicals such as antiobiotics used to cure or prevent fish diseases, and excess food), which can have a wider negative effect on coastal waters. In September 1995, a group of Texan shrimp farmers faced a class-action lawsuit because of the estuarine pollution they had allegedly caused. Because mariculture fisheries are located in areas such as estuaries or bays, they are themselves more susceptible to a variety of forms of water pollution draining from the land. In 1988, 370,000 people in Jiangsu Province, China, became infected with hepatitis A after eating clams contaminated by wastewater, and Chinese shrimp production had fallen by around 70 percent by the mid-1990s, due to pollution and other water-related problems. However, some types of mariculture can actually reduce pollution; seaweeds, for example, remove nutrients from water and produce dissolved oxygen, thereby increasing the quality of coastal waters, possibly for other types of mariculture.

But mariculture itself has other negative impacts on the environment. At best, mariculture pens may be unsightly. At worst, they have often been constructed by destroying natural coastal habitats such as mangroves. In Thailand, for example, it is estimated that about a third of the country's mangrove forests [some 65,000 hectares (161,000 acres)] had been destroyed for shrimp farming by 1993. In countries as diverse as the United States and India, environmental resistance to new mariculture pens has prevented expansion of the industry in some areas.

Environmental impacts such as this might be easier to rationalize if mariculture were truly "feeding the world." But as some researchers point out, mariculture can be regarded as an extremely inefficient way of producing fish protein, given that two to four times more protein is consumed during the mariculture process as

233

produced in salable fish at the end. Yet from the farmer's viewpoint, this is not necessarily a negative argument if low-value fishmeal and fish oil is turned into high-value salmon and shrimp for which there is a buoyant and growing market.

Where ocean ranching is practiced, considerable concern has been expressed over the contamination of wild species when farmed species are released into the wild (farmed salmon produced by ocean ranching now represent 40 percent of salmon caught in the North Atlantic). The use of genetically modified organisms (GMOs) in mariculture has heightened concerns that the biodiversity of natural species is increasingly under threat from the smaller gene pool of "artificial species."

External environmental costs such as this are seldom factored into the equation when mariculture farmers set up their fish farms, although the costs of pollution may eventually feed back negatively into the farmers' own operations. Also, whereas the "polluter pays principle" suggests either the farmers or the consumers of mariculture products should pay these environmental costs, inevitably, as with other forms of pollution, it is the planet that pays a long-term price through the degradation of the "commons"—reduced biodiversity, habitat loss, and ocean pollution.

Future of Mariculture

Increasing pressure on natural fish stocks and a growing human population suggest that an expanded global mariculture industry is practically a certainty. Yet the environmental costs of producing food in this way must somehow be borne by the industry if such dramatic growth is ever to take place. Some argue for pollution taxes or reforms of world trade to take account of environmental sustainability; others suggest that public health concerns act as a form of precautionary regulation, such as when world opinion turned drastically against the production of genetically modified foods in 1999. Greater interest in preserving areas such as mangroves for ecotourism and greater general awareness of environmental issues will also help to ensure that in solving one set of (economic) problems, mariculture doesn't simply create a different set of (environmental) problems.

Chris Woodford

FURTHER READING
Bongaarts, John. "Can the Growing Human Population Feed Itself?" *Scientific American,* March 1994, p. 36.
De Silva, Sena, ed. *Tropical Mariculture.* San Diego: Academic Press, 1998.
Hagler, Mike. *Shrimp: The Devastating Delicacy.* Washington, D.C.: Greenpeace USA, 1997.
Mukerjee, Madhusree. "Pink Gold." *Scientific American,* July 1996, p. 16.
Naylor, Rosamond, et al. "Nature's Subsidies to Shrimp and Salmon Farming." *Science,* Vol. 282, 30 October 1998, p. 883.
Pillay, T. *Aquaculture: Principles and Practice.* Oxford, and Cambridge, Mass.: Fishing News Books, 1993.
Plunkett, Donald, and Donald Winkelmann. "Technology for Sustainable Agriculture." *Scientific American,* September 1995, p. 148.
Raloff, J. "Downtown Fisheries?" *Science News,* 13 May 2000, p. 314.
Shepherd, Jonathan, and Niall Bromage. *Intensive Fish Farming.* Cambridge, Mass.: Blackwell, 1992.
Shueller, Gretel. "Testing the Waters." *New Scientist,* 2 October 1999, p. 34.

RELATED ARTICLES
Fisheries; Ocean Thermal Energy Conversion

Marine Biology

Marine biology is the scientific study of ocean life. Life probably began in water, and for most of Earth's history the dominant forms of life on our planet have been marine organisms. Although biologists have discovered more land-living animal species than marine species, the oceans are home to a much greater diversity of higher animal groups, such as phyla. The job of the marine biologist is to study and make sense of this vast diversity of ocean life, from the tiniest microbes to the largest animals on Earth.

History of Marine Biology

Human knowledge of marine life dates back to prehistoric times. Archaeological finds show that people were using harpoons and hooks to catch fish and other sea animals in the Stone Age, and piles of shells—the remains of "clambakes"—indicate that shellfish have long been an important source of protein to people. As hunter-gatherers, early humans probably harvested seafoods by wading out to sea to harpoon fish and collect mollusks, a practice that continues to this day in many parts of the world. Some anthropologists believe that prehistoric human migrations out of Africa and into Asia may have followed a coastal route, since the skills and knowledge required to live off seafood are applicable over vast geographical areas.

Although early cultures built up a store of practical knowledge about sea animals, the systematic, scientific study of marine biology did not begin until later. One of the first marine biologists was the Greek philosopher Aristotle (384–322 B.C.), who was fascinated by the diversity of animals found in the sea, particularly crabs, lobsters, and other crustaceans. Aristotle kept a detailed catalog of every type of marine animal he could find, and he made several important findings, including his discovery that gills are the breathing organs of fish. He divided all forms of life into two kingdoms: plants and animals. As such, he was one of the first people to practice taxonomy, the scientific classification of living organisms. Biologists now classify all forms of life into five kingdoms: animals, plants, fungi (previously classified as plants), and two kingdoms of microscopic organisms (protists and monera).

Despite Aristotle's contribution to marine biology, the science made little progress for centuries. A major breakthrough came in the seventeenth century, when the development of glass microscopes led to the discovery that aquatic habitats are home to innumerable forms of life invisible to the naked eye. The Dutch scientist Antonie von Leeuwenhoek (1632–1723) became world famous for his discovery of such "animalcules." Von Leeuwenhoek was one of the first people to see microscopic plankton, the minute organisms that are found in huge numbers in ocean surface waters. He also discovered that marine invertebrates such as mussels do not arise spontaneously from sand, as people once thought, but grow from microscopic larvae that emerge from eggs.

Although people had known for thousands of years that a great diversity of animals can be found in coastal waters, it was not until the nineteenth century that scientists discovered the realm of life that inhabits the seafloor. The British naturalist Edward Forbes (1815–54) carried out dredgings of the seafloor from a ship while sailing around the British Isles in the 1840s and 1850s and discovered many previously unknown species as a result. Forbes also found that different types of organisms lived at different depths. Another notable British seafarer and naturalist was Charles Darwin (1809–82), whose famous voyage on HMS *Beagle* partly inspired his theory of evolution. Darwin's theory revolutionized all fields of biology by explaining how such a tremendous diversity of species has come to exist and how each species becomes superbly adapted to its own position in nature. Darwin also made an important contribution to marine geology with his theory of coral atoll formation, which is now widely accepted.

After Edward Forbes's death, other scientists continued to explore the oceans. The British naturalist Charles Wyville Thomson (1830–82) led the most important oceanographic expedition of the nineteenth century on a specially equipped warship, HMS *Challenger*. The *Challenger* expedition was to have an enormous influence on marine science because the scientists on board gathered a vast amount of data in a meticulous and scientific manner. *Challenger*'s three-and-a-half-year voyage, starting in 1872, investigated the Atlantic, Pacific, and Indian Oceans. Detailed observations were made of marine life, sea temperature, ocean currents, seafloor contours, and many other phenomena. The data took years to publish and filled 50 books.

Systematic expeditions to study the oceans continued in the twentieth century. One notable example was the Danish *Galathea* expedition of 1950–52, which was undertaken to study marine life in the unexplored deep-ocean trenches. The *Galathea*'s dredges came up teeming with a variety of fish and invertebrates, including many species that had never been seen before, much to the fascination of the team of more than 50 scientists onboard. Among the discoveries was "Prince Axel's wonder-fish" (*Thaumatichthys axeli*), a strange fish trawled from a depth of 3590 meters (11,778 feet) in the Atlantic Ocean.

Ocean expeditions caused great interest among biologists because many of the organisms discovered were new to science or had previously been thought extinct. However, the specimens were often dead by the time they reached land, so biologists began to set up permanent coastal stations where marine organisms could be studied alive. The first permanent marine laboratory was the Stazione Zoologica in Naples, Italy. The first American laboratory was the Marine Biological Laboratory at Woods Hole, Massachusetts, which is now one of the world's foremost marine biology research sites.

The twentieth century brought important advances in underwater exploration technology, allowing biologists to observe marine life in the natural environment. The most important innovation was the scuba tank, invented in 1943 by French marine explorer Jacques Cousteau (1910–97) and engineer Émile Gagnan. Scuba (self-contained underwater breathing apparatus) allows divers to explore shallow waters while breathing from a tank of compressed air. The development of small submersibles, or bathyscaphes, later allowed scientists to explore the ocean depths. In 1977, scientists from the Woods Hole Oceanographic Institute, on board the now-famous submersible *Alvin*, discovered very unusual ecosystems on the Pacific floor that depend entirely on energy released from volcanic vents (black smokers) and have no need for sunlight.

Marine Biology Today

Although taxonomy remains important, marine biology now has a much broader scope than it did in the nineteenth century. It not only involves a very wide range of biological disciplines but overlaps with other sciences as well. Marine geology, for instance, is difficult to separate from biology because living organisms have had a profound influence on the physical structure of the oceans. The sedimentary rocks and ooze that make up much of the ocean floor consist largely of skeletons of dead marine organisms, and coral reefs and atolls are built from the accumulated skeletons of tiny coral polyps. Similarly, the chemistry of the oceans is inextricably linked to the organisms that live within them.

One of the most important branches of modern marine biology is ecology: the study of habitats, the populations of organisms that live within them, and the way these organisms interact. Marine ecology is of great importance to people because it helps us to exploit marine resources, such as fish and other seafood, while minimizing damage to the marine environment. Marine ecology also helps us to understand how the oceans absorb pollution and how they affect the global climate and nutrient cycles.

Ecologists divide ocean life into three major categories according to habitat and lifestyle: plankton (small organisms that drift in the surface waters), nekton (active swimmers), and benthos (organisms of the seafloor). These different categories are interlinked in many complex ways. Many members of the plankton, for example, are larvae (immature forms) of animals that are benthic (bottom dwelling) as adults.

Ben Morgan

FURTHER READING

Banister, Keith, and Andrew Campbell. *The Encyclopaedia of Underwater Life.* London: Allen and Unwin, 1985.

Brusca, Richard C., and Gary J. Brusca. *Invertebrates.* Sunderland, Mass.: Sinauer, 1990.

Carson, Rachel. *The Sea Around Us.* Oxford: Oxford Paperbacks, 1997.

Castro, Peter, and Michael E. Huber. *Marine Biology.* St. Louis, Mo.: Mosby Year Book, 1991; 3rd ed., Boston: McGraw-Hill, 2000.

Fish, J. *A Student's Guide to the Seashore.* London and Boston: Unwin Hyman, 1989; 2nd ed., Cambridge and New York: Cambridge University Press, 1996.

Levinton, Jeffrey. *Marine Biology: Function, Biodiversity, Ecology.* New York and Oxford: Oxford University Press, 1995.

Nybakken, James W. *Marine Biology: An Ecological Approach,* 5th ed. San Francisco: Benjamin Cummings, 2001.

Sumich, James. *An Introduction to the Biology of Marine Life.* Dubuque, Iowa: Wm. C. Brown, 1976; 7th ed., New York: McGraw-Hill: 1999.

RELATED ARTICLES

Benthos; Biodiversity; Biosphere; Cousteau, Jacques-Yves; Darwin, Charles Robert; Deep-Sea Exploration; Ecology; Ichthyology; Nekton; Nutrient; Plankton

Marine Fungi

Although much less obvious to the observer than their terrestrial counterparts, the members of the Kingdom Fungi living in the ocean and brackish waters play a crucial role in the recycling of nutrients.

Of the more than 200 species of filamentous fungi and nearly 200 species of single-celled yeasts found in salt water, about three-fourths are *ascomycetes.* These fungi produce their sexual spores, known as ascospores, in sacs called *asci.* Most of the rest of the marine species are *basidiomycetes,* the club fungi, which produce their sexual spores, called basidiospores, at the tips of club-shaped filaments called *basidia.* The few remaining marine species produce only asexual spores and belong in the artificial category called *deuteromycetes.* Although these advanced ascomycetes and basidiomycetes are more important in recycling nutrients, the primitive chytrids have a role as well. In addition, species in at least eight genera of chytrids are parasitic on red and green algae.

Marine fungi occupy a variety of ecological roles. Some are parasites on such higher plants as surf grasses, some attack macroalgae, and some parasitize animals. Other marine species have taken up a symbiotic existence with microscopic algae or photosynthetic prokaryotes to form lichens. Still other species are saprobes that live on dead organic matter. Over 100 fungal species live on *Spartina,* a flowering plant of salt marshes in temperate regions. Those adapted to the marine environment occur regularly on submersed lower parts of the plant. Other marine fungi live in the deep sea. If sufficient oxygen is present, they cause "soft rot" of wood that sinks to the ocean floor. Yet other marine fungal species grow in the small water-filled spaces between sand grains on beaches, where their spores accumulate and concentrate in the sea foam.

In tropical and semitropical waters, fungi colonize mangrove bark, wood, dropped leaves, and seedlings. They even colonize mangrove seedlings. These floating seedlings may provide transoceanic dispersal of marine fungi. If oxygen is available, every untreated piece of wood, whether it has washed into the sea naturally or was placed there by humans, will be attacked by marine fungi. The fungi appear to "predigest" the wood surfaces and pave the way for larval settlement of wood-boring molluscan bivalves. These bivalves are the major cause of damage to wood in the oceans.

Other marine fungi weaken manila hemp rope and break down tunicin, the animal cellulose produced by tunicates. In some cases fungi will attack molted chitin exoskeletons of crabs and the waterproofing protein keratin in the tubes of polychaetes. Some marine fungi even penetrate the calcium carbonate in the cell walls of algae, empty shipworm tubes, tests of barnacles, and shells of intertidal molluscs. In the latter, the fungus is probably ignoring the calcium carbonate and using conchyolin, the organic matrix of the shells, as a food source. Fungal filaments have even been found inside the byssal threads that attach the mussel *Mytilus* to the substrate.

Filamentous fungi are important in marine food chains because they increase the nutritional value of marsh plant detritus. At least one stylet-bearing nematode feeds by draining the cytoplasm from marine fungal cells. Many marine molluscs graze preferentially on the parts of large marine algae infested with fungal parasites. Boring isopod crustaceans, known as *gribbles*, can live on sterile wood but will not reproduce unless they have marine fungi in their diet. Only the open ocean waters are a filamentous fungal desert. However, even there, single-celled yeasts and small chytrids can live attached to plankton and pelagic animals.

Bette H. Nybakken

FURTHER READING
Alexopoulos, C. J., C. W. Mims, and M. Blackwell. *Introductory Mycology*, 4th ed. New York: Wiley, 1996.
Carroll, G. C., and D. T. Wicklow. *The Fungal Community: Its Organization and Role in the Ecosystem*. New York: Marcel Dekker, 1992.
Kohlmeyer, J., and E. Kohlmeyer. *Marine Mycology: The Higher Fungi*. New York: Academic Press, 1979.
Raven, P. H., R. F. Evert, and S. E. Eichhorn. *Biology of Plants*, 6th ed. New York: W. H. Freeman, 1999.
Sieburth, J. M. *Sea Microbes*. New York: Oxford University Press, 1979.

RELATED ARTICLES
Lichen

Marine Geology

Marine geology includes all studies that focus on the nature of Earth beneath the sea, including its history and the processes that shape its evolution. It is an important field because so much of Earth's surface is covered by water (approximately 70 percent), and much of what lies beneath the water is poorly understood. Furthermore, ocean basins are changing constantly. Slow changes occur from seafloor spreading at mid-ocean ridges, extrusions from underwater volcanoes, and addition of sediments from skeletal remains of small marine plants and animals. On the other hand, very rapid changes occur in shallow water where rivers enter the ocean and in deeper water when sediments are transported episodically offshore through submarine canyons. Although currents throughout much of the ocean are considered to be sluggish, much sediment can nevertheless be moved from one location to another over long periods of time. Recent fundamental advances in our understanding of marine geology have been exceedingly important to petroleum and seafloor mining industries, defense mapping agencies, the shipping industry, and for unraveling the geological record of global climate change.

Marine geologists typically work from ships, using a variety of sampling, seismic, and drilling tools. Systematic study of the seafloor has been made possible by revolutionary advances in swath sonar and multichannel seismic mapping techniques to examine, respectively, the surface and subsurface of the seafloor. The seafloor now can even be mapped by satellite using radar altimeters. Ocean drilling serves as a way to obtain samples from deep within Earth's layers of sediment and rock and to aid in the geological interpretation of large-scale mapping efforts. For more than three decades, the Deep Sea Drilling Project and the Ocean Drilling Program (ODP) have led more than 100 deep-sea drilling cruises, fostered international cooperation, and enhanced our understanding of the history of Earth. Much of marine geology is also carried out in the laboratory, using sophisticated instruments that measure chemical composition, organic constituents, and radioactive elements in both sediments and rock.

Brief History of Marine Geology

The historical foundation for marine geology began, as it did generally for other areas of marine sciences, with the HMS *Challenger* expedition in the late nineteenth century (1872–76). During the expedition, extensive deep soundings of the ocean basins were made, the major types of ocean sediments were identified, and microfossil assemblages were differentiated on the basis of latitude. Fifty years later, another important expedition was that of the German ship *Meteor*, which mapped the extent of the mid-Atlantic Ridge using an early 1930s version of the echo sounder. Some especially dramatic developments in marine geology occurred during World War II. For example, the first principles of beach dynamics were established at this time because of their importance to amphibious landings. Additionally, pioneering work on characterizing seafloor sediments was undertaken because of the effects of sediments on the behavior of sound and thus on the importance to antisubmarine warfare. Seafloor bathymetry was imaged with fathometers that were used on ships to measure depth.

Following World War II, the U.S. Office of Naval Research and the National Science Foundation began supporting significant efforts in marine geological research for civilian purposes. Rapid advances in the 1950s and 1960s were made in seismic reflection techniques, deep-diving capabilities, and technology for obtaining gravity and piston cores in very deep water. In the early 1960s, revolutionary new ideas concerning seafloor spreading were introduced and later confirmed by studies of magnetic reversals on mid-ocean ridges and subsequent deep-sea drilling of those anomalies and dating the oldest sediments and underlying rocks. By the 1980s, side-scan sonar and multichannel seismic systems were widely available to scientists. During the 1990s, mapping capabilities increased significantly, owing to the availability and accuracy of the global positioning system (GPS), and data-processing capabilities increased significantly, owing to unprecedented advances in computer technology.

The Seafloor and Its Sediments

Even today, more than a century after the HMS *Challenger* expedition, the seafloor is still being mapped. The floor of the ocean can be broadly divided into continental margins, deep-ocean basins, and mid-ocean ridges. Continental margins are the areas adjacent to land; they consist of the continental shelf, which is the submerged part of a continent, the continental slope, which is the steep and relatively narrow incline that leads to the continental rise, a region with a more gradual incline that merges with the deep-ocean basin or abyssal plain. The abyssal plain is a flat, featureless region where thick accumulations of sediment have buried most of the topographic relief. Isolated volcanic peaks that rise from the ocean floor are called *seamounts*, and deep structural incisions into the ocean crust are called *deep-ocean trenches*. An interconnected mid-ocean ridge system extends as a prominent, mountain-like feature down the center of ocean basins, in places rising as much as 3000 meters (9840 feet) above the surrounding ocean floor. Island and continental volcanic arcs rise above subduction zones where seafloor is being consumed along convergent margins.

Most of the ocean floor is covered by a blanket of sediments. Sediments can be broadly classified as terrigenous, biogenous, and hydrogenous. *Terrigenous sediments* are land-derived mineral and rock fragments or clasts that are delivered primarily by rivers. Most terrigenous sediments are trapped on the continental margins. Red clays are fine-grained sediment particles, stained by iron, that are carried to the deep ocean basins by winds. *Biogenous sediments* are derived from the skeletal remains of mostly microscopic marine plants and animals. They are referred to as calcareous (calcium carbonate) oozes and siliceous (silica) oozes. Hemipelagic sediments are sediments, typically on the outer continental margin, that contain mixtures of terrigenous and biogenous material. *Hydrogenous sediments* are precipitated directly from seawater. Well-known examples are pyrite and manganese nodules. The composition of marine sediments provides important clues about their origin and the history of the region in which they are found.

Sediments on the ocean floor contain vast mineral resources that are vitally important to a growing world population. Most are created so slowly that for human purposes, they are considered to be fixed in quantity and thus nonrenewable. Although petroleum and natural gas are the most obvious resources, the shallow seafloor also contains sand and gravel, tin, gold, titanium, and diamonds. In the deep ocean, sulfide deposits form from circulation of seawater when it comes in contact with hot volcanic magma in certain regions of the ocean's uppermost layer, the crust. Sulfur, iron, copper, and zinc are leached from the crust and later precipitated to form massive metallic deposits.

Seismic Stratigraphy and Paleoceanography

Seismic stratigraphy is a relatively new and important approach to studying sedimentary strata under the seafloor. It involves the correlation and interpretation of seismic reflection profiles of the subbottom sediments and sedimentary rocks. The geometry, thickness, composition, and age relations of sedimentary sequences are determined using acoustic energy that is reflected from interfaces between sedimentary layers. This information then allows marine geologists to interpret sea-level history, types of depositional events, and basin history. Paleoceanography, the study of ocean history, integrates the changes in ocean waters with the deep-sea geologic record contained within the sediments of the ocean basins. Important topics in paleoceanography include surface- and bottom-water circulation patterns, biogeographic distribution of marine organisms, global ice volume, and changes in oxygen isotope and carbon cycles. These topics may aid in understanding former "ice age" oceans and the causes for extinctions, even important terrestrial extinctions such as the Cretaceous–Tertiary boundary that marked the disappearance of the dinosaurs and many other fauna and flora approximately 65 million years ago.

Marine Processes

The geology of the seafloor is affected by marine processes that transport sediments. These processes range from imperceptibly slow in the case of deep-ocean circulation to catastrophically fast in the case of turbidity currents that sweep through steep submarine canyons. Continental margins, especially where water depths are sufficiently shallow to allow both waves and currents to move the sediments, display depositional features such as ridges and underwater dunes, and erosional features such as furrows and marginal channels. In deep waters of the lower continental margin and of the abyssal plain, sediments can also be transported by bottom currents, and extremely dense (compared to seawater) sediment concentrations close to the bottom, called *nepheloid layers*, are evidence of this process. Many of the new frontiers in marine geology seek to combine not only physical but also chemical and biological processes, with knowledge of sedimentary deposits to explore questions of global change. Some of the most pressing global societal issues concern the role of marine sediments in carbon storage and export, the role of sea-level change on coastal erosion, and the impact of human activities on benthic marine habitats such as coral reefs.

John T. Wells

FURTHER READING
Ballard, Robert. *Exploring Our Living Planet.* Washington, D.C.: National Geographic Society, 1983; rev. ed., 1988.
Hamblin, W. Kenneth. *Earth's Dynamics Systems: A Textbook in Physical Geology.* Minneapolis, Minn.: Burgess, 1975; 9th ed., with Eric H. Christiansen, Upper Saddle River, N.J.: Prentice Hall, 2001.
Kennett, James. *Marine Geology.* Englewood Cliffs, N.J.: Prentice Hall, 1982.
Seibold, Eugen, and Wolfgang H. Berger. *The Sea Floor: An Introduction to Marine Geology.* Berlin and New York: Springer-Verlag, 1982; 3rd rev. and updated ed., 1996.
Tarbuck, Edward J., and Frederick K. Lutgens. *The Earth: An Introduction to Physical Geology.* Columbus, Ohio: Charles E. Merrill, 1984; 6th ed., Upper Saddle River, N.J.: Prentice Hall, 1999.

RELATED ARTICLES
Abyssal Plain; Continental Margin; Continental Shelf; Continental Slope; Deep Sea Drilling Project; HMS *Challenger*; Marine Geophysics; Mid-Ocean Ridge; Ocean Basin; Ocean Drilling Program; Paleoceanography; Seafloor Spreading; Seamount; Seismic Stratigraphy; Subduction Zone; Turbidity Current

Marine Geophysics

Marine geophysics is a field of study that explores the origin, composition, structure, and development of the ocean basins. Major areas of inquiry include Earth's gravity and magnetic fields, the sedimentary framework of its ocean basins, the shape and rotation of Earth, and the concentric layers that make up Earth's interior. Advances in instrumentation over the past several decades have also made it possible for geophysicists to measure the rate at which heat and electricity pass through the seabed and to measure the radioactivity in rocks and sediments under the oceans. Geophysical measurements are important because of our demand for petroleum and minerals, a need for better maps of the bottom, and the desire for a better understanding of the evolution of ocean basins. Marine geophysics is a relatively young field, and virtually all of the major advances have occurred since the 1950s.

Navigating at Sea
Geophysical measurements in the ocean are of little value if locations of those measurements cannot be determined accurately. Traditional forms of celestial, compass, and land-referenced navigation have now been replaced by electronic navigation systems, developed in part as a result of military needs. Modern navigation systems use technology based on electromagnetic waves (radar, Loran-C), sonar (acoustic transponders), and satellites (global positioning system). By far the most innovative advance in navigation has been the global positioning system (GPS), which provides continuous fixes at any location in the world using orbiting satellites. GPS has been the principal means of navigation for geophysical mapping since the early 1990s. However, certain types of geophysical work (e.g., drilling or conducting repeated surveys) use arrays of acoustic transponders on the seabed to provide extremely accurate positioning of a vessel's range and bearing relative to the fixed transponders.

Tools of Geophysics
Technological developments such as microelectronic devices, fiber-optic cables, and new ceramics and alloys have been important to the field of geophysics. Imaging by sonar is one of the primary tools of geophysics. This technique, which uses acoustic signals, allows high-resolution mapping of seafloor morphology. An echo sounder is a simple surveying device that

records the depths beneath a ship and thus provides a profile of the bottom along a course of travel. More sophisticated acoustic systems are able to image detailed seabed morphology in regions not only beneath, but also to the side, of the ship, thus creating what is referred to as *multibeam swath bathymetry*. Side-scan sonar systems, based on intensity of backscattering (also out to the sides), provide shaded images of the seafloor that can be used to identify different bottom types as well as variations in grain size. For deepwater applications, side-scan sonar systems have been developed that will allow operation in heavy seas. One such system, GLORIA (Geological Long Range Inclined Asdic), was used in mapping the Exclusive Economic Zone (EEZ) in U.S. waters.

Seismic exploration of the bottom involves measuring the time required for a pulse of transmitted energy to return to a ship after being reflected and refracted from sedimentary or rock layers with different physical properties. It differs from sonar imaging in that the vertical structure (layers) can be seen. The pulses or waves can be sent out from many different types of sources, each with particular characteristics, referred to variously as air guns, water guns, sparkers, boomers, and even chemical explosives. Underwater detectors, such as hydrophones and geophones, are towed behind the ships to detect the signals that are returned to the surface. Perhaps the most common technique, multichannel seismic reflection profiling, reveals thickness and geometry of sedimentary layers to great depths (thousands of meters) beneath the seafloor and can be used to aid in interpreting the composition of sedimentary deposits, their origin, and the location of geological hazards such as unstable slopes. Seismic refraction studies, which traditionally have been conducted using explosives and a second ship (or sonobuoys) for receiving the returned signals, led to our early understanding of the oceanic crust, the rigid outermost layer under the oceans of Earth.

Other tools in marine geophysics include magnetometers for determining the magnetic field and magnetic anomalies, and thermistors and needle probes for determining heat flow in sediments. Earth's magnetism is highly variable. Paleomagnetism, the study of magnetism at the time that rocks were formed, can be used to help understand magnetic reversals and thus the structure and history of the oceans. In a similar fashion, measurements of thermal gradients and conductivity offer important clues for understanding evolution of ocean basins, such as the history of sinking or subsidence, as well as how magma is generated for volcanic activity. Finally, offshore drilling and geophysical well logs have been used for more than half a century to search for petroleum and to unravel the detailed variations in sediment that can be used to help understand important global issues such as climate change. Cores returned to the laboratory can be characterized by their electrical resistivity, natural radiation, water content, and density.

Magnetic Reversals and Evolution of the Ocean Basins

One of the most significant of all geophysical discoveries, seafloor spreading (now encompassed in the more unified theory of plate tectonics), was confirmed by the study of magnetic reversals. The early hypothesis of seafloor spreading was that new ocean crust was formed periodically at mountainlike ocean ridges from extrusion of molten material from deep within Earth. Spreading was thought to occur symmetrically to both sides of the ocean ridges. Using magnetometers, researchers discovered alternating stripes of magnetic variation in crust that occurred parallel to ocean ridges. Because each magnetic stripe reflects the polarity of Earth's magnetic field at the time the material is extruded, a record of spreading chronology is created. By establishing dates of magnetic reversals, the rates of ocean basin spreading have been determined to be 2 to 20 centimeters (0.8 to 8 inches) per year.

Mapping the Seafloor from Space

Measurements of ocean properties such as temperature, turbidity, and chlorophyll content, and ocean dynamics such as currents, waves, and small changes in sea-surface elevation, are now routinely undertaken with satellites. Geophysicists can even make maps of the seafloor by using orbiting spacecraft. Referred to as *satellite radar altimetry,* this technique is based on the tight relationship between the surface of the ocean and the topography of the seafloor. The shape of the sea surface mimics the shape of the seafloor because of variations in gravitational attraction that can pile up water over elevated features and leave depressions over troughs or other low areas in the bottom. A satellite measures the amount of time for a pulse of emitted radar to be reflected from the ocean surface back to the satellite. This, in turn, provides a measure of the sea-surface elevation relative to the satellite, which has its own elevation measured accurately by lasers. Satellite altimetry is especially useful for mapping bottom topography in remote locations, such as the South Pacific Ocean.

John T. Wells

FURTHER READING

Alexandrov, A. A. "Study of Sea Bottom Characteristics by Side-Looking Sonar." *Oceanology,* Vol. 23 (1983), pp. 378–381.

Franchetean, J. "The Oceanic Crust." *Scientific American,* Vol. 249 (1983), pp. 114–129.

Hoffman, K. A. "Ancient Magnetic Reversals: Clues to the Geodynamo." *Scientific American,* Vol. 258 (1988), pp. 76–83.

Jones, E. J. W. *Marine Geophysics.* Chichester, England, and New York: Wiley, 1999.

Kennett, James. *Marine Geology.* Englewood Cliffs, N.J.: Prentice Hall, 1982.

Laughton, A. S. "Exploitation or Responsible Use of the Ocean." *Underwater Technology,* Vol. 20 (1994), pp. 32–39.

RELATED ARTICLES

Acoustic Oceanography; Global Positioning System; Loran; Marine Geology; Navigation; Plate Tectonics; Seafloor Spreading; Seismic Refraction; Sonar

Marine Mammal Protection Act

The Marine Mammal Protection Act (MMPA) was enacted in 1972 to protect and manage marine mammals and the use of their products. The governmental agencies responsible for implementing the act are the U.S. Fish and Wildlife Service (FWS) and the National Marine Fisheries Service (NMFS). The U.S. Fish and Wildlife Service manages walruses, polar bears, sea otters, dugongs, marine otters, and West Indian, Amazonian, and West African manatees. The National Marine Fisheries Service manages whales, porpoises, seals, and sea lions.

The MMPA established the Marine Mammal Commission, whose duties involve reviewing laws and international conventions relative to marine mammals, studying the condition of these mammals, and making recommendations to federal representatives that should be taken for the protection of marine mammals.

The Marine Mammal Protection Act Amendments of 1994 reauthorized the Marine Mammal Protection Act (MMPA) of 1972. Changes were made to many of the act's provisions, which incorporated contributions from commercial fishers, conservation groups, scientific researchers, governmental agencies, animal protection groups, and the Alaska Native community. Some of the provisions of the amendments included:

1. Program improvement to reduce the incidental taking of marine mammals during commercial fishing operations.

Marine Mammal Protection Act – 1996 Marine Mammal Stock Assessments

Species	Stock area	Potential Biological Removal	Total annual mortality	Annual fisheries mortality	Primary source of mortality
North Atlantic right whale	W, North Atlantic	0.4	2.5	1.1	Collisions with ships
Harbor porpoise	Gulf of Maine/Bay of Fundy	483	1,834	1,834	Northeast multispecies sink gillnet fishery
Common dolphin	W. North Atlantic	40	234	234	Atlantic large pelagics drift gillnet fishery
Atlantic spotted dolphin	W. North Atlantic	16	22	22	Atlantic large pelagics drift gillnet fishery
Pantropical spotted dolphin	W. North Atlantic	16	22	22	Atlantic large pelagics drift gillnet fishery
Cuvier's beaked whale	W. North Atlantic	8.9	9.7	9.7	Atlantic large pelagics drift gillnet fishery
Mesoplodont beaked whale	W. North Atlantic	8.9	9.7	9.7	Atlantic large pelagics drift gillnet fishery
Pilot whale, short-finned	W. North Atlantic	3.7	42	42	Atlantic large pelagics drift gillnet fishery
Bottlenose dolphin	W. North Atlantic, coastal	25	29	29	Undetermined fisheries interactions, suspected of being from mid-Atlantic coastal gillnet fishery
Pilot whale, short-finned	CA/OR/WA	5.9	13	13	CA/OR thresher shark/swordfish drift gillnet fishery
Mesoplodont beaked whale	CA/OR/WA	11	9.2-13	9.2-13	CA/OR thresher shark/swordfish drift gillnet fishery
Sperm whale	CA to WA	1.8	4.5	4.5	CA/OR thresher shark/swordfish drift gillnet fishery
Humpback whale	California/Mexico	0.5	1.8	1.2	CA/OR thresher shark/swordfish drift gillnet fishery
Minke whale	CA/OR/WA	1.0	1.2	1.2	CA/OR thresher shark/swordfish drift gillnet fishery
Steller sea lion	Western U.S.	383	447	35	Subsistence harvest
Beluga	Cook Inlet	15	40	0	Subsistence harvest

Source: 1996 Marine Mammal Stock Assessment reports as repeated in Marine Mammal Protection Act of 1972 Annual Report – January 1, 1998 to December 31, 1998

This table, taken from the 1998 annual report of the Marine Mammal Protection Act of 1972, outlines threats to the population of various marine mammal groups.

2. Defining two levels of harassment. *Level A harassment* is defined as any act of pursuit, torment, or annoyance that has the potential to injure a marine mammal or marine mammal stock in the wild. *Level B harassment* is defined as harassment having the potential to disturb a marine mammal or marine mammal stock in the wild by causing disruption of behavioral patterns, including, but not limited to, migration, breathing, nursing, breeding, feeding, or sheltering.

3. Restricting scientific research to level B harassment.

4. Adding a new category of permits for photography of marine mammals in the wild for educational or commercial purposes.

5. Encouraging cooperative agreements between Alaska Native organizations and federal agencies with the idea of marine mammal conservation and coordinated management efforts regarding subsistence issues.

6. Encouraging the NMFS and FWS to protect marine mammal rookeries, mating grounds, and areas of similar ecological significance.

7. Promoting the establishment of Regional Scientific Review Groups, in consultation with the Marine Mammal Commission

(MMC), to advise the NMFS and FWS on actual, expected, or potential impacts of habitat destruction on marine mammal stocks.

NMFS was directed to create and implement research plans that assess the health and stability of ecosystems where marine mammals live. Specific activities include a regional workshop for the Gulf of Maine to assess human-caused factors affecting ecosystem health and stability; development of a research plan to monitor the health and stability of the Bering Sea ecosystem; and an

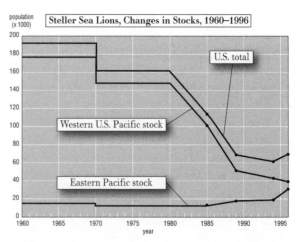

Stock of the Steller sea lion, protected under the Marine Mammal Protection Act. Note the rise in the eastern stock at the end of the 1990s. [Adapted from Report on the Status of U.S. Living Marine Resources *(U.S. Department of Commerce, 1999.)]*

assessment of the impact that California sea lions and Pacific harbor seals have on salmonids and ecosystem stability in the coastal ecosystems of Washington, Oregon, and California.

Anne Beesley

FURTHER READING

Barnes, Robert. *Invertebrate Zoology.* Philadelphia: W. B. Saunders, 1963; 6th ed., by Edward Ruppert, Fort Worth, Texas: Saunders College Publishing, 1994.

Gross, M. Grant. *Oceanography: A View of the Earth.* Englewood Cliffs, N.J.: Prentice Hall, 1972; 7th ed., Upper Saddle River, N.J.: Prentice Hall, 1996.

Regulations implementing MMPA are found in Title 50 of the *Code of Federal Regulations* (CFR), Parts 13, 18, 216, and 229.

USEFUL WEB SITES

Marine Mammal Protection Act, United States Code. Title 16, "Conservation." Chapter 31, "Marine Mammal Protection."
<http://www.nmfs.noaa.gov/prot_res/laws/MMPA/MMPA.html>

National Oceanic and Atmospheric Administration.
<http://www.noaa.gov>.

U.S. Fish and Wildlife Service; Division of Congressional and Legislative Affairs. "Digest of Federal Resource Laws of Interest to the U.S. Fish and Wildlife Service: Table of Contents."
<http://laws.fws.gov/lawsdigest/indx.html>.

RELATED ARTICLES

Fisheries

Marine Optics

Marine optics deals with the physical behavior of light on the surface and within the volume of the sea. It is also concerned with how light enters into biological, chemical, and physical processes in the ocean. Finally, marine optics is concerned with the transmission of information via optical signals above and within the sea. The most important source of light is solar radiation, but light in the sea can also be generated by both biological and chemical means, as well as by light sources introduced by humans. The behavior of light in the ocean affects not only the heating of the upper layer but also the growth of plants. Light has marine applications for charting, for measuring bioluminescence, or for finding fish, submarines, and mines.

Optical Properties of Seawater

Seawater has both inherent and apparent optical properties. This allows the properties of seawater to be considered separately from those of the light source. If the light source is suspended and other particles are not affected by its removal from the sea, inherent properties can be measured in the laboratory. Apparent properties must be measured in situ. For a parallel, monochromatic light beam, the inherent properties include the attenuation coefficient c, the volume absorption coefficient a, and the volume scattering coefficient b, where $c = a + b$. The *beam absorption coefficient* is the measure of the reduction of the energy flux density in the direction of propagation of the light. The *beam scattering coefficient* describes the loss of flux due to the redirection of light out of the beam by the process of scattering. The ratio of the energy flux for a parallel, monochromatic light beam at 1 meter (3.3 feet), I_1, to that at the source, I_0, is $I_1/I_0 = e^{-c}$.

The inherent optical properties for pure seawater depend only weakly on temperature, salinity, and pressure. Large changes in the optical properties of ocean waters are due entirely to the presence of biological populations and their waste products, but nearshore suspended sediment and organic materials from land runoff are also important. Sediments are most pronounced near rivers, as is another class of optically active organic compounds, which are called *gelbstoffe* or yellow substance. The effects are largely separable, so it is possible to expand the attenuation coefficient to include a number of terms: For example, $c = c_\lambda = a_{\lambda w} + a_{\lambda d} + a_{\lambda p} + b_{\lambda w} + b_{\lambda d} + b_{\lambda p}$, where the subscript w indicates pure water; d, dissolved matter; and p, suspended particles. Attenuation is a strong function of wavelength, λ.

Apparent Properties

Apparent properties include the radiance, L (watts per square meter), and the diffuse attenuation coefficient for downwelling irradiance, $k_\lambda^\downarrow$ per meter, which are also both strongly wavelength dependent. The *radiance* is a measure of the radiation incident on a surface or emitted from a source. The *irradiance* is the flux of radiant energy normal to the horizontal plane. The downwelling irradiance attenuation, $k_\lambda^\downarrow(z)$, where z is depth, better represents the depth to which a lidar (a light radar) can detect an object than does $c_\lambda(z)$. It is always true that $a_\lambda < k_\lambda < c_\lambda = a_\lambda + b_\lambda$. A good estimate of the "water-leaving" irradiance $L_w(z)$ can be obtained from satellite observations of the sea surface. The apparent properties are connected to the inherent properties via the radiative transfer equation.

The wavelengths of principal interest range from 300 to 1000 nanometers. Outside this range, the ocean is nearly opaque to electromagnetic radiation. The underwater light field due to natural illumination is locally homogeneous in the horizontal but varies rapidly in the vertical. At any given depth there is a difference between the intensity of the downwelling and upwelling light, both because of the surface distribution of the light source as well as the attenuation of that source due of to oceanic absorbers and scatterers.

Within the ocean, light is mostly absorbed but is also scattered, by both seawater and particles within the water, including plankton. Absorption results in heating of the water. The *euphotic zone* is the upper layer of the ocean, in which the intensity of light is greater than 1 percent of its value at the sea surface. Within the euphotic zone, light is also converted to chemical energy by photosynthesis and reemitted as fluorescent radiation by chlorophyll *a*. Below 300 meters (about 980 feet), the strongest light is bioluminescence.

Color

In terms of clarity, waters may be classified as coastal (types 1 to 9) or oceanic (types I to III).

For oceanic waters, blue light (400 to 500 nanometers) is transmitted to the greatest depth, whereas coastal waters favor transmission of green-yellow light (580 to 650 nanometers) because plankton and organic compounds absorb blue light and water absorbs red. The wavelengths of light in water are only about three-fourths of those in air because the refractive index of seawater is about 1.34 and the speed of light is slowed proportionally. But since color is determined by frequency, it is not affected by the refractive index. Color is affected by wavelength-selective attenuation, and objects take on a blue or green tint because of water's strong absorption of red.

Refraction of Light

As light enters or leaves the sea, it is refracted. The speed of light in seawater is about 2.24×10^8 meters (7.35×10^8 feet) per second. The index of refraction for light entering seawater from the atmosphere is given by the ratio of the speed of light in air to the speed of light in seawater, which is 1.34. This varies by about 1 percent and is a function of the temperature and salinity of the water and the wavelength of light. Refraction causes distortion when looking across the air–sea interface as well as in underwater vision (photography) since there is air on one side of the faceplate (camera lens) and seawater on the other. Objects appear closer and larger than they actually are to the diver. To someone looking up through the surface, objects appear farther away than they actually are and objects never appear lower than 48° from the vertical.

Instrumentation

Marine optical instruments measure both apparent and inherent properties. The beam transmissometer projects a parallel beam of monochromatic light through a fixed length of water [typically 0.25 to 1 meter (about 0.8 to 3.3 feet)]. The ratio of the detected beam intensity is a measure of the total attenuation coefficient *a*, an inherent water property.

Irradiance meters are generally used to collect downwelling natural light fields (sunlight) through horizontal, flat, and translucent collectors. The absolute light intensity *E* (watts per square meter per nanometer) is measured at various wavelengths. Some instruments use six wavebands through the visible spectrum using filters. More sophisticated radiometers use up to 512 wavebands with diffraction grating spectrographs. Radiance meters collect highly directional light essentially through telescopes and typically measure upwelling radiance for application to satellite remote sensing. Thus, radiance *L* (watts per square meter per nanometer per steradian) is a measure of the light flux through a solid angle with units of steradians. These radiometers may collect light at one depth or may be used as free-fall profiling instruments, measuring radiance from the water surface to the base of the euphotic zone. Biological oceanographers often use irradiance collectors that measure photosynthetically active radiation (PAR) between 400 and 700 nanometers. This broad wavelength band is that absorbed by plant pigments.

Satellite Measurements of Ocean Color

Within the past two decades the field of marine optics has grown markedly, due principally to the use of ocean color satellites. These satellites (CZCS, MODIS, and SeaWiFS) measure the color of light reflected from the upper layer of the sea using detectors with several wavebands in the blue, green, yellow, and red parts of the visible spectrum. As explained above, phytoplankton pigments largely determine the spectrum of light reflected from the upper water column. Satellite images, corrected for large atmospheric effects and coupled with empirical algorithms, are now used to convert satellite ocean color information into plant pigment (largely chlorophyll) concentrations. In turn,

phytoplankton abundance, distribution, and variability are important globally in terms of the ocean food web and climate change. The maturation of marine optics and ocean color satellites coupled with rigorous shipborne biological sampling has allowed oceanographers for the first time to see worldwide distribution and changes in phytoplankton populations.

Curtis A. Collins

FURTHER READING

Jerlov, N. G. *Marine Optics.* New York: Elsevier, 1976.

Mobley, Curtis D. *Light and Water: Radiative Transfer in Natural Waters.* San Diego: Academic Press, 1994.

Preisendorfer, R. W. "Secchi Disk Science: Visual Optics of Natural Waters." *Limnology and Oceanography,* Vol. 31 (1986), pp. 909–926.

Robinson, Ian S. *Satellite Oceanography, an Introduction for Oceanographers and Remote-Sensing Scientists.* Hemel Hempstead, England: Ellis Horwood, 1991.

RELATED ARTICLES

Light Attenuation; Phytoplankton Pigment Fluorescence

Marine Sanctuary

The concept of marine protected areas (MPAs) has led to the designation and management of discrete areas in the coastal and marine environment akin to more traditional land parks and reserves. As on land, MPAs are designated for a variety of purposes; the IUCN–World Conservation Union recognizes six broad categories. As of 1994, there were over 1300 MPAs across the world, ranging from small zones such as Mafia Island off Tanzania to immense areas like the Great Barrier Reef Marine Park in Australia. The United States contains several different kinds of MPAs, including national parks, national wildlife refuges, national estuarine research reserves, and national marine sanctuaries. National marine sanctuaries (NMS) are less restrictive, multiple-use MPAs designated to serve either a specific function or meet a variety of goals while accommodating compatible uses within their boundaries.

In the United States the National Marine Sanctuary Program (NMSP) is responsible for the designation and management of NMS. Created under the landmark Marine Protection, Research, and Sanctuaries Act of 1972, the NMSP has led to the identification and protection of 13 unique marine and coastal areas, ranging in size from the tiny Fagatele NMS [0.65 square kilometer (0.25 square mile)] in American Samoa to the 13,800-square-kilometer (5328-square-mile) Monterey Bay NMS off central California.

Under the NMSP guidelines, sanctuaries are created by either administrative designation or congressional action. Sanctuaries are selected in areas of the marine environment with nationally significant aesthetic, ecological, historical, or recreational value; the primary objective of sanctuary management is resource protection while facilitating all public and private uses compatible with the marine areas (such as resource extraction and recreational activities). Once designated, a sanctuary is subject to a number of public hearings and administrative reviews; only after it has passed this rigorous and lengthy process is the sanctuary implemented. In the past, government officials managed sanctuary operations and affairs; more recently, there has been increased public input in the management process. For example, since 1992, all new sanctuaries are to contain a public advisory body called the Sanctuary Advisory Council, which assists officials in the management process and provides information to the public on sanctuary affairs.

The NMS sites vary in resources and size within the NMSP. The first sanctuary designated in 1975, the Monitor NMS, was created to protect the wreck site of the USS *Monitor*, a Civil War ship that sank in 1862 off Cape Hatteras, North Carolina. The sanctuary prevented illegal salvaging and destructive activities such as anchoring and fishing, and it concentrated efforts on the

rehabilitation and maintenance of the USS *Monitor*. Similarly, other sites selected in the 1970s and 1980s—such as the Key Largo NMS in the upper Florida Keys, the Channel Islands NMS off the southern California coast, Gray's Reef NMS off southern Georgia, among others—were designated for narrow, well-defined objectives relating to resource protection measures.

However, managers and scientists recognized the need to protect more than just the small, single sites, and this led to the development of larger, ecosystem-based sanctuaries. In 1990, the U.S. Congress designated the Florida Keys NMS, which then became the largest sanctuary, at over 9500 square kilometers (3668 square miles); this was followed in 1992 with the designation of the aforementioned Monterey Bay NMS (now the largest site). Both sanctuaries embraced the role of ecosystem management and emphasized an integrated approach to stewardship. Also, the Florida Keys NMS introduced a new form of resource management by establishing no-fishing zones, a concept that has since been considered in other sanctuaries. Stellwagen Bank NMS, off the Massachusetts coast, and Hawaiian Humpback NMS, around the main islands of the Hawaiian chain, were two other sanctuaries designated in the 1990s to protect extensive marine mammal and fish habitats.

The newest sanctuary, Thunder Bay NMS, was designated in October 2000. It represents yet further evolution of the NMSP process: Thunder Bay NMS is the first Great Lakes, freshwater site. It is located in Lake Michigan, off the Alpina, Michigan, shoreline, and it was designated to protect the more than 100 shipwrecks within its boundaries.

Manoj Shivlani

FURTHER READING

Agardy, Tundi. *Marine Protected Areas and Ocean Conservation.* San Diego: Academic Press/Austin, Texas: R. G. Landes, 1997.
Kelleher, Graeme, Chris Bleakley, and Sue Wells, eds. *A Global Representative System of Marine Protected Areas.*

Canberra, Australia: Great Barrier Reef Marine Park Authority/Washington, D.C.: World Bank/Gland, Switzerland: IUCN, 1995.

National Academy of Public Administration. *Protecting Our National Marine Sanctuaries.* Washington, D.C.: NAPA, 1999.

National Oceanic and Atmospheric Administration. *Florida Keys National Marine Sanctuary Final Management Plan/Environmental Impact Statement,* Vol. 1. Silver Spring, Md.: SRD/OCRM/NOS/NOAA, 1996.

National Research Council. *Striking a Balance: Improving Stewardship of Marine Areas.* Washington, D.C.: National Academy Press, 1997.

Salm, Rodney, and John Clark. *Marine and Coastal Protected Areas. A Guide for Planners and Managers.* Gland, Switzerland: IUCN, 2000.

Suman, D. O. "The Florida Keys National Marine Sanctuary: A Case Study of an Innovative Federal–State Partnership in Marine Resource Management." *Coastal Management,* Vol. 25 (1997), pp. 293–324.

World Commission on Protected Areas of IUCN. *Guidelines for Marine Protected Areas,* ed. by Graeme Kelleher. Cambridge: IUCN, the World Conservation Union, 1999.

USEFUL WEB SITES

National Marine Sanctuaries Program Home page. <http://www.sanctuaries.nos.noaa.gov>.

RELATED ARTICLES

Great Barrier Reef

Marine Snow

Marine snow is a generic term for aggregates of detritus, fecal matter, algae, microorganisms, and debris in the water column of the ocean larger than 0.5 millimeter (0.02 inch) in diameter. Called marine snow after the "stupendous snow-fall" of sedimenting material described by Rachel Carson in the classic book *The Sea Around Us,* these ubiquitous large particles are visible to the eye and superficially resemble large snowflakes. Because of their large size, they sink much more rapidly in seawater than do microscopic particles and are central to ocean carbon cycling and

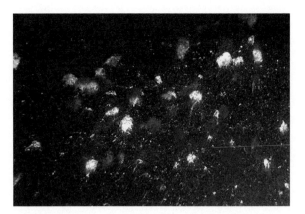

Very dense blizzard of marine snow in Puget Sound, Washington. The largest aggregates are 1 centimeter (0.39 inch) in diameter. (Courtesy, Alice Alldredge)

sedimentation processes. Marine snow is also a locus for enriched biological activity and a food source for organisms in the water column.

Characteristics of Marine Snow

The term *marine snow* encompasses aggregates of highly diverse origins and characteristics. Most are loose associations of smaller particles that form amorphous spheres or comets ranging from 0.5 to about 50 millimeters (0.02 to 2 inches) in diameter. Others are robust gelatinous feeding webs of zooplankton, and a few are large, flocculent, porous fecal pellets. The microbial communities attached to marine snow are diverse and include bacteria; living phytoplankton, especially diatoms and dinoflagellates; protozoans; and even small crustaceans and larvae. These organisms occur on marine snow at abundances two to four orders of magnitude higher than those found in the surrounding seawater. The interstitial fluid within the aggregates is a rich organic soup containing dissolved organic molecules, including amino acids and carbohydrates, which occur at concentrations 10 to 30 times higher than those in the surrounding seawater. Dissolved molecules are produced by the decomposition of the particulate organic matter within the particles. The organic matter in marine snow supports an abundant and actively growing population of bacteria, which are fed upon in turn by small flagellated protozoa and ciliates. This microbial community regenerates nutrients, especially nitrogen in the form of ammonium, within the aggregates and provides favorable conditions for living alga cells within the marine snow to photosynthesize actively if sunlight is also present. Phosphate and nitrate are also elevated within the marine snow microenvironment, further facilitating photosynthesis. The intense microbial activity within marine snow also depletes oxygen and may provide a microenvironment suitable for microbial processes, such as sulfate reduction and methanogenesis that occur without oxygen.

Marine snow is most abundant in coastal waters, where it averages from tens to several hundreds of aggregates per liter. Open ocean and deep-sea abundances are typically 2 to 10 times lower. As one descends vertically, aggregates tend to reach peak abundances where the density of seawater changes abruptly, such as at the thermocline. Despite their abundance, marine snow makes up less than 0.01 percent of the water column by volume, largely because of its small size.

Formation of Marine Snow

Although variable in composition, size, and appearance, most marine snow is formed by two major pathways; aggregation and de nova production by zooplankton. Aggregation occurs when the small particles in the water column, especially chain-forming diatoms, fecal pellets, and flakes of organic debris, collide. Collision is facilitated by physical mixing processes in seawater, including turbulence and convection, that help bring small particles together. Once collided, these small particles stick together to form aggregates. Sticking and aggregation are greatly enhanced by the presence of transparent exopolymer particles (TEPs) in the seawater. TEPs are ubiquitous, abundant gel-like particles produced from polysaccharide molecules exuded by phytoplankton, especially diatoms. These gels facilitate

aggregation by forming a gluelike matrix to which more robust particles adhere.

Marine snow is also produced by zooplankton as cast-off feeding webs and houses. Appendicularians, abundant tadpole-shaped pelagic tunicates, are herbivorous zooplankton found throughout the world's oceans. They feed by producing a balloonlike mucous structure, or "house," with which they strain microscopic particles from the water. Appendicularians build four to six houses per day, which when discarded become marine snow. Although most houses are less than 1 centimeter (0.4 inch) in diameter, those of some deep-sea species reach over 1 meter (3.3 feet). Planktonic snails also produce mucous-feeding structures that can contribute to marine snow.

Ecological Significance of Marine Snow

Marine snow plays a significant role in ocean ecology. First, these large particles serve as food for zooplankton and fish. Small planktonic crustaceans, including copepods and juvenile krill, swim from aggregate to aggregate, scraping particulate food off their surfaces. Others, such as adult krill, salps, flat fish larvae, herring, and coral reef and kelp bed fishes consume aggregates whole. The rain of marine snow to the seafloor also provides a major source of food for bottom-dwelling animals, particularly in the deep ocean. Episodic aggregation of diatom blooms at the surface produces large flocs of marine snow that settle to the seafloor rapidly and are consumed by bottom-dwelling organisms within a few days.

The second major role of marine snow is as a locus for processes of decomposition, nutrient recycling, and remineralization (conversion of organic matter to inorganic forms). Marine snow aggregates are akin to large, rich, particulate islands in a three-dimensional fluid medium where particulate matter is generally scarce. They provide physical surfaces for the attachment of microorganisms and contain concentrated particulate substrates that microorganisms can utilize for energy, growth, and metabolism. Microbial decomposition occurs at rates several orders of magnitude higher on marine snow than in an equal volume of ambient seawater. Microbial communities are very dynamic on marine snow, undergoing rapid successional changes on scales of hours to days. Decomposition processes slowly consume aggregates as they sink. This, and consumption by zooplankton, result in an exponential decrease in the quantity of marine snow with increasing depth in the ocean. Nutrients, such as nitrogen and phosphorus, are regenerated within sinking aggregates, which diffuse to the surrounding seawater, where they may be used by free-living microorganisms.

Third, marine snow is central to the ocean carbon cycle. It serves as a transport vehicle carrying particulate matter generated in surface waters to the deep sea. Although most of the contents of sinking aggregates and fecal pellets are decomposed and utilized as they sink, about 0.1 to 5 percent of the carbon fixed by photosynthesis at the ocean surface reaches the seafloor, mostly as marine snow. On the seafloor some is consumed by organisms in the sediments, but some remains and accumulates over time. Thus, marine snow is an important component of what is known as the *biological pump*, a process significant for climate change on Earth. In the biological pump, photosynthetic phytoplankton near the ocean surface fix carbon dioxide, which is a major greenhouse gas, thus helping remove it from the atmosphere. This fixed carbon makes its way into fecal matter and algal debris and eventually aggregates to form marine snow. It then sinks to the deep seafloor, where some of it becomes sequestered in deep-sea sediments, essentially removing it from the global carbon pool. Although increasing the photosynthesis of algae near the ocean surface and the subsequent sedimentation of carbon-rich marine snow to depth is unlikely to alter atmospheric carbon dioxide on short time scales of years, there is evidence that the biological pump may have an impact on global climate on scales of hundreds of thousands of years. Thus, an understanding of the mechanisms by which marine snow is formed and destroyed is important in understanding how the ocean mediates climate.

Alice Alldredge

FURTHER READING
Alldredge, A. L. "Marine Snow in Oceanic Cycling." In William A. Nierenberg, ed., *Encyclopedia of Earth System Science.* San Diego: Academic Press, 1992; pp. 139–147.
Alldredge, A. L., and M. W. Alldredge. "Silver Characteristics, Dynamics and Significance of Marine Snow." *Progress in Oceanography,* Vol. 20 (1988), pp. 41–82.
Lampitt, R. S. "Snow Falls in the Open Ocean." In C. P. Summerhayes and S.A. Thorpe, eds., *Oceanography: An Illustrated Guide.* New York: Wiley, 1996.

RELATED ARTICLES
Detritus; Particulate Organic Carbon; Photosynthesis; Phytoplankton

Marine Terrace, see Coastal Morphology

Marsh, see Salt Marsh

Mass Extinction

A mass extinction is an event in which a significant fraction of the diversity of more than one geographically widespread group of organisms (taxon), such as dinosaurs or trilobites, becomes extinct within a geologically short period of time. For practical purposes, the loss of a majority of the species on Earth within a period of 1 to 10 million years qualifies as a mass extinction. There have been at least five very severe mass extinctions and about a dozen smaller ones during the last 600 million years. Mass extinctions usually do not affect all ecological niches equally: Some mass extinctions may be more pronounced in the ocean than on land, or vice versa; some kinds of organisms may be completely wiped out, whereas other groups may be completely unaffected. Mass extinctions have many causes. They may be due to systemic changes in Earth's climate and geography, massive environmental changes due to volcanic eruptions or impacts by extraterrestrial objects, or even by random coincidence of natural cycles of extinction among many groups. One or many of these factors have been implicated for each of the mass extinctions.

Evidence

We recognize mass extinctions in the geological record by younger strata of sedimentary rocks that contain significantly fewer kinds of fossils than in immediately subjacent, older strata. This relationship must be observed in many localities that were globally distributed during the time interval in question. For example, in limestones all around the world, there is a drastic reduction in the diversity of plankton (especially calcareous nannoplankton and planktonic foraminifera) from the strata representing the Maastrichtian Stage of the Cretaceous System to the Danian Stage of the Paleocene Series.

Fossils are evidence of past life; they may be preserved body parts, impressions of body parts, or evidence of changes in the environment from life activities (trace fossils). Our knowledge of biodiversity during Earth's history is based on fossils, but not all organisms are equally likely to leave fossil evidence behind. Active organisms with hard body parts living in areas of net sediment deposition, such as a burrowing marine clam, are much more likely to be noticed in the fossil record than inactive, soft-bodied organisms living in areas of net erosion, such as a mushroom growing in a mountain forest. As many as one-third to one-half of the kinds of organisms in the

biologic communities of today's oceans are unlikely to be preserved as fossils. Although the fossil record does not capture the full range of biodiversity that has existed during any particular span of Earth's history, we may infer that a loss of diversity among organisms that were fossilized reflects general losses of diversity in the larger biosphere. During the most severe mass extinction events, entire families and orders disappeared from the fossil record, never to reappear.

The study of mass extinction has accelerated substantially since the early 1980s, when Jack Sepkoski, then at the University of Chicago, began to compile an internally consistent database of fossil biodiversity as a function of geologic time. This evolving database allows more precise understanding of the exact victims of extinction events, which in turn allows more precise speculation about the events that may have claimed them.

The Five "Big Ones"

The most severe mass extinctions occurred (1) at the end of the Ordovician Period, about 439 million years ago; (2) between the Frasnian and Fammenian Ages, near the end of the Devonian Period, about 362.5 million years ago; (3) at the end of the Permian Period, about 247.5 million years ago; (4) at the end of the Triassic Period, about 206 million years ago; and (5) at the end of the Cretaceous Period, about 65 million years ago. The end-Permian event was the most severe; half of all marine families and about 96 percent of marine species disappeared. This event marks the end of the Paleozoic Era of Earth's history. In contrast, the end-Cretaceous event was the least severe of the five "Big Ones." Although the dinosaurs (the most charismatic of all megafauna) expired, only 15 percent of marine families were eliminated. This event, often dubbed the K-T event because it falls at the boundary between the Cretaceous (from the Greek kreta, chalk) and Tertiary periods, marks the end of the Mesozoic Era. The other three big events removed about 20 to 22 percent of the families from the oceans of their times.

Mechanisms

A wide variety of mechanisms has been proposed for mass extinctions. These mechanisms generally fall into two categories: those dependent on the diversity of species (diversity dependent) and those that act on all species equally (diversity independent).

The first category includes origination rate of species, crises at the bottom of the food chain, and decreased diversity of habitats. If the rate at which new species originate should slow down while the rate of extinction remains constant, the overall diversity of species should decline. If some factor causes a crash in primary productivity in the oceans—for example, if upwelling does not recycle nutrients from the deep ocean as happens locally and episodically during El Niño—higher levels of the food chain will suffer. If the variety of environmental provinces declines, the diversity of species that will be adapted to the different provinces should also decline. Such a reduction could be controlled by climate: for example, if higher concentrations of carbon dioxide in the atmosphere reduced the difference in temperature between the poles and the equator. Environmental variability can also be reduced by plate tectonics. The assembly of Pangea, for example, reduced the area of shallow-marine and continental-shelf environments that previously surrounded the continental fragments that were incorporated into the supercontinent.

The second category includes drastic environmental changes due to extraterrestrial causes such as impact by a comet, increased flux of cosmic dust, or increases in cosmic radiation; global climate changes, either warming or cooling; global oceanographic changes, such as changes in sea level, salinity, trace element content, oxygenation,

or circulation; and widespread volcanism. These are all rapid global disruptions that would so unbalance the environment that species could not persist under the new conditions.

Almost every possible mechanism has been invoked to explain the Permian event, the largest of all mass extinctions, at the end of the Paleozoic Era. The most persuasive analyses suggest that many of them played a role simultaneously. On the other hand, the single cause of an impact by an extraterrestrial body has overshadowed all other explanations for the K-T event at the end of the Mesozoic Era that eliminated the dinosaurs. The Ordovician extinction is attributed to a rise in sea level and a reduction in oxygen levels. The Late Devonian extinction was probably due to global cooling, but the cause of the cooling is not conclusively established. An increase in rainfall on the continents and associated changes in the delivery of sediment and nutrients to the oceans have been implicated in the Triassic extinction.

W. A. Heins

FURTHER READING

Carlisle, D. B. *Dinosaurs, Diamonds, and Things from Outer Space.* Stanford, Calif.: Stanford University Press, 1995.
Courtillot, V. *Evolutionary Catastrophes: The Science of Mass Extinction.* Translated by Joe McClinton. Cambridge and New York: Cambridge University Press, 1999.
Erwin, D. H. *The Great Paleozoic Crisis: Life and Death in the Permian.* New York: Columbia University Press, 1993.
McGhee, G. R. *The Late Devonian Mass Extinction: The Frasnian–Famennian Crisis.* New York: Columbia University Press, 1996.
Officer, C., and J. Page. *The Great Dinosaur Extinction Controversy.* Reading, Mass.: Addison-Wesley, 1996.
Raup, D. M. *Extinction: Bad Genes or Bad Luck?* New York: W. W. Norton, 1991.
Sepkoski, J. J. "Extinction and the Fossil Record." *Geotimes,* Vol. 39 (1994), pp. 15–17.
———. "What I Did with My Research Career: or How Research on Biodiversity Yielded Data on

Extinction." In William Glen, ed., *The Mass Extinction Debates: How Science Works in a Crisis*. Stanford, Calif.: Stanford University Press, 1994.

Ward, P. *The End of Evolution: On Mass Extinctions and the Preservation of Biodiversity*. New York: Bantam Books, 1994.

RELATED ARTICLES
Geologic Time; Paleoceanography; Trilobite

Mass Stranding

A mass stranding is usually defined as three or more living cetaceans (whales, dolphins, or porpoises) coming ashore simultaneously at the same location. The stranded animals are unable to return to the water—at least until the tide rises and covers them again—and in many cases, most or all of the stranded animals die unless there is human intervention. Mass strandings most commonly occur among certain species of toothed whale (odontocete) that live in social groups. Most mass strandings involve fewer than 15 animals, but among pilot whales, false killer whales, and melon-headed whales, mass strandings of 50 to 150 or more may occur.

What causes whales to strand *en masse*? There are several hypotheses and one or more may apply in a particular situation. The common denominator appears to be that when one animal strands, strong social cohesion within the pod (social group) causes other group members to stay in the vicinity and strand alongside. In at least some instances, one or more animals in the pod may be weakened by disease, starvation, or old age, and swim or drift ashore, and are followed by healthy individuals. Assisting a member of the pod may override all

Some of the 200 pilot whales stranded on rocks are rescued by volunteers near Dunsborough, West Australia, 21 August 1996. (Associated Press, West Australia)

other considerations, including the danger of close proximity to shore. In many instances, however, all stranded members of the pod appear to be healthy.

Among the species that mass strand most commonly are social whales that normally live in deeper water—among them, pilot whales, sperm whales, and false killer whales. Once inshore, the navigational skills of these deepwater species may be poorly suited to shallow water. Gently sloping beaches may deflect upward rather than return the sound beam of echolocation systems, thus giving a false reading of open water. Certain combinations of shoreline configuration, food availability, currents, and weather conditions may draw whales into shallow waters. Onshore winds or currents, heavy seas, and a falling tide can hamper escape to deeper water.

There is some strong circumstantial evidence that certain cetaceans navigate using Earth's magnetic field. Research published by Michael Walker and others in the *Journal of Experimental Biology* in 1992 showed fin whales following lows in geomagnetic intensity or gradient during migration. Studies in the United Kingdom and United States have shown a high incidence of live strandings of various species—including pilot whales, striped dolphins, sperm whales, and fin whales—in places where local lows in the geomagnetic field intersect a coast or island. It is feasible that whales using geomagnetic cues for navigation could be led astray in such circumstances.

Since the 1970s, stranding networks have been established in many countries. These groups assist stranded animals where possible. They identify the species of stranded individuals, and some groups systematically record biological information using agreed upon protocols. Collected tissue samples enable analysis of the condition of the animal at the time of its stranding and death. Such samples can be preserved for years until techniques and resources are available for their analysis. For example, between 1981 and 1991—within a 32-kilometer (20-mile) radius of Cape Cod, Massachusetts—a total of 476 long-finned pilot whales were stranded on 10 separate occasions. In the previous 20 years there had been only one record of a mass stranding incident. Preserved tissue samples implicated infection with morbillivirus in at least some of the 1980s strandings.

Mass strandings can be an invaluable source of data on the life history, health, genetics, and population size and structure of the animals involved. To gather the best information requires highly organized response teams. The Marine Mammal Health and Stranding Response Act passed by the U.S. Congress in 1992 makes monitoring the health of marine mammals a national policy in which stranding networks can play a key role.

Trevor Day

FURTHER READING
Darling, James D., C. Nicklin, K. S. Norris, H. Whitehead, and B. Wursig. *Whales, Dolphins, and Porpoises.* Washington, D.C.: National Geographic Society, 1995.
Hoyt, Erich, Mark Cawardine, Ewan Fordyce, and Peter Gill. *Whales, Dolphins, and Porpoises.* Alexandria, Va.: Time-Life Books, 1998.
Reynolds, John E., and Sentiel A. Rommel, eds. *Biology of Marine Mammals.* Washington, D.C.: Smithsonian Institution Press, 1999.
Twiss, John R., Jr., and Randall R. Reeves, eds. *Conservation and Management of Marine Mammals.* Washington, D.C.: Smithsonian Institution Press, 1999.

USEFUL WEB SITES
American Cetacean Society home page. <http://www.acsonline.org>.
Institute of Cetacean Research home page. <http://www.icrwhale.org>.

RELATED ARTICLES
Cetacea

Maury, Matthew Fontaine

1806–1873

*Superintendent of U.S. Navy Depot of Charts
and Instruments and Observatory*

American marine meteorologist and physical geographer Matthew Fontaine Maury was interested in the practical aspects of marine and navigation science during a long but turbulent career with the U.S. Navy. He compiled and synthesized vast amounts of data from ships' logbooks on wind and ocean currents, allowing navigators to choose more efficient routes. He standardized a system for recording these, as well as meteorological data, that became widely recognized for its utility. He produced a bathymetric map of the Atlantic seafloor based on sounding surveys as part of a new field that he called "the physical geography of the sea."

Maury was born on 14 January 1806 into a large family near Fredericksburg, Virginia. He grew up near Franklin, Tennessee, graduated from Harpeth Academy in 1825, and then entered the U.S. Navy, where he rose through the ranks to

Matthew Fontaine Maury. (From the collections of the Library of Congress)

become master of the sloop-of-war USS *Falmouth* in 1831. He married Ann Herndon in 1834, eventually fathering eight children. During his first naval appointment, Maury became acutely concerned about the lack of reliable information regarding wind and ocean currents, and he began to ponder ways of consolidating the vast pool of individual mariners' knowledge of the sea. By the time he returned from a long voyage in 1834, Maury had written an article, "On the Navigation of Cape Horn," for the *American Journal of Science and Arts,* and he had drafted a major treatise on navigation that was published in 1836.

After being transferred to an appointment surveying harbors of the southern United States, Maury suffered a serious injury to his right leg in a stagecoach accident in October 1839, thus curtailing his prospects as a career naval officer. As he recovered from this injury over the next three years, Maury wrote a series of pseudonymous and rather polemical essays for the *Southern Literary Messenger* in which he addressed prospects for naval reform, especially in regard to the means of then-current naval education. Maury was critical of the lack of a formal academy for midshipmen and insisted on standardized naval education. Apparently, these writings instigated the establishment of a naval school in Annapolis, Maryland, for which Maury gained some notoriety once he revealed himself as the author.

On 1 July 1842, Maury was recalled to duty and appointed superintendent of the Depot of Charts and Instruments of the Navy Department, an organization that quickly expanded to include an astronomical observatory. By 1844, Maury became superintendent of the U.S. Naval Depot and Observatory. (He held this position until the outbreak of the U.S. Civil War in 1861, when he resigned to serve the Confederacy.) During this time, Maury was far more interested in the sea and atmosphere than in astronomical matters, undertaking one of his most impressive projects—the systematic compilation of wind and weather observations from military and merchant marine craft into a series of *Wind and Current Charts.* Beginning in 1847, these charts, which divided frequently traveled portions of the sea into squares 5° to a side, were widely disseminated and continually revised. After 1850, they were accompanied by additional sailing directions. Maury gleaned his data from the vast number of logbooks stored at the depot, with the insight that oceanic and wind conditions might follow predictable patterns that could be determined and mapped through a statistical treatment of accumulated empirical data. The project also allowed Maury to develop a standard system of recordkeeping for tracking such information, as well as meteorological data, a system that he quickly put into use on navy vessels. Maury's genius was in allowing private merchant sea captains to obtain copies of his charts, as long as they were willing to contribute their own ongoing oceanic and meteorological records according to his system.

Maury's efforts paved the way for an international effort to standardize marine meteorological data, outlined in detail at an International Maritime Meteorological Conference in Brussels in 1853. Here the famous German naturalist Alexander von Humboldt (1769–1859) proclaimed Maury to have founded "the science of the sea," which both men came to call "the physical geography of the sea." Maury envisioned extending his system to land meteorology as well, but this idea was opposed most notably by Joseph Henry (1797–1878), director of the Smithsonian Institution, which had its own network for such data collecting. Henry's influence within American scientific circles was more than powerful enough to ensure that Maury's work remained limited to marine affairs.

Maury did far more than collate data. Between 1849 and 1854, the depot received two modest research vessels by act of Congress. Maury first sent out the *Taney* and then the *Dolphin* on successive voyages into the Atlantic with the principal aim of testing and utilizing a number of sounding devices for determining ocean depths. The *Dolphin* was more thoroughly outfitted with thermometers, water samplers, and special devices for obtaining samples of ocean floor sediments. The results of these soundings allowed Maury in 1854 to produce a *Bathymetrical Map of the North Atlantic Basin with Contour Lines Drawn in at 1,000, 2,000, 3,000, and 4,000 Fathoms.* It was the first such topographic depiction of an entire ocean basin, in many ways marking a significant shift in oceanographic science from a focus on navigation and coastal charting to interest in the seafloor itself. Knowledge of these murky depths was indispensable to officials of the Atlantic Telegraph Company, which laid the first transatlantic telegraph cable between Newfoundland and Ireland in 1858 based on Maury's map.

In Maury's own words, the *Wind and Current Charts* series arose, as did most of his work, from a concern "for the improvement of commerce and navigation." Above all else, he was an eminently practical man, interested in making ocean navigation by sail more efficient, and therefore more profitable, in the face of competition by developing steam technology.

Maury did, however, indulge in theory, which he most fully articulated in *The Physical Geography of the Sea* (1855). This book was both successful and controversial, bringing together thoughts Maury had scattered throughout earlier works, such as the sailing directions that accompanied the *Wind and Current Charts. Physical Geography* was written in an oratorical style that suited a popular audience. It thus sold well and went through numerous editions and translations. Maury wrote from the perspective of natural theology, the belief that nature operates according to physical laws set in motion by, and reinforcing belief in the existence of, God. He repeatedly invoked the "argument from design," for instance by likening the atmosphere to a complex mechanism that could exist only by virtue of a Divine Creator. For the most part, however, such viewpoints had fallen out of favor within an increasingly organized mainstream scientific community by midcentury. Furthermore, Maury neglected to incorporate up-to-date evidence in his speculations, venturing beyond his competency into the realms of geophysics and fluid dynamics. Maury was thus subject to numerous critiques for greatly underemphasizing the role of winds in generating ocean currents such as the Gulf Stream in favor of thermohaline forces generated by the differential density of masses of water. His idea that atmospheric circulation was due to terrestrial magnetism was even more unanimously opposed as outdated. Criticism aside, *Physical Geography* sparked healthy scientific debate, and it contained much practical information for navigators.

With the outbreak of the Civil War in 1861, Maury seceded along with his home state of Virginia and served in the Confederate Navy, inventing an electric torpedo for harbor defense. Serving as agent in England for the Confederacy in 1862–65, he next served Emperor Maximilian of Mexico after the collapse of the Confederacy. In 1866, he joined his family, which had moved to England. Eventually, the Maurys were allowed to return to the United States, where he became physics professor at Virginia Military Institute. Maury died on 1 February 1873.

Maury's work, beginning especially with the *Wind and Current Charts* in 1847, represented a significant step in the standardization of knowledge about oceanic and atmospheric conditions. It was a vital development given the growing economic context of oceanic commerce and navigation. Largely because of Maury, the "physical geography of the sea" emerged as a coherent research program in the nineteenth century.

J. Conor Burns

BIOGRAPHY
- Matthew Fontaine Maury.
- Born 14 January 1806 near Fredericksburg, Virginia.
- He entered the U.S. Navy in 1825.
- He was appointed superintendent of the Depot of Charts and Instruments of the Navy Department in 1842 and superintendent of the U.S. Naval Depot and Observatory in 1844.
- He compiled and published the first of the *Wind and Current Charts* in 1847 and published *Bathymetrical Map of the North Atlantic Basin,* the first contour map of an ocean basin, in 1854 based on soundings taken from depot research vessels.
- In 1855, he published *The Physical Geography of the Sea.*
- He served the Confederate cause during the Civil War, 1861–65, and became professor of physics at Virginia Military Institute in 1868.
- Died 1 February 1873.

SELECTED WRITINGS
Maury, Matthew Fontaine. "On the Navigation of Cape Horn." *American Journal of Science and Arts,* 26 July 1834, pp. 54–63.
———. *Elementary, Practical, and Theoretical Treatise on Navigation.* Philadelphia: Biddle, 1845.
———. *Explanations and Sailing Directions to Accompany the Wind and Current Charts.* Washington: Alexander, 1850 et seq.
———. *The Physical Geography of the Sea.* New York: Harper, 1855.

FURTHER READING
Cotter, Charles. "Matthew Fontaine Maury (1806–1873): 'Pathfinder of the Seas.'" *Journal of Navigation,* Vol. 32 (1979), pp. 75–83.
Leighly, John. "Introduction." In *The Physical Geography of the Sea and Its Meteorology,* by Matthew Fontaine Maury. Cambridge: Harvard University Press, 1963.
Schlee, Susan. *The Edge of an Unfamiliar World: A History of Oceanography.* New York: Dutton, 1973.

RELATED ARTICLES
Ocean Wind System

Maxillopoda

The class Maxillopoda includes a diverse range of small crustacean species, some of which form a major part of the marine plankton. Like other crustaceans (such as crabs, shrimp, and lobsters), maxillopods have a segmented body, an external skeleton, and a number of jointed appendages (limbs). However, maxillopods are generally smaller than other crustaceans and typically have shortened bodies with a head of five segments, a thorax of six segments, an abdomen of four segments, and a reduced number of limbs. The class Maxillopoda is commonly divided into six subclasses (although some authorities recognize more, including several extinct subclasses): Cirripedia, Copepoda, Branchiura, Ostracoda, Mystacocarida, and Tantulocarida.

Members of the subclass Cirripedia are better known as barnacles. Although free-swimming as larvae, adult barnacles live permanently attached to solid objects such as rocks, boats, or whales. They feed by extending their feathery limbs into the water to trap drifting particles of organic matter. Some barnacles have stalks, but most are fastened to their home by a flattened base. A sessile barnacle's external skeleton consists of overlapping plates of calcium carbonate (chalk) and forms a hard, protective shell that encloses and protects the animal completely when exposed at low tide or disturbed by a predator. Stalked barnacles do not have the stalk covered with plates. Barnacles are externally so unlike other crustaceans that biologists once classified them as mollusks.

The subclass Copepoda includes some 9000 species of minute, shrimplike animals. Most copepods live in the ocean plankton, where they feed on microscopic algae and use their thoracic appendages to swim through the water. They are usually less than 2 millimeters (0.079 inch) long and typically have a single simple eye. Copepods are incredibly numerous—according to some estimates, they are the most common animal in the world. Free-living copepods in the oceans are the main herbivores of diatoms and dinoflagellates and are fed upon by many other animals, including some commercially important fishes.

Copepods are also common in freshwater rivers and lakes, and many species are parasites.

Also known as fish lice, branchiurans are parasites that live on the skin or on the gills of fish. They use tiny suckers to hold on to their victims and piercing mouthparts to feed on blood and body fluids. There are about 130 species.

There are about 8000 species of ostracods, or mussel shrimps. These tiny crustaceans are like miniature clams, with hinged shells that can open or close. The head of an ostracod takes up most of its body. There are few segments and only three pairs of legs at most. Most species live on the seafloor and feed on organic matter in sediment.

There are only 10 recognized species of mystacocarids. All are minute animals that live between sand grains in the intertidal and subtidal zones. They are thought to feed by using their mouthparts to scrape organic matter off sand. Also, they are considered to be among the most primitive of the subphylum Crustacea.

Tantulocarids (about 12 species) live as tiny parasites on other crustaceans, usually in deep water. They are typically less than 0.5 millimeter (0.0197 inch) long and have piercing mouthparts to pierce their host's external skeleton.

Ben Morgan

FURTHER READING
Brusca, Richard C., and Gary J. Brusca. *Invertebrates.* Sunderland, Mass.: Sinauer, 1990.
Fish, J. *A Student's Guide to the Seashore.* London and Boston: Unwin Hyman, 1989; 2nd ed., Cambridge and New York: Cambridge University Press, 1996.
Nybakken, James W. *Marine Biology: An Ecological Approach,* 5th ed. San Francisco: Benjamin Cummings, 2001.
Pechenik, Jan A. *Biology of the Invertebrates.* Boston: Prindle, Weber and Schmidt, 1985; 4th ed., Boston: McGraw-Hill, 2000.

RELATED ARTICLES
Arthropoda; Barnacle; Copepod; Crustacea; Mystacocarida

Mediterranean Outflow

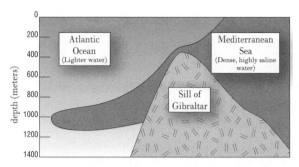

Cross section of the Mediterranean outflow. [Adapted from J. A. Knauss, Introduction to Physical Oceanography (Prentice Hall, 1997.)]

The Mediterranean outflow is one of the most prominent hydrographic features of mid-depths in the northeastern Atlantic. It originates from the relatively warm but salty water that flows out into the North Atlantic through the bottom of the Strait of Gibraltar.

The dry Mediterranean climate results in more water evaporating from the surface of the sea than is added either by rainfall or from river outflows. During the last 40 years the river outflows have decreased by nearly 50 percent as a result of major dam projects such as the Aswan Dam in Egypt. Therefore, inside the Mediterranean, seawater is getting progressively saltier and sea level is falling. Each year about 55,000 cubic kilometers (13,200 cubic miles) of water flows in through the Strait of Gibraltar. This inflow is partially balanced by the net evaporative loss but also by an outflow of about 50,500 cubic kilometers (12,100 cubic miles) at the bottom of the Strait of Gibraltar. The water inside the Mediterranean at the sill depth of the strait is much denser than the water outside in the Atlantic, which causes it to cascade out through the strait and down the slope outside. Every second an average of 700,000 cubic meters (0.18 billion gallons) of water flows out. As it cascades down the slope it mixes with the ambient Atlantic water so that its volume is increased nearly fourfold but its density decreases. Eventually, at a depth of about 1000 meters (3280 feet), it loses its buoyancy and begins to flow and spread laterally. In the northeastern Atlantic the outflow water is easily identified in hydrographic profiles as a thick layer of anomalously warm and salty water at depths of 650 to 1650 meters (2130 to 5415 feet). Under the influence of Earth's rotation (Coriolis force), its flow is turned clockwise and flows northward along the flank of the Iberian Peninsula. Within about a month, the water mass reaches the Bay of Biscay at the northern tip of Spain, where its

speed slows and it begins to dissipate through lateral spread and vertical mixing.

As it flows northward it also spreads laterally into the North Atlantic, but even more dramatically it spawns eddies, particularly where it rounds the southwestern tip of Portugal. These eddies, known as *Meddies*, are lenses (spinning ovoid bodies of water within the water column) of water that spin clockwise. They are 40 to 100 kilometers (25 to 62 miles) in diameter and up to 1 kilometer (3280 feet) thick. Being deeply embedded within the water at depths of 500 to 1500 meters (1640 to 4920 feet), they are difficult to find and track. However, they generally move in a southwestern direction and do not dissipate quickly because the water in them does not mix readily with the surrounding ocean water. Many Meddies collide with seamounts and dissipate; those that do not may persist for up to five years and some have been found as far away as the Bahamas.

The Mediterranean outflow water has an important influence on the physical oceanography of the North Atlantic. The density gradient within the upper 1000 meters (3280 feet) of the northeast Atlantic is less than that in other oceans, so during winter the density becomes almost uniform to considerable depths. As a result, in places vertical mixing can extend to depths of greater than 500 meters (1640 feet), whereas in the North Pacific it is restricted to less than 200 meters (656 feet). It also displays an unusual mechanism of vertical mixing, called *double diffusion* or *salt fingering.* Since heat diffuses faster than salt, when two layers of water of similar density come into contact—one warm and salty and the other cool and less salty—narrow vertical columns (fingers) of rapidly rising or sinking water develop that quickly mix the two layers unexpectedly.

Martin Angel

FURTHER READING

Baminger, Molly O'Neill, and James Price. "Mixing and Spreading of the Mediterranean outflow." *Journal of Physical Oceanography,* Vol. 27 (1997), pp. 1654–1677.

Pingree, Robin. "The Droguing of Meddy Pinball and Seeding with ALACE Floats." *Journal of the Marine Biological Association of the United Kingdom,* Vol. 75 (1995), pp. 235–252.

Richardson, Phillip. "Tracking Ocean Eddies." *American Scientist,* Vol. 81 (1993), pp. 261–269.

Richardson, Philip, A. S. Bower, and Walter Zenk. "A Census of Meddies Tracked by Floats." *Progress in Oceanography,* Vol. 45 (2000), pp. 209–250.

Zenk, Walter, and Lawrence Armi. "The Complex Spreading Pattern of Mediterranean Water off the Portuguese Coast." *Deep-Sea Research I,* Vol. 37 (1990), pp. 1805–1823.

RELATED ARTICLES

Bathypelagic Zone; Mediterranean Sea; Strait of Gibraltar

Mediterranean Sea

Physical Geography

The Mediterranean is a semienclosed marginal sea that connects with the rest of the world ocean through the narrow Strait of Gibraltar. With a mean depth of 1500 meters (4920 feet), it represents just 0.7 percent of the global ocean's area and just 0.3 percent of its total volume. The Mediterranean Sea is divided into a series of deep basins separated by narrow straits, some of which have quite shallow sills. The main division is between the western and eastern basins, which are linked via the Sicily Strait. The western basin is shaped like a right-angled triangle with the African coast representing its longest side. The islands of Sardinia and Corsica create a north–south divide separating the Tyrrhenian Sea, located between the islands and the western coast of Italy, from the larger western basin. The eastern basin is even more complex. There are two main basins, the Ionian and Levantine. To the north of the Ionian basin, the Otranto Strait opens into the Adriatic Sea, which separates Italy from the Balkans. Much of the northern Adriatic is quite shallow, and because it receives large quantities of agricultural runoff from the large Italian rivers such as the Po, it is suffering from eutrophication. To the northeast of the Ionian basin is the beginning of an arc of islands including Crete and Rhodes that partially separates the Aegean Sea from both the Ionian and Levantine basins. In the far northeast corner of the Aegean is a series of two straits that lead first to the Sea of Marmora and then to the Black Sea via the Bosporus. This complicated morphology results in an equally complicated physical circulation. However, because it is such an enclosed sea, it is almost free of tides.

Geological History and Context

Geologically, the Mediterranean, Black, and Caspian Seas are remnants of the Tethys Sea, a much larger sea that separated the ancient continents of Laurasia and Gondwanaland. The African Plate moving northward resulted in the building of the Alps and the Carpathian Mountains and the subduction of most of the Tethys. The African Plate is currently sliding beneath the Eurasian Plate at a rate of 1 to 3 centimeters (0.39 to 1.18 inches) per year beneath the Hellenic Arc that extends from western Greece to southern Turkey. Hence much of the Mediterranean region is tectonically active. There are volcanoes such as Vesuvius and Etna in Italy and on Sicily. On the seabed in deep water are mud volcanoes and brine lakes. The Cretan island arc and the Adriatic region are notoriously prone to earthquakes. About 3500 years ago the island of Santorini suddenly exploded, bringing the Minoan civilization on the island of Crete to an abrupt and catastrophic end. This devastating explosion and the resulting tsunami (seismic sea wave) has also been linked to the Israelites crossing the Red Sea when they were escaping from servitude in Egypt. There have also been extensive movements in land levels, with some of the harbors of the ancient world now several feet either above or below sea level. This volcanic and seismic activity results from the juxtaposition and relative movement of the African and Eurasian Plates and some smaller plates along the northern boundary of the eastern basin. During the Miocene Epoch, starting about 11 million years ago, the movements of the plates resulted in the repeated opening and closing of the Strait of Gibraltar. This resulted in a succession of six or seven events during which the entire Mediterranean alternately dried up, laying down vast beds of rock salt, then subsequently reflooded. The global sea levels have risen and fallen nearly 70 meters (230 feet) each time.

Climate and Circulation

At middle latitudes climates tend to be arid, and the climate of the Mediterranean region has always been relatively dry. As a result, rainfall and river runoff fail to compensate for the quantities of water lost through evaporation from the sea's surface. Evaporation is estimated generally to lower the Mediterranean's sea level by 60 centimeters (24 inches) per year. This loss of water is largely compensated by a constant inflow of water from the Atlantic through the Strait of Gibraltar. The evaporation, however, also increases the saltiness of the sea's water, so that inflowing water from the Atlantic has a salinity of about 36.5 practical salinity units (psu) [i.e., 1 kilogram (2.2 pounds) of seawater contains 36.5 grams (1.29 ounces) of salt], whereas in the eastern Mediterranean, the salinity can exceed 39. Since the density of seawater is determined by both its salinity and temperature, during the winter when cold winds blow from the

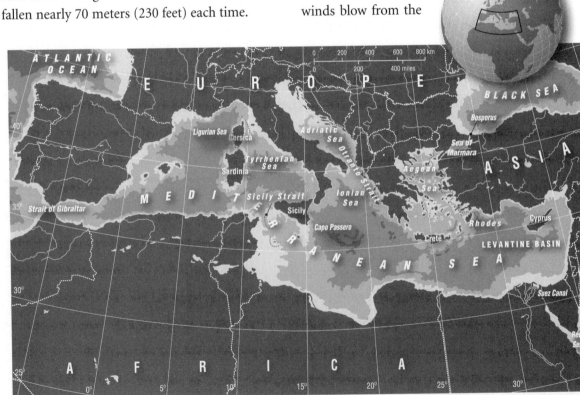

Mediterranean Sea.

262

north, the density of the entire water column can become uniform and mixes from top to bottom. As a result, the Mediterranean is one of the few seas where the temperature is almost uniform below a depth of 250 to 300 meters (820 to 984 feet) to the bottom. The deep water in the western basin has a temperature of around 12.7°C (55°F) and a salinity of 38.4, and in the eastern basin the values are 13.8°C (57°F) and 38.8, respectively. As a result, the Mediterranean is much denser and cascades out through the bottom of the Strait of Gibraltar. Each year about 53,000 cubic kilometers (12,700 cubic miles) of water flows in at the surface and about 50,500 cubic kilometers (12,100 cubic miles) flows out at the bottom of the strait. The water in the Mediterranean is exchanged completely every 80 to 100 years.

Primary Productivity

This circulation results in an export of nutrients to the Atlantic. Since there are relatively few major rivers (Ebro, Rhone, Po, and Nile) flowing into the Mediterranean, supplies of nutrients to the deeper Mediterranean come mainly from the inflow of water from the Atlantic, while some come from dust blown in from the Sahara Desert. Since the water flowing in from the Atlantic has had most of its nutrients stripped out before it even enters the Strait of Gibraltar, the Mediterranean has low productivity and is oligotrophic. This oligotrophy becomes even more extreme in the eastern basin, where as a result of the extremely low concentrations of nitrogenous and phosphatic nutrients, it has only a third the productivity of the poorly productive, northwestern region off Spain and southern France. Hence the waters of the Mediterranean are very clear and blue, attracting sun-seeking tourists.

Under such oligotrophic conditions, the majority of primary production is by picoplankton, phytoplankton, and bacteria that are less than 2 micrometers (0.079 inch) in size. Since they are so small, they can be eaten only by protozoan (mostly ciliates) grazers, which are not much bigger and are too small to contribute to sedimentation. The organic material produced by these tiny plant cells flows through a microbial food web and is utilized and recycled near the surface. Very small quantities become incorporated into the food chain that leads to the larger planktonic grazers, such as copepods, that eventually become the food for fish. This is also the food chain that generates the particles of organic matter that sink into deep water and feed deep-living communities. In addition, not only is this flux of sedimentary material unusually low, but also what there is becomes degraded as it sinks very rapidly because the warm temperatures in the deep water stimulate the metabolism of the bacteria in the water. Consequently, the deep-living populations in the water and on the seabed are exceptionally small.

These extreme oligotrophic conditions are in sharp contrast with the local conditions around the estuaries of the few major rivers. Here water outflow has been reduced (by damming and extracting water for irrigation), but what does run off contains substantially elevated concentrations of agricultural fertilizers and other chemicals, which greatly boost productivity in the local inshore waters. This excessive primary production, or *eutrophication*, increases the incidence of massive blooms of nuisance and toxic algae (red tides) and encourages excessive growth of benthic algae and floating macrophytes. The local waters become discolored and unhealthy. The decay of the excessive amounts of plant biomass produced can strip all oxygen from the warm water, resulting in dead fish and copious amounts of hydrogen sulfide and methane, which are effects similar to those resulting from the discharge of excessive amounts of sewage into coastal waters. Thus conditions in the Mediterranean can be both extremely oligotrophic and, as a result of human activity, eutrophic.

Biodiversity

The semi-isolated nature of the Mediterranean Sea offers ideal conditions for *speciation*, the evolution of new species, to occur. During the glacial eras, the last of which ended about 18,000 years ago, boreal, cold-water species were swept into the sea, whereas today they are more subtropical warm-water species. Thus the fauna and flora of the sea consists of four elements: species that are relicts and that have persisted since the time of the Tethys Sea; glacial relicts, the cold-water species that were carried in during the glacial eras; species that are shared with the North Atlantic; and species that have invaded the eastern Mediterranean through the Suez Canal. Each time a species is swept in through the Strait of Gibraltar, a set becomes isolated from its parent stock. Thus the glacial relict species, such as the northern krill *Meganyctiphanes norvegica* and the lantern fish *Benthosema glaciale*, are not only isolated but also survive in very different environmental conditions and are likely to become different species. Hence it is not surprising, given the extreme alteration in environmental conditions in recent geological eras, that a large number of species occur only in the Mediterranean (i.e., are endemic). Thus the shallow-living assemblages of marine animals and plants are highly variable and diverse, and this diversity has been enhanced (not always advantageously) by the introduction of alien species and migrations through the Suez Canal.

In deeper water the extreme oligotrophic nature, particularly in the eastern basin, keeps the populations extremely low and probably contributes to the poor assemblages of species. Unlike more productive oceans, there is no bathypelagic fauna, and standing crops of pelagic animals below depths of 500 meters (1640 feet) are less than a tenth of those at similar latitudes in the North Atlantic. Interestingly, the Mediterranean is on the migration route of large fishes and whales such as bluefin tuna and fin whales. Thus populations of large scavengers (sharks and amphipods) on the seabed do not appear to be similarly depleted.

Anthropogenic Impacts

Humankind has a major impact on the Mediterranean, and the sea can be considered a microscosm of the environmental problems facing the global ocean. The development of early farming in the Fertile Crescent that subsequently led to the emergence of Western civilization also resulted in extensive anthropogenic changes to the coastal morphology of the region. As metal tools became available during the Bronze Age, large areas of the forests covering the slopes of the steep hills that fringed the coastline were cleared. Without the forests to conserve the soils, sheet erosion took place, which stripped the topsoil from the slopes and deposited it in the coastal seas. As a result, the ancient city of Troy, which in its heyday had been a flourishing port, is now over 16 kilometers (10 miles) from the coast.

The construction of the Suez Canal provided a seawater link between the eastern Mediterranean and the Red Sea. Initially, some highly saline lakes (e.g., the Bitter Lakes) provided a barrier to the movement of organisms through the canal. But over the years their salinity has declined and over 300 species, including dangerous sharks and noxious algae, are known to have undertaken Lessepsian migrations from the Red Sea via the Suez Canal. There have been significant introductions of alien species in the ballast water of large bulk carriers; the most notorious example is the introduction of a ctenophore, *Mnemiopsis*, into the Black Sea, which has devastated the local fisheries. Another accidental introduction has been the seaweed *Caulerpa taxifolia*, which escaped from a marine aquarium in Monaco and has proved to be so aggressively invasive that it is changing the ecology of shallow waters in the region.

Another anthropogenic influence is that more and more of the outflows from the rivers are being intercepted for irrigation. The outflow of the Nile in particular has been reduced by construction of the Aswan High Dam. These activities have had two important impacts on the ecology of the Mediterranean. First, the supplies of some key nutrients have been reduced substantially. The damming of the Danube River reduced supplies of silicate reaching the Black Sea and ultimately the Mediterranean by 50 percent. Silicate is an essential nutrient for the growth of diatoms, and as a result the phytoplankton blooms tend to be dominated by other more noxious species. The building of the Aswan Dam destroyed the sardine fishery in the Nile Delta, which had been producing 50,000 tons of fish a year. The second impact is a 10 percent increase in the Mediterranean's freshwater deficit. This has resulted in an increase of deepwater salinity and temperature in the eastern basin; this effect is already being transmitted into the western basin. These changes not only threaten local changes in climate, making the region drier and hotter, but also in the long run changes of the ocean's circulation in the North Atlantic.

Future

Human population is currently estimated to be 360 million in the countries surrounding the Mediterranean. It is predicted that it will grow to around 550 million by 2025, with the coastal population growing to over 200 million, mostly in the North African countries. Coping with all these people will require 45 million tonnes of meat, 250 million tonnes of cereals, and 1000 million tonnes of oil. In addition, the resident population will swell annually by 200 million tourists, who will visit coastal resorts and add to the environmental pressures on the region. Demands for food, water, and energy in these arid regions will inevitably increase. Water shortages, forest clearance, and fire will exacerbate problems of desertification. Pollution by nonbiodegradable litter will become increasingly serious. Marine fisheries, already suffering from overexploitation, will

become more degraded because of pollution of the inshore waters and the impact of climate change. What happens in the Mediterranean in the next few decades will be a prelude to what will probably happen in the global ocean by the end of the twenty-first century.

Martin Angel

FURTHER READING

Bethoux, J. P., and B. Gentili. "Mediterranean Sea, Coastal and Deep-Sea Signatures of Climatic and Environmental Change." *Journal of Marine Systems*, Vol. 7 (1996), pp. 383–394.

Fowler, M. *The Solid Earth: An Introduction to Global Geophysics.* New York: Cambridge University Press, 1990

Lipiatou, E., et al., eds. "Progress in Oceanography of the Mediterranean Sea." *Progress in Oceanography,* Vol. 44 (1999), pp. 1–468.

Rohling, E.J., and H. L Bryden. "Man-Induced Salinity and Temperature Increases in the Western Mediterranean Deep-Water." *Journal of Geophysical Research,* Vol. 97 (1992), pp. 191–198.

Wallman, K., et al. "Salty Brines on the Mediterranean Sea Floor." *Nature,* Vol. 387 (1997), pp. 31–32.

RELATED ARTICLES
Aegean Sea; Bosporus; Flushing Time; Mediterranean Outflow; Oligotrophic; Primary Productivity; Salinity; Strait of Gibraltar

Medusa

The life cycle of certain cnidarians (jellyfish and hydroids) often includes a free-swimming stage with a body form known as a *medusa*. Medusae are umbrella-shaped, with a ring of tentacles on the outer edge of the umbrella and a central mouth that faces downward; a typical example is a jellyfish. Some cnidarians exist as medusae throughout most of their lives; others alternate between medusae and a body form known as a *polyp*; and still others exist only as polyps. Polyps live anchored to the seafloor with their mouths and tentacles facing upward, and they cannot swim.

The anatomy of a medusa is relatively simple. The body wall consists of two layers of cells, between which is mesoglea, a jellylike filling. Inside the body is a hollow space where food is digested. Medusae catch food with their tentacles, which in many species are armed with stinging cells. When prey has been subdued, the tentacles contract and the meal is swallowed. The mouth is the body's only opening, so it also serves as an anus. The body wall of a medusa contains muscle fibers for movement and a simple nerve net to coordinate the muscles, but there is no brain. Jellyfish move by gentle pulsations of the cup-shaped body, which squeezes out water and propels the animal forward.

In all cnidarians where it is present, the medusa serves as the sexual stage in the life cycle. Male jellyfish release sperm cells into the water, which fuse with egg cells either in the female's body or in the open water to form an embryo. The embryo grows into a free-swimming larva, which eventually attaches itself to the seafloor and turns into a polyp. The polyp then reproduces asexually, producing many tiny buds that break off and swim away as new medusae. Other cnidarian species exist as polyps throughout most of the life cycle, but produce sexually, reproducing medusae as a way of dispersing to new habitats. Cnidarians of the class Anthozoa (corals and sea anemones) have eliminated the medusa stage of their reproductive cycle altogether, and exist only as polyps.

The name *Medusa* comes from one of three sisters in Greek mythology, whose heads were covered with snakes, rather like the tentacles of cnidarians.

Ben Morgan

FURTHER READING

Brusca, Richard C., and Gary J. Brusca. *Invertebrates.* Sunderland, Mass.: Sinauer, 1990.

Pechenik, Jan A. *Biology of the Invertebrates.* Boston: Prindle, Weber and Schmidt, 1985; 4th ed., Boston: McGraw-Hill, 2000.

RELATED TOPICS
Cnidaria; Coral; Jellyfish; Polyp

Megaplankton

Megaplankton are comprised of the largest free-floating organisms in the plankton family and include organisms over 20 centimeters (about 8 inches) in size, such as jellyfish, some ctenophores, and the algae *Sargassum*. Sargassum is a brown algae that can grow to over 600 millimeters (2 feet) in length. The Sargasso Sea was named after the algae because of the large numbers that float within its water. As it drifts on the surface of the ocean it provides a habitat for an entire community of other organisms.

Erin O'Donnell

FURTHER READING

Brusca, Richard C., and Gary J. Brusca. *Invertebrates.* Sunderland, Mass.: Sinauer, 1990.

Buchsbaum, Ralph, Mildred Buchsbaum, John Pearse, and Vicki Pearse. *Animals Without Backbones.* Chicago: University of Chicago Press, 1938; 2nd ed., 1976.

Nybakken, James W. *Marine Biology: An Ecological Approach,* 5th ed. San Francisco: Benjamin Cummings, 2001.

Raymont, John E. G. *Plankton and Productivity in the Oceans,* Vol. 2, *Zooplankton.* New York and Oxford: Pergamon Press, 1980.

RELATED ARTICLES
Ctenophora; Jellyfish; Plankton

Meiobenthos

Meiobenthos are bottom-living or benthic animals that pass through 0.5-millimeter (0.02-inch) mesh but are retained on mesh. They are sampled by taking core samples of the sediment and subjecting the sediment to one of several extraction methods, such as elutriation, freshwater shock, and anesthetizing with a solution of magnesium chloride. The size criterion that characterizes meiobenthos is somewhat arbitrary, but it may have some functional significance in that the different meiofaunal taxa respond differently to the varying extraction methods. The abundant meiofauna taxa include the protozoan group Ciliata and metazoans such as Nematoda, Turbellaria, Polychaeta, and Harpacticoid copepods. It includes a small number of other groups, including Ostracoda, Kinorhyncha, Bivalvia, Gastropoda, Tanaidacea, Gastrotricha, Loricifera, Mystacocarida, and Tardigrada. The dominant groups are the Ciliata, Turbellaria, and Nematoda.

Meiofaunal assemblages are very rich in species. For example, nematodes collected from close to the shelf break in the Bay of Biscay in the North Atlantic included 79 genera from 35 families, virtually all of them new species, but nematodes have so few characteristics useful for species identification that it has not been possible to estimate the numbers of species in the collection. Taxonomy is a major, unresolved problem when trying to deal with these tiny animals. Small core samples of sediment just 10 square centimeters (1.55 square inches) in area from the North Atlantic may contain up to 2500 nematodes, 90 polychaete worms, 500 harpacticoid copepods, and 200 to 300 of the other groups.

The meiofauna biomass decreases with increasing depth, but its decline is slower than that of the macro- and megabenthos, so its contribution to benthic biomass increases with depth. However, the dominant factor that seems to control its biomass is the availability of food, and the best single indicator seems to be the quantities of chlorophyll and chlorophyll degradation products in the surficial layer of the sediment.

The fauna also shows a clear vertical structure within the sediment. Some meiofaunal organisms attach themselves to structures that project above the sediment–water interface, such as stones, the tubes of polychaetes and ascidians, and the tests of sponges and larger foraminifers. They also occur attached to hard substrates such as rock faces and manganese nodules. Within the sediment they typically have vertical profiles with over 40 percent of the specimens in the top 1 centimeter (0.4 inch) of the sediment, diminishing to just over 6 percent at depths of 4 to 5 centimeters (1.6 to 2.0 inches). Once again this reflects the availability of organic matter within the sediment. An important implication of this fauna being concentrated at, or close to, the sediment interface is that many benthic samplers, such as box corers, that have a bow wave will "blow" aside a large proportion of the fauna as it is landing on the bottom. Therefore, some data on meiofauna underestimate abundances by up to 50 percent.

The biomass of the meiofauna in just one of these cores may range from 80 to 1800 micrograms (0.0028 to 0.063 ounce), and the variation results from patchiness from localized physical, chemical, and biological variables. For example, at the large scale a benthic storm may strip the surficial sediment off an area of seabed, removing with it most of the local meiofauna. At small scales the mounds and bumps created by burrowing infauna result in very fine scale variations in the pattern of sedimentation and hence the organic content of the sediment. For instance, a feeding holothurian sucks up the surface layers of sediment, and with it the meiofauna.

Very little is known about the population and metabolic dynamics of this rich fauna. There are opportunistic species that are able to respond quickly to the seasonal deposition of phytodetritus, which consists of organic-rich aggregates. Phytodetritus arrives at abyssal depths after the collapse of the spring bloom in the North Atlantic and various upwelling regions. In some years it arrives in large enough quantities to carpet the seabed entirely. The opportunistic species, mostly nematodes, move out of the sediment and invade the interstices of the aggregates. There they consume bacteria and phytoplankton cells contained in the matrix of the aggregate and multiply quite rapidly. There are times when these species from abyssal depths look visibly green because of the quantities of chlorophyll they have consumed.

The majority of the meiofauna do not appear to be so active. They feed mainly on the nanobiota, the even smaller bacteria, yeast, and protozoans that are responsible for the breakdown of much of the recalcitrant organic matter that arrives on the seafloor. Relatively few seem to be predators. Evolutionary theory would suggest that the rich variety of meiofaunal species indicates that there is considerable partitioning of the available resources, but in such a limited environment the majority of species are likely to consume anything they can. So the diversity of meiofaunal assemblages remains an enigma.

Martin Angel

FURTHER READING

Gage, John D., and Paul A. Tyler. *Deep-Sea Biology: A Natural History of Organisms at the Deep-Sea Floor.* New York: Cambridge University Press, 1991.

SCOR Working Group. "Suggested Criteria for Describing Deep-Sea Benthic Communities; The Final Report of SCOR Working Group 76." *Progress in Oceanography,* Vol. 34 (1974), pp. 81–100.

Soltwedel, T. "Metazoan Meiobenthos along Continental Margins: A Review." *Progress in Oceanography,* Vol. 46 (2000), pp. 59–84.

Vincx, M., J. Bett, A. Dinet, T. Ferrero, A. J. Gooday, P. J. D. Lambshead, O. Pfannkuche, T. Soltwedel, and A. Vanreusel. "Meiobenthos of the Deep Northeast Atlantic." In J. H. S. Blaxter and A. J. Southward, eds., *Advances in Marine Biology,* Vol. 30 (1994), pp. 2–88.

USEFUL WEB SITES

International Association of Meiobenthologists. <http://www.meiofauna.org>.

RELATED ARTICLES

Benthos; Bivalvia; Gastropoda; Gastrotricha; Kinorhyncha; Loricifera; Meiofauna; Mystacocarida; Nematoda; Polychaeta; Spring Bloom; Upwelling

Meiofauna

Most biological investigations, especially those prior to the twentieth century, begin with the study of the larger, more obvious, and easily seen animals. At the same time, these animals were often abundant enough to provide sufficient material for observational data, and often of some practical significance to humankind. Similarly, investigators begin to concentrate on ecosystems or habitats in order to better focus their studies. Those studying aquatic ecosystems found it effective to consider two distinct areas: the water column and the life associated with it, and the substrate or bottom, such as mud, sand, pilings, and rocks and the life adapted thereto. The animals living in the water column were called *pelagic fauna* and the animals living in association with the bottom or other substrate were called *benthic fauna.* Each group had its specialized adaptations for successful existence in these habitats. The pelagic fauna could be divided into two additional groups: one group of animals, usually strong swimmers not drastically affected by water currents, were called *nekton* (e.g., tuna), and a second group of smaller, often microscopic animals, which were carried along by the currents, were called *plankton* (e.g., most jellyfish). Similarly, the benthic fauna consisted of two groups. The larger animals, such as flounder, large polychaete worms, clams, and barnacles, constituted the macroscopic animals, and the second group consisted of microscopic animals, ones who, unlike the others, could not be seen or recognized according to their major taxonomic classification without the use of optical magnification. The larger benthic animals became known as the *macrofauna,* and the smallest of the benthic fauna were given the name *meiofauna* in 1952.

Techniques

Although recognizably abundant, the meiofauna were the most difficult to collect and the most difficult to separate from the sediment and process for the mandatory microscopic examination to determine their primary classification. Until the mid-twentieth century, sediment usually collected by dredges or sediment cores was sieved through a 1-millimeter (0.039-inch) mesh sieve to retain and make the macrofauna easier to see and collect; the meiofauna were generally washed back into the sea with the finer sediment particles and conveniently forgotten.

At first, only a few very patient investigators studied this microscopic component of benthic animals because there were many difficulties in the extraction of sufficient material for study. A further complication involved the recognition of some of the meiofauna that represented the youngest stages of macrofaunal animals, temporary meiofauna, as opposed to those never exceeding the size limits [about 1 millimeter (0.039 inch)], called *permanent meiofauna*. The lower size limit established for meiofauna was set at 62 micrometers (0.0024 inch), although some investigators use a smaller, 42-micrometer (0.001653-inch) mesh sieve. Using fine sieves takes much time and requires numerous steps, including the sieving, the removal of each specimen, the mounting for microscopic examination, and often the identification, since many of the specimens are undescribed taxa and few specialists are available for help. Occasionally, a scanning electron microscope must be used to see certain critical characters to ensure proper identification. Sediment samples are commonly dyed to make living or formerly living tissue red in color. Nonetheless, many new kinds of organisms were seen for the first time, and investigators became aware of the significance of this fauna.

Significant Discoveries of New Major Groups

In addition to the discovery of thousands of new species, some of these meiofauna represented new, higher taxonomic categories such as new families, orders, classes, and even phyla. Of the several phyla of animals discovered in the past century, two have been represented exclusively by meiofaunal animals: the Gnathostomulida and the Loricifera. In addition to these, three previously discovered animal phyla, all members of the Tardigrada, Gastrotricha, and Kinorhyncha, are meiofauna. Of the 30 or so animal phyla generally recognized today, the meiofauna include all the members of the phyla above as well as the smallest members (those meeting the definition of meiofauna) of 15 other phyla, including Cnidaria, Mollusca, and Annelida, that we usually think of as being dominated by relatively large organisms. Some phyla (e.g., the Brachiopoda and the Sipuncula) may have only one or two species that can be considered meiofauna; other phyla are represented by numerous benthic species meeting the criteria of meiofauna.

Distribution

Meiofauna are widely distributed, from pole to pole, from freshwater to marine habitats, and from intertidal zones to the deepest parts of the oceans. Meiofauna are tolerant of warm [at least 40°C (104°F)] and cold water [to -4°C (25°F)]. Some live on or in other macrofaunal animals or plants. They are sometimes associated with bryozoan colonies, sponges, and even holdfasts of large algae. But they must always live where sufficient food and dissolved oxygen are present. In the case of sediment as a habitat, meiofauna usually remain in the upper centimeter of silty to muddy substrates, whereas those associated with sand may venture deeper, along with the available oxygen. In marine beach sand where pounding waves create a habitat of medium to coarse sand, meiofauna may be found as deep as 1 meter (3.3 feet). Over 80 percent of the meiofauna biomass consists of copepod crustaceans and nematodes.

Adaptations

Various kinds of meiofauna are adapted to burrow through fine sediment, making their own space by pushing aside mud particles as they feed on other meiofauna or various marine microalgae. Some have adaptations, commonly a cylindrical shape like the nematodes, to live between sediment particles, usually medium to coarse sand that occurs most commonly on marine beaches where strong wave action is present. These meiofauna may be referred to as *interstitial fauna*. They feed on other members of the community, microalgae, and probably much of the plankton brought in by each successive wave. Sometimes the interstices become filled with fine silt and those meiofauna present and able to burrow through this modified habitat are survivors. Still another assemblage of meiofauna remains at the surface of the sediment or other substrates, including rock, macroalgae, or larger benthic animals. Meiofauna is fed upon by both fish and macrofaunal invertebrates as well as other meiofauna.

One of the most fascinating features of meiofauna is their many adaptations to survive in these habitats, especially the sandy beach habitat. Here, the coarser the sand, the stronger the current necessary to maintain this habitat. Meiofauna must have adaptive morphology or habits that keep them from being washed out of this habitat. One of the most common and more interesting adaptations is the development of a duo-gland adhesive system such as that found in many rotifers, platyhelminthes, and gastrotrichs. In a special organ often at the base of a tube, one gland is capable of secreting a very effective adhesive substance; adjacent to it is a releasing gland capable of secreting a substance that dissolves the adhesive. Some organisms develop strong claws on their feet in order to hang on to a particle of sand, and others have toes that create mechanically a suction similar to that on the feet of the Gekko lizard. Strong exoskeletons protect the meiofaunal animal against the abrasive action of shifting sand.

Numerous features of the meiofauna make them a subject of study for more and more contemporary scientists. Many are certain that better understanding of meiofuanal species and communities will lead to better ways of detecting pollutants and offer early warnings of changes in the environment. Other features give scientists better criteria for assessing the evolutionary relationships of animal groups.

Robert P. Higgins

FURTHER READING

Giere, Olav. *Meiobenthology: The Microscopic Fauna in Aquatic Sediments.* Berlin: Springer-Verlag, 1993.

Higgins, Robert P., and Hjalmar Thiel, eds. *Introduction to the Study of Meiofauna.* Washington: Smithsonian Institution Press, 1988.

Morell, Virginia. "Life on a Grain of Sand." *Discover,* April 1995, pp. 78–86.

Nybakken, James W. *Marine Biology: An Ecological Approach,* 5th ed. San Francisco: Benjamin Cummings, 2001.

RELATED ARTICLES
Annelida; Benthos; Brachiopoda; Cnidaria; Gastrotricha; Gnathostomulida; Kinorhyncha; Loricifera; Mollusca; Sipuncula; Tardigrada

Mendocino Triple Junction

The boundary between two plates may be a spreading center, a transform fault, or a subduction zone. A triple junction occurs where three plate boundaries meet. A triple junction is either stable or unstable. Stable triple junctions occur at the intersection of three spreading ridges, where all boundaries are accretionary (where new oceanic lithosphere is created) and therefore relatively stable, whereas the most unstable triple junctions occur at the intersection of three subducting plates. All other triple junctions are relatively unstable. Triple junctions are characterized by the type of plate boundaries that are in contact with each other. The Mendocino Triple Junction is an unstable fault–fault–trench junction.

The Mendocino Triple Junction is located off the coast of northern California. It began forming about 29 to 25 million years ago, when a spreading center collided with the North American

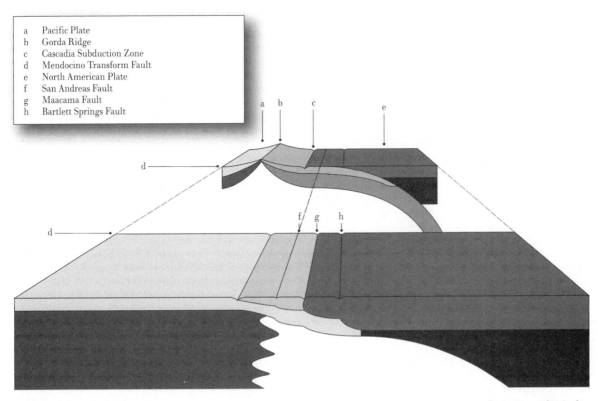

a   Pacific Plate
b   Gorda Ridge
c   Cascadia Subduction Zone
d   Mendocino Transform Fault
e   North American Plate
f   San Andreas Fault
g   Maacama Fault
h   Bartlett Springs Fault

Plate interactions in the region of the Mendocino Triple Junction. [Adapted from J. A. Knauss, Introduction to Physical Oceanography *(Prentice Hall, 1997.)]*

Plate. The Mendocino Triple Junction has continued its northward migration since then. At the Mendocino Triple Junction the Gorda Plate is being obliquely subducted eastward along the Cascadia Subduction Zone beneath the North American Plate. The boundary between the Gorda Plate and the Pacific Plate is the right-lateral Mendocino Fracture Zone, which is a transform fault. The Pacific Plate and the North American Plate meet along a complex right-lateral fault system that includes the San Andreas Transform Fault and the Maacama and Bartlett Springs Faults. The northern extension of the San Andreas Transform Fault, the Mendocino Transform Fault, and the Cascadia Subduction Zone terminate at this triple junction.

The tectonic character of northern California changes abruptly at the Mendocino Triple Junction. The crust becomes thicker at the junction of these three plates and thins away from the junction. As the Mendocino Triple Junction migrates northward the rocks are greatly deformed and leave a trail of deformation like the wake of a boat. North of the Mendocino Triple Junction, the motion changes to subduction. The Gorda slab dips shallowly inland as part of the Cascadia Subduction Zone and earthquakes define a Wadati–Benioff zone. The relative plate movements south of the triple junction are predominantly dextral strike-slip.

Recent seismic studies indicate that the San Andreas, Maacama, and Bartlett Springs Fault zones extend through the crust and into the upper mantle. The deep extension of these faults suggests that the processes controlling crustal deformation are generated within the mantle. Understanding the effects of triple junction migration on the crust and upper mantle allows scientists to evaluate seismic hazards associated with the Mendocino Triple Junction and the plate boundaries associated with it.

David L. White

FURTHER READING

Furlong, K. P. "Lithospheric Behavior with Triple Junction Migration: An Example Based on the Mendociono Triple Junction." *Physics of Earth and Planet Interior,* Vol. 36, No. 213 (1984).

Kennett, James. *Marine Geology.* Englewood Cliffs, N.J.: Prentice Hall, 1982.

Trehu, Anne M., and the Mendocino Working Group. "Pulling the Rug Out From Under California: Seismic Images of the Mendocino Triple Junction." *Eos,* Vol. 76, No. 38 (1995), pp. 369, 380, 381.

RELATED ARTICLES

Cascadia; Gorda Plate; Pacific Plate; Plate Tectonics; Subduction Zone; Transform Fault

Meroplankton

Plankton is a broad descriptive term that comprises the free-floating or weakly swimming organisms that drift with the currents of the ocean. Scientists categorize members of this diverse assemblage of organisms based on taxonomy, size, or life history characteristics. *Meroplankton* is a term based on life history characteristics; it describes those organisms that spend only a short part of their life in the plankton. Holoplanktonic organisms, in contrast, spend their entire lives in the plankton.

Larvae and eggs of *benthic* (bottom-dwelling) animals and *nektonic* (free-swimming) animals constitute the meroplankton, and the assemblage of meroplanktonic organisms found in the oceans is even more diverse than that of the holoplankton. Meroplankton diversity is great, because larvae of almost every animal phylum and from every oceanic habitat can be found in the plankton. Some benthic species produce planktotrophic (feeding) larvae and others produce lecithotrophic (nonfeeding) larvae, but both types spend time in the plankton. In addition, the number of larval forms found in the plankton far exceeds the number of species that produce them—the larvae of many species pass through multiple larval stages before leaving the plankton and metamorphosing into adults. For example, crustaceans have the greatest number of larval types; most species have more than one larval form and some species go through up to 18 different larval stages.

The composition, abundance, and diversity of meroplankton in a given water sample depend on where in the ocean a sample is taken. Coastal waters often offer a rich meroplanktonic assemblage, because of their proximity to shallow inshore sources of larvae (i.e., intertidal and subtidal benthic communities). A coastal plankton sample might contain larvae of phyla that do not have any holoplanktonic representatives, such as the bryozoans (cyphonautes larva), phoronids (actinotroch larva), and brachiopods (lingulid larva). Larvae of echinoderms (e.g., echinopluteus, bipinnaria, brachiolaria, auricularia, and ophiopluteus), sipunculids (pelagosphaera), sponges, and hemichordates (tornaria) are also commonly found in coastal water samples. The phyla annelida (trochophore larvae in polychaetes), nemertea (pilidium larva), mollusca (trochophore and veliger larvae), cnidaria (planula and actinula larvae), chordata (e.g., tadpole larva in tunicates), and of course, crustacea (e.g., megalops, zoea, nauplius, cyprid larval forms) all contain holoplanktonic representatives; determining if a particular larval form was produced by a benthic or a pelagic adult can be difficult for these groups. Nektonic organisms also contribute to the diversity found in the meroplankton; many fish species spawn eggs and/or have larval forms that spend time in the plankton.

Lynn L. Lauerman

FURTHER READING

Fraser, James. *Nature Adrift: The Story of Marine Plankton.* London: Foulis, 1962.

Nybakken, James W. *Marine Biology: An Ecological Approach,* 5th ed. San Francisco: Benjamin Cummings, 2001.

Smith, Deboyd L. *A Guide to Marine Coastal Plankton and Marine Invertebrate Larvae.* Dubuque, Iowa: Kendall/Hunt, 1977; 2nd ed. with Kevin B. Johnson, 1996.

RELATED ARTICLES
Holoplankton; Lecithotrophic Larvae; Plankton; Planktotrophic Larvae

Mesopelagic Zone

The mesopelagic zone is a twilight zone that extends from around 250 to 1000 meters (820 to 3280 feet) deep and lies between the well-lit epipelagic zone and the permanently dark bathypelagic zone. It is sometimes called the *dysphotic zone.* There is never enough light for phytoplankton to photosynthesize, and autotrophic organisms are absent. The only options for feeding are either detritivory or carnivory. However, many of the species that reside at mesopelagic depths by day migrate up into the epipelagic zone at night to feed and return to the original zone at dawn. This daily vertical migration behavior enables the migrants to enjoy the better feeding conditions near the surface, while still reducing the risks of predation from hunting predators.

The zone can often be subdivided into a shallow and a deep layer based on the characteristics of the fish and decapod crustaceans that inhabit them. In the upper mesopelagic zone the decapod crustaceans (prawns and shrimps) are partly transparent and partly pigmented, with red and orange carotenoid pigment. Because of the absence of red light in these depths, the pigment is functionally black. It also has its maximum absorption of light at blue-green wavelengths, which is the color not only of the residual daylight that penetrates to these depths, but also of most bioluminescence (the light produced by the animals themselves). Carotenoids are plant pigments that cannot be synthesized by the animals and have to be derived second- or third-hand

from the contents in their diets. In the deep mesopelagic the decapods are totally red, and again the pigments are carotenoids.

In the shallow mesopelagic zone, the fishes are even more amazing. Their backs are black but their flanks are highly silvered, and their bellies are lined with light organs (photophores). From the side, their mirrorlike sides reflect light of exactly the same intensity as the background, making them invisible. From below, the light from the photophores along their bellies breaks up their silhouettes against the light coming from directly overhead. Lantern fish also have photophores along the flanks arranged in patterns that are species-specific and probably signal an individual's identity to other fish, particularly during mating. In the deep mesopelagic the fishes still have photophores arranged along their bellies but no longer have the mirrorlike sides.

Martin Angel

FURTHER READING
Childress, James J. "Are There Physiological and Biochemical Adaptations of Metabolism in Deep-Sea Animals?" *Trends in Ecology and Evolution,* Vol. 10 (1995), pp. 30–36.
Harris, Roger, et al. *ICES Zooplankton Methodology Manual.* San Diego and London: Academic Press, 2000.
Marshall, Norman B. *Developments in Deep-Sea Biology.* Poole, England: Blandford Press, 1979.
Ormond, Rupert F. G., John D. Gage, and Martin V. Angel. *Marine Biodiversity: Patterns and Processes.* Cambridge and New York: Cambridge University Press, 1997.
Randall, David J., and Anthony P. Farrell. *Deep-Sea Fishes.* San Diego: Academic Press, 1997.

RELATED ARTICLES
Dysphotic Zone; Pelagic; Photophore; Phytoplankton; Vertical Migration

Mesoplankton

Plankton, the organisms that drift passively in the oceans, are classified into various size groups.

Mesoplankton is the term used to describe the plankton that are caught in nets with mesh sizes of 60 to 200 micrometers, a thousandth of a millimeter (0.0000394 inch). Their lengths range from 0.2 to 20 millimeters (0.008 to 0.8 inch). Mesoplankton is most abundant in the upper few hundred meters of the ocean and is dominated, both numerically and in terms of biomass, by small species of copepods, but it includes the early larval stages of many other types of animals. Predominantly, mesoplankton species tend to be either herbivorous or detritivorous. The growth and survival of the early larval stages of many species of commercial fish is determined by the abundances of mesoplankton they encounter and feed upon.

Martin Angel

FURTHER READING
Harris, Roger P. *Ices Zooplankton Methodology Manual.* San Diego: Academic Press, 2000.

USEFUL WEB SITES
"Bigelow Laboratory for Ocean Sciences FlowCAM." <http://www.bigelow.org/flowcam/>.

RELATED ARTICLES
Plankton

Mesozoa

The mesozoans are all parasites of marine invertebrates with a very simple body structure comprising an outer layer of multiciliated cells that enclose an internal mass of reproductive cells. These animals lack any organ systems. Despite the simplicity of the body structure, these animals have very complex life cycles. There are two very different groups of organisms that comprise the mesozoa. Both groups were formerly included in the phylum Mesozoa, but most invertebrate zoologists now consider the two to be separate phyla.

Perhaps the better known of the two taxa are those included in the phylum Rhombozoa.

Most rhombozoans are grouped in the class Dicyemida, all of which are parasites in the nephridia of benthic-dwelling cephalopod mollusks such as octopods and squids, where they apparently feed on the metabolites occurring in the urine of the host. Although they are extremely abundant in their hosts and almost universally present, they do not cause any detectable pathology. In the life cycle the adult dicyemid central internal cell, the axial cell, either produces asexually young of the same form as the parent, which serves to build up the infection, or forms a hermaphroditic gonad in which the egg is fertilized by sperm from the same gonad. The fertilized egg then develops into an infusiform larva that is passed out of the host. Its fate is still unknown, but it is believed that it somehow infects a new cephalopod host without an intermediate host.

In the phylum Orthonectida the dioecious adults consist of a similar outer layer of ciliated cells enclosing a mass of sperm or egg cells. In reproduction males and females are released from the host simultaneously and the sperm are then released from the males outside the host and penetrate the bodies of the females fertilizing the eggs. Development of the fertilized eggs produces a ciliated larva that is subsequently released to infect a new host. Within the host the ciliated larva gives rise to a multinucleate, amoebalike plasmodium that may divide asexually and spread the infection. Certain nuclei in the plasmodium divide to give rise to sexual adults, completing the life cycle.

James W. Nybakken

FURTHER READING
Brusca, R. C., and G. J. Brusca. *Invertebrates.* Sunderland, Mass.: Sinauer, 1990.
Ruppert, E. E., and R. D. Barnes. *Invertebrate Zoology.* 6th ed. New York: Saunders College Publishing, 1994.

RELATED TOPICS
Parasitism

Metamorphosis

Many different marine phyla undergo a strikingly rapid change or metamorphosis from larval to adult form. For example, ciliated nemertine or bryozoan larvae are entirely different from their benthic adults. The larvae of many phyla are specialized for life in the food-rich surface layers and lead a free-floating planktonic life there while also permitting dispersal of the species. These specializations may include sense organs and ciliated locomotor systems absent from the adult, like the velum of molluscan veligers, as well as spines and extensions of the body, enabling them to float in the plankton. Larval planktonic life may be short, less than one hour in some ascidians, where the chordatelike larva (often with special eyes and sense organs) does not feed and it is totally different from the sessile saclike adult. It may also be prolonged, with the larvae feeding and growing in the plankton for weeks or even months before being transformed into the adult. The changes during metamorphosis can be extremely rapid (one minute or less), such as with the transformation of the actinotrocha larvae of phoronids, which then sink to the bottom as minute adults.

Some echinoderm larvae metamorphose differently, for the metamorphosis is less rapid and results in a small adult growing within the larval form for some time before breaking out as a juvenile—in a sense, the adult is a parasite on the larva. Although most free-swimming or floating larval forms arise from benthic adults, all larval-to-adult metamorphoses are not linked necessarily to dispersal of a benthic form. The surface-dwelling Portuguese man-of-war *Physalia* arises from deep-dwelling pelagic larvae, and the pelagic doliolids have chordatelike pelagic larvae, as do three-fourths of all marine teleost fish. In many larvae, metamorphosis is induced by chemical triggers, best known in economically important forms such as biofouling species (e.g., barnacles).

All planktonic larvae share special buoyancy adaptations, and this is also true of fish larvae, which often have the remnants of oil globules that cause the eggs to float and long extensions of fin rays. Although fish larvae are sometimes unlike the adult, their metamorphoses are less drastic than that of many invertebrates. For example, echinoderm and molluscan larvae are entirely different in structure and form from the adults and undergo drastic remodeling at metamorphosis.

Quentin Bone

FURTHER READING
Hadfield, M. G., and M. R. Strathmann. "Variability, Flexibility and Plasticity in Life Histories of Marine Invertebrates." *Oceanologica Acta*, Vol. 19 (1995), pp. 323–334.
Nybakken, James W. *Marine Biology: An Ecological Approach*, 5th ed. San Francisco: Benjamin Cummings, 2001.

RELATED ARTICLES
Larvae; Planktotrophic Larvae

Methane Seep

Methane seeps are a particular type of cold fluid seeping out of the seafloor at water depths ranging from 400 to 6000 meters (1310 to 19,700 feet), in which the fluid is methane rich. Similar to the more generic cold seeps, methane seeps are important because they (1) affect the recycling of carbon, (2) alter the topography of the seafloor, (3) result in the destruction and formation of minerals, (4) can support chemosynthetic communities (e.g., tube worms), and (5) affect the chemistry of the ocean.

Methane is generated by the bacterial breakdown of organic matter in sediments. In addition, in more deeply buried sediments, methane also forms during petroleum generation by the thermal breakdown of organic material. These hydrocarbons migrate to the seafloor from their site of formation, which is accomplished via a variety of mechanisms largely dependent on the geologic setting. In general, gas-charged fluids escape directly into seawater by diffuse flow or by focused venting, often along faults and fractures.

Methane seep sites support diverse benthic chemosynthetic communities. Unlike life in the upper reaches of the ocean and on land that derives its energy from the Sun (photosynthesis), chemosynthetic organisms are believed to derive their energy from carbon and/or sulfur, with the help of symbiotic bacteria. Far removed from the Sun in the deep ocean, seep sites act as seafloor oases of life. Not surprisingly, methane-seep communities generally resemble hydrothermal vent chemosynthetic communities, with organisms such as tube worms, mussels, and clams. The chemosynthetic-dependent creatures, in turn, attract other ocean life (e.g., fish and crabs), forming a dense community that is well out of the photic zone.

The exit of methane-rich fluid from the seafloor can affect the local seafloor topography in both constructive and destructive ways. Rapid escape of gas-charged fluid in soft fine-grained sediments can form hollow depressions, typically about 50 to 100 meters (165 to 330 feet) in diameter and 2 to 3 meters (6.6 to 10 feet) deep, called *pockmarks*. Seepage through steep-sided carbonate platforms like the west Florida escarpment is believed to help shape the morphology of the escarpment by solution undercutting and steepening. Dissolution from seep fluids also has been attributed to playing a role in the formation of submarine canyons in a process called *spring sapping*. In contrast to pockmark formation, the escape of fluid in very muddy sediments has been shown to form positive features called *mud volcanoes* or *mud diapirs*. Other positive topographic features are related to precipitation of minerals at or near the seafloor, especially carbonate minerals such as calcite and dolomite. In general, carbonate minerals precipitate when methane is oxidized at or near the seafloor. Depending on the

pressure and temperature conditions at the seafloor, natural gas hydrates have also been described associated with methane seeps (e.g., Gulf of Mexico). Gas hydrates are icelike compounds composed of water and gas, frequently methane, which form under high-pressure and low-temperature conditions.

Mitchell J. Malone

FURTHER READING
Hovland, M., and A. G. Judd. *Seabed Pockmarks and Seepages: Impact on Geology, Biology, and the Marine Environment.* London and Boston: Graham and Trotman, 1988.
Pain, S. "Extreme Worms." *New Scientist,* Vol. 159, No. 2143, 25 July 1998.
Paull, C. K., et al. "Biological Communities at the Florida Escarpment Resemble Hydrothermal Vent Taxa." *Science,* Vol. 226 (1984), pp. 965–967.
Sibuet, M., and K. Olu. "Biogeography, Biodiversity, and Fluid Dependence of Deep-Sea Cold-Seep Communities at Active and Passive Margins." *Deep-Sea Research II,* Vol. 45 (1998), pp. 517–567.
Suess, E., G. Bohrman, et al. "Flammable Ice." *Scientific American,* November 1999, pp. 76–84.

RELATED ARTICLES
Chemosynthesis; Cold Seep; Gas Hydrate; Hydrothermal Vent; Symbiosis; Tube Worm

Microbenthos

Microbenthos refers to communities of microscopic organisms that live on or in substrata in the sea, such as sediments, rocks, plants, and artificial structures. Most commonly the term is used for microorganisms living on the sediment surface and in the interstitial spaces between sediment particles. Microbenthos displays a high diversity and a great variety of adaptations and comprises *prokaryotes* (bacteria, cyanobacteria) and *unicellular eukaryotes* (protists), including microalgae and unicellular fauna (Protozoa). Sometimes, *meiofauna* [multicellular animals; 0.62 micrometer to 0.5 millimeter (0.000024 to

0.02 inch)] are included in the microbenthos. The density of cells in microbenthic communities is orders of magnitude higher than it is in the water column, and they often form visible biofilms or microbial mats. In the topmost 1 cubic centimeter of shallow-water sediments, typical densities of individuals are 10^{10} bacteria, 10^6 microalgae, and 10^2 ciliates. Microbenthos plays a key role in the production and cycling of carbon and the turnover of nutrients, particularly in shallow coastal waters.

Where light reaches the bottom, the microbenthos is often dominated by microalgae (*microphytobenthos*, i.e., photoautotrophic organisms, comprising both prokaryotes and eukaryotes). Microphytobenthos provides half or more of the total primary production in shallow estuaries, being an important food source for micro-, meio-, and macrofauna. *Diatoms* (Bacillariophyceae) and *cyanobacteria* (Cyanophyceae) are the commonest groups of microphytobenthos, although various flagellates, such as *dinoflagellates* (Dinophyceae), *cryptomonads* (Cryptophyceae), *euglenoids* (Euglenophyceae), and *haptophytes* (Haptophyceae) are also found. The algal cells live either attached to sediment particles (*epipsammic*) or move on the surface of the substratum (*epipelon*) or within the sediment (*endopelon*). While moving, diatoms secrete mucilage (extracellular polymeric substances) that binds together particles, thereby stabilizing sediments. Cells that are attached to rock surfaces are referred to as *epilithic*.

Benthic bacteria include many different functional groups that are either heterotrophic or autotrophic, aerobic or anaerobic. Like microalgae, they constitute an important food source for benthic fauna. They are responsible for the degradation of organic material and play a key role in the turnover of nitrogen through processes such as *nitrification* (the process whereby ammonium and nitrite are oxidized to nitrate) and *denitrification* (the process whereby nitrate is turned into

nitrogen gas). Anaerobic bacteria that reduce sulfate to sulfide, and bacteria that produce methane gas (methanogens), are also important. There are several types of chemolithotrophic bacteria (using inorganic compounds as an energy source), such as aerobic nitrifiers and anaerobic sulfide-oxidizing bacteria.

The microbenthic fauna (*microfauna*) consist of Protozoa, such as ciliates (Ciliophora), foraminiferans (Foraminifera), and heterotrophic flagellates, the latter belonging to several groups, such as dinoflagellates and euglenoids. Like bacteria, protozoan species possess adaptations to different oxygen concentrations, showing chemosensory behavior. The protozoa feed on bacteria and microalgae, and several species of ciliates have algae and bacteria as endosymbionts.

Benthic microbial mats and biofilms are stratified systems with steep physical, chemical, and biological gradients, on the scale of micro- and millimeters. This stratification of organisms and processes depends primarily on how deep oxygen penetrates into the substratum. Electrochemical and optical microsensors have made it possible to analyze the microenvironment of the gradients and measure the rate of microbial metabolism with high spatial precision. In the photic zone [1 to 3 millimeters (0.04 to 0.12 inch) in sediments], sometimes a visible three-layered system of photosynthetic organisms is found, with a brown layer of diatoms on the top, followed by a blue-green layer of cyanobacteria, and a purple layer of oxygen-sensitive sulfur bacteria. Below the narrow photic, oxygen-producing zone, oxygen decreases rapidly and a sequence of anaerobic respiration processes follows, depending on available electron acceptors. Close to the oxygen-producing zone, nitrification occurs, followed deeper down by anaerobic respiration processes, such as denitrification, reduction of Mn^{4+} and Fe^{3+}, sulfate reduction, and finally, methane production.

Kristina Sundbäck

FURTHER READING

Fenchel, T. "What Can Ecologists Learn from Microbes: Life beneath a Square Centimetre of Sediment Surface." *Functional Ecology*, Vol. 6 (1992), pp. 499–507.

Stal, Lucas J., and Caumette Pierre, eds. *Microbial Mats: Structure, Development and Environmental Significance*. NATO ASI Series G, Ecological Studies, Vol. 35. New York, Berlin, and Heidelberg: Springer-Verlag, 1994; p.463.

RELATED ARTICLES

Cyanobacteria; Diatom; Meiofauna

Microbial Loop

The microbial loop is a part of the oceanic food web in which microorganisms recycle carbon back into the larger classical planktonic food web. The loop, which works alongside the classical phytoplankton–zooplankton–fish food web, explains the significant role of heterotrophic bacteria and nanozooplankton grazers in recovering organic material that was once thought to be lost from the upper layers of the ocean. Historically, researchers thought that microorganisms such as bacteria, viruses, and nanozooplankton played a minor role in the oceanic ecosystem. Development of the concept of the microbial loop in the 1980s was a breakthrough in understanding marine food webs.

Classical Planktonic Food Web

The classical marine planktonic food web consists of a system in which minerals and energy flow upward from primary producers that fix carbon to increasingly larger organisms. It generally consists of a phytoplankton to zooplankton to fish transfer. Thus, net phytoplankton, which are algal-like protists such as diatoms and dinoflagellates, fix carbon by photosynthesis. Phytoplankton cells are grazed upon by tiny herbivores such as copepods and other crustaceans. Grazers are consumed by larger crustaceans, invertebrates, and small fish that are in turn eaten by a succession of predators such as large fishes, cephalopods, marine mammals, sea birds, and humans in higher trophic levels. In this scenario, the role of bacteria is limited to degrading and remineralizing material.

Theoretically, the classical food web results in a large amount of wasted energy. Approximately one-fourth of the carbon fixed by photosynthesis is lost to the surrounding water as dissolved organic matter (DOM) and is potentially lost from the upper ocean system. DOM includes compounds such as amino acids, simple sugars, carbohydrates, proteins, and nucleic acids, and it is extremely abundant in the upper layers of the ocean. In fact, seawater is one of the largest reservoirs of organic carbon [in the form of dissolved organic carbon (DOC)] on Earth. DOM comes from both phytoplankton and zooplankton. Phytoplankton cells naturally exude a portion of DOM derived from photosynthesis and zooplankton naturally excrete DOM. Zooplankton–phytoplankton interactions also release DOM. When feeding, herbivorous zooplankton break phytoplankton cells, and DOM is lost in the process; this source of DOM is referred to as *sloppy feeding*.

Microbial Loop

While the traditional food web remains a basic framework for understanding energy transfer in marine systems, improvements in technology beginning in the mid-1970s illustrated that a large part of the picture was missing. New tools, such as better staining techniques, epifluorescence microscopy, adenosine triphosphate (ATP) assays, nucleopore filters, scanning electron microscopy, transmission electron microscopy, the development of molecular biology assays, and improved methods for measuring minute amounts of chemicals, led to a number of findings that resulted in the concept of the microbial loop. As researchers developed new techniques for detecting and counting bacterioplankton and nanoplankton and for measuring uptake and release of chemical compounds by these organisms, they found that the role of microbes in the oceanic ecosystem is to recycle much of the DOM released by phytoplankton and zooplankton so that it is not lost from the upper layers of the ocean.

Researchers discovered that the smallest members of the oceanic ecosystem were much more abundant than previously imagined. For example, coastal waters can harbor as many as 5×10^6 cells per milliliter of water. Viruses can be found at an abundance of 10^7 particles per milliliter of seawater. In some locales at certain times of the year, bacterial biomass can equal or exceed

phytoplankton biomass. Most of these bacteria are free living, heterotrophic, and less than 0.4 micrometers in diameter.

The microbial loop consists of several trophic levels. DOM is supplied at varying rates by phytoplankton and zooplankton, and bacteria are the only organisms that can effectively use it. Heterotrophic bacteria convert DOM into bacterial biomass, and they can do so at varying levels (10 to 80 percent) of efficiency. Bacteria, which have recovered DOM lost from the classical planktonic food web, are too small to be efficiently grazed by copepods. Instead, nanozooplankton such as flagellates consume bacteria, and larger nanoplankton such as ciliates consume the flagellates. The nanozooplankton are then

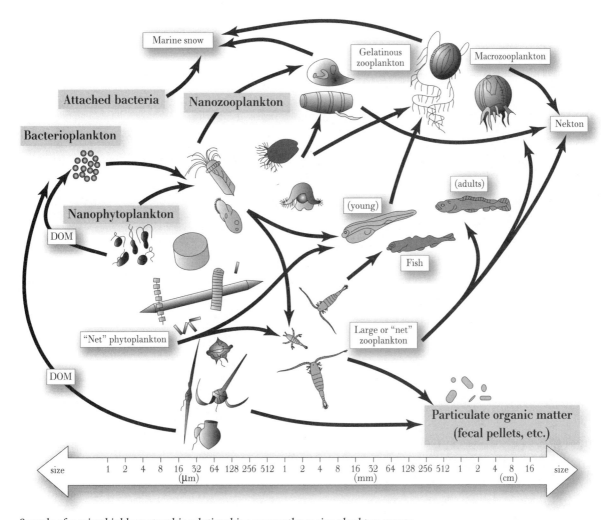

Sample of a microbial loop: trophic relationships among the major plankton groups.

eaten by copepods and the loop reenters the traditional food web.

Scientists have known of the existence of marine viruses since the 1960s, but the role of viruses in the microbial loop and in the larger oceanic ecosystem is still largely unknown. Viruses are thought to infect bacteria primarily and may affect bacterial species composition. Viruses may act to keep bacterial abundance at a fairly constant level so that populations do not explode and utilize all available nutrients at the expense of primary producers.

Heterotrophic bacteria and nanozooplankton also affect the oceanic ecosystem in another way: They can affect the availability of nutrients such as nitrogen and phosphorus that are crucial to growth and reproduction of photosynthetic organisms. These nutrients are recycled rapidly by the smallest members of the community. Grazers often excrete phosphorus as phosphate and nitrogen as ammonium, and in doing so they can provide nutrients to phytoplankton even when nutrient-rich water is absent. On the other hand, when nitrogen and phosphorus are limited, bacteria compete with phytoplankton for these nutrients. The great abundance of bacterial cells and their large surface-to-volume ratio make them successful competitors.

Role of the Microbial Loop in the Oceanic Ecosystem

Much of the material and energy (in the form of DOM) previously considered lost from the epipelagic zone is actually returned to the classical food web by the microbial loop. Direct uptake of DOM by heterotrophic bacteria can equal 50 percent of the annual production by phytoplankton. The relative importance of the microbial loop in the large-scale oceanic system, however, varies from place to place and season to season. Bacterial biomass ranges from 5 percent to more than 100 percent of phytoplankton biomass, and it often is greater than the biomass of zooplankton. In some

locales, bacteria efficiently utilize DOM, grazers feed efficiently, and the microbial loop acts as a link for transferring a substantial amount of energy to higher trophic levels. In other places, the microbial loop transfers a minor amount of carbon to higher levels.

In oligotrophic waters such as in the central gyres of the oceans, which typically are low in nutrients and exhibit low productivity, bacterial biomass often exceeds that of phytoplankton. As a general rule, oligotrophic waters are dominated by the microbial food web; this food web includes the microbial loop and primary production by autotrophic bacterioplankton. In contrast, well-mixed waters such as those found in coastal areas and in areas of upwelling are dominated by net phytoplankton and the classical food web.

Lynn L. Lauerman

FURTHER READING

Azam, F., T. Fenchel, J. G. Field, J. S. Gray, L. A. Meyer-Reil, and F. Thingstad. "The Ecological Role of Water-Column Microbes in the Sea." *Marine Ecology Progress Series*, Vol. 10 (1983), pp. 257–263.

Fuhrman, J. "Bacterioplankton Roles in Cycling of Organic Matter: The Microbial Food Web." In P. G. Falkowski and A. D. Woodhead, eds., *Primary Productivity and Biogeochemical Cycles in the Sea.* New York: Plenum Press, 1992; pp. 361–383.

NATO Advanced Research Institute on Microbial Metabolism and the Cycling of Organic Matter in the Sea. In J. E. Hobbie and P. J. LeB. Williams, eds., *Heterotrophic Activity in the Sea.* New York: Plenum Press, 1984.

Kiorboe, T. "Turbulence, Phytoplankton Cell Size and the Structure of Pelagic Food Webs." In J. H. S. Blaxter and A. J. Southward, eds., *Advances in Marine Biology*, Vol. 29. New York: Academic Press, 1993; pp. 1–72.

Nybakken, James W. *Marine Biology: An Ecological Approach*, 5th ed. San Francisco: Benjamin Cummings, 2001.

Pomeroy, L.R. "The Ocean's Food Web: A Changing Paradigm." *Bioscience*, Vol. 24 (1974), pp. 499–504.

RELATED ARTICLES
Dissolved Organic Matter; Food Chain; Food Web

Microplankton

Planktonic organisms have either little or no ability to move on their own and rely on water currents for transportation. Larger plankton, known as *net plankton,* can be collected using plankton nets, which are fine meshed nets that allow water to pass through while retaining planktonic organisms. The microplankton range in size from 20 to 200 micrometers (about 787 microinches to 0.00787 inch) and include most diatoms and dinoflagellates.

Erin O'Donnell

FURTHER READING
Nybakken, James W. *Marine Biology: An Ecological Approach,* 5th ed. San Francisco: Benjamin Cummings, 2001.
Raymont, John E. G. *Plankton and Productivity in the Oceans,* Vol. 1, *Phytoplankton.* New York and Oxford: Pergamon Press, 1980.

RELATED ARTICLES
Diatom; Dinoflagellate; Net Plankton; Plankton

Mid-Atlantic Ridge

The Mid-Atlantic Ridge is a string of volcanic seamounts that runs approximately along the central Atlantic Ocean, from Iceland in the north to Bouvet Island (1000 miles off Antarctica) in the south. Situated primarily 3 to 5 kilometers (1.9 to 3.1 miles) below the ocean surface, the ridge covers over 15,000 kilometers (9320 miles) and is part of a larger, pan-oceanic ridge system that extends almost 60,000 kilometers (37,285 miles). By contrast, the longest mountain range on land, the Andes, covers 8000 kilometers, slightly more than half the distance of the Mid-Atlantic Ridge. The seamounts on the Mid-Atlantic Ridge are located on either side of a deep valley. The valley, referred to as the *central rift,* is between 30 and 50 kilometers (19 to 31 miles) wide, and it ranges in depth from 1500 meters (4920 feet) to more than 3000

meters (9840 feet). The seamounts are equally imposing, rising as high as 3 kilometers (1.9 miles) from the seafloor and measuring up to 1500 kilometers (930 miles) in width. Even though the Mid-Atlantic Ridge is such an immense and impressive physical feature, it was virtually unknown until the nineteenth century and has only been explored in greater detail since the 1950s.

Discovery of the Mid-Atlantic Ridge
The invention of the telegraph led to a scheme of improving communication systems between Europe and the United States by laying submarine cables across the North Atlantic Ocean to connect the two continents. Depth recordings taken as preparation for laying the first transatlantic cable revealed hills

Mid-Atlantic Ridge.

and valleys and a rise in the central North Atlantic Ocean. This rise, later named *Telegraph Plateau*, demonstrated that the central ocean was not flat or deep as previously thought. In 1874, a cable laying ship landed a large chunk of basalt, a common volcanic rock, from the North Atlantic floor.

By the end of World War II, sonar technology had improved significantly to reveal more detailed images of the ocean floor. Between 1956 and 1960, scientists discovered a continuous mid-ocean ridge, a vast submarine mountain system lying along the middle of the oceans. In 1962, Harry Hammond Hess (1906–69) published a paper titled "History of Ocean Basins," in which he proposed the process of seafloor spreading. This theory served as the basis for the larger, unifying theory of plate tectonics, and it helped explain the evolution and workings of the Mid-Atlantic Ridge (and other spreading centers).

Plate Tectonics and the Evolution of the Mid-Atlantic Ridge

According to the theory of plate tectonics, Earth's outer layer, the lithosphere (crust and uppermost mantle), is composed of a number of plates. The plates, on which continents rest, are either being created or destroyed due to a series of complex geological processes. The ultimate source for the plate activity is the heat generated in Earth's core. The heat is transferred from the core to the mantle by a series of convection currents. The lithosphere, which sits on top of the mantle, is subject to the underlying heat, pressure, and convection currents. It fractures in locations such as mid-ocean ridges to form divergent plate boundaries. Once fractured, molten rock material (magma) oozes out and creates new seafloor. The older seafloor moves away from the spreading center in both directions and is destroyed when it sinks back into the mantle at a convergent plate boundary. The Mid-Atlantic Ridge is a spreading center and a divergent plate boundary. Its central rift represents the fractured crust, and its volcanic seamounts and

lava plains are created by molten rock upwelling from within the underlying mantle.

It is believed that the Atlantic Ocean began forming over 170 million years ago after a rift occurred within the supercontinent of Pangea in the current position of the Caribbean Sea. This rift separated the regions of North America, northwest Africa, and Eurasia, creating the North Atlantic Ocean. After 50 million years of rifting, the North Atlantic Ocean was bisected by an active mid-ocean ridge system that produced new crust as the plates carrying the surrounding continents separated. By 80 million years ago, the North Atlantic was a fully developed ocean, and 20 million years after, the Mid-Atlantic Ridge progressed into the Arctic Basin, separating Greenland from Europe. Greenland fully separated from North America and Eurasia 57 million years ago, opening up the North Atlantic. During this period, South America continued to separate from Africa, opening up the southern Atlantic Ocean. Finally, only about 3 million years ago, the continents of North and South America connected, closing the Pacific from the Atlantic Ocean.

Topography and Features of the Mid-Atlantic Ridge

Although mostly submarine, parts of the Mid-Atlantic Ridge break the ocean surface and form islands or groups of islands. Iceland, Azores, Canary and Cape Verde Islands, Ascension Island, Saint Helena, Tristan da Cunha, and Bouvet are all volcanic islands located on the Mid-Atlantic Ridge. They were created as a result of seamount volcanoes that grew high enough to break through the ocean's surface. Iceland is a broad volcanic plateau that rose out of the ocean 16 million years ago. The elevated topography of the plateau extends for approximately 1400 kilometers (870 miles) in each direction, and over a third of the plateau lies above sea level. Iceland straddles the spreading ridge system, and the central rift occurs as a fault-bounded and flat-floored valley that traverses the entire northern part of the island. The valley is flanked by numerous volcanoes, making Iceland one of the most volcanically active regions on Earth. Among the other islands, the Azores were created by a mantle plume (hotspot), and the Saints Peter and Paul Islands were formed as fragments of the mantle that were uplifted.

The spreading ridge system of the Mid-Atlantic Ridge is not continuous from the north to the south. Instead, it is broken into a series of small, straight sections. As the plates spread apart in opposite directions, the resulting stress and strain on the seafloor create a series of transform faults that occur every 30 to 100 kilometers (19 to 62 miles) along the ridge. These faults offset the ridge east to west from a few miles to several hundred miles, creating independent fracture zone segments with ridges and valleys in a step shape. Each segment is fully independent, with its own volcanic sources. One of the largest such features in the Atlantic Ocean is the Romanche Fracture Zone. Located near the equator, the fracture zone is almost 1000 kilometers (620 miles) long, matching the continental bends of Africa and South America.

The spreading rate at the Mid-Atlantic Ridge averages 3 centimeters (a little over 1 inch) per year, adding 5 cubic miles (20.5 cubic kilometers) of new basalt (volcanic rock) to the seafloor. However, this rate is considered "slow" compared to faster spreading centers, such as the East Pacific Rise in the Pacific Ocean, which spreads 5 to 10 times faster than the Mid-Atlantic Ridge. But the slower spreading rate provides the Mid-Atlantic Ridge with more relief and elevation. Moreover, there is considerable variation in the phases of growth and stretching along the ridge system.

Hydrothermal Vents: Chemosynthesis in the Mid-Atlantic Ridge

Sites within the Mid-Atlantic Ridge contain hydrothermal vents that host a variety of unique species living under extreme conditions. Hydrothermal vents are geysers on the ocean floor that spew hot [up to 400°C (750°F)], mineral-laden water. Most are found in deep water in areas of seafloor spreading and near active seamount volcanoes on mid-ocean ridges. The vents are formed when water seeps into the cracks in the lithosphere, becomes superheated by the underlying molten rock, changes its mineral content on its way back up, and then rises through holes in the seafloor.

In 1977, during a submersible expedition near a spreading center in the Galápagos Islands region of the Pacific Ocean, scientists discovered hydrothermal vents rich in unique marine life. These animals included strange tube worms, giant clams, and blind crabs living in superheated waters in complete darkness. A few years later, researchers determined that these rich communities exist on a chemical source of energy instead of sunlight. That process, known as *chemosynthesis*, is driven by sulfur-oxidizing bacteria that serve as the basis for the community's food chain. Further research in the Mid-Atlantic Ridge and other vent-rich areas has led to the discovery of various new species previously unknown to science, as well as studies into the origins and ecology of these communities.

Manoj Shivlani

FURTHER READING

Cone, Joseph. *Fire Under the Sea: The Discovery of the Most Extraordinary Environment on Earth—Volcanic Hot Springs on the Ocean Floor.* New York: Morrow, 1991.

Hess, H. H. "History of Ocean Basins." In A. E. J. Engel et al., eds., *Petrological Studies: A Volume in Honor of A. F. Buddington.* Boulder, Colo.: Geological Society of America, 1962; pp. 599–620.

Kearey, P., and F. J. Vine. *Global Tectonics.* Oxford and Boston: Blackwell Scientific, 1990; 2nd ed., Oxford and Cambridge, Mass.: Blackwell Science, 1996.

Nicolas, Adolphe. *The Mid-oceanic Ridges: Mountains below Sea Level.* Translated by Thomas Reimer. Berlin and New York: Springer-Verlag, 1995.

Seibold, Eugen, and Wolfgang H. Berger. *The Sea Floor: An Introduction to Marine Geology.* Berlin and New York: Springer-Verlag, 1982; 3rd rev. and updated ed., 1996.

USEFUL WEB SITES
United States Geological Survey. "Exploring the Deep Ocean Floor: Hot Springs and Strange Creatures." <http://pubs.usgs.gov/publications/text/exploring.html>.

RELATED ARTICLES
Atlantic Ocean; Chemosynthesis; Convergent Plate Boundary; Divergent Plate Boundary; Hydrothermal Vent; Mid-Ocean Ridge; Pangea; Plate Tectonics; Seafloor Spreading; Seamount; Transform Fault

Midlittoral Zone

The intertidal, or littoral, zone is the shallow area of seafloor closest to land that lies between the highest high and lowest low tides. In areas of the world where the shoreline is rocky, ecologists divide the intertidal zone into three bands: the uppermost supralittoral fringe, the midlittoral zone, and the lowermost infralittoral fringe. Of these zones, the midlittoral is the broadest in extent: It lies between mean high and low tide and is covered by seawater at least once a day. Researchers sometimes subdivide the midlittoral zone into upper, middle, and lower bands because the zone can be quite broad; sometimes its upper and lower reaches can experience different physical and environmental conditions. Because rocky intertidal zones throughout the world exhibit similar patterns of zonation (prominent horizontal bands composed of similar types of organisms), the distribution of organisms can also be used to define the boundaries of these zones. Under this zonation scheme, the midlittoral zone lies between the highest point inhabited by barnacles and the highest point at which large laminarian kelps grow.

The midlittoral zone and its tide pools (areas of rocky shore that retain seawater when the tide goes out) can host a great variety of organisms, including anemones, chitons, hermit crabs, limpets, mussels, snails, and many types of algae. These organisms spend time both under water and in air and are exposed to drastic environmental and physical stresses that accompany the ebb and flow of the tide. However, the inhabitants of the midlittoral zone are well adapted to face the fluctuations in temperature and salinity and the threat of desiccation (drying out) and dislodgment by wave action that they experience on a daily basis. For example, to prevent desiccation during low tide, anemones retract their tentacles and barnacles and mussels close their shells. To avoid dislodgment by wave action, snails, limpets, and chitons use their muscular foot to clamp themselves firmly to the rock surface. Mussels use byssal threads to anchor themselves into rock crevices.

Lynn L. Lauerman

FURTHER READING
Nybakken, James W. *Marine Biology: An Ecological Approach,* 5th ed. San Francisco: Benjamin Cummings, 2001.
Ricketts, Edward F., and Jack Calvin. *Between Pacific Tides,* 5th ed. rev. by Joel W. Hedgpeth. Stanford, Calif.: Stanford University Press, 1985.

RELATED ARTICLES
Infralittoral Fringe; Intertidal; Littoral Zone; Supralittoral Fringe

Mid-Ocean Ridge

The largest and most continuous mountain ranges on Earth are the extensive systems of ridges, rifts, fault zones, and volcanic constructs that make up the globe-encircling mid-ocean ridge (MOR). This approximately 60,000-kilometer (37,280-mile)-long submarine chain is formed as a consequence of seafloor spreading and marks the location where new oceanic crust is created and Earth's tectonic plates diverge at rates of 1 to 16 centimeters (about 0.4 to 6 inches) per year. The undersea mountains and rift zones that comprise the MOR form as a result of the complex interactions between magmatic (i.e., eruptions of lava on the surface of the seafloor and intrusion of magma at depth within the oceanic crust and upper mantle) and tectonic (i.e., faulting, thrusting, and rifting of the solid portions of the outer layer of Earth) processes. Although rarely explosive or exposed above sea level (Iceland is an exception), they are the most volcanically active regions of our planet; 60 percent of Earth's magma production occurs at the MOR. This magmatism is believed to be a consequence of the upwelling of hot mantle material that partially melts to form basaltic magma as it rises from depths around 100 kilometers (about 62 miles) or less. Exploration of mid-ocean ridges by human-operated submersibles (HOVs), remote-operated vehicles (ROVs), deep-sea cameras, and other remote sensing devices has provided clear evidence that MORs are associated with volcanic eruptions, earthquakes (seismic activity), hot springs (hydrothermal vents), and unique biological communities.

Ridge Segmentation

Although the ridge system is a globe-encircling feature, it is broken up into segments that vary from long, first-order segments [about 400 to 600 kilometers (249 to 373 miles)] bounded by major transform faults or fracture zones, to short, fourth-order segments [about 10 kilometers (6.2 miles)] defined by subtle bends or offsets in the linearity of the ridge crest. Ridge axis discontinuities that occur at locally deep areas along ridges can be long-lived, substantial tectonic features such as transform faults (first order), smaller [0.5 to 30 kilometers (0.3 to 18.6 miles)] overlapping spreading centers (second and third order), or subtle [< 1 kilometer (3280 feet)], short-lived and mobile deviations from axial linearity called *devals* (fourth order). All of these discontinuities appear to reflect breaks in the volcanic plumbing systems that feed the axial zone of magmatism where volcanism is concentrated.

Transform faults are tectonically active zones that offset major MOR segments at roughly right angles and are characterized by narrow, deep troughs where faulting is common, lower crustal rocks are often exposed, and volcanism and hydrothermal activities are very rare. The traces of these fault zones extend as prominent fracture zones for hundreds to a few thousands of kilometers (about 100 to 2000 miles) beyond the axis of the MOR. Recent studies suggest that the shallowest and widest portions of ridge segments correspond to areas of robust magmatism, whereas deep, narrow zones are relatively magma-starved. Elevated and wide segments of some ridges (e.g., south of Iceland, central portion of the Galápagos Rift, Mid-Atlantic Ridge near the Azores) are influenced by nearby island formation related to mantle plumes or hotspots that generate voluminous magma deep within Earth.

Major differences in the morphology, structure, and scale of magmatism along the MOR vary with the rate of spreading (see figure). Slowly spreading or diverging plate boundaries [1 to 4 centimeters (< 2 inches) per year total divergence from the axis], which have low volcanic output, are dominated by faulting and the brittle rupture of the crust, whereas fast-spreading boundaries [8 to 16 centimeters (about 3 to 6 inches) per year] are controlled more by volcanic processes. Intermediate-spreading-rate [4 to 8 centimeters (about 1.6 to 3 inches) per year] ridges are transitional in that they may be dominated by volcanism during some time periods and then by tectonism as magmatic activity wanes. Whereas slow-spreading ridges typically have deep and wide fault-bounded valleys (graben) with rugged flanking morphology, fast-spreading MORs have elevated, dome-shaped cross sections (rises) with smoother flanking morphology.

The region along the MOR within which volcanic eruptions and high-temperature

285

hydrothermal activity (vents, black smokers, white smokers, sulfide chimneys) are concentrated is called the *neovolcanic zone*. The part of the ridge crest that encompasses the neovolcanic zone has variously been described as the axial valley, rift valley, inner valley floor, median valley, elongate summit depression, axial summit graben, axial summit caldera, and axial summit collapse trough. The width of the neovolcanic zone, its structure, and the style of volcanism within it vary considerably with spreading rate. The continuous spectrum of MOR axial morphologies that are observed is a function of two competing processes that vary in time and space: volcanic activity, which results in the construction of relatively smooth features on the seafloor, and faulting/rifting, which results in the creation of rough, linear features that range from small fractures to larger fissures and steep escarpments that can have hundreds of meters (>300 feet) of relief. In all cases, the neovolcanic zone on the MOR is marked by a roughly linear depression or trough, similar to volcanic rift zones on land (e.g., East African Rift Valley, East Rift Zone on Hawaii), but quite different from the circular craters and calderas associated with typical terrestrial volcanoes (e.g., Crater Lake). These fault-bounded valleys or troughs are called *graben*. Not all MOR volcanism occurs along the neovolcanic zone. Relatively small [<1 kilometer (<3280 feet) high] near-axis seamounts are common within approximately 10 to 40 kilometers (6 to 25 miles) of fast and intermediate spreading ridges, and some off-axis volcanism may occur up to a few kilometers from the axis as pillow mounds and ridges, or associated with faulting and the formation of linear ridges called *abyssal hills* that parallel the MOR axis.

Many features on the MOR vary with spreading rate—the width of the neovolcanic zone, the overall morphology of the ridge crest, the size and frequency of eruptions, and the morphology of lava flows—all of which appear to be fundamentally related to whether or not a steady-state magma reservoir or chamber is maintained. Where a steady-state magma reservoir exists, volcanism can keep pace with or dominate over tectonism; where magma reservoirs are intermittent, tectonism tends to dominate.

Slow-Spreading Ridges

Slow-spreading ridges such as the Mid-Atlantic Ridge (see figure), which extends down the center of the Atlantic Ocean, have large, discontinuous axial valleys [8 to 20 kilometers (5 to 12 miles) wide and 1 to 2 kilometers (3280 to 6560 feet) deep], and the neovolcanic zone can extend across the entire axial valley floor [5 to 12 kilometers (3 to 7.5 miles) wide] because magmatism there is relatively unfocused, both across and along the axis. Lava morphology on slow ridges is dominantly pillow lava, which tends to construct hummocks, hummocky ridges, or small circular seamounts that often coalesce or overlap one another to form axial volcanic ridges along the inner valley floor. The prevalence of small seamounts in the neovolcanic zone of slow-spreading ridges is in marked contrast with fast-spreading ridges, where virtually no seamounts or large constructional forms are found in the neovolcanic zone, and at intermediate ridges, where seamounts are only rarely associated with the neovolcanic zone.

The inner valley floor of slow-spreading MORs is more faulted and fissured and large earthquakes (indicating major faulting events) occur more commonly than on fast-spreading ridges. These features, rough topography and large axial valleys, reflect the dominance of extensional faulting and tectonism over volcanism at slow ridges. Lower magma supply, thicker crust, and greater cooling of the crust due to deeper circulation of seawater all lead to volcanic events being relatively infrequent. In addition, slow-spreading ridges probably do not maintain long-lived magma reservoirs or chambers in the shallow crust, so that volcanic episodes tend to be limited in extent and longevity.

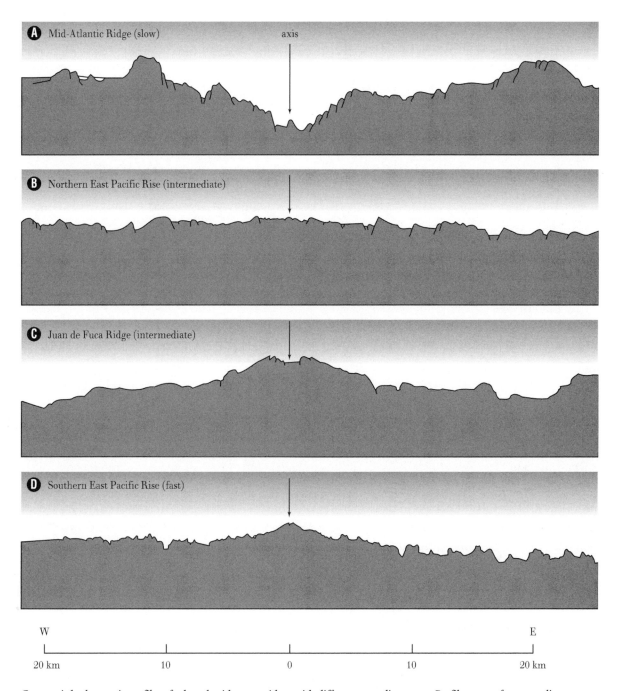

Cross-axis bathymetric profiles of selected mid-ocean ridges with different spreading rates. Profiles across fast-spreading (Southern East Pacific Rise) and slow-spreading (Northern Mid-Atlantic Ridge) ridges show the morphologic contrast between a narrow axial high and a wide rift valley, whereas intermediate-spreading ridges (Juan de Fuca Ridge) have transitional features. Location of the axis where volcanism and spreading are commonly focused is shown as an arrow on each profile.

On the other hand, tectonic faulting events are more frequent than at fast-spreading ridges, because there is more opportunity for tensional stresses (i.e., extensional pull) perpendicular to the ridge to build up over long periods of gradual plate divergence without interruption from volcanic intrusions. This faulting leads to the exposure of plutonic rocks (magmas that have been intruded into the crust and cooled slowly to form large crystals) and peridotites (ultramafic rocks rich in magnesium and iron that are residues of mantle melting) that make up the deep crust and upper mantle, and the development of strong geologic and structural asymmetry in the axes at some slow-spreading ridges. During nonmagmatic periods, tectonic stretching and thinning of the crust creates numerous low-angle listric or detachment faults that extend down to a ductile (plastic) zone in the oceanic crust. This faulting results in the formation of megamullions—broad exposures of deep-level crustal rocks similar to core complexes in highly extended continental rift zones.

Fast-Spreading Ridges

There is no rift valley or prominent axial valley or graben on fast-spreading MORs, but along most of the axial crest, there is a narrow, linear depression or trough, which is typically 5 to 40 meters (16.4 to 130 feet) deep and 40 to 250 meters (130 to 820 feet) wide, that marks the locus of the neovolcanic zone. The most striking characteristic of the neovolcanic zone at fast-spreading ridges such as the Southern East Pacific Rise is that it is very narrow [generally, <2 kilometers (<1.24 miles)], indicating that narrow, elongate igneous intrusions (dikes) that feed magma to the seafloor are focused beneath the ridge in a linear fashion. This focusing of magmatism along the axis is apparently the direct consequence of the fast rate of plate spreading, greater magma supply, a shallower and more steady-state magma reservoir or chamber, and more frequent intrusive events than at slow-spreading centers.

Observations indicate that the axial summit trough forms as a series of elongate and irregularly shaped collapse features forming over drained lava ponds and channels over zones of primary fissuring and diking. There are essentially no seamounts within the neovolcanic zone at fast-spreading ridges, although lava domes are known to form at the ends of volcanic segments. Lavas erupted within the trough are dominantly fluid sheet flows that vary from remarkably flat

and thin [<4 centimeters (1.5 inches)] to ropy and jumbled varieties with chaotically folded and deformed surfaces that can be tens of centimeters thick. The textures of some sheet flows are similar to the fluid pahoehoe flows erupted on land from basaltic volcanoes such as in Hawaii. Smoother, more bulbous flows known as *lobate lavas* are also common at fast-spreading MORs and typically develop an extensive collapse zone surrounding the axis where lavas have flooded and overflowed the axial trough.

Intermediate-Spreading Ridges

The ridge morphology and neovolcanic zone at intermediate-spreading ridges have morphological characteristics that are transitional between those at fast and slow ridges (see figure). However, individual ridge segments on an intermediate ridge can be significantly different in character from one another—some closer to one end member or the other. The morphology of intermediate ridges is variable, but generally consists of a small axial valley 1 to 5 kilometers (about 0.6 to 3 miles) wide, with bounding faults 50 to 1000 meters (164 to 3280 feet) high. Well-studied intermediate ridges include the Juan de Fuca and Gorda Ridges in the Northeast Pacific, the Galápagos Ridge, the northernmost East Pacific Rise at 21°N, and the Southeast Indian Ridge.

Future Research

MOR studies are trending toward multidisciplinary, multiscale research and long-term monitoring of specific segments. Future focus will be on determining the relationships between volcanic and tectonic processes and the origin and development of hydrothermal systems, as well as on life in the deep sea. This research will rely on systematic studies of various MORs that utilize mapping, dating, sampling, geophysics, and arrays of crustal drill holes. Deep-ocean oceanographic research in the coming decades will require the development of new sensors, deep-submergence vehicle systems, and seafloor observatory complexes.

Michael Perfit

FURTHER READING

Carbotte, Suzanne, and Ken Macdonald. "Comparison of Seafloor Tectonic Fabric at Intermediate, Fast, and Superfast Spreading Ridges: Influence of Spreading Rate, Plate Motions, and Ridge Segmentation on Fault Patterns." *Journal of Geophysical Research*, Vol. 99 (1994), pp. 13,609–13,631.

Fornari, Daniel, and Robert Embley. "Tectonic and Volcanic Controls on Hydrothermal Processes at the Mid-ocean Ridge: An Overview Based on Near-Bottom and Submersible Studies." In Susan E. Humphris, ed., *Seafloor Hydrothermal Systems: Physical, Chemical, Biological, and Geological Interactions*. Geophysical Monograph 91. Washington, D.C.: American Geophysical Union, 1995; pp. 1–46

Fox, Paul J., Nancy Grindlay, and Ken Macdonald. "The Mid-Atlantic Ridge (31°S–34°30'S): Temporal and Spatial Variations of Accretionary Processes." *Marine Geophysical Researches*, Vol. 13 (1991), pp. 1–20.

Karson, Jeffrey, and Peter Rona. "Block-Tilting, Transfer Faults, and Structural Control of Magmatic and Hydrothermal Processes in the TAG Area, Mid-Atlantic Ridge 26°N." *Geological Society of America Bulletin*, Vol. 102 (1990), pp. 1635–1645.

Macdonald, Ken. "The Crest of the Mid-Atlantic Ridge: Models for Crustal Generation Processes and Tectonics." In P. R. Vogt and B. E. Tucholke, eds., *The Geology of North America: The Western North Atlantic Region*. Boulder, Colo.: Geological Society of America, 1986; pp. 51–68

———. "Linkages between Faulting, Volcanism, Hydrothermal Activity and Segmentation on Fast Spreading Centers." In W. R. Buck, P. T. Delaney, J. A. Karson, and Y. Lagabrielle, eds., *Faulting and Magmatism at Mid-Ocean Ridges*. American Geophysical Monograph 106. Washington, D.C.: American Geophysical Union, 1998, pp. 27–58.

Mutter, John, and Jeffrey Karson. "Structural Processes at Slow-Spreading Ridges." *Science*, Vol. 257 (1992), pp. 627–634.

Nicolas, Adolphe. *The Mid-Oceanic Ridges: Mountains below Sea Level*. Translated by Thomas Reimer. Berlin and New York: Springer-Verlag, 1995.

Perfit, Michael, and William Chadwick, Jr. "Magmatism at Mid-ocean Ridges: Constraints from Volcanological and Geochemical Investigations." In W. R. Buck, P. T. Delaney, J. A. Karson, and Y. Lagabrielle, eds., *Faulting and Magmatism at Mid-ocean Ridges*. American Geophysical Monograph 106. Washington, D.C.: American Geophysical Union, 1998; pp. 59–115.

Scheirer, Daniel, and Ken Macdonald. "Variation in Cross-Sectional Area of the Axial Ridge Along the East Pacific Rise: Evidence for the Magmatic Budget of a Fast Spreading Center." *Journal of Geophysical Research*, Vol. 98 (1993), pp. 7871–7885.

Smith, Deborah, and Johnson Cann. "Mid-Atlantic Ridge Volcanic Processes: How Erupting Lava Forms the Earth's Anatomy." *Oceanus*, Vol. 41 (1998), pp. 11–14.

RELATED ARTICLES

Abyssal Hill; Gorda Ridge; Hydrothermal Vent; Juan de Fuca Ridge; Mid-Atlantic Ridge; Plate Tectonics; Seafloor Spreading

Midwater Trawl

Midwater trawls are used to catch pelagic animals living in the water column between the upper ocean and the seabed. Commercial midwater trawls are used to catch fish such as herring and mackerel and invertebrates such as krill. They are nets with large trawl doors rigged to act as hydroplanes—both keeping the net open and dragging it down. The trawlers use sonars to locate the shoals and target them with the net. When successful, such trawls can catch tens of tons of fish on each tow, although in recent years overfishing and climate change have reduced the catchability of many stocks of fish.

When used for scientific purposes, midwater trawls ideally provide both qualitative and quantitative information about the depth distributions and abundances of invertebrate and vertebrate species. The aim is to catch a representative sample of the animals from a known depth range. However, there are problems with this approach. Large animals tend to be less frequent than smaller ones and can usually swim faster. As the depth of fishing increases, the species composition changes and their abundances decline.

Finer-meshed nets catch more but have greater drag and lower filtering efficiency than do coarser-meshed nets. Conversely, coarse-mesh nets extrude more animals and inflict more damage on those that are retained.

Because of these obstacles, scientific midwater trawls are compromises seeking to optimize the sampling of the targeted species. Those designed to capture zooplankton [0.5 to 10 millimeters (0.02 to 0.4 inch) long] have fine meshes, commonly 200 to 500 nanometers, have relatively small mouth areas of 0.5 to 1 square meter (5 to 11 square feet), and are towed at speeds of about 3.54 kilometers per hour (2 knots). To study depth distributions the nets have to be opened only at the sampling depths. Those designed to sample micronekton [1 to 20 centimeters (0.4 to 8 inches) long)] mostly have meshes of 1 to 5 centimeters (0.4 to 2 inches), mouth areas of 5 to 10 square meters (54 to 108 square feet), and are towed at speeds of 3.54 to 8.85 kilometers per hour (2 to 5 knots). They also either need to be opened and closed or fitted with codends (i.e., the end of the net that retains the catch), which segregate the catch caught at the target depth. To catch large animals such as fish and squid, commercial-sized trawls are used. These tend to have enormous mouth openings [up to 100 square meters (1075 square feet)] but cannot be opened and closed.

The opening and closing mechanisms vary in sophistication. Early mechanical or pressure-activated releases have been replaced by either acoustically or electrically operated releases. Increasingly the trawls are fitted with sensors that measure environmental parameters such as depth, temperature, and speed. Speed is important to measure since the speed and direction of currents can differ greatly between the surface and the depth of tow. On the Equator, for example, the equatorial current near the surface may be 2.66 kilometers per hour (1.5 knots) and be underlain by a countercurrent flowing at 1 knot in the opposite direction. So a trawl being towed behind a ship steaming at 3.54 kilometers per hour (2 knots) may either be going backward or moving at 7 to 8.8 kilometers per hour (4 to 5 knots).

Despite all this sophistication, trawl samples provide a skewed impression of what is in the water. Fast-swimming animals such as squid and large fish can escape from the net. Others may detect its approach either by feeling its vibrations or seeing the glowing luminescence of animals already in the net. Many gelatinous species are too fragile to be collected in nets and can only be collected using *slurp guns* on manned submersibles or remote operated vehicles (ROVs). Large carnivores can either eat other animals in the nets or damage them, making them unidentifiable. Nonetheless, midwater trawls are likely to remain the main technique for studying animal communities in the water.

Martin Angel

FURTHER READING

English, H. R., and J. E. Tumulty. "Catching Methods for Pelagic Fish." In J. R. Burt, R. Hardy, and K. J. Whittle, eds., *Pelagic Fish: The Resource and Its Exploitation.* Oxford: Fishing News Books, 1992.

Harris, Roger P., et al., eds. *IECS Zooplankton Methodology Manual.* San Diego: Academic Press, 2000.

Murphy, Brian R., and David W. Willis. *Fisheries Techniques.* Bethesda, Md.: American Fisheries Society, 1983; 2nd ed., 1996.

Omori, Makoto, and Tsutomu Ikeda. *Methods in Marine Zooplankton Ecology.* Malabar, Fla.: Krieger Publishing, 1992.

RELATED ARTICLES
Pelagic; Plankton Net; Trawl

Minamata Disease

(*Note*: Minamata is the usual spelling of the English translation, although the spelling Minimata is seen occasionally.)

Minamata disease gained its name from the fishing town of Minamata on Kyushu Island,

Japan. Minamata is the site of the first well-documented example of marine heavy-metal pollution. The incident resulted in dozens of human deaths. Minamata disease is caused by the consumption of mercury-contaminated food. Mercury attacks the human nervous system. Small doses may cause headaches and irritability; larger doses may produce brain damage, with convulsions and blindness, and ultimately, coma and death.

In 1952, the Shin-Nihon Chisso Hiryo chemical factory in Minamata Bay began manufacturing acetaldehyde and vinyl chloride for use in making plastics. The factory used mercury compounds in the manufacturing process and began discharging mercury-contaminated wastewater into Minamata Bay.

In 1953, local physicians began to recognize unusual symptoms among local inhabitants. Initially, physicians suspected that a contagious form of meningitis was the cause. This was later discounted. Investigators noted that those who became ill frequently ate Minamata Bay fish, as did local cats, which were demonstrating similar symptoms. Heavy-metal contamination of fish was suspected. The full story—linking the wastewater discharge to the signs and symptoms appearing in local inhabitants—emerged only gradually.

In 1957, local authorities banned fishing in Minamata Bay. It took an additional two years to confirm that mercury was the toxic heavy metal involved in causing the symptoms. It was not until 1960 that the Chisso factory wastewater was identified as the source of the contamination. Even so, the Japanese chemical company refused to accept responsibility for the onset of Minamata disease. Only in 1969—sixteen years after the disease first appeared—was the Chisso factory forced to stop discharging mercury-contaminated wastewater.

The Minamata tragedy was a classic example of methyl mercury poisoning. Methyl mercury, unlike inorganic mercury, is not excreted from the human body and thus accumulates. It passes across the blood–brain barrier and damages brain tissue progressively and irreversibly. About 5 percent of the mercury in Chisso factory wastewater was methyl mercury, and of the remainder, some would have been converted to methyl mercury by bacterial action within Minamata Bay. Mercury, especially methyl mercury, is a particularly deadly toxin because it *biomagnifies* (reaches higher concentrations in the tissues of organisms at successive trophic levels in the food web). Local plankton contained 5 parts per million (ppm) mercury, intertidal bivalves 10 to 39 ppm dry weight, and fish, 10 to 55 ppm, with most of this in the methylated form. The local fishermen and their families were eating the fish and shellfish, and as a result, mercury compounds were accumulating inside their bodies. The problem was exacerbated by their seafood-rich diet. Japanese families in fishing communities often eat 20 times more seafood than in the diet of a typical North American or European family.

Governments in most developed countries recognize the risk to human and environmental health posed by uncontrolled release of mercury. They enforce legislation to prohibit discharge of mercury-contaminated wastewater, and in many cases, forbid or restrict the use of mercury in industrial processes. Vigilance is necessary to restrict the consumption of mercury-contaminated fish flesh. Most technologically advanced countries regard the acceptable upper level of mercury in fish tissue as being 0.5 to 1 ppm wet weight (about 2.5 to 5 ppm dry weight).

By 1974 about 800 cases of methyl mercury poisoning were confirmed in Minamata. Of these, more than 100 died and many of the remainder lived with the disease's highly debilitating effects. At least 26 babies were born with cerebral palsy-like symptoms characteristic of mercury poisoning. It is likely that many cases of Minamata disease went unreported.

Trevor Day

FURTHER READING

Clark, R. B., Chris Frid, and Martin Attrill. *Marine Pollution*, 4th ed. Oxford and New York: Clarendon Press, 1997.

Mishima, Akio. *Bitter Sea: The Human Cost of Minamata Disease.* Translated by Richard L. Gage and Susan B. Murata. Tokyo: Kosei, 1992.

U.N. Joint Group of Experts on the Scientific Aspects of Marine Pollution (GESAMP). *The Review of the Health of the Oceans.* Reports and Studies 15. Geneva: UNESCO, 1982.

RELATED ARTICLES
Biological Magnification; Pollution, Ocean

Mississippi Fan

The Mississippi Fan is a sedimentary feature that fans out and over the continental slope, dominating the floor of the Gulf of Mexico. It is the result of millions of years of transported sediments spilling out over an area of 78,000 square kilometers (30,120 square miles). The point source is the Mississippi River, which drains the Interior Lowlands and Great Plains of North America. The Mississippi Canyon, a submarine canyon, connects the river and the submarine fan. The apex of the Mississippi Fan is a few hundred feet below sea level, at the place thought to be the mouth of the Pleistocene (1.64 million years to about 10,000 years ago) Mississippi River.

Sediments from the present Mississippi River now form the delta and are also deposited on the adjacent continental shelf. In the Pleistocene Epoch, during lower sea levels caused by continental glaciation, the river sediments were transported directly into the Mississippi Canyon, which fed the Mississippi Fan. Now the fan is inactive because sediments are again trapped in the delta and on the shelf. A prominent feature of the Mississippi Fan is the Mississippi Channel, which is a channel and levee complex reaching approximately 500 kilometers (310 miles) from its apex with the mouth of the submarine canyon to the outer parts of the

submarine fan complex. The Mississippi Channel is, for the most part, fed by sediments that are transported by turbidity currents from the submarine canyon. Elongate outer fan lobes form in succession from the main channel and reflect positions of active accumulation through time. These channels appear much as rivers do on land; however, they were formed under as many as 3200 meters (10,500 feet) of water.

Mass wasting (slumping) of the upper fan occurs on an enormous scale, resulting in outer fan lobes that are hundreds of meters thick and hundreds of kilometers long. The youngest lobe is composed of eight sublobes, each 150 kilometers (93 miles) long, 50 kilometers (31 miles) wide, and 10 to 40 meters (33 to 131 feet) thick. The channel that feeds the outer lobe is approximately 120 kilometers (75 miles) from the base of the Mississippi Canyon to where it branches into many smaller channels. These, in turn, form multiple splays.

Levees and channels form the only major relief. Levee height is variable, but in one study site a levee rose 15 to 30 meters (50 to 98 feet) above a channel floor that stretched 400 meters (1310 feet) wide. Sand and silt are transported across gradients of as little as 1 meter per kilometer (5 feet per mile) for over 100 kilometers (62 miles) as long as the sediments remain channeled. Otherwise, deposition occurs over a short distance. Core samples of sublobes expose deposits of sandy turbidites, chaotic silts, and hemipelagic muds (mixture of terrigenous sands and, in this case, inorganic clays).

Gas and oil exploration continues in the Gulf of Mexico as the petroleum industry looks to the gulf's deep waters. This new frontier extends westward through the Mississippi Fan Fold Belt, the Alaminos Canyon, and the Perdido Fold Belt. Current exploration is concentrated on reservoirs, probably Miocene (about 23 million to 5 million years old) in age, in the Mississippi Fan Fold Belt structures located beneath the upper and middle Mississippi Fan. The fold belt extends 300 kilometers (186 miles) eastward from the Mississippi Fan and is approximately 50 kilometers (31 miles) wide.

Dense assemblages of animals called *chemosynthetic communities* live off oil and gases that seep and vent from the ocean floor. Bacteria thrive on the chemicals associated with seeping hydrocarbons. Larger animals, such as clams and tube worms, have developed a symbiotic relationship with the bacteria. In 1997, a new species of ice worm was discovered in gas hydrates, which are ice with gas trapped inside. Studies of these communities, spurred by the development of the offshore oil and gas industry, are required to protect the fragile communities from the physical effects of continental slope exploration and production.

Deanna Madison

FURTHER READING
Gardner, James V., Michael E. Field, and David C. Twichell, eds. *Geology of the United States' Seafloor: The View from GLORIA.* Cambridge, Mass.: Cambridge University Press, 1996.
Normark, William R. "Growth Patterns of Deep-Sea Fans." *American Association of Petroleum Geologists Bulletin,* Vol. 11, No. 54 (1970), pp. 2170–2171, 2181–2192, 2194–2195.
Stanley, Daniel Jean, and George Moore, eds. *The Shelfbreak: Critical Interface on Continental Margins.* Special Publication 33. Tulsa, Okla.: Society of Economic Paleontologists and Mineralogists, 1983.
Worzel, J. L., W. Bryant, et al. *Initial Reports of the Deep Sea Drilling Project,* Vol. 10. Washington, D.C.: U.S. Government Printing Office, 1973.

RELATED ARTICLES
Continental Slope; Delta; Gas Hydrate; Submarine Canyon; Submarine Fan; Turbidity Current

Mixed Layer

Also known as the *surface mixed layer* or the *surface layer*, the mixed layer is the uppermost layer of the ocean, comprising about 2 percent of the total ocean volume. This thin, sun-lit layer is usually between 10 and 200 meters (between 33 and 660 feet) thick and is so thoroughly mixed that the difference in temperature at the top and bottom of this layer typically does not exceed 0.1°C (0.2°F). The sunlight that penetrates the mixed layer allows photosynthesis to occur, especially when nutrients are also present, making it a very important zone for the marine biosphere. In addition to a constant temperature, mixing in the surface layer produces a constant salinity from the top to the bottom of the layer.

Mixing of the surface layer is achieved through the action of winds. The mixed layer is thickest in late winter, when turbulence caused by winter storms reaches new depths. In the summer, when winds weaken, the mixed layer is sometimes only a few meters deep. Heat from the sun also affects the thickness of the mixed layer because it reduces the density of the surface water. Extra work is needed to mix a warmer, lighter layer with a denser, colder layer that lies beneath it.

In addition to seasonal variations there are regional differences in the thickness of the mixed layer. For example, the winter mixed layer tends to be thicker in the saltier North Atlantic than in the fresher North Pacific Ocean. The fresher surface layer of the North Pacific is too light to displace the denser water underneath, resulting in a thinner mixed layer.

Sonya Wainwright

FURTHER READING
Pinet, Paul R. *Oceanography: An Introduction to the Planet Oceanus.* St. Paul, Minn.: West Publishing, 1992.

RELATED ARTICLES
Mixing Processes

Mixed Tide

Tides in the ocean are caused by a slight imbalance between two forces, the gravitational pull of the Sun and the Moon, and the force required to keep the waters of the world's oceans moving along with the rest of Earth, called the *centripetal force*. When gravitational forces exceed centripetal forces, ocean waters pile up in the direction of the gravitational forces, producing a slight bulge in the ocean surface. Periodic fluctuations in the forces that produce the tides occur due to continuous changes in the position of Earth with respect to the Sun and the Moon. As a result, tidal bulges become tidal waves that travel around Earth in very predictable ways. Measurements of the height of the tide at many locations around the world have shown that the form of the tide or its pattern of rise and fall varies at different locations due to the shapes of the ocean basins and the latitude. The tides can be broken down into three main categories: tidal variations with a period of about 12 hours, which are called *semidiurnal*; tidal variations with a period of about 24 hours, which are called *diurnal*; and tidal variations with periods significantly longer than 24 hours. Thus, when there are two high tides and two low tides per day, the tide is semidiurnal, and when there is one high tide and one low tide per day the tide is diurnal. However, in many locations the tide is a combination of a semidiurnal contribution and a diurnal contribution. When the tides contain both semidiurnal and diurnal components, they are called *mixed tides*. Tides along the coast of San Francisco, for example, are mixed. A precise classification of mixed tides, however, depends on the amplitudes of the various components involved.

Laurence C. Breaker

FURTHER READING

Defant, Albert. *Ebb and Flow: The Tides of Earth, Air, and Water.* Ann Arbor, Mich.: University of Michigan Press, 1958.
Godin, Gabriel. *The Analysis of Tides.* Toronto and Buffalo, N.Y.: University of Toronto Press, 1972.

RELATED ARTICLES
Diurnal and Semidiurnal Tide

Mixing Processes

Within the ocean, mixing of temperature, salinity, and kinetic energy occur at a wide variety of scales. For temperature and salinity at the very smallest scale, the continuous movement of molecules will result in the transfer of flux across a property gradient. This process is called *molecular diffusion* and the rate of transfer is proportional to the gradient. The coefficient of molecular diffusivity of salt is 2.0×10^{-9} square meter [m^2; 22×10^{-9} square foot (ft^2)] per second and the coefficient of thermal diffusivity is two orders of magnitude greater, 1.4×10^{-7} m^2 (15×10^{-7} ft^2) per second. The corresponding quantity for kinetic energy, *kinematic viscosity*, is 1.5×10^{-6} m^2 (16×10^{-6} ft^2) per second. The rates of transfer of heat, salt, and kinetic energy due to molecular processes are much too small to explain the mixing that is observed in the ocean.

Eddies and turbulence are responsible for the larger mixing rates that are observed in the

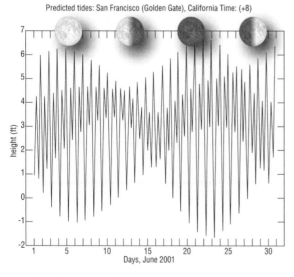

Predicted tides at Golden Gate (San Francisco, California). The figure shows the mixed tide having unequal high and unequal low tides through a month. The tidal range follows the phases of the moon. (Graphics courtesy of William Broenkow)

ocean. With respect to mixing, eddies can be thought of as similar to molecules, and modeled as eddy diffusion or eddy mixing coefficients. It is more difficult for these processes to work against gravity, so different values are given for horizontal and vertical eddy coefficients. Values for horizontal eddy diffusion range from 10^{-1} to 10^3 m^2 (11×10^{-1} to 11×10^3 ft^2) per second and for horizontal eddy viscosity range from 10^2 to 10^5 m^2 (11×10^2 to 11×10^5 ft^2) per second. Vertical eddy diffusion and viscosity are six orders of magnitude less than these horizontal values. The range of values for these coefficients reflects the wide range of scales associated with turbulent eddies in the ocean, from tens of kilometers to centimeters.

The energy for mixing comes from the large-scale forcing of the ocean by solar energy (winds and differences in temperature and salinity) and gravitational (tidal) forces. As these act to accelerate ocean currents, frictional forces must develop to impede further acceleration. The frictional forces are aided by a cascade of energy from large scales to small scales that produce eddies and turbulence. The energy causing the turbulence may be either *kinetic energy* (the energy due to motion) or *potential energy* (the energy due to the distribution of mass). The energy for mixing may also be characterized as coming from outside the ocean boundaries (such as wind stress on the sea surface) or internal to the ocean. Ultimately, a steady state is reached where forcing and dissipation are in balance.

Boundary Mixed Layers

A number of mixing processes act on the upper layer of the ocean. Here the energy needed for mixing is supplied by heat exchange or wind stress. The wind stress creates a strong velocity gradient and turbulence develops. Waves also add energy and turbulence, especially if they break, and Langmuir cells can also develop. Heat exchanges at the surface of the ocean may result

in surface waters becoming cooler and saltier. In this case, the waters become denser than those immediately below, so that they are not gravitationally stable and overturn (this is called *convective overturning*). The result of both processes (mixing by the wind and waves and convective overturning) is a characteristic mixed layer at the sea surface. In this layer, temperature and salinity do not vary with depth.

At the seafloor, a velocity gradient is created between the moving water and the fixed bottom that can generate turbulence. In shallow water, when the bottom is rough or the velocity strong, the entire water column may mix. The empirical criterion for this situation is that $H/U^3 < 70$ per square meter per cubic second, where H is water depth and U is current velocity. Density gradients can also create turbulent bottom flows. This occurs when sediment is stirred into the water or when dense bottom waters flow out of a basin. An example of the latter is the flow of dense Mediterranean waters into the Atlantic at the Strait of Gibraltar.

Away from boundary layers, continuous recording instruments have revealed mixed layers separated by strong gradients in vertical profiles of temperature and salinity. These features resemble steps and have vertical scales from decimeters to many meters. Strong velocity shear (a change in the direction or speed of ocean currents with depth) occurs across the steps, and internal waves develop on the interface and become unstable and break, resulting in intense mixing.

The different rates of molecular diffusion of heat and salt can enhance mixing at the centimeter-to-meter scales through a process known as *double diffusion*. One type of double diffusive mixing, called *salt fingering*, occurs when warm salty water lies above cool fresh water that is slightly denser. Heat will diffuse across this interface much faster than salt. As a result, the upper layer will lose and the lower layer will gain heat faster than the lower layer will gain and the upper layer will lose salt. The result is that lower layer waters will become slightly less dense than those above and overturn. This process has been duplicated in laboratory experiments with layered fluids; salt fingers a few millimeters across and up to 25 centimeters (about 10 inches) long develop. Lateral diffusion between the fingers results in subsequent development of a uniform layer.

A second type of double diffusion known as *layering* has been observed in Arctic regions. In this case, a layer of cold fresh water is above a layer of warmer, saltier water. Again, the temperature diffuses more rapidly than the salt, so the water above the boundary tends to get lighter and rise, while that below the boundary gets heavier and sinks. This results in fairly homogeneous layers separated by thinner regions of high gradients of temperature and salinity.

A final mixing process is caused by the nonlinear relationship between temperature, salinity, and density of seawater. When two parcels of equal density but differing temperatures and salinities mix, the density of the resulting mixture is greater than that of the original parcels. Called *cabbeling,* this is an important process in the formation of Antarctic Bottom Waters.

Tidal Mixing
Direct measurements of energy dissipation have yielded results in agreement with theories of the structure of oceanic boundary layers, but measurements in the ocean thermocline yield mixing rates that are too low. This means that the ocean should fill to near the top with cold water, shutting down the meridional circulation (the conveyor belt). Oceanographers, measuring tides from a satellite, recently found intense patches of tidally driven mixing deep within the open ocean located along the ridge joining the Hawaiian Islands, the Mid-Atlantic Ridge, and the ridges of the southwest Pacific. Preliminary estimates suggest that this open ocean tidal mixing could account for enough energy dissipation

to keep the ocean conveyor belt running. It also suggests that rearrangement of continents and seafloor ridges alters tidal mixing, the way in which the conveyor belt operates, and contributes to climate change.

Curtis A. Collins

FURTHER READING
Gregg, Michael C. "A Study of Mixing in the Ocean: A Brief History." *Oceanography,* Vol. 4 (1991), pp. 34–45.
Kantha, L. K., and C. A. Clayson. *Small Scale Processes in Geophysical Fluid Flows.* San Diego: Academic Press, 2000.
Schmitt, R. W. "Double Diffusion in Oceanography." *Annual Review of Fluid Mechanics,* Vol. 26 (1994), pp. 255–86.
Turner, J. S. "Small Scale Mixing Processes." In B. A. Warren and C. Wunsch, eds., *Evolution of Physical Oceanography.* Boston: MIT Press, 1981.

RELATED ARTICLES
Eddy; Langmuir Circulation; Mixed Layer

Mollusca

The phylum Mollusca is the second largest group of invertebrates after the arthropods (insects, crustaceans, and their relatives). Mollusks are most familiar to us as the snails and slugs that live on land, but they are also common in fresh water and the oceans, where they exist in an astonishing variety of forms, including mussels, limpets, oysters, squids, and octopuses. Typically, mollusks have a soft and compact body with a muscular foot, and many are protected by shells. They are of great importance both to humans and to marine life as a source of food.

Diversity
There are about 100,000 living species of mollusks and thousands more known only as fossils, thanks to their well-preserved shells. Scientists divide the living species into seven classes. The largest is the class Gastropoda, which includes

snails, slugs, limpets, whelks, and periwinkles, and most move by creeping along on a muscular foot (although sea butterflies use their winglike foot to swim). The class Bivalvia includes mollusks with a shell in the form of two lateral valves hinged together on the dorsal side and has forms such as mussels, clams, cockles, oysters, and scallops. Squids, octopuses, and cuttlefish are placed in the class Cephalopoda and are distinguished by their long, muscular arms, parrotlike beaks, and often reduced or absent shells.

The remaining four mollusk classes are made up of less familiar species: Polyplacophora includes the chitons, small mollusks with the shell in eight plates that live clinging to rocks; Scaphopoda includes the tusk shells, which burrow in soft sediments and live in tubular shells, open at both ends and looking rather like elephants' tusks; Monoplacophora includes about 20 species of very deep-living, limpetlike animals with serially arranged gills, kidneys, and muscles; and Aplacophora comprises mainly deep-living, wormlike animals that have an outer layer of spicules rather than a shell.

Anatomy

Mollusks are so varied that it is difficult to make generalizations about their anatomy, and many species have lost typical molluscan features during their evolution or adapted them for different purposes. Nevertheless, there are some distinctive features that are present across most of the phylum. The majority of mollusks have a soft, moist body, with a separate head (lost in bivalves) that bears a

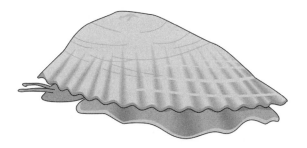

Patella, *part of the phylum mollusca.*

mouth and sense organs. The mouth contains an organ unique to all mollusks (except bivalves) called a *radula*, which is covered with minute teeth that rasp away at food like a cheese grater.

Internal organs—including the heart, stomach, intestine, and digestive glands—are packed together in a part of the body called the *visceral mass*, below which there is usually a single muscular foot used for clinging to surfaces like a sucker (as in limpets), for sliding along (as in slugs and snails), or for burrowing (as in many bivalves). In cephalopods the foot has evolved into a ring of arms and tentacles covered with suckers for grasping prey.

In all mollusks, the visceral mass is covered by a special fold of tissue called the *mantle*. In many species the mantle secretes the mineral calcium carbonate, which forms a protective outer shell. Mollusk shells are incredibly diverse and range from delicate, polished spirals to spectacular pronged conches and the colossal shells of giant clams; all the seashells that wash up on beaches are derived from mollusks, mostly from bivalves and gastropods. Species that lack shells rely on other strategies to defend themselves against predators. Octopuses and squids can squirt a cloud of ink at attackers to confuse them long enough to make a getaway, and some species can change color dramatically to startle enemies. Land slugs secrete a foul-tasting slime to repel predators, and the brilliantly colored nudibranchs, or sea slugs, often have toxic chemicals in their mantles. Some sea slugs eat sea anemones and incorporate the anemones' stinging cells into their own skin.

Between the mantle and the visceral mass is a water-filled cavity containing the gills. In terrestrial snails and slugs—the only mollusks to have conquered land—the mantle cavity has evolved into a lung, its wall having developed hundreds of tiny blood vessels to absorb oxygen from the air. Cephalopods have adapted the mantle cavity to squirt out a powerful jet of water through the exit tube or siphon. This gives them a sudden burst of speed, enabling them to dart toward prey or escape from enemies.

Feeding

Mollusks are as varied in their feeding strategies as in their anatomy. Most species, with the notable exception of bivalves, use the distinctive molluscan radula to feed. Ancestral mollusks probably fed by grazing algae on rocks, using the radula to scrape up matter, and many species continue to feed this way today, including limpets and periwinkles. Terrestrial snails and slugs are mainly herbivores that graze on leaves, whereas many of their aquatic relatives are predators or carrion feeders. The dog whelk (*Nucella lapillus*), a type of sea snail, preys on bivalves and can smell prey by drawing water through its siphon and over a special chemical sense organ called an *osphradium*. When it finds a victim it uses its radula to bore through the shell and tear at the flesh within. But the most advanced predators of the gastropod world are the cone snails, which are inhabitants of tropical reefs. The cone snail's radula has been modified by evolution to form a hollow, harpoonlike dart through which flows a nerve toxin so potent that some species have been known to kill humans. Cone snails' usual victims are invertebrates or fish. When the cone finds a prey item, usually detected by the osphradium, the cone extends its proboscis with the venom-charged tooth at the end and injects it into the prey. The tip is snagged like a harpoon so that the victim cannot wriggle free. After the venom takes effect, the cone shell draws in its catch, envelops the meal with its mouth, and then swallows it whole and starts to digest it.

In bivalves the gills have evolved into feeding as well as breathing organs. Water is drawn into the mantle cavity through the siphon and across the gills, which filter out tiny food particles. The food is then carried toward the mouth by tiny beating hairs or cilia. Many bivalves bury themselves in sand or mud and reach up to the water level with their siphons to feed and breathe; in some burrowing species, the siphons can be as long as 1 meter (3 feet 3 inches). Other bivalves, such as oysters, secrete shell material to cement themselves to rocks or to each other and live permanently fastened to a solid surface, filter-feeding when submerged. Not all bivalves are filter-feeders, however. A few are predaceous; others are symbiotic, living on other organisms or in their burrows; and the shipworm (*Teredo norvegica*) burrows into ship hulls and eats wood.

Cephalopods are brainy hunters that use their prehensile tentacles and arms to grasp prey such as fish or crustaceans. Their radulas are comparatively small, but their mouths are equipped with sharp, parrotlike beaks for tearing flesh apart. To help them hunt, cephalopods have keen senses, a well-developed nervous system, and a sophisticated brain, making them the most intelligent of the invertebrates.

Reproduction

Most mollusk species have separate sexes, although some are hermaphrodites. Many marine mollusks, like most aquatic animals, usually reproduce by releasing sex cells into the water, allowing fertilization to take place outside the parents' body (external fertilization). Female giant clams (*Tridacna gigas*), for instance, release huge clouds of egg cells into the water, and males must release their sperm at the same time to ensure that fertilization takes place. Male cephalopods produce their sperm in special packets called *spermatophores*, which are then deposited in the female's mantle cavity. The sperm are released when the female is ready to lay her eggs.

Most mollusks have first a trochophore and then a veliger larval form. The larvae of marine mollusks usually join the zooplankton as free-swimming creatures. They live as plankton for varying times, some feeding on microscopic algae. When mature, they sink to the seafloor and undergo metamorphosis into the adult form.

Ben Morgan

FURTHER READING

Banister, Keith, and Andrew Campbell. *The Encyclopaedia of Underwater Life.* London: Allen and Unwin, 1985.

Barnes, Robert. *Invertebrate Zoology.* Philadelphia: Saunders, 1963; 6th ed., by Edward Ruppert, Fort Worth, Texas: Saunders, 1994.

Brusca, Richard C., and Gary J. Brusca. *Invertebrates.* Sunderland, Mass.: Sinauer, 1990.

Fish, J. *A Student's Guide to the Seashore.* London and Boston: Unwin Hyman, 1989; 2nd ed., Cambridge and New York: Cambridge University Press, 1996.

Nybakken, James W. *Marine Biology: An Ecological Approach,* 5th ed. San Francisco: Benjamin Cummings, 2001.

Pechenik, Jan A. *Biology of the Invertebrates.* Boston: Prindle, Weber and Schmidt, 1985; 4th ed., Boston: McGraw-Hill, 2000.

Postlethwait, John. *The Nature of Life.* New York: McGraw-Hill, 1989; 3rd ed., 1995.

Purves, William, et al. *Life: The Science of Biology.* Sunderland, Mass.: Sinauer/Boston: Grant Press, 1983; 5th ed., Sunderland, Mass.: Sinauer, 1998.

RELATED ARTICLES

Aplacophora; Bivalvia; Cephalopoda; Gastropoda; Monoplacophora; Nautilus; Polyplacophora; Scaphopoda

Monoplacophora

The Monoplacophora, or *single-shell bearers,* comprise a class of the phylum Mollusca with about 20 species in three genera (*Vema, Neopilina, Monoplacophorus*). In the fossil record, there are two subclasses: the Cyclomya, with a planospiral shell, and the Tergomya, with a caplike shell.

The class was thought to be extinct since the Devonian (400 million to 360 million years ago) until several specimens of *Neopilina galatheae* were discovered in 1952. They were dredged from depth off the Pacific coast of Costa Rica during the Danish *Galathea* Expedition, for which the "living fossil" was named.

In addition to their single, cap-shaped shell, living members of this class are characterized externally by their large, central muscular foot. This limpetlike form is also reflected in their habit, as they live attached to hard surfaces, usually in the deep ocean. Monoplacophorans are usually found at depths over 2000 meters (6562 feet) and are usually quite small, less than 1 millimeter to approximately 3 centimeters (less than 1.18 inches).

Their enigmatic status is enhanced by their bizarre internal anatomy, displaying a repetition of organ systems unusual for mollusks: typically five or six pairs of gills, eight pairs of pedal retractor muscles, six pairs of kidneys, two pairs of auricles, one pair of pericardial spaces, and two pairs of gonads. This repetition is reminiscent of the seriality found in the molluscan class Polyplacophora (chitons) and the metamerism in annelid worms, and rekindled discussion and research on the evolutionary relationships of the Monoplacophora and of the entire phylum Mollusca. One extremely small species, *Micropilina arntzi* [<1 millimeter (0.04 inch) maximum length], shows only three pairs of ctenidia, three pairs of kidneys, and a single pair of hermaphroditic gonads; both heart and pericardium appear to be absent, but eight retractor muscles are still present. Relatively little is currently known about the biology of living monoplacophorans.

Patrick D. Reynolds

FURTHER READING

Barnes, Robert. *Invertebrate Zoology.* Philadelphia: W. B. Saunders, 1963; 6th ed., by Edward Ruppert, Fort Worth, Texas: Saunders College Publishing, 1994.

Pechenik, Jan A. *Biology of the Invertebrates.* Boston: Prindle, Weber and Schmidt, 1985; 4th ed., Boston: McGraw-Hill, 2000.

RELATED ARTICLES

Annelida; Mollusca; Polyplacophora

Monsoon

The word *monsoon* entered the English language from Dutch (*monssoen*) and is derived originally from an Arabic word, *mawsim*, which means a season that brings the same kind of weather every year. Seasonal changes in the direction of the prevailing winds were important to Arab traders, whose ships took them along the western coast of India during the summer and along the eastern coast of Africa during the winter.

There are two monsoon seasons. The winter monsoon is marked by very dry weather, and the summer monsoon brings heavy rain. Yangôn (Rangoon), the capital of Myanmar (Burma), has a typical monsoon climate. The city receives an average of about 2620 millimeters (103 inches) of rain a year. Of this total, 146 millimeters (5.7 inches) falls between November and April, during the winter monsoon, and 2474 millimeters (97.4 inches) falls between May and September.

Winter Monsoon

During the winter, cold air subsides over Siberia and produces high atmospheric pressure over a large area of northern and central Asia. There is also high pressure over the Indian subcontinent. The Intertropical Convergence Zone (ITCZ), where the trade wind systems of the northern and southern hemispheres meet, moves northward, and the jet stream blows from west to east at 25 to 30°N, above the Himalaya Mountains. Air flows outward from regions of high pressure. The combination of high pressure and the location of the ITCZ and jet stream carries air from the interior of the continent toward the oceans, where the atmospheric pressure is lower. Strong winds blow from the land across the Pacific Ocean and South China Sea, to the north of the Himalayas. The winds are weaker on the southern side of the mountains, but nevertheless, air moves from the land toward the sea. Air from the continental interior is dry, and it produces very dry weather in the lands over which it moves. This is the winter monsoon.

Summer Monsoon

In summer the situation reverses. As the land warms, air warmed by contact with the surface expands and rises. This produces relatively low pressure over the continental interior, but pressure remains high over the Tibetan Plateau. The oceans warm much more slowly, so in late spring the air over the oceans is cooler than the air over the land, and the pressure is higher over the oceans.

The ITCZ moves southward, reaching about latitude 25°N by the middle of summer. At that point there is a large difference in pressure between north and south, with low pressure associated with the ITCZ and high pressure over Tibet. A marked difference in temperature at high altitude also develops as warm air rises from the Tibetan Plateau. The jet stream breaks down and the clockwise flow of air at high level around the Tibetan high-pressure area combined with the sharp difference in temperature generates the tropical easterly jet. This wind blows from east to west between latitudes 15 and 40°N at a height of about 15 kilometers (9 miles). The prevailing surface winds change direction and southern Asia and the Indian subcontinent start to receive air that has crossed the Pacific and Indian Oceans and the Arabian Sea. Warm and moist, the wind from the sea brings increasingly humid, oppressive weather. The clear sky of the winter monsoon darkens as it fills with towering clouds, until at last the clouds release heavy rain that lowers the air temperature.

As the summer monsoon draws to a close, the contrast in temperature between the land and sea decreases, thereby weakening the onshore winds. At the same time the westerly winds of middle latitudes extend southward, causing replacement of the tropical easterly jet by winds that blow from west to east. As the land cools in northern Asia, high pressure becomes established over Siberia. Conditions are then set for the start of the winter monsoon.

It does not rain all the time during the summer monsoon, and some rain falls during the winter monsoon. There are periods of relatively wet and dry weather during both monsoon seasons. Typically, these spells of weather last for about 40 days in cycles that begin over the oceans and then move over land.

Burst of Monsoon

Both monsoon seasons begin abruptly. The onset, called the *burst of monsoon*, occurs when the wind changes direction and strengthens. A belt of offshore winds arrives from the north to mark the start of the winter monsoon, and in summer a belt of onshore winds arrives from the south. The arrival of the monsoon winds varies. If the burst of the summer monsoon is late, it usually indicates that there will be less rain than average over the entire season.

The monsoons burst at different times in different places. The summer monsoon rains begin first in Myanmar (Burma), where they arrive in May. In southeastern India, where southwesterly winds bring the monsoon rains, the summer monsoon winds usually arrive in June, but the rain does not arrive until October. In Assam, in the far northeast of India, the rainy season lasts from June until October, and in Tourane (formerly Da-Nang), Vietnam, the heaviest rains fall between July and January. The summer monsoon also begins in June over southern China and Japan.

Although southern Asia experiences the most dramatic monsoons, much gentler monsoons also affect tropical Africa, especially West Africa, and the United States. A type of monsoon circulation brings dry summers to those regions of the United States lying to the west of the Rockies and wet summers to the eastern United States. The dry summers in the west are caused by the northward movement of high pressure along the Pacific coast. Wet summers in the east are produced by

winds flowing outward from a region of high pressure centered over the Azores.

Parts of northern Australia also have a monsoon climate. The Australian monsoon region extends from Darwin, Northern Territories, to approximately Brisbane, Queensland. Winter in Darwin lasts from April to October. During this time the city receives an average of 182 millimeters (7 inches) of rain, with none at all falling in July. Rainfall during the summer monsoon between November and March averages 1310 millimeters (51.6 inches). Brisbane has an annual total of 1136 millimeters (44.7 inches) of rain. Some rain falls in every month, but 689 millimeters (27 inches), about 60 percent of the yearly total, falls between November and March.

Cost of a Late or Failed Monsoon

In Asia, however, the monsoons bring extremes of both drought and rain, and departures from the normal weather can mean catastrophe. Sometimes the summer monsoon arrives late, and occasionally it fails to arrive at all. There is then insufficient water for the irrigation of farm crops, and in countries with no reserves of stored food this can lead to famine. Thanks to the improved varieties of wheat and rice introduced during the so-called Green Revolution, agricultural output has risen dramatically in India. Famine is much less likely now than it used to be. Monsoon failures between 1876 and 1879 caused famines in which between 14 million and 18 million people died in India and China. More than 1 million people died in the early 1970s when the monsoon failed to arrive in India and Bangladesh. If the summer monsoon bursts early, or the winter monsoon bursts late, the increased rainfall can cause severe flooding. Floods also destroy farm crops, as well as bringing disease and contaminating everything touched by the water.

In 1904, while trying to find a way to predict the arrival and intensity of the Asian monsoons, Gilbert Walker, head of the Indian Meteorological

Service, discovered the changes that produce El Niño. Famine had followed a failure of the 1899 monsoon and Walker was seeking a way to provide the authorities with advance warning of such failures. What he discovered was a movement of tropical air, now known as the *Walker circulation*, and a periodic change in the distribution of pressure that he named the *Southern Oscillation*. It is the Southern Oscillation that produces the El Niño effect, although Walker failed to make the connection, and El Niño–Southern Oscillation events are the most frequent cause of delayed or failed summer monsoons over the whole of southern Asia and Australia. Meteorologists are now able to predict quite accurately the amount of rain that will fall during the summer monsoon.

Michael Allaby

FURTHER READING

Barry, Roger G., and Richard J. Chorley. *Atmosphere, Weather and Climate.* London: Methuen, 1968; 7th ed., London and New York: Routledge, 1998.

Henderson-Sellers, Ann, and Peter J. Robinson. *Contemporary Climatology.* London: Longman Scientific & Technical/New York: Wiley, 1986; 2nd ed., Harlow, England: Addison Wesley Longman, 1999.

Hidore, John J., and John E. Oliver. *Climatology: An Atmospheric Science.* New York: Macmillan/Toronto: Maxwell Macmillan Canada/New York: Maxwell Macmillan International, 1993.

Kendrew, W. G. *Climates of the Continents.* Oxford: Clarendon Press, 1922; 5th ed., 1961.

RELATED ARTICLES
El Niño; Intertropical Convergence Zone

Monterey Canyon

Monterey Canyon is one of the world's largest submarine canyons. It is not the largest, however, but nearly equivalent in size to the Grand Canyon of the Colorado River (see figure). Its head is located in Monterey Bay, immediately offshore of

Moss Landing, a small fishing and research village located on the coast between the towns of Santa Cruz and Monterey, California, approximately 150 kilometers (about 93 miles) south of San Francisco. This major offshore physiographic feature of the western North American continental margin has a maximum rim to floor relief of 1700 meters (5580 feet), a maximum rim-to-rim width of approximately 12 kilometers (about 7.5 miles), and a length, including its associated fan valley, of 470 kilometers (292 miles). Monterey Canyon drops in depth from about 100 meters (328 feet) at its head to over 4300 meters (14,100 feet) at its terminus on Monterey Fan. The canyon head is located at 56°48′N latitude and 121°48′W longitude and the end of the fan valley is located on the Monterey Fan at 34°30′N latitude and 123°30′W longitude.

Physiography, Biology, and Geology

This spectacular canyon is the dominant physiographic feature of the Ascension–Monterey canyon system, a two-canyon system comprised of a series of six submarine canyons that notch or cross the continental shelf in the central California region. The sinuous upper reaches of Monterey Canyon have as many as 10 distinct incised meanders. Along this canyon segment the axis has a fairly flat floored thalweg that is approximately 250 meters (820 feet) wide with a down canyon gradient of 1.8° and local wall gradients as steep as 33 to 35° but with typical wall slopes between 10 and 25°. Landslides have altered much of the canyon. Spectacular first- and second-generation slumps are present (see figure).

Not only does Monterey Canyon exhibit extraordinary geomorphology, but it also supports a prolific biology. Its walls of differentially eroded rock types provide refuge to a multitude of rockfish, bottom fish, sharks, and rays. Extensive chemosynthetic communities that thrive on sulfide-rich fluids abound. Examples of past and present-day fluid seeps along its walls are evidenced by the presence of sculptured and filigree carbonate deposits and autotrophic organisms such as *Calyptogena* clams and vestimentiferan tube worms.

Monterey Canyon cuts through over 1700 meters (5577 feet) of Cretaceous [144 million to 65 million years ago (M.a.)] basement and Tertiary (65 to 1.64 M.a.) to Quaternary (1.64 M.a. to present) sedimentary rocks. Walls of the upper canyon expose Pleistocene (about 1.64 to 0.01 M.a.) sand dune deposits (the Aromas Red Sands) and Holocene (last 10,000 years) deltaic deposits. Exposed along the wall of the meanders in the middle part of the canyon are Neogene (23.3 to 1.64 M.a.) sedimentary rocks of the middle Miocene (about 10 M.a.) Monterey Formation and the Pliocene to Pleistocene (about 5.2 to 0.01 M.a.) Purisima Formation. The lower part of the canyon has walls with the Neogene (about 12 to 1.64 M.a.) sedimentary rocks unconformably overlying the Cretaceous (about 145 to 135 M.a.) granitic basement rocks.

Discovery and Origin

Monterey Bay was first charted in 1786 by Jean-François de Galoup (1741–88), who made no mention of the existence of a submarine canyon. The first indication of the existence of a submarine canyon in Monterey Bay came in 1853 when the first U.S. Coast and Geodetic Survey hydrographic map showed that depths greater than 120 fathoms (720 feet) occur near shore in the central part of the bay. Although the origin of Monterey Canyon is not known for certain, several geologists have offered speculations upon its formation, which included (1) erosion by bottom currents; (2) stream or river erosion, possibly from the Sacramento River during the Pleistocene epoch when sea level was lower; and (3) turbidity current erosion.

The origin and modification of Monterey Canyon can be placed in the context of plate

An artificial Sun-shaded bathymetric image of the seafloor in the Monterey Bay region formed by using a computer mapping system. (Norman M. Maher, © 2001 MBARI)

tectonics. The headward part of the canyon is located within the western transform boundary of the Pacific and North American Plates, along the San Andreas fault system, and upon an exotic allochthonous tectonic block known as Salinia that has moved, due to plate motion, northward (right laterally) in the past 20 million years or so. Monterey Canyon may have originated some 300 kilometers (186 miles) south of its present location. At this location, approximately where the town of Santa Barbara is situated today, a shallow inland sea existed in pre-Miocene time and low islands and peninsulas extended into this sea. Here Monterey Canyon may have initiated as an onshore creek or submarine channel eroded by tidal flow in and out of the inland sea, along an east/west-oriented fault that facilitated easy erosion of the granitic basement rocks of the Salinian block. Through tectonic movement, both laterally and vertically, the ancestral Monterey Canyon was elevated and moved into erosional environments. This yo-yo effect deepened the canyon both through erosion by turbidity currents and up-building of the walls by sediment deposition. Exhumation of the canyon fill with active scouring of its floor is shaping the canyon today. The meanders are the result of deformation and weakening of rock along the Monterey Bay and Palo Colorado–San Gregorio fault zones, the western part of the San Andreas fault system. Gravity and earthquakes mobilize sediment near the canyon head to form turbidity currents that erode and enlarge the canyon.

H. Gary Greene

FURTHER READING

Dill, Robert, Robert Dietz, and H. Stewart, Jr. "Deep-Sea Channels and Delta of the Monterey Submarine Canyon." *Geological Society of America*, Vol. 65 (1954), pp. 191–194.

Greene, Gary. "Monterey Submarine Canyon." *California Geology*, 1977, pp. 112–113.

Greene, Gary, and Karen Hicks. "Ascension–Monterey Canyon System: History and Development." In Robert Garrison, Gary Greene, Karen Hicks, Gerald Weber, and Thomas Wright, eds., *Geology and Tectonics of the Central California Coastal Region: San Francisco to Monterey, Pacific Section*. Tulsa, Okla.: American Association of Petroleum Geologists, 1990, pp. 229–250.

McHugh, Cynthia, Ryan William, Steve Eittreim, and Donald Reed. "The Influence of the San Gregorio Fault on Morphology of Monterey Canyon." *Marine Geology*, Vol. 146 (1997), pp. 63–91.

Shepard, Francis, and K. O. Emery. "Submarine Topography off the California Coast: Canyons and Tectonic Interpretation." Special Paper 31. Boulder, Colo.: Geological Society of America, 1941.

Starke, G., and Arthur Howard. "Polygenetic Origin of Monterey Submarine Canyon." *Geological Society of America*, Vol. 79, No. 7, 1968, pp. 813–826.

RELATED ARTICLES

Continental Margin; Submarine Canyon; Submarine Fan; Turbidity Current

Moon, Tidal Effect of, see Sun and Moon, Tidal Effect of

Mud Volcano

A mud volcano is an accumulation, usually conical, of mud and rock ejected either by volcanic gases or by escaping petroliferous gases such as methane and ethane. It is essentially a mud diapir formed by sedimentary and volcanic processes. Mud diapirs (volcanoes) are common along convergent plate margins. Most often they are found in forearc basins and accretionary prisms. These chaotic mixtures resemble, and are sometime mistaken for, debris flows and melange deposits.

Sedimentary volcanism or *diapirism* is caused by either high-pressure gas release or eruptions of water-charged mud or shale. Desiccation of overlying clay units and dehydration cause cracks to form, and overpressurized fluid rises through these channel ways. The vertical release of these mud slurries may fracture consolidated lithologies (mostly fine-grained sedimentary rocks) and incorporate them as xenoliths, extruding them on the surface.

In areas where organic material is decomposing, methane forms and is confined under high pressure in the lower sedimentary pile. Diapirism is controlled primarily by the local structure of the basement rocks and the regional structural setting. Large-scale regional compression and faulting release significant volumes of methane and initiate diapiric movement.

Mud volcanoes are confined primarily to regions that are underlain by hydrous clay, shale, sand, boulders, submarine landslides, slump deposits, or other unconsolidated material. Mud volcanoes are found in the countries of Burma, India, Romania, Malay Archipelago, Trinidad, Venezuela, the Crimean–Caucasian province of Russia, and along the Gulf coast of Texas in the United States. The association between mud volcanism and hydrocarbon reservoirs is very strong. In the early part of the twentieth century, over 70 percent of the oil production in Russia was related to sedimentary volcanism.

The geometric form of extruded mud flows may be either planar or cylindrical. Many of the planar mud volcano flows and features are associated with faults and fractures. Clastic dikes are composed of the sediment that fills the planar channels. In fact, the presence of clastic dikes is a good indication that mud volcanoes are nearby. Sedimentary "eruptions" often bring stratigraphically older blocks (xenoliths) to the surface, similar to an igneous volcano. A cylindrical mud volcano forms at the intersections of two or more planar channels or faults.

Thick sequences of sediments along continental margins can give rise to overpressurized units that become liquefied and produce wet sediment injections and mud diapirs. Mud diapirs are found in the Lesser Antilles accretionary prism, Timor Trough, and Barbados Basin. Mud diapirs occur on all scales; some of the largest have a matrix of mud and shale that includes blocks of lithified and semilithified rock. Liquefaction forms from seismic-induced stress associated with faulting, a fast rate of sediment accumulation, hydrocarbon buildup causing methane hydrates, dehydration during compaction, and unstable density inversions. Following the sedimentary eruption, the volume decreases in the source area and the overlying sediment collapses, creating a landform that is similar to the structure of an igneous caldera.

David L. White

FURTHER READING

Freeman, P. S. "Exposed Middle Tertiary Mud Diapirs, South Texas." In Jules Braunstein and Gerald D. O'Brien, eds., *Diapirs and Diapirism.* Menasha, Wis.: American Association of Petroleum Geologists, 1968.

Pickering, K. T., R. N. Hiscott, and F. J. Hein. *Deep Marine Environments.* London and Boston: Unwin Hyman, 1989.

RELATED ARTICLES

Diapir; Methane Seep

Multibeam Sonar

Multibeam sonar is important for a broad range of geological and biological studies. This instrument uses sound waves to generate both bathymetry (depth of seafloor) and sidescan (backscatter intensity) images. Because multibeam sonar can map wide swaths of the seafloor at a time, it is an efficient tool for scientists to use as they endeavor to image the entire ocean bottom. During the last 10 to 15 years, use of multibeam bathymetry in hydrographic mapping has become increasingly common and accepted. Initially fraught with considerable accuracy and precision issues, multibeam sonar technology has improved vastly, and rigorous testing has established its reliability. The ability to acquire *denser* sounding data while surveying *fewer* tracklines (with greater spacing between lines), and simultaneously acquiring backscatter imagery using the same sensor, has made multibeam a popular tool among oceanographers. Using this technology, however, requires attention to a number of considerations that are less crucial when using single-beam technology. Multibeam depth sounders, as their name implies, acquire bathymetric soundings across a swath of seabed using a collection of acoustic beams, as opposed to a single beam, which measures depth only in the area directly below the transducer. The number of beams and arc coverage of the transducer varies among makes and models and determines the swath width across which a multibeam sounder acquires depth measurements in a given depth of water. The potential swath width w for a given multibeam sounder with angular coverage ϕ in water depth z can be calculated as follows:

$$w = 2z \tan\left[\frac{\phi}{\sqrt{2}}\right]$$

It is important to note that effective swath width is often somewhat less than potential swath width, as data from the outermost beams are often unusable due to large deviations induced by ship roll, refraction errors, and interference from bottom features such as pinnacles. The potential swath width for a given sonar may be realized only under calm conditions over a relatively flat bottom. Swath width is depth dependent, requiring closer line spacing in shallower water if full coverage is to be maintained. The mechanics and physics of how the beams are formed vary as well among makes and models and may be a consideration of importance if extremely high resolution, precision, and accuracy are required.

For the multibeam system to calculate accurate x, y, and z positions for soundings from all off-nadir (nonvertical) beams (every beam other than the center beam), precise measurement of ship and transducer attitude is required. This includes measurement of pitch, roll, heading, and (preferably) vertical heave. Thus a motion sensor must be interfaced to the unit so that its output may be used to adjust and correct the multibeam depth sounding data in either real time or during postprocessing.

In addition, because of longer travel times for off-nadir beams, variations in the speed of sound in water (SOS) can induce relatively large errors in these beams, especially if temperature stratification exists in the water column. For this reason, sound velocity profiling should be conducted on site during a survey, so that the SOS profile data may be used to adjust depth soundings. Controlling for variations in SOS is of increasing importance as depth increases. Multibeam surveying also requires more rigorous system calibration to account for systemic variations in, and improve the accuracy of, heading, roll, and pitch sensor values, as well as any adjustment to navigation time tags that will reduce timing errors between navigation and sonar data. This calibration, known as a *patch test,* is typically conducted by running a series of survey lines over the same area with relative orientations that allow assessment of the variables listed above.

Multibeam bathymetric surveying generates orders of magnitude more data than single-beam

surveying, resulting in greater storage requirements, longer processing times, and the need in some cases for greater processing power. Gigabytes of data may be generated daily, as opposed to megabytes in single-beam surveys, especially if backscatter imagery is being recorded as well. The removal of bad sounding data during the editing process is, accordingly, a much larger task in multibeam than in single-beam surveys, although some processing packages allow some degree of automation of this process.

The considerations and requirements listed above make multibeam surveying a much more complex and expensive undertaking relative to single beam, but the benefits in cost per unit effort and resolution can well outweigh the hardships, especially if extensive surveying is planned. Survey speeds of up to 6 meters per second (12 knots) are now possible with some systems. Minimal costs for setting up a multibeam system range from U.S.$75,000 to U.S.$150,000 for equipment alone, not including vessel, installation, and maintenance costs. Higher-precision equipment with greater capabilities and more features can cost substantially more.

Pat J. Iampietro

FURTHER READING

Blondel, Philippe, and Bramley J. Murton. *Handbook of Seafloor Sonar Imagery.* New York: Wiley, 1997.

Fish, John Perry, and H. Arnold Carr. *Sound Underwater Images: A Guide to the Generation and Interpretation of Side Scan Sonar Data.* Orleans, Mass.: Lower Cape Publishing, 1990.

Ingham, A. E. *Sea Surveying.* New York: Wiley, 1975.

Ingham, A. E., and V. J. Abbott. *Hydrography for the Surveyor and Engineer,* 3rd ed. Boston: Blackwell Scientific, 1993.

Milne, P. H. *Underwater Engineering Surveys.* Houston; Texas: Gulf Publishing, 1980.

Urrick, Robert J. *Principles of Underwater Sound.* New York: McGraw-Hill, 1967; 3rd ed., 1983.

Various contributors. *Five Hundred Years of Nautical Science, 1400–1900: Proceedings of the 3rd International Reunion for the History of Nautical Science and Hydrography Held at the National*

Maritime Museum. Greenwich, London: National Maritime Museum, 24–28 September 1979.

RELATED ARTICLES
Sonar

Murray, John
1841–1914
Marine Geologist and Director of Challenger *Expedition Commission*

John Murray accompanied the voyage of the HMS *Challenger* (1872–76) as one of its civilian scientific staff and began intensive geological investigations of seafloor deposits during the expedition. When *Challenger* Expedition Commission scientific director Charles Wyville Thomson died in 1882, Murray took over the immense project of overseeing publication of the 50-volume *Challenger* Reports (1880–95).

John Murray was born in Cobourg, Ontario, Canada, on 3 March 1841 to Scottish immigrant parents. He moved to Scotland at age 17. After high school, Murray began medical studies at the University of Edinburgh. In 1868, before completing his studies, he sailed on the whaler *Jan Mayen* as surgeon for a seven-month voyage to the Arctic. This voyage allowed Murray to indulge a blossoming predilection for marine biology and geography. He collected organisms and made observations of ocean currents and temperatures. Immediately after the *Jan Mayen* excursion, Murray returned to the University of Edinburgh. He abandoned medicine and studied broadly in the sciences, never taking any degree. This sort of jack-of-all-trades approach to science education, not uncommon among the British gentleman-scholars of the day, suited Murray well, as he developed research interests that did not fit easily within existing disciplinary categories. At Edinburgh, Murray also worked in the physical laboratory of Peter Tait (1831–1901), a professor of natural

philosophy, and he spent his vacations practicing marine biology, participating in dredging excursions along the Scottish coast using weighted nets to collect specimens from the seafloor.

In 1872, Tait recommended Murray to Charles Wyville Thomson (1830–82), a professor of natural history at the University of Edinburgh and director of the scientific staff for the upcoming expedition of the HMS *Challenger.* This costly venture was supported by both the British Admiralty and the Royal Society of London, one of the premier scientific organizations in the world. It became a model of naval and civilian cooperation in virtually all aspects of ocean science on a large scale. The ship itself was a specially outfitted 2300-ton steam-powered corvette with a total crew of 240, and the journey, which began on 7 December 1872, lasted three and a half tedious years.

Initially, Murray helped only to prepare scientific apparatus for the voyage but was asked to go

John Murray. (© The Natural History Museum, London)

along when a vacancy opened. He was one of four principal assistant scientists to Thomson. Henry Mosely (1844–91) and Rudolph von Willemoes-Suhm (1847–75) were also naturalists, and John Buchanon (1844–1925), another Edinburgh colleague was a chemist. The scientists collected marine and terrestrial biological specimens and water and sediment samples as the *Challenger* circumnavigated the globe slowly and methodically. Some analysis was conducted in a special laboratory on the ship, but most samples were stored away for later work. Depth soundings were taken, along with serial temperature and ocean current readings and the standard battery of meteorological and nautical recordings. Some sediment samples were recovered from unheard-of depths, such as those from almost 10 kilometers (6.2 miles) down in the area now known as the Mariana Trench, by using winches outfitted with hemp line and weighted sinkers that drove sampling tubes into the seafloor before being cranked back up to the surface.

From a scientific perspective, what marked the *Challenger* expedition from others was its focus on deep-sea phenomena. Since midcentury, scientists had become increasingly interested in studying life at the bottom of the ocean through a combination of factors. Sounding surveys for cable telegraph companies began determining optimal routes for laying transoceanic telegraph lines, and in sampling the ocean floor, many strange new organisms were uncovered from ever-greater depths. Such discoveries challenged the belief that life could not possibly exist at these deepest levels. Charles Darwin's (1809–82) *Origin of Species* (1859), furthermore, stimulated a great deal of scientific interest in the potential evolutionary significance of deep-sea organisms. Thomson was one of the first scientists to devote himself fully to the study of this astonishing new realm for biology.

As the expedition progressed, Murray became responsible, possibly by default, for supervising the collection of seafloor deposits and biological specimens from the surface and intermediate depths. He noted a close correlation between protozoa living in the upper levels of the water and the composition of various oozelike deposits that cover the ocean floor. He realized that as the organisms die, their remains sink to the bottom, decompose, and form oozes that differ geographically (and chemically) according to the range of protozoan species above. Aware of this dynamic process, Murray classified the radiolarian, diatom, and pteropod oozes in addition to the previously identified globigerina ooze. He further recognized that the globigerina ooze was by far the most abundant and geographically widespread. It was composed primarily of the decomposing calcareous shells of protozoa belonging to the large genus *Globigerina*. Curiously, Murray found that in certain very deep areas of the ocean, the floor appeared to be an ooze-free muddy red clay, an intriguing fact considering that species of *Globigerina* lived in the waters far above. Buchanon and Thomson helped solve this puzzle, determining that the concentration of carbonic acid increased with depth, to the point that it simply dissolved the shells normally composing globigerina ooze.

The *Challenger* returned home on 24 May 1876 with over 13,000 animal and plant specimens that needed to be sorted and classified, hundreds of water samples and seafloor deposits to be analyzed, and volumes of depth, temperature, and ocean current data meticulously collected from 362 sounding stations. At first, Thomson supervised the distribution of these materials to numerous specialists around the world for analysis from the new *Challenger* Expedition Commission in Edinburgh. This office served a major centralizing role in the production and dissemination of oceanographic knowledge after 1876. Publication of the *Report on the Scientific Results of the Voyage of H.M.S. Challenger during the Years 1873–1876* (1880–95) had barely begun when Thomson died in 1882, leaving Murray in charge of a project that expanded far beyond its initial scope, ultimately resulting in a 50-volume work that cost the British Treasury £100,000 and Murray a considerable amount of his own money. He was a persistent editor and doggedly pushed his many authors to finish their work. To the *Challenger* report itself, Murray personally contributed a two-volume summary (1895) and coauthored (with geologist Alphonse Renard) an 1891 volume, *Report on Deep-Sea Deposits*, in which the major sediment types for the entire ocean were classified and mapped for the first time.

Murray somehow found time to pursue his own studies, conducting research aboard the *Knight Errant* (1880) and the *Triton* (1882) and directing dredging projects along the coast of Scotland from the *Medusa* (between 1883 and 1894). In 1880 he published a controversial theory of coral reef formation that contradicted one articulated by Darwin in 1842. Darwin's theory relied on the geological subsidence of volcanic islands. As the islands slowly sank, Darwin thought, the fringing corals continued to grow upward, maintaining a constant depth below the surface. Murray's extensive firsthand experience with ocean sediments, on the other hand, gave him immense respect for the slow but powerful forces of deposition continually at work in the sea. He believed that layers of sediments accumulated atop existing underwater mountains. These gradually built up to a depth at which coral would grow after being colonized by larvae. Murray's explanation has not proved as durable as Darwin's, but it did stimulate important reef research well into the twentieth century.

In 1889, Murray married Isabel Henderson, sole daughter of a wealthy shipowner, and by 1900 he had begun to profit from phosphate mining ventures on Christmas Island, a British possession in the Indian Ocean south of Java. Murray used his wealth to endow oceanographic research

and to keep the *Challenger* office open. He served as the British government's representative for the 1899 founding of the International Council for the Exploration of the Sea. In 1912 he coauthored (with Johan Hjort) *The Depths of the Ocean*, an account of the *Challenger* project that served as the principal textbook of oceanography for three decades. Murray was killed in an automobile accident in 1914.

Murray's principal contributions to the oceanographic sciences arose from his role in the *Challenger* expedition, both as a practicing scientist and as director of the Expedition Commission. This project was an important episode in the history of oceanography because it became a model of naval and civilian cooperation in deep-sea science that many countries emulated immediately afterward. The expedition generated an immense amount of scientific data about life in the sea. This information would have been of little value to anyone had Murray not personally invested in the publication of the *Challenger* Reports.

J. Conor Burns

BIOGRAPHY

- John Murray.
- Born 3 March 1841 in Cobourg, Ontario, Canada.
- After sailing on a voyage to the Arctic in 1868, he abandoned medical studies at the University of Edinburgh in favor of marine biology.
- He was staff naturalist for expedition of HMS *Challenger*, 1872–76, where he began intensive studies of ocean floor sediments.
- In 1882, he became editor of the 50-volume *Report on the Scientific Results of the Voyage of H.M.S. Challenger during the Years 1873–1876* (1880–95).
- He was granted a lease from the British government in 1891 for phosphate mining on Christmas Island.
- In 1912 he coauthored an oceanography textbook, *The Depths of the Ocean*, with Johan Hjort.
- Died in a car accident, 16 March 1914.

SELECTED WRITINGS

Murray, John. "Preliminary Reports . . . on Work Done on Board the *Challenger*." *Proceedings of the Royal Society of London*, Vol. 24, No. 170 (1875), pp. 471–544.

———. "On the Structure and Origin of Coral Islands." *Proceedings of the Royal Society of Edinburgh*, Vol. 10 (1880), pp. 505–518.

Murray, John, and Johan Hjort. *The Depths of the Ocean*. London: Macmillan, 1912.

Murray, John, and Alphonse Renard. *Report on Deep-Sea Deposits*. In *Report on the Scientific Results of the Voyage of H.M.S.* Challenger *during the Years 1873-1876*. London: Her Majesty's Stationery Office, 1891.

FURTHER READING

Deacon, Margaret. *Scientists and the Sea, 1650–1900: A Study of Marine Science*. London and New York: Academic Press, 1971; 2nd ed., Aldershot, England, and Brookfield, Vt.: Ashgate, 1997.

Schlee, Susan. *The Edge of an Unfamiliar World: A History of Oceanography*. New York: Dutton, 1973; London: Hale, 1975.

RELATED ARTICLES

Darwin, Charles Robert; HMS *Challenger*; Thomson, Charles Wyville

Musicians Seamounts

One of many groups of Cretaceous age (144 million to 65 million years ago) seamounts in the western Pacific Ocean, the Musicians Seamounts are a diffuse cluster of about 65 extinct undersea volcanoes and volcanic ridges located north of the Hawaiian Islands. They stretch northwest approximately 1400 kilometers (870 miles) from 25°N, 157°W to 34°N, 167°W. Most are small, 30 to 80 kilometers (19 to 50 miles) across, and average 3000 meters (9843 feet) in height. The shallowest is Liszt Seamount, which rises to 1582 meters (5190 feet). About 17 of the larger seamounts comprise a prominent northwest-trending line, while most others are associated with 8 to 10 east-trending ridges in the eastern part of the province.

Basaltic rocks dredged from the seamounts yield radiometric dates from about 96 million to 75 million years ago. Dates in the northwest line become progressively younger to the south,

leading scientists to believe that they were formed as the Pacific Plate drifted northwest over a hotspot (mantle plume). The volcanic ridges are thought to have formed along cracks and fracture zones as the hotspot moved beneath the spreading ridge separating the Pacific and Farallon Plates about 75 million years ago.

Apparently the name *Musicians Seamounts* was used informally at Scripps Institution of Oceanography in the late 1950s, when many Pacific seamount groups were formally recognized. Scripps oceanographer William Menard (1920–86) urged that colleagues give Pacific seamounts noble names and probably first instituted the name in his 1964 book, *Marine Geology of the Pacific*. Most individual seamount names were bestowed by David K. Rea (1942–), who made maps of geophysical data from the region during the late 1960s and happened to have season tickets to the Seattle Symphony.

William W. Sager

FURTHER READING

Menard, Henry William. *Marine Geology of the Pacific*. New York: McGraw-Hill, 1964.

Pringle, Malcolm S. "Age Progressive Volcanism in the Musicians Seamounts: A Test of the Hot Spot Hypothesis for the Late Cretaceous Pacific." In Malcolm S. Pringle, William W. Sager, Willam V. Sliter, and Seth Stein, eds., *The Mesozoic Pacific: Geology, Tectonics, and Volcanism*. Washington, D.C.: American Geophysical Union, 1993.

Rea, David K., and Frederic P. Naugler. "Musicians Seamount Province and Related Crustal Structures North of the Hawaiian Ridge." *Marine Geology*, Vol. 10 (1971), pp. 89–111.

RELATED ARTICLES

Hotspot; Mantle Plume; Seamount

Mutualism

Symbiosis is a close, long-lasting association between members of different species. Various types of symbiosis occur in the oceans, and they are categorized by whether the relationship is beneficial or harmful and whether one or both partners are affected. Mutualism is a type of symbiosis in which both organisms, called *symbionts*, benefit from the association. In some cases it is difficult to determine whether an association is truly mutual or whether it is commensal; in *commensalism*, one partner benefits while the other neither benefits nor is harmed.

Mutualistic associations between algal cells and invertebrates are particularly common in the tropics but are also found in other well-lit areas of the marine environment. Symbiotic algal cells, called *zooxanthellae*, are associated with members of many phyla, including cnidarians, mollusks, sponges, and flatworms. Some invertebrates ingest green algae and transport chloroplasts from the digestive tract to other tissues; in this case mutualism occurs between the invertebrate and the organelle. Mutualism also occurs between zooxanthellae and protists such as ciliates, foraminiferans, and radiolarians. Mutualistic associations with zooxanthellae involve the reciprocal transfer of nutrients; algal cells receive nitrates and phosphates from their partner, which in turn receives organic compounds (i.e., energy) derived from photosynthesis.

Mutualistic associations also occur between various invertebrate species. Examples include crabs and sea anemones, anemones and anemone fish, large fish and cleaner organisms, and luminescent bacteria and fishes and squids. In crab–anemone associations, the anemone provides defense and gathers food for the crab while the crab provides substrate, movement, and food fragments for the anemone. Anemone fish, which are protected by the anemone, may bring food to and/or attract prey to their partner and deter the predators of the sea anemones. Cleaner fish and shrimp remove ectoparasites from larger fish, thereby obtaining a food source. Luminescent bacteria receive food from their partner, and the partner uses bacteria-produced light for camouflage, defense, or predation.

Lynn L. Lauerman

FURTHER READING
Nybakken, James W. *Marine Biology: An Ecological Approach*, 5th ed. San Francisco: Benjamin Cummings, 2001.
Paracer, Surindar, and Vernon Ahmadjian. *Symbiosis: An Introduction to Biological Associations.* Hanover, N.H.: University Press of New England, 1986; 2nd ed., Oxford and New York: Oxford University Press, 2000.
Smith, David C., and Angela E. Douglas. *The Biology of Symbiosis.* London and Baltimore: Edward Arnold, 1987.

RELATED ARTICLES
Commensalism; Symbiosis; Zooxanthellae

Mystacocarida

Mystacocarids (subclass Mystacocarida) are tiny crustaceans that live between sandgrains in the littoral and sublittoral zones along the coast. Only 10 species are known, divided into two genera: *Ctenocheilocaris* and *Derocheilocaris*.

Most mystacocarids are less than 0.5 millimeter (0.02 inch) in length, although some reach as long as 1 millimeter (0.04 inch). Like other crustaceans, they have a segmented body, an external skeleton, and a number of jointed appendages (limbs). However, adults lack the compound eyes seen in other crustaceans and they have no carapace (shell). The long, slender body is divided into two main regions: a cephalon (head) and a 10-segmented trunk of uniform width along its length. The cephalon is divided into two parts by a deep cleft and bears appendages, which are nearly identical and are used for feeding, touch, and for crawling through sand. The last trunk segment bears a pair of pincerlike caudal rami, which characterize the group.

Mystacocarids are sometimes described as sandgrazers or sandlickers because they are thought to feed by brushing organic matter off sand grains with their bristly mouthparts. Their diet consists of organic detritus and microorganisms such as diatoms.

Relatively little is known about the reproductive biology of mystacocarids. They reproduce sexually and the sexes are separate. Eggs are apparently laid free and hatch into free-swimming larvae that disperse in the plankton. The larvae develop into adults by passing through a series of molts.

Mystacocarids were first discovered near Woods Hole, Massachusetts, in 1943 and have since been found in western and southern Africa, the Gulf of Mexico, and the eastern coast of North America, Chile, and the Mediterranean Sea. Their simple, segmented bodies led some scientists to speculate that these creatures might be the most primitive members of the Crustacean subphylum. However, others have argued that the apparently primitive features seen in the mystacocarids might have arisen by retention of larval characteristics into adulthood as they adapted to their interstitial habitat.

Ben Morgan

FURTHER READING
Brusca, Richard C., and Gary J. Brusca. *Invertebrates.* Sunderland, Mass.: Sinauer, 1990.
Nybakken, James W. *Marine Biology: An Ecological Approach,* 5th ed. San Francisco: Benjamin Cummings, 2001.
Pechenik, Jan A. *Biology of the Invertebrates.* Boston: Prindle, Weber and Schmidt, 1985; 4th ed., Boston: McGraw-Hill, 2000.

RELATED ARTICLES
Crustacea; Maxillopoda

Mysticeti

The suborder Mysticeti, in the order Cetacea, is a group of marine mammals that have baleen instead of teeth. The baleen whales have a pair of blowholes at the top of their head from which they breathe, streamlined bodies for swimming through water, and a pair of flukes at the tail end used for propulsion. They all have flippers instead of individual fingers, and lack hair. Depending on the species, they have a very arched jaw, no dorsal fin, and no throat grooves (family Balaenidae or right whales); a moderately curved upper jaw, a dorsal ridge with bumps, and two to four throat grooves (family Eschrichtiidae or gray whales); or a fairly straight upper jaw, a dorsal fin, and multiple throat grooves (family Balaenopteridae or rorqual whales). The blue whale, which can reach 29 meters (95 feet) in length and 72 tonnes (80 tons), is the largest animal that has ever lived.

Mysticetes feed by filtering prey from the water using their baleen plates as a sieve, and their large tongue is used to move the water out of the mouth and captured food into the throat. Right whales usually feed on small zooplankton, such as copepods, that swarm in large numbers near the ocean's surface. Right whales swim through plankton swarms skimming the prey from the water. Gray whales generally feed on benthic crustaceans by swimming to the ocean's bottom, turning on their side, and sucking a portion of the sediments and prey into their mouth. As they begin to come to the water's surface they use their tongue to force out the sediments and water, retaining the food in their mouth. Rorqual whales are much more aggressive in obtaining their prey. These whales actively search for schools or swarms of fish or euphausiids (krill). They swim rapidly through the schools and engulf their prey by expanding their large mouths with the help of the throat grooves. Humpback whales will sometimes use air expelled from their blowhole to create a circle of bubbles around fishes, which seems to corral the fishes as the humpback whale comes to the surface to capture the tightly grouped fishes.

Jim Harvey

Further Reading

Berta, A., and J. L. Sumich. *Marine Mammals: Evolutionary Biology.* San Diego: Academic Press, 1999.

Ellis, Richard. *The Book of Whales.* New York: Knopf, 1980.

Haley, Delphine, ed. *Marine Mammals of Eastern North Pacific and Arctic Waters.* 2nd rev. ed. Seattle: Pacific Search Press, 1986.

Leatherwood, Stephen, and Randall R. Reeves. *The Sierra Club Handbook of Whales and Dolphins.* San Francisco: Sierra Club Books, 1983.

Slijper, E. J. *Whales.* Translated by A. J. Pomerans. New York: Basic Books, 1962.

Related Articles

Baleen; Cetacea

Myxini

The Myxini (from the Greek *myxa*, "slime") is the taxonomic group comprising the 40 or so species of hagfishes. The Myxini is usually regarded, as in Joseph S. Nelson's *Fishes of the World* (1994), as a class within the superclass Agnatha (agnathans or jawless fishes). Prevailing opinion considers the hagfish lineage to be an early offshoot of the vertebrates (subphylum Vertebrata), dating back to the Cambrian Period (at least 500 million years ago).

Hagfishes are superficially similar to lampreys, the members of the other class of living agnathans (Cephalaspidomorphi). Both hagfishes and lampreys are slimy, eel-like, and without jaws and paired fins. On closer examination, however, the two groups are quite different anatomically and physiologically.

Hagfishes have poorly developed eyes. The head bears three pairs of sensory (tactile) barbels surrounding the mouth and single nostril. The mouth is ventral (on the underside) and is relatively inconspicuous. It is armed with a tongue that bears four rows of keratinized "teeth." Together with a cartilaginous dental plate, this arrangement forms a jawlike structure that can tear chunks of flesh from dead or dying fish. The hagfish's nostril serves for water intake. It

provides the animal with a sense of smell and empties into the pharynx to deliver oxygenated water for gas exchange. Along the hagfish's flanks are 1 to 16 gill openings (depending on species).

Hagfishes have several key features that may be unique among living vertebrates. Among these are blood hemoglobin (oxygen-carrying pigment) that has unusual composition and properties, a nervous system that lacks myelin (a fatty insulating layer around the nerve fibers), and a large liver that is tubular rather than lobular. Because hagfishes lack true bone and vertebrae, yet have the notochord characteristic of chordates (phylum Chordata), some authorities do not regard them as vertebrates but incorporate them in a separate chordate subphylum, the Myxini.

The concentration of salts in hagfish tissues is similar to that of seawater, and it is commonly assumed that hagfishes have always lived in seawater. However, some kidney features are similar to those of freshwater fishes, and some authors suggest that hagfishes might have had a freshwater phase in their early evolutionary history. They may have been anadromous (spawning in fresh water and maturing in the sea), as are present-day lampreys.

Little is known of the reproductive habits of hagfishes. Females produce 20 to 30 large, leathery eggs that bear hooklike structures that in some species cause the eggs to link together in rosette-shaped clusters. Males do not have obvious copulatory structures and eggs may be fertilized externally, although the presence of a tough case on eggs suggests otherwise. Hagfishes, unlike lampreys, do not have a larval phase.

Hagfishes are widely distributed in the world's ocean system. They are typically found in water deeper than 25 meters (82 feet) and many are deepwater species living at depths in excess of 1500 meters (4920 feet). They commonly occur on soft bottoms, where they burrow and hunt for soft-bodied invertebrates. They also scavenge on dead and dying fishes and other medium-sized animals. Usually, they enter the animal through the mouth, anus, gill slit, or a wound in the body wall, and consume the body from the inside.

The hagfish's main form of defense against potential predators appears to be its eel-like contortions and the production of copious amounts of unpalatable slime. The hagfish has the ability to tie itself in a single sliding knot by which it can slough off a layer of slime. This knotting facility also offers extra leverage when a hagfish is tearing flesh from a large prey item. In some localities, hagfishes have developed a reputation for boring into fish caught on hooks or gill nets set by fishers. In this way, hagfishes are sometimes landed with the normal catch. However, hagfishes have now become targets themselves. Their tough skins are used to make a common form of "eel skin," a type of leather.

Trevor Day

FURTHER READING

Conniff, R. "The Most Disgusting Fish in the Sea." *Audubon*, Vol. 93, No. 2 (March 1991), pp. 100–108.

Jørgensen, Jørgen Mørup, Jens Peter Lomholt, Roy E. Weber, and Hans Malte, eds. *The Biology of Hagfishes*. London and New York: Chapman and Hall, 1998.

Moyle, Peter B., and Joseph J. Cech. *Fishes: An Introduction to Ichthyology*. Englewood Cliffs, N.J.: Prentice Hall, 1982; 4th ed., Upper Saddle River, N.J.: Prentice Hall, 2000.

Nelson, Joseph S. *Fishes of the World*. New York: Wiley, 1976; 3rd ed., 1994.

Paxton, John R., and William N. Eschmeyer, eds. *Encyclopedia of Fishes*. San Diego: Academic Press, 1995; 2nd ed., 1998.

RELATED ARTICLES
Agnatha; Cephalaspidomorphi

Nanoplankton

Free-floating or weakly swimming organisms that live in the water column and drift with the ocean's currents collectively are called *plankton*. Scientists often categorize planktonic organisms by their size (specifically by their ability to pass through or be collected on various sizes of nets or filters). The term *nanoplankton* comprises planktonic organisms that range in size from 2 to 20 micrometers (μm; 0.000079 to 0.00079 inch). These minute organisms are mostly members of the kingdom Protista. The most common members (in absolute numbers, diversity, and biomass) of the nanoplankton are autotrophic and heterotrophic flagellates; the former are microscopic photosynthesizers and the latter are grazers. Nanoplankton are too small to collect with plankton nets; collecting organisms this small would require a mesh size through which water could not pass. To collect nanoplankton, researchers usually collect a volume of water and then pass it through very fine meshed filters (such as Millipore filters), centrifuge it, or simply allow the organisms to settle out of the water sample.

Photosynthetic members of the nanoplankton, which sometimes are called *microalgae* or *nanophytoplankton*, make a significant contribution to oceanic primary productivity. Haptophytes are abundant members of the nanoplankton and exist in all oceans. External plates composed of calcium or organic material are characteristic of this group of organisms. Of the haptophytes, the coccolithophores are the most common and widespread and are major contributors of primary productivity in many locales. Other autotrophic nanoplankton groups include the silicoflagellates, cryptomonads, and some forms of motile green algae. In addition, some diatoms and dinoflagellates are smaller than 20 μm and thus fall into the nanoplankton category. The most abundant types of nanozooplankton (generally animal-like protists) are the flagellates and the ciliates.

Since the late 1960s, researchers have become increasingly aware of the importance of nanoplankton (and even smaller size categories) in oceanic food webs. Autotrophic nanoplankton and picoplankton (0.2 to 2.0 μm) dominate the epipelagic phytoplankton assemblage in many areas of the ocean (particularly in temperate and tropical locales); they are less abundant in coastal and upwelling areas. These smaller photosynthesizers exhibit less seasonal variability than do their larger phytoplankton counterparts, at least in part because their small surface-to-volume ratio allows them better survival in low-nutrient conditions. Some scientists suggest that the nanoplankton and picoplankton may perform 80 percent of the photosynthesis and contribute 75 percent of the biomass in the open ocean. Nanozooplankton, which are the primary consumers of nanophytoplankton, in turn, may consume most of the energy fixed by photosynthesis in the oceans.

Lynn L. Lauerman

FURTHER READING

Fraser, James. *Nature Adrift: The Story of Marine Plankton.* London: Foulis, 1962.

Nybakken, James W. *Marine Biology: An Ecological Approach,* 5th ed. San Francisco: Benjamin Cummings, 2001.

Parsons, Timothy R., and Masayuki Takahashi. *Biological Oceanographic Processes.* Oxford and New York: Pergamon Press, 1973; 3rd ed., with Barry Hargrave, 1984.

Pierce, Robert W., and George F. Hart. *Phytoplankton of the Gulf of Mexico: Taxonomy of Calcareous Nannoplankton.* Baton Rouge, La.: School of Geoscience, Louisiana State University, 1979.

RELATED ARTICLES

Microbial Loop; Plankton; Plankton Net; Zooplankton

Nansen, Fridtjof

1861–1930

Oceanographer, Polar Explorer, Statesman, and Humanitarian

Norwegian oceanographer and polar explorer Fridtjof Nansen led the famous *Fram* expedition (1893–96) that drifted close to the North Pole. The voyage established that the Arctic was an ocean basin, not a shallow sea. Nansen invented and improved oceanographic sampling equipment, and his observations led to important theoretical developments in physical oceanography.

Fridtjof Nansen, was born near Christiania (now Oslo), Norway, in 1861, the son of a lawyer. From an early age, Fridtjof loved the outdoors and as a teenager he won several prizes in national skiing competitions. When he began his studies at the University of Christiania in 1880, he was initially interested in physics and mathematics, but changed his specialty to zoology. He predicted, rightly, that this subject would provide greater opportunity for investigations in the wild.

In 1882, Christiania's professor of zoology, Robert Collett, encouraged Nansen to join a four-month sealing expedition aboard the vessel *Viking.* The voyage proved a pivotal influence. This was Nansen's introduction to the harsh conditions of the Arctic. The *Viking* sailed west and froze fast in ice, drifting south for several weeks, close to Greenland's eastern shore. Nansen recorded his observations and impressions in writing, drawings, and sketches. On Nansen's return, Collett arranged for Nansen to take up the post of curator at the Bergen Museum. Nansen chose to study myzostomes, a rather obscure group of parasitic and commensal polychaete worms. His findings, published in 1885, have become a standard reference and in 1886 earned Nansen the Joachim Friele Gold Medal.

In 1886, Nansen traveled to Italy and Germany, visiting the marine biological station at Naples and Camillo Golgi's (1843–1926) laboratory where he observed the technique for impregnating nerve cells with silver to render them visible for microscopy. In 1888, Nansen received his doctorate at Christiania for his studies of nerve fibers in the vertebrate spinal column. That year, Nansen organized an expedition to ski across Greenland. He was interested in settling the argument, one way or the other, as to whether central Greenland was ice-bound or had a mild climate. Many believed the latter. Nansen and his party of five completed a 40-day, east-to-west trip across Greenland. During the trip, they traversed the 2740-meter (8990-foot)-high central plateau, endured thick fog, snowstorms, and night temperatures as low as -50°C (-58°F), without any possibility of rescue. They arrived on the west coast, where they were stranded overwinter, making friends with local Inuit. Their expedition confirmed that central Greenland was ice-covered all year.

Nansen returned to Norway in 1889, taking up the post of curator at the University of Christiania. He soon planned to raise funds for an expedition to test a new theory. In 1879, a U.S. expedition headed by George Washington DeLong had sought to sail through the Bering

Fridtjof Nansen. (Hulton/Archive)

Strait between Alaska and Russia. Their vessel, the *Jeanette*, became locked in ice and was crushed. Five years later, the *Jeanette*'s remains were found in ice on the Greenland side of the North Pole. In 1888, Nansen had noted that driftwood on Greenland's east coast seemed to be of Siberian origin. Nansen surmised that there was an ice-carrying current that crossed the Arctic from Siberia to Greenland. If so, this suggested that the North Pole might not harbor a continent, but was an ice-covered ocean. To test this notion, Nansen proposed to use a vessel that could become locked in ice without being crushed.

Despite criticism from Arctic explorers, Nansen succeeded in gaining funding from the Norwegian Geographic Society and the Royal Geographical Society in London to support an expedition. The *Fram* was commissioned to Nansen's design. This novel, three-masted schooner had a hull shaped to rise up out of the ice. On 24 June 1893, the *Fram* with its

13-person complement sailed from Christiania and on 22 September became locked in sea ice north of the New Siberian Islands. The *Fram* emerged from the ice north of Spitsbergen nearly three years later, having drifted across the Arctic Circle as far north as 85°57'. Meanwhile, Nansen with a companion, F. H. Johansen, and a team of sledge dogs, had tried for the North Pole. They were forced to turn back at 86°14', the closest to the North Pole anyone had reached. They overwintered and on their way back met up with an English expedition and returned to Norway in triumph.

The voyage of the *Fram* led to several major oceanographic discoveries. First and foremost, it helped establish that the Arctic Ocean did not surround a polar continent. Soundings taken through holes cut in the ice showed that the Arctic was an ocean basin, sometimes exceeding 3000 meters (9840 feet) in depth, not the shallow sea that others had expected. Temperature readings revealed a layer of water at about 1.5°C (35°F) and at depths of 150 to 900 meters (490 to 2950 feet) sandwiched between cooler layers. Nansen concluded—correctly as was later shown—that the layer of warm water was Atlantic water penetrating below Arctic water diluted by melting ice. Temperature and salinity readings also suggested the existence of an underwater ridge between Svalbard and Greenland, whose existence was later proved, and the feature became the Nansen Ridge. Nansen also described the *dead-water phenomenon*, where boundary waves between a top layer of brackish water and an underlying layer of full-strength seawater take up the propulsive energy of a boat's propeller, causing the boat to move sluggishly.

Nansen noted that sea ice typically drifted at 20 to 40° to the right of wind blowing across its surface. He explained this as an effect of Earth's rotation, and on his return, suggested that Swedish physicist Vagn Walfrid Ekman

(1874–1954) investigate the phenomenon mathematically. The *Ekman spiral*—a highly influential model describing wind-generated water movement at different depths—was the outcome.

Nansen devised or improved several sampling devices and measuring instruments. The *Nansen bottle,* a seawater sampler, was in use in modified forms until the 1960s, when electronic measurement of salinity largely replaced chemical methods.

On his return from the *Fram* expedition in 1896, Nansen took a professorship in zoology at Christiania. During the period from 1896 to 1917, Nansen continued his scientific work, his appointment as professor of oceanography in 1908 reflecting his change in interest.

In 1900, Nansen initiated an oceanographic study of the Norwegian Sea, joining the vessel *Michael Sars* on its voyage before handing over to his assistant Bjørn Helland-Hansen (1877– 1957). Their monograph on the Norwegian Sea became a model of its kind. Between 1910 and 1914, Nansen joined various cruises, from the Azores in the Atlantic to the Barents and Kara Seas in the Arctic, writing his findings in a series of articles, sometimes in collaboration with Helland-Hansen.

Early in the 20th century, Nansen participated in the establishment of the International Council for the Exploration of the Sea (ICES), at one period directing the council's headquarters in Christiania. From 1905, Nansen increasingly took on political roles. A passionate nationalist, Nansen was influential in the negotiated separation of Norway from Sweden. In 1917, Nansen was appointed head of the Norwegian commission to the United States. From 1920, he headed the Norwegian delegation to the League of Nations and played a lead role in this organization until his death in 1930. He spearheaded initiatives for the humanitarian treatment and resettlement of refugees and prisoners of war. Organizations such as the Nansen International Office for Refugees, founded in 1931, continued this work after his death. In 1922, Nansen was awarded the Nobel Prize for Peace.

Trevor Day

BIOGRAPHY

- Fridtjof Nansen.
- Born 10 October 1861 near Christiania (now Oslo), Norway.
- He trained as a zoologist and took his doctorate at University of Christiania in 1888.
- He led an expedition across Greenland in 1888 and then headed the *Fram* expedition (1893–96), which reached close to the North Pole and established that the Arctic was an ocean basin.
- He made developments in physical oceanographic sampling methods.
- His observations on wind-generated water movements and the dead-water effect led to important advances in physical oceanography.
- Professor of zoology at Christiania (1896–1908), then professor of oceanography (1908–17).
- From 1905, he became increasingly involved in political and humanitarian issues and was awarded the Nobel Prize for Peace in 1922.
- Died 13 May 1930 at Lysaker, near Oslo.

SELECTED WRITINGS

Nansen, Fridtjof. *Farthest North.* New York: Modern Library, 1999.

Nansen, Fridtjof, and B. Helland-Hansen. *The Norwegian Sea: Its Physical Oceanography Based upon the Norwegian Researches, 1900–1904.* Kristiania, Norway: Det Mallingske bogtrykkeri, 1909.

Nansen, Fridtjof, ed. *Norwegian North Polar Expedition, 1893–96: Scientific Results.* 6 vols. London: Greenwood Press, 1971.

FURTHER READING

Huntford, Roland. *Nansen.* London: Duckworth, 1997.

Shackleton, Edward. *Nansen the Explorer.* London: Witherby, 1959.

Sörenson, Jon. *The Saga of Fridtjof Nansen.* New York: W. W. Norton, 1932.

Vogt, Per, ed. *Fridtjof Nansen; Explorer–Scientist–Humanitarian.* Oslo: Dryers Forlag, 1961.

RELATED ARTICLES

Amundsen, Roald; Arctic Ocean; Ekman, Vagn Walfrid; *Fram;* Helland-Hansen, Bjørn; Nansen Bottle; Salinity

Nansen Bottle

A Nansen bottle is a flask used for collecting samples of seawater from different depths for later analysis in a laboratory. The bottle was invented in the late nineteenth century by Norwegian explorer and oceanographer Fridtjof Nansen (1861–1930) and is built to a standard specification. Usually, it is a cylindrical brass flask with a capacity of 1.25 liters (42.3 fluid ounces), an inert lining, and valves at either end that admit water in one position and block it from escaping in another.

In order to take samples from a particular location, a series of bottles (usually, 10 or more) are attached at set lengths along a wire and winched down into the water until the bottles are at the required depths. The bottles are anchored to the hydro wire at both ends. To close the bottles a messenger weight is released down the wire. When it hits the top attachment, the bottle flips over, its valves seal, and water is trapped inside. This action releases another messenger weight, which slides farther down the wire to trigger the next bottle.

Once hauled to the surface, the bottles can be emptied and their contents analyzed. Other instruments, such as a reversing thermometer, can be attached to the side of a bottle. These record conditions in the water at the moment the sample is taken and help to map the temperature, salinity, and density variations in the sea. Through these measurements, oceanographers can deduce the direction and strength of ocean currents both near the surface and in the deep sea. Because of contamination problems caused by the metal in the bottles, traditional Nansen bottles have been widely replaced for use in oceanographic work by modern plastic samplers.

Giles Sparrow

FURTHER READING
Grasshof, Klaus, Klaus Kremling, and Manfred Ehrhardt, eds. *Methods of Seawater Analysis.* Weinheim, Germany, and New York: Verlag Chemie, 1976; 3rd ed., Weinheim, Germany, and New York: Wiley-VCH, 1999.
Thurman, Harold V., and Alan P. Trujillo. *Essentials of Oceanography.* Columbus, Ohio: Charles E. Merrill, 1983; Upper Saddle River, N.J.: Prentice Hall, 1992; 6th ed., Upper Saddle River, N.J.: Prentice Hall, 1999.

RELATED ARTICLES
Nansen, Fridtjof; Reversing Thermometer

Nauplius

Nauplius is the name given to the distinctive, free-swimming larva produced by a diverse range of crustaceans, including copepods, barnacles, ostracods, and branchiopods. Although the adult forms of these crustaceans are very different, their nauplius larvae are similar. Nauplii are very common in ocean plankton and provide food for many other marine animals.

A nauplius has a simple body protected by a hard outer casing called a *carapace*. The body bears a single eye and three pairs of appendages (limbs), which are used for swimming. The three pairs of appendages eventually become the antennae and mouthparts of the adult crustacean. Nauplii periodically shed their outer carapace as they grow, a process known as *molting*. With each molting the nauplius changes slightly, for instance by acquiring a new body segment or a new pair of appendages. As a result, the nauplius gradually takes on the adult form as it grows. The appearance of the fourth pair of functioning limbs marks the end of naupliar development.

In some crustaceans the nauplius develops into a distinct type of larva before becoming an adult. For example, copepods pass through six naupliar stages before turning into larvae known as *copepodites*. These pass through five subsequent moltings to become adults. The nauplii of barnacles undergo an even more dramatic transformation. They develop into shelled larvae called *cyprids*. When a cyprid locates a suitable rock or other solid object on which to settle, it glues itself headfirst to the object and metamorphoses into an adult barnacle, its appendages turning into feathery filters for catching food.

Some crustaceans hatch into a slightly more advanced state of development known as a *metanauplius*. Others, such as crabs and lobsters, do not produce nauplius larvae at all. Instead, their eggs hatch into advanced larvae called *zoea*. These drift away in the plankton and slowly change into megalopa larvae, which resemble tiny lobsters, before settling on the seafloor and molting to take on the adult form.

Ben Morgan

FURTHER READING
Brusca, Richard C., and Gary J. Brusca. *Invertebrates.* Sunderland, Mass.: Sinauer, 1990.
Pechenik, Jan A. *Biology of the Invertebrates.* Boston: Prindle, Weber and Schmidt, 1985; 4th ed., Boston: McGraw-Hill, 2000.

RELATED ARTICLES
Branchiopoda; Copepod; Crustacea

Nautilus

The chambered or pearly nautilus (genus *Nautilus*) is a large swimming mollusk that lives in deep water adjacent to landmasses and possesses a distinctive planospiral shell that contains internal chambers. A relative of octopuses and squids (class Cephalopoda), it is the only living cephalopod with an external shell. There are four to six nautilus species, classified as members of the subclass Nautiloidea.

The shell of an adult nautilus measures about 25 centimeters (10 inches) across and has a smooth, pearly surface with brown and white stripes. The shell's interior possesses up to 30 to 40 chambers in adults and is arranged in a spiral. The body of the animal always occupies the large outermost chamber, and the inner chambers contain air or liquid. By adjusting the amount of air in its shell, a nautilus can control how quickly it rises or sinks in the water. As a nautilus grows, it adds new chambers to the shell, each slightly larger than the last. In the face of danger, a nautilus withdraws quickly into its shell and covers its soft flesh with a tough fold of tissue called a *hood*.

Most mollusks are slow movers, but cephalopods are an exception. By squirting a jet of water out of a special tube called a *siphon*, they can swim quickly through the water to capture prey. Nautiluses have 80 to 90 muscular tentacles that protrude from the open end of the shell. These are used for grasping prey, such as shrimp. A sharp, pincerlike beak is used to dismember meals, and a rasping tongue scrapes food into the mouth, like a cheese grater.

The living nautilus species are the only surviving members of ancient groups of animals (Nautiloidea) that were much more common millions of years ago. Scientists have identified more than 17,000 species of fossil nautiloids, and these fossils now provide an important means of dating rock strata.

The "paper nautilus" (Argonauta) is not a nautilus but a type of octopus. Females brood their eggs within a thin, fragile "shell" formed from folds of skin from the arms.

Ben Morgan

FURTHER READING
Banister, K., and A. Campbell. *The Encyclopaedia of Underwater Life.* London: Allen and Unwin, 1985.
Barnes, Robert. *Invertebrate Zoology.* Philadelphia: W. B Saunders, 1963; 6th ed., by Edward Ruppert, Fort Worth, Texas: Saunders College Publishing, 1994.
Brusca, Richard C., and Gary J. Brusca. *Invertebrates.* Sunderland, Mass.: Sinauer, 1990.
Pechenik, Jan A. *Biology of the Invertebrates.* Boston: Prindle, Weber and Schmidt, 1985; 4th ed., Boston: McGraw-Hill, 2000.

RELATED ARTICLES
Cephalopoda; Mollusca

Navigation

The word *navigation* derives from the Latin words *navis* (ship) and *agere* (to direct) and refers to the various methods used for locating an object's position on Earth or guiding it successfully from one place to another. Modern navigation applies equally to airplanes, automobiles, spacecraft, guided missiles, and indeed to anything that needs to find its way across the Earth or through space.

The basic principle of ocean navigation is to get from one place to another by following a particular course between two points on a map (usually, the shortest possible course, taking into account winds, ocean currents, dangerous waters, and so on). This involves regularly establishing a ship's position (or *fix*) and knowing how far it has traveled, in which direction it is moving, and at what speed, so that it can be kept on course. A variety of scientific instruments and maps and charts of known regions of the oceans make this a much more accurate process than in ancient times, and electronic methods have now largely replaced many of the older techniques.

Methods of Navigation

The seafarer uses four main methods of navigation: pilotage, dead reckoning, celestial navigation, and electronic navigation. *Pilotage* involves steering a course according to known landmarks. At its simplest, this involves using visual indicators such as lighthouses to navigate through rocky coastal areas or following buoys (floating markers) that indicate shipping channels. Pilotage also involves keeping watch for other ships and altering the course accordingly. A more complex form of pilotage uses landmarks to fix the ship's position precisely by a process known as *taking bearings*. This entails working out a *line of position* (LOP; a line somewhere on which the ship must be located) by using either a sighting device called a *sextant* and a known landmark, a radio, or radar

bearings. The process is then repeated once or twice more and the fix (the ship's actual position) lies at the intersection of the LOPs.

A less accurate method of finding a ship's position, known as *dead reckoning*, involves estimating where a ship is at any time by calculating how far (and in which direction) it has traveled since the previous fix. Dead reckoning is much less accurate than pilotage because it assumes steady speed in a straight line, and inaccurate measurements plus the effects of ocean currents, winds, and stormy weather can introduce errors. Nevertheless, dead reckoning gives the navigator an immediate (albeit approximate) picture of where the ship is and what course it is following.

The navigators of ancient times were more closely attuned to winds, ocean currents, and the positions of stars in the sky than are today's navigators, and something of their skill survives in *celestial navigation*. Before the invention in the eighteenth century of chronometers, accurate clocks that could precisely calculate longitude, astronomy provided the only reliable means of navigation on long voyages by comparing the relative positions of the Sun, Moon, stars, and planets. In practice, celestial navigation involves using a sextant to measure the position of a celestial body at a particular time. Using this information and a large set of tables called the *Nautical Almanac*, which lists the positions of celestial bodies at different times of day for every day of the year, the latitude and longitude of the ship can be calculated.

Navigational Instruments

Navigational instruments have changed dramatically from when Polynesian sailors used bamboo sticks to make two-dimensional wooden maps of the oceans around their islands. Today, hand-held global positioning system (GPS) receivers use satellite signals to produce a digital reading of latitude (north–south position on Earth's surface) and longitude (east–west position) to within a few feet. Navigational instruments help the navigator fix the position of a ship as accurately as possible. GPS receivers now do this automatically and almost instantaneously, but previously, navigators worked out their position by piecing together information from a number of less sophisticated instruments. In navigational terms, a fix gives the position of a ship by the intersection of two or more LOPs, which are determined by any one of several methods.

Compasses, for example, indicate direction. The navigator determines the compass bearing of charted landmarks as one or more LOPs. The navigator draws straight lines from the charted landmarks on a nautical chart. The ship's position is given by the intersection of these lines. Magnetic compasses point toward Earth's magnetic north pole, and the true north (the actual direction of north) can be calculated from this point if the magnetic declination (the angle of difference between true north and magnetic north) is known. Other types of compasses are also used because the presence of magnetism in a ship and nearby iron and steel objects can affect the accuracy of a magnetic compass.

Gyrocompasses depend on the properties of a spinning gyroscope, since a gyroscope always points in the same direction, even aboard a pitching and rolling ship. The gyrocompass is set to point northward; as the ship turns, the gyrocompass readouts indicate the ship's direction. Gyrocompass bearings toward land features can be used to obtain LOPs. Most large ships use a gyrocompass to control their inertial guidance (automatic pilot) system. Another type of compass called a radio direction finder (RDF) or radiocompass uses an antenna onboard the ship to establish the direction of a known radio beacon. Bearings between the ship and the radio station also establish one LOP.

Whereas radio compasses simply help to establish a ship's direction, other radio-based navigational instruments can be used to fix a ship's position. The loran (long-range navigation) system uses a master radio transmitter and several secondary transmitters to send out signals to a receiver onboard ship. The ship's position relative to the transmitters causes slight differences between the master and secondary signals, which can be used to work out where the ship is to an accuracy of about 50 to 500 meters (164 to 1640 feet). Although Loran is effective only in certain areas (the Loran-C system is used primarily in U.S. coastal waters, for example), various other radio-based aids provide coverage in other areas. For example, the Omega system fixes a position less accurately [to within around 3.2 kilometers (2 miles)], but provides worldwide coverage from eight transmitting stations around Earth.

Another type of radio-based navigation aid, radar (radio direction and ranging), works in the opposite way to radio beacons. It sends out a high-frequency radio signal from a transmitter onboard a ship and monitors the signals reflected back to work out the position, direction of movement, and speed of nearby obstacles. The ship's position is determined by the distance between the ship and charted features on shore or by radar bearings. Sonar (sound navigation ranging) is a similar system that uses sound waves instead of radio waves to determine water depth and to locate obstacles underwater. It is one of the main navigation instruments onboard submarines. Near shore, water depth determined by sonar gives another LOP because all ships carry charts showing water depth.

Before the advent of GPS and radio, navigators worked out their ship's latitude and longitude using a sextant. Looking through the eyepiece of the sextant at a known star, sun, or planet, the navigator moves a mirror until the reflected image of the star is superimposed on the horizon. The amount by which the mirror has moved is read off the bottom of the sextant as an angle in degrees. This "altitude" (the angle between the star and the horizon) gives one LOP. If another star sight is determined and the exact time of these sights are compared to the time at Greenwich in London, England, the ship's position can be calculated. Accurate celestial navigation requires good visibility, a sextant, an accurate chronometer, and extensive astronomical tables.

When the Sun is sighted at noon, the ship's latitude is given by the Sun's altitude, and the longitude is determined by the time difference between local noon and noon at Greenwich, where longitude is 0°. Every hour's difference in time from Greenwich corresponds to a difference in longitude of 15°. Thus New York City, about five hours west of Greenwich, has a longitude of 75°W. In the eighteenth century, the invention of chronometers that were sufficiently robust to keep time during the trials of an ocean voyage allowed for the accurate calculation of longitude, thereby solving what had been known as the *longitude problem*.

Other navigational aids include dividers, compasses, rulers for marking charts, and logs (mechanical devices of various kinds that measure the ship's speed through the water). Measurements of ocean depth are also useful for navigation if the seabed is well charted where the ship is sailing. Once made by hand leads (heavy weights hung from lines to measure ocean depths in relatively shallow waters), depth is now measured by echo sounders (which measure depth by calculating the time it takes for a sound wave to reflect from the seabed).

Electronic methods of navigation, such as Loran and GPS, have made earlier methods of navigation largely obsolete. But navigators are still trained in the traditional methods of navigation as well as the most modern. A worldwide failure of the GPS system in autumn 1999, when it switched over to a new date and time system, confirmed that the old methods of navigation remain just as valuable today as they were in ancient times.

Chris Woodford

FURTHER READING

Bowditch, Nathaniel. *The American Practical Navigator: An Epitome of Navigation.* Washington, D.C.: Government Printing Office, 1900; Bethesda, Md.: Defense Mapping Agency Hydrographic/Topographic Center, 1995.

Herring, Thomas. "The Global Positioning System." *Scientific American,* May 1996, p. 32.

Heyerdahl, Thor. *Early Man and the Ocean: A Search for the Beginnings of Navigation and Seaborne Civilizations.* Garden City, N.Y.: Doubleday, 1979.

Mellor, John. *The Art of Pilotage.* Dobbs Ferry, N.Y.: Sheridan House, 1991.

Sobel, Dava. *Longitude: The True Story of a Lone Genius Who Solved the Greatest Scientific Problem of His Time.* New York: Walker, 1995.

Williams, J. E. D. *From Sails to Satellites.* New York and Oxford: Oxford University Press, 1992.

RELATED ARTICLES

Chronometer; Compass; Global Positioning System; Loran; Magnetic Declination; Radar Altimeter; Sextant; Sonar

Nazca Plate

One of 12 major lithospheric plates that have been identified and mapped by Earth scientists since about 1965, the Nazca Plate is a small but significant plate that is entirely oceanic. Its convergence with the South American Plate has created (and is continuing to create) significant geological features along the South American continent and within the Pacific Ocean. The Nazca Plate is located off the west coast of South America and is roughly defined as a quadrilateral with vertices (0°, 100°W); (5°, 85°W); (45°S, 75°W); (33°S, 110°W). The Nazca Plate is bounded by the Cocos Plate to the north, the South American Plate to the east, the Antarctic Plate to the south, and the Pacific Plate to the west.

The East Pacific Rise on the west and the Galápagos Spreading Center on the north create new oceanic lithosphere of the Nazca Plate, which moves southeast, away from the Cocos and Pacific Plates, at the geologically rapid rate of approximately 67 millimeters (2.6 inches) per year. Because of this movement, the Nazca Plate is colliding with the western edge of the South American Plate, where it forms a convergent plate boundary with an attendant subduction zone. Upon collision, the denser oceanic Nazca Plate is forced underneath the less dense continental crust of the South American Plate. As the Nazca Plate descends deep into the mantle, parts of it and the overlying plate melt to form magma, which works its way back to the surface to form volcanoes. This geological process is continuing to build the young volcanoes that cap the Andes Mountains along the western coast of South America. The "crumpling" of the South American Plate as it rides over the descending Nazca Plate tectonically raises the land into this spectacular mountain belt. Violent earthquakes, some as large as magnitude 9.0, are associated with the destructive Nazca/South American Plate margin as well. These large earthquakes can cause great destruction and economic consequences for the people of South America.

In addition to creating the Andes Mountains, the southeast movement of the Nazca Plate is directly responsible for many of the characteristics associated with the Galápagos Islands chain. Charles Darwin formulated a large part of his famous theory on evolution by observing the fauna and flora of the Galápagos Islands. Below the Nazca Plate is a fixed hotspot that sends molten mantle material directly to Earth's surface. The molten material burns through the crust and forms an underwater volcano that eventually grows into an island. As the Nazca Plate moves over the fixed hotspot, subsequent islands are created and the island chain grows. The Galápagos Islands continue to expand in this manner.

Other important geological features are located along the boundary between the Nazca and Cocos Plates. For example, the first hydrothermal vents in the ocean were found in 1977 at a 2500-meter (8200-feet) depth along the Galápagos seafloor-spreading center, the divergent plate boundary between the Nazca and Cocos Plates. These vents are gentle warm-water hydrothermal springs where mineral-charged water emerges from the seafloor at temperatures 6 to 20°C (11 to 36°F) above the ambient bottom water (1 to 2°C or 34 to 36°F). The analysis of these vents led to the hypothesis and ensuing discovery of hydrothermal vent black smokers and associated chemosynthetic biological communities.

Daniel Schuller

FURTHER READING

Kulm, L., J. Dymond, E. J. Dasch, and D. M. Hussong, eds. "Nazca Plate: Crustal Formation and Andean Convergence." *Geological Society of America Memoir,* Vol. 154 (1981).

Open University Course Team. *The Ocean Basins: Their Structure and Evolution,* Oxford and New York: Pergamon Press/Milton Keynes, England: Open University, 1989; 2nd ed., prepared by John Wright and David A. Rothery, Oxford: Butterworth-Heinemann in association with Open University, 1998.

———. *Ocean Chemistry and Deep-Sea Sediments.* Oxford and New York: Pergamon Press/Milton Keynes, England: Open University, 1989.

RELATED ARTICLES

Cocos Plate; Convergent Plate Boundary; Farallon Plate; Galápagos Spreading Center; HotSpot; Hydrothermal Vent; Pacific Plate; Subduction Zone

Neap Tide

Neaps are those tides with the smallest tidal range (height between high water and low water) that occur within a lunar month (about 29.5 days). Neap tides take place when the Moon is at first or third quarter. On these dates, the Moon and Sun are positioned at 90° relative to Earth. During spring tides the time of maximum solar tide corresponds to the time of the maximum lunar tide, but during neap tides the time of the maximum solar tide is about six hours later than that of maximum lunar tide. That is, during neap tides the solar and lunar tides are out of phase. The relative height of the solar tide is about 46 percent of the lunar tide, and the tidal range of a neap tide may be about 20 percent smaller than the "average" tidal range for the month.

As a general rule, the tidal range is small in the deep ocean, rarely exceeding 0.5 meter (about 1.6 feet), but it increases in shallow water in a superficial manner similar to the way an ocean wave builds when it approaches the shore. However, tidal ranges in coastal waters vary enormously from one location to the next. In the Bay of Fundy, Canada, a neap tide may exceed 10 meters (about 33 feet) in tidal range, whereas along much of the Mediterranean Sea coast a neap is less than 0.5 meter (1.6 feet).

Trevor Day

FURTHER READING
Garrett, C., and L. R. M. Mass. "Tides and Their Effects." *Oceanus*, Vol. 36, No. 1 (1993), pp. 27–37.
Open University Course Team. *Waves, Tides and Shallow Water Processes*. Oxford and New York: Pergamon Press, in association with the Open University, Milton Keynes, England, 1989; 2nd ed., Boston: Butterworth-Heinemann, in association with the Open University, 1999.
Redfield, Alfred C. *Introduction to Tides*. Woods Hole, Mass.: Marine Science International, 1980.

RELATED ARTICLES
Spring Tide; Tide

Nekton

Nekton is a descriptive term that encompasses all of the fast-swimming organisms that travel at will through the water column. Most nektonic organisms are large vertebrate species such as bony fishes, sharks, and marine mammals. Unlike free-floating or weakly swimming planktonic organisms that drift with the ocean's currents, nekton can swim against the prevailing water motion and many species range over vast distances.

Oceanic (or open ocean) nekton inhabit the upper (epipelagic or photic) layers of the oceans and roam throughout a huge three-dimensional volume. This habitat exposes nekton to a variety of challenges that have resulted in adaptations (e.g., for buoyancy, swimming, and camouflage) that are similar among very different groups of animals. The term *nekton* is used most commonly to refer to species inhabiting the open ocean. Nektonic animals, however, also inhabit many other environments, including the middle depths of the ocean, the waters just above the deep-sea floor, and coastal habitats such as coral reefs and kelp beds. Inshore nekton and deep-sea nekton exhibit adaptations to their particular habitats that differ from the common adaptations found in oceanic nekton.

Types of Nekton
Nekton is composed almost exclusively of vertebrates: Some species of squid and octopus (phylum Mollusca, class Cephalopoda) are the only invertebrate nekton. The bony fishes (class Osteichthyes) and cartilaginous fishes (class Chondrichthyes) are the most abundant nektonic organisms in terms of number of species and individuals. All vertebrate classes, however, except Amphibia have nektonic representatives; lampreys and hagfish (class Agnatha), sea turtles and sea snakes (class Reptilia), sea birds (class Aves), and marine mammals (class Mammalia) all are considered nekton.

OCEANIC NEKTON
Scientists often classify open ocean fishes (bony and cartilaginous) into two groups. *Holoepipelagic nekton* are those species that spend their entire lives in the upper layers of the ocean and are most abundant in the tropics and subtropics. This group includes bony fishes such as bream, flying fish, marlin, oarfish, ocean sunfish, saury, skipjack, swordfish, and tuna and cartilaginous fishes such as blue shark, mackerel shark, thresher shark,

and white tip shark. Holoepipelagic bony fishes often produce floating eggs and have epipelagic larvae. *Meroepipelagic nekton* spend only part of their life in the epipelagic zone. A common pattern for members of this group is to live in the open ocean as adults but to migrate to inshore waters (where they are still nekton) to spawn. Dolphin, halfbeaks, herring, and whale sharks are examples of meroepipelagic nekton. Salmon, which migrate to fresh water to spawn, also fall into this category of oceanic nekton. Other meroepipelagic species spend only the juvenile part of their life in surface waters, and many species of mesopelagic (midwater) fishes migrate to surface waters only at night.

Whales, dolphins, porpoises, seals, and sea lions comprise the marine mammal component of oceanic nekton, and sea turtles represent the class Reptilia. Penguins, which do not fly, are the only true nektonic birds. Many seabird species, however, fly vast distances over the open ocean and swim on the ocean's surface, and many species can dive to considerable depth (e.g., several hundred feet) to feed. Thus, seabirds are important members of the open ocean ecosystem.

NEKTON IN OTHER HABITATS

Inshore waters host numerous species of bony fishes, sharks, and rays. Marine mammals that inhabit coastal waters include dugongs and manatees, sea otters, and dolphins and porpoises. Many whale species also spend time close to shore. Sea turtles migrate to inshore waters and ultimately lay eggs on land, and sea snakes often inhabit tropical coastal waters in the Indian and Pacific Oceans. Marine iguanas and saltwater crocodiles live in shallow water and stay near land. Many bird species venture out over inshore waters, but stay close to land as well.

Many nektonic species also inhabit the mesopelagic (midwater) zone and the waters close to the seafloor. Midwater nekton include angler fish, gulper eels, hatchetfish, lantern fish,

and squid. Midwater fish often are silvery gray or black, have large mouths, large eyes, and light organs, and undergo a daily vertical migration. The more primitive fishes dominate the deep-water assemblage, and most species are slow moving or fairly sedentary. Many lack pigment and have small or absent eyes. The most common deep-sea forms are the rat tails, brotulids, liparids, and some species of eels.

The agnathans are difficult to place into a specific habitat category. Hagfish are marine scavengers that inhabit cold water areas and often are found in deep water. Even though they live at the seafloor and burrow into the sediments, they are considered nekton because they travel through the water to feed on dead and disabled prey. Many lamprey species are parasites that attach to other fish and feed on their blood and soft tissues.

Adaptations to Nektonic Life

Nektonic animals inhabit a three-dimensional world that lacks solid substrate and shelter from predators. Nekton have successfully adapted to the challenges posed by this environment by developing methods to stay afloat, avoid predators, find food, and find each other.

One of the most significant challenges of nektonic life is to maintain buoyancy. Nektonic animals are relatively large and without special adaptations would be more dense than the water in which they live. Many fish species have a swim (gas) bladder, and they use it to regulate their buoyancy. Sharks and bony fishes that lack a swim bladder deposit large amounts of lipid in various parts of the body; lipids provide buoyancy because they are less dense than seawater. Marine mammals use lipids (stored as blubber), gas-filled cavities in their lungs, and/or air trapped under their fur to stay afloat. Air sacs in the lungs, air channels in bones, and air trapped under feathers provide buoyancy for seabirds. Squids use chemical means to ensure neutral buoyancy; they exchange light ammonium ions for the heavy sodium ions normally found in body fluids. Nekton also employ hydrodynamic mechanisms, such as pectoral fins, flippers, or a heterocercal tail (in which the top half is larger than the bottom half), to provide lift.

In a shelterless environment, nektonic animals must be able to move quickly to evade predators and to catch prey. Seawater is, however, a dense medium, and it requires great energy to move through it, especially at high speed. Thus, nektonic animals generally show adaptations to reduce surface resistance and drag. Most nektonic animals, for example, have streamlined bodies and structures that protrude from the body are modified (e.g., fins retract into grooves, eyes are not raised from the body, scales are reduced or absent, and hair is either short or absent).

In addition to speed, many nektonic species depend on camouflage as a defense against predators. Some species bear a ventral keel that helps eliminate a shadow when viewed from below. Others use cryptic coloration as camouflage. Many fishes, for example, exhibit countershading: Their dorsal surfaces are blue or green, making them invisible from above, and their ventral surfaces are white or silver, making them invisible from below.

Some groups of nektonic animals also have developed sophisticated sensory systems that allow them to navigate over vast distances, avoid predators, locate prey, and/or locate each other. Sea turtles and many species of marine mammals, seabirds, and fishes undertake extensive horizontal migrations. Many cartilaginous fishes use electroreception to find prey. Marine mammals may use a geomagnetic system for navigation, and cetaceans use echo location to avoid predators, catch prey, and communicate with each other.

Ecology

Little is known about many nektonic organisms; they are hard to study in situ and most do not survive captivity. Thus, much of what is known about the ecology, life history, and physiology of nekton is inferred from animals caught in nets or sampled with submersibles or remote-operated vehicles (ROVs).

Nekton play an important role in the ecology of the open ocean and understanding that role is a major goal of fisheries biologists and oceanographers. Nektonic animals are primarily carnivores and they are found at many trophic levels; some are top predators (e.g., sharks and killer whales), most are intermediate predators (e.g., predatory fish, seals, and sea lions that feed on other nekton), and still others are plankton feeders (e.g., baleen whales, flying fish, salmon, and whale sharks) that consume small herbivores. Many species also are important to humans and are the object of intense international fisheries. The potential for depleting fish (bony and cartilaginous), marine mammal, sea turtle, and seabird populations, either by overfishing or by destruction of habitat, has been realized in many locales. Because nektonic organisms are integral members of the oceanic food web, the effects of depletions or extinctions may reverberate throughout the ecosystem.

Lynn L. Lauerman

FURTHER READING

Aleyev, Yu G. *Nekton.* Translated from the Russian by B. M. Meerovich. The Hague: Junk, 1977.

Arseniev, V. A. *Atlas of Marine Mammals.* Neptune City, N.J.: T.F.H. Publications, 1986.

Bjorndal, Karen A., ed. *Biology and Conservation of Sea Turtles: Proceedings of the World Conference on Sea Turtle Conservation,* Washington, D.C., 26–30 November 1979. Washington, D.C.: Smithsonian Institution Press in cooperation with World Wildlife Fund, 1982.

Brodeur, Richard D., Harriet V. Lorz, and William G. Pearcy. *Food Habits and Dietary Variability of Pelagic Nekton off Oregon and Washington, 1979–84.* Seattle, Wash.: U.S. Department of Commerce, National Oceanic and Atmospheric Administration, National Marine Fisheries Service, 1987.

Dunson, William A., ed. *The Biology of Sea Snakes.* Baltimore: University Park Press, 1975.

Ellis, Richard. *The Book of Sharks.* New York: Knopf, 1989.

Freon, Pierre, and Ole Arve Misund. *Dynamics of Pelagic Fish Distribution and Behaviour: Effects on Fisheries and Stock Assessment.* Oxford: Fishing News Books, 1999.

Hardy, Alister. *The Open Sea: Its Natural History,* Vol. II, *Fish and Fisheries.* Boston: Houghton Mifflin, 1965.

Howe, Marshall A., Roger B. Clapp, and John S. Weske. *Marine and Coastal Birds.* Albany, N.Y.: New York Sea Grant Institute, 1978.

Nybakken, James W. *Marine Biology: An Ecological Approach,* 5th ed. San Francisco: Benjamin Cummings, 2001.

Parker, Steve, and Jane Parker. *The Encyclopedia of Sharks.* Buffalo, N.Y.: Firefly Books, 1999.

Scheffer, Victor B. *A Natural History of Marine Mammals.* New York: Scribner's, 1976.

RELATED ARTICLES
Cephalopoda; Cetacea; Cryptic Coloration; Food Web; Pelagic; Seal; Shark; Swim Bladder

Nematocyst

Nematocysts are microscopic hollow threads that are enclosed in a capsule and found in vast numbers on the tentacles of members of the phylum Cnidaria. They are used primarily to capture and subdue prey.

Anyone who has been stung by a jellyfish knows that nematocysts are potent weapons. Although they are minute (much less than a tenth of a millimetre in size), the combined effect of many can be extremely painful. Moreover, the nematocysts of many cnidarians are laced with a cocktail of venomous chemicals, including nerve toxins intended to paralyze and kill prey. The sting of the Portuguese man-of-war (*Physalia*) can overwhelm an adult mackerel and cause serious injury to humans. The sting of the Australian box jellyfish *Chironex* and *Chiropsalmus* (sea wasps) contains a toxin that is more powerful than cobra venom; it can kill a person in minutes.

Nematocysts are housed within special cells called *cnidocytes*, which are found on a cnidarian's tentacles and body. They are most concentrated on the tentacles, where they sometimes occur in wartlike clusters called *nematocyst batteries.* Each nematocyst consists of a tightly coiled hollow tube held within a capsule inside the cnidocyte. A microscopic bristle or hair serves as a trigger. When a prey animal activates the trigger—either by touching it or by causing vibrations in the water—the tube is discharged. The hollow tube everts itself like a sock being pulled inside out. It turns inside out with a twisting motion, drilling its way into the prey's body with the help of tiny spines arranged in a spiral pattern along its length. Venom is injected through the tube, and backward-pointing barbs at the base of the tube snag in the flesh, holding the prey.

Nematocysts vary from one species to another and different types of nematocyst can be found in one individual. Some serve to penetrate flesh; others stick to or tangle around the prey. As well as helping to capture food, nematocysts help ward off predators, although some predators seem to be immune to their effects.

Ben Morgan

FURTHER READING
Brusca, Richard C., and Gary J. Brusca. *Invertebrates.* Sunderland, Mass.: Sinauer, 1990.

Nybakken, James W. *Marine Biology: An Ecological Approach,* 5th ed. San Francisco: Benjamin Cummings, 2001.

Pechenik, Jan A. *Biology of the Invertebrates.* Boston: Prindle, Weber and Schmidt, 1985; 4th ed., Boston: McGraw-Hill, 2000.

RELATED ARTICLES
Cnidaria; Jellyfish

Nematoda

Nematodes (phylum Nematoda; also known as roundworms or threadworms) are small cylindrical worms with unsegmented bodies. They are one of the most widespread phyla of animals on Earth and are found in vast numbers in an enormous range of habitats, including the sea, coastal mud, soil, fresh water, and in the bodies of both plants and animals, where they commonly live as parasites. A rotting apple may contain as many as 90,000 nematodes, and a shovelful of soil may contain 1 million. Some nematode species are found in a range of habitats, but others are highly specific—one is known to live only in beer mats in certain parts of Europe, for instance.

There are more than 15,000 named species of nematodes, but the true number of species may be more than 1 million. They range in size from a thousandth of a millimeter long to parasites of whales that can reach 7 meters (23 feet) in length. Parasitic species are the largest but most free-living nematodes are small or microscopic. They typically have thin, cylindrical bodies that are transparent and taper to a point at both ends. Unlike earthworms, nematodes do not have body segments and their muscles are aligned only lengthwise. They never inch along like segmented worms (phylum Annelida); instead, they move with a characteristic thrashing motion that makes them easy to recognize under the microscope.

Nematodes have a simple nervous system but no circulatory or respiratory system; oxygen is absorbed through the skin from the watery environment in which they live. At the front of the body is the mouth, which in predatory species may be equipped with a set of vicious teeth. Some parasites have a ring of hooks around the mouth to anchor themselves to the host's body. The mouth leads to a muscular pharynx, designed for sucking in food, and to a simple digestive tract that runs in a straight line through the body, without loops or coils. Unlike flatworms, which are hermaphroditic, most nematode species have separate male and female sexes. After mating, the female releases eggs into her environment. Some species reproduce at an incredible rate—females have been known to lay 200,000 eggs a day.

Scientists know a great deal about parasitic nematodes because many cause human diseases, including trichinosis, toxocariasis, and intestinal worms (hookworms). However, less is known about free-living marine species, although nematodes are abundant in every type of marine habitat, from sandy beaches to abyssal depths. One study found 236 nematode species in just 0.065 liter (2.2 fluid ounces) of coastal mud, and there may be an even greater diversity of nematodes in deep-sea sediment. Free-living marine nematodes play an important role in benthic ecology by helping to recycle the nutrients in sediment, and many provide food for fish, crustaceans, and other animals. Other marine nematodes live as parasites, and a few species live symbiotically in the gills of fish.

The phylum Nematoda is divided into two classes: Adenophorea and Secernentea. Most free-living and marine species belong to the class Adenophorea, whereas most parasites and terrestrial species are placed in the class Secernentea.

Ben Morgan

FURTHER READING

Brusca, Richard C., and Gary J. Brusca. *Invertebrates.* Sunderland, Mass.: Sinauer, 1990.

Margulis, Lynn. *Five Kingdoms: An Illustrated Guide to the Phyla of Life on Earth.* San Francisco: W. H. Freeman, 1982; 3rd ed., New York, 1998.

Pechenik, Jan A. *Biology of the Invertebrates.* Boston: Prindle, Weber and Schmidt, 1985; 4th ed., Boston: McGraw-Hill, 2000.

Postlethwait, John. *The Nature of Life.* New York: McGraw-Hill, 1989; 3rd ed., 1995.

Purves, William, et al. *Life: The Science of Biology.* Sunderland, Mass.: Sinauer/Boston: Grant Press, 1983; 5th ed., Sunderland, Mass.: Sinauer, 1998.

RELATED ARTICLES
Benthos; Meiobenthos; Meiofauna ; Parasitism

Nemertea

Nemerteans, commonly called *ribbon worms,* are soft-bodied nonsegmented worms. Some have strikingly beautiful colors and color patterns.

Approximately 1200 species are described, with many additional species not yet named. Most nemerteans are marine, although there are a few freshwater and terrestrial species. Most species are benthic; about 100 pelagic species live in the water column of deep-sea areas. A few species live on or in other animals. They range in size from a few millimeters to several meters (less than 0.25 inch to several yards) in length. The longest animal ever recorded (*Guinness Book of Records*) was a 54-meter (177-foot) specimen of the nemertean *Lineus longissimus* found off Scotland in 1864. Nemerteans have long been considered to be relatives of flatworms (Platyhelminthes); however, molecular and electron microscopic studies of the past 15 to 20 years indicate that they are coelomate protostomes, related to such groups as annelids and mollusks.

The easily recognized unique feature of nemerteans is the presence of a tonguelike structure called the *proboscis*, enclosed in a fluid-filled coelomic cavity (rhynchocoel) dorsal to and separate from the digestive tract. The proboscis is used primarily for prey capture. In classification, nemerteans are divided into two classes, Anopla and Enopla. In the Enopla, the proboscis is armed with a needlelike stylet or pad bearing several small stylets and contains toxin; anoplan proboscides are simple tubes. Most nemerteans are predators on crustaceans, polychaete worms, or clams. When a nemertean senses the presence of a prey organism, it quickly everts the sticky proboscis and wraps it around the prey, and, if an enoplan, paralyzes the prey via the toxins that enter after the stylet makes a hole in the prey. Prey such as polychaetes are swallowed whole; those enoplans that feed on crustaceans make a hole in the prey's skeleton, then suck out the prey's internal fluids. Nemerteans can have substantial effects on prey populations and can be of importance to humans. For example, *Carcinonemertes*, which lives on host crabs and feeds on developing crab embryos, can wipe out entire clutches of eggs. *Carcinonemertes* has been suggested as a factor in the decline in abundance of some commercially important crab species. In addition to the toxins found in the proboscis of enoplans, nemerteans typically have toxins in their skin. A few nemerteans have even been found to harbor tetrodotoxins. These toxins deter most types of animals from feeding on nemerteans.

Most nemerteans have separate sexes. Both ovaries and testes are usually located in spaces between lateral branches of the digestive tract along both sides of the body. In pelagic nemerteans, however, testes of males are located in clusters near the brain. Fertilization is external in most nemerteans, with gametes being shed into the sea; in gelatinous strings or masses; or into secreted cocoons, burrows, or tubes of the adults. Enoplans and some anoplans have direct development, although developing young living in the water column are called *larvae*. Other anoplans have indirect development, with larvae (e.g., the pilidium) that undergo metamorphosis into worms.

Pamela Roe

FURTHER READING
Barnes, Robert. *Invertebrate Zoology.* Philadelphia: W. B. Saunders, 1963; 6th ed., by Edward Ruppert, Fort Worth, Texas: Saunders College Publishing, 1994.
Gibson, Ray. *Nemerteans.* London: Hutchinson, 1972.
MacGinitie, George E., and Nettie MacGinitie. *Natural History of Marine Animals.* New York: McGraw-Hill, 1949; 2nd ed., 1968.

RELATED ARTICLES
Benthos; Pelagic

Neopterygii

The Neopterygii (from the Greek *neos*, "new," and *pteryx*, "fin") is a major subclass of bony fishes within the class Actinopterygii (ray-finned fishes). The fossil record suggests that

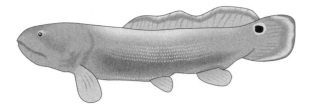

Example of the subclass neopterygii, *of the order* amiiformes, *of the family* amiidae *(bowfins).*

neopterygians evolved from a line of the original ray-finned fishes (Chondrostei) by the late Permian Period (290 to 247.5 million years ago). Today, the relict chondrosteans—sturgeons, paddlefishes, and the bichir—all live in fresh water and are represented by only 36 species. Neopterygians, on the other hand, are amazingly diverse and abundant today, live in marine and freshwater habitats, and include approximately 24,000 described species.

Neopterygians diversified during the Mesozoic era (247.5 to 65 million years ago) and ultimately gave rise to two lineages (or groups): the *nonteleosts* (formerly known as *holosteans*, the Holostei) and the *teleosts* (Teleostei). The nonteleost neopterygians are today represented by only two surviving genera, both living in fresh water: the gars, *Lepisosteus* (order Semionotiformes), and the bowfin, *Amia* (order Amiiformes). The modern lineage of neopterygians is the incredibly diverse group, the teleosts. According to Joseph S. Nelson's *Fishes of the World* (1994), the teleosts are represented by 38 living orders, 426 families, and almost 24,000 species (the status of the Teleostei, and allocation of subgroups within it, varies according to authority). The major evolutionary trend within the neopterygians is toward fishes that have greater maneuverability, wider dietary choices, and improved respiratory efficiency than the chondrosteans.

Trevor Day

FURTHER READING
Long, John A. *The Rise of Fishes.* Baltimore: Johns Hopkins University Press, 1995.

McFarland, William N., et al. *Vertebrate Life.* New York: Macmillan, 1979; 5th ed., edited by Harvey F. Pough, Christine M. Janis, and John B. Heiser, Upper Saddle River, N.J.: Prentice Hall, 1999.

Moyle, Peter B., and Joseph J. Cech. *Fishes: An Introduction to Ichthyology.* Englewood Cliffs, N.J.: Prentice Hall, 1982; 4th ed., Upper Saddle River, N.J.: Prentice Hall, 2000.

Nelson, Joseph S. *Fishes of the World.* New York: Wiley, 1976; 3rd ed., 1994.

Paxton, John R., and William N. Eschmeyer, eds. *Encyclopedia of Fishes.* San Diego: Academic Press, 1995; 2nd ed., 1998.

RELATED ARTICLES
Actinopterygii; Chondrostei; Teleostei

Neritic Zone

The water filling the oceans constitutes the pelagic environment (in contrast to the *benthic*, or bottom, environment). Scientists divide the vast pelagic environment into two major provinces: the neritic zone and the oceanic zone. The *neritic zone* encompasses the water overlying the continental shelf (the undersea extension of the continent); this zone begins at the low water mark and ends when water depth reaches 200 meters (656 feet). The continental shelf represents only about 7 to 8 percent of the seafloor; thus the vast majority of seawater is found in the oceanic zone.

The *oceanic zone* extends from the sea surface to the deepest trenches of the ocean and can be subdivided into several zones based on depth and changing physical and biological characteristics. The shallow coastal waters of the neritic zone, on the other hand, comprise only an *epipelagic zone*, which by definition ranges from the sea surface to about 200 meters (656 feet) deep. The lower boundary of the *euphotic* (lighted) *zone* is usually between 100 and 200 meters (328 to 656 feet); thus primary productivity occurs throughout most of the neritic zone. Inshore waters are rich in nutrients and plant life and support a great diversity of animal life, including many neritic species of fish and invertebrates that are the basis of some of the world's greatest fisheries.

Lynn L. Lauerman

FURTHER READING

Lalli, Carol M., and Timothy R. Parsons. *Biological Oceanography: An Introduction.* Oxford and New York: Pergamon Press, 1993; 2nd ed., Oxford: Butterworth-Heinemann, 1997.

Nybakken, James W. *Marine Biology: An Ecological Approach.* 5th ed. San Francisco: Benjamin Cummings, 2001.

RELATED ARTICLES

Continental Shelf; Epipelagic Zone; Euphotic Zone; Oceanic Zone; Primary Productivity

Net Plankton

Plankton is the term describing both the plant and animal species that drift passively in the water. They are sampled either by taking water samples or by towing nets that filter them out of the water. *Net plankton* is the term used to describe the organisms that are caught in nets. The nets may be hauled vertically or towed either obliquely or horizontally. They may be lowered open, or closed and then opened and closed again to sample selected depths. The size of the nets' meshes determines the size of the organisms retained; the finer the mesh, the smaller the organisms retained. The drag of the net, however, increases as the mesh gets finer, so that the fine mesh nets have to be hauled more slowly. The smaller organisms are also much more abundant than the larger ones, and smaller nets are needed to collect a representative sample. The fine-meshed nets, however, tend to clog more rapidly and can be towed only short distances if quantitative samples are being collected.

The mean size of the plankton increases with depth, and at the same time the overall biomass of plankton decreases. At a depth of 1000 meters (3280 feet) the biomass is about a tenth of that near the surface, and it declines to a hundredth at a depth of 4000 meters (13,120 feet); thus the deeper the sampling, the more water that needs to be filtered to obtain a meaningful sample.

Net plankton is usually dominated by copepods, but other groups of organisms form swarms and dominate the catches locally. The numbers of species caught increase from the high latitudes toward the tropics and also with depth to a maximum of 1000 meters (3280 feet).

Martin Angel

FURTHER READING

Harris, Roger P. *Ices Zooplankton Methodology Manual.* New York: Academic Press, 2000.

RELATED ARTICLES

Copepod; Plankton; Plankton Net

Neuston

Neuston are the varied planktonic organisms that float at or on the sea surface or live in the upper layer just below it. Neuston (from the Greek *neo,* to swim) are also known as *pleuston* (from the Greek *pleo,* to float). Since some members of the neuston swim while others float and there are marine water skaters that simply stand on the sea surface, both terms can be considered accurate.

It was only slowly realized that the organisms of the neuston were different from those in the sea below. The concept of a unique neuston ecosystem was first generally accepted in the mid-1950s, when the work of the pioneer Soviet scientist A. I. Savilov made it clear that the neuston was a special group of organisms, adapted to the somewhat hostile sea-surface conditions such as high ultraviolet-B radiation and changing salinity and temperature.

The biology of the neuston is closely linked to the chemistry and physics of the surface layers. In particular, the pico- [< 2 micrometers (0.00008 inch)] and microneuston [2 to 200 micrometers (0.00008 to 0.008 inch)] are involved in geochemical cycling processes within the micrometer-thick surface microlayer, and by releasing particulates such as dimethyl sulfoxide and influencing bubble dispersion of material into the atmosphere, they are involved directly in cloud formation over the oceans. Since clouds play a critical role in modulating the global radiation balance, global climate is in part regulated by the neuston. Both pico- and microneuston are abundant [almost 30 percent of the biomass as carbon is in organisms < 2 micrometers (0.00008 inch)] and play a crucial role in the neuston food web.

The larger macrozooneuston include copepods, and larger predators such as the Portuguese man-of-war *Physalia* and other cnidarians, as well as many larval forms that are benthic as adults. The smaller macrozooneuston provide food for the larvae of important fish species such as cod and sole.

Quentin Bone

FURTHER READING
Liss, P. S., and R. A. Druce, eds. *The Sea Surface and Global Change.* Cambridge: Cambridge University Press, 1997.
Nybakken, James W. *Marine Biology: An Ecological Approach,* 5th ed. San Francisco: Benjamin Cummings, 2001.
Savilov, A. I. "Pleuston of the Pacific Ocean." In *Biology of the Pacific Ocean,* ed. by L. A. Zenkevitch. Moscow: NOO translation no. 487, 1969.

RELATED ARTICLES
Benthos; Cnidaria; Copepod; Plankton

New Hebrides Island Arc

The New Hebrides Island Arc is located in the southwest Pacific, 500 to 1500 kilometers (310 to 930 miles) southeast of the Solomon Islands Arc, about 500 kilometers (310 miles) northeast of New Caledonia, and 1000 kilometers (620 miles) due west of Fiji between approximately 11°30' and 23°10'S latitude and 166°45' and 172°10'E longitude. The arc includes islands of both the Solomon Islands (Santa Cruz Group) and the Republic of Vanuatu and New Caledonia (Matthew and Hunter Islands). Vanuatu occupies most of the arc, extending from the Torres group of islands in the north to Matthew Island in the south, a distance of almost 700 kilometers (435 miles).

The landmass is a narrow chain of Tertiary through Holocene (about 50 million years ago to present) volcanic islands and extends some 1000 kilometers (620 miles) from Nendo Island in the north to Hunter in the south. The island chain can be divided into three major parts:

1. The narrow northern part, comprising the major islands of Nendo, Utupua, and Vanikolo (the Santa Cruz Group), the Torres Islands, Vot Tande, Ureparapara, Mata Lava, Vanua Lava, Mata, Merig, Santa Maria, and Mere Lava
2. The broader Central Basin part, comprising the islands of Espritu Santo, Maewo, Aoba, Malakula, Pentecost, and Ambrym
3. The narrow southern part, comprising the major islands of Lopevi, Epi, Tongoa, Efate Erromango, Aniwa, Tanna, Futuna, Tanna, Anatom, Matthew, and Hunter.

Many smaller islands, too numerous to name here, are also part of the New Hebrides Island Arc.

Physiography

The New Hebrides Island Arc is the product of active and past subduction and consists of three major physiographic components: trench, arc platform complex with an active volcanic chain, and back-arc region. The trench is a linear depression that generally parallels the western margin of the arc and is well developed southwest of the island of Malakula and northwest of Espiritu Santo Island, where it averages 6000 meters (19,685 feet) in depth, with isolated areas as deep as 7000 meters (22,970 feet). North of the Torres Islands, depths of more than 9000 meters (29,530 feet) have been recorded. However, the trench is active in the central area, where the D'Entrecasteaux zone of ridges meets the arc. The arc platform complex is a broad region of complicated topography and geology that contains the active volcanic chain—a sinuous, generally north/northwest-trending series of active or recently active volcanic islands. The width and form of this complex varies considerably along the arc, although the active volcanic chain lies generally 150 kilometers (93 miles) east of the trench. Within the arc platform complex and bounded on the east by the back-arc zone is an intra-arc sedimentary basin, the Central Basin. Under the physiographic Central Basin, this intra-arc basin includes the North Aoba and South Aoba sedimentary basins. The backarc, which is characterized by irregular seafloor at a water depth of 2000 to 3000 meters (6560 to 9840 feet), is continuous eastward with the North Fiji Basin.

Geology

The New Hebrides Arc is part of a narrow chain of Tertiary [about 50 million to 1.6 million years ago (Ma)] and Quaternary (about 1.6 to 0.01 Ma) volcanic island arcs extending from Papua New Guinea and the Solomon Islands, through Fiji, Tonga, and the Kermadec Islands to New Zealand. The New Hebrides Arc is a partly emerged ridge with an average width of 200 kilometers (124 miles). This ridge is underlain by an east-dipping subduction zone that is fairly continuous along the length of the arc and marks the site of collision of the Australia–India Plate with the Pacific Plate. The trace of plate convergence is morphologically expressed by the New Hebrides Trench. Near the islands of Matthew and Hunter, the trench passes eastward into a complex basin and ridge feature known as the Hunter Fracture Zone.

The earliest known geologic observations in the arc are attributed to the explorer Queiros, the first European to visit the islands, in 1606. He is quoted as having seen smoke rising from the now-extinct Mere Lava volcano in the Banks Islands. Over 150 years later in 1774, Captain James Cook (1728–79), on his second voyage of exploration to the Pacific, landed at Port Resolution on the island of Tanna, where he sampled the hot springs and witnessed an eruption of Yasur volcano. In the next 100 years or so, accounts of volcanic activity by early Christian missionaries and descriptions of rock specimens collected during naval visits were reported.

Sir Douglas Mawson (1882–1958), who visited most of the islands in 1903, made the first systematic geologic investigations. He recognized the essentially volcanic nature of the archipelago and the presence of raised coral platforms in many areas. Mineral prospecting in the 1930s, in particular by the French geologist Aubert de la Rue, led to reconnaissance accounts of the general geology and volcanism of individual islands. However, it was not until after World War II that the first geologic maps were produced. These maps largely were based on research instigated by French mining companies. Modern mapping of the arc was undertaken during the rule of the British-French Condominium of the New Hebrides and since 1989 by the Department of Mines, Geology and Rural Water Supply of Vanuatu.

H. Gary Greene

Further Reading

Carney, John, and Alexander Macfarlane. "Geological Evidence Bearing on the Miocene to Recent Structural Evolution of the New Hebrides Arc." *Tectonophysics*, Vol. 87 (1982), pp. 147–175.

Greene, H. Gary, Jean-Yves Collot, and Laural Stokking, et al. *Proceedings of the Ocean Drilling Program*, Vol. 134, *Scientific Results*. Washington, D.C.: U.S. Government Printing Office, 1994.

Greene, H. Gary, and Florence Wong, eds. *Geology and Offshore Resources of Pacific Island Arcs, Vanuatu Region*. Earth Science Series, Vol. 8. Houston, Texas: Circum-Pacific Council for Energy and Mineral Resources, 1988.

Mawson, D. "The Geology of the New Hebrides." *Linnean Society of New South Wales, Proceedings*, Vol. 30, No. 3 (1905), pp. 400–485.

RELATED ARTICLES
India Plate; Island Arc; Pacific Plate; Plate Tectonics; Subduction Zone

Ninetyeast Ridge

On any map showing the Indian Ocean seafloor, Ninetyeast Ridge is an unusual, eye-catching feature. It is a long, narrow, linear volcanic ridge that stretches north–south across almost the entire Indian Ocean and is one of the longest volcanic chains in the world. Were it on the surface of another planet, its unusual linearity might have suggested to some that it was built by "little green men." Indeed, its fortuitous location at almost exactly 90°E longitude (hence its odd name) might well fuel such speculation.

Ninetyeast Ridge extends more than 4000 kilometers (2490 miles) from 31°S to 5°N, where it disappears beneath the Bengal Fan (a thick pile of sediments dumped on the ocean floor from the mouths of the Ganges and Brahmaputra Rivers), about 550 kilometers (342 miles) west of the northwest tip of the island of Sumatra. Geophysical data indicate that it continues another 1000 kilometers (621 miles) northward beneath the fan. The ridge is not aligned perfectly with the 90°E meridian; it trends slightly east of north and it crosses 90°E longitude near the equator. In width, Ninetyeast Ridge varies little along its length, from about 100 to 200 kilometers (62 to 124 miles). On average it stands 2000 meters (6562 feet) above the surrounding seafloor and its summit depths range from about 2000 meters (6562 feet) at its southern end to almost 3000 meters (9840 feet) on its north end. Near the middle of the ridge at 14°S, Osborn Knoll, a 200-kilometer (124-mile)-diameter seamount, sticks out as an appendage on the west flank of the ridge. At its southern terminus, Ninetyeast Ridge merges with Broken Ridge, another volcanic edifice that stretches 1300 kilometers (808 miles) eastward, to form a giant "L" on the seafloor.

Although unusual in appearance, Ninetyeast Ridge is constructed of normal ocean rocks—basalt lavas to be exact. Samples drilled by the Deep Sea Drilling Project during the early 1970s and by the Ocean Drilling Program during the late 1980s recovered basalt from beneath a variable cover, typically 100 to 300 meters (328 to 984 feet) of pelagic sediments collected on the ridge summit. Because it is a large, long, linear edifice, Ninetyeast Ridge is an unusual volcanic feature. Most geologists think that it formed from hotspot (mantle plume) volcanism but with complications due to the volcanic source interacting with a fracture zone. As the Australia–India Plate drifted northward during the Cretaceous (142 to 65 million years ago) and Tertiary (65 million years to present) periods, it passed over a mantle plume, leaving a linear volcanic trace, the Ninetyeast Ridge. This progression is supported by ages of volcanic rocks from the ridge, which decrease southward, from 82 million years on the north to 38 million years near the intersection with Broken Ridge on the south. Because the ridge is so straight and because it does not precisely follow the trends of other hotspot ridges in the Indian Ocean, the volcanism may have been steered by a north/south-trending fracture zone (the scar of a transform fault on the Southeast Indian spreading ridge). This fracture may have acted as a weak zone, providing a conduit for magma to rise to the seafloor. Volcanism on Ninetyeast Ridge seems to have stopped 38 million years ago when the Southeast Indian Ridge drifted over the hotspot and subsequent volcanic eruptions occurred on the Antarctic Plate, to the south of the spreading ridge.

William W. Sager

FURTHER READING

Duncan, Robert A. "Age Distrubution of Volcanism along Aseismic Ridges in the Eastern Indian Ocean." In Jeffrey K. Weissel, et al., eds., *Proceedings of the Ocean Drilling Program, Scientific Results*, Vol. 121. College Station, Texas: Ocean Drilling Program, 1991.

Kennett, James. *Marine Geology*. Englewood Cliffs, N.J.: Prentice Hall, 1982.

Luyendyk, Bruce P. "Deep Sea Drilling on the Ninetyeast Ridge: Synthesis and a Tectonic Model." In James R. Heirtzler, et al., eds., *Indian Ocean Geology and Biostratigraphy*. Washington, D.C.: American Geophysical Union, 1977.

Royer, Jean-Yves, John W. Peirce, and Jeffrey K. Weissel. "Tectonic Constraints on the Hot-Spot Formation of Ninetyeast Ridge." In Jeffrey K. Weissel, et al., eds., *Proceedings of the Ocean Drilling Program, Scientific Results*. Vol. 121. College Station, Texas: Ocean Drilling Program, 1991.

RELATED ARTICLES
Hotspot; India Plate; Mantle Plume; Seamount

Nitrogen

Nitrogen is a difficult element to study because it exists in the ocean in many forms, under a variety of oxidation states, and shows great spatial and temporal variations. It is the ninth-most-abundant element in seawater at approximately 1.4×10^{13} tonnes (1.5×10^{13} tons) total nitrogen. Nitrogen can exist as inorganic and organic species and as dissolved or particulate forms of the latter species. The various forms of nitrogen in the ocean are controlled primarily by oxidation and reduction reactions involving bacteria and phytoplankton. The marine nitrogen cycle, involving the atmosphere, water column, and sediments, is closely linked to other elemental cycles. Currently, human activities are perturbing the nitrogen cycle and may have the potential to affect global climate, oceanic circulation, and sea level.

Some important species of dissolved inorganic nitrogen (DIN) in the ocean include dimolecular nitrogen gas (N_2), nitrate ion (NO_3^-), nitrite ion (NO_2^-), ammonia gas (NH_3), and ammonium ion (NH_4^+). Approximately 95 percent of nitrogen in the ocean exists as dissolved dimolecular nitrogen gas. This is due to equilibration between the ocean and atmosphere, which is almost 80 percent N_2. Most of this form of nitrogen is biologically unusable due to the strong nitrogen–nitrogen triple bond. However, some nitrogen-fixing organisms such as cyanobacteria can break this bond and form biologically useful forms of nitrogen such as nitrate.

Nitrate (NO_3^-) is the second-most-abundant form of nitrogen in the ocean. It is an important nutrient that phytoplankton require for the formation of amino acids, the building blocks of proteins. Nitrate and other nutrients show large vertical and horizontal segregation in the ocean based on biological, physical, and chemical processes. Other DIN species, such as ammonia gas and ammonium ion, can also be biologically assimilated (absorbed) to form amino acids and other nitrogen–organic complexes. The form of ammonia (gas or ion) is controlled by the pH of seawater. In oxygenated waters, some bacteria oxidize ammonia to nitrate, a process called *nitrification*. Nitrite ion (NO_2^-) is an intermediary in the stepwise nitrification process and a major reservoir of nitrogen in the ocean.

Organic nitrogen can be found in either dissolved or particulate forms. Phytoplankton assimilate DIN to form amino acids and other nitrogen–organic complexes that are thought to be used largely for cellular osmoregulation. When phytoplankton die, their cells and release dissolved organic nitrogen (DON). DON is bacterially degraded or consumed by protozoans and zooplanktons in the photic zone. Dissolved organic nitrogen (DON) is the major form of organic nitrogen and is the third-largest reservoir of nitrogen in the ocean, behind N_2 and NO_3^-.

Particulate organic nitrogen (PON) is found primarily as sinking organic particles (fecal pellets) produced by phytoplankton grazers. Sinking PON particles are the primary method of transporting organic nitrogen out of the photic zone. Most PON particles are bacterially respired to DIN in the oxygen minimum zone; hence DIN goes through a maximum in this region The recycling of nitrogen between the different forms of DIN, DON, and PON is one crucial fraction of the marine nitrogen cycle.

Currently, humans are adding major amounts of DIN to the ocean and may be perturbing the nitrogen cycle. Industrial processes are fixing large quantities of atmospheric nitrogen to make (primarily) nitrate fertilizers that eventually end up in the ocean via groundwater and stormwater runoff. In some areas this has increased coastal nitrate concentrations and stimulated productivity. To respire elevated amounts of organic matter, bacteria respond by utilizing all available oxygen and can cause basins to become anoxic, which is harmful to marine life. This has happened recently to Chesapeake Bay in Maryland. In anoxic waters denitrification can occur. Denitrification is a bacterial process in which organic matter is respired using nitrate ion as the electron acceptor instead of oxygen. This ultimately converts nitrate ion back into dimolecular nitrogen. An important by-product of the denitrification process is nitrous oxide (N_2O), a greenhouse gas.

Clearly, complex positive feedback loops link the biogeochemical cycle of nitrogen with other elemental cycles, such as carbon, oxygen, phosphorus, and sulfur. These feedback loops are not very well understood; therefore, human perturbations of the nitrogen cycle may have the potential to alter biological and chemical conditions of seawater, which can in turn significantly alter global climate and thus oceanic circulation, and sea-level position.

Daniel Schuller

FURTHER READING
Libes, Susan M. *Marine Biogeochemistry.* New York: Wiley, 1992.
Millero, Frank J. *Chemical Oceanography.* Boca Raton, Fla.: CRC Press, 1992; 2nd ed., 1996.
Open University Course Team. *Ocean Chemistry and Deep-Sea Sediments.* Oxford and New York: Pergamon Press/Milton Keynes, England: Open University, 1989.

RELATED ARTICLES
Biogeochemical Cycle; Carbon Cycle; Cyanobacteria; Nitrogen Cycle; Oxygen Minimum Zone; Photic Zone; Phytoplankton

Nitrogen Cycle

Nitrogen is the most abundant element in the atmosphere and a vital ingredient in amino acids, proteins, and nucleic acids—necessary components of all living material. The nitrogen cycle describes the flow of nitrogen, in its various forms, through the natural environment. Nitrogen is removed from the atmosphere and transformed by microorganisms (bacteria) into forms that pass through terrestrial and oceanic food webs. The nitrogen cycle is closed by other microorganisms, which transform nitrogen into a form that replenishes the atmosphere. Even though the nitrogen cycle is controlled primarily by biological organisms, human impacts are causing great changes in the flows of nitrogen between the land, ocean, atmosphere, and sediments.

Nitrogen Species
Nitrogen in the environment is found naturally in a variety of forms, or chemical species. In the marine environment, these include nitrate, nitrite, and ammonium ions (dissolved inorganic nitrogen); nitrogen, nitrous oxide, and nitrogen oxide gases; and organic nitrogen compounds, including biomolecules such as amino acids, proteins, and chlorophyll.

Even though nitrate is the equilibrium-predicted form of nitrogen in the presence of oxygen, most nitrogen is found as nitrogen gas—a molecule containing two nitrogen atoms joined by a triple bond. Only a very few bacteria species can utilize this form of nitrogen by breaking the triple bond through the process of nitrogen fixation. All other organisms must use nitrogen in an available form (such as nitrate, nitrite, or ammonia). Nitrate, for example, is supplied to seawater by rainfall and river runoff. Oceanic distributions of nitrogen vary greatly both geographically and seasonally. Since primary production of organic matter can be limited in ocean regions containing low nitrogen, it is considered a biolimiting element.

Nitrogen Fixation

The greatest quantity of nitrogen in the atmosphere and the oceans is found as nitrogen gas. These large reservoirs of nitrogen can be utilized only if the nitrogen is fixed. This process requires substantial energy input and is accomplished in nature by only a few bacteria and algae species (biological fixation) and lightning (atmospheric fixation). Human-driven processes that fix nitrogen include production of fertilizers and burning of fossil fuels in internal combustion engines. In fact, these anthropogenic (caused by humans) sources produce nearly twice as much fixed nitrogen as do natural sources.

Marine Nitrogen Cycle

Although cycling of nitrogen also occurs between the atmosphere, terrestrial plants, and soils, the primary focus of this section is on nitrogen cycling through the oceans—the marine nitrogen cycle. The basic components of this cycle include assimilation (uptake) by phytoplankton, transfer through food webs, degradation by bacteria (regenerating dissolved inorganic nitrogen), nitrification, denitrification, and nitrogen fixation.

Marine phytoplankton—plants that are the primary producers of the ocean—absorb fixed forms of nitrogen to meet their needs for photosynthesis. Phytoplankton can take up nitrate, nitrite, ammonia, and/or urea that are dissolved in the water. Once inside the cell wall, these forms of nitrogen are changed into substances used in the plant's metabolism. The process whereby phytoplankton reduce nitrate to a form they can utilize is called *assimilatory nitrate reduction*. Since energy is required, assimilatory nitrate reduction occurs only in the euphotic zone (the depth zone through which light penetrates).

Phytoplankton produce organic matter, which contains a form of solid nitrogen often called particulate organic nitrogen (PON), which has two possible fates. The organism may die and its PON dissolves, or it is remineralized into dissolved organic nitrogen (DON). DON can be degraded by bacteria into dissolved inorganic nitrogen (DIN), which can again be used by phytoplankton for primary production. A second possibility is that phytoplankton are eaten by other organisms, which in turn excrete and/or die. This returns DON to the system, again to be degraded by bacteria to DIN and ultimately reused by phytoplankton.

Heterotrophs (organisms that cannot synthesize organic matter) can transform nitrogen in several ways. As mentioned above, heterotrophic bacteria degrade DON, producing ammonia. The ammonia reacts with seawater to form ammonium (a positively charged ion) through a process called ammonification. Other biomolecules, including proteins, can then be made by organisms.

Ammonium ions generated by the decomposition of organic matter can be transformed by certain species of marine bacteria (*Nitrosomonas* and *Nitrobacter*) into nitrite and nitrate through the process of *nitrification*. This process regenerates nitrate and occurs only in oxygenated seawater, as the reactions are aerobic (requiring oxygen).

If seawater has low oxygen concentrations or is anoxic (lacking oxygen), denitrification can occur. Certain heterotrophic bacteria species respire (metabolize) organic matter, changing nitrate into nitrogen gas (some ammonium is also produced). Since this transformation makes a form of nitrogen unavailable to most living organisms (including those bacteria that formed the nitrogen gas as a by-product of respiration), denitrification is also termed *dissimilatory nitrate reduction*. Areas favorable for denitrification include oxygen-minimum zones in the water column and shallow sediments.

Nitrogen fixation is the process of breaking the triple bond of nitrogen gas to produce forms of nitrogen useful to organisms. Nitrogen fixation is very energy expensive and is accomplished in seawater by only a few bacteria species. The light energy found in the euphotic zone helps power the reaction, but a low- or no-oxygen zone is also necessary to allow the enzyme-catalyzing nitrogen fixation to function. Probably the most important nitrogen-fixing organisms in the marine environment are species of blue-green algae living in tropical sunlit surface waters. As the algae grow, thick mats are formed that provide low-oxygen regions that allow nitrogen fixation.

Human Impact

The fluxes (flows) of nitrogen through the nitrogen cycle are affected by human activities. Fossil-fuel burning, land clearing, burning practices, and some agricultural practices result in the production of two nitrogen-containing gases: nitric oxide and nitrous oxide. Nitric oxide catalyzes the formation of smog and combines with other molecules to form ozone—both of which are detrimental to human health. Nitrous oxide is a greenhouse gas 200 times more powerful than carbon dioxide. This gas can trap heat in the atmosphere, leading to increased global temperatures.

Humans also increase the nitrogen flux into the ocean by sewage discharge and fertilizer application. Runoff from agricultural lands and sewage, both containing high quantities of nitrates, build up levels in aquatic ecosystems to the point of a nutrient overload. This leads to *eutrophication*, an overgrowth of phytoplankton that impedes gas exchange across the air–water interface. The ensuing oxygen depletion in the water below the surface algal bloom can kill fish and other organisms.

Several methods have been proposed to lessen or mediate anthropogenic nitrogen production. These include more efficient fertilizer use (less runoff and evaporation), restoration of wetlands, which can act as "nutrient sponges," and cutting emissions from fossil-fuel burning.

Carmyn Priewe

FURTHER READING
Carpenter, Edward J., and Douglas G. Capone, eds. *Nitrogen in the Marine Environment.* New York: Academic Press, 1983.
Libes, Susan M. *Marine Biogeochemistry.* New York: Wiley, 1992.
Millero, Frank J. *Chemical Oceanography.* Boca Raton, Fla.: CRC Press, 1992; 2nd ed., 1996.
Vitousek, Peter M., et al. "Human Alteration of the Global Nitrogen Cycle: Causes and Consequences." *Issues in Ecology,* No. 1 (1997).

RELATED ARTICLES
Biogeochemical Cycle; Food Web; Photosynthesis; Phytoplankton

Nonconservative Element

The most abundant ions in seawater—chloride (Cl^-), sodium (Na^+), magnesium (Mg^{2+}), sulfate (SO_4^{2-}), calcium (Ca^{2+}), potassium (K^+), and dissolved gases (N_2 and Ar)—are found in remarkably constant proportions throughout the open ocean. These materials are termed *conservative* and their distribution through the ocean is controlled largely by physical processes such as mixing and the addition or removal of water. The

EXAMPLES OF NONCONSERVATIVE CHEMICAL SPECIES DISSOLVED IN SEAWATER

Category	Examples
Major nonconservative ions	Bicarbonate (HCO_3^-), carbonate (CO_3^{2-})
Nutrients	Nitrate (NO_3^-), nitrite (NO_2^-), ammonium (NH_4^+), phosphate (PO_4^{3-}), dissolved silicate (H_4SiO_4)
Gases	Oxygen (O_2), carbon dioxide (CO_2)
Trace metals	Iron (Fe), manganese (Mn), zinc (Zn), copper (Cu)

major ions comprise more than 99.8 percent of the mass of the solutes dissolved in seawater.

By contrast, many of the remaining elements in seawater are *nonconservative* (see table). Their oceanic concentrations vary markedly in space and time because of their biological or chemical reactivity (such as uptake and use by living organisms, chemical precipitation, and photochemical reactivity). Nonconservative chemicals compose less than 0.2 percent of the total mass of substances dissolved in seawater. Their importance belies this statistic, because some nonconservative chemicals are vital to living organisms and their occurrence helps determine the abundance and distribution of marine life.

The rate of growth of phytoplankton and seaweeds—the living matter on which most marine organisms ultimately depend—is limited by the availability of light and nutrients such as nitrate (NO_3^-), phosphate (PO_4^{3-}), and reactive silicate (H_4SiO_4). Nitrogen (N) and phosphorus (P) are key elements in biologically active molecules such as enzymes, coenzymes, and nucleic acids. Silicon (Si) is needed by some organisms, notably diatoms, for the construction of an external casing (frustule). Primary production removes such nutrients from the surface waters. When organisms die or excrete nutrient-rich waste, the biological material sinks through the water column and is gradually decomposed, releasing the nutrients and carbon dioxide while consuming dissolved oxygen. Silica in the frustules of diatoms gradually dissolves without biological decay, releasing silicate.

Nutrients are eventually returned to surface waters by the gradual ascent of deep-ocean currents, by coastal upwelling, and by diffusion. The overall result is that the vertical profiles of nutrients are characterized by low concentrations in surface waters (where rates of biological utilization exceed supply) and high concentrations in deeper water (where, in the absence of light for photosynthesis, decomposition rates or dissolution exceed uptake). Because the thermohaline circulation aerates the deep and bottom waters with oxygen-rich and nutrient-poor water, vertical profiles in latitudes between 40°N and 40°S show nutrient maxima in the region of the oxygen minimum zone.

Elements that dissolve as ions and have a small ionic size but carry a relatively large charge tend to attach (adsorb) to particle surfaces, a process known as *scavenging*. Scavenged elements such as aluminum (Al), iron (Fe), and lead (Pb) tend to show the reversed vertical profile of concentration from that of nutrients. Scavenged elements are in greatest abundance in surface waters, where they often enter the marine environment as wind-blown particles or with freshwater discharge by rivers, and are in lower concentration at depths. Their concentration may rise near the seafloor as a result of diffusion from the chemical-reducing environment in sediments.

Lead levels in seawater, as mirrored by the lead content of newly formed coral skeletons, rose dramatically between the 1950s and 1980s as a result of atmospheric lead pollution from automobile exhaust emissions. Iron, despite exhibiting scavenged behavior only recently, has been shown to act as a limiting nutrient for phytoplankton productivity. Much remains to be discovered about the chemistry and biochemistry of other nonconservative trace elements.

Trevor Day

FURTHER READING

Andrews, J. E., P. Brimblecombe, T. D. Jickells, and P. S. Liss. *An Introduction to Environmental Chemistry.* Oxford and Cambridge, Mass.: Blackwell Science, 1996.

Beer, Tom. *Environmental Oceanography: An Introduction to the Behaviour of Coastal Waters.* Oxford and New York: Pergamon Press, 1983; 2nd ed., Boca Raton, Fla.: CRC Press, 1997.

Burton, J. D. "The Ocean: A Global Geochemical System." In C. P. Summerhayes and S. A. Thorpe, eds., *Oceanography: An Illustrated Guide.* London: Manson Publishing, 1996; pp. 165–181.

Libes, Susan M. *An Introduction to Marine Biogeochemistry.* New York: Wiley, 1992.

Millero, Frank J. *Chemical Oceanography.* Boca Raton, Fla.: CRC Press, 1992; 2nd ed., 1996.

RELATED ARTICLES

Nutrient; Primary Productivity; Seawater, Composition of; Trace Element

Nonpelagic Development

Marine invertebrates may develop according to three possible paths: planktotrophic, lecithotrophic, and nonpelagic. In the case of the first two, the eggs hatch as larvae and usually must spend some time in the plankton before they metamorphose into the adult. In nonpelagic development the eggs are endowed with large amounts of yolk and undergo a lengthy development in a protective capsule using the abundant yolk as an energy source. In some cases the egg capsule is furnished with nurse eggs that do not undergo development but are there for the developing animal to consume as an energy source. Larval stages, if there are any, are passed in the capsule and the animal hatches as a juvenile anatomically similar to the adult but smaller. In this type of development there is no free-swimming larval stage.

The advantages of nonpelagic development are that the young are protected in a capsule and are not subjected to the heavy predation that occurs in the plankton. One disadvantage of this form of development is that given a finite amount of energy, the number of eggs that can be produced is much smaller than in planktotrophic or lecithotrophic development, so there are always fewer young. A second disadvantage is that because there is no planktonic phase, the ability of the species to disperse to other habitats is very limited.

Over the last half of the twentieth century there have been a number of attempts to explain under what conditions one would expect to see each of the three types of development. One of the first was that there would be a latitudinal gradient in the proportions of the three types, with planktotrophy predominating in the tropics and lecithotrophy and nonpelagic development becoming more common in temperate and polar waters. Yet another hypothesis suggested that small animals would have nonpelagic development because they were not big enough to allocate a large amount of energy to produce large numbers of eggs and therefore to ensure the survival of the few they would brood. Still another model suggested that the type of larvae produced could be predicted by the relative abundance of suitable substrates for the adults. In this model, animals that colonized abundant habitats would have less need for planktotrophic larvae, while those that inhabited rare habitats would benefit from long-lived planktotrophic larvae that could search out the rare habitats. Lately, more research and surveys of existing data have revealed discrepancies in all of the models, such that many factors may be of importance and that energy considerations alone are inadequate to account for the different strategies.

James W. Nybakken

FURTHER READING

Nybakken, James W. *Marine Biology: An Ecological Approach,* 5th ed. San Francisco: Benjamin Cummings, 2001.

Obrebski, S. "Larval Colonizing Strategies in Marine Benthic Invertebrates." *Marine Ecological Progress Series 1* (1979), pp. 293–300.

Strathmann, R. R. "Egg Size, Larval Development, and Juvenile Size in Benthic Marine Invertebrates." *American Naturalist*, Vol. 111 (1977), pp. 373–376.

——. "Evolution and Loss of Feeding Larval Stages of Marine Invertebrates." *Evolution*, Vol. 32 (1978), pp. 899–906.

Thorson, G. "Reproductive and Larval Ecology of Marine Bottom Invertebrates." *Biology Review*, Vol. 25 (1950), pp. 1–45.

Underwood, A. J. "On Models for Reproductive Strategy in Marine Benthic Invertebrates." *American Naturalist*, Vol. 108 (1974), pp. 874–878.

Vance, R. "Reproductive Strategies in Marine Benthic Invertebrates." *American Naturalist*, Vol. 107 (1973), pp. 339–352.

RELATED ARTICLES
Larvae; Lecithotrophic Larvae; Planktotrophic Larvae

Nonskeletal Carbonate

Nonskeletal carbonate is the carbonate component formed by nonbiogenic processes and is commonly referred to as *inorganic carbonate*. The raw materials to form inorganic carbonate are present in the seawater and the seawater–atmosphere interface. Calcium ions saturate the ocean water, but absence of the carbonate ion prevents the precipitation of calcium carbonate. The inorganic source of carbonate in calcium carbonate is carbon dioxide. Carbon dioxide is in turn generated at the air–seawater interface and is included as a dissolved gas in seawater.

Carbon dioxide and carbonate are exclusive of each other in seawater. Where carbon dioxide is present in large amounts, carbonate is present in small amounts. In the upper water level, photosynthesis removes carbon dioxide during plant production. Once the carbon dioxide is removed, the result is an increase in carbonate ion concentration. The carbonate ion combines with calcium ions and precipitates as calcium carbonate

The ocean maintains a constant pH of 8.1. The ocean achieves this by precipitating calcium carbonate when there is excess carbonate in the water and dissolving calcium carbonate when there is a shortage of carbonate in the seawater. This process, termed *buffering*, is summarized by the following equations:

$$H_2O + CO_2 \rightarrow H_2CO_3 \rightarrow H^+ + HCO_3^-$$

(Water plus carbon dioxide forms carbonic acid, which dissociates to the hydrogen ion plus the bicarbonate ion.)

$$HCO_3^- \leftrightarrow H^+ + CO_3^{2-}$$

(Bicarbonate ion dissociates to the hydrogen ion and the carbonate ion.)

$$CO_3^{2-} + Ca^{2+} \leftrightarrow CaCO_3$$

(This is a reversible reaction. The calcium ion is available from the seawater. The carbonate ion joins with calcium ions in the water to form calcium carbonate.)

Water temperature influences the concentration of dissolved carbon dioxide. Warm water holds less carbon dioxide, whereas cold water will retain more of the dissolved gas. Since the deep ocean water is cold, it holds more carbon dioxide. Water combined with carbon dioxide forms carbonic acid, which lowers the pH of the water and makes the water slightly acidic. To counteract this effect, the water is neutralized by the carbonate tests of microorganisms as they settle to the bottom. This helps maintain a normal pH value for the ocean.

Presently, limestone is forming from the precipitation of inorganic carbonate in several locations. Low-latitudinal areas with shallow water near continental margins or islands generally characterize these regions. The Bahama Banks near Florida are characterized by warm water; algal photosynthesis removes carbon dioxide from the water, resulting in carbonate precipitation. In addition to the Bahama Banks, other areas of limestone precipitation include the Great Barrier Reef of Australia and the Persian Gulf.

Carbonate rocks other than limestone, such as tufa and travertine, form from nonskeletal carbonate.

Tufa is carbonate that precipitates at continental springs, in lakes, or in groundwater. Travertine usually is found either in caves or near hot springs.

David L. White

FURTHER READING

Kennett, James P. *Marine Geology.* Englewood Cliffs, N.J.: Prentice Hall, 1982.

Plummer, Charles C., David McGeary, and Diane H. Carlson. *Physical Geology.* Dubuque, Iowa: Wm. C. Brown, 1992; 8th ed., Burr Ridge, Ill.: McGraw-Hill Higher Education, 1998.

Thurman, Harold V. *Essentials of Oceanography.* Columbus, Ohio: Charles E. Merrill, 1983; 6th ed., with Alan P. Trujillo, Upper Saddle River, N.J.: Prentice Hall, 1999.

RELATED ARTICLES
Carbonate Platform; Great Barrier Reef

North Atlantic Drift

The North Atlantic Drift, or North Atlantic Current, is an ocean current that breaks away from the Gulf Stream at 40°N 60°W, to the southeast of the Grand Banks, off Newfoundland. Driven by the prevailing westerly winds of middle latitudes, the North Atlantic Drift flows in a northeasterly direction. It crosses the western North Atlantic and divides at about 30°W in winter and at about 40°W in summer.

One branch turns southward. It becomes the Canary Current and continues southward to join the North Equatorial Current, thus completing the North Atlantic gyre. The Canary Current may therefore be regarded as a branch of the North Atlantic Drift. The other branch continues in a northeasterly direction. At about 50°N and about 20°W in winter and 30°W in summer, the drift divides once more, this time into three branches. One of these branches curves in an anticlockwise direction and flows past the southern coast of Iceland and around the southernmost tip of Greenland. This is called the *Irminger Current,*

and when it reaches the western side of Greenland it is called the West Greenland Current. Despite mixing with water from Baffin Bay, this branch of the North Atlantic Drift can be detected as far as 65°N by its high salinity.

A second branch flows through the English Channel into the North Sea. On the eastern side of the North Sea it turns and heads northward, passing the southwestern coast of Norway and entering the Norwegian Sea. There it joins the third branch, which passes to the west of the British Isles. When the two branches have joined they are known as the Norway (or Norwegian) Current. This divides again, one branch flowing past the North Cape and into the Barents Sea and the other heading northward into the Greenland Sea and then turning southward to become the East Greenland Current, which flows parallel to the eastern coast of Greenland.

All the parts of the North Atlantic Drift are broad and slow-moving, with an average speed of about 0.4 kilometer (0.25 mile) per hour. This is much slower than the main section of the Gulf Stream, which flows at 2 to 10 kilometers (1.2 to 6.2 miles) per hour, and sometimes the drift is difficult to detect because of shallow surface currents that are produced temporarily by winds that depart from the prevailing direction. The water is also more saline than that of the adjacent ocean water. This is because of the high rate of evaporation from the warm surface of the Gulf Stream. The salinity of Gulf Stream water is about 36 practical salinity units (psu), compared with the average salinity of the Atlantic, which is 34.9 psu.

Airmasses move in an easterly direction across the North Atlantic. Consequently, air must cross the North Atlantic Drift before it reaches northwestern Europe. It is warmed by contact with the surface water, giving the British Isles and coastal regions of northwestern Europe climates that are markedly milder than those in similar latitudes on the western side of the ocean. London, England, is at about 51.50°N. Its average annual temperature is 10.1°C (50.2°F). The average temperature in the warmest month (July) is 17.2°C (63.0°F), and in the coldest month (January) it is 4.2°C (39.6°F). Belle Isle, Newfoundland, is located near 52°N, but instead of the warm North Atlantic Drift, its climate is influenced by the cold Labrador Current. Its average annual temperature is -0.6°C (30.9°F). The average temperature in the warmest month (August) is 10.4°C (50.7°F), and in the coldest month (January) it is -11.3°C (11.7°F).

Michael Allaby

FURTHER READING

Cunningham, Stuart A. "Circulation and Volume Flux of the North Atlantic Using Synoptic Hydrographic Data in a Bernoulli Inverse." *Journal of Marine Research*, Vol. 58, No. 1 (2000), pp. 1–35.

King, Cuchlaine A. M. *Introduction to Physical and Biological Oceanography.* London: Edward Arnold/New York: Crane, Russak, 1975.

Schneider, Stephen H., ed. *Encyclopedia of Climate and Weather,* 2 vols. New York: Oxford University Press, 1996.

RELATED ARTICLES

Canary Current; Equatorial Currents, North and South; Gulf Stream; Gyre

North Equatorial Current, see
Equatorial Currents, North and South

North Pacific Drift

The North Pacific Drift (NPD), sometimes called the North Pacific Current (NPC), is a broad eastward transoceanic current that carries relatively warm and salty waters from Japan to North America's west coast. The NPD originates as a downstream extension of the Kuroshio after its separation from the coast of Honshu Island at approximately 35°N. The Kuroshio Extension appears less coherent as it flows eastward, broadens, and becomes more diffuse. This is where the

term NPD (NPC) fully applies, although some authors prefer to use the "Kuroshio Extension" term all the way across the North Pacific Ocean.

The NPD (Kuroshio Extension) is a deep current that penetrates down to at least 2000 meters (6562 feet). In the middle of the ocean (at 179°E), the NPD is located at 35 to 36°N and is about 150 kilometers (93 miles) wide. In situ observations, numerical models, and satellite data show that the Kuroshio Extension weakens significantly after passing over the Emperor Seamounts at approximately 170°E. Upstream of the Emperor Seamounts, the Kuroshio Extension is a jetlike current, whereas downstream the Kuroshio Extension (NPD) sometimes cannot be distinguished as a single eastward jet. The maximum surface speed of the current is between 60 and 70 centimeters per second (1.2 and 1.4 knots), decreasing to 10 centimeters per second (0.2 knot) at 600 meters (1969 feet) and to a few centimeters per second in the deep layers, toward the bottom. The current carries approximately 30 Sverdrup (Sv; 1 Sv = 106 cubic meters per second) eastward at 179°E. This amount decreases to the east so that shortly before the NPD becomes the California Current it transports only 10 Sv.

The NPD is sometimes considered as the northern limb of the Subtropical Gyre, a huge anticyclonic (clockwise) circulation that encompasses the entire subtropical North Pacific. The NPD represents an important biogeographical boundary between the subtropical and temperate realms. At the same time, this relatively broad zone (up to several hundred kilometers in the north–south direction, especially in the central and eastern North Pacific) is an ecotone per se, featuring a number of species that are endemic to the NPD.

Igor M. Belkin

FURTHER READING:

Roden, G. I. "Flow and Water Property Structures between the Bering Sea and Fiji in the Summer of 1993." *Journal of Geophysical Research*, Vol. 105, No. C12 (2000), pp. 28,595–28,612.

Schmitz, W. J., Jr. *On the World Ocean Circulation*; Vol. 2, *The Pacific and Indian Oceans: A Global Update.* Technical Report WHOI-96-08. Woods Hole, Mass.: Woods Hole Oceanographic Institution, 1996.

RELATED ARTICLES
Gyre; Kuroshio

North Sea

The North Sea is the major shelf sea off northwestern Europe, opening into the Norwegian Sea in the north and into the Atlantic Ocean via the English Channel to the southwest. In the northeast, it connects with the Baltic Sea via the Skaggerak. Its surface area is about 570,000 square kilometers (220,000 square miles) and its volume is about 94,000 cubic kilometers (22,550 cubic miles). Its depth is generally less then 200 meters (656 feet). Its maximum depth is 700 meters (2297 feet) in the Norwegian Trench, which lies in an arc around Norway and extends into the Skaggerak. It is a very young sea; only 7000 years ago the English Channel and southern North Sea consisted of swampy land.

The tidal ranges often exceed 2 meters (6.6 feet) and the currents generated often exceed 1 meter per second (2.24 miles per hour). There are three major inflows from the Norwegian Sea that enter to the north of Scotland near the Shetland Islands, from north of the Orkneys, and along the southwestern edge of the Norwegian Trench. These inflows of water originating from the Atlantic feed a counterclockwise circulation that is quite intense

North Sea.

in the north but weakens over the shallower areas in the south. A weak inflow also enters via the English Channel. A strong outflow hugs the southern coastline of Norway.

All the coastal states bordering the North Sea are densely populated, intensively farmed, and heavily industrialized. Thus it receives considerable quantities of industrial and sewage effluents, agricultural runoff, and atmospheric fallout. There are acute problems of eutrophication in the east (e.g., the Wadden Sea and German Bight), where exchanges of water are limited. Its shipping lanes are among the busiest in the world, and in the last 20 years there has been extensive exploitation of offshore hydrocarbon reserves. Despite all this industrialization, the waters of the North Sea are highly productive; its fisheries annually yield over 3 million tons.

Martin Angel

FURTHER READING

Hardisty, J. *The British Seas: An Introduction to the New Oceanography and Resources of the North-West European Continental Shelf.* New York: Routledge, 1990.

Holligan, P. M., T. Aarup, and S. B. Groom. "The North Sea Colour Atlas." *Continental Shelf Research,* Vol. 9 (1989), pp. 665–765.

Oslo and Paris Commission. *Quality Status Report for Region II: The North Sea.* London: OSPAR, 2000.

Otto, L., J. T. F. Zimmerman, G. K. Furnes, M. Mork, R. Saetre, and G. Becker. "Review of the Physical Oceanography of the North Sea." *Netherlands Journal of Sea Research,* Vol. 26 (1990), pp. 161–238.

USEFUL WEB SITES

NorthSeaNet Home page.
<http://www.northseanet.co.uk>.

RELATED ARTICLES

Baltic Sea; Norwegian Sea; Offshore Oil Technology; Petroleum

Norwegian Sea

The Norwegian Sea lies between Norway and Greenland. To the south it is bounded by shallow sills located between Greenland, Iceland, the Faroes, and Scotland that form a continuous barrier below a depth of 840 meters (2756 feet) but are intersected by narrow channels scoured by strong currents. To the north it is bounded by the Nansen Ridge, located between northern Greenland and Spitsbergen (at about 80°N), and the Barents Sea, located between Spitsbergen and the Northern Cape of Norway. Its total area is about 2.6 million square kilometers (1 million square miles), and its volume is 4.1 million cubic kilometers (0.98 million cubic miles). Relatively warm water flows in at the surface from the North Atlantic to the north of Scotland and then flows northeastward along the Norwegian coastline. This inflow maintains a much milder climate in Norway than is experienced in Alaska at a similar latitude. It also keeps the eastern half of the Norwegian Sea and the Arctic Ocean to the east of Spitsbergen almost totally free of ice. The southward flow of the East Greenland Current to the west carries pack ice and icebergs (one of which sank the *Titanic*) calved from the glaciers of eastern Greenland into the Labrador Sea.

The upper few hundred meters of the sea are relatively warm, but below about 500 to 750 meters (1640 to 2460 feet), water temperatures plummet to 0 to -1°C (32 to 30°F). This very cold water cascades through the narrow channels into the North Atlantic, where it mixes rapidly with the ambient deep water to form North Atlantic Deep Water, the water mass that pervades the global ocean. So any climate change affecting the Norwegian Sea is likely to affect climate throughout the global ocean.

Another feature of the Norwegian Sea is the Storegga Flow. Five to ten thousand years ago, the continental slope off Norway failed catastrophically; in three stages, massive underwater landslides shifted about 5000 cubic kilometers (1200 cubic miles) of sediment into the deep basins. Archaeological evidence has been found indicating that the tsunamis (seismic sea waves) generated by these catastrophic slips overwhelmed Bronze Age settlements on several islands.

Martin Angel

FURTHER READING

Arctic Monitoring and Assessment Programme. *AMAP Assessment Report: Arctic Pollution Issues.* Oslo: AMAP, 1998.

Hansen, B., and S. Østerhus. "North Atlantic–Nordic Seas Exchanges." *Progress in Oceanography,* Vol. 45 (2000), pp. 109–208.

Hurdle, B. G., ed. *The Nordic Seas.* New York: Springer-Verlag, 1986.

RELATED ARTICLES

Arctic Ocean; Barents Sea; Bottom Water Formation; Continental Slope; Labrador Sea; Seismic Sea Wave (Tsunami)

Nutrient

A nutrient is defined as a dissolved inorganic molecule or compound taken up by phytoplankton for photosynthesis needs. The most important nutrients are fixed nitrogen in the form of nitrate (NO_3^-), phosphorus in the form of phosphate (PO_4^{3-}), and silicon in the form of silicic acid ($Si(OH)_4$). These nutrients, together with light, are essential for phytoplankton growth. Nitrate, phosphate, and silicic acid are used up until they become limiting, and further growth is prohibited. These salts are considered biologically active or biolimiting nutrients due to their non-conservative status throughout the ocean. Although potassium (K^+) is needed by phytoplankton for growth, it is not considered a biolimiting nutrient because it is essentially unlimited in the ocean (by the principle of constant proportions), and therefore its concentration is not affected by phytoplankton use.

Organisms use nitrate for the formation of amino acids, which are the basic building blocks of proteins. Phosphorus is required for the formation of ATP, the molecule that stores cellular energy. Some organisms, such as diatoms, have siliceous hard parts and therefore require silicon. Biological oceanographers have noticed that the ratio of nutrients in marine organic matter is broadly constant. Nitrate and phosphate are assimilated from seawater in a 16:1 ratio as phytoplankton grow.

Because phytoplankton need a combination of a certain intensity of light and nutrients for photosynthesis, they are usually confined to the upper 100 meters (330 feet) of the ocean, where the light is sufficient for photosynthesis. This zone is variously called the *photic, euphotic,* or *epipelagic zone.* Nutrients are taken up in the photic zone. They are regenerated or returned back into their dissolved forms by metabolic processes of organisms or by decay of the bodies of organisms. The nutrient cycle can be thought of as an internal oceanic biological pump:

- Dissolved nutrients are upwelled to the surface oceans.
- They are assimilated by photosynthetic organisms and turned into solid organic molecules such as carbohydrates and proteins.
- Grazers and predators consume these molecules and may excrete some of the nutrients as particulate matter (fecal pellets) that sink out of the photic zone under the influence of gravity. Other nutrients are released through the death and decay of the organisms.
- Particulate matter is acted upon by microorganisms that release the nutrient back into their dissolved state, where they may become available to photosynthetic organisms when returned to the photic zone.

As a result of these processes, there is a strong vertical nutrient concentration gradient throughout the world's oceans. Nutrients are depleted in photic zone waters due to phytoplankton uptake. Below the photic zone, nutrient concentrations increase sharply with increasing depth as they are returned back into biologically useful salts. At about 1000 meters (3280 feet) depth, nutrient concentrations level off and remain relatively constant to the seafloor. Deepwater nutrient concentrations are typically six to 10 or more times higher than surface water concentrations. The deep Pacific Ocean is enriched in nutrients compared to the deep Atlantic Ocean, due to thermohaline circulation. Upwelling of deep waters brings new nutrients to the surface, where they can be utilized biologically by phytoplankton. Areas of intense upwelling, such as the Peruvian coastline, support large fisheries, due to food chains based on phytoplankton blooms, which are caused by the constant influx of nutrients from the deep.

It is important to note that some transition metals, such as iron, zinc, cobalt, and manganese, are also essential for growth. All of these transition metals play central enzymatic roles in organisms. These metals are not traditionally considered nutrients because phytoplankton growth is not limited by their concentration. However, it is thought that iron may serve as a limiting nutrient in areas of the ocean where nitrate, phosphate, and silicon are in high concentrations. These areas, such as the Southern Ocean and the eastern equatorial Pacific, are known as *high-nutrient low-chlorophyll* (HNLC) regions.

Daniel Schuller

FURTHER READING

Broecker, W. S., and Tsung-Hung Peng. *Tracers in the Sea.* Palisades, N.Y.: Lamont-Doherty Geological Observatory, Columbia University, 1982.

Lalli, Carol M., and Timothy R. Parsons. *Biological Oceanography: An Introduction.* Oxford and New York: Pergamon Press, 1993; 2nd ed., Oxford: Butterworth-Heinemann, 1997.

Millero, Frank J. *Chemical Oceanography.* Boca Raton, Fla.: CRC Press, 1992; 2nd ed., 1996.

Open University Course Team. *Ocean Chemistry and Deep-Sea Sediments.* Oxford: Pergamon Press in association with Open University, 1989.

Spencer, C. P. "The Micronutrient Elements." In J. P. Riley and G. Skirrow, eds., *Chemical Oceanography.* Vol. 2, 2nd ed. New York: Academic Press, 1975.

RELATED ARTICLES
Biogeochemical Cycle; Constant Proportions, Principle of; Nitrogen; Nitrogen Cycle; Particulate Organic Carbon; Phosphorus; Photic Zone; Photosynthesis; Photosynthesis and Iron Limitation; Phytoplankton; Primary Productivity; Thermohaline Circulation; Upwelling

Nutrient Limitation

Autotrophs are organisms that can use water, carbon dioxide, and other nutrients to make their own food (i.e., organic macromolecules such as sugars and proteins) using energy from sunlight or from certain high-energy chemical compounds. Production of organic matter by marine autotrophs, a process called *primary production,* is critical because it forms that basis of the food chain on which all higher organisms depend. Primary production by autotrophs such as microscopic marine algae, known as *phytoplankton,* can be limited either by lack of energy (e.g., sunlight) or by lack of raw materials (e.g., nutrients). The major nutrients needed for primary production include carbon, nitrogen, and phosphorus. The average ratio of these three nutrients in freshly produced marine organic matter is 105:15:1 (called the *Redfield ratio*). In other words, for every phosphorus molecule used by phytoplankton, an average of 15 molecules of nitrogen and 105 molecules of carbon are needed. If a nutrient is present in a lower amount than this ratio, it is said to be a limiting nutrient because it restricts the rate of primary production.

Carbon, which is a component of all organic macromolecules generated by autotrophs, is generally present in sufficient quantities throughout the ocean and is rarely limiting. Nitrogen and phosphorus availability, however, are often a bottleneck in the production of organic matter. In fact, nitrogen is the most commonly limiting nutrient in the ocean, while phosphorus is the most frequently limiting in estuaries. Nitrogen is needed to generate proteins, and both nutrients are needed to create nucleic acids. Sulfur, which is a component of some proteins, can also be limiting, as can silicon, which is used in the structural material of some phytoplankton. Other trace elements that can limit primary production under certain circumstances include iron, manganese, cobalt, zinc, and copper. For example, photosynthesis by phytoplankton in some remote, open-ocean areas (e.g., the equatorial Pacific, the subarctic Pacific offshore from Alaska, and the Southern Ocean around Antarctica) is limited by the availability of iron.

The occurrence of nutrient limitation in the marine environment varies with space and time. Availability of nutrients tends to be highest near the margins of continents, where erosion and input from rivers keep nutrient concentrations high, and to decline with increasing distance from shore. The availability of nutrients also varies with depth in the water column. Nutrients are used up by phytoplankton in the surface layer of the ocean, where there is sufficient light for photosynthesis (the photic zone). As the newly produced organic matter sinks through the water column, it is decomposed (mainly by bacteria), and the nutrients are released again. However, much of this decomposition takes place in water deeper than the photic zone. Thus, for the recycled nutrients to be returned to the surface where they are needed for photosynthesis, the deep water must be able to mix with the surface water through the motion of winds and tides. Whether this mixing can take place depends greatly on

latitude and season. At middle (i.e., temperate) latitudes in late spring and summer, there is very little mixing of deep water into the surface layer because of density differences between the warm surface water and cold deeper layers. Thus, nutrients become limited at the surface in warm weather at temperate latitudes. In the fall, the surface cools and the nutrient-rich deep water can mix again with surface water. At polar latitudes, availability of nutrients generally does not limit primary production. The water column here is of relatively uniform temperature year-round; thus, wind mixing tends to keep nutrients plentiful at the surface. At tropical latitudes, on the other hand, most areas are continuously nutrient-limited. Intense tropical heat leads to a permanent thermocline and little mixing of the water column. With a few notable exceptions (e.g., coral reefs, upwelling zones), the clear blue water of the tropics is essentially a marine desert and is a result of nutrient limitation.

Mary E. Clark

FURTHER READING
Nybakken, James W. *Marine Biology: An Ecological Approach*, 5th ed. San Francisco: Benjamin Cummings, 2001.
Oremland, R. S. "Microorganisms and Marine Ecology." *Sea Frontiers*, Vol. 22 (1976), pp. 305–310.
Thurman, Harold V. *Essentials of Oceanography.* Columbus, Ohio: Charles E. Merrill, 1983; 6th ed., with Alan P. Trujillo, Upper Saddle River, N.J.: Prentice Hall, 1999.

RELATED ARTICLES
Nutrient; Photosynthesis; Phytoplankton

Ocean

Oceans cover 71 percent of Earth's surface and account for 97 percent of its water. They play a profound role in Earth's geologic, hydrologic, and biologic cycles. Oceans support marine life, provide commercial fisheries, and contain compounds that are important in medicine and industry. They store and release heat, thereby affecting weather patterns, while slowing rates of climate change. Oceans also exchange gases, especially carbon dioxide, with the atmosphere and are a major source of water vapor that eventually becomes rain and snow on the continents. Finally, because ocean waters are constantly in motion, they redistribute sediments and alter bottom habitat; however, over long periods of time, ocean sediments can generate petroleum and concentrate important minerals such as titanium. Study of the oceans is thus a truly interdisciplinary endeavor.

The world's oceans can be divided into four main water bodies: the Pacific, Atlantic, Indian, and Arctic Oceans. A fifth, the Antarctic Ocean (also referred to as the Southern Ocean), is usually considered a southern extension of the Pacific, Atlantic, and Indian Oceans. The Pacific Ocean, which occupies more than one-third of Earth's surface and contains more than one-half of its water, has an average depth of 4500 meters (14,765 feet). The margins of the Pacific Ocean are surrounded by active volcanoes and earthquake-prone land surfaces. The Atlantic Ocean is long and narrow and has an average depth of 3600 meters (11,810 feet). It receives abundant terrigenous sediments from many large rivers. The Indian Ocean, confined mostly to the southern hemisphere, has an average depth of 3900 meters (12,795 feet). It is influenced significantly by the warm saline waters from the Red Sea and the Arabian Gulf. The Arctic Ocean, smallest of the four, has an average depth of 1300 meters (4265 feet). Most of its surface is covered with ice.

Salinity and Temperature

Seawater is a chemical solution that contains small amounts of dissolved salts. The major constituents are sodium (Na^+) and chloride (Cl^-), but seawater contains many other dissolved substances in minute quantities. Salinity of seawater, a measure of the total dissolved salts, varies with the amount of freshwater input from rainfall, rivers, and melting glaciers, and with the rate of freshwater loss from evaporation. Typical salinities of the open ocean are 33 to 37 practical salinity units (psu). The salinity of seawater is considered to be in a steady-state equilibrium. This is because the residence time of the ionic components in the water (defined as mean time between introduction and removal of substances from the water) is hundreds of millions of years.

Water has a great capacity to store and release heat. Although ocean temperature decreases with

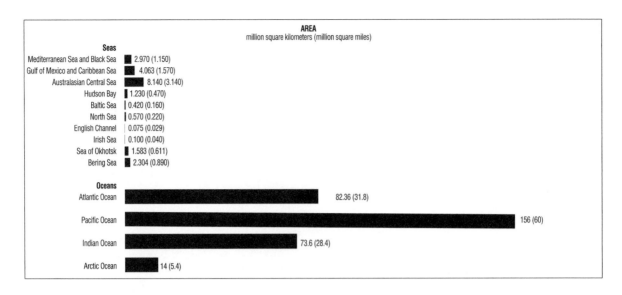

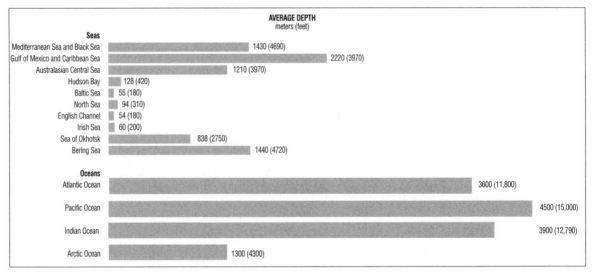

Area and average depth of selected marginal seas and oceans.

depth, the oceans have a layered thermal structure. Surface waters form a thin upper layer [approximately 100 meters (330 feet) thick] that is warm and has low density in the tropics and subtropics but is variable in the temperate zones. Winds, waves, and currents tend to keep this upper layer well mixed, and it is through this layer that exchange with the atmosphere occurs. Below the surface layer, temperatures decrease sharply within the thermocline, a permanent transition zone throughout most of the ocean between depths of 200 and 1000 meters (656 and 3280 feet). Cold deep water, which occurs beneath the

thermocline, has higher density and does not readily mix with the upper surface layer. In polar regions, even the surface waters are very cold, and sea ice covers as much as 15 percent of the world's oceans at any time.

Ocean Circulation

Circulation in the deep ocean, although slow, is continuous. It is driven by density gradients that are produced by differences in water temperature and salinity. This thermohaline circulation moves large masses of water at mid-depths and near the bottom. Cold waters that originate in polar regions sink toward the ocean bottom and are transported for great distances before eventually resurfacing at lower latitudes. Bottom topography controls movement of the waters through the ocean basins. Water masses that are driven by thermohaline circulation are rich in nutrients. Deep ocean water can rise by the process of coastal upwelling. Under certain combinations of wind direction and coastal orientation, surface waters move away from the coastline, causing cold deep water to rise and take its place. Areas of upwelling, for example along the west coasts of South America and Africa, have especially productive fisheries because of nutrients driving primary productivity.

Circulation in the upper (surface) layer of the oceans is driven primarily by wind (tides and waves are important very close to the coast). Prevailing currents are set up by persistent wind patterns at different latitudes, such as the trade winds between 30°N and 30°S and the prevailing westerlies at higher latitudes. Rotation of Earth creates the *Coriolis effect*, which also influences motion of the currents. The result is well-defined gyres in the Pacific, Atlantic, and Indian Oceans, and smaller gyres in polar and subpolar regions. Each gyre has a strong and narrow flow toward the pole on the west side and toward the equator on the east side (in both hemispheres). Western boundary currents, such as the Gulf Steam in the Atlantic, are the strongest currents in the ocean.

Living Resources

Organisms that live in the ocean can be classified as *planktonic* (drifting), *nektonic* (swimming), and *benthic* (bottom dwelling). Plankton are abundant in the surface layer of the open ocean and include phytoplankton (e.g., diatoms) and zooplankton (e.g., copepods). Plankton are very small and unable to swim against ocean currents; zooplankton, on the other hand, have the ability to swim but are still

influenced by strong currents and by turbulence. All higher forms of life, including zooplankton, rely on phytoplankton for food. Biologists have found that both phytoplankton and zooplankton exhibit patchiness in spatial distribution that appears to be caused by changes in physical conditions, grazing (consumption) patterns, and reproduction. For reasons that are not fully understood, some zooplankton have been noted to descend vertically through the water, sometimes hundreds of meters, during the day, only to return to the surface at night.

Nekton include swimming fish but also marine mammals and reptiles. Commercial species include herring, cod, tuna, swordfish, as well as flounder, sharks, and whales. Fisheries provide about 10 percent of the animal protein consumed by humans. However, many of the world's fisheries began to collapse in the 1980s and are now heavily depleted. Overfishing, loss of water quality, and habitat degradation are some of the main causes. Abundance and distribution of nekton can also display tremendous natural year-to-year variations. Unlike petroleum and natural gas, fisheries resources are renewable, and depleted fisheries stock can eventually recover.

Benthic organisms include those that are attached to the bottom (coral reefs, oysters), live on the bottom (crabs, lobsters), and live within the bottom (flatworms, gastropods). Seaweeds and grasses, often less noticed than marine animals, are also important in the marine environment. Benthic organisms must compete for food and for space on the bottom. Deposit feeders ingest sediment in order to obtain microorganisms that are associated with the sediments. The margins of the ocean basins support many shallow-water benthic species that are commercially feasible, such as oysters, clams, and scallops.

Observations from Space

High-resolution satellite images have revolutionized our understanding of the oceans. Satellites are able to capture images at different wavelengths and different scales, thereby allowing them to be useful for a wide range of applications: fisheries oceanography, weather prediction, tracking pollution, and measurement of particulate matter in the atmosphere and the ocean. Some satellites orbit so that they cover the entire surface of Earth with pictures each day; others are equipped with radar that can be used to map the surface of the ocean and even the seafloor. Perhaps the most important aspect of satellite sensors is their ability to make observations as they happen. Satellites have tracked eddies and meanders of the Gulf Stream off North America and identified timing and extent of important upwelling events off South America. Satellites are also providing valuable information on El Niño events, where changes in wind patterns and ocean currents cause significant variations in water temperatures and weather.

John T. Wells

FURTHER READING

Hamblin, W. Kenneth. *Earth's Dynamic Systems: A Textbook in Physical Geology.* Minneapolis, Minn.: Burgess, 1975; 9th ed., with Eric H. Christiansen, Upper Saddle River, N.J.: Prentice Hall, 2001.

Karleskint, George, Jr. *Introduction to Marine Biology.* Philadelphia: Saunders College Publishing, 1998.

Kunzig. R. "In Deep Water." *Discover,* Vol. 17 (1996), pp. 86–96.

Open University Course Team. *Seawater: Its Composition, Properties, and Behavior.* Oxford: Pergamon Press/Milton Keynes, England: Open University, 1989; 2nd ed., rev. by John Wright and Angela Colling, Oxford and New York: Pergamon Press, 1995.

Pinet, Paul R. *Oceanography: An Introduction to the Planet Oceanus.* St. Paul, Minn.: West Publishing, 1992.

Tarbuck, Edward J., and Frederick K. Lutgens. *The Earth: An Introduction to Physical Geology.* Columbus, Ohio: Charles E. Merrill, 1984; 6th ed., Upper Saddle River, N.J.: Prentice Hall, 1999.

RELATED ARTICLES

Arctic Ocean; Atlantic Ocean; Earth, Rotation of; El Niño; Gyre; Indian Ocean; Ocean Basin; Ocean circulation; Pacific Ocean; Salinity; Seawater, composition of; Southern Ocean; Temperature, distribution of; Upwelling

Ocean, Water Budget of

A water budget is simply an accounting of the water in a region and the relationships between water entering and leaving the region. The volume of water on Earth is 1.399×10^9 cubic kilometers. Almost all water (97.4 percent) is in the oceans, and most of the rest (2.0 percent) is ice. The remainder is groundwater (0.58 percent), water in lakes and rivers (0.02 percent), and water in the atmosphere (0.001 percent). The oceans cover 71 percent of Earth's surface and the mean depth is 3795 meters (12,450 feet). If the entire surface of Earth were covered with water, the volume of ocean water would provide a mean water depth of 2643 meters (8671 feet). The water from land and ice would add another 46 meters (151 feet) to the water depth.

Reservoirs

The places where water resides (the oceans, lakes, ice, rivers, atmosphere, and ground) are called *reservoirs.* Water is constantly moving from one reservoir to another. Water leaves the surface of the ocean as water vapor entering the atmosphere through evaporation. Water leaves the atmosphere as snow and rain through precipitation. When this occurs over land, the rain and snow fill rivers and lakes and the water percolates into Earth to replenish groundwater supplies. The water eventually flows back into the sea. The movement of water from one reservoir to another is called the *hydrologic cycle.* Although water is constantly moving between reservoirs, the total amount of water in each reservoir remains about the same.

The distribution of evaporation and precipitation over the ocean is one of the least understood elements of the climate system. Most discussions of the water cycle focus on the much smaller terrestrial component, due to the impact on agriculture and human activities. But since 86 percent of global evaporation and 78 percent of global precipitation occurs over the oceans, it is important to improve our understanding of the ocean hydrologic cycle. For example, if less than 1 percent of the rain falling on the Atlantic Ocean were to fall over the central United States, the discharge of the Mississippi River would double.

During ice ages, a significant transfer of water from the ocean to land ice occurs. In this case, the ocean volume is decreased by 6.5 percent and the volume of land ice increases by 400 percent. The loss of ocean volume corresponds to a drop in sea level of 250 meters (820 feet).

Major Ocean Basins

The water in the ocean is divided among the Atlantic, Pacific, and Indian Oceans. The Southern Ocean connects these three oceans but is considered divided along meridians so as to fall into one of these three oceans. The Arctic Ocean and the Mediterranean and Black Seas are considered part of the Atlantic. The smallest of the oceans is the Indian Ocean, which contains 0.29×10^9 cubic kilometers of water and has a mean depth of 3897 meters (12,785 feet). The Indian Ocean lies mostly in the southern hemisphere. The Atlantic Ocean contains 0.35×10^9 cubic kilometers and has a mean depth of 3332 meters (10,932 feet). The Pacific Ocean is larger than the sum of both the Indian and Atlantic Oceans, with 0.72×10^9 cubic kilometers and a mean depth of 4028 meters (13,215 feet). Since 70 percent of Earth's land is in the northern hemisphere, the climate of the southern hemisphere is more moderate at most latitudes.

Relationship between Evaporation and Surface Salinity

The net effect of evaporation is to remove water from the ocean. When seawater evaporates, it leaves the salt behind, so that the surface waters become saltier. Water is added to the oceans through precipitation and river runoff, diluting the surface waters of the sea and reducing their salinity. Regions with high precipitation and large river runoff such as the Baltic have low surface salinity, whereas regions with few rivers and little rainfall such as the Red Sea have high surface salinity. Similarly, in subtropical latitudes of the open ocean where evaporation exceeds precipitation, the surface salinity is higher than it is in the tropics and subpolar regions, where the reverse is true.

Conservation of Mass or Salt

The principle of conservation of mass or salt can be used to help understand the differences between changes in salinity or mass. These principles state simply that there can be no change in salinity or mass in a fixed volume except by a flux of material in or out of the box. For example, consider an estuary, which is connected to the ocean. The amount of water entering the estuary from the sea (V_i) and from river runoff (R) and precipitation (P) must equal the amount of water leaving the estuary as evaporation (E) and flow to the sea (V_o). This can be written as an equation: $V_i + R + P = V_o + E$. If this balance does not occur, the level of water in the estuary must change. Similarly, the amount of salt carried into the estuary (S_i) from the ocean by V_i must equal the salt carried out of the estuary (S_o) to the sea by V_o, so $V_i S_i = V_o S_o$. If this salinity balance does not occur, the mean salinity of the estuary must change. These balances may not hold during short periods of time such as spring floods or fall droughts, when water levels and salinity change, so it is important to apply these conservation principles over time periods and areas where they are applicable.

These relationships can be applied to ocean basins. In the Pacific, precipitation averages 1.29 meters (about 4.2 feet) per year, evaporation 1.2 meters (about 3.9 feet) per year, and river runoff

0.07 meter (about 0.2 foot) per year, so that the freshwater balance, $X = R + P - E$, is 0.16 meter (about 0.5 foot) per year. For the Indian and Atlantic Oceans, the freshwater balance is minus 0.18 meter (0.6 foot) per year. Since the sea level of these oceans is not changing, water must flow from the Pacific to the Atlantic and Indian Oceans. The required freshwater transport, 28 cubic kilometers per year, is four orders of magnitude greater than the flow of the largest river.

It is possible to determine the water budget for individual ocean basins. In the North Atlantic and the North and South Pacific, fresh water is transported southward. In the South Atlantic and the Indian Ocean, fresh water is transported northward. Improved measurements of precipitation and evaporation for the ocean will allow refinement of these water budgets.

Residence Time

A second concept that can be applied to elements of the hydrologic cycle or individual ocean basins is that of *residence time*, the amount of time that water spends in any one reservoir. It is equal to the amount of water divided by the rate at which water is added. About 1.2 meters (about 3.9 feet) per year evaporate from the ocean each year, and the mean depth of the ocean is 3795 meters (12,450 feet), so the residence time of the ocean as a whole would be 3162 years. The residence time of water in the atmosphere is much less, 14 days.

Curtis A. Collins

FURTHER READING
Schmitt, R. "The Ocean Component of the Global Water Cycle." U.S. National Report to the I.U.G.G., 1991–1994. *Reviews of Geophysics*, Vol. 33, Suppl. (1995).
Weller, R. A., and P. K. Taylor. *Surface Conditions and Air Sea Fluxes.* CCCO-JSC Ocean Observing System Development Panel. College Station, Texas: Texas A&M University, 1993.

RELATED ARTICLES
Hydrologic Cycle; Residence Time; Salinity

Ocean Basin

The oceans of the world can be broadly divided into the Pacific Basin, Atlantic Basin, Indian Ocean Basin, and the marginal ocean basins. The Pacific is the largest and deepest, covering over one-third of Earth's surface and containing over one-half of its water. Much of the Pacific Basin is rimmed by rugged mountains, and the interior is dotted by volcanic islands, often occurring in chains called *island arcs*. The Atlantic Basin, which connects the Arctic and Antarctic Oceans, is relatively narrow and shallow by comparison. However, it receives enormous amounts of water and sediments from large rivers, such as the Amazon and Congo. The Indian Basin, smallest of the three main ocean basins, also receives large volumes of sediment from rivers, such as the Ganges and Indus. This basin occurs mostly in the southern hemisphere, has relatively few islands, and receives warm waters from the Red Sea and Arabian Gulf. Marginal ocean basins are isolated from the main ocean basins by landmasses, submarine ridges, or island arcs. Examples include the Mediterranean Sea, Gulf of Mexico, and Gulf of California.

Mapping of ocean basins using sonar began in the 1920s. Since then it has become obvious that if the water were removed, the basins of the world's oceans would have impressive features that resemble those on continents: high mountains, deep canyons and trenches, and flat plateaus. Moreover, many of the same geologic processes and agents that operate on land also operate in the oceans: earthquakes, volcanoes, landslides, sediment scour and deposition, and chemical precipitation and dissolution. Ocean basins are covered by a blanket of sediment that ranges from a few centimeters to thousands of meters thick. The sediments are important sources of petroleum and minerals, and the type and amount of sediments are important to the organisms that inhabit the marine environment.

Topographic Features of the Oceans

The topography of the oceans can be delineated into thee major units: continental margins, deep-ocean basins, and mid-ocean ridges. The continental margins are transition regions that extend from the continents to the seafloor of the deep ocean. The continental shelf, the landward-most part of the continental margin, was exposed terrestrially during the peak of glaciation about 18,000 years ago. It has remnants of river channels, beaches, deltas, and wave-cut platforms. The continental slope is a steep and narrow incline that extends from the continental shelf down to the continental rise, where the topography then grades more gently into the deep ocean. The abyssal plain is a vast, remarkably flat region within the deep-ocean basins where thick sedimentary sequences have covered almost all of the topographic relief. The mid-ocean ridges are broad, highly fractured, but nearly continuous features that extend around the globe through the centers of the ocean basins. They mark spreading centers from which new slabs of seafloor are added by extrusion of magma from deep within Earth.

Other significant topographic features include submarine canyons, trenches, seamounts, and coral reefs. Submarine canyons are incised into the continental slope and rise, in some cases forming seaward extensions of river channels. Ocean trenches are spectacular, long and narrow features that form the deepest reaches of the oceans. Many are located in the Pacific Ocean, oriented parallel to the trend of the continents; their depths can exceed 10,000 meters (32,800 feet). In contrast, seamounts are volcanic peaks that rise hundreds of meters above the surrounding ocean floor. They also occur primarily in the Pacific and most are associated with ocean spreading centers. Some may become islands. Finally, coral reefs are common in warm, clear waters of the Pacific and Indian Oceans. These complex biological communities are made of hard corals and certain types of algae. Coral reefs can form atolls, or doughnut-shaped islands, when they colonize and grow upward on the margins of volcanic islands that have subsided beneath the surface of the ocean.

Evolution of the Ocean Basins

Ocean basins have evolved as a result of seafloor spreading and plate tectonics. There is considerable scientific evidence to show that approximately 200 million years ago a single supercontinent, Pangea, began to break apart into smaller plates or continents. These plates were part of the outermost rigid layer of Earth, called the *lithosphere*, which moved by convection cells over a weaker region below. Seven major plates and numerous smaller plates formed over a period of approximately 160 million years. As the plates moved, changing in size and shape, the ocean basins formed. The plates are still in motion. Mid-ocean ridges delineate regions where plates are moving apart at rates of 2 to 6 centimeters (0.8 to 2.4 inches) per year; these are *divergent plate boundaries*. Trenches and subduction zones delineate regions where plates are colliding, with one plate moving beneath the other; these are *convergent plate boundaries*. Volcanoes and earthquakes tend to be concentrated around the margins of convergent plates. A third type of plate boundary, the *transform fault boundary*, delineates regions where plates move past each other without creating or destroying lithosphere. Although most transform faults occur in ocean basins, the well-known San Andreas Fault in California is an example of a continental transform fault.

Sediments in the Ocean Basins

Sediments in the ocean basins and along their margins are derived from rivers, glaciers, coastal erosion, wind transport, and from the remains of microscopic marine organisms. The global distribution of ocean sediments depends primarily on distance from land and depth of the water. Continental margins trap much of the land-derived or terrigenous sediment; however, a small amount bypasses the margins and moves to the deep ocean basins by sliding downslope (slumping) or by transport through submarine canyons as turbidity currents. Sediments on the upper continental margins are subject to widespread erosion, transport, and deposition from tidal currents, wind-driven currents, storm waves, and variations in sea level.

Pelagic sediments dominate toward the centers of the ocean basins. These deposits are comprised of very small particles, both organic and inorganic, that have settled from the water over long periods of time. The organic (or biogenous) sediments are called *oozes* and are composed of the skeletal remains of small marine plants and animals. Pelagic oozes that are composed of calcium carbonate are very soluble at great depths or in cold water. As a result, they cannot accumulate when the ocean floor is shallower than the CCD (carbonate compensation depth) and thus rarely occur in water depths greater than 5000 meters (16,400 feet). The main inorganic pelagic sediment is red clay, comprised of extremely small particles [less than 1 micrometer (0.00004 inch) in size] that appear to be transported by wind. Globally, about 62 percent by area of the pelagic sediments are oozes and 38 percent are red clays.

Long-term rates of sediment accumulation vary tremendously. The highest rates are close to continents where terrigenous sources are dominant. Here, sedimentation rates of 5 centimeters (2 inches) per 1000 years are typical, although short-term rates can be even higher [up to 10 centimeters (4 inches) per year]. The slowest rates, less than 1 centimeter (0.4 inch) per 1000 years, are in regions of the ocean dominated by red clay. The accumulation rates of oozes are intermediate at about 1 to 3 centimeters (0.4 to 1.2 inches) per 1000 years. Long periods of sediment deposition (millions of years), even at seemingly slow rates, produce thick sequences of sedimentary strata that contain a detailed history of the ocean basins.

Minerals from the Seafloor

Ocean basins hold vast mineral resources on which society depends. In addition to petroleum and natural gas, the shallow seafloor contains sand and gravel, titanium, tin, gold, and even diamonds. Deep-ocean basins contain chemically precipitated minerals such as manganese nodules and metallic sulfide deposits, and bacterially produced methane or gas hydrates (icelike solids). All of these resources are nonrenewable, and many are in limited supply.

John T. Wells

FURTHER READING

Bonatti, E. "The Rifting of Continents." *Scientific American,* Vol. 256 (1987), pp. 96–103.

Heath, G. R. "Manganese Nodules: Unanswered Questions." *Oceanus,* Vol. 25 (1982), pp. 37–41.

Heirtzler, J. R., and W. B. Bryan. "The Floor of the Mid-Atlantic Rift." *Scientific American,* Vol. 233 (1975), pp. 78–91.

McGregor, B. A. "The Submerged Continental Margin." *American Scientist,* Vol. 72 (1984), pp. 275–281.

Seibold, E., and W. H. Berger. *The Sea Floor.* Berlin: Springer-Verlag, 1993.

Tarbuck, E. J., and F. K. Lutgens. *Earth.* Upper Saddle River, N.J.: Prentice Hall, 1999.

RELATED ARTICLES

Continental Margin; Ocean; Pangea; Plate Tectonics; Submarine Volcanism

Ocean Circulation

The movement of the ocean's waters is referred to as the circulation of the ocean. It consists of a wide range of spatial and temporal scales of motion. The largest scale is that of oceanic gyres, which span thousands of kilometers and have variability that ranges from seasons to centuries. The next important scale is the mesoscale, which spans 50 to 200 kilometers (about 30 to 125 miles) with time scales of about one month. The ocean circulation has an important role in maintaining global balances of heat, fresh water, and carbon dioxide. It also determines where productive fisheries will occur.

Solar energy drives the ocean circulation in two different ways. The first is the wind. The second is by differences in heating and evaporation. Oceanographers refer to the first as the wind-driven circulation and the second as thermohaline circulation. In addition to these forcing mechanisms, the circulation is also controlled by the rotation of Earth and the shape of the ocean basins. The average of the circulation over many years is called the *general circulation of the ocean.*

One way of classifying currents is by their depth. Currently, oceanographers recognize four circulation levels: surface, intermediate, deep, and bottom. Prior to 1940, oceanographers used only two levels, stratosphere and troposphere, adopting terminology from meteorology where the stratosphere referred to the deep and bottom circulation and the troposphere referred to surface and intermediate-level currents. Another way of classifying ocean currents is by their forcing mechanisms. Wind-driven circulation is mostly the *surface circulation,* and intermediate, deep, and bottom circulation is the *thermohaline circulation.* Although these classification schemes are useful for an introduction to the circulation of the ocean, they can be misleading if taken too literally. For example, the Gulf Stream and the Antarctic Circumpolar Current are part of the wind-driven circulation, yet both extend to the bottom of the ocean. Although the general pattern of the surface circulation can be deduced by assuming that wind is the only driving force, heating and evaporation are important factors as well. The distinction between intermediate, deep, and bottom circulation is based on the origin of the water masses involved and does not correspond to a fixed depth level.

It is useful to compare the circulation to that of the atmosphere. The principal difference between the two is the presence or absence of lateral boundaries. The atmosphere has no lateral boundaries due to landmasses, so it is possible to describe its circulation by taking zonal averages around Earth. In the ocean, with the exception of the circumpolar current, the oceans have lateral boundaries due to landmasses. As a result, circulations are turned or forced to other depths by continental blocking. The boundaries also result in westward intensification and support coastal trapped waves. The types of mean circulations in the atmosphere include vertical circulation cells, called *Hadley* or *Ferrel* cells, and jet streams that are driven by meridional temperature gradients. Within the ocean, the wind-driven circulation is organized into gyres as well as a thermohaline-driven meridional overturning, part of which is sometimes referred to as the *oceanic conveyor belt.*

Wind-Driven Circulation

In 1905, Vagn Walfrid Ekman (1874–1954) produced a theory that explained the relationship between winds and the surface circulation of the ocean. His theory was motivated by Fridtjof Nansen's (1861–1930) observation that ice drifted to the right of the wind in the Arctic Ocean. For more than 40 years, this was the only quantitative theory of ocean circulation. Ekman assumed that the frictional stress of the winds was balanced by the rotation of Earth, and he showed that the transport of ocean waters was 90° to the right (left) of the wind stress in the northern (southern) hemisphere. This surface layer, moving orthogonally to the wind stress, is called the *Ekman layer* by oceanographers.

Since the trade winds are northeastward at low latitudes (0 to 30°) and westward winds prevail at higher latitudes (40 to 60°), Ekman's theory predicts northward flow at low latitudes and southward flow at high latitudes. These result in a convergence of flow, and since the water does not pile up, it must escape downward, a process called *Ekman pumping* by oceanographers. A typical rate for Ekman pumping at subtropical latitudes is 30 meters (about 98 feet) per year. This creates a pool of warm water in the middle of the subtropical gyre. Geostrophic flow, which involves a balance between horizontal pressure gradients and the rotation of Earth, causes water in the northern (southern) hemisphere to flow so that the warmer water is on the right (left). This creates a system of ocean gyres.

Variations in gyre-scale circulation can occur over various periods of time. Two examples for the North Pacific Ocean are El Niño and the Pacific Decadal Oscillations (PDO). El Niño events involve warming of Eastern Tropical Pacific and coastal California Current waters, which persists for 6 to 18 months. PDO involves a pattern of cooling (warming) in the northwestern Pacific Ocean and warming (cooling) in the eastern tropical Pacific Ocean. PDO eras persist for 20 to 30 years at a time. Cool PDO regimes prevailed from 1890 to 1924 and from 1947 to 1976 and warm PDO regimes occurred from 1925 to 1946 and from 1976 through the early 1990s.

Oceanic Conveyor Belt

Thermohaline circulation is caused by density differences. Dense fluid will sink and flow toward regions of lower density, whereas lighter fluid will rise and flow on the surface toward the region of density increase. Density increases are caused by cooling or an increase in salinity (evaporation or ice formation). Density decreases are caused by heating or a decrease in salinity (runoff, precipitation, or ice melting). Because it is cold at the poles and warm at the equator, surfaces of constant density are deep at the equator and shoal toward the poles. Oceanographers have been able to infer the flow of intermediate, deep, and bottom currents by examining the patterns of temperature, salinity, and other ocean tracers (e.g., dissolved oxygen, nutrients) on surfaces of constant density.

At low latitudes, heat flows into the ocean, warming surface waters that do not mix deeply. At high latitudes, a net heat loss produces cooler water, which sinks and moves equatorward.

The waters that sink must be replaced by the horizontal advection of warm waters from equatorial regions. Sinking is localized to areas of deep and bottom water formation—the former in the northern North Atlantic and the latter mostly in the Weddell Sea. Separating the warm surface and deep cold waters is the thermocline. Continuity requires that if waters are sinking at one location, they must rise at another location. The rising takes place throughout the interior of the ocean as a slow upward flow of cool water that can be thought of as supporting the thermocline.

The sinking of deep and bottom waters occurs at a rate of 30×10^6 meters per second The overturning and circulation of the deep waters in the North Atlantic has been linked to a global circulation that is called the *oceanic conveyor belt*. After sinking in the North Atlantic, these waters flow southward as a deep western boundary current into the Circumpolar Current. The Circumpolar Current transports the deep waters to the east, from where they flow northward into the Indian and Pacific Oceans. They return to the North Atlantic as a surface current, originating in the Pacific Ocean, flowing through the Indonesian Archipelago to the Indian Ocean, and then south of Africa into the South and North Atlantic Oceans. Conditions at high latitudes in the North Atlantic drive this conveyor belt: The colder and saltier the water, the greater the rate of formation of deep water and the faster the conveyor belt will move.

In practice, both the wind-driven and thermohaline circulation act together to produce the general circulation. The upper layers respond to exchanges of heat, fresh water, and momentum with a relaxation time of weeks. The depth of reaction increases with time interval so that, by definition, the seasonal thermocline at 100 meters (about 328 feet) is the reaction depth for seasonal changes in the atmosphere. The behavior of deep ocean is the result of atmospheric coupling over hundreds and thousands of years.

Mesoscale Eddies

If the general circulation is ocean climate, mesoscale eddies are ocean weather. Most of the kinetic energy of the ocean, perhaps as much as 99 percent, resides in these mesoscale motions. Mesoscale variability is particularly strong near western boundary currents as well as in the Circumpolar Current. Eddies have characteristic velocities of 0.04 to 0.4 meter per second (0.078 to 0.78 knots) and are generated by meanders and instabilities in the gyre-scale circulation. The extent to which the energy of mesoscale eddies feeds back into the large-scale general circulation is not clear, nor is their role in transporting heat, fresh water, and ocean properties.

Paleoocean Circulation

Because the ocean plays a key role in climate change, scientists examining the history of Earth have used ocean circulation models to try to explain how the climate of Earth changes from an ice age to an interglacial period or a period when there is no glacial ice on land (called a *greenhouse climate*). Two forcing mechanisms for climate change are tectonic movements and orbital changes. *Tectonic changes* are movements of Earth's crust that change the shape and configuration of the ocean basins as well as the continents. *Orbital changes* are changes in the tilt of Earth and its distance from the Sun.

Tectonic-Scale Climate Change

A single super continent, Pangea, was created by a sequence of continental collisions between 350 and 250 million years ago. Pangea began to break up 180 million years ago, and the continents have gradually moved to their present positions. Beginning about 55 million years ago, Earth began a profound cooling at both poles and across lower latitudes that continues to the present. The climate changes might be explained by opening or closing critical oceanic gateways. Two examples of ocean gateways are the opening of circulation around Antarctica and the emergence of the Isthmus of Panama, which joined North and South America.

The last of the present continents were connected to Antarctica at the beginning of this period. A chronology for subsequent events is: Australia moves away from Antarctica 40 million years ago, the first Antarctic ice occurred 35 million years ago, and Drake's Passage between South America and Antarctica opened about 25 million years ago, surrounding Antarctica with the circumpolar ocean. Oceanographers have hypothesized that before the continents separated from Antarctica, Australia and South America diverted warm ocean currents poleward from low latitudes, bringing enough heat to Antarctica to prevent glaciation. Clearly, opening just one passage, south of Australia, was enough to begin the glaciation, as the later opening of Drake's Passage was not correlated with changes in Antarctic glaciers.

The second case involved the closing of the Central American seaway caused by the emergence of the Isthmus of Panama. Final closure occurred just before 4 million years ago and was followed by the first large-scale glaciation of North America. Prior to closure, the tropical Pacific and Atlantic Oceans could exchange water, resulting in warmer water in the Pacific and fresher water in the Atlantic. Closure forced the tropical Atlantic waters to feed the Gulf Stream, bringing more heat and salinity to high latitudes in the North Atlantic. This meant that less sea ice and more moisture from the ocean was available to nearby landmasses, triggering the growth of ice sheets. The higher salt also contributed to an increase in deep-water formation in the North Atlantic.

Orbital-Scale Climate Change

Small but significant changes in the pattern of the Sun's radiation are caused by variations in the tilt of Earth and the orbit of Earth around the Sun. The axis of rotation of Earth is presently inclined by 23.5° to the plane of rotation of Earth about the Sun, but it varies from 22 to 24.5° with a period of 41,000 years. A second variation is called the *precession of the equinoxes* and has a period of 22,000 years. This refers to the fact that at the present time Earth is closest to the Sun in July and 11,000 years from now, Earth will be closest to the Sun in December. A third orbital parameter is the eccentricity of the Earth–Sun ellipse, which varies from more ellipsoid to more circular with a period of 100,000 years.

Two oceanic circulation patterns have been associated with orbital climate change. The first is a strengthening of the Atlantic Southwest Monsoon, which occurs over a 22,000-year period. When the monsoon is stronger, the westward trade-wind flow along the equator is weaker. This reduces the intensity of upwelling, so the thermocline is deepened and the layer of water over the thermocline is warmed.

A second pattern is associated with ice growth when summer insolation is low in high northern latitudes. This happens both when Earth's orbital tilt is small, so its poles are pointed less directly at the Sun, as well as when northern hemisphere summer solstice occurs and Earth is farthest from the Sun. This has 100,000-year cycles and is accompanied by a slow buildup of ice followed by a rapid deglaciation, which takes only about 10,000 years. In 1920, a Serbian astronomer, Milutin Milankovitch (1879–1958), made detailed calculations of the orbital changes and their consequence on Earth's radiation budget and proposed that they would be reflected in Earth's climate. Only in the past 20 years have geologists been able to confirm these predictions.

Deep circulation in the Atlantic Ocean is entirely different during periods of glaciation. North Atlantic deep water is replaced in most of the deep Atlantic basin by water from southern sources, which can dissolve calcium carbonate much more rapidly.

About 20,000 years ago during the peak of the last ice age, ocean temperatures were warm when the ice sheets were small; they were cold when the ice sheets were large. The formation of deep water in the Atlantic slowed during times when ice sheets were large. For example, 20,000 years ago the oceanic conveyor belt had a circulation period of 675 years, and today it has a period of 350 years. This means that the deep Atlantic water was replaced more slowly at the glacial maximum than today.

Millennial-Scale (1000 years) Climate Change

Millennial-scale climate changes may be controlled by a mechanism referred to as a *natural salt oscillator*. When ice sheets are present, the salt forced out of the ice increases the salinity of surface waters, which sink into the deep ocean, forming deep water. This removes the salt from the sea surface, but the ocean heat is handed off to the atmosphere where the deep water forms, then melts nearby coastal margins of ice sheets. This melting gradually increases the delivery of fresh meltwater, reducing the salinity of the sea surface so that no deep water forms. This means that no heat is handed off to the atmosphere, so ice forms, salt is introduced into the surface layer of the ocean, and the cycle begins again.

Curtis A. Collins

FURTHER READING

Broecker, Wallace. "The Great Ocean Conveyor." *Oceanography*, Vol. 4 (1991).

Broecker, Wallace, and George Denton. "What Drives Glacial Cycles." *Scientific American*, January 1990, p. 49.

Garrison, Tom. *Oceanography*. Belmont, Calif.: Wadsworth Publishing, 1993; 3rd ed. 1998.

Knauss, John A. *Introduction to Physical Oceanography*. Englewood Cliffs, N.J.: Prentice Hall, 1978; 2nd ed. rev., Upper Saddle River, N.J.: Prentice Hall, 2000.

Neumann, Gerhard. *Ocean Currents*. Amsterdam and New York: Elsevier, 1968.

Pickard, G. L., and W. J. Emery. *Descriptive Physical Oceanography: An Introduction,* 5th ed. Elmsford, N.Y.: Pergamon Press, 1990.

Ruddiman, William F. *Earth's Climate, Past and Future.* New York: W. H. Freeman, 2001.

Stommel, Henry M. *A View of the Sea.* Princeton, N.J.: Princeton University Press, 1987.

Warren, Bruce. "Deep Circulation of the World Ocean." In *Evolution of Physical Oceanography.* Cambridge, Mass.: MIT Press, 1981; pp. 6–41.

RELATED ARTICLES

Antarctic Circumpolar Current; Bottom Current; Climate Change; Earth, Rotation of; Eddy; Ekman Layer; El Niño; Gulf Stream; Gyre; Hadley Cell; Thermohaline Circulation

Ocean Current

Ocean currents are organized systems of flow that occur on many different scales throughout the world's oceans. These currents often transport large volumes of water over great distances. Ocean currents have been observed and charted for hundreds of years. The majority of information on ocean currents has been obtained from observations of ship drift. Ship drift is usually calculated as the difference between the actual position of a ship and its position predicted 24 hours earlier. Although ship drift is affected by both wind and currents, it is usually assumed that the primary source of drift is currents. Although the method is not precise, most of what we know today about circulation of the world's oceans has been obtained in this manner. When observations of ship drift are averaged over many years, a picture emerges of the mean circulation over the world's oceans.

Different types of currents exist. Currents occur in coastal areas adjacent to land boundaries and in the deep ocean away from any land influence. Major currents are found in Arctic and Antarctic as well as equatorial regions. Many currents are primarily surface flows that extend down to depths of only a few hundred meters. Other currents are deep, existing entirely below the ocean surface at

depths as great as 1000 meters (3280 feet) or more. Some of the more well-known currents are better characterized as current systems because they may include countercurrents that flow in opposition to the primary flow and undercurrents that are found near the primary current but at some depth below the surface. Some currents exist throughout the year whereas other currents, such as the Davidson Current off California, occur for only several months during the year. Some currents, such as the Gulf Stream, are intense, deep, and jetlike, with speeds up to 2 meters per second (4 knots). Other currents, such as the California Current, are broad and diffuse and have much weaker mean flows.

Forces That Produce Ocean Currents

The circulation of the surface ocean is primarily wind-driven. Winds blowing over the ocean surface exert a stress on the water that produces shallow circulation referred to as *wind drift*. Based on the difference in density between air and seawater, a simple rule of thumb is that the current speed should be roughly equal to 3 percent of the wind speed. This 3 percent rule is very approximate and under some conditions can give misleading results. If the effects of Earth's rotation are taken into account, theoretical calculations (called *Ekman currents*) show that the surface drift is deflected 45° to the right in the northern hemisphere and 45° to the left in the southern hemisphere. Proceeding deeper into the water column, the currents continue to rotate to the right (in the northern hemisphere) and decrease in strength, forming a spiral known as the *Ekman spiral*. Because of other forces at work, it has been difficult in practice to verify this theory. When transport due to wind drift is summed up vertically, the total transport (i.e., the *Ekman transport*) is directed at right angles to the wind. Next to a coastline, if the coast lies to the left of the wind direction (in the northern hemisphere), the surface waters are driven offshore through the process of offshore Ekman transport, and colder waters from below rise to the surface to

OCEAN CURRENT

replace them. This process, referred to as *coastal upwelling*, occurs along the western boundaries of many continents.

When the apparent force due to Earth's rotation is balanced by downslope gravitational forces that result from small changes in elevation of the ocean surface, the type of current motion that results is called *geostrophic*. Slopes in the sea surface that result from changes in surface elevation, although relatively small [usually less than 100 centimeters (39 inches) over distances of a few kilometers or more], come about through changes in the internal density structure of the ocean that are due to changes in temperature and salinity. These very small changes in surface slope can now be measured directly from space using instruments called *satellite altimeters*. Most major ocean currents, such as the Gulf Stream and the Kuroshio, are considered to be in geostrophic balance, at least approximately.

Tidal currents are produced by forces associated with the gravitational attraction of the Sun and the Moon. In the open ocean, tidal currents usually rotate due to the rotation of Earth (i.e., the speed and direction as both change from hour to hour). They are also usually small, in the neighborhood of 2 to 5 centimeters (0.8 to 2.0 inches) per second. In coastal areas, tidal currents vary from one location to another, depending on the character of the tide, the water depth, and the shape of the coastline. As the tide approaches the shore and water depth decreases, tidal flows become more intense and tend to parallel the coastline. To predict tidal currents in any given coastal area, a series of tidal current measurements must first be made.

How Ocean Currents Are Defined and Measured

Ocean currents are defined according to their speed and direction, as are *vectors* (quantities that have both direction and magnitude). As a result, a coordinate system of reference must be chosen.

The usual convention for ocean currents is to use a right-handed coordinate system with the positive x-axis pointing horizontally to the east and the positive y-axis pointing horizontally to the north. Unlike the wind, which is defined by the direction *from which* it blows, ocean currents are defined according to the direction *toward which* they flow. Current speeds are usually measured in centimeters per second, kilometers per day, or nautical miles per hour (knots). The transport of water by currents or volume flow is measured in millions of cubic meters per second. The Gulf Stream south of Nova Scotia, for example, transports roughly 150 million cubic meters (5295 million cubic feet) of water per second compared to the Mississippi River, which transports about 0.02 million cubic meters (0.7 million cubic feet) of water per second.

The field of motion in the ocean can be determined through direct measurement, or indirectly through measurements of temperature and salinity. The internal distribution of temperature and salinity determines the distribution of density, and changes in density over distance generate the forces required to produce currents. Using this approach, the motion relative to some deeper level in the ocean where the actual velocity is known or assumed can be estimated.

There are basically two ways to measure water motions directly, the Eulerian approach and the Lagrangian approach. In the application of *Eulerian methods*, the velocity of flow (i.e., speed and direction) past a fixed point is measured as a function of depth and time. In using *Lagrangian methods*, the paths followed by tagged water particles are tracked with respect to time. Eulerian methods are often used in theoretical studies, whereas Lagrangian methods are most frequently used to describe the large-scale circulation of the oceans. Eulerian measurements are made typically using current meters attached to moored arrays that are anchored to the ocean bottom. These instruments, much like the anemometers that

364

measure winds in the atmosphere, are rotary devices that count the number of rotations over a given time period of a propeller that is mounted in the instrument. This information is either stored for later retrieval or telemetered back to the surface so that it can be accessed in real time. The current meter, with refinements over the years, has been a mainstay in making current measurements in the ocean. However, in recent years new techniques using underwater sound have become increasingly popular. One technique employs sound waves that are backscattered to a listening device by particles in the water. The frequency of the sound waves emitted and received is shifted slightly due to the motion of the water itself (i.e., Doppler shift) and thus provides a method of estimating currents. A number of other methods are also used in making current measurements using the Eulerian approach.

In making Lagrangian measurements, different types of floating devices have been used, including drift cards, drift bottles, and other drifting objects. More recently, remotely tracked drifting buoys have been developed whose locations can be monitored using satellites. Lagrangian subsurface measurements are also made using neutrally buoyant floats whose density is adjusted so that they move at a predetermined depth along with water of comparable density. These floats transmit acoustic signals that allow a ship to track their path. In each case the trajectories of these devices are used to estimate the motion that results from their displacement over time. Chemical and radioactive tracers have also been used to infer patterns of circulation. However, the use of tracers to estimate the flow tends to be more difficult because the distribution of the tracer must be observed over space and time, and tracer concentrations must also be measured.

Ocean Currents around the Globe

The global ocean circulation is made up of many currents; some are primarily surface currents, whereas others are located at intermediate and deeper levels. Here, the best known major ocean currents are described. In some cases, these currents are deep and may extend all the way to the ocean bottom. The circulation of the Atlantic and Pacific Oceans are generally similar. In both cases the circulation is dominated by large rotating systems of circulation called *gyres*. In the northern hemisphere, the gyres rotate clockwise and in the southern hemisphere, they rotate counterclockwise. In each case they are driven by torque from the surface wind field. The gyres in each hemisphere are separated by currents that flow in an east–west direction at low latitudes near the equator. In both hemispheres there are relatively strong, narrow currents flowing toward the poles along the eastern boundaries of the continents (called *western boundary currents* because they are located along the western boundaries of the oceans). Conversely, weaker currents tend to occur along the western boundaries of the continents (called *eastern boundary currents* because they are located along the eastern boundaries of the oceans), which flow toward the equator.

Two of the best-known western boundary currents are the Gulf Stream, which is located in the North Atlantic, and the Kuroshio, located in the North Pacific Ocean. These currents appear to be somewhat more intense than their counterparts in the southern hemisphere. The Gulf Stream extends all the way from the Gulf of Mexico, around Florida, and hugs the coast up to Cape Hatteras, where it separates from the coast and crosses the Atlantic, approaching the coast of Europe. After leaving the coast, the path of the Gulf Stream varies and sizable meanders develop downstream. These meanders often break off and become eddies, which are found on both sides of the Gulf Stream. The width of the Gulf Stream is between 100 and 150 kilometers (62 and 93 miles). The maximum velocities approach about 2.5 meters per second (5 knots).

After it leaves Cape Hatteras, the Gulf Stream becomes very deep and reaches the bottom. The amount of water transported by the Gulf Stream increases as it flows downstream past Cape Hatteras. Maximum transport has been estimated to be as high as 150 million cubic meters (196 million cubic yards) per second. The Kuroshio is similar to the Gulf Stream in most respects. However, it has one important difference; it develops a large, semipermanent meander off the coast of Japan that can last for years. Thus, the Kuroshio appears to have two states, one with the meander and one without, and both can last for several years or more.

Along eastern boundaries (i.e., the western boundaries of continents), currents flow toward the equator. These currents tend to be broad, weak, and shallow compared to western boundary currents. The California Current is an eastern boundary current that flows southward off the west coast of the United States. Because the mean southward flow is weak, it is sometimes difficult to observe because of the inherent variability in the flow. The California Current is at most 500 meters (1640 feet) deep and probably transports less than 15 million cubic meters (19.6 million cubic yards) of water per second. In regions where eastern boundary currents occur, coastal upwelling and countercurrents are often found. These features are related to the California Current itself, but the details of this relationship are not well understood.

Near the equator in the Atlantic and Pacific Oceans between about 10°S and 20°N, a complex system of currents, countercurrents, and undercurrents exists. These currents flow parallel to the equator and are directly related to the trade winds that are found in this region. The North and South Equatorial Currents that are located north and south of the equator, respectively, flow to the west. Just north of the equator, flowing between these currents to the east, is the North Equatorial Countercurrent. Finally, at the equator itself is a subsurface current called the Equatorial Undercurrent, which flows eastward. These currents collectively make up the Equatorial Current System.

The Antarctic Circumpolar Current is located at high southern latitudes surrounding Antarctica. This current flows eastward and extends to the bottom. It is the largest current in the world, with a transport of roughly 200 million cubic meters (262 million cubic yards) per second. The driving force behind the Antarctic Circumpolar Current is the prevailing westerly winds, which occur at high southern latitudes.

Ocean currents are important to ships at sea. By sailing with the current, the time spent at sea can be reduced, resulting in significant fuel savings. Coastal currents have a significant impact on the weather in coastal areas. Some of the worst storms to hit the east coast of the United States have intensified rapidly over the warm waters of the Gulf Stream. The cool waters of the California Current, together with coastal upwelling, help to maintain a comfortable climate along the west coast of the United States. Finally, ocean currents provide essential pathways for redistributing heat from lower latitudes to higher latitudes over the world's oceans. In so doing, currents help to regulate the thermal climate of the entire planet.

Laurence C. Breaker

FURTHER READING

Fairbridge, Rhodes W., ed. *The Encyclopedia of Oceanography, Encyclopedia of Earth Sciences,* Vol. 1. New York: Reinhold, 1966.

Knauss, John A. *Introduction to Physical Oceanography.* Englewood Cliffs, N.J.: Prentice Hall, 1978; 2nd ed. rev., Upper Saddle River, N.J.: Prentice Hall, 2000.

Neumann, Gerhard. *Ocean Currents.* Amsterdam and New York: Elsevier, 1968.

Wells, Neil. *The Atmosphere and Ocean: A Physical Introduction.* London and Philadelphia: Taylor and Francis, 1986; 2nd ed., Chichester, England, and New York: Wiley, 1997.

Ocean Drilling Program

The Ocean Drilling Program (ODP), successor to the highly successful Deep Sea Drilling Project (DSDP), is an international partnership of scientists and research institutions formed to continue the exploration of the portion of Earth beneath the sea. ODP began in 1983 and is scheduled to end in 2003.

Following the reconnaissance drilling of DSDP, ODP represents a more focused approach to fundamental scientific questions. Drill sites are selected both to gain basic information about the geology of the ocean floor and to obtain data critical to the solution of specific problems. Topics addressed by the program can be grouped into two broad themes: the dynamics of Earth's environment and the dynamics of Earth's interior. Environmental questions include Earth's changing climate and ocean circulation, as recorded in the oceanic sedimentary record; the history of changing sea level; the subseafloor biosphere; and the occurrence of gas hydrates in deep-sea sediments. Issues concerning Earth's interior encompass hydrothermal mineralization, deformation and fluid flow in the lithosphere, the nature and origin of large igneous provinces, and the deep crust. In all these areas ODP results are causing Earth scientists to refine and reevaluate their concepts of Earth's structure and evolution.

Overall management of ODP rests with Joint Oceanographic Institutions (JOI), a consortium of major U.S. marine science research institutions, which has subcontracted with Texas A&M University (TAMU) for science operations and with Lamont-Doherty Earth Observatory (LDEO) for wireline services (well logging) and for operation of the site survey database. In addition to directing the operations of the drillship, TAMU is responsible for maintaining and staffing state-of-the-art scientific laboratories on the ship, publishing the scientific results of the program, and maintaining a database of scientific data and core repositories located at Scripps Institution of Oceanography in California, LDEO in New York, TAMU in Texas, and the University of Bremen in Germany.

JOIDES Resolution

The centerpiece of ODP is the 143-meter (470-feet)-long dynamically positioned drillship, *JOIDES Resolution*, owned by TransOcean Sedco-Forex. Built in 1978 in Halifax, Nova Scotia, and first operated as an oil exploration vessel, *JOIDES Resolution* was converted for scientific drilling in 1984. The ship is equipped to drill in water up to 8 kilometers (26,247 feet) deep, recover core samples of the rocks, and make in situ measurements of crustal properties to depths of more than 1 kilometer (3280 feet) below the seafloor. The cores are described and analyzed in the shipboard laboratories while the ship is at sea. An ice-strengthened hull permits operations at high latitudes. A recent modification installed of the world's largest active heave compensation system, designed to decouple the drill string from the vertical motion of the ship and reduce variations in the weight on the drill bit at the bottom of the hole. The deepest hole drilled to date extends 2 kilometers (6562 feet) below the seafloor, on the East Pacific Rise. As of October 2000, almost 1200 sites have been occupied by either *JOIDES Resolution* or her DSDP predecessor, *Glomar Challenger*. These span all the oceans (except the Arctic) and many of the major seas.

JOIDES Resolution uses open-circulation drilling; that is, seawater is pumped down the drill pipe to remove cuttings and cool the bit, the cuttings being swept up the annulus between the drill string and the walls of the hole and out onto the seafloor. Although less complex than closed-circulation drilling, which uses a conductor pipe (riser) to carry drilling fluid and cuttings back to the surface, open circulation has a disadvantage because drilling mud cannot be used to improve drilling conditions and maintain control over the downhole environment. Although many cores are cut using "conventional" wireline rotary tools, ODP has made significant improvements in coring and sampling tools and techniques. In soft sediment, rotary coring destroys the integrity of the cores. The Advanced Piston Corer (APC), a further evolution of a device developed by DSDP, uses hydraulic pressure to drive the core barrel through and ahead of the bit into soft sediment, retrieving essentially undisturbed cores. In alternating hard and soft material, an extended core barrel pushes ahead of the bit in soft sediment

and then retracts within the drill string when the bit is needed to cut through harder material. A pressure core barrel can be used to retrieve cores at near bottom-hole pressures.

In addition to drilling and coring, *JOIDES Resolution* carries a logging unit provided by Schlumberger Technology Corporation, and LDEO, in conjunction with Schlumberger, operates a logging program designed to measure in situ rock properties in the drillhole. Basic tool suites developed for oilfield use are deployed, as well as special tools developed by scientists, which include a temperature probe, a deep-sensing resistivity tool, and a downhole fluid sampler.

Some Results from the Ocean Drilling Program

Space precludes a comprehensive account of the results of ODP, which by now fill many thousands

JOIDES Resolution, *a scientific drillship. (Courtesy, ODP, John Beck)*

of pages of books and papers. Following are a few selected examples.

HIGH-RESOLUTION STRATIGRAPHY

Drilling with the APC in Santa Barbara Basin, offshore of southern California, ODP recovered an undisturbed, highly detailed record extending back to 160,000 years ago. The sediments occur as thin laminae reflecting the alternating seasonal dominance between river input from land during the rainy season and marine input from surface biological productivity during the dry season. Individual laminar pairs can be examined and counted and can be correlated with the tree ring dating record from land. Furthermore, the Santa Barbara cores show changes in oxygen isotope ratios and levels of oxygenation of the basin that can be matched with short-lived climatic excursions recorded in cores from the Greenland ice sheet, suggesting global-scale climatic linkages.

Sediment cores obtained with the APC have made it possible to construct an astronomically tuned geologic timescale, which can now be extended back several million years, with resolution at the century to millennial scale. The timescale is based on the discovery that many sediment properties (bulk density, magnetic susceptibility, color reflectance, and oxygen isotope ratios) not only vary coherently between closely spaced sites but can also be correlated with variations in solar insolation, calculated from astronomical observations. Thus the response of climate and ocean circulation to variations in Earth's orbit is recorded with extraordinary sensitivity in subtle variations in sediment properties. The astronomically tuned timescale provides a reliable absolute timescale to which the seafloor magnetic anomaly scale, the oxygen isotope record, the seismic stratigraphy of the Pacific and Atlantic Oceans, and other aspects of the sedimentary record can be related. It can also be used to calibrate biostratigraphy, opening the way to examine quantitatively species distribution, and

rates of cycling of carbon and other biologically important nutrients, and to relate these to changes in atmospheric and ocean circulation. Such studies add constraints to climatologists' models of past and future climates, as well as enhance our understanding of past ocean environments and their biota.

SUBSEAFLOOR BIOSPHERE

It was long thought that life is restricted to Earth's surface and the uppermost 5 to 10 meters (16 to 33 feet) of the solid Earth, both on land and under the oceans. However, ODP cores reveal bacteria living in sediments to depths of at least 800 meters (2625 feet) below the seafloor. Similar observations have been made in boreholes on land. Bacteria have also been found within voids and cracks in volcanic rock formed at mid-ocean ridges. Bacteria in this deep biosphere are adapted to survive in extreme temperatures and pressures and in fluids of unusual compositions. Together with research revealing the role that bacteria play in global biogeochemistry, this discovery affects ideas about biomineralization, biomagnetization, nutrient cycling, and biological adaptation. Some bacterial populations appear to be able to survive on buried organic matter for millions of years. Studies of the deep biosphere, accessible only by drilling, open new avenues for bioremediation, waste treatment, enhanced oil recovery, and perhaps, economic concentrations of biominerals.

TERMINAL CRETACEOUS EVENT

Scientists now recognize that Earth's history is punctuated by rare, but catastrophic events, the best known of which occurred at the end of the Cretaceous Period (65 million years ago). The event is recorded in an iridium-enriched clay layer, which apparently exists worldwide and is thought to provide evidence of a major bolide (meteorite or comet) impact. The end of the Cretaceous is also a time when about 70 percent of existing species became extinct. Debates on the "terminal Cretaceous event" and its possible connection to the mass extinction invariably raise the question: Where was the impact site? The Chicxulub crater, lying partially on the Yucatán Peninsula and partially offshore, is frequently cited. Recent geophysical evidence indicates that the Chicxulub crater is indeed the result of an impact by a very large object, perhaps as wide as 16 kilometers (10 miles) across. Such an impact would have had a dramatic effect on the Caribbean and Gulf of Mexico, producing tsunamis that would have devastated low-lying coastal regions, including much of Florida. This is confirmed by ODP cores collected from the Atlantic, 483 kilometers (300 miles) off northern Florida, which show a 15-centimeter (6-inch)-thick layer of meteoritic debris at the Cretaceous–Tertiary boundary, presumed to have come from Chicxulub. Above the meteoritic debris is an interval of sediment deposited in an ocean apparently almost devoid of life, overlain by sediments recording the gradual repopulation of the region in the earliest Tertiary.

FLUID CIRCULATION AND SULFIDE ORES

Like groundwater flow beneath the continents, fluid flow is ubiquitous beneath the ocean floor. Such flow occurs at high-temperature vents associated with spreading centers, as tectonically forced fluid expulsion in subduction zones, and as low-temperature hydrothermal circulation throughout much of the ocean floors. Drilling into a volcanic-hosted sulfide mound situated in the median valley of the Mid-Atlantic Ridge provided insights into hydrothermal activity associated with young oceanic crust. This particular site is important because it serves as a modern analog to massive (and economically important) sulfide deposits such as those found on Cyprus. More recent drilling in Middle Valley, the sediment-covered portion of the northern Juan de Fuca Ridge, penetrated an

active hydrothermal system, obtaining samples and well logs in rock temperatures approaching 300°C (572°F). The composition of this active hydrothermal field was demonstrably linked to convective circulation of seawater and controlled by subseafloor metamorphism of the overlying rocks.

Scientists working in collaboration with ODP engineers have developed a device known as a CORK (Circulation Obviation Retrofit Kit). This consists of a data recording package (the CORK) designed to fit tightly into the opening of a seafloor drill hole, isolating the hole from the seafloor environment. Beneath the CORK hangs a string of sensors to measure in situ conditions (temperature, pressure) within the borehole, and a fluid sampler that can gather water for chemical analysis. Measurements made by the sensors are recorded by the datalogger in the CORK, which can be serviced periodically by a submersible or a remote-operated vehicle (ROV). CORK experiments are providing hard data about seafloor permeabilities, rates of fluid circulation, fluid compositions, and so on. Such data are of interest not only for basic research but also for the mining industry, as it refines exploration strategies. A new generation of advanced CORK (A-CORK) will be deployed in 2001. The A-CORK allows portions of the borehole at different depths to be isolated for separate studies.

DEEP CRUST AND UPPER MANTLE

Most of our knowledge of the deep crust and upper mantle of Earth comes from geophysical measurements (seismic refraction) and from examination of rocks exposed on land that are believed to have originated at such depths (ophiolites). However, on the Southwest Indian Ridge, east of the Atlantis II Fracture Zone, faulting has brought rocks that are certainly from the lower crust within reach of the drill. Here, ODP has sampled gabbro from 1.5 kilometers (4921 feet) beneath the seafloor. The rocks sampled consist of four units of relatively primitive olivine gabbro and troctolite, from 200 to 700 meters (656 to 2297 feet) thick, each with its own internal chemical and petrological coherence. Interestingly, the sequence of rocks sampled by drilling incorporates some features unlike those found in well-studied ophiolites. In this case drilling has provided both important new information and a tantalizing reminder of how little we know about the deep crust and upper mantle of Earth.

The presence of the oceans results in large gaps in the global network of geophysical observatories. This limits the sensitivity of seismic observations, prevents reliable mapping of the core–mantle boundary, and introduces bias into studies of mantle convection. The International Ocean Network (ION) program seeks to address this problem by installing seismic stations in oceanic areas. In the summer of 1999, ODP, in collaboration with a U.S.–Japanese team of scientists and engineers, successfully installed two complete seafloor observatories in boreholes off Japan in water depths of 2180 meters (7152 feet) and 2680 meters (8793 feet), respectively. Each observatory contains a strainmeter, tiltmeter, and two broadband seismometers cemented into place 1000 meters (3281 feet) beneath the seafloor. Data from these sensors are recorded in dataloggers at the seafloor and recovered periodically by submersible. Eventually, one of these observatories will be linked by fiber-optic cable to observatories on land, allowing real-time monitoring of the instruments. In 2000, in support of the ION program, a third successful installation was completed in the West Pacific in 5500 meters (18,045 feet) of water, northwest of Shatsky Rise.

Legacy of Ocean Drilling

Each drilling cruise has specific objectives, but ODP is building a legacy that has impacts far beyond those immediate goals. The results of ODP, and its predecessor DSDP, recorded in hundreds of scientific papers and volumes of published reports, databases, and core repositories, which now house more than 240 kilometers (150 miles) of core material, form priceless resources for future study. These resources are available to scientists from all countries. In addition, ODP materials provide the foundation of undergraduate and graduate courses at colleges and universities worldwide.

Beyond the simple acquisition of new knowledge, ODP results have affected the perceptions of petroleum and mineral exploration companies regarding resource potential and exploration strategies. Following ODP drilling, several new sedimentary basins with previously unknown hydrocarbon potential have been found offshore of Australia and within island chains of the southwest Pacific. Drilling results from active hydrothermal areas on mid-ocean ridges have provoked much excitement in the mining community and provided new models to be applied in the exploration for ore bodies on land. Thus, while ODP is a basic geologic research endeavor, its results, through its impact on exploration concepts, lead to economic benefits.

Finally, in addition to such tangible results, ODP has been cited as an outstanding example of international scientific collaboration. Despite the high costs, the program remains driven by the needs and desires of the Earth science community. Joint Oceanographic Institutions for Deep Earth Sampling (JOIDES), an international planning and advisory structure composed of scientists from academia, government agencies, and industry, provides scientific direction. The total annual budget is approximately U.S.$44 million, provided through the U.S. National Science Foundation (NSF), but with roughly one-third coming from more than 20 international partners. Scientists who sail aboard the ship are selected from the scientific communities of the contributing partners. Each cruise involves a group of about 25 scientists from different countries and varying specialties. They include scientists from small colleges and universities and from large research universities and government agencies. They range in experience from graduate students to senior professors, united in pursuit of the scientific objectives of the cruise. By working together, and socializing together, ideas are exchanged and new and productive scientific and personal collaborations develop, enriching participants' future professional careers and fostering deeper understanding of the Earth on which we live.

Thomas A. Davies

FURTHER READING

Proceedings of the Ocean Drilling Program. College Station, Texas: Publications Distribution Center, Ocean Drilling Program. (Detailed scientific results from the Ocean Drilling Program can be found in this continuing series.)

Behl, R. J., and J. P. Kennett. "Brief Interstadial Events in the Santa Barbara Basin, N.E. Pacific, During the Past 60 kyr." *Nature*, Vol. 379 (1996), pp. 243–246.

Davies, T. A. "Scientific Ocean Drilling." *Marine Technology Society Journal*, Vol. 32 (1988), pp. 5–16.

Davis, E. E., and K. Becker. "Studying Crustal Fluid Flow with ODP Borehole Observatories." *Oceanus*, Vol. 36, No. 4 (1993), pp. 82–86.

Humphris, S. E., et al. "The Internal Structure of an Active Seafloor Massive Sulphide Deposit." *Nature*, Vol. 377 (1995), pp. 713–716.

Joint Oceanographic Institutions. *ODP's Greatest Hits: Contributions from the U.S. Scientific Community.* Washington, D.C.: JOI, 1997.

Norris, R. D., B. T. Huber, and J. Self Trail. "Synchroneity of the K-T Oceanic Mass Extinction and Meteorite Impact: Blake Nose, Western North Atlantic." *Geology*, Vol. 27 (1999), pp. 419–422.

Parkes, R. J., et al. "Deep Bacterial Biosphere in Pacific Ocean Sediments." *Nature*, Vol. 371 (1994), pp. 410–413.

Winterer, E. L. "Scientific Ocean Drilling, from AMSOC to COMPOST." In *50 Years of Ocean Discovery: National Science Foundation, 1950–2000.* Washington, D.C.: National Academy Press, 2000; pp. 117–127.

RELATED ARTICLES
Deep Sea Drilling Project; Gabbro; Geologic Time; Mass Extinction; Ophiolite; Seismic Refraction

Ocean Floor Resource

Oceanographers often comment that *Earth* is a particularly inappropriate name for a planet whose surface is covered mostly by water. The oceans contain an estimated 80 percent of the planet's mineral resources, located mostly on or beneath the ocean floor. According to some estimates, that makes the oceans worth trillions of dollars, yet those riches remain largely intangible. Not only is the precise extent of most ocean floor resources unknown, the economic feasibility of extracting them is also uncertain.

Types and Locations of Resources

By far the most economically important ocean floor resource is petroleum (both oil and natural gas), which accounts for over 95 percent of the value of nonbiological resources extracted from the oceans. *Gas hydrates* (a term usually referring to methane gas trapped inside the crystalline structure of ice) are expected to become another valuable energy resource in the future as production of petroleum begins to decline. The salt domes (salt deposits forced upward) beneath and around which petroleum is trapped can also produce sulfur deposits through a set of chemical reactions involving anhydrite (calcium sulfate), petroleum, bacteria, calcite (calcium carbonate), and oxygen. Most often, ocean floor resources are grouped into four categories: loose sediments, metallic minerals in placer deposits, hydrothermal deposits, and hydrogenous deposits.

Many floor resources are formed through sedimentary processes, of which the four commonly recognized kinds are *biogenous* (formed from the hard parts of marine organisms), *hydrogenous* (precipitated from seawater), *lithogenous* (eroded from rock materials and transported to the oceans by rivers, glaciers, wind, and gravity), and *cosmogenous* (originating from outer space, for example, through meteor impacts). These various types of sediment mix in different proportions in different regions of the ocean; lithogenous sediments typically dominate coastal (neritic) deposits, whereas biogenous sediments are present in greater proportions in deep-sea (pelagic) deposits.

Loose sediments, such as aggregates (including sand and gravel that in places consist of seashell material) represent the largest volume of material (by weight) extracted from the oceans and the second greatest in value. They provide immense volumes of material for the construction industry and also for the control of marine erosion (through beach nourishment). Some industrial minerals (such as clays) are also deposited in this way. Very large deposits of phosphorite (a source of phosphorus used to make fertilizers) exist on the continental margins, but are currently too expensive to extract compared to land-based sources. Calcium carbonate (used to make agricultural lime and concrete) occurs in the shallow waters of some continental margins, although most is quarried from limestone bodies on land.

Metallic minerals, such as gold, cassiterite (a source of tin), rutile (from which titanium is extracted), diamonds, and platinum, are often found in placer deposits. The action of moving water on a beach or in a stream removes lighter sediments (those with less specific gravity) and leaves behind heavier minerals. When the sea level changes, relic beaches may be preserved that are rich in the heavier minerals. As their name suggests, hydrothermal deposits are formed in areas of volcanic activity, such as the hydrothermal vents near mid-ocean ridges. They include metal-rich sulfides of copper, zinc, iron, lead, nickel, silver, and gold.

Hydrogenous means "formed from water." Hydrogenous deposits were initially dissolved in seawater, but a physical change of some kind, such as an increase in their concentration or a decrease in temperature, means that they are no longer stable in this form, so they precipitate (crystallize out of solution) as metals and salts. Resources formed in this way include manganese nodules (lumps of minerals consisting mainly of manganese and iron, with smaller quantities of nickel, copper, and cobalt), cobalt crusts (encrustations rich in cobalt that are found, for example, on the slopes of seamounts), gypsum, and halite.

These resources, formed by different geological processes, are located in various parts of the oceanic realm. Petroleum has so far been recovered mostly from the continents themselves and the continental shelves, although the trend is toward production from deeper and deeper waters, even from the continental slope in some areas. Loose sediments are produced mostly from the continental margins (aggregates typically form just offshore in the shallowest part of the continental shelf), and materials such as phosphorite exist on the continental shelf and slope. Placer deposits are typically located near coastal regions. Deeper parts of the ocean, the continental rise and the abyssal plain, are home to hydrogenous deposits and manganese nodules. The most recently formed part of the ocean floor, the mid-ocean ridge system, contains hydrothermal deposits.

Different ocean floor resources have been recovered from all around the world. Sulfur deposits associated with salt domes are common in the Gulf of Mexico and the eastern Mediterranean, which provide about 5 percent of the world's sulfur. Aggregates (sands and gravels) are dredged in large quantities off the coasts of Japan, Canada, the United Kingdom, Iceland, Israel, and Lebanon. Calcium carbonate has been mined in coastal regions off the Bahamas. Placer deposits are mined for gold in Alaska, and offshore diamond deposits have been recovered off the coasts of Namibia and South Africa. Although manganese nodules attracted intense interest as an ocean floor resource from the 1960s through the 1980s, thus far they have been recovered only in small quantities; a number of exploration licenses have been issued for the area between Hawaii and Central America. Partly because of the location of hydrothermal deposits (at great depths and in the middle of the ocean) and partly because of environmental and scientific concerns about the preservation of their remarkable ecosystems, they remain largely unexploited.

Extraction

Recovering minerals from the ocean floor is necessarily a more difficult undertaking than recovering them from land; different techniques are used to recover minerals from various parts of the ocean. Although offshore deposits of petroleum are typically recovered using oil rigs of several kinds mostly on the continental shelf, it is also possible to recover shallow water resources from land-based rigs by drilling more or less horizontally outward. Coal and placer deposits have also been recovered in this way.

Ocean floor sediments (such as aggregates and industrial minerals) are typically recovered by dredges using either mechanical or hydraulic methods. Mechanical dredges use a dragline, clamshell bucket, or conveyor chain of buckets to scoop material physically from the ocean floor to a waiting barge, which then carries it ashore. Hydraulic dredges, by contrast, are more like giant vacuum cleaners, sucking sediments off the ocean floor as a slurry (mixture of sediment and water), screening or filtering out the valuable minerals, and storing them in the ship's hold before ejecting the wastewater back to the sea. Environmental concerns, including fears that dredged channels contribute to coastal erosion, now typically mean that dredges operate farther offshore than in the past.

Placer deposits are usually recovered by mining (mostly dredging) in relatively shallow coastal waters. Diamonds were dredged off the coast of South Africa in waters up to 40 meters (131 feet) deep until several dredges were lost in storms in the early 1970s. Today, mining companies find it more economical to use scuba divers to dredge diamonds (which exist only in small quantities) using suction equipment.

Of all the mineral recovery methods used for offshore resources, those devised for retrieving manganese nodules have perhaps attracted the most interest. Reclusive U.S. billionaire Howard Hughes built a ship called the Hughes *Glomar Explorer,* supposedly to recover manganese nodules in the 1970s. It was subsequently revealed (and later confirmed by the Central Intelligence Agency) that the ship had really been built to recover the remains of a Soviet submarine, which had sunk in very deep water in the western Pacific Ocean. In an ironic twist, the *Glomar Explorer* was eventually used to test the feasibility of harvesting manganese nodules from the ocean floor. Ocean Minerals Company used it to drag a sled along the seabed, which raked up nodules and washed them before passing them by suction to the ship above.

Economics

Although the vast mineral resources of the oceans are estimated to be worth many billions or even trillions (billions of billions) of U.S. dollars, relatively little of this great wealth has so far been exploited. This reflects the greater difficulty of extracting minerals from the ocean at feasible prices as well as environmental and other concerns. Chronic shortages of minerals, famously forecast by the *Limits to Growth* report of the Club of Rome in 1972 and others, have consistently failed to materialize; indeed, although more minerals were extracted and consumed between 1950 and 2000 than in the sum total of human history up to that point, world reserves of most minerals continued to increase during the same period. Abundance of this type hardly favors recovering minerals from extreme and remote environments, such as mid-ocean ridges.

However, this generalized picture conceals a more pressing need to discover other mineral deposits: Not all countries are equally favored with mineral wealth. Even the United States, the world's largest producer of minerals, is totally dependent on imports for some of its needs, including columbium and manganese (essential for steel production), mica (essential for electronic components), aluminum ore, niobium, graphite, strontium, and thallium, and almost entirely dependent on imports of industrial diamonds (for cutting and grinding machinery), tungsten, platinum-group metals (used in catalytic converters), chromium, and tin. Over 80 percent of U.S. cobalt—a mineral described as essential to national security because of its use in aerospace alloys—is imported from countries such as Zambia, Congo, and Norway. Thus it makes sense for the United States and other industrialized nations to explore offshore sources of some of these minerals, perhaps for political reasons, even if their exploitation is not currently economically feasible. Because it can take a decade or more to develop an economical extraction process, it is wise to establish methods of extracting minerals offshore far in advance of actually needing to use them.

Another reason for the relative lack of offshore exploitation is the sheer scale of the area that must be explored, and the cost of doing so at a time when mineral prices are relatively depressed. Since the ratification of the United Nations Convention on the Law of the Sea (UNCLOS), coastal nations have been able to claim an Exclusive Economic Zone (EEZ), giving them economic rights to ocean resources 360 kilometers (194 nautical miles) off their coast. The vast coastline of the United States (and its numerous territories, notably in the Pacific) has thus produced the world's largest EEZ, about 1.6 billion hectares (4.0 billion acres) in total, more than doubling U.S. territory. However, the EEZ concept and the UNCLOS created a long-running political dispute. The suggestion that mining companies should transfer technology to developing nations and share profits with the United Nations caused the United States to refuse to sign the agreement until 1994, an action that was credited as the main reason for the collapse of interest in manganese nodule mining.

For ocean floor resources to be economically feasible, they must necessarily be more advantageous to mine than similar resources on land. Greater environmental awareness and increased recycling has dramatically affected the economics of mining metals such as aluminum and steel (about 40 percent of which metals are now recycled, saving 95 percent of energy use in the case of aluminum and 60 percent in the case of steel). Land-based mines seldom operate at maximum capacity (typically, mines extract at only 50 to 80 percent of their possible rate), which also reduces the incentive to seek offshore sites.

Nuclear Waste

Although the ocean floor has attracted most interest as a place from which minerals might be extracted, it has also long been of interest as a place where unwanted materials generated onshore—notably radioactive waste—might be stored. In other words, using the ocean floor as a resource for storing waste materials that have been generated on land is the opposite of extracting materials from the ocean floor to use on land. The idea of long-term storage of nuclear waste under the ocean floor differs radically from indiscriminate dumping of radioactive pollution into the sea, as currently practiced by a number of nuclear power and fuel reprocessing plants. Charles Hollister of the Woods Hole Oceanographic Institution advocated the use of *sub-seabed disposal* as early as 1973 because he argued that concentrations of fine-grained (clay) sediments found beneath the ocean floor have a unique ability to trap radioactive contaminants and prevent them from spreading into the ocean itself. Provisional experiments suggest burial at a depth of only 10 meters (33 feet) would be sufficient to bind radioactive wastes safely for millions of years.

Despite the attractions of using the ocean as a nuclear waste repository, the idea has long been opposed by environmentalists; Rachel Carson (1907–64) was referring to nuclear disposal at sea in 1960 when she wrote: "It is a curious situation that the sea, from which life first arose, should now be threatened by the activities of one form of that life. But the sea, though changed in a sinister way, will continue to exist; the threat is rather to life itself." Environmental concerns aside, in countries such as the United States, sub-seabed disposal has effectively been rejected by the adoption of land-based programs for storage of nuclear waste. But the vast quantities of high-level waste generated both by nuclear power programs and nuclear weapons production and strident objections to its disposal anywhere near populated places suggest that the ocean floor might one day be exploited as a very different type of resource.

Remaining Issues

The protracted international arguments over the UNCLOS, drafted in 1982 but not effectively adopted until significant revisions had been agreed to in 1994, illustrate the complexity of exploiting ocean floor resources. Economic and environmental considerations must be balanced by political and legal considerations; it must be possible to extract resources without harming the environment and without causing international disputes between neighboring nations. Although the UNCLOS and its EEZ concept solve some of the difficulties, it leaves others unresolved. Who, for example, owns potentially valuable resources

on mid-ocean ridges well beyond the limits of any nation's EEZ?

Issues such as this are the responsibility of the International Seabed Authority (ISA), founded through the UNCLOS in 1994 and fully operational since 1996. Until large-scale commercial exploitation of the seabed begins, the ISBA's role is to monitor mineral explorations, developments in technology, and the economic and environmental impacts of mining, and to continue to refine the regulatory framework introduced by the UNCLOS.

With the exception of petroleum and aggregates, little of the ocean's vast mineral resources have been mined. The relative abundance of economically important minerals in land-based deposits will not last indefinitely, however. As environmental legislation becomes more stringent and the public increasingly values environmental assets as much as economic ones, mineral exploration and recovery—and the environmental problems associated with them—may be driven offshore. Similar concerns may increase pressures to use the ocean floor as a "resource" for disposal of land-based wastes. Ultimately, abundant ocean floor resources present humankind with a choice: to use the last 30 to 40 years of awareness of land-based environmental problems to help secure the future of the oceans and to manage their economic exploitation in a sustainable way, or simply transfer current environmental problems from the land to the ocean.

Chris Woodford

FURTHER READING

Barkenbus, Jack. *Deep Seabed Resources: Politics and Technology.* New York: Free Press, 1979.

Borgese, Elisabeth. "The Law of the Sea." *Scientific American,* March 1983, p. 28.

Carson, Rachel. *The Sea Around Us.* New York: Oxford University Press, 1951; rev. ed., 1961.

Committee on Seabed Utilization in the Exclusive Economic Zone, Marine Board, Commission on Engineering and Technical Systems, National

Research Council. *Our Seabed Frontier: Challenges and Choices.* Washington, D.C.: National Academy Press, 1989.

Hodges, Carol. "Mineral Resources, Environmental Issues, and Land Use." *Science,* 2 June 1995, p. 1305.

Independent World Commission on the Oceans. *The Oceans: Our Future.* Cambridge and New York: Cambridge University Press, 1999.

Nadis, Steven. "The Sub-seabed Solution." *Atlantic Monthly,* October 1996, p. 28.

Ross, David. *Introduction to Oceanography.* New York: HarperCollins College Publishing, 1995.

RELATED ARTICLES

Energy from the Sea; Exclusive Economic Zone; Petroleum; Phosphorite Nodule; Placer Deposit

Oceanic Crust

Earth's crust, the outermost shell of Earth, overlies Earth's mantle above the Mohorovicic discontinuity (Moho). The most prominent morphological feature of the oceanic crust is the globe-encircling mid-ocean ridge and transform fault system, which are areas of crustal accretion and two of Earth's major plate boundaries. Another major morphologic expression of the oceanic crust is the trench–island arc system, which includes regions of crustal subduction, and is another one of Earth's major plate boundaries. This plate boundary is observed mostly around the rim of the Pacific Ocean; it is also observed in the Indian Ocean (Indonesian trench–island arc system) and surrounding the Caribbean and Scotia Seas in the Atlantic Ocean. All of the plate boundaries are associated with earthquake activity; the mid-ocean ridge axes and trench–island arc systems are associated with volcanic activity. Other major morphologic features of the ocean crust include the seamount chains and aseismic ridges.

Our knowledge of the nature of the oceanic crust comes from direct sampling, geophysical measurements, satellite observations, and comparisons with ophiolites observed on land.

Oceanographic research vessels and deep-ocean submersibles such as *Alvin* are used to sample the seafloor's near-surface sediments and hard rock [generally less than 30 meters (about 98 feet) beneath the seafloor] by direct sampling, piston coring, or dredging. The research vessels also take photographs of the ocean floor. The Ocean Drilling Program (ODP) and its predecessor program, the Deep-Sea Drilling Project (DSDP), have utilized scientific ocean drill ships (*JOIDES Resolution* in ODP and *Glomar Challenger* in DSDP) to sample the ocean crust at over 1150 sites in the world's oceans at depths beneath the seafloor not obtainable by sampling gear or conventional oceanographic research vessels. The deepest hole thus far drilled and sampled in the deep ocean for a scientific purpose is about 2100 meters (6890 feet) beneath the seafloor. Geophysical measurements such as seismic reflection and refraction, gravity, magnetics, and heat flow are remote sensing techniques whose interpretation gives important information about the ocean crust with respect to its layering and the layers' physical properties, such as their seismic velocity, density, magnetization, and conductivity. Satellite altimetry uses radar to measure sea surface heights or the marine geoid and yields information with respect to thickness and density changes in the crust. Finally, ophiolites such as the Troodos Complex in Cyprus are believed to be remnants of the ocean floor that have been uplifted and thrust onto the land surface. Thickness measurements of the ophiolite layers' physical properties compare favorably with those obtained by direct sampling of the ocean crust and remote sensing techniques.

Earth's crust differs considerably in age, thickness, and composition beneath the oceans and continents. Ocean crust is generally much younger and has a less complex geologic history than continental crust. Age determinations in the oceans and continents tell us fundamentally different things. The age of a piece of continental crust is often the last time it has experienced an episode of magmatism or metamorphism. In some cases it may be the time of formation of the particular piece of continental crust, but generally it is not. The age of the oldest continental rocks is about 3.8 billion years. Ocean crust, on the other hand, is formed by processes of seafloor spreading and plate tectonics and is geologically ephemeral. The age of a piece of oceanic crust gives us the time of its formation at a spreading ridge. Oceanic crust is created by upwelling and partial melting of the mantle beneath the mid-ocean ridges. As the ocean grows wider with creation of new ocean crust, the older ocean crust moves away from either side of the mid-ocean ridge to make room for more magma. Thus, the ocean crust increases in age outward from either side of the mid-ocean ridge axes. The age of the ocean crust has been determined by ODP and DSDP sampling and interpretation of magnetic anomalies for large expanses of the world's oceans. The age ranges from the present at mid-ocean ridge axes to 180 to 200 million years old at regions distant from the ridge axes such as in the western Pacific Ocean and bordering the margins of the central Atlantic Ocean. The Red Sea is an example of a relatively young ocean that appears to be opening from the south.

Seismic refraction measurements show the crust beneath the continents to be between about 30 and 70 kilometers (18.6 to 43.5 miles) thick. Generally, the thickest continental crust is located beneath the mountain belts associated with continental collision zones such as the Himalayas and Swiss Alps. The thinnest continental crust is observed in coastal plains and continental rift zones, such as the Basin and Range Province of western United States and the East African Rift Valley. The surface rocks on the continents consist of diverse suites of sedimentary, igneous, and metamorphic rocks. Its igneous crust is primarily granitic in composition and is rich in low-density minerals such as quartz and feldspar. Beneath the

oceans, however, Earth's crust is much thinner and basaltic in composition. The average ocean crustal thickness is about 7 kilometers (about 4.3 miles); it does reach a thickness of 24 kilometers (14.9 miles) in elevated areas of the ocean floor such as near Iceland. The igneous ocean crust, as discussed below, is basaltic in composition and is rich in minerals such as olivine, pyroxene, and plagioclase feldspar.

Geoscientists have divided the ocean crust into three main layers based primarily on a seismic velocity structure. Layer 1, the uppermost layer of the seafloor, is composed of sediments and is characterized by compressional wave velocities in the approximate range 1.8 to 4.0 kilometers (about 1.1 to 2.5 miles) per second. The thickness of ocean crust Layer 1 ranges from near zero in the regions of the mid-ocean ridge axes, where new ocean crust is being formed, to 1 to 2 kilometers (about 0.6 to 1.2 miles) in older ocean crust at long distances from the mid-ocean ridge axes. The predominant sediment types comprising Layer 1 are calcareous oozes (48 percent), siliceous oozes (14 percent), and abyssal clays (38 percent). The calcareous oozes, predominantly foraminiferal oozes, are dominant in the Indian and Atlantic Oceans. Siliceous oozes, with diatoms and radiolaria as major components, are dominant in the sub-Antarctic and equatorial Pacific regions. The abyssal clays, dominant in the Pacific Ocean, consist primarily of continentally derived particles that have been carried to the open sea by wind or ocean currents. The Pacific Ocean tends to be deeper than other oceans and tends to have less sediment (Layer 1). Large segments of its seafloor lie below the carbonate compensation depth (CCD), preventing deposition of calcareous oozes in these locations. In addition, the Pacific Ocean is surrounded in large part by trenches. Therefore, turbidity currents, which can deposit large amounts of sediment from the continental margins to the deep ocean basins, deposit most of their load in the trenches without reaching the deep ocean.

Early seismic models of the igneous part of the oceanic crust showed a 5-kilometer (about 3.1-mile) per second Layer 2 with thickness in the range 1 to 2 kilometers (0.6 to 1.2 miles) overlying a 6.8-kilometer (about 4.2-mile) per second Layer 3 with a thickness of about 5 kilometers (3.1 miles). With additional detailed seismic measurements, Layer 2 was subdivided into a three-layer model called Layers 2A, 2B, and 2C and characterized by compressional wave velocities in the approximate range 3.5 to 6.2 kilometers (2.2 to 3.9 miles) per second. These subdivisions are not always observed in seismic experiments. Using modern seismic techniques, geophysicists have modified the earlier models of Layer 2 to show that there are no definite seismic discontinuities and that changes in velocity gradients replace the layered model. In the vicinity of the mid-ocean ridge, the upper part of Layer 2 consists of 500 meters (about 1640 feet) of pillow lavas, massive basalt flows, and rubble zones with many fractures and voids. With depth the voids tend to be filled with alteration minerals and the pillows are less fractured. The lower part of Layer 2 consists of about 1 to 1.5 kilometers (about 0.6 to 0.9 mile) of basaltic sheeted dykes. The seismic velocities of Layer 2 tend to increase with distance from the mid-ocean ridge crest (i.e., with age). This may be a result of cementation and lithification of the rubble zones and the filling of the voids and fractures with alteration minerals that result from the interaction of seawater with the basalt. The boundary between Layers 2 and 3 is also characterized by a change in velocity gradient, not by a discrete change of seismic velocity. Beneath the basalts, Layer 3 consists of gabbro with a thickness in the range 3 to 5 kilometers (about 1.9 to 3.1 miles) and characterized by compressional seismic velocities in the range of about 6.2 to 7.0 kilometers (3.9 to 4.3 miles) per second. The chemical and mineralogical characteristics of Layers 2 and 3 are virtually the same. They are composed of the minerals olivine, pyroxene, and plagioclase feldspar, in order of increasing abundance. Layer 3 is situated above the mantle (Layer 4). The boundary between Layers 3 and 4 is associated generally with an abrupt change in seismic velocity, to about 7.0 to 8.1 kilometers (4.3 to 5.0 miles) per second. This velocity increase is caused by a change in chemical and mineralogical composition from gabbroic rocks in Layer 3 to peridotite, with its major minerals olivine and pyroxene in the upper mantle.

The amount of heat escaping from the ocean crust decreases with age as we proceed from the axes of the mid-ocean ridges to the deep ocean basins. Much of the heat loss is by conduction, in which the heat from Earth's interior diffuses upward; a significant component of heat loss is by convection, a process in which heat is transferred by movement of seawater called *hydrothermal circulation*. The relatively newly formed rocks near the mid-ocean ridge crest are highly fractured and permeable. This permeability allows seawater to penetrate into the hot oceanic crust and circulate back to the surface as hot mineral-laden water. The fluid temperatures emerging from the crust are greater than 350°C (662°F). This process is not only a significant heat exchange between the interior of Earth and the seafloor, but black smokers that are hydrothermal vents emerge from the seafloor through chimneys up to 10 meters (about 32.8 feet) high composed of iron, copper, and zinc sulfides. In the vicinity of the black smokers, exotic life, such as 2-meter (about 6.6-feet)-long tubeworms, thrive in total darkness of the deep sea and rely on sulfur and the process of chemosynthesis as the energy source and mechanism to support life. These communities are different from all other living systems on Earth, which are dependent on the Sun as their source of energy.

The physiographic characteristics of ocean crust are related to seafloor spreading rates. For significant parts of their geologic history, the

Atlantic and Indian Oceans have exemplified slow spreading [about 1 to 3 centimeters (0.4 to 1.2 inches) per year]. In this slow-spreading environment, the top of the igneous ocean crustal layer (Layer 2) is characterized by very rough block-faulted topography, and a prominent rift valley is observed at the ridge crest, generally 30 to 50 kilometers (about 18.6 to 31.1 miles) wide and 1500 to 3000 meters (about 4920 to 9840 feet) deep. The Pacific Ocean is an example, for the most part, of intermediate to fast spreading [about 5 to 10 centimeters (2 to 4 inches) per year]. Here, the top of the igneous ocean crustal layer is characterized by relatively smooth topography and, in general, no rift valley.

Not all of the igneous part of the oceanic crust is formed at mid-ocean ridges. Numerous seamounts and aseismic ridges are formed away from the axes of mid-ocean ridges. These have no earthquake activity associated with them. Examples of aseismic ridges include the Walvis Ridge and Rio Grande Rise in the South Atlantic Ocean and the very linear Ninetyeast Ridge in the Indian Ocean. The Hawaiian Island and Emperor Seamount chains in the Pacific Ocean are well-known linear chains of volcanic islands and seamounts. These volcanic lineaments are aligned northwest to southeast with a general decrease in ages of individual volcanoes from older to younger progressing southeast along the chain. This has led to the formation of the hotspot concept, in which each linear chain is formed as a result of the plate moving over a narrow heat source or mantle plume that is fixed in location deep within Earth's mantle. The hotspots can thus be used as fixed reference points that allow us to determine the direction and speed (once we determine the age of the individual volcanoes) of the plates that are moving above them. These ocean island basalts contain small but significant amounts of sodium, potassium, and aluminum suggesting that they originate from a deep part of the mantle that has not been depleted of these elements. About 20 to 25 hotspots are active today in the ocean basins, and about another 10 to 15 are active on the continents. The Hawaiian Island chain is a relatively recent manifestation of hotspot activity. The oldest island of the chain, Kauai, is about 3.8 to 5.6 million years old. The "Big Island," Hawaii, is presently experiencing eruptions, and to its southeast, Loihi seamount, whose still submerged summit rises about 4400 meters (about 14,435 feet) above the seafloor, will perhaps be the next island formed in the Hawaiian chain. The volcanoes tend to be circular in plan and several have some of Earth's greatest relief. For example, the base of Mauna Loa in the Hawaiian Island chain is about 100 kilometers (62 miles) across, with a summit about 9000 meters (29,500 feet) above the surrounding seafloor, making it about as high above its base as Mount Everest. Some oceanic volcanic islands have been eroded to sea level and subsided to become flat-topped features called *guyots*.

Scientists have made great strides over the last few decades in their knowledge of the morphology of the ocean crust and its layering. However, much of this knowledge comes from indirect means, such as remote sensing geophysical techniques. We have only one deep hole in the ocean crust, which extends about 2100 meters (6890 feet) below the seafloor, and very few others that penetrate greater than 500 meters (about 1640 feet) into the igneous ocean crust. Much deeper samples of "normal" ocean crust in the various ocean regimes (i.e., in slow- and fast-spreading regimes of different ages) must be obtained for scientists to gain a better understanding of the ocean crust.

Philip Rabinowitz

FURTHER READING

Davidson, Jon P., Walter E. Reed, and Paul M. Davis. *Exploring Earth: An Introduction to Physical Geology.* Upper Saddle River, N.J.: Prentice Hall, 1997.

Emiliani, C., ed., *The Sea*, Vol. 7, *The Oceanic Lithosphere*, New York: Wiley, 1981.

Fowler, C. M. R. *The Solid Earth: An Introduction to Global Geophysics.* Cambridge: Cambridge University Press, 1990.

Houtz, R., and J. Ewing. "Upper Crustal Structure as a Function of Plate Age." *Journal of Geophysical Research*, Vol. 81, No. 14 (1976), pp. 2490–2498.

Kearey, P., and F. J. Vine. *Global Tectonics.* Oxford and Boston: Blackwell Scientific, 1990; 2nd ed., Oxford and Cambridge, Mass.: Blackwell Science, 1996.

Kennett, James. *Marine Geology.* Englewood Cliffs, N.J.: Prentice Hall, 1982.

RELATED ARTICLES

Emperor Seamounts; Hawaiian Islands; Magnetic Anomaly; Marine Geophysics, Mid-Ocean Ridge; Ocean Basin; Ocean Drilling Program; Oceanic Volcanic Rock; Ophiolite; Plate Tectonics; Seafloor Spreading; Transform Fault; Trench

Oceanic Island

An island is an area of land surrounded by water. If the area of an island is too small for it to be inhabitable it is usually considered to be a rock or a reef, whereas a very large island such as Greenland is regarded as a minicontinent. Oceanic islands have two basic origins. A few islands, which consist of granites and sedimentary rocks, originated as fragments of continents that broke off during the process of continental drift. Madagascar and the Seychelles were left behind during the fragmentation of Gondwanaland about 100 million years ago, as what ultimately became the Indian subcontinent drifted across the Indian Ocean and collided with the Asian continental landmass.

Volcanic Origins

The majority of oceanic islands are volcanic in origin, and many are much younger than the ocean crust on which they now sit. Most have formed where there were weaknesses in the oceanic crust, such as along transform fault lines or where tectonic plates meet in a triple junction.

The Azores in the North Atlantic formed at the junction between three plates. They are still volcanically active and the islands at the extreme ends of the archipelago are gradually moving farther apart. Alternatively, a number of island chains have formed where there is a hotspot in the mantle underlying the crust. The hotspot in the mantle remains at about the same position on Earth's surface, but because the ocean crust is constantly moving over it, linear chains of islands develop. The best example is the Hawaiin–Emperor Volcanic Chain in the North Pacific, which is 3500 kilometers (2175 miles) long. This linear island and seamount chain has a remarkable bend, showing that the direction of Pacific Plate movement changed in the geological past. Currently, the hotspot is close to Loihi Seamount, which lies southeast of the island of Hawaii. Moving along the island chain away from the hotspot, the islands become progressively older. For example, the island of Kauai is about 5 million years old, Laysan Island [1848 kilometers (1148 miles) farther along the chain] is 20 million years old, and Midway Island [2460 kilometers (1529 miles) away] is nearly 28 million years old.

Island Building

As soon as volcanic activity builds an island, the sea begins to erode away the rock. If the volcanism results in the production of copious lava flows, the island building continues. If the volcano is producing mainly ash by the time it breaches the surface, erosion is very rapid. Hence many newly formed islands are rapidly eroded away. The island of Surtsey near the main island of Iceland, which appeared in the 1960s in a series of dramatic eruptions, is being eroded away quite rapidly. The ultimate fate of many new islands, therefore, is to become guyots or flat-topped seamounts. The depth of a guyot indicates an old sea level. When volcanism ceases, the volcanic islands cool and sink. In equatorial parts of the oceans, a progression of coral reefs forms around the island as it sinks: fringing reef, barrier reef, and finally an atoll. Charles Darwin (1809–82) was first to propose that the origin of coral atolls is related to subsiding islands.

Slope Failures

Volcanoes are typically conical, yet many volcanic islands are triangular in outline. For example, the island of Hawaii has been formed from a series of shield volcanoes, yet its outline is very angular. This is because some of its sides have suffered massive structural failures. In some places the entire side of the island has slipped away in a massive underwater landslide, and trails of hundreds of cubic miles of debris are strewn along the pathway taken by the slide for hundreds of miles. Similar slides have been reported around the Canary Islands in the North Atlantic.

Islands and Ocean Currents

Islands form physical barriers to the flow of ocean currents, and in some places they are areas of high primary productivity because of upwelling. These areas not only attract a wide variety of fishes, but also are used as staging posts for migrating animals. They provide seabirds and marine mammals with the resources they need to use the islands for breeding. The Galápagos Islands that sit astride the equator in the eastern Pacific act as a barrier to equatorial currents such as the Cromwell Current. They physically enhance the equatorial upwelling, so the water that surrounds them is usually cold and rich in nutrients. Even though the islands at sea level are deserts, they support vast numbers of marine mammals and seabirds, and the surrounding ocean waters are feeding grounds for large numbers of whales and other sea mammals.

Islands as Centers of Evolution

Islands like the Galápagos are important in evolutionary terms. Colonization of a newly formed island depends on the distances the colonizers have had to travel. It is easier to make the journey when helped by prevailing winds and currents. Most benthic marine species have a dispersal phase during their life cycles, and the longer this phase lasts, the farther such larvae can disperse. The "phyllosoma" larvae of lobsters stay in the plankton for many months and thus can survive the long transit time of drifting across an ocean. The endemic lobster of Tristan da Cunha, for example, has been found on the Vema Seamount over 3000 kilometers (1864 miles) away from its normal home. Other animals and plants have quite brief dispersal phases and have to hitch a lift on floating logs, turtles, or even the feet of migrating birds. Both on land and in shallow water, island faunas and floras tend to originate from assemblages of species that are either well adapted to long-distance dispersal or have made the journey through a series of chance events. Being isolated from any gene flow from the parent stock, they tend to speciate, so that islands become a source of endemic species. The rich variety of tortoises and finches on the Galápagos Islands are thought to have given Darwin the inspiration for his theory of natural selection.

Martin Angel

FURTHER READING

Nunn, Patrick D. *Oceanic Islands*. Oxford and Cambridge, Mass.: Blackwell, 1994.

Watts, A. B. "The Growth and Decay of Oceanic Islands." In M. A. Summerfield, ed., *Geomorphology and Global Tectonics*. Chichester, England, and New York: Wiley, 2000.

Whittaker, Robert J. *Island Biogeography: Ecology, Evolution and Conservation*. Oxford and New York: Oxford University Press, 1999.

RELATED ARTICLES

Coral Reef; Hawaiian–Emperor Bend; Hotspot; Mantle Plume, Ocean Current; Oceanic Volcanic Rock; Plate Tectonics; Upwelling

Oceanic Microfossil

Most of the world's past and present biodiversity and biomass is microscopic. Oceanic microfossils are smaller than 5 millimeters (approximately 0.2 inch) with skeletal hard parts typically of calcite, aragonite, or opaline silica preserved in the fossil record in oceanic sediments. They can be divided into microplanktonic floating forms, including phytoplankton (plant) and zooplankton (animal), and benthonic (bottom-dwelling) forms such as mollusks and ostracods. Along with the ultramicroscopic picoplankton, algae particularly have always been an important autotrophic component, the primary source of food as well as of oxygen to the atmosphere.

Marine planktonic microfossils and nannofossils occur in Precambrian to Recent rocks (4.5 billion years). The fossil record encompassing some 3.5 billion years includes some of the oldest known forms, which began the carbon–oxygen cycle in our atmosphere. Most of the earliest ocean wanderers, bacteria, and blue-green and other algae and fungi that lived before 600 million years ago have disappeared without trace. Nevertheless, the oldest microfossils from the Iapetus and Palaeotethys oceans include 1000-million- to 3000-million-year-old blue-green algae from the Bitter Springs chert of Australia, the Gunflint chert of Ontario, Canada, and the Fig Tree chert of South Africa.

Microorganisms make up the largest percent by volume of many sediments, particularly oceanic oozes. These pelagic deep-sea sediments from the ocean floors are formed by slow accumulation mainly of skeletons of various

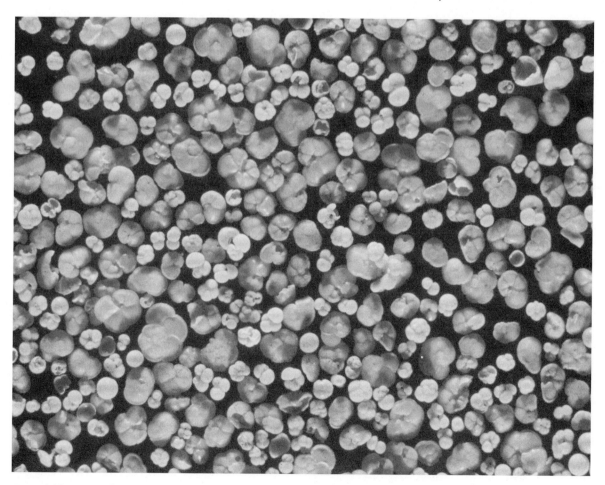

Foraminiferan ooze from 1200 meters (about 3900 feet) at 9°N in the western Atlantic. (© Peter Herring/Natural Visions)

plankton that settle from surface waters into the bathyal and abyssal realms. Deep-sea calcareous oozes are composed mostly of foraminifera; coccolithophores, siliceous diatoms, sponge spicules, radiolaria, and nannoplankton form siliceous oozes, some of which become chert. The solubility of calcium carbonate in seawater increases with depth, and below about 5000 meters (16,404 feet), almost all calcareous sediment dissolves. Mobilization and eventual redeposition of silica after burial is believed to result in radiolarian chert. Accumulation depends on complex, interrelated processes affecting their productivity in the water and their transfer to the ocean bottom.

Micropaleontology (the study of microfossils) provides an exploratory tool for use in applied geology and the economic development of oil and gas fields, an indicator of ocean water masses, circulation, and climate. Oceanic microfossils are important for biostratigraphy where fossils help determine the age of a rock and aid in correlation, matching one particular rock with another. Fossil phytoplankton (algae, flagellates such as coccoliths, dinocysts, and siliceous diatoms) and zooplankton (protozoans, radiolarians, metazoa such as pteropods, sponge spicules, conodont elements, fish scales, and teeth) are used extensively in biostratigraphy. High-resolution biostratigraphy, sometimes in conjunction with paleomagnetic reversal studies in deep-sea drilling projects to provide substantiating age data, aims to reduce time constraints to a few thousand years.

The fossil size, 5 millimeters (0.2 inch) and less and mostly within the magnification zone of 200 to 1000 times, requires special methods of study, collecting, and examination. Light and scanning electron microscopy help gauge morphological and ultrastructural characteristics of specimens. Although the groups currently in favor for detailed biostratigraphy may vary, stratigraphic paleontology grows with the development of new technologies and concepts, and thus microfossils will always be present to provide age data and often, evidence of paleogeography and paleoclimatology.

Microfossils have distinct advantages because of their small size, so that even a small sample can provide many thousands of fossils. This abundance makes it possible to analyze distribution better. In addition, fast-evolving forms that distribute themselves widely as plankton in oceanic currents and have a short vertical range in the fossil record (i.e., a genus with a fast species turnover) provide excellent microfossil marker or zone fossils. These help underpin standard stratigraphic schemes of sedimentary rocks accepted worldwide. Microfossil, magneto-, isotopic, and sequence stratigraphy can establish the geological age of a given bed or section, and stratigraphic datum points or marker beds in relation, for instance, to oil-bearing strata, which aids in drilling wildcat wells in unproven territory. Stratigraphic correlation among wells and countries is possible using zone fossils. The ecological significance of microfossils can be inferred by comparing fossil to modern equivalents. Changes related to major global events are seen from study of taxon extinction and recovery—first and last appearances (FAD and LAD) being very important—and response to *Milankovich cycles,* cycles in Earth's orbit that influence the amount of solar radiation striking different parts of Earth at different times of year, which can affect Earth processes such as periodic changes in sea level (eustasy). Microfossils also reflect the sedimentary environment in which a bed or sequence was deposited. Tectonic activity in a sedimentary basin, as reflected by oscillation of water depth, can also be determined; a resulting oscillation chart can be compared with sea-level curves. Heat applied is estimated by checking the state and color alteration indices of the fossils (e.g., conodonts and microvertebrates).

Calcareous Microfossils

Calcareous phytoplankton comprises nannofossils, including discoasters (Paleocene–early Quaternary, 64 million to 2 million years ago) and the Coccolithophorida, golden brown algae with a sphere of calcareous surface scales formed of low-magnesium calcite and ranging in diameter from 2 to 10 micrometers (0.00008 to 0.0004 inch). These coccoliths, which appear in the Late Triassic (about 210 million years ago) Tethyan epicontinental seas, are the primary contributor to calcareous ooze and chalk deposits generally restricted to lower latitudes. Their abundance and biodiversity are controlled by the seasonal supply of coccolithophorids and by the tidal influence in the overlying water column. They are widely used biostratigraphic tools, especially in deep-sea sediments, and help track cooling episodes.

Foraminifera (Ordovician, about 450 million years ago, to Recent) are diverse shell-bearing protozoans comprising planktonic and benthonic families mostly enclosed in a calcium carbonate skeleton that probably evolved for protection and stability. They range in size typically from 50 to 400 micrometers (0.002 to 0.016 inch) and contribute to deep-sea calcareous ooze formation in all latitudes and oceans. Foraminifera have a long history of use, especially in Tertiary biostratigraphy, often being used to record past fluctuations in ocean depths. Early Cretaceous (140 million years ago) to Holocene planktonic foraminifera are utilized to check periodicity in evolution, defining a 26-million- to 30-million-year cycle of turnover as background to more intense diversity fluctuations of 3 million to 10 million years after major extinction events. Deep-water forms provide important data in North Sea oil basin studies.

Marine benthonic Ostracoda are small [0.5 to 2 millimeters (0.02 to 0.08 inch)] specialized crustacea with bivalved carapaces usually of chitinous-rich calcite incorporating up to 5 percent $MgCo_3$. Planktonic forms have organic-walled tests, which do not preserve. Classification is based on carapace morphology, growth series, and sexual dimorphs, with females outnumbering males as preserved fossils from the early Ordovician onward. They are important especially for mid-Paleozoic biostratigraphy and for indicating paleodepth, paleoenvironment, and paleoecology, deeper forms having intricate ornamentation. Population biodiversity and density decreases in deeper-sea environments. Today, bathyal and abyssal psycrospheric assemblages occur in depths greater than 500 meters (1640 feet) and in high latitudes and upwelling sites, while thermospheric forms inhabit warmer water layers above 10°C (50°F).

Molluscan microfossils, pteropods, and heteropods, the winged sea butterflies, had aragonitic shells in the size range 0.3 to 5 millimeters (0.012 to 0.2 inch). They live in the upper few hundred meters of the ocean, with some bathypelagic species at depths greater than 500 meters (1640 feet). Their cone-shaped shells form oozes from Eocene (about 55 million years ago) to Recent with doubtful Mesozoic records, mostly restricted to Quaternary sediments from subtropical to tropical areas in less than 2500 meters (8202 feet) (because of dissolution beyond the aragonite compensation depth). They provide restricted paleoclimatic data.

Siliceous Microfossils

Siliceous microfossils date back to the Precambrian. Chitinozoans had a test made up of a chamber and an oral tube. They were important in mid-Paleozoic oceans, evolving rapidly in Ordovician through Devonian times (some 100 million years). Because they occur in a wide range of sedimentary rocks, they are biostratigraphically useful despite their exact phylogenetic position being unclear.

Diatoms are eukaryotic solitary or colonial algae with a rigid bivalved opaline test or frustule. They are known from Jurassic time to the present, being increasingly important for Cenozoic biostratigraphy. Generally, frustules vary in size from 10 micrometers to 2 millimeters (0.0004 to 0.08 inch) but chains can be longer. They produce nearly 50 percent of organic matter and 70 to 90 percent of silica in oceans, plus some 9 billion tonnes (10 billion tons) of carbon per year. Diatom preservation is favored in areas of high sediment accumulation and upwelling; they also attach to sea ice at high latitudes. Their end-Cretaceous productivity collapse 65 million years ago, along with that of other planktonic microfossils, led to what has been called the "Strangelove Ocean."

Dinoflagellates appear first in abundance in the Triassic, about 240 million years ago. Their uses include stratigraphic correlation as indicators of paleoecology, including water depth and shoreline position, ocean current circulation patterns, sea-level changes (eustasy), and paleotemperature. The earlier Acritarchs might represent true dinoflagellate forerunners. This group appears in the Precambrian, reaches its maximum abundance in late Silurian–early Devonian time, and has a severe post-Paleozoic decline.

Radiolaria are pelagic, marine protozoans with symbiotic dinoflagellates (zooxanthellate algae) to provide chlorophyll for photosynthesis. Clothed in breathtakingly beautiful globelike skeletons of either silica or strontium sulfate, in the size range 50 to 400 micrometers (0.002 to 0.016 inch), they are strong and durable. The opaline silica polycystine taxa that inhabited surface waters are common deep-sea microfossils in many siliceous and some calcareous, argillaceous, and phosphatic rocks. An astounding biodiversity of over 7000 fossils known from distinct provinces related to water masses includes deep-sea forms with more massive, heavier, and coarser skeletons than those of shallow water forms. The early history is poorly known, coming from the Early Ordovician (about 490 million years ago) of

Spitsbergen, Kazakhstan, and Nevada, as well as Late Ordovician deeper-water slope limestone clasts in Australia.

Phosphatic Microfossils

Whereas recent discovery of complete conodont animals has stimulated research on the early chordates, there is still no consensus on whether the phosphatic conodont elements, which span the Cambrian to Triassic (over 300 million years), are true teeth or parts of a pharyngeal basket. Nevertheless, the elements are used successfully as zone fossils in Paleozoic rocks. In addition, they provide evidence of earth processes—fluctuations such as sea-level changes and possible oceanic transgressive episodes and major events related to climate change. Deeper-water communities are recognized.

Vertebrate microfossils (ichthyoliths) comprise fish scales, teeth, and other hard-tissue remains composed of apatite. Fish microfossils can be an important component of oozes when fish kills at nutrient-rich upwelling sites create phosphatic bonebeds. Overabundance of motile dinoflagellates and cyst assemblages can lead to lethal blooms with toxic red and brown tides, which result in mass death sites. Such deposits are linked to sapropelic oil formation. Diatoms are also implicated in mass deaths of fish, dolphins, and whales in the ocean margins of Antarctica. Recent research is considering pelagic associations of shark teeth in the Devonian and Tertiary, and Ocean Drilling Program studies have used a fish-based stratigraphy.

Susan Turner

FURTHER READING
Blome, Charles D., Patricia M. Whalen, and Katherine M. Reed. *Siliceous Microfossils.* Short Courses in Paleontology, No. 8. Knoxville, Tenn.: Paleontological Society, 1995.
Bosence, Dan W. J., and Peter A. Allison, eds. *Marine Palaeoenvironmental Analysis from Fossils.* London and Tulsa, Okla.: Geological Society, 1995.

Hailwood, Ernest A., and Robert B. Kidd, eds. *High Resolution Stratigraphy*. London and Tulsa, Okla.: Geological Society, 1993.

Jenkins, David G., ed. *Applied Micropalaeontology.* Dordrecht, the Netherlands, and Boston: Kluwer Academic, 1993.

Kennett, James. *Marine Geology.* Englewood Cliffs, N.J.: Prentice Hall, 1982.

Singer, Rod, ed. *Encyclopedia of Paleontology,* 2 vols. Chicago: Fitzroy Dearborn, 1999.

RELATED ARTICLES

Algae; Diatom; Dinoflagellate; Flagellate; Foraminifera; Ooze; Phytoplankton; Plankton; Pteropoda; Upwelling; Zooplankton

Oceanic Volcanic Rock

The sparkling crystals of clear quartz and milky feldspars of a polished granite countertop are the stuff of continents. They formed deep in the Earth beneath some ancient volcano that in its day resembled Mount St. Helens, Popocatepetl, or Fuji-san—well-known features of our modern Ring of Fire.

The stuff of the ocean basins is basalt, dark and brittle lava that is rarely used for decoration. Basalt is the most ordinary of earthly materials, and only when it erupts as incandescent lava, such as in Hawaii, does it have much aesthetic appeal. It is denser than granite, when not full of bubbles, and richer in iron and magnesium. Its density is partly why continents stand higher than ocean basins, and its iron-richness is why basalt is so much darker than granite.

Like granite, basalt can be sliced thin with a rock saw, glued to a glass slide, and polished down until light shines through most of the minerals. Then, under a microscope, its true glory can be seen and the minerals identified. Depending on how quickly it cooled, especially when quenched under water on the seafloor, it can take on myriad and quite extraordinary forms, emphasized by the brilliant but artificial colors induced by placing a slide between crossed polarizing plates. Under water, the actual edges of lava flows, which are usually lobate, tubular structures called *pillows*, quench to glass, and minerals crystallize only in the pillow interiors.

Powders of the lava, whether dissolved, fused, or pressed into pellets, can be analyzed for their chemical compositions, including measurement of dozens of elements present only in trace amounts (at concentrations of a few hundred parts per million or less). Isotopes of some trace elements have radioactive parents, and mass spectrometers can be used to measure the ratios of the different isotopes of an element in order to determine, for example, the ages of lavas, or attributes of their sources that have existed for many hundreds of millions of years, or may even date from times near that of the origin of Earth itself. To the igneous petrologist or geochemist, then, basalt, that most widespread and ordinary of materials, is a vehicle used to explore the inner and ancient workings of Earth.

Near Uniformity of Volcanic Rocks on the Seafloor

At least 60 percent of Earth's rocky surface is covered with basalt that erupted under water at spreading ridges. Almost all of this volcanism is presently confined to the narrow traces of the ridge axes, but seafloor spreading ensures that frozen basalt is carried away to either side of the ridges, eventually to pave the entire ocean floor, which is veneered only thinly with sediment. A few other lava types have been found, but most of these are related to basalt by a process called *magmatic differentiation*. Even so, these are far less than 1 percent of all the rocks that have been sampled at several thousand locations along the spreading ridges.

Add to this the overwhelmingly basaltic mass of all seamounts and large volcanic islands that build on top of the ocean crust. The basalt of volcanic islands has a slightly different composition than that of the spreading ridges, but it shares a commonalty of origin that actually makes the slight contrast both amenable to scientific evaluation and important to understand. Similarly, we can compare the geochemistry of basalt from ridges and islands to that of ancient volcanoes on land, and of all earthly basalt to that of the lunar Maria, meteorites from the asteroid belt, and some few that have reached Earth as meteorites from Mars.

Magmatic Differentiation and the Structure of the Ocean Crust

Basalt consists mainly of two silicate minerals, plagioclase, which has sodium, calcium, and aluminum in its structure, and pyroxene, which has calcium, magnesium, and iron in its structure. Much basalt also contains olivine, a silicate with iron and magnesium in its structure. When such lava cools or quenches rapidly under water, olivine is the first of these to form, followed by plagioclase and calcic pyroxene. All basalt also contains a still-later-crystallizing mineral called *titanomagnetite*, in amounts of 1 to 3 percent. This is not a silicate but an oxide, with mainly iron and titanium in its structure. Titanomagnetite is magnetic, and when the lava quenches, titanomagnetite crystals align themselves in the direction of Earth's magnetic field at the time of eruption. This makes basalt the fundamental tape recorder that charts reversals of Earth's magnetic field and the principal source of the magnetic stripes that record seafloor spreading.

Crystallization influences the composition of basalt, especially when it is slow, and the minerals can separate from the remaining liquid, because of gravitational forces. This process is termed *magmatic differentiation*. Slow crystallization, thus magmatic differention, occurs when basaltic magma is trapped in pools in the crust. At spreading ridges, this appears to take place mainly in a widespread layer of rock that has been detected by seismic techniques and lies between about 1.6 and 7 kilometers (1 to 4.3 miles) below the seafloor. Beneath the waters of the ocean itself and a carapace of eruptive basalt, this is termed the *third layer,* or *Layer 3,* of the ocean crust. This directly overlies the mantle, across a seismic transition that is marked by a sharp downward increase in the velocity of sound called the *Mohorovicic discontinuity*, or *Moho* (named for its discoverer, a Croatian seismologist who worked early in the twentieth century). At some places, mainly fracture zones that offset spreading ridges, faulting has exposed material of Layer 3, and there it can be sampled both by dredging and drilling. The main rock type has been found to be gabbro, a fairly high-density material that consists of the accumulated crystals that separated from molten basalt during magmatic differentiation.

Primary Magma and the Origin of Basalt in the Ocean Basins

Using gabbro and basalt together, we can take the effects of magmatic differentiation into account and establish the original composition and even the temperature of the molten material that escaped the mantle, and the conditions in the mantle under which it was produced. This is called *parental* or *primary basalt*, and estimates of its composition vary depending on modeling. Primary magma is somewhat fictive in that no seafloor basalt ever sampled has escaped some degree of magmatic differentiation. Nevertheless, primary basalt is described as being derived from the upper mantle, over a range of pressure and temperature, by a process called *partial melting.*

The rock that partially melts is an olivine-rich mantle rock called *peridotite.* The melt separates, leaving behind an even more olivine-rich residuum, also a peridotite. The melt, being buoyant, makes its way upward to the ocean crust, where some of it ponds in the lower ocean crust and some of it erupts. Faulting along fracture zones has also exposed samples of the residual peridotite in addition to gabbro. Such rock is almost invariably altered and hydrated to a form called *serpentinite*, which makes it rather difficult to study, but the unaltered equivalent has the appropriate density and sonic velocity to be the rock of the upper mantle that lies just beneath the Moho. The extraction of basaltic magma from mantle peridotite, its ponding and differentiation in layer 3, and its eruption together build the ocean crust and are the most important factors in producing its seismic layering. This layering can be traced all over the ocean basins using modern techniques of seismic reflection and refraction.

Trace-Element and Isotopic Geochemistry

Variable concentrations of certain minor and trace elements, such as potassium, uranium, thorium, and some of the rare-earth elements, together with variations in radiogenic isotopes of strontium, neodymium, and lead, reveal subtle but important differences between types of basalt erupted along spreading ridges and those found on ocean islands, volcanic arcs, and continents. At some time in the past, a large-scale partial melting event or events depleted a large zone of mantle rock in the radioactive parents to the daughter isotopes. This stopped the buildup of radiogenic isotopes in the residual rock, but buildup prior to the melting event had left them higher in concentration than could have been produced by decay of the amount of radioactive parents those peridotites still contained. The rocks are thus described as depleted. The zone of mantle with the depleted, residual peridotite now resides at shallow levels immediately beneath many spreading ridges and is the source for their basalts, which are, consequently, also termed depleted. Some places along the ridges, however, such as

Iceland and many ocean islands, have basalts that come from less depleted, or even enriched, mantle sources compared with a presumed original undifferentiated mantle.

The sources of the enriched components of many of these latter basalts are believed to reside at deep levels in the mantle. The enrichments reflect recycling of ancient ocean crust and varieties of ancient sediment that once were on the seafloor but which were subducted and subjected to complex processes as they descended in lithospheric slabs beneath ancient volcanic island arcs and beyond. These have now reemerged at the end of a complex convective process after first having traveled to great depths in the mantle. Whether some material actually transited the entire thickness of the mantle from the vicinity of the core–mantle boundary is a subject of current intensive investigation.

James H. Natland

FURTHER READING
Condie, Kent C. *Plate Tectonics and Crustal Evolution.* New York: Pergamon Press, 1976; 4th ed., Oxford and Boston: Butterworth-Heinemann, 1997.
Cox, Allan, and R. B. Hart. *Plate Tectonics: How It Works.* Oxford: Blackwell Scientific, 1986.
Floyd, Peter A., ed. *Oceanic Basalts.* London: Blackie and Sons, 1991.
Kearer, Philip, and Frederick J. Vine. *Global Tectonics,* 2nd ed. Oxford: Blackwell Scientific, 1996
Plummer, Charles C., David McGeary, and Diane H. Carlson. *Physical Geology.* Dubuque, Iowa: Wm. C. Brown, 1979; 8th ed., Boston: McGraw-Hill, 1999.
Tarbuck, Edward J., and Frederick K. Lutgens. *Earth.* Columbus, Ohio: Charles E. Merrill, 1984; 6th ed., Upper Saddle River, N.J.: Prentice Hall, 1999.
Thurman, Harold V. *Essentials of Oceanography.* Columbus, Ohio: Charles E. Merrill, 1983; 6th ed., with Alan P. Trujillo, Upper Saddle River, N.J.: Prentice Hall, 1999.

RELATED ARTICLES
Gabbro; Pillow Lava; Plate Tectonics; Seafloor Spreading; Seamount; Submarine Volcanism; Volcanic Ridge

Oceanic Zone

The pelagic environment of the ocean is the vast three-dimensional space created by the water itself. Oceanographers divide the pelagic environment into the oceanic and neritic zones. Most of the ocean is in the oceanic zone; it comprises water covering the ocean basins, or the sea floor deeper than 200 meters (656 feet). In contrast, the neritic zone is the wedge of water that extends from land's end to a water depth of 200 meters (656 feet); this volume of water covers the continental shelf.

Scientists subdivide the oceanic zone into ecological zones based on depth and biological and physical characteristics. The epipelagic zone extends from the sea surface to about 200 meters (656 feet). The lower boundary of this layer generally delineates the lower limit of photosynthesis and often coincides with the bottom of the mixed layer and the seasonal thermocline. The mesopelagic zone ranges from 200 to 1000 meters (656 to 3280 feet); its lower boundary is variable but usually represents the 10°C (50°F) isotherm in the tropics. The mesopelagic zone may contain an oxygen minimum zone between 500 and 1000 meters (1640 and 3280 feet). The bathypelagic zone extends from 1000 to 4000 meters (3280 feet to 2.5 miles), the abyssopelagic zone ranges from 4000 to 6000 meters (2.5 to 3.7 miles), and the hadal zone comprises water deeper than 6000 meters (3.7 miles).

Oceanographers also subdivide the oceanic zone based on light penetration. The euphotic zone is the uppermost lighted area of the oceans, where primary production occurs. It ranges from the sea surface to the depth at which light cannot support photosynthesis, which usually occurs between 100 and 200 meters (328 and 656 feet). The epipelagic zone and euphotic zone are generally synonymous. The dysphotic zone extends from the bottom of the euphotic zone to the depth at which light disappears completely, which usually occurs at the bottom of the mesopelagic zone. The aphotic zone describes the permanently dark depths of the ocean.

Lynn L. Lauerman

FURTHER READING
Lalli, Carol M., and Timothy R. Parsons. *Biological Oceanography: An Introduction.* Oxford and New York: Pergamon Press, 1993; 2nd ed., Oxford: Butterworth-Heinemann, 1997.
Nybakken, James W. *Marine Biology: An Ecological Approach,* 5th ed. San Francisco: Benjamin Cummings, 2001.

RELATED ARTICLES
Abyssopelagic Zone; Bathypelagic Zone; Dysphotic Zone; Epipelagic Zone; Euphotic Zone; Hadal Zone; Mesopelagic Zone; Oxygen Minimum Zone; Thermocline

Oceanographic Research Vessel

One of the more complicated aspects of studying the ocean is that humans are land-dwelling creatures, ill suited by nature to traveling on or under the sea for any length of time. In the early stages of their civilization, humans developed boating technology to exploit the ocean for food and for transportation, but studying the ocean, as opposed to merely using it, continues to pose a variety of challenges to engineers and oceanographers. Before oceanographers began undertaking regular research cruises in the late nineteenth century, scientists would simply take equipment onboard a ship and hope the ship's officers would allow them to study the ocean environment. Once large-scale research cruises became the norm, ships were outfitted with extensive amounts of built-in equipment that made them true research vessels.

The earliest oceanographic research vessels were simply commercial or naval ships or even yachts refitted with oceanographic equipment, a practice that continues today for economic reasons. Although some of these ships—such as the HMS *Challenger*, a refitted naval vessel that circumnavigated the globe in the 1870s—were quite seaworthy, the quality of the ships varied widely. All too often, the ships made available for oceanographic research by governments were navy cast-offs that could barely stay afloat and were a hazard to their crews. Luckily, oceanography attracted such wealthy benefactors as Prince Albert I of Monaco (1848–1922) and Alexander Agassiz (1835–1910), who used their funds to outfit yachts as research ships that they made available to other scientists.

Eventually, as oceanography became established, governments and private organizations began to build ships designed specifically for research use. One of the earliest ships built expressly for oceanographic research was the Norwegian vessel the *Fram*, built for the Arctic explorer and oceanographer Fridtjof Nansen (1861–1930). Nansen had the daring idea of deliberately allowing a ship to get frozen into the Arctic ice pack in order to study the Arctic Ocean. To ensure that the ship would not get crushed by the pressure of the ice, the *Fram* was built with an extra-thick, reinforced hull. The hull was also bowl-shaped, so that pressure on its sides from the expanding ice would force it up and the ship would rest safely on top of the ice pack. The *Fram* expedition, which lasted from 1893 to 1896, was a resounding success, and its design was copied for other Arctic research vessels.

In modern times, ships built for oceanographic research are developed to fulfill the special demands of scientists. Oceanographic research ships need to be able to stay at sea for long periods of time and to be stable and quiet, so that observations can be made from one place for several hours or days. This requirement resulted in the development in the 1960s of the floating instrument platform, or FLIP, by the Marine Physical Laboratory of the Scripps Institution of Oceanography in California. The FLIP, which

looks like the front half of a ship attached to a submarine, is towed to the location where observations need to be made. Then the tanks in the submarine portion are flooded with water, sinking half the ship and raising the other half to a vertical position. When FLIP is vertical, it is extremely stable despite the up-and-down motion of the waves around it. After the observations are made (FLIP is used predominantly for underwater acoustics), the water is forced out of FLIP's tanks, it returns to the horizontal position, and it is towed back to shore.

Another sort of specialized oceanographic research vessel is the drilling ship, used to extract core samples of the ocean floor. While oil companies use drills on ships, for oceanographic research the drills need to extend much deeper. The first oceanographic drilling ship, the *Glomar Challenger*, was built for the Deep Sea Drilling Program, lead by Scripps, in 1968. The *Challenger* drilled more than 1000 holes during its 15-year career, providing vital material to confirm the theory of ocean-floor spreading. The *Challenger* was eventually replaced by the *JOIDES Resolution*, an extensively refitted oil-drilling vessel. The *Resolution* carries a special positioning system that is so precise the ship can pull a drill out of a hole in the ocean floor miles below, then put the drill back into the same hole.

Although important to oceanography, ships are limited in the study of the sea surface. A variety of sophisticated submersible vessels have proved quite useful to oceanography. Unlike research ships, almost all research submersibles are built specifically for research. Conventional submarines have made some contribution to oceanography—most notably when the USS *Skate* surfaced the North Pole in 1959—but research submersibles are often required to travel to inhospitable depths and to perform specialized tasks such as gathering samples and taking photographs that conventional submarines simply cannot perform.

Humans have been experimenting with submersibles for centuries—classical Greek literature mentions diving bells, and a crude submarine was tested for use in warfare during the American Revolution. But the first submersible used expressly for marine research was not developed until the twentieth century. A small, spherical vessel called a *bathysphere* was dropped into the ocean from a ship in 1930. The bathysphere was tethered to the ship by a line and carried two scientists, who could only look out the vessel's thick window as the sphere dropped thousands of feet below the surface of the water. Nonetheless watching deep-sea creatures in their natural environment was both an exciting and an instructive experience. The basic bathysphere concept reached a climax of sorts in 1960, when the *Trieste* touched down at the bottom of the 10,912-meter (35,800-foot)-deep Challenger Deep in the Pacific Ocean, the deepest spot on Earth. The *Trieste*'s searchlights promptly picked out a swimming fish and proved that life could exist even at the greatest depths.

As valuable as such observations are, research submersibles became even more useful in 1964 when the U.S. Navy built *Alvin*, a vessel operated by the Woods Hole Oceanographic Institution. The titanium submersible could carry a team of scientists 4 kilometers (2.5 miles) below the surface and featured cameras and a pair of maneuverable arms for capturing sea creatures and taking samples. Later submersibles have incorporated many more features, including airlocks that allow divers to exit the vessel and explore the area. Some submersibles are built to be extremely quiet, allowing marine biologists to observe sea life unobtrusively.

The danger and expense of taking people underwater led in the late 1970s to the development of robotic submersibles that are tethered either to research ships or to manned submersibles. Perhaps the most famous of these remote-operated vehicles (ROVs) is *Argo*, which located the wreck of the ocean liner *Titanic* in 1985, more than 70 years after the ship collided with an iceberg and sank. While ROVs are tethered to manned vehicles and require human control, autonomous underwater vehicles (AUVs) operate independently. First built in 1979, AUVs can follow a preprogrammed route and take pictures and samples. Like ROVs, AUVs can operate underwater for long periods of time, so they are often used for surveying.

Mary Sisson

FURTHER READING

Barton, Robert. *The Oceans.* New York: Facts On File, 1980.

Beebe, William. *Half Mile Down.* New York: Harcourt, Brace, 1934.

Piccard, Jacques, and Robert Dietz. *Seven Miles Down: The Story of the Bathyscaph* Trieste. New York: Putnam, 1961.

Ross, David A. *Introduction to Oceanography.* New York: Appleton-Century-Crofts, 1970; 4th ed., Englewood Cliffs, N.J.: Prentice Hall, 1988.

Wallace, Joseph. *The Deep Sea.* New York: Gallery Books, 1987.

RELATED ARTICLES

Agassiz, Alexander Emmanuel Rodolphe; Albert I, Prince of Monaco; *Alvin*; Autonomous Underwater Vehicle; Deep Sea Drilling Project; FLIP; *Fram*; *Glomar Challenger*; HMS *Challenger*; Nansen, Fridtjof; Submersible; *Trieste*

Oceanography

Oceanography is the science of understanding the oceans, how they work, how they came into existence, how they affect our daily lives, the creatures that live in them, and how they may be affected by changes caused by human influences. Oceanography is concerned not only with the oceans, but with all the edges of the oceans as well, where the oceans interact with the other components of our planet. These include the coastlines, estuaries, and marshes, where fresh water enters the oceans continually; the surface of the ocean, where weather is made and dust settles down; and the deep, dark, cold ocean bottom, which has springs of hot water and where chemicals and even lava spew out from deep within Earth's crust.

Oceanography and society are intimately linked. The ocean covers more than 70 percent of the surface of Earth and is vital to the health of our planet. Oceans play a critical role in global systems that control Earth's environment. Physical, chemical, and biological processes that take place in the oceans and modulate the environment are tightly linked. These processes control life in the seas, affect large transfers of energy, and drive the pulse of climate change. They also affect the surrounding landmasses and respond to perturbations taking place outside the oceanic sphere. The ocean sustains life ranging from the largest whales, which are bigger than any dinosaur, to the tiniest one-celled floating plants, which harness the energy of sunlight and feed the rest of the creatures. It contains the largest and least explored habitat for life on Earth. It provides routes for commerce and sites for recreation. It contains food and energy resources that are in great demand by society. The movement of ocean plates builds spectacular undersea mountain ranges but is also the cause of earthquakes and volcanoes that wrench the margins of ocean basins. As the human impact on Earth's environment increases, the need to gain a fuller understanding of these processes becomes all the more urgent.

The goal of oceanographers is to improve our understanding of the ocean. The ocean is difficult to observe, and much of the scientific progress that has been made has depended on improvements in instrumentation that allow oceanographers to glimpse ocean processes. These processes are complex, and the body of knowledge that comprises oceanography is inherently multidisciplinary, requiring a breadth of scientific expertise. This has led to the division of oceanography into four basic subdivisions: physics, biology, chemistry, and geology, which are described below. In practice, many of the problems that oceanographers are trying to solve defy disciplinary classification.

Physical Oceanography

Physical oceanography is the study of the physical structure, motion, and mixing of ocean waters. Physical oceanography problems are solved using a variety of approaches, including field experiments, analysis of historical data, numerical ocean modeling, laboratory studies, and theoretical modeling. Physical oceanographers have mapped the global ocean current system and are now trying to understand how this system responds to climate change as well as how ocean currents transport heat, momentum, fresh water, and dissolved chemical constituents. They also study tides and surface and internal waves. Mixing processes, including double diffusion, convection, and turbulence, and small-scale transport processes such as diffusion and conduction are important to physical oceanographers. Research areas also include the dynamics of coastal and estuarine circulation and the physical properties of seawater.

Biological Oceanography

Biological oceanographers study the relationships among marine organisms and their interactions with the geochemical and physical environment. They study not only the plants and animals that live in the water column, but also benthic communities that live in the seabed. Areas of research include (1) productivity of plankton; (2) the distribution, abundance, physiology, and life history of marine organisms from coastal, oceanic, and deep-sea ecosystems; (3) processes that structure food webs in both the water column and benthic regimes; (4) the population ecology of marine organisms; and (5) interactions, adaptations, and behaviors of marine organisms.

Chemical Oceanography

Chemical oceanographers study the chemical components, reaction mechanisms, and geo-chemical pathways within the ocean and at its interfaces with the solid Earth and the atmosphere. They provide insights into oceanic processes at molecular scales. There has been a consistent history of development of chemical understanding of the oceans followed by application and transfer of techniques to other ocean disciplines. For example, ocean physics depends on a variety of chemical tools, including accurate salinity determination as well as measurement of extraordinarily low concentrations of water-mass tracers. Understanding ocean biological productivity patterns depended on the evolution of chemical measurements: Early nutrient measurements at 10^{-6} mole per liter explained many phenomena, and more recent assays of ultratrace nutrients at 10^{-10} mole per liter are beginning to elucidate long-standing and perplexing problems in plankton distributions. Measurements of even lower levels of various elements and isotopes have developed tools critical to understanding the geological evolution of Earth.

Marine Geology and Geophysics

Geological oceanographers study not only the sediments on the ocean floor but also try to understand the movement and structure of the plates that form the crust of Earth under the ocean as well as the forces and causes of the topographic features under the sea. Geological oceanographers have determined the history of the movement of all major ocean basins and have developed a robust model for the variation of seafloor depth with age. Systematic studies of seismic profiles have shown that sea-level changes on regional and global scales have been correlated: Few crustal margins are truly stable and local sea level is a function of many factors. Detailed mapping and sampling at mid-ocean ridges have shown a complex relationship between biology, chemistry, and physics in the ocean. Seawater flushing through the mid-ocean ridge systems pumps a variety of elements, vital to vent communities and the ocean's overall chemical budget, into the oceans along with a large amount of heat. Microbial communities, discovered in both the shallow crust at mid-ocean ridges and at depths of up to 800 meters (about 2625 feet) in seafloor sediments, may have implications for the origin of life on Earth as well as the potential for life on other planets. Measurements of isotopes of oxygen in the shells of microscopic organisms that are preserved in sediments have linked orbital forcing to Pleistocene climate change.

Instruments

Modern technology has provided an array of instrumentation that oceanographers use. Both government and universities maintain a fleet of research vessels that are capable of operating in most weather conditions and have special facilities for launching and retrieving instruments, making observations while underway, maintaining precise positions, and carrying modern scientific laboratories. Shipboard instruments include current meters, CTD profilers, plankton nets, and midwater trawls, which are in widespread use. Some vessels have high-resolution sonar systems and multichannel seismic systems that allow oceanographers to view the seabed as well as the structure of Earth beneath the seabed. Drilling ships are capable of drilling into the oceanic lithosphere and providing samples of rock and sediment. Manned submersibles, remote-operated vehicles (ROVs), and autonomous underwater vehicles (AUVs) provide unique observations of the structure of the ocean. A class of inexpensive AUVs is currently being deployed to provide global observations of the structure of the thermocline, and future versions will be able to measure mixing processes, biological production, and the optical properties of water. Satellites provide global sampling for sea surface temperature, color, height, waves, and sea ice. Oceanographers also use mass spectrometers, microprobes, sub-sea observatories, and cabled arrays of scientific instruments, including hydrophones.

Oceanographers

The most important element for advancing our understanding of the oceans is individual creativity. Making students aware of the challenges of the ocean, and attracting and retaining them, are critical for progress. Although a few universities offer undergraduate majors in ocean sciences, most oceanographers specialize in biology, chemistry, geology, or physics as undergraduates. Oceanography is typically a graduate program, and good programs are available at universities in all coastal (and Great Lakes) states in the United States. The largest program on the west coast is at the Scripps Institution of Oceanography, University of California, in San Diego, and, on the east coast, large programs are located at the Woods Hole Oceanographic Institution in Woods Hole, Massachusetts, and the Lamont-Doherty Geological Observatory, Columbia University, in Palisades, New York. Oceanographers work for a wide range of employers, including academic organizations. The largest government employers are the U.S. Navy and the National Oceanic and Atmospheric Agency (NOAA) of the Department of Commerce. The largest private employers include the oil industry and aquaculture. Professional societies for oceanographers include the American Geophysical Union, the American Society of Limnology and Oceanography, and the Oceanography Society.

Curtis A. Collins

FURTHER READING

Ballard, Robert. *Exploring Our Living Planet.* Washington, D.C.: National Geographic Society, 1983; rev. ed., 1988.

Duxbury, Alison B., and Alyn C. Duxbury. *Fundamentals of Oceanography.* Dubuque, Iowa: Wm. C. Brown, 1996.

Duxbury, Alyn C., and Alison B. Duxbury. *An Introduction to the World's Oceans.* 4th ed. Dubuque, Iowa: Wm. C. Brown, 1994.

Hamblin, W. Kenneth. *Earth's Dynamics Systems: A Textbook in Physical Geology.* Minneapolis, Minn.: Burgess, 1975; 9th ed., with Eric H. Christiansen, Upper Saddle River, N.J.: Prentice Hall, 2001.

Jones, E. J. W. *Marine Geophysics.* Chichester, England, and New York: Wiley, 1999.

Kennett, James. *Marine Geology.* Englewood Cliffs, N.J.: Prentice Hall, 1982.

National Science Foundation. *Ocean Sciences at the New Millennium.* Washington, D.C.; NSF, 2001.

Thurman, Harold V. *Introductory Oceanography,* 8th ed. Upper Saddle River, N.J.: Prentice Hall, 1997.

RELATED ARTICLES

Climate Change; Marine Biology; Marine Geology; Marine Geophysics; Paleoceanography

Ocean Plateau

An ocean plateau is a large and broad submarine feature that has high relief, a thick crust, a relatively thick sedimentary section compared to that of nearby and deeper seafloor, and no seismic activity. Within a generous definition, ocean plateaus include aseismic ridges, which are elongate features that have geologic histories similar to those of ocean plateaus; the sizes and shapes of aseismic ridges merge with those of ocean plateaus. The term *ocean rise* is synonymous with *ocean plateau.* Therefore, discussions of ocean plateaus generally include aseismic ridges and ocean rises.

Ocean plateaus are topographically, structurally, and petrologically distinct from most other seafloor tectonic features. Lava flows that form the pedestals of many ocean plateaus are studied to understand magma source regions and differentiation processes. Ocean plateaus may possess sedimentary sections that have remained above the regional calcite compensation depth (CCD), thereby recording data of scientific interest that are interpreted to answer questions about such things as evolutionary trends of planktonic (floating pelagic) organisms, mass extinctions, and paleoclimates.

Description

The crustal thickness of ocean plateaus is more than double the thickness of normal ocean crust. Geophysical data indicate that crusts of ocean plateaus range in thickness from 20 to 40 kilometers (12.4 to 25 miles). The greater thickness of ocean plateaus that form on the deep ocean floor is caused by a buildup of lava flows and intrusive masses that occurs above mantle plumes (hotspots), at the intersection of transform faults and spreading ridges, and above subduction zones where two or more plates converge. Ocean plateaus near continents generally have thick crusts of continental character. Most ocean plateaus remain below sea level, but some, including the Seychelles Bank, Bahama Platform, and Kerguelen Plateau, are decorated with islands.

Oceanic plateaus are free of earthquake activity. They have distinct geophysical (gravity, magnetic, seismic reflection, and seismic refraction) characteristics. They may be solitary or contiguous with adjacent landmasses or even with a spreading ridge. Nearly 50 percent of all ocean plateaus and aseismic ridges lead away from hotspots.

An excellent example of an oceanic plateau is the Ontong Java Plateau in the southwestern Pacific Ocean. It may be the largest flood basalt province in the world. The plateau's broad and relatively flat surface stands approximately 3 kilometers (1.9 miles) above the surrounding seafloor and is underlain by as much as 25 kilometers (15.5 miles) of igneous crust that is composed mostly of lava flows about 90 million years old. The Ontong Java Plateau caused a change in subduction direction below the Solomon Islands Arc when those two features collided during the Miocene Epoch, about 20 million years ago.

Distribution

Within the very broad grouping of ocean plateaus, aseismic ridges, and ocean rises these submarine features represent about 10 percent of the ocean floor. More than 100 are known; they are particularly abundant in the western Pacific Ocean, where they move relentlessly toward the continents and island arcs, with the threat of future collisions.

Some major ocean plateaus and aseismic ridges are the following.
- *Atlantic Ocean*: Agulhas Plateau, Azores Ridge, Bahama Platform, Rio Grande Rise, Rockall Bank, Sierra Leone Rise, Vöring Plateau, and Walvis Ridge
- *Arctic Ocean and Bering Sea*: Bowers Ridge, Lomonosov Ridge, Shirshov Ridge, and Umnak Plateau
- *Indian Ocean*: Broken Ridge, Chagos–Laccadive Ridge, Crozet Plateau, Exmouth Plateau, Kerguelen Plateau, Naturaliste Plateau, Ninetyeast Ridge, Madagascar Ridge, Mascarene Plateau, and Seychelles Bank
- *Pacific Ocean*: Campbell Plateau, Chatham Rise, Hess Rise, Kyushu–Palau Ridge, Lau Ridge, Lord Howe Rise, Magellan Rise, Manahiki Plateau, Norfolk Ridge, Ontong Java Plateau, Queensland Plateau, Shatsky Rise, Stalemate Ridge, Tasman Plateau, and Three Kings Rise

Origin

Several explanations have been given for the origin of oceanic plateaus and aseismic ridges. They may be either isolated fragments of continental crust; extinct and subsided linear volcanic features such as fracture zones, spreading ridges, and island arcs; or heads of mantle plumes (hotspots), especially where they intersect spreading ridges, transform faults, and island arcs. Uplifted, normal oceanic crust is a rare explanation for the origin of ocean plateaus. Many ocean plateaus are fragments of continents that have broken off and drifted away from a parent. These are often referred to as microcontinents. Examples are the Seychelles Bank and Mascarene Plateau of the western Indian Ocean, Agulhas Plateau south of Africa, Rockall Bank and Vöring Plateau in the North Atlantic Ocean, and Lord Howe Rise and Campbell Plateau near New Zealand.

Extinct linear features are aseismic ridges. These include abandoned spreading ridges (Hess Rise), island arcs (Kyushu–Palau Ridge and Lau Ridge), and fracture zones such as Louisville Ridge and Stalemate Ridge. Intraplate volcanism causes the growth of seamounts and islands, often above a hotspot. Although most result in chains because of movement by a lithospheric plate, some may concentrate their volcanic activity over only a short period of time and form an ocean plateau upon sinking (subsidence). The Ontong Java Plateau, Manahiki Plateau, and Shatsky Rise are among Earth's largest igneous provinces and are commonly believed to have formed above mantle plumes.

Geological Significance

Collisions of ocean plateaus (and aseismic ridges) with plate boundaries are common, especially along subduction zones. A large ocean plateau can greatly affect a convergent margin because it resists subduction; the subduction process cannot swallow the plateau and the only alternative is to either stop the subduction process or scrape the plateau off and attach it to the upper plate. Collisions of aseismic ridges with subduction zones are in part responsible for the arcuate shape of island arcs. For example, the Mariana Islands Arc was rotated and bent by colliding with the Caroline and Marcus Ridges. Furthermore, volcanic gaps in arc systems commonly occur at points of collision. Along the west coast of South America and Central America, the impingement of the Cocos, Tehuantepec, Nazca, Carnegie, and Juan Fernandez Ridges has affected the onshore volcanism by creating gaps in the active volcanic

chain. Seismic gaps, where earthquakes are absent, may also occur near points of collision, indicating that the subduction zone is plugged up and that the downgoing slab has stopped moving.

Ocean plateaus and aseismic ridges have undergone significant long-term subsidence since their formation. They subside at about the same rate as normal ocean floor. Evidence for subsidence is derived from detailed studies of calcareous sediments that cap many ocean plateaus. Marine sedimentation begins in shallow water followed by the deposition of progressively deeper-water sediments as the plateaus sink.

Shatsky Rise and Hess Rise show histories of vertical subsidence and lateral movement within their sediment sections. Their pedestals were built by volcanism in the southern hemisphere; Shatsky Rise formed about 145 to 140 million years ago and Hess Rise formed about 110 to 105 million years ago. Subsequently, they moved on the back of the Pacific Plate and subsided. During their journeys north, the plateaus passed under the equatorial divergence (where upwelling of nutrient-rich water occurs), thereby increasing the productivity of calcareous and siliceous planktonic organisms. Thick piles of these biogenous sediments accumulated and with time were converted to chalk, limestone, and chert.

Ancient Ocean Plateaus

Earth scientists have studied most ocean plateaus in the world's oceans and have speculated about their importance in the geologic past. Apparently, ocean plateaus have greatly affected convergent margins throughout geologic time. Some ocean plateaus were either obducted (scraped off the lower plate within a subduction zone and emplaced on the upper plate) or otherwise accreted and are now locked in mountain ranges. An outstanding example of an accreted ocean plateau is the Wrangellia terrane of Vancouver Island, southeastern Alaska, and eastern Oregon.

Tracy L. Vallier

FURTHER READING

Condie, Kent C. *Plate Tectonics and Crustal Evolution.* New York: Pergamon Press, 1976; 4th ed., Oxford and Boston: Butterworth-Heinemann, 1997.

Ito, Garrett, and Peter D. Clift. "Subsidence and Growth of Pacific Cretaceous Plateaus." *Earth and Planetary Science Letters,* Vol. 161 (1998), pp. 85–100.

Kennett, James P. *Marine Geology.* Englewood Cliffs, N.J.: Prentice Hall, 1982.

Pringle, Malcolm, William Sager, William Sliter, and Seth Stein, eds. *The Mesozoic Pacific: Geology, Tectonics, and Volcanism.* Washington, D.C.: American Geophysical Union, 1993.

Seibold, Eugen, and Wolfgang H. Berger. *The Sea Floor: An Introduction to Marine Geology.* Berlin and New York: Springer-Verlag, 1982; 3rd ed., 1996.

Vallier, Tracy, Walter Dean, David Rea, and Jörn Thiede. "Geologic Evolution of Hess Rise, Central North Pacific Ocean." *Geological Society of America Bulletin,* Vol. 94 (1983), pp. 1289–1307.

RELATED ARTICLES

Bering Sea; Fracture Zone; Hess Rise; Hotspot; Mantle Plume; Ontong Java Plateau; Pacific Plate; Plate Tectonics; Shatsky Rise; Terrane

Ocean Thermal Energy Conversion

Ocean thermal energy conversion (OTEC) is one of the least publicized methods for extracting energy from the world's seas, yet it is also one of the most practical and economically feasible. OTEC makes use of the temperature difference between the sea's surface and its depths to generate clean, "green" electrical power. Although it is generally more expensive than traditional sources of energy, it costs less than wave or tidal power schemes and is particularly effective on small islands, where importing traditional fuels is expensive, and the geography of the surrounding seabed lends itself particularly well to OTEC.

How OTEC works

OTEC uses the temperature difference between warm surface water and cold deep waters to boil a working fluid. The vapor produced by this fluid is used to spin electricity turbines, and the fluid is then recondensed. In practice, there are two main types of OTEC: closed cycle and open cycle. In *closed-cycle OTEC,* the working fluid is a liquid, typically ammonia, with a low boiling point. Warm water is collected from the sea surface and passes through heat exchangers inside the plant (a heat exchanger is a network of narrow pipes with a large surface area, which allows heat to be transferred efficiently between a fluid inside the exchanger and another fluid surrounding it). The heat exchangers are used to warm the working fluid so that it boils, and the expanding vapor is used to turn the turbines. The working fluid then passes over another set of heat exchangers, which are filled with cold water pumped from the deep ocean. The temperature drop causes the fluid to recondense, and the cycle can repeat.

In *open-cycle OTEC,* the warm seawater actually becomes the working fluid. After it enters the plant, it is pumped into a vacuum chamber, where the low air pressure causes it to boil at a temperature lower than 100°C (212°F). This produces steam, which spins the turbines and is then passed over heat exchangers filled with cold deep seawater. The steam condenses and is pumped back into the sea, or is used as a supply of desalinated water. The pressure drop created as the steam recondenses is used to create the partial vacuum needed to evaporate more warm water at the start of the cycle.

OTEC in Practice

The most important practical limitation on the use of OTEC comes from the need for a sufficient temperature difference between the warm and cold water used in the system. Experiments have shown that a temperature difference of at least 20°C (68°F) is needed and that OTEC is practical only if the cold water can be pumped from depths of less than about 1 kilometer (3280 feet). This makes OTEC practical in those regions where the sea surface receives the most heat from the sun, largely within a band 20 to 30° north and south of the equator. Within this region, tropical islands offer the best prospects for inexpensive development of OTEC; they frequently have steep ocean shelves, allowing deep-sea cold water close to shore. Islands are also often reliant on expensive fuel imports, which makes OTEC even more economically sensible.

Uses of OTEC

As well as generating electricity, OTEC has a number of useful by-products. Desalination is one of the most important and is particularly useful on isolated islands. Either type of OTEC cycle can produce desalinated water. The open-cycle process is described above, but in a closed-cycle plant, the cold water used to condense the working fluid can be passed on through another set of heat exchangers to condense smaller amounts of water out of the humid tropical atmosphere. (A third variation, called the *hybrid cycle,* evaporates and recondenses warm seawater to produce desalinated water, but uses the steam to boil a separate closed-cycle working fluid.)

Even after it has passed through the complete OTEC cycle, deep-sea water remains very cold and rich in nutrients. Rather than simply returning it to the ocean floor, it can be useful in a variety of applications. In mariculture, for example, cold water from an OTEC plant provides an ideal breeding ground for plankton and algae as a source of food for farmed fish. The cold water can even be used directly to provide an environment for rearing salmon, trout, and other fish not normally found in the tropics.

Cold OTEC water can also be used for refrigeration and air-conditioning plants. Although it contains nutrients and microorganisms, experiments have shown that introducing just small, environmentally safe amounts of chlorine into the water will prevent the bacteria in it from breeding and clogging pipes. Another long-term goal for OTEC plants is to extract minerals from seawater chemically. At present, "mining" of seawater is uneconomical, but this can change if the seawater is already being brought to the surface for another purpose. In Japan, for instance, experiments for extracting uranium from seawater are already under way.

History of OTEC

OTEC has a surprisingly long history—the technique was invented by French engineer Jacques d'Arsonval (1851–1940) in 1881. D'Arsonval developed the closed-cycle system but was unable to put it into practice. However, his student Georges Claude (1870–1960) took things a step further, devising the open cycle and building two prototype plants, one in Cuba and one on board a cargo ship off the coast of Brazil. Both plants were destroyed by the weather before Claude could demonstrate their ability to produce more energy than was needed to run them. Another French project, begun in the 1950s on the west coast of Africa, failed because of competition from cheaper hydroelectric power.

In the early 1980s the prospects for OTEC began to improve. Japan demonstrated a working plant capable of generating around 30 kilowatts of electricity on the Pacific island of Nauru, and experiments proved that aluminum could be used to replace the expensive titanium previously used in OTEC heat exchangers. Improvements in the heat exchanger design also meant that it was possible to extract more energy from a less expensive plant. From 1979 onward, the U.S. Natural Energy Laboratory of Hawaii (NELHA) began to build a series of test facilities to demonstrate and improve OTEC technology. NELHA has also demonstrated many of the useful by-products of OTEC, ranging from desalination to mariculture. The current record for electricity generation by an OTEC plant is held by NELHA's open-cycle plant at Keahole Point,

Hawaii, which generated 50 kilowatts in continuous tests in May 1993. At present, most OTEC research is directed toward improving turbine designs to make the electricity generation process even more efficient.

Future Prospects

Today, there are still no commercial OTEC plants in existence. The major obstacle to their development is the high initial cost of building such a plant, but improvements in design and cost-effectiveness mean that the possibility of economically feasible OTEC is getting closer. Because the oceans absorb so much solar energy every day, there is potentially a huge resource waiting to be tapped, offering billions of watts of clean, renewable power. Over the next few years, OTEC plants are likely to be built in small island groups such as those of the Pacific Ocean. These would have to generate only around 1 megawatt of power, and when coupled to desalination plants they could be economically feasible because of the high costs of fuel imports. As fossil-fuel prices continue to rise, larger OTEC plants will become a more feasible energy source for larger island groups, such as Hawaii. Surveys have shown that in the long term, more than 70 developing nations are situated in regions where they could take advantage of OTEC.

More ambitious plans for the future would involve using large *plantships* that could float off the continental shelves of the Americas or Australia. The power that plantships could generate would either be sent back to shore by submarine cables or used in onboard factories for energy-intensive manufacturing processes such as the making of hydrogen, ammonia, or methanol.

Giles Sparrow

FURTHER READING
Avery, William H., and Chih Wu. *Renewable Energy from the Ocean.* New York: Oxford University Press, 1994.

Cohen, R. "Energy from the Ocean." *Philosophical Transactions of the Royal Society of London, Series A: Mathematical and Physical Sciences,* Vol. 307, No. 1499 (1982), pp. 405–437.

Dunbar, L. E. "Potential for Ocean Thermal Energy Conversion as a Renewable Energy Source For Developing Nations." Washington, D.C.: Science Applications International Corporation, 1981.

Johnson, F. A. "Energy from the Oceans: A Small Land-Based Ocean Thermal Energy Plant." *Proceedings, EEZ Resources Technology Assessment,* Honolulu, Hawaii, January 1988.

Marine Board–National Research Council. *Ocean Engineering for Ocean Thermal Energy Conversion.* Washington, D.C.: National Academy Press, 1982.

Penney, T. R., and D. Bharathan. "Power from the Sea." *Scientific American,* Vol. 256, No. 1 (January 1987).

Seymour, Richard J., ed. *Ocean Energy Recovery: The State of the Art.* New York: American Society of Civil Engineers, 1992.

RELATED ARTICLES
Energy from the Sea

Ocean Wind System

Current knowledge of ocean surface winds, the trade winds, the westerlies, the polar easterlies, and the monsoons, is often taken for granted. Coming to understand these airflows and their underlying physics involves some of the most recognized names in science. Mariners have been aware of the ocean winds for millennia, but that knowledge was often a well-guarded trade secret. Much of the systematic data archiving in marine meteorology and sea surface oceanography can be credited to a dedicated U.S. naval officer, Matthew Fontaine Maury (1806–73), in the nineteenth century.

The ancient Greeks knew Earth to be a sphere with three climatic zones: torrid, temperate, and frigid. Aristotle's *Meteorologica* (c. 330 B.C.) contains references to the winds, but it was not until 1686 that Edmond Halley (1656–1742) related the primary ocean winds to ocean currents. Although thermometers were known at the end of the sixteenth century, the sealed liquid-in-glass thermometer was not invented until 1654, barometers until 1643, and hygrometers until the late eighteenth century. In 1735, George Hadley (1685–1768) used conservation of momentum to explain the trade winds, and in 1775, Pierre Laplace (1749–1827) derived the hydrodynamic equations, including horizontal Coriolis terms. Following these developments, in 1806, Francis Beaufort (1774–1857) devised the 0 to 12 category marine wind scale, and in 1853, James Coffin (1829–1911) first observed the relationship between wind and pressure, which became known as *Buys Ballot's law,* after the chief of the Dutch Meteorological Services, Christoph Buys Ballot (1817–90).

The ocean wind system is highly seasonal, driven by the annual migration of the Sun. Three millennia ago, Arab sailors in the Indian Ocean steered reed ships from Africa to India and beyond, following the yearly cycle of the Northeast and Southwest Monsoons. In their discovery of North America, Vikings appreciated the variations in the polar easterlies and established a thriving intercontinental maritime trading system 500 years before the voyages of Christopher Columbus. Polynesian mariners in magnificent double-hulled sailing vessels colonized the entire Pacific Ocean using only their knowledge of the stars, seasonal winds, and ocean waves to navigate distances unimaginable to European explorers of the early fifteenth century.

Although the seasonal nature of the ocean wind system is a continuum, the months of January and July will be used to illustrate the changing structure of the air flowing over the ocean's surface (see figure). The vectors shown in the figure can be considered to be those of the average surface wind during winter (upper panel) and summer (lower panel) in the northern hemisphere. In many ways, the figure is the culmination of Maury's dream of systematic, quality-controlled, volunteer observations.

Wind is a vector and thus has both direction and magnitude. Winds are named for the direction from which they are blowing, whereas ocean currents are named for the direction toward which they flow. On average, surface winds over the ocean are stronger than those over land and demonstrate a more nearly zonal flow (i.e., in an east–west direction). The low-latitude easterly trade winds and the midlatitude westerlies are easily discernible in both the January and July panels of the figure. Globally, ocean surface winds are stronger in January than in July, a consequence of the distribution of land surface area in the northern hemisphere exceeding that in the southern hemisphere.

Northeast Trades and Southeast Trades

In the "torrid zone," as the ancients would have called it, the surface winds are named the Northeast Trades and the Southeast Trades. The region near Earth's equator where they converge is known as the Intertropical Convergence Zone (ITCZ). The ITCZ moves northward with the Sun and can be found between 10 and 15°N in July and close to the equator in January. The mean position of the ITCZ is about 5°N, again a consequence of the asymmetric land distribution between hemispheres. Earth's "meteorological equator" is approximately coincident with the mean ITCZ position. An important consequence of the mean ITCZ location is that the Southeast Trades generally blow across the equator, leading to oceanic upwelling of cool water, a phenomenon known as *Ekman divergence.*

As shown in the figure, the Northeast Trade Winds are stronger than the Southeast Trade Winds. Average January wind speeds in the Northeast Trades are up to 10 meters per second (m/s; about 20 knots) in the Caribbean Sea and along the coast of Southeast Asia, whereas the Southeast Trade Winds tend to average 5 to 7 m/s (10 to 14 knots) except in local regions, notably the eastern Pacific and Indian Oceans. In July both the Northeast and Southeast Trades weaken over the open ocean and tend to average 6 to 8 m/s (12 to 16 knots) except in two locales: the eastern Caribbean Sea and the western Indian Ocean. Both exceptions are associated with a monsoonal circulation of the atmosphere.

Monsoons

Monsoons are examples of what will be called a *coupled land–air–sea system* (CLASS) occurrence. A CLASS is observed on various space and time scales, from the diurnal sea-breeze/land-breeze flows famous over the Florida peninsula in summertime, to the annual monsoon of the Indian subcontinent. CLASS occurrences are driven by differential heating between the sea and the land, there being a difference factor of 5 in the specific heat of seawater and the juxtaposed land. Note also that there is a relationship between the time and space scales of the wind system. Short-duration events (e.g., daily) such as a sea breeze occur over small areas (e.g., 100 kilometers; 62 miles), whereas a monsoon occurs over annual time periods and thousands of kilometers.

During the boreal summer, the air over India warms much more than the air over the Arabian Sea, resulting in a large surface temperature difference. From the perfect gas law for the atmosphere, $p = \rho rt$, where p is air pressure, ρ is air density, R is the gas constant for air, and T is air temperature, it is seen that large temperature differences (ΔT) imply large pressure differences (Δp). Horizontal pressure differences formed as the CLASS evolves seasonally lead to strong winds that characterize the Indian Monsoon. In July, surface winds blow from the southwest onto India that average 15 m/s (29 knots), carrying enormous amounts of moisture evaporated from the western Indian Ocean. This moisture eventually precipitates out and is central to the agriculture that feeds some 1 billion humans.

Characteristically, in boreal winter (as represented by January in the figure) the lands of India have lost their heat five times more rapidly than has the nearby sea, and the Monsoon wind reverses direction. January winds over the western Indian Ocean are from the northeast but average approximately 8 m/s (16 knots). Weaker northwest monsoonal winds are due to smaller values of ΔT in January than in July, and hence smaller pressure differences. These reversing winds cause a 180° reversal in the direction of the Somali Current, the only such major current cycle in the ocean. Many other areas of Earth experience monsoons, notably Southeast Asia and central North America, where it is called the American Monsoon.

Seasonal precipitation patterns in the tropics are associated with the ITCZ, but these should not be confused with monsoons. In a global sense, the annual migration of the ITCZ can be appreciated from a CLASS perspective, but the dynamics are different. Tropical meteorology is focused on the *Hadley Cell,* one of Earth's three meridional (north–south) vertical circulations. In midlatitudes the vertical circulation (say, between 30 and 60° latitude) is called the *Ferrel Cell,* and in high latitudes it is called the *Polar Cell.* The horse latitudes of weaker winds and subsiding air from aloft at about 30°N and 30°S mark the transition between the Hadley and Ferrel Cells and the associated change from low-latitude easterly winds to midlatitude westerlies. These surface transition areas are readily discernible in the figure as regions of weak winds.

Midlatitude westerlies are studied extensively because of the vigorous maritime commerce in the northern hemisphere. The winter North Atlantic is infamous for deadly storms. Nautical protection associations such as the American Bureau of Shipping require merchant ships to leave the largest margin of safety when navigating the North Atlantic Ocean in winter. Stories of the ferocity of the winds and the waves they create in this season are a continuing source of great literature.

The surface air pressure difference between Iceland and the Azores (or Bermuda) is often used

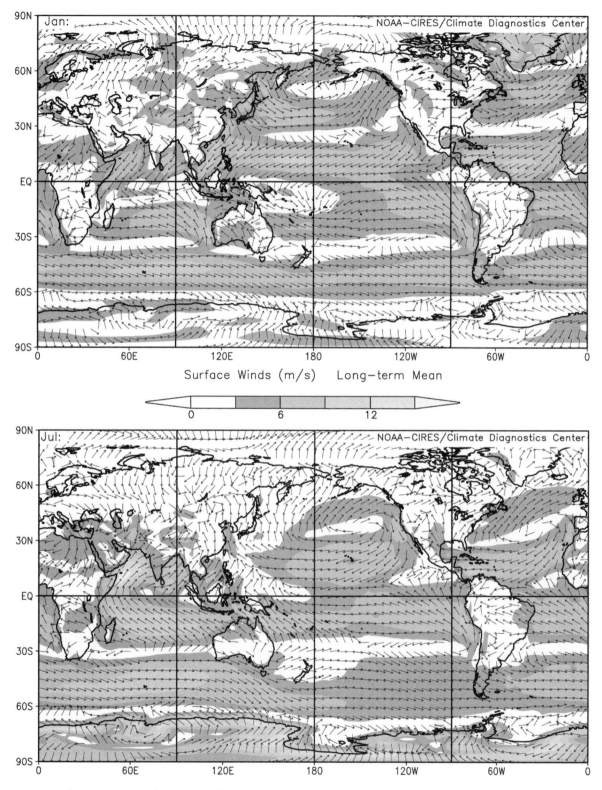

Average surface wind vectors for northern hemisphere winter (upper panel) and summer (lower panel), based on the 1968–96 long-term mean of the National Center for Atmospheric Research/National Center for Environmental Prediction global reanalysis project. (Courtesy, George Maul)

403

to quantify the strength of the westerlies over the North Atlantic Ocean. These north–south pressure gradients give rise to east–west winds, a consequence of the Coriolis effect. Geostrophic calculations show average winds in January of approximately 10 m/s (20 knots) and summer values of half as much (see figure).

The interannual change in the pressure difference between Iceland and the Azores results in interesting changes in the North Atlantic winds. Temporal variations in this surface air pressure difference have been named the North Atlantic Oscillation (NAO). Spectral analysis of the NAO shows a significant period of approximately 14 years. That is, seven years after a year or so of strong westerlies, there follows a few years of weaker westerlies, and so on. A similar oscillation in the North Pacific Ocean is called the Pacific Decadal Oscillation (PDO), but the PDO seems to have a cycle of about 20 to 30 years. Before addressing the most famous of these coupled ocean–atmospheric cycles, the El Niño–Southern Oscillation, the polar easterlies and the westerlies merit discussion.

Polar Easterlies and the Westerlies

In 1893, Norwegian explorer and scientist Fridtjof Nansen (1861–1930) purposefully froze his specially built research vessel the *Fram* into the Arctic Ocean. One of his goals was to show that the sea ice moved in the same direction as the polar winds. Three years later, the *Fram* emerged from the ice having circumnavigated the Arctic. Thus the polar easterlies were shown to drive the frozen Arctic Ocean. In the Antarctic the polar easterlies are strong coastal winds, and can be seen in the figure to be substantially stronger than the Arctic winds, averaging 12 to 14 m/s (23 to 27 knots). Averages, of course, hide the fact that individual Arctic and Antarctic storms can easily have sustained winds of hurricane force [33 m/s (64 knots)] or greater. Integrated into the surface winds of the polar areas is the *Polar Cell*, which

describes a vertical circulation of rising air at about 60°N or 60°S latitude and sinking air at 90°. The sinking air is dry and Earth's poles are deserts for the same reason that sinking air at 30°N or 30°S latitude causes the great deserts of Africa, Asia, and Australia.

While studying the high-latitude winds in the figure, note that the westerlies in the southern hemisphere are substantially stronger than in the North Atlantic or the North Pacific Oceans. These winds blow around the Southern Ocean between 40 and 50°S, virtually unimpeded by land, and can be seen to have January averages exceeding 10 m/s (20 knots). They are aptly named the "roaring forties." The wind system of trades, westerlies, and polar easterlies is the result of semipermanent surface high-air-pressure cells centered at 30 and 90° latitudes, and of semipermanent lows at 0 and 60° latitudes. These pressure patterns of low–high–low–high every 30° or so of latitude are surface expressions of the Hadley, Ferrel, and Polar Cells. They are the fundamental cause of the quasi-geostrophic winds seen in the figure.

El Niño–Southern Oscillation

An ocean wind system of global proportions is the El Niño–Southern Oscillation (ENSO). The name *El Niño*, a Spanish term meaning "the (Christ) child," stems from the observation by natives of the west coast of South America of an ocean warming off the coasts of Ecuador and Peru, often at Christmas. *Southern Oscillation* is an equatorial analog of the NAO or PDO except that its surface air pressure differences are in an east–west direction. *ENSO* became the joint scientific term when it was realized that an El Niño is related to a Pacific Ocean scale rearrangement of the tropical atmosphere. The strong coast-parallel winds of the normal (neutral ENSO or average) conditions are seen in both panels of the figure. These shore-parallel winds, which cause an Ekman upwelling of cold nutrient-rich waters off tropical South America, provide another example of CLASS behavior.

With the advent of global observing systems brought on by the satellite era, ENSO has been recognized as a short-term modulation of Earth's entire climate. ENSO occurs every four to seven years on average, with a very strong event every 14 years or so. ENSO involves changes in monsoonal strengths, precipitation and weather pattern changes at great distance from the tropical Pacific Ocean—a phenomenon called *teleconnections*—and substantial weakening or reversing of the trade winds. For example, the Southeast Trades normally cross the equator, causing an Ekman divergence that results in cold water along the eastern Equatorial Pacific. When the trades weaken, this divergence ceases and the sea surface temperature of the eastern Pacific (in particular) warms by 3 to 5°C (5.4 to 9°F). This warming causes a positive feedback from the ocean to the atmosphere, and areas with little normal rainfall experience floods and attendant loss of human life. Indeed, ENSO even seems related to the NAO, hurricanes, and typhoons by modulating the upper atmospheric winds in low latitudes.

Tropical Storms

Hurricanes, typhoons, and cyclones are all common names for the same CLASS phenomenon: the tropical storm. Many tropical weather disturbances start over western Africa and migrate into the Atlantic Ocean. Easterly waves, north–south surface air pressure disturbances that appear as horizontal waves on weather charts, move across the ocean from east to west. Some intensify in response to the positive feedback of warm sea surface temperatures, growing cumulus convective systems, adequate atmospheric moisture, and moderate increase of wind speed from the surface to the tropopause (the upper limit of the troposphere, a layered band of atmosphere lying just below the stratosphere). Some hurricanes form in the Atlantic and cross Central America to re-form in the eastern Pacific. Others form in the central Pacific and devastate the coasts of Southeast Asia, where they are called *typhoons*. In the Indian Ocean, these storm systems are called *cyclones*, and one event in 1971 that came ashore in Bangladesh is estimated to have killed over 300,000 people.

Tropical storms rotate around a small radius of curvature, and their equations of motion include centrifugal force as well as the geostrophic force. Because of centrifugal force, the pressure in the storm center can reach very low values. Hurricane Gilbert in 1988 had a central pressure of 888 hectopascal (888 millibar), sustained winds in excess of 58 m/s (113 knots), and up to 85 m/s (165 knots) in gusts near the eye wall at a radius of 25 kilometers (16 miles) from the storm center. A few typhoons have been estimated to exceed this Atlantic Ocean record storm.

Although tropical storms bring wind and storm-surge damage, they also bring much needed precipitation to the land. In some cases it is understood that these storms also help cleanse the seafloor of accumulated debris, and are a positive part of the natural marine ecosystem. From a human perspective, the wind does most of the damage to coastal infrastructure, but most lives are lost by drowning from the storm surge or landslides. Hurricane Mitch is blamed for over 11,000 deaths from mudslides in Central America in 1998.

Conclusion

Much has yet to be learned about the ocean wind system. Many of the oscillations discussed (the NAO, the PDO, ENSO) and others not mentioned probably have links to each other. Analysis of improved global data sets, such as the winds shown in the figure, will undoubtedly reveal additional teleconnections. As computers improve, numerical models will reveal additional understanding. How all this will evolve in time to improve understanding of global climate is the wondrous challenge for coming generations of scientists. Perhaps even more profound is how the knowledge will be used by engineers and managers to mitigate natural disasters, and by physicians to improve public health by forecasting disease vectors, plagues, and famine. Integrated thinking in a CLASS perspective seems the best approach of linking the ocean wind system to the biosphere and geosphere and to human activities.

George A. Maul

FURTHER READING

Barry, Roger G., and Richard J. Chorley. *Atmosphere, Weather and Climate.* London: Methuen, 1968; 7th ed., London and New York: Routledge, 1998.

Diaz, Henry F., and Vera Markgraf. El Niño: *Historical and Paleoclimatic Aspects of the Southern Oscillation.* Cambridge and New York: Cambridge University Press, 1992.

Henderson-Sellers, Ann, and Peter J. Robinson. *Contemporary Climatology.* London: Longman Scientific and Technical/New York: Wiley, 1986; 2nd ed., Harlow, England: Addison Wesley Longman, 1999.

Hidore, John J., and John E. Oliver. *Climatology: An Atmospheric Science.* New York: Macmillan/Toronto, Canada: Macmillan Canada, 1993.

Wells, Neil. *The Atmosphere and Ocean: A Physical Introduction.* London and Philadelphia: Taylor and Francis, 1986; 2nd ed., Chichester, England, and New York: Wiley, 1997.

RELATED ARTICLES

El Niño; Monsoon; Ocean Current; Pressure; Trade Winds

Ochrophyta

Walk along any rocky ocean shore in the temperate, subpolar, or polar regions and you will see large brown algae covering the rocks. These members of the class *Phaeophyceae* in the phylum *Ochrophyta* often dominate the rocky intertidal and subtidal environment in these areas. Although many of the species are golden-brown (ocher) in color, others range from olive green to dark brown. The new phylum name reflects the color of the majority. (These organisms have also been placed as a class in the phylum *Heterokontophyta* and before that in their own phylum, *Phaeophyta.*)

The class *Phaeophyceae* contains over 1500 species in more than 250 genera. They range in structure from microscopic filamentous forms to the giant kelps such as *Nereocystis* that can grow to over 30 meters (about 100 feet) in length. The large brown algae, such as the kelps, have significant specialization of cells, tissues, and organs. The thallus or body is typically divided into broad blades, a long stipe, and a rootlike holdfast system for attaching the organism to the substrate. Some large browns are annual, but others can live up to 15 years.

Brown algae can also be found in subtropical and tropical waters. Among these is a free-floating species of the genus *Sargassum*, which gave its name to the Sargasso Sea. In their natural environment, the large browns dominate the complex ecosystem of the kelp forest, creating a world that is predominantly brown in color. This is in contrast to the green leafy terrestrial environment familiar to humans. The kelps shelter sea otters, fishes, and many kinds of invertebrate animals.

Brown algal cells carry the green pigment chlorophyll *a*, which is necessary for photosynthesis. They also contain two forms of chlorophyll *c*, beta-carotene, violaxanthin, and relatively large amounts of fucoxanthin. The latter is the pigment responsible for the brown color of these organisms. These cells produce a carbohydrate storage product known as laminarin as a result of photosynthesis. Another product of photosynthesis, the six-carbon sugar alcohol mannitol, is important in moving food around in the thallus. It makes up about 65 percent of the sap translocated in these kelp cells specialized for transporting food.

Mannitol's low molecular weight may decrease the freezing point of the living cytoplasm in the cells. This is particularly valuable for kelps growing in cold ocean waters.

The life histories of most brown algae are very similar to one another. They have flagellated reproductive cells. Many of these cells have the typical two heterokont flagella: a long, forward-pointed flagellum with two rows of stiff hairs and a shorter smooth flagellum. The life cycles of these brown algae alternate between two generations: a gametophyte generation of organisms that produces the flagellated gametes, which must fuse before giving rise to the sporophyte generation, which produces flagellated zoospores. These settle down to produce a new gametophyte. An exception to this pattern occurs in *Fucus* and its relatives, which have life cycles very similar to those of humans, with egg and sperm as the only reproductive cells.

The cell walls of brown algae contain up to 10 percent cellulose, polysaccharides such as fucans, and large amounts of alginic acids and their mineral salts, the alginates. Alginates make up 20 to 40 percent of the dry weight of brown seaweeds. They provide flexibility for the algal thallus and help prevent desiccation.

The large brown seaweeds are harvested into barges by a cutting device mounted at the front end of a conveyor belt. After processing, the alginates extracted are used in printing textiles and in making dental creams, shoe polish, and drilling muds. They also thicken ice cream, puddings, sauces, salad dressings, custards, fillings, and decorations for baked goods.

In addition to harvesting for alginates, browns are used by humans in a number of other ways. In China, humans have harvested wild seaweeds for over 2000 years and still use at least four genera for food today. The Chinese, Japanese, Koreans, and others cultivate *Laminaria japonica* for food. It is high in iodine, the element necessary to the human body for synthesis of the thyroid hormone thyroxin, making it a valuable addition to the diet.

Bette H. Nybakken

FURTHER READING

Bold, H. C., and M. J. Wynne. *Introduction to the Algae,* 2nd ed. Englewood Cliffs, N.J.: Prentice Hall, 1985.
Graham, L. E., and L. W. Wilcox. *Algae.* Upper Saddle River, N.J.: Prentice Hall, 2000.
Lembi, Carol A., and J. R. Waaland. *Algae and Human Affairs.* Cambridge: Cambridge University Press, 1988.
Raven, Peter H., Ray F. Evert, and Susan E. Eichhorn. *Biology of Plants,* 6th ed. New York: W. H. Freeman, 1999.

RELATED ARTICLES
Algae

Odontoceti

The Odontoceti are a suborder of the order Cetacea, a group of marine mammals that are highly developed for ocean life. Odontoceti are the toothed whales, using their teeth generally for grasping their fish and squid prey before swallowing them. Like baleen whales, tooth whales are very hydrodynamic in shape: They have no or few hairs on the body, internalized reproductive organs, no hind limbs, smooth fusiform shape, flippers, and a single blowhole (air passage) located at the top of the head (baleen whales have two blowholes). These traits make odontocetes excellent swimmers and divers. The toothed whales include 10 families of marine mammals, with the following traits.

The odontocetes are a diverse group of cetaceans with adaptations that allow them to exploit different environments and prey types. The sperm whale (family Physeteridae) is the largest odontocete [adults are 11 to 19 meters (36 to 62 feet) in length]; they have a large bulbous head to accommodate the spermaceti organ, and the upper jaw often is without functional teeth. This species can dive deep in pursuit of deepwater squids. The smaller pygmy sperm whales (family Kogiidae) are 2.7 to 3.4 meters (9 to 11 feet) in length, with small, sharp teeth in the lower jaw. The shape of the lower jaw and pigmentation that resembles gills give these animals the look of a shark. The beaked whales (family Ziphiidae) are moderate in size [adults are 5 to 8 meters (16 to 26 feet) in length] with a slender rostrum, flukes not deeply notched, and few teeth (males with one or two pairs of teeth; teeth of females generally do not erupt). The river dolphins (families Platanistidae, Iniidae, Lipotidae, and Pontoporiidae) are 1.6 to 2.5 meters (5 to 8 feet) in length, with a narrow beak and broad flippers. River dolphins typically are found in tropical freshwater river basins. The narwhal and beluga (family Monodontidae) are in the same family, but their appearance is different. Male narwhals have a distinctive tusk (left incisor tooth) that grows to 2.5 meters (8 feet) in length, whereas the beluga, which is completely white, has 40 well-developed teeth in both jaws. Both are Arctic species often found near pack ice. The dolphins (family Delphinidae) as adults are 2 to 9 meters (6.6 to 29.5 feet) in length depending on species, with numerous peglike teeth in both jaws and a dorsal fin that may be absent (northern right whale dolphin) or large and recurved. Different species of dolphins are distributed throughout the world's oceans. The porpoises (family Phocoenidae) are relatively small [adults 1.5 to 2 meters (5 to 6.5 feet) in length] cetaceans with spatulate-shaped teeth, a triangular dorsal fin, and short snout. Porpoises are distributed mostly in subarctic to tropical waters.

Toothed whales typically have teeth present as adults (however, many female beaked whales have no functional teeth), one external blowhole, an asymmetrical skull, and five digits in the flipper. This is different from the baleen whales, which have baleen instead of teeth, two external blowholes, a symmetrical skull, and four digits in the flipper. All the toothed whales tested have demonstrated the ability to echolocate, which allows them to locate prey and sense their surroundings. Some odontocetes may stun their prey during capture using blasts of sound, which may explain how some toothed whales with no functional teeth (i.e., female beaked whales) can catch fast-swimming squids. All odontocetes probably communicate partially using acoustical signals. Male odontocetes are usually larger than females of the same age. All toothed whales are adept divers; male sperm whales can dive deeper than 1000 meters (3280 feet) and for greater than 90 minutes' duration.

Jim Harvey

FURTHER READING

Berta, A., and J. L. Sumich. *Marine Mammals: Evolutionary Biology.* San Diego: Academic Press, 1999.

Ellis, Richard. *Dolphins and Porpoises.* New York: Knopf, 1982.

Haley, Delphine, ed. *Marine Mammals of Eastern North Pacific and Arctic Waters*, 2nd rev. ed. Seattle: Pacific Search Press, 1986.

Leatherwood, Stephen, and Randall R. Reeves. *The Sierra Club Handbook of Whales and Dolphins.* San Francisco: Sierra Club Books, 1983.

Pryor, K., and K. S. Norris, eds. *Dolphin Societies: Discoveries and Puzzles.* Berkeley: University of California Press, 1991.

Slijper, E. J. *Whales.* Translated by A. J. Pomerans. New York: Basic Books, 1962.

RELATED ARTICLES
Cetacea; Echolocation; Mass Stranding

Offshore Oil Technology

Petroleum (crude oil) is such an economically important resource that it is feasible to extract even from the world's harshest environments. It was first drilled from beneath the ocean off Santa Barbara, California, in 1896 using simple wooden piers; and the first modern-style offshore platform was built in just 7 meters (23 feet) of water off the Gulf of Mexico in 1947. Today, offshore technology makes an important contribution to the world's oil supply. Major offshore fields have now been drilled in such places as the Gulf of Mexico, the North Sea, the Arctic Ocean, and off the coasts of Africa and South America. Although offshore oil recovery can cost 10 times more than drilling oil on land, increasingly sophisticated technology has reduced the cost of offshore wells and allowed oil companies to exploit ever-deeper offshore resources.

Exploration

Geologists locate profitable oil deposits using a range of sophisticated techniques, the most important of which is seismic surveying (measuring the geological nature of an area with sound). Improved technologies are constantly enhancing the accuracy of oil exploration. Supercomputers enable three-dimensional models of an area's geology to be built up from seismic surveys. The most advanced (and expensive) surveys extend the models into four dimensions, showing where oil and gas deposits are located and suggesting where they will move to in the future. Regions that were once "no-go" areas are now yielding valuable secrets. In some places salt and basalt rock under the deep ocean floor block seismic waves and prevent accurate surveys. But other geophysical techniques, such as *gravimetrics* (measuring variations in the strength of Earth's gravity) and *magnetics* (measuring changes in Earth's magnetic field) complement seismic surveys and help to reveal what is under the seafloor in inaccessible places such as this.

Initially, oil companies use limited survey information to bid for commercial licenses allowing them to explore areas of the seabed using more precise techniques, such as the drilling of exploration wells. The technology used for drilling exploration wells depends on the depth of the ocean: In shallow water, mobile platforms called jack-up rigs are erected temporarily over the drill site on retractable legs. In deeper water, semisubmersibles (small-scale

floating platforms anchored to the seabed) may be used. Alternatively, drilling rigs can be mounted on ships that use global positioning system (GPS) satellite navigation and hull-mounted thrusters to "hover" precisely in place above the test sites. Riser systems, which circulate well cuttings and fluids to the ground or ship surface, and blow-out preventers, which are used to contain highly charged fluids, are necessary to ensure that the ocean is not polluted by oil.

Once a test well has been drilled, geologists have enough information to calculate the size of the reservoir and whether it is worth constructing a full-scale production well to extract the oil. That decision depends on a variety of factors, including the predicted price of oil for the lifetime of the well, the technical difficulties of extracting it, and the availability of new technology that may change the viability of the well in the future.

Production

Sinking an offshore oil well is a considerable engineering challenge. In the North Sea, the sheer hostility of the environment means that rigs must be designed to withstand gale-force winds of up to 180 kilometers (112 miles) per hour, the constant buffeting of waves 30 meters (100 feet) high, corrosion from saltwater, and in some regions, damage from floating ice. A fixed oil platform (a traditional oil rig) is an expensive investment; today's most advanced production platforms can cost several billion dollars. Constructed on top of a number of legs or piles driven into the seabed, a platform is designed and positioned for maximum flexibility so that many wells can be drilled from it over the productive lifetime of the oil deposit.

No matter how large, sophisticated, or remotely located they are, oil platforms work in much the same way. A rotating drill bit is suspended from the familiar high tower or derrick. It cuts deeper and deeper through the seafloor and into the underlying sediments and rocks on the end of lengths of pipe that are screwed together to form what is known as the *drill string*. In traditional platforms, the entire drill string is rotated from the surface, since it is difficult to drill anything other than almost vertical wells. Modern drill strings have motors near the drill bit, which means that the drill string can bend around corners and even cut horizontally. The latest technique uses smart, geosteering drill bits fitted with sensors that can automatically dig the best route toward the buried oil. The oil corporation Exxon estimates that such advanced technology has helped to reduce the cost of exploration by around 85 percent over the last decade.

Advanced Production Techniques

Given the difficulty and cost of extracting oil from beneath the seabed, it is vital for offshore oil technology to be able to recover as much oil as

Shell Oil drilling platform in the Gulf of Mexico off the coast of Louisiana. (© Philip Gould/Corbis)

possible. Initially, oil flows to the surface under its own pressure and through the pressure of the natural gas released at the same time. But this recovers only about 25 to 30 percent of the oil in the reservoir. A variety of techniques, collectively known as *enhanced recovery*, are used to extract more of the remaining oil. These include pumping water, steam, and carbon dioxide down one well to force the oil up through a second, nearby well. One example is the $4 billion Hibernia well, built on a huge concrete platform off Newfoundland in Canada in the 1990s, which is designed to recover large amounts of oil using water and gas injection.

Sometimes, technology can expand the capacity of an existing field with relatively little extra investment. BP-Amoco's Wytch Farm oil field in Dorset, on the south coast of England, is the largest onshore oilfield in Western Europe, but half the reserves extend offshore. Although the company originally planned to construct a $260 million artificial island off the coast to extract the offshore deposits, the development of advanced horizontal drilling technology enabled it to drill out to the offshore deposit from its existing onshore complex at less than half the cost. It has since set several world records for "extended reach" oil recovery, drilling out more than 11 kilometers (7 miles) into the reservoir from the onshore complex.

No matter how sophisticated the drilling technology, there is only so much oil that can be extracted from a given well before other less conveniently located wells must be explored. An increasingly important technique known as *subsea production* makes it possible to recover oil from much deeper waters than with a traditional rig. The world's deepest subsea well is around 1.7 kilometers (1.1 miles) below sea level in the Marlim field off Brazil. In a subsea complex, there is no oil platform; the *wellhead* (the top of the well through which oil emerges) is constructed on the seabed itself and oil is either piped to a nearby oil rig or to a ship on the surface. Surface vessels of this type are replacing smaller oil platforms altogether. Floating production storage and offloading vessels (FPSOs) can perform all the functions of a traditional platform, from injecting oil and gas to remove oil to storing oil and transporting it elsewhere.

Future of Offshore Oil

With a permanent decline in world oil production expected to begin in the next two decades and the rate of oil consumption two to three times higher than its discovery, improvements in the technology for extracting oil from deeper and deeper offshore waters is becoming increasingly important. Beyond the present era of cheap and plentiful oil, a future of dwindling production and gradually increasing prices will make it economically feasible to employ more sophisticated technologies for offshore exploration and production. For example, although four-dimensional seismic modeling can boost production costs by a quarter, and injecting gas or carbon dioxide to remove more oil from wells can double costs again, declining production will make such techniques increasingly feasible. But although advanced technologies such as this will extend the life of some fields, they cannot reverse the inevitable long-term decline in oil discovery and production.

Chris Woodford

FURTHER READING
Anderson, Roger. "Oil Production in the 21st Century." *Scientific American,* March 1998, p. 69.
Campbell, Colin, and Jean Laherrère. "The End of Cheap Oil." *Scientific American,* March 1998, p. 60.
Cooper, George. "Directional Drilling." *Scientific American,* May 1994, p. 56.
Howarth, Stephen. *A Century in Oil: The "Shell" Transport and Trading Co. 1897–1997.* London: Weidenfeld and Nicolson, 1997.
Hyne, N. J. *Geology for Petroleum Exploration, Drilling, and Production.* New York: McGraw-Hill, 1984.
Ramage, Janet. *Energy: A Guidebook.* Oxford and New York: Oxford University Press, 1983; 2nd ed.,1997.
Upton, David. *Waves of Fortune: The Past, Present and Future of the United Kingdom Offshore Oil Industries.* Chichester, England, and New York: Wiley, 1996.

RELATED ARTICLES
Petroleum; Seismic Profiling

Oligotrophic

The term *oligotrophic* refers to nutrient-poor areas in the marine ecosystem that have low levels of biological production. For example, the centers of many ocean gyres typically have low levels of nutrients and are therefore oligotrophic. The oceanic condition of oligotrophy can be seasonal or permanent.

In seasonal oligotrophy, factors such as upwelling (the process of mixing nutrient-laden deep water with the surface layer) and changes in currents or circulation patterns cause an increase in the supply of nutrients to surface water layers. This, in turn, results in increased primary production or unusually high concentrations of phytoplankton. This seasonal occurrence is called a *spring bloom*, and during this process phytoplankton deplete the nutrients in the surface water layer.

Permanent oligotrophy occurs when a water column does not undergo the process of mixing during the winter, and thus sufficient nutrients are not available to support a spring bloom. The ecosystem enters a state of permanent oligotrophy and has low annual new production—the fraction of annual primary production that can be attributed to nutrients mixed up into the surface water layer during the previous winter. Therefore, it also experiences a decline in ecosystem productivity.

Anne Beesley

FURTHER READING
Gross, M. Grant. *Oceanography: A View of the Earth.* Englewood Cliffs, N.J.: Prentice Hall, 1972; 5th ed., 1990.

Kennish, Michael J. *Practical Handbook of Marine Science.* Boca Raton, Fla.: CRC Press, 1989; 2nd ed., 1994.

RELATED ARTICLES
Microbial Loop; Primary Productivity; Spring Bloom

Ontong Java Plateau

Centered at about 0°N, 158°E in the western Pacific Ocean, Ontong Java is the world's largest submarine plateau, a broad undersea mountain range. Its name derives from Ontong Java Island, an atoll (low coral island with a central lagoon) that formed atop a volcanic peak on the plateau summit. Viewed from above, the plateau's shape is like that of a kidney, with its convex side pointing southwest toward the nearby Solomon Islands. In cross section, the plateau appears as a broad dome with low flank slopes of 1 to 2°. With a width and length of approximately 1300 by 2400 kilometers (808 by 1491 miles), the plateau has an area of 1.5 million square kilometers (579,165 square miles), roughly equivalent to Alaska. Despite its large size and the fact that it stands roughly 2 to 3 kilometers (6600 to 9800 feet) above the surrounding abyssal seafloor, the plateau summit reaches no higher than 1.7 kilometers (5600 feet) below sea level. Like an iceberg, most of the plateau's bulk lies out of sight, deep beneath the seafloor.

The structure and composition of the Ontong Java Plateau are similar to those of other oceanic plateaus, especially those in the Pacific and Indian Oceans. Like many, its layering is similar to ocean crust, albeit much thicker. Beneath the central plateau, the Moho (the Mohorovicic discontinuity, the boundary between crust and mantle) is depressed to a depth of more than 42 kilometers (26 miles), approximately 30 kilometers (19 miles) deeper than normal. Although virtually all of Ontong Java Plateau lies beneath the ocean, a small sliver has been thrust above sea level. Situated at the edge of the Pacific Plate, where the plate underthrusts the Solomon Islands, the plateau's crust is too thick and buoyant to be drawn easily down the subduction zone. Instead, slivers of the plateau have been obducted (thrust onto land) on the islands of Malaita and Santa Isabel.

As are many plateaus, Ontong Java is mantled with a sedimentary layer, in places more than 1 kilometer (3280 feet) in thickness. These sediments are derived largely of shells from microscopic plankton (coccolithophores, foraminifera, and radiolarians) that once lived in the surface waters. The shells were able to accumulate to great thickness because seawater at shallower depths, atop the plateau, does not readily dissolve these shells as do deeper waters.

The mechanism that forms ocean plateaus is not certain, but many scientists believe that they are created when the bulbous head of a new mantle plume rises through the mantle and arrives at the base of the ocean plate. Heat and magma from the plume head migrate through the lithosphere to produce enormous volcanic eruptions that are the oceanic equivalent of continental flood basalt eruptions. Samples from Malaita and basalt drill cores obtained offshore by the Ocean Drilling Program and Deep Sea Drilling Project yield radiometric dates that cluster around 90 and 122 million years. The latter value is particularly common and occurs in samples from other volcanic eruption sites in the surrounding Pacific Basin. Consequently, many scientists believe that Ontong Java Plateau formed mainly about 122 million years ago at the center of an extraordinarily large episode of volcanic eruptions that affected much of the western Pacific. Samples that give dates around 90 million years ago imply that a second, smaller eruptive period followed after a hiatus. Since 90 million years ago, Ontong Java Plateau became dormant, subsided slowly, and drifted northward with the Pacific Plate to its present-day equatorial latitude.

William W. Sager

FURTHER READING

Coffin, Millard F., and Olav Eldholm. "Large Igneous Provinces." *Scientific American,* Vol. 269 (October 1993), pp. 42–49.

Coffin, Millard F., and Lisa M. Gahagan. "Ontong Java and Kerguelen Plateaux: Cretaceous Icelands?" *Journal of the Geological Society,* Vol. 152 (1995), pp. 1047–1052.

Larson, Roger L. "Latest Pulse of the Earth: Evidence for a Mid-Cretaceous Superplume." *Geology,* Vol. 19 (1991), pp. 547–550.

Neal, Clive R., John J. Mahoney, Loren W. Kroenke, Robert A. Duncan, and Michael G. Petterson. "The Ontong Java Plateau." In John. J. Mahoney and Millard F. Coffin, eds., *Large Igneous Provinces: Continental, Oceanic, and Planetary Flood Volcanism.* Washington, D.C.: American Geophysical Union, 1997.

RELATED ARTICLES
Mantle Plume; Ocean Drilling Program; Ocean Plateau

Oolite

Oolite, originally termed *oolith,* is a sedimentary rock. It is usually inorganic limestone composed of small spherical grains called *ooids* that are cemented together. Oolites form in marine and fresh waters, and today they can be found in the Bahamas. Aragonite comprises the cortex in young oolites and calcite comprises the cortex in older deposits, suggesting either that aragonite undergoes diagenetic changes or that calcite was the original material.

Ooids are easily recognizable and resemble fish roe. Oolites form from calcite or aragonite in warm, shallow waters with strong bottom currents; deposition of aragonite or calcite occurs in concentric layers (cortex) around a central nucleus. The nucleus may be a fecal pellet, a piece of skeletal material, a sand grain, or another ooid. Ooids are well sorted and form in places where strong bottom currents exist, such as tidal bars or deltas. There the ooids are subject to rolling by waves and tides and are washed free of mud. The tidal setting is important, as a grain may be moved periodically but must remain in the same depositional setting for a time long enough to develop an oolitic coating. The coating is a product of a complex process that involves the transport, burial, and exhumation of the grain in carbonate-saturated water. Thickness of the coating indicates the length of time the grain has been subjected to the process. Ooliths with a high magnesium calcite or aragonite composition are dissolved by seawater, forming vugs.

Composition of ooids is variable; they are usually composed of calcite or aragonite, but other minerals also form ooids. Siderite, chamosite, and hematite may form oolitic ironstone, usually in lagoons or shoals due to the oxygen required to oxidize the iron. In phophate-rich waters, collophane ooids form, and in calcium-rich waters, aragonite and calcite form oolitic limestone. Glauconitic rocks rarely form ooliths.

Mary White

FURTHER READING

Blatt, Harvey, Gerard Middleton, and Raymond Murray. *Origin of Sedimentary Rocks.* Englewood Cliffs, N.J.: Prentice Hall, 1972; 2nd ed., 1980.

Williams, Howell, Francis J. Turner, and Charles M. Gilbert. *Petrograph: An Introduction to the Study of Rocks in Thin Section.* San Francisco: W. H. Freeman, 1954; 2nd ed., 1982.

RELATED ARTICLES
Bottom Current

Ooze, see Oceanic Microfossil

Ophiolite

An ophiolite is a suite of rocks that comprise the oceanic lithosphere and is generally found on continents and island arcs. The suite forms at a spreading center, travels across a closing ocean basin, and is emplaced tectonically along convergent plate boundaries. An ophiolite represents the lithosphere and upper asthenosphere (mantle) at the time of the rocks' formation.

The ophiolite suite consists of the following units: (1) basal, foliated ultramafic (rock composed of magnesium- and iron-rich minerals) tectonite; (2) cumulate gabbro and ultramafic rock assemblage; (3) noncumulate gabbro, plagiogranite, and dunite; (4) sheeted diabase dike complex with one-way chill zones (fine-grained minerals formed by rapid cooling), indicating intrusion at an axial rift; and (5) pillow basalt or hyaloclastic breccia (glassy, fragmented submarine lava).

While moving across the closing ocean basin, the ophiolite accumulates, capping sediments of abyssal, pelagic, and volcanic arc origins. Abyssal sediments consist of pelites and siltstone; pelagic sediments contain ribbon chert, limestone, and metal-rich sediments; volcaniclastic sediments include locally derived arc detritus, turbidites, limestone, and greywacke. When the suite reaches the ocean basin edge, it is scraped onto a convergent plate boundary. During emplacement, the suite acquires a basal melange consisting of a chaotic mixture of clasts encased in a serpentinite matrix.

Three mechanisms cause ophiolite emplacement: (1) the ophiolite is obducted onto a passive continental margin at a convergent plate boundary; (2) the ophiolite is split, with the upper part obducted while the lower part is subducted; and (3) the ophiolite is added into an accretionary prism in a volcanic arc system. Two types of mineral deposits are associated with ophiolites: one is Cyprus-type Cu–Fe massive sulfide bodies formed by hydrothermal solutions at spreading centers that create stratiform deposits in pillow basalts; the second type is podiform chromite formed by fractional crystallization in the gabbro–ultramafic section.

David L. White

FURTHER READING
Coleman, R. G. *Ophiolites.* Berlin and New York: Springer-Verlag, 1977.

Condie, Kent C. *Plate Tectonics and Crustal Evolution.* New York: Pergamon Press, 1976; 4th ed., Oxford and Boston, Butterworth-Heinemann, 1997.
Plummer, Charles C., David McGeary, and Diane H. Carlson. *Physical Geology.* Dubuque, Iowa: Wm. C. Brown, 1979; 8th ed., Boston: WCB/McGraw-Hill, 1999.

RELATED ARTICLES
Accretionary Prism; Continental Margin; Convergent Plate Boundary; Gabbro; Pillow Lava

Ophiuroidea

The Ophiuroidea, the most diverse class of echinoderms, includes over 2000 species of brittlestars and basket stars. Living from the poles to the tropics, sometimes in densities exceeding 1000 per square meter (93 per square foot), they are the most numerous large organisms in many ocean habitats. Over two-thirds of the species occur at depths shallower than 1000 meters (3281 feet), and a few are found below 6000 meters (19,685 feet). Although generally restricted to marine conditions, some species survive in brackish water. Ophiuroids are the most active and agile echinoderms. Where they are abundant, ophiuroids strongly influence ecosystem ecology. They are widely preyed upon, frequently parasitized, and are themselves consumers at many levels in the aquatic food chain.

The smallest ophiuroids are less than 1 centimeter (0.4 inch) in size; the largest, exceeding 1 meter (3.3 feet) in diameter, are basket stars with complex, branching arms. Living ophiuroids resemble asteroids (sea stars) only superficially, but the similarity of extinct ophiuroids and asteroids suggests that the two groups share a common ancestor. The central part of the ophiuroid body (disk) contains the gonads, the thin-walled sacs (bursae) used in respiration and reproduction, and a digestive system with a pouch-shaped stomach and without an anus. The arms, typically five in number (up to 10 in certain species), are slender and flexuous and consist of numerous nearly solid joints. At the core of the arm is a series of articulating bones ("vertebrae") resembling the elements of a spinal column. Bones connected to the vertebrae bear movable spines. Penetrating each vertebra and protruding from the arm are muscular, hydraulically powered tube feet.

Ophiuroid lifestyles and body forms are highly varied. Some species are bioluminescent; their glow is thought to repel predators. Some change color and thereby regulate the light focused by crystalline lenses in the skeleton on internal light receptors. Others can rapidly stroke their arms and swim. The ophiuroids that nestle in sand and mud have very long, slender arms that undulate, pumping oxygenated water through a mucus-lined burrow. Some species live symbiotically on sea whips or in sponges, cleaning the host and gaining protection and food. Most shallow-water species emerge from shelter only at night, but many deep-sea species do not conceal themselves. Ophiuroids move and feed by coordinated activities of arms, spines, tube feet, and jaws, and detect food by sensing minute amounts of water-borne chemicals. Their bodies and behaviors are specialized for suspension feeding or deposit feeding on small particles and scavenging or preying on large items.

Ophiuroids are known as *brittlestars* because they can autotomize (voluntarily break off) parts of their arms. Some species do so with little provocation, others only after harsh stimulation

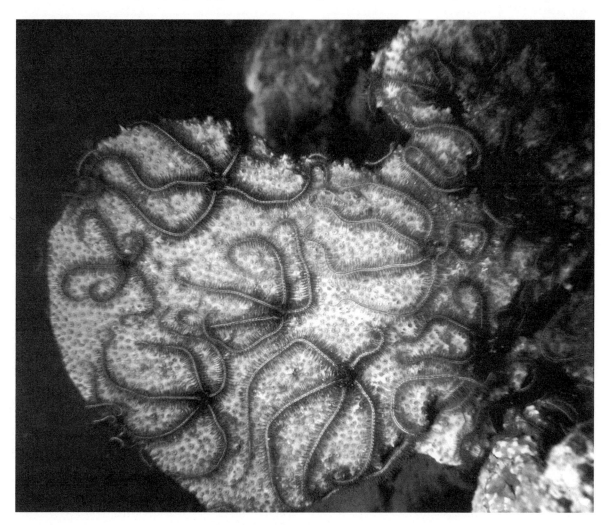

Brittlestars on coral in the Caribbean. (© Ian Took/Natural Visions)

such as that caused by predators. In some species the disk can be autotomized and discarded with its digestive and reproductive organs. Along with a capacity for autotomy and susceptibility to injury, ophiuroids have remarkable capabilities for regeneration. The incidence of animals with regenerating arms is often 50 percent or more. In certain species, disks with gonads and stomach are replaced in less than one month; arms can take more than several months to re-grow.

Individuals of some small, specialized ophiuroid species periodically reproduce asexually by splitting across the disk. The two incomplete animals that arise regenerate the disk and the missing complement of arms. Most ophiuroids, including asexually reproducing species, reproduce sexually. Their fertilization is external. Species with rapidly developing, nonfeeding larvae produce small numbers of large eggs. Those with feeding larvae that can take a month or more to develop may release hundreds of thousands of tiny eggs. Other species, usually small and frequently hermaphroditic, nurture crawl-away young within their bursae.

Gordon Hendler

FURTHER READING

Aizenberg, Joanna, et al. "Calcitic Microlenses as Part of the Photoreceptor System in Brittlestars." *Nature*, Vol. 23 (August 2001), pp. 819–822.

Clark, Ailsa M. *Starfishes and Their Relations.* London: Trustees of the British Museum, 1962; 3rd ed., as *Starfishes and Related Echinoderms,* London: Trustees of the British Museum/Neptune City, N.J.: T.F.H. Publications, 1977.

Grober, Matthew S. "Starlight on the Reef." *Natural History* (October 1989), pp. 72–80.

Hendler, Gordon, et al. *Sea Stars, Sea Urchins, and Allies: Echinoderms of Florida and the Caribbean.* Washington, D.C.: Smithsonian Institution Press, 1995.

Hyman, L. H. *The Invertebrates: Echinodermata.* Vol. 4. New York and London: McGraw-Hill, 1955.

RELATED ARTICLES

Asteroidea; Benthos; Brittlestar; Crinoidea; Echinodermata; Echinoidea; Holothuroidea

Organic Geochemistry

Organic geochemistry is the study of organic (carbon-containing) material in sediments, rocks, and the environment. Organic geochemistry is important because rocks and sediments provide a significant reservoir in the global carbon cycle, and organic matter plays a major role in ocean chemistry. Reactions involving organic matter in sediments and rock create coal and petroleum, substances that are combusted to create energy and fuel for most of the world. Hence, the study and understanding of organic geochemistry has tremendous economic implications. Moreover, scientists study organic matter in sediments and rocks to gain insight on past Earth climates and to examine anthropogenic organic pollutants and their effect on nature.

Organic material is present in natural waters as dissolved organic matter (DOM), suspended particulate organic carbon (POC), colloidal material, and adsorbed compounds. Dissolved organic matter exists at an average concentration of 1 part per million in the oceans and 4 parts per million in freshwater sources. Eventually, some of this organic matter sinks through the water column and finds its way to sediments where it can undergo a variety of chemical changes. Organic matter in pelagic sediments varies in abundance from near 0 up to 5 percent by weight and includes particulate organic matter, clay materials, and components of inorganic rock matrices.

The sources of all organic matter in rocks and sediments are plants and animals, which are composed of proteins, lipids, carbohydrates, pigments, and lignins. These organic compounds decompose into a broad spectrum of other complex organic compounds as well as simpler molecules such as carbon dioxide (CO_2) and methane (CH_4). Sediment and rock organic matter can be divided into bitumens (soluble in carbon disulfide) and pyrobitumens (insoluble in carbon disulfide). Crude oil is an example of liquid bitumen, whereas asphalt is an example of solid bitumen. Kerogen and coal are the most important pyrobitumens.

Most organic matter in rocks is *kerogen*, which is a diagenetic (microbial breakdown) product of recently deposited organic matter. Kerogen is a complex and little understood material that is an integral component of inorganic rock–mineral matrices. Thermal alteration of kerogen ultimately produces petroleum (crude oil and natural gas), which is utilized to provide energy for human industries. Hence, the organic geochemistry of petroleum formation has been studied thoroughly and is now well understood. Important factors in the determination of petroleum formation include temperature, abundance, and type of kerogen, the rock/mineral matrix, and time. Kerogen-rich rocks such as oil shales can yield up to 379 liters (100 gallons) of oil per ton of rock when heated.

Coal, which is greater than 65 percent carbon, is formed from the accumulation and decomposition of plant debris. However, the exact organic compounds that make up coal are not well known. Coalification (coal formation) starts with the development of peat from the diagenetic alteration of lignin and cellulose in plant tissues. After this primary biochemical stage, metamorphic changes involving temperature and pressure ultimately yield coal.

The field of organic geochemistry also includes the study of preserved organic compounds in the geological record to better our understanding of past Earth climates. For example, paleoceanographers analyze organic matter in pelagic ocean sediments to calculate past ocean temperatures. These analyses include amino acid racemization and degree of unsaturation in long-chain ketones.

Recently, organic geochemists have begun studying the negative impact on the environment of human beings. These scientists study the environmental behavior of anthropogenic organic compounds, including carbon dioxide and polycyclic aromatic hydrocarbons (PAHs), from fossil-fuel burning, nutrient pollution from fertilizers, and hydrocarbon pollution from oil spills. Scientists are also focusing their attention on synthetic organic molecules such as DDT and polychlorinated biphenyls (PCBs). These are *xenobiotic* (entirely human-made; no natural source) organic substances that have been released to nature in significant quantities and have a negative impact on the environment.

Daniel Schuller

FURTHER READING

Brownlow, A. H. *Geochemistry.* Englewood Cliffs, N.J.: Prentice Hall, 1979; 2nd ed., Upper Saddle River, N.J.: Prentice Hall, 1996.

Chester, Roy. *Marine Geochemistry.* London and Boston: Unwin Hyman, 1990; 2nd ed., Malden, Mass.: Blackwell Science, 2000.

Killops, S. D., and V. J. Killops. *An Introduction to Organic Geochemistry.* Harlow, England: Longman Scientific and Technical; New York: Wiley, 1993.

Libes, Susan M. *Marine Biogeochemistry.* New York: Wiley, 1992.

RELATED ARTICLES

Carbon Cycle; DDT; Dissolved Organic Matter; Particulate Organic Carbon; Petroleum

Osmoconformer

An osmoconformer is a marine organism whose body fluids are in osmotic equilibrium with seawater; this means that the concentration of solutes (dissolved substances) in the body of an osmoconformer equals the concentration of solutes in the surrounding seawater. Therefore, if the salinity, or total salt concentration, of seawater increases or decreases, the solute concentration of an osmoconformer's internal fluids also increases or decreases. Although the total concentration of solutes inside and outside an osmoconformer is the same, the chemical composition of the solutes in each environment can be quite different. Many osmoconformers use high concentrations of organic molecules such as amino acids and sugars to maintain equilibrium with the surrounding seawater.

Maintaining osmotic equilibrium is one method of keeping water from flowing in or out of an organism and its cells, which would otherwise happen due to osmosis; osmosis is the process by which water diffuses through a semipermeable membrane from a more dilute to a more salty solution. If an organism's internal fluids were more dilute than seawater (hyperosmotic stress), the organism would shrink as water diffused out of the animal; under opposite conditions (hypoosmotic stress), the animal would swell. Osmoregulation is another strategy for dealing with osmotic stress; osmoregulators are organisms that can maintain a fairly constant internal solute balance regardless of the salinity of their environment.

Osmoconforming marine species include algae, bacteria, most marine invertebrates, and some vertebrates (e.g., hagfish, sharks, rays, and skates). Osmoconformers that inhabit environments where they are subject to osmotic stress, such as estuaries and the intertidal, are adapted to withstand salinity changes. For example, intertidal barnacles and mollusks close their shells to prevent osmosis and desiccation (drying out), and many estuarine invertebrates burrow into the mud, where salinity changes are minimal compared to the overlying water.

Lynn L. Lauerman

FURTHER READING
Nybakken, James W. *Marine Biology: An Ecological Approach,* 5th ed. San Francisco: Benjamin Cummings, 2001.
Solomon, Eldra P., Linda R. Berg, Diana W. Martin, and Claude Ville. *Biology*. Philadelphia: W. B. Saunders, 1985; 5th ed., Fort Worth, Texas: Saunders College Publishing, 1999.

RELATED ARTICLES
Osmoregulator; Osmosis

Osmoregulator

Osmoregulators are organisms that have the physiological ability to maintain their internal salt and fluid balance regardless of fluctuations in the salinity of the surrounding seawater. Unlike osmoconformers, whose internal salt and fluid concentrations vary with external salinity, osmoregulators keep their internal salinity within a narrow range that allows metabolic processes to function optimally at a particular concentration of solutes (dissolved substances). Marine organisms that osmoregulate are *hyporegulators*; they keep their internal osmotic concentration below that of seawater. Freshwater organisms are *hyperregulators*; they maintain an internal solute concentration that is higher than that of the surrounding water.

Marine osmoregulators inhabit environments that experience extreme fluctuations in salinity, such as estuaries. Many estuarine invertebrates (e.g., crustaceans, mollusks, and polychaete worms) and vertebrates (e.g., bony fishes, birds, reptiles, and mammals) are osmoregulators. When exposed to large changes in salinity, an organism must be able to control its internal solute concentration, or osmosis would severely stress or kill the organism. Osmosis is the process by which water diffuses through a semipermeable membrane from a more dilute to a more salty solution. Marine organisms are subject to osmosis because their body wall acts as a semipermeable membrane that separates their internal fluids from the surrounding seawater. Without the ability to osmoregulate, a marine organism moved from high to low salinity (hypoosmotic stress) would swell as water moved into the animal. Under hyperosmotic stress (a move from low- to high-salinity water), an animal would shrink. Osmoregulators maintain their internal osmotic concentration by transporting water or by replacing lost solutes. New solutes can be manufactured internally or they can be actively transported into an animal from the surrounding seawater. Animals may use specialized cells or excretory organs such as kidneys to regulate their internal solute concentration.

Lynn L. Lauerman

FURTHER READING
Nybakken, James W. *Marine Biology: An Ecological Approach*, 5th ed. San Francisco: Benjamin Cummings, 2001.
Solomon, Eldra P., Linda R. Berg, Diana W. Martin, and Claude Ville. *Biology*. Philadelphia: Saunders, 1985; 5th ed., Fort Worth, Texas: Saunders College Publishing,1999.

RELATED ARTICLES
Osmoconformer; Osmosis

Osmosis

Osmosis describes the diffusion or movement of fluid through a semipermeable membrane. The fluid particles diffuse across the membrane until the concentrations on either side of the membrane are equal, a state known as *equilibrium*. Therefore, osmosis requires a concentration gradient, or difference in salt concentrations on either side of the membrane, to occur. It is the concentration of the solute that provides the concentration gradient and drives fluid movement across a membrane. The osmotic pressure of a solution is the pressure that is required to halt osmosis, stopping the movement across a membrane. The osmotic pressure is dependent on the concentration of solute molecules in a solution.

Electrolytic solutions, such as water with dissolved salt ions, provide excellent examples of osmosis. The contraction of muscles in the human body is driven by the concentration gradient in muscle cells. Osmosis results in the movement of salt ions in the muscle cell from an area of higher concentration to an area of lower concentration. Therefore, if there is a higher concentration of calcium ions on the inside of a cell,

the calcium ions will diffuse across the cell membrane to the outside of the cell, until equilibrium is achieved. When equilibrium exists on either side of a membrane, the membrane is described as depolarized.

Osmoregulation is the process that marine organisms use to regulate their internal salt balances to control the loss or gain of water from osmosis. (Marine organisms that do not have the ability to regulate their salt content are called *osmoconformers.*) Since marine fish species generally have an internal salinity of about 14 practical salinity units (psu), the opportunity for water movement from the organism to the saltwater environment (about 35 psu), via osmosis, would lead to dehydration. Anadromous species, which live in both fresh and marine environments (e.g., salmon) have highly specialized excretory systems to selectively eliminate or retain salts in order to control fluid balance in both fresh- and saltwater systems. Species that reside in salt water tend to have only organ systems that retain salts, to minimize fluid loss, via osmosis, to the saline external environment.

Alison Kelley

FURTHER READING
Ebbing, Darrel D. *General Chemistry*. Boston: Houghton Mifflin, 1984.
Scanlon, Valerie C., and Tina Sanders. *Essentials of Anatomy and Physiology*. Philadelphia: F. A. Davis, 1999.

RELATED ARTICLES
Osmoconformer; Osmoregulator

Osteichthyes

The term *Osteichthyes*, from the Greek *osteo* (bone) and Latin *ict* (fish), is used to designate the bony fishes. It was, until recently, considered one of three classes of extant fishes, the others being the Agnatha (jawless fishes) and

Chondrichthyes (cartilaginous fishes). However, based on changes in Joseph S. Nelson's most recent edition of *Fishes of the World* (1994), most ichthyologists have abandoned the use of Osteichthyes as a class and instead adopted use of the term *Teleostomi* as a grade that contains all the remaining vertebrates. Teleostomi includes the classes Acanthodii (an extinct group of primitive jawed fishes termed *spiny sharks*), Sarcopterygii (lobe-finned fishes and tetrapods), and Actinopterygii (ray-finned fishes). This new designation is based on Nelson's assertion that *Osteichthyes*, as used conventionally, did not designate a monophyletic group, whereas the teleostomes do share a common ancestor. The term *Osteichthyes* is therefore no longer used to designate a taxon; rather, it is used as vernacular to denote those members of Sarcopterygii that are considered fishes plus the actinopterygians.

Primitive osteichthyans share certain characteristics with the classes Elasmobranchii and Placodermi, including a heterocercal caudal fin, spiracles, a spiral valve intestine, a valvular conus arteriosus, and a cloaca—the primitive placement of the anus between the base of the pelvic fins. Typically, however, the caudal fin is homocercal, the spiracles, conus arteriosus, and cloaca are absent, and the anus is usually located just anterior to the anal fin. No single feature distinguishes the Osteichthyes, but the most distinctive elements of the osteichthyan structural pattern are the presence of lungs or swim bladders (which may be secondarily lost in some species), an ossified endoskeleton with dermal bones occurring in the head region, bony scales, and lepidotrichia (soft fin rays). An operculum also covers the gills in these fishes, and the gill septa are reduced.

The monophyletic teleostomes with three classes contain about 47,239 extant valid species. Within the paraphyletic osteichthyans, there are some 45 orders, 435 families, 4079 genera, and approximately 23,500 species. The number of species has been increasing at the rate of approximately 200 species per year. This is due primarily to the discovery of new fishes in previously unexplored environments (i.e., the deep sea and some tropical freshwater and reef systems) and the designation of new species from those previously considered monospecific (a result of advancements in genetic analysis). About half of the world's vertebrates are considered osteichthyans, as is any living fish that is not jawless (class Agnatha) or shark- or raylike (class Chondrichthyes).

Joseph J. Bizzarro

FURTHER READING
Bond, Carl E. *Biology of Fishes.* New York: Saunders College Publishing, 1979; 2nd ed., 1996.
Carroll, Robert L. *Vertebrate Paleontology and Evolution.* New York: W. H. Freeman, 1988.
Helfman, Gene S., Bruce B. Collette, and Douglas E. Facey. *The Diversity of Fishes.* Malden, Mass.: Blackwell Science, 1997.
Moyle, Peter B., and Joseph J. Cech. *Fishes: An Introduction to Ichthyology.* Upper Saddle River, N.J.: Prentice Hall, 2000.
Nelson, Joseph S. *Fishes of the World.* New York: Wiley, 1994.

RELATED ARTICLES
Acanthodii; Actinopterygii; Elasmobranchii; Fins; Placodermi; Sarcopterygii; Swim Bladder; Teleostei

Osteoglossomorpha

Fishes in the subdivision Osteoglossomorpha are commonly referred to as bony tongues (from the Greek *osteo*, bony, and *glosso*, tongue). These fishes represent the earliest morphological features characteristic of the division Teleostei, specifically the presence of specialized bones, called *uroneurals*, used to support the upper portion of the caudal fin, resulting in greater swimming ability. There are two orders in the Osteoglossomorpha: the extinct Ichthyodectiformes and the extant

Osteoglossiformes. The oldest known fossil record of Osteoglossomorpha comes from the middle Jurassic (170 million years ago) and belongs to the Ichthyodectiformes. This order was composed of marine fishes and is represented in the fossil record through the upper Cretaceous (85 million years ago). These fishes were large, up to 5 meters (16 feet), and were probably predatory, based on their high number of teeth. The extant Osteoglossiformes appeared in the lower Cretaceous (115 million years ago) and invaded fresh water during the middle Cretaceous (100 million years ago). There are currently six families in this order, with 29 genera and about 217 species, all of which live in fresh and brackish waters.

The family Osteoglossidae contains seven species, including the arapaima (*Arapaima gigas*) of South America, which reaches up to 3 meters (10 feet) in length. The two species within the family Hiodontidae, referred to as the mooneye (*Hiodon tergisus*) and goldeye (*Hiodon alosoides*), are characterized by the presence of a tapetum lucidum located in the retina of fishes, which increases their ability to visualize under nocturnal conditions. There are eight species of knifefishes in the family Notopteridae. Knifefishes have compressed bodies with an elongated anal fin confluent with a reduced caudal fin and are capable of air breathing. The single species in the family Pantodotidae (butterflyfish), *Pantodon buchholzi* of tropical Africa, is also capable of air breathing, but unlike notopterids, butterflyfish have distinct anal and caudal fins and greatly enlarged pectoral fins. The family Mormyridae contains approximately 200 species of elephant fishes. These fishes possess electric organs, used for orientation, communication, and locating prey. The family Gymnarchidae also possesses electric organs, but unlike mormyrids, lack anal, caudal, and pelvic fins and have an elongate dorsal fin, which is used for locomotion.

Jeffrey M. Field

FURTHER READING
Long, J. A. *The Rise of Fishes: 500 Million Years of Evolution.* Baltimore: Johns Hopkins University Press, 1995.
Moyle, P. B., and J. J. Cech, Jr. *Fishes: An Introduction to Ichthyology,* 4th ed. Upper Saddle River, N.J.: Prentice Hall, 1996.
Nelson, J. S. *Fishes of the World,* 3rd ed. New York: Wiley, 1994.

RELATED ARTICLES
Elopomorpha; Euteleostei; Teleostei

Otolith

Otoliths (from the Greek *oto*, ear, and *lith*, stone) are hard, calcified structures found in the inner ear, or paired labyrinth system, of most bony fishes (Osteichthyes). They are situated within membranous sacs located among cranial bones and respond to sound-wave vibrations, changes in physical orientation, and gravitational forces. Otoliths are commonly used in studies of aging because they exhibit concentric rings that often grow in a predictable pattern throughout a fish's life.

The three semicircular canals and sacs of the inner ear (the sacculus, utriculus, and lagena) are filled with fluid (endolymph) and lined with an epithelium (macula) consisting of thousands of sensory hair cells. Within each sac, an otolith lies suspended in the endolymph, coupled mechanically to the macula by a thin outer membrane. Hair bundles, protruding from the hair cells of the macula, lie in direct contact with the otolith. Since the density of otoliths is far greater than that of surrounding tissue, they lag somewhat behind the movements of the fish. This causes displacement of the hair cells and stimulates sensory neurons, signaling changes in spatial orientation and movement. These functions are performed primarily by the *pars superior,* which consists of the semicircular canals and utriculus, containing the utricular otolith.

Hearing in fishes is accomplished in much the same matter by the *pars inferior*, which consists of the sacculus and lagena and their respective otoliths (sagitta and lapillus). Sound vibrations stimulate otoliths for a longer period of time than surrounding tissue, due to their greater densities. The difference in vibration between the otolith and the hair cells stimulates the sensory hair bundles and activates the neurons of the auditory nerve, which transmits messages to the brain.

Otoliths are excellent sources of age information since they form early in development, grow throughout life, and are not subject to loss or chemical modification. Of the three otoliths, the sagitta is typically the largest and therefore most useful for aging studies. Otoliths grow via accretion of layers of fibroprotein and calcium carbonate crystals. In many fishes, this deposition occurs on a regular basis and is represented by concentric markings called *circuli*. These concentric rings can be counted like tree rings to determine a fish's age. Together, these rings form bands (called *annuli* when they are verified to occur annually) consisting of many circuli that are either translucent (usually formed during faster, summer growth) or opaque (usually formed during slower, winter growth). Although individual circuli may be counted to age larval fishes on the order of days and months, annuli are typically used in determining yearly age.

The temporal nature of band formation must be verified for each species studied in order to arrive at accurate conclusions. The antibiotic oxytetracycline, when injected into a fish, deposits in calcifying structures and forms a fluorescent marker ring in the otolith of known date that can be used to verify banding periodicity. The temporal periodicity of ring deposition can be validated through the use of tagging and recapture methods.

In some species, concentric rings can be viewed simply with the aid of a dissecting microscope. However, otoliths often must be enhanced to allow rings to be more easily interpreted. Otoliths are typically thin-sectioned through the nucleus (which records the first year of growth) and stained using a suite of available techniques to enhance banding. Another sectioning technique involves breaking and burning the otolith to improve ring resolution. Alternatively, radiometric age determination can be used alone or combined with traditional methods to confirm longevity estimates. This technique uses the ratio of naturally occurring radioisotopes (typically, radium-226 and lead-210) of a known decay series to determine age.

Age and growth data can be combined with reproductive and abundance information to establish demographic parameters for fish species that are critical to their sustainable management. Indeed, many species that exhibit long life spans and late ages at maturity (i.e., rockfishes and the orange roughy) have suffered precipitous declines in abundance due to absent or inaccurate aging information. In addition, because sizes and shapes of otoliths are distinct and highly variable between species, they can be used for identification, especially in feeding studies. Trace elements incorporated into the otolith can also mark significant events in a fish's life. For example, strontium concentrations (higher in marine environments) can be studied in diadromous fishes to determine their temporal movements between fresh and salt water. Birth location and stock discrimination can also be determined by comparing the chemical composition of otoliths to that of different aqueous environments. Recently, bomb-generated radioactive carbon has been used to validate the ages of long-lived fishes, as the precise dates of past nuclear explosions are known.

Joseph J. Bizzarro

FURTHER READING

Bond, Carl E. *Biology of Fishes*. New York: Saunders College Publishing, 1996.

Cailliet, Gregor M., Milton S. Love, and Alfred W. Ebeling. *Fishes: A Field and Laboratory Manual on*

Their Structure, Identification, and Natural History.
Prospect Heights, Ill.: Waveland Press, 1986.

Evans, David H., ed. *The Physiology of Fishes.*
Boca Raton, Fla.: CRC Press, 1998.

Helfman, Gene S., Bruce B. Collette, and Douglas E.
Facey. *The Diversity of Fishes.* Malden, Mass.:
Blackwell Science, 1997.

Moyle, Peter B., and Joseph J. Cech. *Fishes: An
Introduction to Ichthyology.* Upper Saddle River, N.J.:
Prentice Hall, 2000.

RELATED ARTICLES
Osteichthyes

Oxygen

Oxygen (O_2) is a reactive gas that is essential to
life; only a few organisms (e.g., anaerobic bacteria) can survive extended periods of time without
it. Oxygen is metabolically important for both
terrestrial and aquatic organisms, but the availability of the gas differs dramatically between
these environments. The concentration of oxygen
in air is 210 milliliters per liter (mL/L). In contrast, only about 5.2 mL of oxygen is dissolved in
1 liter of 20°C (68°F) average salinity [35 practical salinity units (psu)] seawater.

Oxygen is not distributed evenly within the
ocean's depth for a number of physical and biological reasons. The solubility of oxygen in water
increases with decreased temperature and salinity
(i.e., colder, saltier water contains more O_2).
Thus, water masses of different temperatures and
salinities vary in oxygen content. Utilization of
oxygen by organisms also affects the O_2 content
within a given volume of water. Oxygen content
is highest at and just below the sea surface
because of atmospheric input and photosynthetic
activity of phytoplankton. The production of
molecular oxygen by phytoplankton photosynthesis can increase the O_2 concentration to 150
percent of the solubility value.

In the open ocean, an oxygen minimum zone
may be found between 500 and 1000 meters
(1640 to 3280 feet). The oxygen minimum is
best developed in the eastern Pacific. There,
oxygen levels can be close to zero because
organisms consume the available oxygen, which
is not replenished. The relatively large oxygen
concentration found in deep-water masses originally comes from the sea surface; these water
masses are created when cold surface water at
high latitudes (predominantly in the East
Greenland Sea and Weddell Sea) sinks and
spreads throughout the oceans as deep-water
currents. When they sink, this water contains
almost 8 mL/L O_2, whereas surface subtropical
water contain about 5 mL/L. The abundance
and metabolic rates of deep-water organisms
are lower than those of shallow-water organisms; thus the deep-sea biota do not deplete the
oxygen concentration to the low levels found in
the oxygen minimum zone.

Oxygen also plays important roles in the oceans'
chemistry, because oxygen is an integral part of
other molecules. Antoine-Laurent Lavoisier
(1743–94) discovered that water is comprised of
two atoms of hydrogen and one atom of oxygen,
H2O. The consumption of CO_2-producing organic
matter and the release of O_2 is the keystone in the
biochemistry of photosynthesis. Chemically
bound forms of oxygen, such as CO_2 (carbon dioxide), H_2CO_3 (carbonic acid), HCO_3 (bicarbonate),
and CO_3 (carbonate) are intimately involved in the
carbon dioxide–carbonic acid–bicarbonate system, which regulates the ocean pH.

Lynn L. Lauerman

FURTHER READING
Millero, Frank J. *Chemical Oceanography.* Boca Raton,
Fla.: CRC Press, 1992; 2nd ed.,1996.
Nybakken, James W. *Marine Biology: An Ecological
Approach,* 5th ed. San Francisco: Benjamin
Cummings, 2001.

RELATED ARTICLES
Air–Sea Interaction; Anoxia; Deep-Ocean Circulation;
Euphotic Zone; Photosynthesis; Phytoplankton

Oxygen Isotopes

There are no direct records of climatic conditions in the remote past, because no one was there to take measurements and write down observations. Consequently, paleoclimatologists, the scientists who seek to discover the conditions of those ancient climates (paleoclimates), must rely on indirect evidence. Changes in air temperature produce effects that can be detected later. One of the most important of these methods relates to the ratio between two isotopes of the element oxygen.

An atom consists of a nucleus surrounded by electrons. The nucleus is made from protons, which carry a positive electrochemical charge, and neutrons, which carry no charge. The electrons carry a negative charge. They are held by the attraction exerted by the positive charge on the protons. It is the number of protons in its nucleus that determines the chemical identity of the atom. Varying the number of neutrons in the nucleus alters the mass of the atom but not its chemical identity. Consequently, many chemical elements have two or more types of atoms that differ in mass because their nuclei have different numbers of neutrons. These different types of atoms are called the *isotopes* of the element.

Natural oxygen is mainly oxygen-16, usually written ^{16}O. The nuclei of its atoms each contain eight protons and eight neutrons. This is the most abundant isotope and accounts for 99.76 percent of natural oxygen. The addition of one more neutron produces ^{17}O, accounting for 0.04 percent of natural oxygen, and adding two more neutrons produces ^{18}O, accounting for 0.20 percent of natural oxygen. There are also three other very short-lived oxygen isotopes, ^{14}O, ^{15}O, and ^{19}O.

Isotope Ratios in Fresh Water and Seawater

The ratio of the two most common isotopes, ^{16}O and ^{18}O, provides an important but indirect clue to the temperature of the air and is used by paleoclimatologists in their reconstructions of past climates. This is possible because of the small difference in the masses of the two isotopes. Both isotopes bond equally well with hydrogen to form water, so the ratio of the two isotopes is the same as their natural abundance. For every 499 molecules of water with the lighter isotope ($H_2^{16}O$) there is one molecule with the heavier isotope ($H_2^{18}O$).

Being lighter, $H_2^{16}O$ molecules evaporate more readily than do molecules of $H_2^{18}O$. Water vapor then either condenses into liquid droplets or freezes into ice crystals and subsequently falls back to the surface as precipitation. When water evaporates, the molecules of vapor consist only of water, H_2O. Any substances dissolved in the water, such as salt, are left behind. Precipitation returns the $H_2^{16}O$ to the sea, with the result that the ratio of the two isotopes remains constant in seawater. On the other hand, fresh water such as rain and snow contains approximately 0.7 percent more $H_2^{16}O$.

The two isotopes are not returned to the sea at the same rate. ^{18}O is heavier, and therefore $H_2^{18}O$ condenses and falls faster than $H_2^{16}O$. When water vapor travels a long distance its composition is gradually altered. Snow falling over Greenland from water vapor that has traveled all the way from the Gulf of Mexico is about 3 percent lighter than seawater because so much of the heavier isotope has already condensed and fallen to Earth's surface.

During ice ages, fresh water, enriched in $H_2^{16}O$, falls as snow and the snow accumulates to form ice sheets and glaciers. When this happens, the fresh water is trapped as ice and does not return to the sea until the ice age ends and the ice sheets and glaciers melt. The snow is made from water containing more than 499 parts of ^{16}O to every 1 part of ^{18}O. Because the water molecules evaporated primarily from the oceans, removing more than 499 molecules of $H_2^{16}O$ for every molecule of $H_2^{18}O$, the proportion of ^{18}O to ^{16}O in seawater increases.

Isotopes Stored in Sediments

Small animals called foraminifera, or forams, are abundant in the oceans. They are tiny, most of them less than 1 millimeter (0.04 inch) in diameter, but they live inside shells that they grow from chemical ingredients present in the water around them. Foraminiferans have existed for at least the last 600 million years. Coccolithophores, which are tiny plants, possess similar shells. These shells are called *coccoliths*. Other animals that precipitate $CaCO_3$, such as clams and corals, can also be used to determine oxygen isotope ratios. The source of water, whether fresh or ocean, that is associated with sediment diagenesis and rock metamorphism is determined through the use of oxygen isotope ratios.

The shells are made from calcium carbonate ($CaCO_3$), which the foraminiferans and coccolithophores synthesize from chemicals they obtain from the surrounding water. The oxygen they use in making the carbonate (CO_3) contains the two oxygen isotopes in the same proportion as that which is present in the water, but there is an additional effect. The colder the water, the higher the proportion of ^{18}O the organisms use. These two effects augment each other. The result is that the colder the water, the greater the proportion of ^{18}O that is incorporated into the shells.

When these organisms die, the soft parts of their bodies decompose and disappear, but their insoluble shells sink to the bottom of shallow water and accumulate. They do not accumulate on the floor of the deep oceans, because $CaCO_3$ dissolves at the low temperature and high pressure found at depths below about 3 to 5 kilometers (2 to 3 miles). The depth at which $CaCO_3$ forms at precisely the same rate at which it dissolves is called the *carbonate compensation depth*.

The shells form part of the sediment on the seabed, where their chemical remains are preserved either as unconsolidated sediment or as sedimentary rock. Samples taken from this sediment or sedimentary rock can be used to determine the near-surface water temperature at the time the shell remains precipitated as $CaCO_3$ from seawater. If the $CaCO_3$ is enriched in ^{18}O, it indicates that at the time it formed, ^{16}O was accumulating in snow and ice and therefore that the ice sheets were becoming thicker and more extensive. Clearly, the climate was growing colder. If the isotope ratio is 499:1, the same as that in the air, it means that water that evaporated was condensing, falling as precipitation, and returning rapidly to the ocean. Snow was not accumulating, so the climate was warm. Shells that were made during an ice age contain about 0.2 percent more ^{18}O than shells produced during a warm period between ice ages.

Dating makes it possible to determine when the foraminiferan shells and coccoliths precipitated. The shells can be dated paleontologically by careful studies related to the changes in the populations through time. The age of the $CaCO_3$ can also be determined by radiocarbon dating of the carbon it contains. This technique is reliable for material tens of thousands of years old. Ages greater than that can be determined by applying other radiometric dating methods to mineral particles.

Isotopes in Ice Sheets

The isotope ratio is also preserved in the ice sheets. All the water molecules in the ice are enriched with ^{16}O, but they are enriched by an amount that depends on the temperature. Although ^{16}O evaporates more readily than ^{18}O, ^{18}O also evaporates, and more of it evaporates the warmer the weather. If the ice contains more ^{18}O than that in ordinary fresh water, it means that the weather was relatively warm when the snow fell. If it contains less ^{18}O than in fresh water, the weather was cooler. This "thermometer" is so sensitive that it can be used to detect the difference between winter and summer temperatures, which helps in counting the annual layers in cores cut from the ice.

Oxygen isotopes are separated and their ratios measured by a mass spectrometer. The technique is routine and is also accurate and reliable. Scientists now have a continuous record of climate changes for the last 60 million years, based on the oxygen isotope ratios of shells found in sediments and sedimentary rocks. Studies of cores of rock drilled from the seabed provide an even more detailed record of climate over about the last 4 million years. The most detailed record of all, over about the last 200,000 years, has been built by analyzing the oxygen isotope ratios in cores of ice cut all the way through the Greenland ice sheet and partway through the Antarctic ice sheet.

Michael Allaby

FURTHER READING

Bryant, Edward. *Climate Process and Change.* Cambridge and New York: Cambridge University Press, 1997; pp. 78–81.

Emiliani, Cesare. *Planet Earth: Cosmology, Geology, and the Evolution of Life and Environment.* Cambridge and New York: Cambridge University Press 1995; pp. 542–543.

"Holocene and Pleistocene Decadal to Millenial Scale Climate Variability: The Marine Record." *Journal of Conference Abstracts,* Vol. 4, No. 1 (1999). Reports from a symposium held in Strasbourg, France, 28 March to 1 April 1999.

USEFUL WEB SITES

National Ice Core Laboratory, Science Management Office at the Climate Change Research Center, Institute for the Study of Earth, Oceans and Space, University of New Hampshire. <http://www.nicl-smo.sr.unh.edu>.

RELATED ARTICLES

Paleoceanography

Oxygen Minimum Zone

An oxygen minimum zone (OMZ) is a layer in the ocean where the concentration of dissolved oxygen is less than the concentration above and below that layer. In the open ocean, the OMZ lies generally between 500 and 1500 meters (1640 to 4921 feet). Oceanographers believe that formation of an OMZ is caused by a combination of several processes.

Nearly all seawater contains dissolved oxygen, which originates from two sources. At the surface, oxygen is absorbed directly from the atmosphere. This keeps surface concentrations near 100 percent saturation. In the photic zone [from the surface to about 100 meters (328 feet)], phytoplankton (microscopic plants) and algae use sunlight to convert inorganic nutrients into organic matter and produce oxygen as a by-product. Both of these oxygen-producing processes occur in surface waters.

Dissolved oxygen is required to support the oxygen respiration needs of fish, zooplankton (microscopic animals), and bacteria that live at all depths in the sea. At one time some thought that because respiration consumes oxygen and because photosynthetic oxygen production occurs only near the surface, the deep ocean would be devoid of animals. They hypothesized that the deep ocean would be an "azoic zone." However, biologists have found that although most animals live near the surface where oxygen is abundant, animals and bacteria are present throughout the water column. Oxygen consumption at intermediate depths [500 to 1500 meters (1640 to 4921 feet)] is sufficient to reduce oxygen concentrations significantly. This leads to the formation of an OMZ, where concentrations can fall from 50 percent to less than 1 percent of the surface concentration.

Early oceanographers did not appreciate that oxygen is continuously supplied to the deep ocean [3000 to 6000 meters (9800 to 19,700 feet)] by the wintertime sinking of cold, oxygen-rich water. The ocean's deep and bottom waters are formed in two places: the North Atlantic between Greenland and Norway, and the South Atlantic in the Weddell Sea. Thus the deep ocean is "ventilated" by the oxygen-rich deep waters. However, the waters at middepth are isolated from oxygen sources above and below the OMZ.

The formation of an OMZ is also affected by the surface productivity. In areas where there is an abundance of life (high primary productivity) in surface waters, the supply of sinking detritus and the vertical migration of fish and zooplankton lead to increased oxygen consumption at depth, hence intensifying the OMZ. Oxygen minimum zones such as in the eastern Pacific Ocean are located in regions of sluggish subsurface currents, which also reduces the supply of dissolved oxygen and contributes to this being the largest and most oxygen-deprived area in the world ocean.

The OMZs in the Atlantic contain higher oxygen concentrations than do those in the Pacific because the Atlantic Ocean has vigorous deep-water sources, whereas the Pacific does not. Surface oxygen concentrations in the ocean are about 5 milliliters of O_2 gas in 1 liter of water (mL/L).

The OMZs in the tropical and subtropical Atlantic Ocean have oxygen concentrations between 3 and 4 mL/L. Two distinct oxygen minima in the Pacific are formed as thin bands extending westward from the Americas centered near 20° latitude both north and south of the equator. In the Pacific Ocean near Central America the oxygen minimum lies within 200 meters (656 feet) of the surface. In these Pacific OMZs, the oxygen concentration may be less than 1/10 mL/L.

Other OMZs include the Arabian Sea in the Indian Ocean and the Alboran Sea in the Mediterranean. The OMZ in the northern Arabian Sea is believed to be caused by normal oxygen consumption rates in waters that already have low oxygen before being advected into the area. The Alboran Sea OMZ is thought to be triggered by the decomposition of large amounts of plankton that grow in nutrient-rich waters originating in the Atlantic. The Black Sea and Cariaco Trench, as well as numerous fjords, are examples of extremely low oxygen conditions. Because these basins are completely cut off from deepwater flow, their depths below several hundred meters contain absolutely no dissolved oxygen. The deep waters of these anoxic basins are characterized by the presence of hydrogen sulfide (which has the smell of rotten eggs), which is poisonous to most fish and zooplankton.

William W. Broenkow

FURTHER READING
Gross, M. G. *Oceanography: A View of the Earth.* Englewood Cliffs, N.J.: Prentice Hall, 1971; 5th ed., 1990.
Open University Team. *Seawater: Its Composition, Properties and Behaviour.* Oxford and New York: Pergamon Press, 1989; 2nd ed., 1995.
Riley, J. P., and R. Chester. *Introduction to Marine Chemistry.* London and New York: Academic Press, 1971.
Sverdrup, H. U., M. W. Johnson, and R. H. Fleming. *The Oceans, Their Physics, Chemistry, and General Biology.* New York: Prentice Hall, 1942.
Thurman, H. V. *Introductory Oceanography.* Columbus, Ohio: Merrill, 1975; 8th ed., Upper Saddle River, N.J.: Prentice Hall, 1997.

RELATED ARTICLES
Anoxia; Primary Productivity

Oyashio

The Oyashio ("parent current"), or *Kuril Current*, is an ocean current that forms part of the North Pacific gyre. It originates mainly in the Sea of Okhotsk, from where it flows southward. Near the southern tip of the Kamchatka Peninsula it joins the merged Alaskan Stream and Kamchatka, or Bering, Current, carrying water from the Bering Sea. The Kamchatka Current is often considered to be the northern section of the Oyashio. The Oyashio continues past the Kuril Islands, and to the south it divides into two sections. One turns eastward and joins the North Pacific Current. The other continues to flow southward, passing the coast of the Japanese islands of Hokkaido and northern Honshu. Finally it meets the Kuroshio and turns eastward to join the North Pacific Current. The southern boundary of the Oyashio, at about 39°N, defines the location of the Polar Front.

The Oyashio flows at less than 2.4 kilometers per second (1.5 miles per hour) and is strongest in spring. The salinity of its water is low, ranging from 33.7 to 34.0 practical salinity units (psu; compared with the oceanic average for seawater of 34.7 psu), and it is cold. At a depth of 100 meters (330 feet) off Hokkaido, the temperature of Oyashio water is a fairly constant 5°C (41°F), but the temperature at the surface is more variable, ranging from 0°C (32°F) in winter to as high as 20°C (68°F) in summer.

The inflow of warm water carried by a deep current through the Kuril Strait produces intense mixing of the water in the Sea of Okhotsk. This maximizes the amount of dissolved oxygen held in the sea and contributes to a high dissolved-oxygen content in Oyashio water. The divergence of the Oyashio produces upwelling rich in nutrients, and the combination of these nutrients and the oxygenated water makes the Oyashio highly productive biologically.

Michael Allaby

FURTHER READING

Kendrew, W. G. *The Climates of the Continents*, 5th ed. Oxford: Clarendon Press, 1961.

Knauss, John A. *Introduction to Physical Oceanography.* Englewood Cliffs, N.J.: Prentice Hall, 1978; 2nd ed. rev., Upper Saddle River, N.J.: Prentice Hall, 2000.

RELATED ARTICLES
Kuroshio; Salinity; Sea of Okhotsk; Upwelling

Ozone Hole

Few things illustrate humankind's ability to damage Earth better than the hole in the ozone layer (the region of the upper atmosphere that protects organisms from the Sun's harmful ultraviolet radiation). Predicted in 1974, the hole was first spotted over Antarctica in 1985 and was followed by a second hole over the Arctic region more than a decade later. *Ozone depletion,* as the reduction in the ozone layer is known, has increased dramatically since then. Apart from promoting human illnesses such as skin cancer and cataracts (a major cause of blindness), increased ultraviolet radiation due to ozone depletion could cause serious disruption to marine life.

Ozone is a type of oxygen gas that exists in the stratosphere, the upper layer of Earth's atmosphere around 19 to 48 kilometers (12 to 30 miles) above sea level. Radiation from the Sun includes a type of ultraviolet light called UV-B that is harmful to living things but normally is screened out by the ozone layer. The use of ozone-depleting chemicals, however, has reduced the thickness of ozone and led to the formation of increasingly large holes in the ozone layer over the polar regions each spring. The largest ozone hole produced so far was discovered over Antarctica by U.S. National Aeronautics and Space Administration scientists in 2000 and covered an area of 28.3 million square kilometers (11 million square miles), three times larger than the land area of the United States.

Ozone-depleting chemicals include chlorofluorocarbons (CFCs), which have been used widely in aerosol propellants, refrigerant gases, and numerous industrial processes since the 1930s. Ironically, CFCs are very inactive gases and were initially thought to be completely harmless. But high in the stratosphere, ultraviolet radiation breaks them into individual chlorine atoms, each of which can destroy thousands of ozone molecules.

The effects of UV-B radiation on living organisms are already well understood. For humans, the probable consequences of a thinner ozone layer are a greater incidence of skin cancer, premature aging of the skin, and cataracts (a clouding of the human eye's lens responsible for half of all cases of blindness). The U.S. Environmental Protection Agency estimates that a 40 percent depletion of ozone (by the year 2075) will produce an extra 154 million cases of skin cancer and 3.4 million more deaths.

But the effects are not confined to humans; marine life could also be seriously affected. Phytoplankton, "the pasture of the oceans," are tiny single-celled plants that float in water, producing food for higher organisms through photosynthesis. But UV-B radiation has been found to reduce phytoplankton photosynthesis, thereby cutting food supplies at the bottom of the ocean food chain. UV-B also disrupts zooplankton, which feed off the phytoplankton, and is known to damage the DNA (genetic material) of small fish, crab larvae, starfish, and urchins. It can slow the growth of fish, damage cellular processes, and ultimately reduce the number of creatures that survive to adulthood. UV-B can also react with organic matter in ocean water to form chemicals dangerous to marine life, such as hydrogen peroxide. The effect that all this damage will have on higher marine life (and humans) is unclear. Some scientists highlight the potentially devastating consequences of disrupting food chains at their lowest point; others suggest that the effects may be significant, but less dramatic, for higher organisms.

An international agreement called the Montreal Protocol has reduced the production of ozone-depleting substances in industrialized nations since 1987, but these substances continue to be produced by developing countries, including India and China, and through a thriving international black market. Scientists are increasingly concerned that natural events, such as the Mount Pinatubo volcanic eruption in 1991 and greenhouse gases linked to global warming, could accelerate ozone depletion. As a result, it could be many decades before ozone depletion is controlled or reversed.

Chris Woodford

FURTHER READING
Kerr, Richard A. "Ozone Loss, Greenhouse Gases Linked." *Science*, 10 April 1998, p. 202.

Leaf, Alexander. "Loss of Stratospheric Ozone and Health Effects of Increased Ultraviolet Radiation." In Eric Chivian, et al., eds., *Critical Condition: Human Health and Environment*. Cambridge, Mass.: MIT Press, 1993.

USEFUL WEB SITES
National Science Foundation, "First Evidence That Ozone Hole Harms Antarctic Fish." *National Science Foundation Press Release*, No. 97-19, 11 Mar. 1997. <http://www.nsf.gov/od/lpa/news/press/pr9719.htm>.

RELATED ARTICLES
Pollution, Ocean; Ultraviolet Radiation

REFERENCE